ACCLAIM FOR

Mayday

by Michael R. Beschloss

"A fascinating reconstruction of the American U-2 program, of relations and attitudes in the intelligence community, of politics and personalities around the Eisenhower White House, of the fit (or lack thereof) between American diplomacy and intelligence, of Soviet-American relations in the Eisenhower-Khrushchev years and a good deal more. Beschloss has done an excellent job of asking good questions, digging for answers wherever he could and making his way through the shoals of complexity and contradiction....The title refers both to the date of the incident and to the code signal for distress. But *Mayday* can also stand as a metaphor for the relationship between the superpowers."
—Alexander Dallin, *New York Times Book Review*

"Mr. Beschloss's modesty makes an engaging frame for his achievement; he has told us more than anyone else so far, and told it with clarity and intelligence....His grand narrative is crowded with well-drawn portraits. It is fascinating to follow great figures moving from headlines into history books....Of all the huge cast, the figure of the pilot touches me most, possibly because what happened to him—or something similar—could happen to any of us."
—Naomi Bliven, *The New Yorker*

"A fast-paced, highly readable history....Beschloss has accomplished the difficult task of making a work of scholarship read like a novel."
—James Bamford, *Washington Post Book World*

"Beschloss weaves together, with remarkable skill, the strands of the story.... He not only explains, with great lucidity, the technology of modern espionage, but, drawing on the private papers of the participants, he reveals the structure of political control behind these missions....Up until this book, the tangled web of public deceit over the U-2 has not been unraveled.... Beschloss's reconstruction of this atmosphere should be required reading by all those concerned with the interpretation of this crucial period of the Cold War....*Mayday* is far more than the intriguing story of the U-2. It is the anatomy of an international crisis that exposes, as few other modern histories do, the subterranean connections between espionage and diplomacy."
—Edward Jay Epstein, *Boston Globe*

"A classic account."   —Robert McNeill, United Press International

"Fascinating, compellingly written...Beschloss is wise enough to understand the subtle interplay between personality and policy at the highest levels. This insight is combined with impeccable scholarship and a knowing sense of how government operates."   —Richard Elias, *Cleveland Plain Dealer*

"*Mayday* has everything—heroes, villains, high drama, low knavery, the grand wash of sweeping tides and the close focus of average people trying to stem those tides or to ride them out."
                                    —Harry Levins, *St. Louis Post-Dispatch*

"A work of history destined to become the definitive book on the U-2 incident...Beschloss tells this story of high intrigue and double-dealing with the literary pacing of a le Carré thriller; he inserts cameo biographies of many of the principal figures of both governments and their allies that show a keen eye for the flaws which aggravated the problem. There is no prejudice evident here....The result is a mix of knowledge and dispassion—a cheery blend for a historian and, even more, for his readers....A genuine page-turner with important lessons for major governments in an age of instant crises."
                                                        —*Kirkus Reviews*

"Absorbing and magnificently researched....*Mayday* is one of the most engrossing books written on Cold War history."
                                —Walter LaFeber, *Bulletin of the Atomic Scientists*

"A fascinating story...Where Beschloss has the facts, his narrative convinces, and where he must surmise—for example, in dealing with the Kremlin's manic-depressive style of politics—he persuades."
                                    —Ed Cray, *Philadelphia Inquirer*

"*Mayday* is a book written in the best historical tradition: the telling of a fascinating story in all its richness and detail, accompanied by humor and pathos....This is history worth the telling and worth the reading."
                                    —Michael M. Boll, *Military Review*

"A very valuable contribution to the history of Soviet-American relations."
                                    —Adam B. Ulam

"Beschloss has told this extraordinary story with the clean pace of a superior thriller....His subtle, understanding portraits of Eisenhower and Khrushchev, and his grasp of the interplay between accident and misunderstanding, give his book the tragic dimension of a Hardy or a Tolstoy novel. It also has the power and precision of classic contemporary history."
                                    —Godfrey Hodgson, *The Independent* (London)

MAYDAY

The U-2 Affair

*The untold story of
the greatest U.S.-U.S.S.R.
spy scandal*

MICHAEL R. BESCHLOSS

Harper & Row, Publishers, New York
Cambridge, Philadelphia, San Francisco, Washington
London, Mexico City, São Paulo, Singapore, Sydney

MAYDAY. Copyright © 1986 by Michael R. Beschloss. All rights reserved. Printed in the United States
of America. No part of this book may be used or reproduced in any manner whatsoever without written
permission except in the case of brief quotations embodied in critical articles and reviews. For
information address Harper & Row, Publishers, Inc., 10 East 53rd Street, New York, N.Y. 10022.
Published simultaneously in Canada by Fitzhenry & Whiteside Limited, Toronto.

First PERENNIAL LIBRARY edition published 1987.

Designer: Sidney Feinberg

Map by George Colbert

Library of Congress Cataloging-in-Publication Data

Beschloss, Michael R.
    MAYDAY : the U-2 affair.

    "Perennial Library."
    Includes index.
    1. U-2 Incident, 1960. 2. Eisenhower, Dwight D. (Dwight David), 1890–1969. 3. Khrushchev, Nikita
Sergeyevich, 1894–1971. I. Title.
E183.8.S65B47   1987   973.921   85-45620
ISBN 0-06-091407-6 (pbk.)

87 88 89 90 91   MPC   10 9 8 7 6 5 4 3 2 1

For Steven Beschloss

I had thought the President sincerely wanted to change his
policies and improve relations. Then, all of a sudden, came
an outrageous violation of our sovereignty. And it came
as a bitter, shameful disappointment. . . . Now, thanks to the
U-2, the honeymoon was over.

—Nikita Khrushchev

If I'd said, "I had nothing to do with this," and picked
some goat below me and canned him, Khrushchev might have
behaved differently in' Paris, but I don't think so. I think
it would have come out the same, once that original mistake
was made of not stopping the flights.

—Dwight Eisenhower

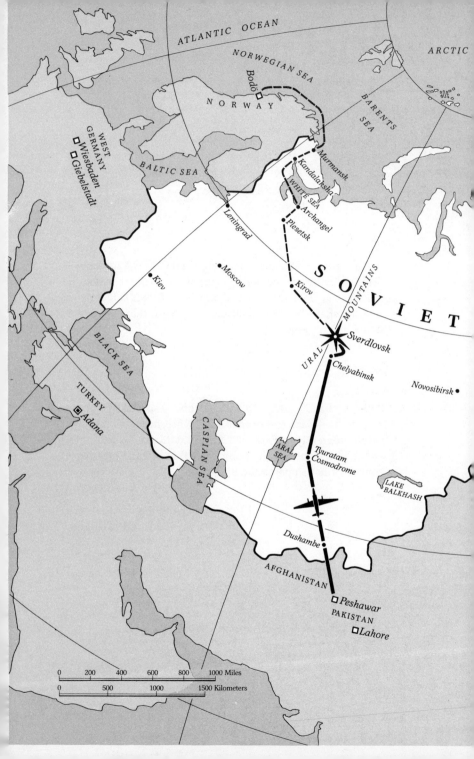

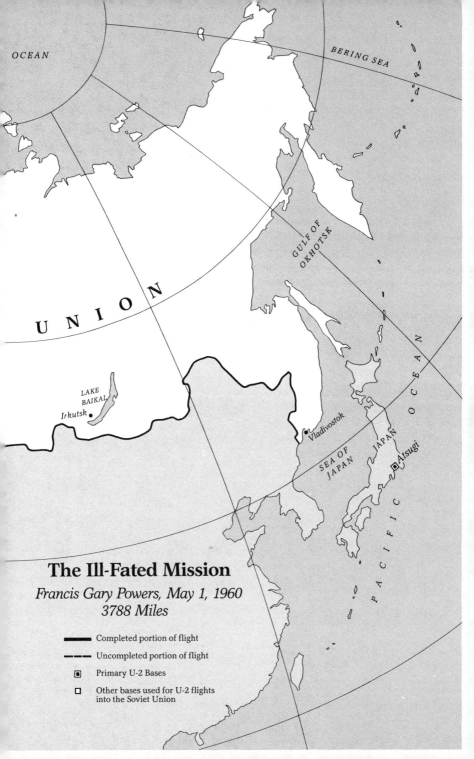

OCEAN

BERING SEA

GULF OF OKHOTSK

U N I O N

LAKE BAIKAL

Irkutsk

Vladivostok

SEA OF JAPAN

JAPAN

Atsugi

PACIFIC OCEAN

The Ill-Fated Mission

Francis Gary Powers, May 1, 1960
3788 Miles

—————— Completed portion of flight

- - - - - - Uncompleted portion of flight

■ Primary U-2 Bases

□ Other bases used for U-2 flights
into the Soviet Union

Preface

For much of the world, the spring of 1960 seemed to hold bright promise for improved relations between the United States and the Soviet Union. Then on May Day, like a clap of thunder, a CIA U-2 spy plane fell from the skies at Sverdlovsk, followed by some of the most perilous years of the Cold War. This book is an effort to explain what happened.

The U-2 episode deserves renewed attention because of the light it sheds on American-Soviet diplomacy and other battles being fought in our own day. The four years of flights into Soviet airspace are an instance of the oft-hidden influence of espionage and covert action on the deeds and emotions that drive nations toward war or peace. The downing of the U-2 was the CIA's first massive public failure, the first time many Americans discovered that their government practiced espionage. May 1960 was the first time many learned that their leaders did not always tell them the truth.

The U-2 provides evidence for the student of historical reputation. Western historians have lately shown new appreciation of Dwight Eisenhower's shrewdness and commitment to curbing the arms race. Some who once saw Nikita Khrushchev purely as the Butcher of Budapest and a careless rattler of missiles have come to view him also as a man committed—however ambivalently—to reducing the harshness of the Cold War.

It is difficult to write with absolute assurance about still-sensitive matters of national security only a generation after they occur. Historical perspective and access to secret documents are more difficult to obtain than after a half-century or more. But history is, among other things, a policy science: the study of issues and institutions that are still vital provides guidance to diplomats, generals, political leaders and, above all, citizens.

This volume draws on Western private diaries and letters, oral history interviews, memoirs and papers, including White House, State Department, Pentagon, FBI and CIA documents, many released under the Freedom of Information Act. Like every history dealing with the Cold War, it suffers from the paucity of Soviet sources open to Western scholars.

The historian of American-Soviet relations Adam Ulam has observed that it is not the rivalry of the superpowers that poses the main threat to peace: "It is the irrational premises and impulses that underlie the policies of both which threaten the world with incalculable dangers." Only when there is a free exchange of information and ideas between West and East can those premises and impulses begin to be swept away.

—MICHAEL R. BESCHLOSS

Washington, D.C.
January 1986

Contents

ILLUSTRATIONS

(*following page 174*)

MAYDAY

Prologue: April 30, 1960

T HERE WAS NO PREMONITION of disaster. On a tranquil Saturday like this, the President's day began in the First Lady's bedroom on the second floor of the White House, where the first beams of sunlight pushed through the floral draperies and fell across the sleeping man and woman.

In the absence of an urgent telephone call, Dwight David Eisenhower was awakened by his valet, a black sergeant named John Moaney who had laid out the General of the Army's clothes in Algiers, London, Frankfurt, New York and Paris. When Moaney knocked, the President usually cried, "Okay!" and reached for a bathrobe, his cheeks pink and fringe of snowy hair ruffled from sleep. To avoid waking his wife, Eisenhower slipped into the adjoining President's bedroom, which he used for changing clothes and naps.

He ordinarily took his morning shower before stirring hot shaving foam in an old-fashioned mug and moving a safety razor up and down the most famous face in the Western world. In the spring of 1960, the image in the mirror looked firmer and graver than the face smiling from the I LIKE IKE banners of his first campaign, as if seven years in the White House had chastened and deepened him. But the actual reason was his diet. Since his heart attack in 1955, the President had obeyed his doctor and forsworn the rich food he loved, to bring himself down to 173 pounds, his football weight at West Point in 1913. Stripped of the extra layer of fat, his features were at once more sensitive and more powerful. Years later, on first meeting Eisenhower, Henry Kissinger was not prepared for the "cold, deep blue, extraordinarily penetrating eyes."

When Moaney yanked the curtains open, the bedroom glowed in sunlight. At the start of the day, the President often took a few swings with a ten-iron before stopping to gaze at his favorite view in Washington—Andrew Jackson's magnolias on the South Grounds, the Washington Monument and Jefferson Memorial, three thousand cherry blossom trees, the flat gray-blue Potomac.

Breakfast was often a lean steak, skim milk, fruit juice and decaffeinated coffee, which the Sergeant served from a tray. Like other Presidents, Eisenhower professed in public to ignore the swing of daily opinion ("I just can't be bothered"), but this did not stop him from reading newspapers alongside his morning meal. He preferred the *New York Herald Tribune,* bible of "modern Republicanism," lately purchased and kept afloat by John Hay Whitney, his friend and envoy to the Court of St. James's. To Eisenhower, the *New York Times* was "the most untrustworthy paper in the world" (at least at one angry moment), but he read it.

In sheer column inches, the most prominent story this morning was the Democratic Presidential campaign: John Kennedy was battling with Hubert Humphrey in the hills and coalfields of West Virginia. The President considered Kennedy an unserious man whose reputation had been inflated by his father's wealth and his own public relations talents. Like Woodrow Wilson's contemplation of Warren Harding forty years earlier, Eisenhower could not believe that the same country that had twice elected him could turn the government over to a man like Kennedy.

He might have felt more serene about Kennedy's nomination had he felt more sanguine about the Republican side of the campaign. His relations with his Vice President, Richard Nixon, were complex and often indecipherable even to the two men themselves. By any test of loyalty, Nixon could not be faulted. For more than seven years, he had skillfuliy foiled the efforts of the press to find and generate conflict between himself and his boss. Still Eisenhower had never felt comfortable with the notion of Nixon as President. Like Franklin Roosevelt, he saw the Presidency as essentially himself in office, and to this Nixon bore little resemblance. Eisenhower often carped that no man of any sense would aspire to the Presidency: the office had to be thrust upon him. Without mentioning names, he said he was inclined to oppose anyone who actively sought the job.

And yet by this final week of April 1960, Nixon had almost a hammerlock on the nomination. With the Republican convention to open in three months, the only remaining alternative was Governor Nelson Rockefeller of New York. All spring, Rockefeller had been charging that the President had been too budget-conscious, shortchanging the Pentagon and America's capacity to defend itself, an accusation calculated to make the Supreme Allied Commander of World War Two see red. Eisenhower may have been angry at Rockefeller, but he knew he might need him. Suspecting that the Governor's presence on the ticket might be the Republicans' only chance for victory, he toyed with urging Nixon and Rockefeller to cut a deal: if Rockefeller ran for Vice President this year and they won, Nixon would retire from the White House in 1964 and endorse Rockefeller as the next nominee.

The President's well-contained enthusiasm for his potential successors made it more painful to leave the White House after twenty years at the center of the world stage. His son John privately agreed with other members of the White House staff that had the Twenty-second Amendment not barred a third term, the President would probably have run for re-election in 1960.

•

Part of Sergeant Moaney's ritual was holding out boxer shorts for the President to step into and slipping socks and well-polished shoes onto the Presidential feet. After he finished dressing, the President walked down the wide hall that served First Families as a private parlor, past the plaque (BLESS THIS HOUSE) which had graced all twenty-seven Eisenhower homes since their marriage in 1916, and into the private elevator. On the ground floor, he nodded to policemen guarding the double white doors dividing the Mansion from the West Wing, the business quarters of the White House. Striding down the outdoor colonnade, he could see his putting green, a gift from the American Public Golf Association.

The President entered his pale green Oval Office and sat down behind the massive dark rosewood desk. John Eisenhower, one of his father's aides, always thought it looked "like a big football field." As he

sat, the President saw the (unused) marble fireplace crowned with
busts of Washington and Franklin, a military flag with battle stream-
ers, an Andrew Wyeth, a naval battle scene and George Cope's "Wild
Duck Hanging on the Wall." When he swiveled his leather chair
about, he looked out through two inches of bulletproof glass onto the
South Grounds, where *Marine One,* the Presidential helicopter, waited
to take him to his home at Gettysburg for the weekend.

General Andrew Jackson Goodpaster, his staff secretary, walked in
to deliver the morning intelligence briefing. Lanky, laconic, unflap-
pable, Goodpaster was a man who gauged the impact of every syllable.
Born in Granite City, Illinois, in 1918, he had finished West Point second in his class. After that, he led a wartime battalion into North
Africa and Italy, took a doctorate in international relations at Princeton and served under General Eisenhower at Supreme Headquarters
Allied Powers Europe in Paris. When the President's first staff secretary, General Paul Carroll, died in 1954, Goodpaster's name was proposed. "I would ask nothing more than for my son to grow up as good
a man as he is," said Eisenhower. That settled the matter. Goodpaster's
relationship with the President was almost filial: the young General
saw the old General more often than almost anyone.

In 1960, Eisenhower had no Bundy or Kissinger or Brzezinski. The
work of later national security advisers was divided between two men.
Gordon Gray, a Democrat, tobacco heir and former president of the
University of North Carolina, held the title but mainly worked on
long-term planning. Goodpaster was the day-to-day man, the President's adviser, note taker, briefer, organizer of meetings and transmission wire to the international side of the government.

Goodpaster reported that there had been no major overnight developments. The friendly regime in Turkey was still teetering amid riots
and strikes and policemen shooting into crowds. Off the coast of Long
Island, American naval intelligence had found that a Soviet trawler
was spying on the nuclear submarine, *George Washington.* Before the
end of his briefing, Goodpaster reminded the President of something
so secret that it was known only to two other key members of the
White House staff*: in West Pakistan, a CIA pilot was waiting to fly
for nine hours to Norway across the forbidden territory of the Union
of Soviet Socialist Republics.

* Gordon Gray and John Eisenhower.

•

Numerous times since July 1956, after scrutinizing the red-blue-green route maps spread across his big desk, Eisenhower had ordered the CIA to fly deep into Soviet airspace. From Norway, West Germany, Turkey, Pakistan, Japan, Alaska and elsewhere, former Air Force pilots soared in specially-designed black, unmarked planes over 70,000 feet above Russian air bases, missile-launching pads, submarine pens, factories, highways, railroads, atomic testing grounds. With sophisticated apparatus they took in Soviet radio and radar signals; with huge state-of-the-art cameras that swung from side to side, they could photograph a Soviet general's license plate from twelve miles overhead. Allen Dulles, Director of Central Intelligence, later boasted, "I was able to get a look at every blade of grass in the Soviet Union."

The new American space agency, the National Aeronautics and Space Administration, had told *Wings, Aviation Week* and other air journals that NASA owned the U-2s and flew them through storms at 55,000 feet to find what dangers lay in store for the Boeing 707, DC-8 and other jet airliners entering service. The press was not told that the U-2 pilots were, in fact, CIA pilots, that in secret they had broken the world's known altitude record, or that they were flying these planes across the Soviet Union.

Parched, cramped, sweating, staggering out of their cockpits after many hours locked in pressurized flight suits, the fliers brought back a king's ransom in film, tape and other material for study by the CIA and other agencies. The CIA's Richard Bissell, father of the program, later said that by 1959, the U-2 was bringing back "ninety percent of our hard intelligence information about the Soviet Union." These findings helped to reassure the President that Soviet boasts about a mammoth bomber and missile buildup were no more than boasts. This helped to persuade Eisenhower to hold down defense spending against almost unbearable public pressure.

Nelson Rockefeller, Senator Stuart Symington, the columnist Joseph Alsop and others who lacked the secret information charged Eisenhower with allowing first a Bomber Gap and then a Missile Gap—failures to keep ahead of the Soviets that endangered every American. Privately the President pounded his desktop and threw offending magazines and newspapers against the Oval Office walls: Alsop was "about the lowest form of animal life on earth." But publicly he bit his tongue and relied on public faith that the old General would not allow his country to be underdefended.

Eisenhower had warned Dulles and Bissell that at any moment the Russians might misinterpret a U-2 plane as the forerunner of an American military invasion. Shortly after the program started, he had taken the flights under his direct control. Dulles or Bissell or both and their aides would arrive at the White House to show him how the Free World's security rested on a U-2 mission from Turkey over Kazakhstan or from Japan across Siberia. The President bent over the maps, his suit bunched up, his India-rubber face changing from curiosity to surprise, skepticism, bafflement. Sometimes he said yes, with a shrug or a pat on someone's shoulder; sometimes he said no, with a violent shake of the head, complaining that the flight's potential gain was not worth the provocation.

For years, the Russians had failed to shoot down the planes. But this weakness could not last forever. By 1959, U-2 pilots saw new silver Soviet fighters rising higher and higher beneath them, firing vainly. The CIA knew that the Russians were building more powerful anti-aircraft weapons and that Eastern bloc secret agents dreamed of sabotaging a U-2 on the ground so that it would fall on Soviet territory.

Through 1959 and into 1960, the President was more reluctant than ever to sanction additional U-2 missions. Not only might there be greater risk of downing, but relations between the United States and the Soviet Union were growing warmer than perhaps at any time since the start of the Cold War.

•

Since January 1953, when he entered office, Eisenhower's chief aspiration had been to build the foundation for an extended improvement in American-Soviet relations. He was uniquely qualified to achieve a détente.* In Congress and among the American public, his military record and vast popularity helped to shield him against charges of selling out to the Russians and gave him authority to show Americans the benefits of reduced tensions. In the Soviet Union, he

---

* Some have taken the word "détente" to mean a state of near-bliss between Washington and Moscow. In fact, it simply means "the easing of strained relations, especially in a political situation" (*The Oxford English Dictionary,* Oxford, 1984). Eisenhower rarely used the term in public, but he did employ it in this sense in private conversations and letters. The term is so used throughout this book.

was fondly remembered as a stalwart of the Grand Alliance who had dealt fairly with his wartime Soviet counterparts.

But Eisenhower's hopes had long been frustrated. In 1959, he complained to aides that with small exception, "we haven't made a chip in the granite in seven years." That September, Nikita Sergeyevich Khrushchev arrived for the first American visit by a Soviet chief of government. After bowing his head at the Lincoln Memorial, riding to the top of the Empire State Building, watching Frank Sinatra and Shirley MacLaine film *Can Can* in Hollywood and trading outlandish compliments and insults with Americans across the land, Khrushchev went to the Presidential retreat at Camp David, Maryland, for two private days with the master of world imperialism.

The two leaders made a chip in the granite. Eisenhower lifted his objections to the full-fledged East-West summit conference that Khrushchev had been seeking for months. Khrushchev lifted his ultimatum obliging the West to promptly sign a German peace treaty and flee Berlin. Back in Moscow, he pronounced himself "captivated" by Eisenhower and praised the President's wisdom and love of peace in terms no Cold War Soviet leader had used before.

The two men would meet in Paris with the leaders of Britain and France. Starting on May 16, 1960, they would address "the major problems affecting the attainment of peace and stability in the world." In June, Eisenhower would go to the Soviet Union, where Khrushchev planned an extravagant welcome. Some in the West scoffed at what the Paris Summit might accomplish. But in fact, negotiators for both sides had drawn close to reaching a limited nuclear test ban treaty, which, if signed, would be the first major accord of the Cold War. Privately Eisenhower told aides that he was "determined" to achieve it.

To his old friend Prime Minister Harold Macmillan he noted that such a treaty would be "a ray of light in a world that is bound to be weary of the tensions brought about by mutual suspicion, distrust and arms races." It might slow the arms competition, prevent new nations from obtaining the Bomb and lead to other accords including a comprehensive ban on all nuclear testing. Eisenhower expected that the American Presidential candidates of 1960 would compete largely on the basis of who could best expand his opening to the Russians: his own party would have the obvious advantage. He told Charles de Gaulle, "What a splendid exit it would be for me to end up . . . with an agreement between East and West!"

●

What if a U-2 crashed on Soviet territory? If the Russians captured a live pilot and spying equipment, they could use it to embarrass the United States with charges of invasion and espionage.

Eisenhower had been troubled by this problem since the start of the program. By his recollection, the CIA and Joint Chiefs of Staff had "assured" him that "it would be impossible, if things should go wrong, for the Soviets to come in possession of the equipment intact—or, unfortunately, of a live pilot. This was a cruel assumption, but I was assured that the young pilots undertaking these missions were doing so with their eyes open and motivated by a high degree of patriotism, a swashbuckling bravado and certain material inducements." The President had been advised that in a crash, the U-2 would "virtually disintegrate."

Each pilot was told that in a mishap, before leaving his plane, he must throw two switches. Then he would have seventy seconds to eject before an explosive blew up cameras and other proof of espionage. After a crash, NASA would issue a cover story announcing that one of its weather planes had apparently strayed over Russia and fallen. Without espionage equipment in good condition or a live pilot, the Soviets could never prove for certain that the American government had deliberately sent the plane into Soviet airspace to spy.

That the Russians would never be able to capture a live pilot was "a *complete* given, a *complete* assumption as far as we were concerned," John Eisenhower later recalled. Would the President have permitted the CIA to fly deep into Russia without such an assurance? "It's very hard to say," Andrew Goodpaster replied years later. "But it would have been much more difficult to give approval to it."

The majority of Eisenhower's counselors predicted that the Russians would never publicize the downing of a plane on their soil. "I'm sure they will never admit it," John Foster Dulles, Secretary of State, told him in 1956. "To do so would make it necessary for them to admit also that for years we have been carrying on flights over their territory while they . . . had been helpless to do anything about the matter."

The President disagreed. He was almost certain that even with a charred mound of debris as the only proof, the Soviets would play up the offense for all it was worth. The winds would blow. A wave of "excitement mounting almost to panic" would sweep the world, along with the "standard Soviet claim of injustice, unfairness, aggression and ruthlessness." But Eisenhower knew that as long as the Russians lacked convincing evidence, he could plausibly deny their accusation.

•

What were Khrushchev and his comrades thinking in Moscow as each hostile aircraft soared overhead? They had issued three protests in 1956 and 1958. Washington had refuted all three. Other quieter protests had trailed off, almost as if the Kremlin had decided to resign itself to the violations until it could down a plane.

Both Eisenhower and Khrushchev had ample reason for public silence about the flights—Eisenhower to preserve the secrecy essential to U-2 operations, Khrushchev to keep his nation from learning that under his leadership Soviet armed forces were too weak to close Soviet skies to enemy planes bearing, for all anyone knew, nuclear weapons.

Khrushchev had not complained about the flights during his talks with Eisenhower at Camp David. From this the President had deduced that the Russians must not think the U-2 such a serious provocation. His own private view was that all nations spied. Tradition dictated that leaders did not complain to each other about it. It was up to the affronted country to expose and defeat the spies. Yet Eisenhower also knew that the U-2 flights hardly fit the definition of traditional espionage. A secret agent working the streets of a hostile capital was not likely to start a world war; an aerial violation had at least a tiny chance of doing so. And might not more flights undermine the improved relations between the United States and the Soviet Union that had begun at Camp David?

On April 9, 1960, after a pause, Eisenhower sent the U-2 back into Russia. Then Dulles and Bissell asked the President to approve another flight. Was this not tempting fate? The Paris Summit was only a month away. After four years of success, perhaps this was the moment to beware the lesson of Icarus and Daedalus.

But Eisenhower was no mystic. He approved the mission and fixed a deadline. Dulles and Bissell could have two weeks to fly. If they couldn't get good weather by April 25, the flight must be canceled: "We don't want to have that thing flying up there while the Summit's on."

A fortnight passed. Clouds and snowstorms concealed much of the route over the Soviet Union. Bissell pleaded for a few more days of grace. After consulting Eisenhower, Goodpaster called Bissell and then wrote a top-secret memorandum:

> After checking with the President, I informed Mr. Bissell that one additional operation may be undertaken, provided it is carried out prior to May 1. No operation is to be carried out after May 1.

By Saturday morning, this final day of April 1960, pilot and plane were still waiting in West Pakistan. If they could not fly tomorrow, there would be no mission at least until after the Summit. And if the Paris conference was successful, there was a chance that the U-2 might never streak into the Soviet Union again.

•

In the Oval Office, the President riffled his papers and then joined his son and portly friend George Allen, businessman and lobbyist, author of *Presidents Who Have Known Me,* who served as Eisenhower's bridge partner, golf partner and Falstaff. They boarded *Marine One* for the sixty-mile hop to Gettysburg. The First Lady would follow by car: the President always joked that she had "never completely convinced herself that an airplane flies."

Thirty-nine minutes later, the chopper landed on the farm the Eisenhowers had purchased after the war, five hundred acres of crop and pasture land once part of the Civil War battleground. The President and Allen drove to the Gettysburg Country Club, where Eisenhower greeted the twelve-year-old grandson after whom he had named the Presidential retreat: "Hello there, Mr. David, how are you doing?"

The President, his son and grandson and the Presidential chum played eighteen holes as Secret Service men followed with submachine guns hidden in their golf bags. That afternoon, Eisenhower and Allen drove south to Camp David, where they fished in a nearby stream.

All gathered for dinner at the Camp—the Presidential couple, George and Mary Allen, John and Barbara Eisenhower and David, Anne, Susan and Mary Jean. After the meal, they watched *April Showers,* starring Jack Carson and Ann Sothern, a sentimental tale made in 1948 about a vaudeville family's rise to Broadway.

That was all right with the President, as long as it wasn't a romance: one screen kiss, and he would be up and out of the room. Eisenhower preferred Westerns, which caused problems for the White House staff because he had seen most of the good ones three or four times. After first viewing *High Noon,* he whistled the theme music for months. His favorite motion picture was *Angels in the Outfield,* a comedy about a baseball manager's struggle to control his temper. This presumably had special meaning for the President, especially after his heart attack. He had the film screened at least eight times.

Motion pictures had lately been on John Eisenhower's mind. He had been asked to choose a film to be dubbed in Russian and presented by the President to Khrushchev in Moscow in June. He ruled out *The Benny Goodman Story* ("I don't see Khrushchev idolizing a jazz man") and *The King and I* ("Dubbing in a musical would be nearly impossible"). *Quo Vadis?* "The religious angle might get a bit heavy for Khrushchev." John chose Mike Todd's *Around the World in 80 Days*: "The only possible disadvantage is that it pokes good-natured fun at the British of the nineteenth century, but, on the other hand, it does the same with Americans."

The sixty-nine-year-old President sat with his family in the darkened room, the changing brightness of the screen lighting their faces as they watched the film. On this evening at Camp David, the scene of his encounter with Khrushchev, Eisenhower looked forward to nine final months in the White House that would be the capstone of his long career: a Soviet-American accord at Paris, the grand tour of Russia and, as he also expected, a Republican victory in November that would be a national ratification of his Presidency.

He could not know that these expectations largely rested on the fate of a young former Air Force lieutenant whose name he had never heard, who was tossing and turning on his cot in a noisy, steaming hangar in West Pakistan.

★

1

"I've Had It Now!"

I N SOUTH ASIA, it was now Sunday, the first of May. Inside the well-guarded hangar at Peshawar, two hours after midnight, Francis Gary Powers rose from his cot and braced himself for his mission—3,788 miles north to Bodö, Norway, bisecting the Soviet land mass at the Urals.

Last Wednesday, at the American base in Adana, Turkey, he had asked his wife Barbara for "a good-sized lunch"; she packed sandwiches, cookies and thermos bottles of soup and coffee into a red plaid case. He took it, kissed her and walked out of their house trailer into the sunshine. With two dozen fellow U-2 pilots, officers and technicians, he took a transport plane to Peshawar, there to cook his meals from rations and wait.

On the Khyber Pass above the old city, hundreds of thousands of tribesmen were climbing to Afghan grazing lands. They were the world that Kipling knew—lean brown men on camels, women staggering under bundles, children, sheep, hens, goats, donkeys. Their forebears had climbed these hills each spring since before the age of Alexander. They were indifferent to the Cold War and the rise and fall of nation-states.

Frank Powers never saw them. He was confined to a small corner of the field that the United States used as a military-intelligence base.

On Thursday before dawn, he was shaken from sleep to make his flight but, after washing and dressing, learned that Soviet weather was bad: no flight that day. On Friday and Saturday, the mission was scrubbed again. He killed time and tried to relax by reading and playing poker with friends, but the false starts made him very nervous.

Finally on this Sunday morning, he was told that this was the day. Like an astronaut before launching, he feasted on eggs, bacon and toast to keep himself alert: he would not eat or drink again until landing in Norway thirteen hours from now.

The false starts were not all that made him nervous. He disliked the plane, Number 360, brought in last night for this mission. Something had always seemed to go wrong: now one of its fuel tanks was reputedly on the blink. And Powers wondered whether the Russians were by now able to shoot down the U-2. When two missions were scheduled for the spring of 1960 after the hiatus, fellow U-2 pilots had guessed that the CIA was trying to jam in as many flights as possible before the Russians shot one down. Powers's superiors had told him that it was "absolutely safe" to fly over the Soviet Union, but he was still anxious: today's route would take him over hostile terrain for seven long hours.

While squeezing into his flight suit, he was asked, "Do you want the silver dollar?" It looked like an ordinary coin with a loop attached for fastening onto a key chain. But inside the two halves of the coin was a tiny pin loaded with a shellfish toxin perfected by the CIA at a reported cost of three million dollars. One jab and death was almost instantaneous.

As Richard Bissell later said, the U-2 pilots were "exhorted but not ordered" to kill themselves if caught by the Russians. Allen Dulles thought there was "more chance of a man's individual nobility prompting him to such an act" if he had not been ordered. If a plane went down and a U-2 pilot was captured, he might well prefer suicide to torture. Powers knew how American prisoners of war had been abused in North Korea: he accepted the lethal coin and dropped it into the pocket of his flight suit.

He would carry other equipment over Russia in case of an accident—a hunting knife, a custom-made .22-caliber pistol with silencer, a parachute that opened at 15,000 feet. His seat pack held survival gear including a collapsible life raft, clothing, water, food, a compass, signal flares, matches, chemicals for starting fires from damp wood, a first aid kit, heavy-duty hunting gear and a large silk banner in fourteen languages:

> I AM AN AMERICAN AND DO NOT SPEAK YOUR LANGUAGE.
> I NEED FOOD, SHELTER, ASSISTANCE. I WILL NOT HARM YOU. I
> BEAR NO MALICE TOWARD YOUR PEOPLE. IF YOU HELP ME,
> YOU WILL BE REWARDED.

The rewards were 7,500 rubles, two dozen gold Napoleon francs, gold rings and watches for men and ladies.

This kind of cache was later immortalized in Stanley Kubrick's classic *Dr. Strangelove* when the redneck pilot portrayed by Slim Pickens read fellow airmen the contents of their survival packs: "In them you'll find one forty-five-caliber automatic, two boxes amma-ni-shun, four days' concentrated emergency rations, one drug isha containin' annabah-yotics, *mor*-phine, *vah*-tamin pills, *pep* pills, *sleep*-in' pills, *trank*-willizin' pills, one minitcher Roo-shin phrase book and Bah-ble, one hundred dollars in rubles, one hundred dollars in gold, five packs o' chewin' gum, one isha prophylactics, three pair o' nah-lon stockin's—

"Shoot, a guy could have a pretty good weekend in Vegas with all *that* stuff!"

•

Powers and the other fliers did not know it, but the main reason for the equipment was not pilot survival but pilot morale—at least from Richard Bissell's point of view. Bissell did not think there was "one chance in a million" that a pilot would survive a mishap. The U-2 was so fragile that when one was buzzed by two curious Canadian jets over West Germany it broke up amid the shock waves. Bissell thought a Russian assault might shatter the plane before the pilot had the chance to even think about bailing out.

In case that did not come to pass, there was the explosive that technicians stowed behind the U-2 pilot's seat before flights into the Soviet Union. Each pilot was told that in an emergency, it was his "duty to ensure the destruction of the aircraft and its equipment to the greatest extent possible." If he had to abandon his plane over hostile territory, he must set off the bomb before using his ejection seat and parachute. After the first switch (ARM) was flipped, the circuits were activated;

after the second (DESTRUCT) was flipped, the pilot would have seventy seconds to bail out before the bomb exploded, or so he was told.

Flying over hostile terrain with a bomb behind the seat would have unnerved anyone. Powers knew that despite safeguards, a spark might ignite an explosion in midair. And from the CIA's "exhortations" to kill themselves if captured, the U-2 pilots knew that the Agency had an interest in ensuring that no flier emerged from a mishap alive: dead pilots told no tales. Some of the men wondered whether the bomb had actually been rigged with a sixty-second delay—or fifty seconds, or ten. Some suspected there was no delay at all: that way, once they flipped the second switch, the bomb would obliterate not only the equipment but them too.

Fliers were invited to supervise the testing of the explosive device before each mission by technicians they knew and liked. But no one could be sure what would really happen until someone actually set off the bomb in midair. "If *my* plane goes down, *I'm* not going to pull the switch," cried one pilot. "I'm *jumping!*"

●

By 5:20 A.M., the Sunday morning sun had been beating down from over the Hindu Kush Mountains for over an hour. With a package of Kents in his pocket, Powers was strapped into the scorching cockpit of Number 360. To keep the U-2 from being traced to the U.S. government, the plane's black skin and the pilot's silver suit were both unmarked. Powers's helmet bore only the number 29.

The CIA had ordered U-2 pilots to strip themselves of personal identification before making their flights. But some wanted to make sure that if they survived a downing in Russia the crash would be publicized and diplomatic efforts made to win their freedom. Like other pilots, Powers broke the rule this morning: in his wallet were two documents authorizing him to use U.S. Air Force facilities, a Social Security card, an American driver's license and a picture of himself dining with his wife in a nightclub. The Soviets later claimed that Powers also carried some "well-thumbed-over erotic literature."

Six o'clock, the assigned moment of takeoff, came and went. The CIA men at Peshawar were evidently waiting for final approval from Washington. Poised on the runway in the open sun, Number 360 was hot to the touch. One of the men stripped off his shirt and held it over the cockpit to shield Powers from the rays, but this did not much help.

Inside the cockpit, sweat rolled down the pilot's face and drenched the long underwear he wore underneath his flight suit. Sealed inside his suit and helmet, he could not wipe his brow.

Six-twenty: still no word. By now Powers was convinced that his mission would be canceled. He could not wait to peel off his water-logged flight suit and leap into a shower.

Then at 6:26 the signal came. The shirt was pulled from his cockpit. He locked his plastic canopy from the inside. The ladder was pulled from his plane.

•

"I knew that flying over the Soviet Union without permission was spying," Francis Gary Powers said much later. "I *knew* that it was. But I really didn't think that in the true sense of the word spy I ever considered myself a spy. I was a pilot flying an airplane and it just so happened that *where* I was flying made what I was doing spying."

His wife called him Gary, but almost everyone else he knew called him Frank. His head was slightly large for the stocky, muscled frame of five-foot-nine and 165 pounds. The brown wavy hair was clipped short: a caricaturist might have noticed that the hairline had the same contour as the overhead silhouette of a U-2's wingspan. When he spoke, the sound came not from his diaphragm but higher in the torso, which gave his voice the languid quality of a Perry Como. His accent did not betray his Appalachian origins, except on words like talk ("towk") and poison ("pawson").

Powers was modest, polite, with a fierce temper usually under control. Had they met, President Eisenhower would probably have thought him a fine young man. But the leader of a country that professed not to stoop to Soviet-style practices like espionage rarely had meetings with American spies—even incidental spies like Frank Powers. The President and top command of the CIA were as remote to the U-2 pilots as the pilots were to them. Some of the fliers knew even Richard Bissell only as "Mr. B."

Powers identified less with the world of his father, a struggling old miner and cobbler, than with the white-collar strivers who were the American heroes of the 1950s. He admired Eisenhower and considered himself a Republican but, like many military men, did not vote. He had once hoped to become a commercial pilot for the high wages, professional camaraderie and the chance to stay aloft but, when his first

Air Force tour ended, discovered that he was over the maximum age for airline trainees.

Had he not joined the U-2 program, he might have applied for Project Mercury: his age, weight, height, looks and background were roughly correct for an astronaut. In April 1959, when he read in *Stars and Stripes* of the unveiling of the first spacemen, he was jealous and thought, *How exciting it would be to be the first man to land on the moon.*

Powers joked and caroused with fellow U-2 pilots but never quite succeeded in shedding the aura of the solitary man. "A dear, sweet man—somewhat retiring," said a colleague's wife. "Outstanding among the pilots for calmness under pressure," said an Air Force flight surgeon. "A naturally pliable type who has a tendency to go through life wanting to satisfy people," said an Air Force study based on who knows what evidence. And "possibly counterphobic"—inclined to prove himself by taking on dangerous missions demanding high courage.

●

He was born two months before the Crash of 1929 in the coal country of Burdine, Kentucky, a region without electricity or telephones or through roads. One of his earliest duties was to walk to a company store each day to find mining work for his father, who had dropped out of school in the fifth grade. Oliver Powers wanted Francis to become a doctor: he had never seen a doctor who had to fight for a living.

But the son had other ideas. The sound of World War Two bombers sent him running to windows, and he searched for books on planes and pilots. At thirteen, after his first flight in a two-seater at a fair, his knees shook with excitement.

Oliver packed him off to Milligan College, a church school in Tennessee, where he waited on tables and sat stone-faced through premedical courses. Only in his junior year did he tell his angry father that he would never be a doctor. Were the next part of the story up to a screenwriter, he might have gone to his nearest Air Force recruiter and sailed into the wild blue yonder. Instead, being Powers, he stuck it out until graduation and spent the summer of 1950 as a lifeguard near Pound, Virginia, where his father had opened a shoe repair store.

In June 1950, North Koreans crossed the thirty-eighth parallel. As Powers later recalled, "I was looking forward to going over, because I wanted to—what do you say?—try yourself in combat. I had never done this and I wanted to see how I would react emotionally—in a good cause, of course." After basic Air Force training, he was schooled in flying and photography in Mississippi. Flying his own plane brought him "the satisfaction of total responsibility, of being dependent solely upon yourself. . . . I was in full control."

Appendicitis delayed his departure for Korea. By the time he recovered, the war was over. As a second lieutenant, he was assigned to a strategic fighter squadron at Turner Air Force Base near Albany, Georgia, to test F-84s. He was taught to load atomic weapons into aircraft and given a target behind the Iron Curtain in expectation of the day that a President of the United States would be compelled to press the Button.

In August 1953, at the base cafeteria, he noticed a nineteen-year-old brunette and told the night supervisor he would "sure like" to meet her. She said, "That shouldn't be very difficult. That's my daughter, Barbara Gay."

•

Barbara Gay Moore, clerk-typist for the Marines and recent graduate of Cleone Morton's Business College for Girls, was as smitten with the Air Force man as he was with her. There was a strong physical attraction. Soon they were engaged. The impetuous and histrionic manner with which Barbara faced life was almost the opposite of her husband's. She resented his frequent departures for places like London and Tokyo. They broke their engagement half a dozen times; once Barbara hurled her ring into a river. But like more than one couple in history, they decided that marriage might solve their problems. In April 1955, when they wed, the new bride bit her husband on the neck: "Now don't you keep flying away from me!"

At Thomasville, Georgia (where Eisenhower often shot quail with Treasury Secretary George Humphrey), the couple spent their wedding night. "It sure made me forget all the apprehensions I had previously entertained about Gary's line of duty," Barbara later wrote. "Lordy, but how that handsome Ridge Runner of mine could make love!"

As an Air Force pilot at Turner, Powers was considered one of the best gunners in his wing. Four hundred dollars a month was more money than he had ever earned. The newlyweds went to Florida to sunbathe and waterski. Still he felt he "hadn't really proved" himself.

In January 1956, he and other pilots were approached about a civilian job offer. This was strange because the Air Force did not normally approach its own men about such jobs, and stranger yet because the meeting with the mystery employer was scheduled off the base and at night.

Curious, he drove as instructed to the Radium Springs Motel, knocked on Cottage One and called out his name. A man opened the door and identified himself as "William Collins": "I'm afraid there's not very much I can tell you. You and several other pilots have been picked to be part of an organization to carry out a special mission. It will be risky but patriotic." The mission would pay more money but would take him abroad for eighteen months without his wife.

Barbara reasoned that the job might help them set a down payment on a house. Back he drove to the Radium Springs, where Collins revealed that he was with the CIA and that for $2,500 per month, Powers would fly a new plane that rose higher than any before: "Your main mission will be to fly over Russia."

By Powers's later account, as he listened to Collins speak, he felt "very proud of my country for having the guts to do this because I had felt—and a lot of people had felt—that we had not been responding the way we should have to threats from the Communist nations, such as Korea and so forth." He told the CIA man, "I'm in! I wouldn't miss it for the world. All my life I've wanted to do something like this!"

●

Soaring on his own over the Soviet Union filled him with a spirit of achievement and purpose he had never known: "It was thrilling to know that you were doing something no one had ever done—just a very few people who flew this particular airplane. Each flight broke an altitude record."

As ordered, he told Barbara that he was stationed in Athens, not Adana, and did not say what he was doing overseas. She suspected he was running guns for revolutionaries. Late in 1956, at the Turkish base, his commander accosted him as he stumbled from his plane after a mission: "Your wife called the Washington number you gave her, Powers, to tell us she's on her way to Athens determined to see you."

Richard Bissell did not want her in the region, but she could not simply be ordered home. The CIA quietly placed her as a clerk-stenographer for an Air Force captain in Athens. There Powers revealed to her that he was actually based in Turkey; he flew in to see her once or twice a month. In the spring of 1957, anti-American rioters turned over cars and raped women on Athens streets: the CIA was evidently chary that Barbara might fall into a situation that would threaten the U-2 program's cover. She was slipped into a new job at Wheelus Air Force Base in Tripoli.

From Athens, her former superior wrote that he had fallen in love with her: there was not much hope for a man "who is away most of the time, working at a job he won't even tell you about." She was saddled with "an ungrateful, self-centered husband who fails to realize that *you* are the one who is getting the short end of the stick!"

Powers arrived in Tripoli by surprise. As he later recalled, his arrival hastened the departure of a man in Barbara's room. Powers noted that she was trying to conceal a letter sticking out of her handbag. She grabbed the letter, fled to another room, slammed and locked the door behind her. Powers kicked it down and took the letter, a marriage proposal from Barbara's former boss.

By the time he finished reading, the Air Police arrived to arrest him. The couple had to explain their behavior to base authorities. Upbraided for his temper, Powers was told that if he had to argue with his wife, they should do it off base. Later Barbara explained that the billet-doux had surprised her: she had only been a "listening ear" for her boss's marital problems. He wanted to believe her. They decided to try to save their marriage.

Barbara became pregnant and miscarried at her mother's home in Milledgeville, Georgia. She was incensed about her husband's absence during the ordeal and puzzled by his continued access to Air Force planes while presenting himself to friends as a civilian pilot. When they asked what he was really doing, she said, "He's making weather reconnaissance flights over Outer Slobbovia when he isn't making mad love to the fifty-year-old daughter of a naked Arab chieftain."

Complaining about the months away from home, U-2 pilots were threatening not to renew their contracts in October 1957. The CIA reluctantly invited the families to Turkey. Recalling movies rendering Istanbul as the "spy center of the world," Barbara was delighted. She did not realize that Adana was not Istanbul. She was indignant about their sand-and-mud flat and about having to carry a pistol at night. For the first time, Powers told her that he was making reconnaissance flights vital to national security.

"Are they dangerous?"

"Not with the kind of equipment we have, honey. And remember, they pay us damned good salaries!" He was saving money in hopes of acquiring a business, perhaps a service station. The couple toured cities they had only read about: Paris, Naples—and Beirut, which they fled as U.S. Marines came ashore on President Eisenhower's order in 1958. The pilot paid $12,000 for a gleaming gray Mercedes convertible.

In the fall of 1959, concerned about security, the CIA moved the U-2 families from houses and flats in town back onto the base, where they lived in twenty-two identical trailers along a black asphalt road. Suburban gardens and manicured lawns were installed on the Turkish plain. The unit hired a butler, a gardener and two maids.

As Powers later recalled, he told his wife that she was drinking too much. At a party in March 1960, someone spun her around too quickly while dancing and she fell and broke her leg. On May 1, 1960, as his U-2 moved down the Peshawar runway, Barbara was not far from his mind: "I worried not only about her excessive drinking but also about what she was apt to do when left alone."

•

He jerked the throttle. The engine screamed and the plane shot into the unforgettable parabola so steep that early U-2 pilots feared that their planes would overturn. The Khyber Pass and the silver peaks of the Hindu Kush fell beneath him. To his east was China in the full brilliance of dawn; to the west, Afghanistan, Iran and the Middle East were emerging from the night.

In no time, he was soaring over 60,000 feet. Up here, without a pressurized flight suit or cockpit, blood would boil and intestines burst. Outside the temperature had plunged 160 degrees. His underwear was still soaked but now he shivered. By his later account, he switched on the autopilot and wrote in his flight log, "Delayed one-half hour."

Sixty minutes into his mission, he neared the air frontier of the Soviet Union. The radio could not be used to let colleagues in Pakistan know: that could alert the Russians. Instead he broadcast two clicks. Peshawar sent back a single click: proceed as planned.

Powers later noted that "there was no abrupt change in topogra-

phy, yet the moment you crossed the border, you sensed the difference. . . . Knowing there were people who would shoot you down if
they could created a strange tension. . . . I wondered how the Russians
felt, knowing I was up here, unable to do anything about it. . . . I could
imagine their frustration and rage."

•

Nikita Khrushchev was asleep. In the dark, workers in Moscow's
Red Square were tacking up bunting and moving bleachers in preparation for the national celebration of May Day, the most venerated
Soviet holiday after the October anniversary of the Russian Revolution. Since his days as a junior member of Stalin's entourage in the
1930s, Khrushchev had loved the pageantry of the workers' jubilee:
unlike more sedate members of the leadership, he whooped when new
rockets and tanks rolled through Red Square.

For weeks, Muscovites had been splashing fresh paint on wooden
houses and apartment blocks, unsealing double windows after eight
months of winter and scouring them with wadded-up copies of *Pravda*.
Tens of thousands of Soviets were streaming into Moscow for the great
day.

Khrushchev had ordered Party officials to eliminate some of the
usual military trappings from this parade: the thaw between East and
West since Camp David called for homage not only to military power
but peaceful coexistence. Floats, placards and uniforms were embla-
zoned with doves of peace. *Pravda* listed the Central Committee's slo-
gans for May Day 1960: PROLETARIANS OF ALL COUNTRIES, UNITE! . . .
MORE MINERAL FERTILIZERS FOR AGRICULTURE! . . . DEMAND THE
SPEEDIEST CONCLUSION OF A GERMAN PEACE TREATY! . . . STRIVE FOR A
COMPLETE END TO THE COLD WAR AND FURTHER RELAXATION OF IN-
TERNATIONAL TENSIONS!

In Khrushchev's bedroom, the telephone rang. As he later recalled,
at the other end of the line was his Defense Minister, Marshal Rodion
Malinovsky. An unidentified plane had crossed the Afghan frontier
into Soviet airspace. Both men knew who had sent the plane.

Khrushchev was furious: bad enough to invade Soviet airspace but
on a national holiday—and fifteen days before the Paris Summit! The
plane must be shot down.

This was easier said than done. Both men knew that for nearly four
years they had failed to strike the American intruder. But Malinovsky

said he had already given the order: "If our anti-aircraft units can just keep their eyes open and stop yawning long enough, I'm sure we'll knock the plane down."

●

Sealed inside his flight suit, a single soul over a ghostly and menacing land, Frank Powers gazed into the midnight blue stratosphere that only a small brotherhood of pilots knew. "Every cell, fluid, muscle of my body is acutely awake," wrote another flier. "Perception is enormously exaggerated. Black is white, white is whiter. Silence is more acute. . . . Time is now. Nothing but this experience is significant now. . . . I have the unshakable feeling that no matter what the instruments read, it will have no effect on the power that is making this ship fly. An independent, supernatural kind of power she has."

Weather below was worse than expected. A frosted eiderdown of clouds covered the Russian landscape. Dead ahead was one of Powers's targets—Tyuratam Cosmodrome, where *Sputnik* and other satellites had been boosted into space. The launch site was hidden by clouds, but the rest of the region was clear. He switched his cameras on and off.

He swept on past the Aral Sea over the long route north to Chelyabinsk. On his left were the ivory-topped Urals, the ancient divider of Europe from Asia. The lowlands on either side of the mountains were green. He relaxed as the skies cleared and he glimpsed the magnificent Russian spring.

At this instant, by his later recollection, the plane pitched nose-up: the autopilot had conked out. He disengaged it, flew the plane manually for a few minutes and then re-engaged it. Soon it conked out again. As he later recalled, he tried once more and then turned it off for good. If he proceeded, he would have to fly the airplane manually.

This could be treacherous: without the autopilot, he would have to keep his wings level and govern the pitch of the airplane himself—all while watching his instruments, computing times, navigating and turning his switches on and off. If the nose pitched too high, airspeed would drop and the engine could flame out. A flameout might require him to plunge the plane to 30,000 feet to restart his engine. At that altitude, the Soviets could easily shoot him down.

Should he turn back? An hour before, the decision would have been automatic. But now he was roughly thirteen hundred miles inside

Russia. He decided to "go on and accomplish what I had set out to do."

•

Next target was Sverdlovsk, where Bolsheviks had murdered Czar Nicholas II and his family in 1918; the tenth largest Soviet city was a center of transportation, mining and heavy industry. In July 1959, on his visit to the Soviet Union, Richard Nixon was touring a factory in Sverdlovsk when he saw a policeman try to stop a woman from applauding. Nixon seized the policeman and shook him as hard as he could: "When the people are happy and want to express themselves, you leave them alone!"

Meanwhile, Pat Nixon and Milton Eisenhower had called on a Sverdlovsk family who said they had never seen Americans before. The wary father was coaxed to bring out his accordion and serenade the guests with Russian folk songs. By the end of the visit, he tearfully gave the President's youngest brother a bear hug. The scene reminded Eisenhower of the moment in *War and Peace* in which the Russian soldier lifts his gun, looks into the doomed Frenchman's eyes and realizes how absurd human conflicts are.

Sverdlovsk was defended by the Soviet Union's new SA-2 Guideline missiles. As Powers later said, he switched on cameras and other equipment, and turned ninety degrees, toward the southwestern edge of the city. He later recalled marking the location on his map and the speed, altitude and time in his logbook.

Now he was more than halfway into his mission. In Washington, it was 1:53 on Sunday morning. Moscow time was 8:53 A.M.

•

The U-2 had set off alarms all over the southern Soviet Union. According to *Pravda* later, the Sverdlovsk anti-aircraft unit flinched and ran to battle stations: "The fighting men in charge of the grim machinery for defending our airspace were ready in an instant." The "pirate plane" was flying at such height that the blips on the radar screen were barely visible.

A target mark was fixed on the aircraft. "Time seems to stand still, so slowly do the seconds before the execution of the battle task flow." In *Pravda*'s rendering, the commander now gave his order: *"Destroy the enemy plane!"*

•

As Powers later recalled, he heard a dull "thump." The plane convulsed and an orange flash lit the cockpit and sky. Knocked back in his seat, he cried, *"My God, I've had it now!"*

Had he been flying in the West, he might have snapped on radio and called out the distress sign corrupted from the French: *"M'aidez!"* But over thirteen hundred miles inside a hostile country, there was no one to ask for help. By his later account, he seized the throttle with his left hand while keeping his right on the steering wheel. The aircraft's nose swung down; when he pulled on the wheel, he found that the plane had gone out of control.

A violent movement shook the plane and flung him about the cockpit. Wings snapped off. With its nose to the heavens, the mangled fuselage spun toward earth.

The destructor switches. As he later recalled, he reached for them and then changed his mind: first he must position himself to eject. Like other pilots, Powers was leery of ejection seats. Activated, they shot pilots through the plastic canopy like human cannonballs. Sometimes men were killed by accidental ejections. Others lost limbs and faces, torn off by the rim of the cockpit or the lethal wall of air. Knowing this, some chose to ride their planes to the ground and certain death.

Powers was so sprawled that he feared that during ejection, his legs might be sheared off by the metal canopy rails overhead. Nevertheless, as he later recalled, he forced both heels into the stirrups of his seat. But he could not force his shoulders back. He later said he was on the edge of panic when he realized that he could simply climb out of the cockpit. He reached up and unfastened the canopy; it sailed into space.

He later testified that he was planning to throw the destructor switches when centrifugal force threw him halfway out of the cockpit. His face plate frosted over. Still tied to the plane by oxygen hoses, by his account, he tried to climb back into the cockpit to set off the destruction device but the G-force, the gravitational force, was overpowering. Unable to thrust his hand under the windscreen to reach the switches, he later recalled thinking, *I've just got to try to save myself now.* Kicking and squirming, he must have broken the hoses because suddenly he was free.

The orange-and-white parachute bloomed overhead. He flicked off his face plate and fresh air blasted his lungs. All was silent and cold as fragments of his plane fell past him. Looking down, he saw green hills, a lake, roads and buildings, It occurred to him that with so much vacant Soviet territory, why did he have to fall here? It looked almost like Virginia—as if by wishing, he could make it so. He shed his gloves, reached into his pocket and tore up a map marked with alternate routes back to Pakistan and Turkey; the pieces fluttered to the ground.

Now the silver dollar: what better emblem of a well-paid capitalist pilot? He unscrewed the tiny loop, tossed away the two halves of the coin and held the poison pin between thumb and forefinger. He knew that when an American plane crashed in Armenia two years earlier, local Russians had almost lynched one of the crewmen from a telephone pole. He slipped the pin into his pocket, just in case.

He tried to drift toward trees for camouflage, but the winds brought him back toward the lake. If his chute tangled and he landed there, weighed down by his heavy seat pack, he might drown. Now he swung above a new-plowed field where one farmer was riding a tractor, another piling brush. A new scare—electric power lines! Plunging fast now, he dropped fatally close to the wires as the earth rushed up to greet him and his head slammed hard against the denied territory of the Soviet Union.

●

Pravda later reported that inside the anti-aircraft unit, the men shouted, *"Target destroyed!"*

When the all-clear siren sounded, there were bear hugs. In *Pravda*'s version, someone cried, "The bandit got what he deserved! That will be the fate of anyone who tries from now on to penetrate the clear Soviet sky!" The men were described gathering around a radio and listening to the distant strains of an orchestra in Red Square. Soon the May Day parade would begin.

●

As Powers later recalled, his ears were ringing, his head pulsing as he looked up at the puzzled Soviet farmer helping him to his feet. The other farmer folded the parachute. Two motorists stopped and helped the farmers pull off the pilot's helmet and parachute harness. About fifty other gaping Soviets crowded around and shouted questions in Russian. The pilot shook his head. They took away his pistol and pushed him into the front seat of the car between the motorists.

As they bounced down the rutted road, his heart pounding, the

Russians examined his pistol. With a tremor, he realized that it bore the letters "U.S.A." One of the Russians traced the letters in the dust on the dashboard and Powers glumly nodded. The Russians perked up.

"I was completely unprepared," Powers said years later. "I presumed that once it was known I was missing, a cover story would be issued. Unfortunately no one had ever bothered to inform us pilots what it would be." He decided to tell his captors that he had been flying a weather plane from Pakistan to Turkey when his compass failed and he had accidentally flown the wrong way. Thirteen hundred miles inside Russia, he doubted that they would believe it.

Allen Dulles later said that the U-2 pilots had been told, if captured, to "delay as long as possible the revelation of damaging information." Each pilot should tell the truth about "those matters which were obviously within the knowledge of his captors as a result of what fell into their hands." But Powers later insisted that the possibility of an accident was never seriously raised in his briefings. A few months before this flight, he had asked, "What if something happens and one of us goes down over Russia? That's an awfully big country and it could be a hell of a long walk to a border. . . . Exactly how much should he tell?"

By his account, the intelligence officer replied: "You may as well tell them everything, because they're going to get it out of you anyway."

Powers had crashed on a state farm. The car pulled up at its headquarters, where he was strip-searched. No one spoke English. People brought in remnants of his plane, including a reel of seventy-millimeter film. After frenzied telephone calls, two soldiers drove him to the center of Sverdlovsk. Streets were filled with crowds and red flags and banners. Some holiday was being celebrated. Only then did Powers realize the date on which he had dropped uninvited into the Soviet Union.

•

In Red Square, row after row after row of soldiers, students, farmers, athletes, drummers, dancers marched past the frieze of Soviet leaders standing atop the red porphyry temple still known in 1960 as the Lenin-Stalin Tomb. "The sky was sunny and beautiful," observed Khrushchev, standing at center stage. "The mood of the working people was joyous."

The Soviet novelist and journalist Ilya Ehrenburg had written in *Pravda* this morning that "May 1960 could become a very great May." Eisenhower, Khrushchev, de Gaulle and Macmillan would soon go to Paris. "Four men with great power and therefore great responsibility will meet. The fate of peoples will depend on what they decide."

As bands played martial music, marchers, rockets and an atomic cannon moved through the square. Great papier-mâché doves moved down the parade route while hundreds of the real thing fluttered overhead, followed by huge solemn portraits of Khrushchev and banners emblazoned with PEACE in Russian, English and Chinese. Atop the mausoleum, Khrushchev cheered and ruffled the hair of boys and girls invited, as in Stalin days, to view the parade with their leader.

Pushing through the crowd atop the tomb was Marshal S. S. Biryuzov, chief commander of Soviet anti-aircraft forces. Perceptive reporters and diplomats suspected that something was amiss because the Marshal was not wearing his dress uniform. He spoke into Khrushchev's ear: the intruder plane had been downed. The pilot had been captured alive and was being questioned. Khrushchev studied a map and congratulated the Marshal on "this wonderful news."

Khrushchev's smile may have taxed his considerable dramatic skills, for this "wonderful news" was unlikely to help him. Despite Western references to the "absolute ruler of the Soviet Union," Khrushchev had actually been almost overthrown in 1957. He had exiled the chief conspirators and tried to surround himself with loyalists, but potential rivals remained, waiting for an opportunity. Now, a fortnight before the Summit he had sought for years, this pirate plane. "As far as we were concerned," he later said, "this sort of espionage was war—war waged by other means." And on *May Day,* no less!

Had the plane not been downed, it might have been possible to confine the information to a relatively small number within the Soviet hierarchy. But Khrushchev knew that it would be almost impossible to conceal American wreckage and a live pilot, even if he wished. Once word spread through the Party, the Army and the KGB, potential foes might seize the violation as evidence of how foolish Khrushchev had been, infatuated with Eisenhower and an Uncle Sam now revealed to be as warlike as ever. The "wonderful news," if not deftly managed, could throw Khrushchev into another struggle for his political life.

●

"Are you an American?"

Frank Powers was startled to hear the first English words he had heard since leaving Peshawar. Few in the crowded room in Sverdlovsk believed his alibi that he had strayed accidentally over the Soviet border. Citizens brought in more items from his plane—a map marked with the route from Pakistan to Norway, the seat pack with its rubles, gold coins, watches, rings and his wallet. His captors pulled out the card that showed him to be a civilian employee of the U.S. Air Force and shouted, "Air Force! Air Force! Air Force! Air Force!" He declared that he was a civilian pilot employed by the CIA.

More telephone calls. Four Russians took him in a limousine to an airfield and rushed him aboard a passenger jet, where they sat in a sealed-off forward compartment. Where were they flying? "Moscow." He was certain that sooner or later he would be executed.

•

Sunlight raced around the globe to bring morning to the Eastern Seaboard of the United States. At the Waldorf-Astoria in New York, Allen Dulles was taking Sunday breakfast with 2,500 members of the New York Police Department's St. George Association to accept their Golden Rule Award for "distinguished government service and dedication to Christian ideals."

As the policemen finished their coffee and sweet rolls, Dulles accepted his prize and warned the audience that Khrushchev would prefer, if possible, to conquer the world by subversion and economic pressure: "He doesn't want to acquire a world in ruins if he can take it intact."

Dulles did not know yet that the U-2 was down, but his people in Washington did. Professional eavesdroppers of the National Security Agency had followed the Powers plane as it soared up the Urals; from listening posts they heard the babble of frantic Soviet officers demanding its interception. CIA men at Bodö airfield in Norway flashed word to Washington that the plane was overdue.

•

Shortly after noon, Hugh Cumming returned from church to his home on Q Street in Georgetown. A white-haired Virginian, son of Warren Harding's Surgeon General, Cumming ran the State Department's Bureau of Intelligence and Research, its chief day-to-day link with the CIA.

A housemaid told him that someone had been calling with an urgent message. Cumming recognized the caller as his CIA contact for the U-2 operation. He dialed the number and heard, *"Our boy isn't there. We don't know what happened to him."*

●

A CIA man also called Thomas Gates, Secretary of Defense: the Pentagon gave the U-2 logistical support and was prime consumer of what the black planes brought back from Russia. Someone also called Hugh Dryden, number-two man at NASA. A scientist and lay Methodist preacher, Dryden had been the head of NASA's predecessor agency in 1956 when Richard Bissell came looking for a cover for the U-2 project. Dryden had agreed. His agency had nothing to do with actual U-2 operations, but the CIA disguised its espionage runs by flying NASA devices on bona fide weather research missions outside the Iron Curtain.

Dryden was anxious about the missing U-2. Unlike its predecessor, NASA had an international charter, and its chief purpose was exploring outer space. This meant obtaining other nations' consent to place ground stations and personnel on their territory. If NASA was exposed as a CIA front, it would threaten the American manned space flight program before it had a chance to begin.

●

In Moscow, the gray stone facade of Lubyanka Prison was barely visible in the moonlight. Before the Revolution, the six-story building had housed the All-Russian Insurance Company. During the Great Purge of the 1930s, its stone cells rang with the cries of the tortured and the doomed. Every day crews had passed through to cleanse blood from the walls and ceilings.

Now these rituals of the Soviet police state were mainly performed elsewhere. In 1960, the prison served as KGB headquarters and jail for political prisoners.

Here Powers was dressed in an overlarge wool double-breasted suit and seated at the end of a long table lined with military and intelligence men. What was his name? Nationality? Rank? Why had he flown into Russia?

By his later account, he improvised. If the Russians asked him something he was sure they already knew, like his route, or something they might discover, like his commander's name, he would tell them.

Establishing his credibility might permit lies about other topics. He presented himself as an airplane jockey paid merely to fly over a given route and throw the switches on and off.

The poison pin had been confiscated and put in a briefcase. While being questioned, Powers noticed that someone had taken the satchel out of the room. His situation was dire enough without adding a murder. He told his captors about the pin; someone ran off to find it. Later the Russians used it to inject a dog, which died within ninety seconds.

After three hours of interrogation, guards took the prisoner to his cell and slammed the steel-and-oak door behind him. A naked light bulb burned overhead; he could not sleep. So far he had survived the ordeal but, as he later recalled, one line of questioning had thrown him slightly off-balance: "Why was this flight flown so close to the Summit meeting? *Was this a deliberate attempt to sabotage the talks?*"

•

In Washington, it was Sunday afternoon. Richard Bissell and his wife had spent the early part of the weekend away from their home near the Washington Cathedral. Allen Dulles had filled in for his subordinate on Saturday by sending the go-ahead signal to Peshawar. Now that Bissell was back in town, he went straight to the office building on the north side of H Street that housed the U-2 project office behind a false front. Two blocks away was the White House; across the street was the Metropolitan Club, where Bissell sometimes lunched. As he walked through the door, he saw the grim face of the colonel who served as his Air Force liaison: Number 360 had not made it to Norway. "You'd better get in there fast."

Bissell hauled his six-foot-three-inch frame onto the elevator (colleagues thought he resembled a great stork) and rushed into the secret office, which CIA men called "the Bissell Center." As Bissell later recalled, Hugh Cumming, intelligence and technical experts were examining a large wall map of the Soviet Union: "There was a lot of turmoil about cranking up the cover story." Silence now might raise suspicions later, so a story must be issued.

"We were quite prepared to say, if the Russians showed photographs of it, either that it wasn't the U-2 or that they had taken the plane and moved it," Bissell later noted. "And we felt that it would be very difficult for them to disprove that. So the whole point of the story was to explain what had happened—that a pilot had inadvertently crossed the border and been shot down and landed inside, and that they had moved the wreckage."

This presupposed a dead pilot.

They pulled out a draft written years ago in anticipation of this day. It stated that a NASA U-2 weather plane had left Turkey on a high-altitude mission and accidentally overflown Pakistan without permission after the pilot had reported mechanical problems by radio.

Cumming asked them to delete mention of Pakistan, whose government was less intimate with the United States and more vulnerable to Soviet military and political retaliation than Turkey—even though the Turkish government was in danger of being toppled. All agreed, but this required contrivance of a new fictional flight plan. The technicians used slide rules, calipers and maps to work out a new cover story within the limits of information about the U-2's performance that was publicly known. They drew a new triangular flight plan that skirted the Soviet frontier but remained entirely within the boundaries of Turkey.

•

"High Tower—*pull!*" A clay pigeon sailed up over the skeet shooting range at Camp David. The President raised his shotgun and fired.

For Eisenhower, this had been a disappointing Sunday. He had planned on early church and eighteen holes of golf, but when he opened his eyes this morning, rain was pounding the roof of Aspen Lodge, the Presidential cottage. "Today the President wanted to play golf very badly," his secretary Ann Whitman wrote on a similar occasion. "He woke to a cold and drizzly rain. He peered out at the sky frequently during the morning and finally, after another excursion to the porch, announced, 'Sometimes I feel so sorry for myself I could cry!' "

After breakfast, the President took his granddaughter Mary Jean and George Allen to the Camp David bowling alley, where he had taken Khrushchev during their talks in hopes of breaking the tension between them.

When the rain stopped in midmorning, Eisenhower and Allen drove to Gettysburg, but the golf course was soggy and they returned within an hour. The President and First Lady had lunch and posed for a group portrait with the Camp David staff. While Sergeant Moaney in white jacket stood by, Eisenhower and Allen hit some golf balls and then walked over to the skeet shooting range.

•

Andrew Goodpaster was spending Sunday with his family in Alexandria when the CIA man called. He picked up his special telephone. The Army Signal Corps put him through to the President at Camp David and he said, "One of our reconnaissance planes on a scheduled flight is overdue and possibly lost"—the news Eisenhower had feared since the start of the U-2 program.

Goodpaster recalled the President's old forecast of what would happen if a U-2 crashed in Russia and predicted that "the winds are going to blow."

"You're probably right," came the reply. The President boarded his helicopter. As it flew toward the White House, he looked down on the farms and tract houses of the Maryland countryside. He had once told his aides that "if one of these planes is shot down, this thing is going to be on my head. I'm going to catch hell. The world will be in a mess."

It would be embarrassing for the United States to rebut Russian charges of aerial espionage but he had the satisfaction of knowing that his government could plausibly deny that the U-2 pilot had deliberately violated Soviet airspace: the CIA and Joint Chiefs had given that assurance that it would be "impossible" for the Soviets to capture a live pilot.

The chopper landed on the South Grounds at 4:26 P.M. Eisenhower walked through the Diplomatic Entrance into the White House. At the same hour, in his prison cell in Moscow, Francis Gary Powers fell asleep for the night.

★

2

Eisenhower's Dilemma

J OHN EISENHOWER WALKED into Andrew Goodpaster's Spartan office in the West Wing. It was Monday morning, the second of May. The office was small but had the advantage of being just a few steps from the President's. Adorning the wall was the formal portrait of Eisenhower that hung in embassies and post offices, but not the usual parchment Presidential commission, for officially Goodpaster was not a Presidential appointee but a Brigadier General attached to the White House.

It might have been trying for the President's son to work for the man the President regarded almost as a son, but the two men managed their relations with tact and civility. Before John moved his family away from Washington publicity to Gettysburg in June 1959, the same White House car had picked up both men at their Alexandria homes. During the morning ride across the Potomac, the two men talked of the day's business—or doubletalked, if state secrets had to be kept from the driver's ears.

When John joined the White House in 1958, he had asked Goodpaster to give him a sphere of responsibility in which he could move with independence. Goodpaster declined—"either for my own education or in order for him to keep his hand in on all issues," as John recalled. Goodpaster did keep his deputy informed. John remembered attending "a hell of a New Year's party the night of December 31, 1958. The next morning, when I had a head the size of a pumpkin, Andy called me and told me that Batista had fallen." The Castro epoch in Cuba had begun. "I thanked him profusely."

The President sometimes used his son as a sounding board. Two weeks before Hiroshima, he had confided in him the secret of the atomic bomb. During a visit to John's house in Alexandria in the fall of 1957, while Mamie played with their grandchildren, the President took him aside and said, "We're making flights now over the Soviet Union to get material."

The next year, as the President's new assistant staff secretary, John went to the CIA for a briefing by Richard Bissell on the U-2: "He showed me all the pictures. . . . He told me about the techniques, which were a real eye-opener, and the fact that the wings were so fragile that you had to have special supports for them once the planes were on the ground."

In the spring of 1960, John had sat in the Oval Office with the President and Goodpaster when the CIA pleaded for more U-2 flights into Russia. More than once, he and Goodpaster had heard Allen Dulles assure the President that if the Soviets ever downed a plane, no pilot would escape alive. This morning, therefore, when Goodpaster told John that a U-2 had been lost, the two men lamented the pilot's death. As John later recalled, "There was not *one scintilla* of doubt in our minds that he was dead."

Goodpaster and his deputy felt sorry for the pilot's family but for these two Army men, there were worse fates than dying in the service of the United States. In 1952, when John said good-bye to his father before leaving to fight in Korea, there were rumors that Chinese and North Korean patrols were plotting to capture John and use the famous prisoner to blackmail the United States. His father said, "If you're captured, I suppose I would just have to drop out of the Presidential race."

John assured his father that he would never be captured alive. He later said, "Had I ever found myself surrounded by Chinese or North Koreans, I had every intention of keeping my promise and using my .45-caliber pistol, taking—I hoped—some of them with me."

•

The President disliked it when staff members tiptoed through the Oval Office door and waited at the threshold. Even the most reserved aides learned to walk in briskly and maintain stride until they reached his desk. At 10:24 A.M., Eisenhower looked up and saw Goodpaster, whose face looked to him like "an etching of bad news." The aide said, "Mr. President, I have received word from the CIA that the U-2 reconnaissance plane I mentioned yesterday is still missing. . . . With the amount of fuel he has on board, there is not a chance of his being aloft."

Eisenhower regretted the presumed death of an American. It was cruel, but he had long ago consoled himself that the U-2 pilots were flying "with their eyes wide open." ("What the hell," a more flippant White House aide said later. "They were paying 'em thirty grand!") On Sunday, Goodpaster had promised that he would "stay in touch with CIA" and "take a look at our cover plan." Since then, a CIA man had brought over the agreed-upon draft of the cover story. The President later recalled having doubts, but he read the document, nodded assent and handed it back to Goodpaster.

•

Robert Amory of the CIA often timed his morning drive to listen to *The CBS World News Roundup* on his car radio. He knew Allen Dulles would be listening to that. CIA headquarters in 1960 was a cluster of manila and gray Georgian buildings up the hill from the State Department. The President had laid the cornerstone for the massive new white complex across the river at Langley, Virginia, but the new building would not be ready for another year. When Amory reached his office, he ran his eyes over a superpriority message on the U-2 and said, "One of our machines is down."

Richard Bissell walked in hopping mad. Before the Powers mission, to preserve secrecy, he had demanded that incoming intelligence on Soviet air defense be sent directly to him. But on Sunday, when tracking stations notified the National Security Agency in Baltimore that the Russians were shooting at an enemy plane, someone erred and disobeyed Bissell's command. An excited technician at NSA had evidently sent the news to nerve centers at the FBI, State Department, Army, Navy, Air Force and CIA.

"I thought I'd shut this thing down!" shouted Bissell. NSA's mistake could make the cover story harder to sell around Washington. When the government publicly announced that it did not know the whereabouts of its stray weather plane, what if someone leaked the fact that NSA had traced it thirteen hundred miles into Russia?

That could cause problems—but not dire ones, so long as the U-2 pilot was dead. In the Director's office, Bissell assured Allen Dulles and colleagues that it was "impossible" for the pilot to have survived the crash.

•

Just after dawn in Turkey, someone pounded on the door of Barbara Powers's house trailer. She dragged her leg with its plaster cast out of bed and hobbled to the door: "This had better be good."

A U-2 pilot told her that her husband was missing: "We have search planes out, but they haven't found him yet."

The base doctor injected her with a sedative. While she slept, the defiant U-2 pilots and their wives tried to forget their anxieties by throwing a party that lasted three days.

•

In Lubyanka Prison, Moscow, an old Russian woman woke up Frank Powers and set down a tin samovar and cup. He worried that the tea was laced with drugs, but drank it to soothe his arid mouth and throat. Guards locked him into a bathroom, where they watched his ablutions through a peephole.

After more interrogation, he was driven through Moscow. Riding in a limousine with six of his captors, Powers peered out at the Kremlin, Moscow University and a city transforming itself for President Eisenhower's visit in June. The Russians asked him friendly questions about his country. He wondered whether they might not allow him to survive after all: perhaps Khrushchev would take him to the Paris Summit and say, "Here, Ike, is something that belongs to you!"

But back in his cell, depression resumed. He considered himself a fool to think the Russians would believe his lies: once they found him out, they would surely put him to death.

•

Tuesday, the third of May. The President flew to Fort Benning, Georgia, for a long-planned six-hour demonstration of the U.S. Army's latest war machines. What went through his mind as he rode in a jeep and stared at a row of photoreconnaissance planes?

At the end of the pageant, Eisenhower gave a speech: "A day like this makes a man quite ready to call all those people mistaken—if not worse—who say that America has become soft and is not capable of defending herself."

While the President was at Benning, NASA handed out the cover story he had secretly approved:

> A NASA U-2 research airplane being flown in Turkey on a joint NASA-USAF Air Weather Service mission apparently went down in the Lake Van, Turkey, area at about 9:00 A.M. (3:00 A.M. E.D.T.), Sunday, May 1.
>
> During the flight in eastern Turkey, the pilot reported over the emergency frequency that he was experiencing oxygen difficulties. The flight originated in Adana with a mission to obtain data on clear air turbulence.
>
> A search is now underway in the Lake Van area. The pilot is an employee of Lockheed Aircraft under contract to NASA. The U-2 program was initiated by NASA in 1956 as a method of making high-altitude weather studies.

Near Pound, Virginia, two men from Washington walked into Oliver Powers's cobbler's shop and told him that his son was missing on a weather flight in Turkey: planes had been searching for three days without success.

•

Wednesday, the fourth of May. Reporters asked NASA for details about the missing "weather plane," but most editors yawned. The *Washington Post* ran a small item on the front page of early editions but dropped it to accommodate a headline about a Washington Senators game.

The President enjoyed a jovial breakfast with sixteen congressmen, signed a wheat agreement with India, saw staff members and drove out to Burning Tree Club in Maryland for eighteen holes. Three days after the U-2's disappearance, the Russians still had not complained. Eisenhower mused that Foster Dulles's prophecy might prove right, after all.

Other evidence suggested the same conclusion. Today's *Pravda* reported that the Soviet Air Force commander, Marshal Konstantin Vershinin, would arrive in Washington in ten days as scheduled for a tour of the United States. At the test ban talks in Geneva, the Russians had agreed to join the United States to explore new detection methods for small underground tests. Would Khrushchev have permitted such concessions if he was planning to disrupt relations over the U-2?

This reasoning made sense if one assumed, as some American officials did, that power in the Soviet Union was wholly centralized in the hands of Khrushchev and his close allies. Eisenhower and his advisers did not fully know that the Kremlin's silence, the failure to cancel Vershinin's trip and the Soviet move at Geneva were all merely holding actions. The internal debate on how to handle the U-2 had evidently been deferred until the fourth of May. In Moscow, at a secret one-day session in the gray building that some Westerners called "the Little Kremlin," members of the Central Committee of the Soviet Communist Party were wrangling over that question at this very moment.

•

For days, Khrushchev had been pondering his decision: should he sweep the U-2 under the rug or reveal it in a propaganda assault that would stir up Soviet and world opinion against the United States?

If he swept the matter under the rug, the Paris Summit and Eisenhower's trip to Russia might proceed. But this would give Khrushchev's enemies a powerful weapon. They would argue that Khrushchev had been so overwhelmed by Eisenhower that he was willing to tolerate even such a grave infraction during a period of supposedly improved relations. What else could they expect from a man who wished to cut the armed forces and take other "reckless" chances with Soviet security?

Dramatic revelation of the U-2 downing and a propaganda attack on the United States would satisfy Khrushchev's critics and would put the Americans on the defensive—especially in the Third World. But as a master propagandist and agitator of more than forty years, Khrushchev knew that once such a storm was started, it could be impossible to control. The period of good feeling which began at Camp David would surely be over. The indignation of Soviet outer circles and the Soviet people might endanger the Paris Summit and compel re-escalation of the Cold War.

Khrushchev was the man who had extolled the American President and peaceful coexistence as no Soviet leader had before. Casting Eisenhower and the Americans as villains now would be a grandiose, humiliating public confession of how wrong he had been. The Soviet people were bound to discover that the United States had repeatedly penetrated Soviet air defenses for four years. Why had Khrushchev allowed such assaults? Unlike the Chinese, the Russians did not set dunce caps on the heads of discredited leaders and send them through jeering mobs, but such confessions were no formula for political survival in the Soviet Union.

Members of the Central Committee talked through the day and into the night. The U-2 was not their only subject: a party reshuffling promoted men who, on the whole, were said to be less loyal to Khrushchev than their predecessors. By the end of the session, it was clear that the U-2 downing would have to be publicized. But how?

Khrushchev proposed a plan. Tomorrow the Supreme Soviet would convene in Moscow. He would inform the parliament's members that the United States had sent a spy plane into Soviet territory. He would reveal that the plane had been shot down, but *not* that the pilot had been captured alive.

As Khrushchev later recalled, "Our intention here was to confuse the government circles of the United States. As long as the Americans thought the pilot was dead, they would keep putting out the story that perhaps the plane had accidentally strayed off-course and been shot down in the mountains on the Soviet side of the border." Later Khrushchev would reveal that, in fact, the pilot was alive and that the Soviets had equipment proving that his mission had been espionage.

By managing the news, Khrushchev could thus present himself not as the timid victim of American spy flights but as the leader of the mighty forces which had defended the Soviet motherland by shooting down the intruder plane. By tricking the Americans into expanding upon their fable that the U-2 was a stray weather plane and then exposing it, he could put them on the defensive as obvious liars guilty of espionage. After that, he might magnanimously accept President Eisenhower's apology and fly into Paris on the heels of a propaganda victory.

That evening, Khrushchev attended a reception at the Czechoslovak Embassy. Sauntering over to a group of diplomats, he revealed that tomorrow at the opening session of the Supreme Soviet, he would have something "stupendous" to say.

●

Thursday morning, the fifth of May. During the workweek, Khrushchev liked to spend the night at his five-room flat in a Moscow apartment block near the Canadian Embassy that housed the elite. The living room was said to be adorned with a large photograph of the Kremlin, books on Lenin, Stalin, Marxism, capitalism, and Khrushchev's favorite hemlock rocking chair. A few minutes away, thirteen hundred Soviets were moving into the white chamber of the Great Kremlin Palace, where they sat down, conversed and scanned *Pravda* and *Izvestia.* Some wore vivid costumes of Uzbekistan and Kazakhstan. Television and newsreel cameramen crouched atop a catwalk.

Llewellyn Thompson, American Ambassador to the Soviet Union, sat in a prominent box at the right of the hall. During the May Day parade, when he saw the commotion as Khrushchev was told of the U-2 downing, he had turned to his wife Jane and said, "Jesus, I wonder what's happening now."

Lean, gray, modest, with sparkling blue eyes, Thompson was the image of a diplomat and a godfather to the improvement in American-Soviet relations. His wife said years later, "You wanted so much with all your heart and soul for there to be an understanding." The Thompsons were sometimes asked to Khrushchev's dacha thirty minutes outside Moscow, where the lord of the manor showed off his corn and horses and told chilling stories about the last days of Stalin. On one such weekend, Khrushchev's Deputy Premier Anastas Mikoyan said, "If Stalin could only see us now, with the American Ambassador here, he'd turn in his grave."

At the end of such visits, the Thompsons would rush back to Moscow, where the envoy hushed his wife as he scribbled out recollections of what Khrushchev had said. Harrison Salisbury of the *New York Times* felt that Thompson was, "in a curious way," closer to Khrushchev than even Khrushchev's colleagues on the Presidium.

Born in 1905, Tommy Thompson had worked his way through the University of Colorado before joining the Foreign Service. During the Second World War, as American second secretary in Moscow, he slept underground in the Metro while German bombers roared overhead. After postings in London, Washington, Rome and Vienna, he returned to the Moscow embassy as top man in 1957. This morning, when a Kremlin guard brought him to his choice box, Thompson was surprised: he was one of the most junior members of the Diplomatic Corps in Moscow. He thought, *There is something funny about this.*

Khrushchev's arrival on stage touched off resounding applause. The leader grinned, clapped his own fleshy hands and the room fell quiet: "Comrade Deputies! This session of the Supreme Soviet has convened in the spring—a wonderful time. Spring is a joyful season and the Soviet people are reinforcing nature's work with their own inspired labor."

For two hours, he gasconaded about the tenfold revaluation of the ruble and the abolition of the Soviet income tax by 1965. After an intermission, he spoke about other domestic issues. Then he turned to the world scene:

"As you know, on May sixteenth, a meeting will take place in Paris involving the leaders of the Soviet Union, the United States, Great Britain and France." Success at the Summit was "essential if a solid basis is to be laid for peaceful coexistence between states with different social systems."

But there was cause for alarm. "Certain ruling circles in the United States have at present not reached the conclusion that a relaxation of tension and the solution of controversial problems through negotiation is necessary. Lately influential forces—imperialist and militarist circles, whose stronghold is the Pentagon—have become noticeably more active in the United States. These aggressive forces stand for the continuation of the Cold War and the arms race. And they have been going in for downright provocation."

Now Khrushchev almost shouted: *"Comrade Deputies!* On the instructions of the Soviet government, I must report to you on aggressive actions against the Soviet Union in the past few weeks by the United States of America.

"The United States has been sending aircraft that have been crossing our state frontiers and intruding upon the airspace of the Soviet Union. We protested to the United States against several previous aggressive acts of this kind and brought them to the attention of the United Nations Security Council. But as a rule, the United States offered formalistic excuses and tried in every possible way to deny the facts of aggression—even when the proof was irrefutable."

The U.S. had sent such a plane on April 9, 1960. "The American military apparently found this impunity to their liking and decided to repeat their aggressive act. The day they chose for this was the most festive day for the working peoples of all countries—*May Day!*

"On this day, early in the morning, at 5:36 Moscow time, an

American plane crossed our frontier and continued its flight deep into Soviet territory. The Minister of Defense immediately reported this aggressive act to the government. The government said, 'The aggressor knows what he is in for when he intrudes upon foreign territory. . . . Shoot down the plane!'

"This assignment was fulfilled. The plane was shot down."

Earsplitting applause from the audience: "Shame to the aggressor! Shame to the aggressor!"

Khrushchev said, "The first investigation showed that this plane belonged to the United States of America—"

"Outright banditry!" someone cried (or so *Pravda* later reported). "How can this be squared with Eisenhower's pious speeches?"

"Just imagine what would have happened had a *Soviet* aircraft appeared over New York, Chicago or Detroit," said Khrushchev. "How would the *United States* have reacted?" He twisted his neck to glare up at Thompson: "What *was* this? A *May Day* greeting?"

Delegates whooped and stamped their feet. Thompson put on his blandest poker face: so this was why he was seated so prominently.

"The question then arises: who *sent* this aircraft across the Soviet frontier? Was it the American Commander-in-Chief who, as everyone knows, is the President? Or was this aggressive act performed by Pentagon militarists without the President's knowledge? If American military men can take such actions on their own, the world should be greatly concerned." Khrushchev charged that "American aggressive circles" were trying to "torpedo the Paris Summit or, at any rate, prevent an agreement for which the whole world is waiting."

Now he capped off the outrage he had so artfully whipped up: "It is understandable that we are seized by feelings of indignation at the American military provocations. But this must not guide our actions. We must be guided not by emotion but reason. . . .

"We address the American people: in spite of these aggressive acts against our country, we have not forgotten the friendly encounters we had during our visit to America. Even now, I profoundly believe that the American people—except for certain imperialist and monopolist circles—want peace and friendship with the Soviet Union. . . . I do not doubt President Eisenhower's sincere desire for peace."

After four hours of oratory, Khrushchev ended his speech with a raspy cry: "Under the banner of Lenin, under the Communist Party's leadership, to new victories in the building of Communism!" A final roar, and the audience leapt to its feet. Western reporters fled the hall for the Central Telegraph Office on Gorky Street.

•

In Washington, it was seven o'clock on Thursday morning. From the White House, Gordon Gray's secretaries called Thomas Gates, Allen Dulles and other members and staff of the National Security Council to go at once to helicopter pads in the District, Maryland and Virginia. George Kistiakowsky, the President's science adviser, was in the shower when his telephone rang. His caller refused to give him time to towel himself but allowed him to dry his hands so that he could jot down instructions.

What made the most powerful men in the Executive Branch rush to helicopters? Not Khrushchev's speech: the text had not yet reached Washington. The exercise was part of a long-planned Doomsday rehearsal to insure government continuity should Washington be destroyed by nuclear attack. The choppers' destination was High Point, a top-secret command post tunneled thirty minutes away in Virginia's Blue Ridge. The previous day, Richard Nixon had called the President from New York and asked if it was "imperative" that he go to High Point. Eisenhower had excused him.

This morning, Gates was driven to his takeoff point in northwest Washington by his wife in her nightgown. He had forgotten his pass; for a while, guards refused to let him through. Kistiakowsky had another problem: a black Cadillac was blocking his driveway in Georgetown. Hovering over the stalled engine was a "highly agitated" Allen Dulles. The scientist helped the CIA Director push the car aside and they rode away together. Dulles could not have helped but think that everything was breaking down on him this week.

•

At 7:36, United Press International's New York bureau sent a message to Washington:

WA
REUTERS SAYING KHRUSHCHEV SED IN SPEECH TDAY TT U.S.
PLANE SHOT DOWN SUNDAY FR VIOLATING SOVIET AIR SPACE.
SUG CK DEF DEPT. SAP.
    NXD JL736A5/5

A UPI man in Washington called a Pentagon spokesman, who said, "It strikes me cold."

•

Hugh Cumming was driving back to the Capital from Charlottesville, Virginia, when he turned on his car radio and heard, "Premier Khrushchev said today the Soviet Union shot down an American plane Sunday inside Soviet territory—" Cumming nearly drove into a ditch. At the first telephone he saw, he screeched to a stop and called the State Department.

•

Near the U-2 base in Atsugi, Japan, Sammy Snider was flying a T-33 and listening to music on Armed Forces Radio. The bulletin came. Snider turned to his co-pilot and said, "One of us is down."

The two men landed the plane, drove back to Atsugi and learned who the missing pilot was. For Snider, there was a sense of "There but for the grace of God go I." He and Frank Powers had served in the same Air Force wing at Turner, gone through U-2 training and served in Turkey together. At the Atsugi base, he found that "everyone was holding his breath to see what would happen."

•

At High Point, helicopters set down like pigeons on a telephone wire. The President and twenty-two others were rushed into the humid air-conditioned hideout. Such rehearsals usually included the Presidential announcement "I declare martial law." Early in the meeting, Allen Dulles reported on the first part of Khrushchev's speech, which had reached High Point by teletype. He said the next item seemed to be a tough statement of some kind on the United States and the Paris Summit.

The CIA's Herbert Scoville and the Pentagon's Herbert York gave a history of Soviet and American long-range missiles, which Kistiakowsky found "boring." As they spoke, staff aides popped in with teletype rippings; the men at the table whispered among themselves. Goodpaster was called to a secure telephone to talk to James Hagerty, the President's press secretary. Hagerty asked about Khrushchev's allegations: the White House press was already breaking down his door. What should he tell them? Goodpaster had a quiet word with the President and told Hagerty he should say nothing until hearing back from him either by telephone or in person.

Scoville and York finished their briefing but the group's attention had turned to the events in Moscow. Eisenhower asked senior officials of State, Defense and CIA to join him in an adjoining lounge. At 10:32 A.M., they sat down on sofas and chairs—Gordon Gray, Dulles, Gates and Douglas Dillon, Acting Secretary of State in Christian Herter's absence. Goodpaster brought in the final portion of Khrushchev's speech.

Someone said they must refute Khrushchev's charges at once. The President disagreed: NASA's release had said enough. They should say nothing now until they learned what Khrushchev would do next. But others wanted an immediate statement: the American government's silence might be taken as tacit admission that Khrushchev's charges were true. Eisenhower relented, and asked Dillon to draft a statement. To avoid confusion, he ordered that all public information about the U-2 be given out by the State Department and no one else.

At 10:45, they rose. The President went to a Signal Corps studio inside the hideout and gave High Point workers a one-minute pep talk on closed-circuit television. With Goodpaster, Gray and other aides, he boarded his chopper. At 11:23, they landed at the White House, where Jim Hagerty was furious. Reporters had been badgering him all morning about Khrushchev's speech and he had not heard back from Goodpaster for more than an hour.

●

With his Irish face and temper, his ever-present cigarette and energetic drinking, Hagerty seemed to some as if he belonged almost anywhere but the Eisenhower White House. Born in 1909, he spoke in the manner of the Bronx, where he grew up the son of the *New York Times*'s chief political correspondent. After graduation from Columbia, he too joined the *Times,* for which he followed the rough-and-tumble politics of Albany. During the war, Governor Thomas Dewey hired him as his press secretary. In 1952, when Eisenhower was looking for a seasoned man to handle the press, Dewey told him, "Take mine—he's the best there is."

Hagerty's hybrid background trained him to think as both reporter and politician, but reporters were badly mistaken if they presumed that Hagerty's client was anyone other than Dwight David Eisenhower. He worked hard to make up for the President's Olympian attitude toward the press; reporters on Presidential trips enjoyed good food, lodging and telephones. He gave the illusion of candor by overwhelming with detail: during Eisenhower's heart attack, he told reporters more than anyone might have ever wished to know about what the President was wearing, eating, drinking, reading, listening to.

During a Presidential trip to Paris, Art Buchwald published a parody of a Hagerty briefing in the Paris *Herald Tribune:* "Q. Jim, whose idea was it for the President to go to sleep? A. It was the President's idea.... Q. What did he say to the Secretary of State? A. He said, 'Good night, Foster.'" Hagerty found this not the least amusing and excoriated Buchwald in the Hotel Crillon lobby in front of other reporters.

The Eisenhower White House sprang few leaks. More than any administration since Hoover's, the Eisenhower people were disinclined to mix with reporters. Interviews were scheduled through Hagerty, and Hagerty was not shy about refusing. Inside the West Wing, "Jim didn't mince words," as his colleague Kevin McCann recalled. "If the entire Cabinet was in favor of something and Jim thought it would not sit well . . . he'd fight and he'd fight hard. He was not afraid of anyone."

As with Goodpaster, the President saw Hagerty as something of a son. If Goodpaster appealed to Eisenhower's ascetic, nonpartisan, West Point side, Hagerty appealed to the more political Eisenhower who made wisecracks, was not unaware of public relations and privately inveighed against difficult figures like Joseph McCarthy and de Gaulle while disdaining public discussion of personalities. At one famous moment, when the President asked him to give a less-than-candid statement to the press, Hagerty demurred and said that reporters would give him hell. The President smiled, walked around his desk, patted him on the back and said, "My boy, better you than me."

•

Hagerty was told that the President was back from High Point. At 11:47, he walked into the Oval Office and crisply told Eisenhower and Goodpaster that Khrushchev's charges were such a major story that the President must speak to the press at once.

This raised Goodpaster's hackles: if the American government was going to hand out a deliberate lie, he wanted the President kept as far away from it as possible. Otherwise, if the lie should be exposed, the President's good name might be tarnished. But Goodpaster was handicapped from fully making his case: the U-2 was so secret that Hagerty was not cleared to know. Even at this crucial moment, as Goodpaster later recalled, he and Eisenhower did not tell him the full truth about the flight. Hence Hagerty persisted in arguing that the President be involved as much as possible with this story.

The cant of the age had it that Eisenhower was too tired or lazy or dumb to take command of his job: while the President toured the nation's golf links, the government was run by faceless White House aides. As John Eisenhower later said, "Nobody wanted to take the Old Man on in a frontal attack. . . . So they would try to walk around saying, 'Ike's a good guy, but he's over the hill. Those evil boys in the government are not telling him what they're doing. And he's sort of a constitutional monarch.' "

Hagerty considered it his sacred mission to demonstrate that his President was always on top of the job. How would it look if the President declined comment on a matter so urgent as Khrushchev's charges? Hagerty fought and he fought hard. He wanted Eisenhower to meet the press and to put reporters in touch with NASA, since NASA (as far as he knew) owned the plane.

The President ruled out meeting the press but agreed to let Hagerty announce that NASA and State were investigating Khrushchev's charges and would publicize the results. Goodpaster was displeased, but not Hagerty. He left the Oval Office at 11:51 to brief reporters.

•

In 1960, roughly fifteen reporters were assigned full-time to the White House—AP, UPI, ABC, CBS, NBC, Mutual, *Time, Newsweek, U.S. News* and a half dozen newspapers. They resided in a small room off of the White House lobby crowded with desks, ancient typewriters, greasy telephones and a poker table where Harry Truman had dropped by for an occasional hand. One of Hagerty's female aides usually called a briefing by opening her door and shouting, "Press!" whereupon reporters entered Hagerty's office and formed a semicircle.

At 12:05 P.M., standing behind his desk and in front of a picture of himself with the President, Hagerty read out a statement on Khrushchev's accusations: "At the direction of the President, a complete inquiry is being made. The results of this inquiry, the facts as developed, will be made public by the National Aeronautics and Space Administration and the Department of State."

Ray Scherer of NBC called his bureau and was told, "Why don't you go over to NASA?" With *Newsweek*'s Charles Roberts and other reporters, he trotted across Pennsylvania Avenue and Lafayette Square to the eighteenth-century home of Dolley Madison that now served as NASA headquarters. Scherer pushed through the front door and called out, "Where's the statement?"

"*What* statement?" asked a secretary.

"The statement that Jim Hagerty said you were going to put out!"

Even Walter Bonney, NASA's information chief, was baffled. As other reporters arrived, he went to his inner office, called Hagerty, returned and announced that he would issue NASA's statement at 1:30 P.M.

For reporters to have arrived and found that NASA did not know what Hagerty was talking about handed the President's critics an irresistible example of administration dysfunction. "I'm not sure whose error it was," Goodpaster said years later. "I would say it probably lay between Hagerty and me. . . . Either Hagerty or I should have seen that these people were well-primed over there. . . . Because we had changed the mode of handling it in the midst of the affair, that's where things come unstrung and this came unstrung."

•

On the fifth floor of the State Department, Douglas Dillon pressed the telephone receiver to his ear and scrawled on a pad. At the other end of the line was Allen Dulles at the CIA. As Dillon later recalled, "We were talking back and forth, trying to draft a statement as to what we were going to say about this damn thing. We were having a *hell* of a time."

The two men felt that the less said, the better. When they finished writing, Dillon called Goodpaster and read him the statement. Goodpaster suggested a few changes and told Dillon that the President had changed his mind about assigning public comment on the U-2 purely to State. NASA would also put out a statement with greater detail. Dillon gave the finished draft to Lincoln White, the State Department spokesman. White was angry that Dillon had not told him about the problem the minute he arrived from High Point. At 12:45 P.M., he met reporters and read out the unsigned handiwork of Dillon and Dulles:

"The Department has been informed by NASA that, as announced May 3, a U-2 weather research plane based at Adana, Turkey, piloted by a civilian, has been missing since May 1. During the flight of this plane, the pilot reported difficulty with his oxygen equipment. Mr. Khrushchev has announced that a U.S. plane has been shot down over the U.S.S.R. on that date. It may be that this was the missing plane.

"It is entirely possible that, having a failure in the oxygen equipment which could result in the pilot losing consciousness, the plane continued on automatic pilot for a considerable distance and accidentally violated Soviet airspace. The United States is taking this matter up with the Soviet government, with particular reference to the fate of the pilot."

"What was the plane doing? Weather reconnaissance?"

"NASA is briefing reporters on the full details of that."

"You say this plane was from Adana, Turkey. Is that the U.S. Air Force base down there?"

"As I say, you better get this information from NASA. . . ."

"Linc, how do you know the pilot was having difficulty?"

"He reported it."

"Linc, do you have any comment on the rest of Khrushchev's speech—his statement that the Summit looks gloomy now because of aggressive American action?"

"No."

●

During the past two days, Richard Bissell had given NASA detailed cover information on the U-2 in question-and-answer form. Now Goodpaster called NASA's administrator, T. Keith Glennan: NASA should put Bissell's material in a written memorandum and issue that as the result of NASA's inquiry. Goodpaster thought a written statement by NASA would be better than "turning the press loose on them."

Walter Bonney worked Bissell's material into a rough statement, which he gave to a secretary. She corrected some of the language, retyped it on a multilith mat and ran off copies. At 1:30, Bonney entered Dolley Madison's ballroom. Thirteen months before, he had presented the seven Mercury astronauts in this room ("These are our astronaut volunteers. Take your pictures as you will, gentlemen.") Now, dreading the prospect of lying to reporters who liked and trusted him, he drew a deep breath and read aloud:

"One of NASA's U-2 research airplanes, in use since 1956 in a continuing program to study gust-meteorological conditions found at high altitude, has been missing since about 9:00 Sunday morning, local time, when the pilot reported he was having oxygen difficulties over the Lake Van, Turkey, area." Planned route: 1,400 nautical miles. Flight time: 3 hours, 45 minutes. Pilot was last heard from flying northeast. Maximum altitude: 45,000 feet. Mission's purpose: gathering information on "clear air turbulence, convective clouds, wind shear, the jet stream and such widespread weather patterns as typhoons."

Why was the plane flying so close to Russia? Weather research was worldwide. Replying to another question, Bonney said that the U-2 had cameras "but they are not reconnaissance cameras. They are cameras to cover cloud pictures." He added that the U-2 "weather missions" had never been classified secret. "We are still searching for the airplane in the Lake Van area. It may be a waste of effort. If the Russians would care to identify the plane as the U-2, a civilian plane carrying no armament and only research equipment, then we could stop looking."

•

At State, Douglas Dillon was on the telephone with Allen Dulles when Lincoln White walked into the room looking stricken. White gave him the text of the NASA statement, just ripped off the teletype. Dillon read the tearing, groaned and told Dulles, "God, get the ticker!"

Dillon had known that NASA would be issuing a more detailed statement but had not expected that the statement would include so much information that the Russians could disprove: "This statement was absolutely crazy because we *knew* the Russians would jump us on it."

•

It was Thursday evening in Moscow. At a Soviet Press Day reception, some Russian journalists invited an attractive young American reporter named Priscilla Johnson to dinner. When she refused, one of the Russians asked, "Why are you always so shy?" and took her by the arm into the private dining hall of the House of Journalists, where hundreds of Soviet editors and reporters ate and drank.

Well into the meal, *Izvestia*'s thirty-six-year-old editor, Alexei Adzhubei, rose and shouted, "Is there an American in the room?" Adzhubei was Khrushchev's son-in-law and the butt of many private jokes: Party members revised the Russian proverb that a hundred friends were better than a hundred rubles to say instead, "Better to be married like Adzhubei than to have a hundred rubles!" A backslapper like his father-in-law, he was said to be much involved with a woman not his wife. Khrushchev was said to have warned him to be more discreet.

When Adzhubei asked his question, all eyes in the room turned to Johnson. He declared that it was easy to see that she was the best-looking American correspondent in Moscow. All right! (He mimicked a plunging plane with his index finger.) What did she think of the incident Nikita Sergeyevich had revealed to the Supreme Soviet?

Someone cried that she must defend her country's honor. Shakily she stood and proposed a toast to peace, friendship and—as Nikita Sergeyevich had so often said—an end to taxes for weapons.

But this only increased the crowd's appetite for more. With hoots and shouts, they compelled her to walk down the long room to drink a toast with Adzhubei. As he touched his glass to hers, he showed off more of his uproarious sense of humor. Johnson looked down and saw a row of Chinese faces grinning back. As she groped her way back to her chair, a Russian stood, held his glass to hers and leered, "Do *you* fly?" A Soviet foreign affairs writer rose and proposed a toast to "our *only* friends, the *Chinese.*"

•

Llewellyn Thompson was attending a more sedate affair held by the Ethiopian Embassy at the Sovietskaya Hotel. Mrs. Thompson had stayed home; her children had the mumps. Within his earshot, the Swedish Ambassador drifted up to the Soviet Deputy Foreign Minister, Jacob Malik: Under what article of the UN Charter were the Soviets going to raise the plane incident?

Malik said they didn't know yet: they were still questioning the pilot. Malik told the Indian Ambassador that the American plane "was flying at sixty thousand feet and had been followed by radar all the way and destroyed deep in Soviet territory when it turned to go back."

Still questioning the pilot? Thompson rushed back to his embassy. Since Khrushchev's speech (as his wife later recalled) he had been trying to telephone the State Department but had not been able to get through to Washington. Now he sent a "MOST URGENT" cable to Dillon in Washington.

Malik's slip of the tongue was the first concrete indication that the Russians might have captured the U-2 pilot alive. Had Thompson's cable reached Washington in time, it might have kept the Americans from releasing the NASA statement that could be so damningly contradicted by a live U-2 pilot. But the cable arrived at 1:34 P.M.—four minutes after Walter Bonney began reading the statement at NASA.

Years later, the defector Arkady Shevchenko wrote that after word of the indiscretion reached Khrushchev, Malik fell to his knees before his leader, weeping, and begged forgiveness. By Shevchenko's account, Khrushchev forced Malik to confess his crime to colleagues at the Foreign Ministry, where he bleated, "Comrades, I have never before revealed state secrets," and they howled with laughter.

That was not Thompson's interpretation. Senior Soviet diplomats simply did not make such extravagant *faux pas*. By his wife's recollection, Thompson believed that Khrushchev was using Malik to get the message to the Americans that they should make no statements that could ultimately jeopardize the Paris Summit and a Soviet-American understanding.

●

After sending his alert to Washington, Thompson wrote a more ruminative cable on Khrushchev's Supreme Soviet speech. As the man who probably knew Khrushchev better than any other American, he took pains to dissuade colleagues in Washington from jumping to the conclusion that Khrushchev had given up on détente. What had impressed Thompson was not Khrushchev's ferocity but his moderation:

> Although showing anger and arousing strong reaction from deputies by his words and manner about the plane incident, the moment shouts started from the floor, he immediately moved to resume his speech and shut off any hostile demonstration.
>
> As I listened to his remarks on the plane incident, it appeared to me that they had been carefully considered in order not—repeat not—to slam any doors. The fact that the Soviets made a move toward our position on the underground test problem at Geneva and the fact that they announced Marshal Vershinin's visit to the U.S. after the facts of the plane incident were known to them would appear to indicate that while they expect to make full propaganda exploitation, they do not wish it to prevent carrying out previous policies and, in particular, wish to proceed with the President's visit.

●

As the sun set in Washington on the long day which had begun with the early-morning flight to High Point, the President was unwinding in the family quarters of the White House. Mamie answered the telephone. John Eisenhower was calling from Denver, where he was seeing his ailing maternal grandmother. He had seen the U-2 headlines and asked how his father liked the news.

The First Lady relayed the question to the President and he barked, "Do you think I *ought* to like it?"

●

Friday, the sixth of May. The American Embassy in Moscow named Francis Gary Powers as the pilot of the missing "unarmed weather research plane" and asked the Soviet Foreign Ministry for "full facts" about the fate of the plane and pilot.

In the Great Kremlin Palace, the Supreme Soviet convened for its second session. Marshal Andrei Grechko, commander of Soviet ground forces, lampooned the American claim that the pilot was unconscious. What about other pilots who had violated Soviet airspace? "Were they unconscious *too?* Are they suggesting that the crews of American planes sent to intrude upon our territory lose consciousness the minute they cross the Soviet border? Really, this is a new problem for medicine!"

Foreign Minister Andrei Gromyko, wartime envoy to Washington, declared, "If the Western powers think we are weak because we show patience, they are miscalculating."

A Byelorussian delegate: "The Soviet people are particularly revolted by this aggressive act of the American military clique after the people of the United States so warmly welcomed the chief of the Soviet state and President Eisenhower proclaimed his love of peace."

Tommy Thompson knew that Supreme Soviet "debates" were usually orchestrated beforehand: he noted that the speakers were following Khrushchev's lead. They denounced American "piracy," but divorced Eisenhower from the "American military clique" and pledged a warm welcome in June:

> Local workers' meetings are being organized throughout the country in connection with the plane incident. The latter procedure is, of course,

customary when any major problem or crisis arises, and the leadership may have felt compelled to follow standard practice in order to support the seriousness with which they view the incident. . . .

I believe there is no question but that the Soviets are genuinely angry at what they consider repeated violations of their territory. They have always reacted strongly to any statement or action which implied military weakness on their part. . . .

It is also possible that Khrushchev is discouraged over prospects for the Summit and wishes to prepare the Soviet public for the failure of this meeting to result in progress toward his goals. Although some of my diplomatic colleagues think the Soviets may have desired to provoke us into cancellation of this meeting in view of dim prospects, I think this unlikely.

•

Friday morning in Washington. Like the Supreme Soviet delegates, United States Senators were outraged—but at the downing of an "innocent American plane." Mike Mansfield, the Democratic whip: "It's a fine thing when the Russians shoot first and complain later." Republican Styles Bridges of New Hampshire demanded that the President boycott the Paris Summit unless Khrushchev gave him a proper explanation.

Almost the entire U.S. Congress was ignorant about the U-2. Allen Dulles had secretly briefed senior members of the House and Senate Armed Services and Appropriations Committees, as he generally did on major intelligence projects, but that was all. J. William Fulbright, chairman of the Senate Foreign Relations Committee, had never heard of the program.

Major American papers in the East generally restrained themselves from condemning the Soviet action. James Reston asked in his *New York Times* column "why it is necessary, a few days before President Eisenhower's last-chance meeting with Khrushchev, to send planes aloft to check weather-data and wind-shear on the Soviet-Turkish border." The *Washington Post* asked, "Why was the plane dispatched so close to Soviet territory that it could stray across the border even by accident?"

The restraint shown by Reston and *Post* editors was not merely preternatural insight. Months ago, they and other American journalists had discovered that the United States was sending spy planes across the Soviet Union. This was a world-important scoop, but every national reporter who learned the secret refrained from publication to keep from harming American national security.

•

At the White House, Richard Bissell and George Kistiakowsky exchanged commiserations on the U-2. As the science adviser recorded, "Dick said that the pilot is apparently alive and is being interrogated which, of course, won't help the situation."

At 9:53 A.M., Douglas Dillon and Goodpaster went to the Oval Office, where the President was "grumbling" over Thompson's cable that the pilot might be alive. "We didn't know whether it was accurate or not, but it gave us pause," Dillon later recalled. "We acted on the assumption from then on that they probably had the pilot and that they probably had a good deal of the plane."

Goodpaster reported that Dulles and Bissell were nervous about the congressmen who were denouncing Khrushchev for shooting down the plane. If the truth came out and the congressmen looked foolish, they might turn their wrath upon the President and CIA. Dulles and Bissell wanted the President to "take Congressional leaders at least partly into his confidence to prevent the building up of indignation in Congress, which would only pour more fuel on the fire."

Eisenhower refused: "These Congressional fellows will inevitably spill the beans."

At noon, the President was driven to the Washington Armory, where he snipped a ribbon opening an AFL-CIO trade show and toured the exhibition with union boss George Meany. At the barbers' booth, he ran into his own barber, Steve Martini, and said, "I don't need him very much. I just say, 'Come in and clip my neck, Steve.'" Catching sight of a Fiberglas boat, he said, "That reminds me: I'm taking to Premier Khrushchev, if I go, a new kind of boat that has no propeller."

If I go? Merriman Smith of UPI, Robert Pierpoint of CBS and *Newsweek*'s Roberts ran for telephones. Hagerty was asked if the President's remark meant he was thinking of canceling his Soviet trip and replied, "No comment." Outside the Armory, the President took off in *Marine One* for a weekend at Gettysburg.

George Allen stood at his side as he whacked a ball over two hundred yards down the first fairway of the Gettysburg golf club. Someone shouted, "There's not a Democrat in the world who can hit a ball like that!" and Eisenhower laughed with the crowd.

●

At Lincoln White's noon briefing, State Department reporters asked whether orders given American planes flying near the Soviet border had been changed. "There is no change to be made," he said. "The gentleman informed us that he was having difficulty with his oxygen equipment. Now our assumption is that the man blacked out. There was absolutely no—N, O—no deliberate attempt to violate Soviet airspace. There never has been."

In Turkey, CIA agents asked a groggy Barbara Powers to pack her bags to fly immediately to the United States. "Where's my husband?" she cried. "I demand to know what has happened to Gary!" But by her account, they told her nothing: "Everything is going to be all right, Mrs. Powers. Now please, just do as we say."

At Lubyanka Prison, Moscow, Francis Gary Powers was learning why he had been driven around the city the previous day—not because the Russians intended to release him, but because they evidently presumed that the excursion might loosen him up for the punishing interrogations that lay ahead. As Powers later recalled, from this point on, his captors were no longer friendly.

●

Saturday, the seventh of May. In Moscow, Khrushchev was scheduled to wind up the meeting of the Supreme Soviet with his own benediction. Having no desire for another cameo appearance in another of Khrushchev's morality dramas, Llewellyn Thompson stayed home and sent a second secretary from the Embassy in his stead.

At one in the afternoon, the man of the hour made his entrance to the usual standing ovation. Khrushchev opened his text and slid the curled earpieces of his rimless reading glasses around his ears. After a preamble, he gripped the sides of the lectern:

"Comrade Deputies! The aggressive act committed by the U.S. Air Force against the Soviet Union has justifiably incensed Deputies and all Soviet people." With a smirk, he read out the most tantalizing portions of the State Department and NASA announcements. Then he dropped his bombshell:

"Comrades, I must let you in on a secret. When I made my report two days ago, I deliberately refrained from mentioning that we have the remnants of the plane—*and we also have the pilot, who is quite alive and kicking!"* Thunderous applause. Outside the Great Kremlin Hall, chauffeurs leaning against Cadillacs, Zils and Bentleys threw back their heads in laughter.

"We did this quite deliberately, because if we had given out the whole story, the Americans would have thought up still another fable. And now, just look how many silly things they have said: Lake Van, scientific research and so on. Now when they learn that the pilot is alive, they will have to think up something else. *And they will!"*

Hoots and more laughter. "First of all, I wish to announce that the pilot of the downed American plane is alive and in good health. He is now in Moscow. The pilot's name is Francis Gary Powers. He is thirty years old. He says he is a first lieutenant in the U.S. Air Force, where he served until 1956—that is, until the day he went over to the Central Intelligence Agency."

Khrushchev reported that the pilot had testified that he had had "no dizziness" or faulty oxygen equipment. Following orders, he had been flying along an assigned route, switching on and off his apparatus for spying on the Soviet Union "until the very moment his pirate flight into this country was cut short."

Khrushchev pulled out large copies of aerial photographs and waved them at the American diplomat. "Here are some of the pictures showing military airfields. Here—*look at this!* Here are the airfields—*here!* Fighters in position on the ground. Two little white strips. *Here they are! Here they are!"* More thunderous applause.*

"Also a tape recording of the signals of a number of our ground radar stations—incontestable evidence of spying. . . . And the people behind this pirate flight could not think up anything better than the stupid story that this was a weather plane and that when the pilot lost consciousness, his plane—literally a runaway horse—dragged him against his will into Soviet territory. *What innocence!"*

In case someone doubted the pilot was really alive, Khrushchev gave out information about Powers's unit in Turkey—his commander, Colonel William Shelton, his NASA disguise, his takeoff not in Turkey but Pakistan, and the curious fact that he had chosen to bail out by

---

* The "U-2 photographs" Khrushchev held up before the Supreme Soviet were actually counterfeit. Having succeeded in halting the mission, he was clearly unwilling to allow even a small sample of its intelligence product to reach Washington.

parachute: "Why did he do this if there was an ejection seat? Maybe because there was an explosive in the plane that was supposed to blow up the plane as soon as the pilot ejected. The pilot knew this and perhaps was afraid that he would be killed in the explosion. Clever enough!

"But this diabolical machine was not the only precaution taken. To cover up his crime, the pilot was told that he must not be captured alive by the Soviets. . . . He was to jab himself with this poison pin, which would have killed him instantly. *What barbarism!*" Holding up a picture of the pin, he cried, "Here it is! The latest achievement of American technology for killing their own people!"

"Shame! Shame! Shame! Shame!" cried the deputies.

"But everything alive wants to live. . . . When he landed, he did not follow the advice of those who sent him . . . . He stayed alive."

Khrushchev revealed that the pilot had also carried a pistol with a silencer: "Why a noiseless pistol? Not to take air samples, but to blow out someone's brains!" Thousands of rubles and French gold francs: "I have seen them with my eyes and you can see them here in this photograph. They are covered with cellophane on both sides—done in a *cultured, American* way." Two gold watches and seven gold ladies' rings: "Perhaps he was supposed to have flown still higher, to Mars, and seduced the Martian ladies!" More laughter, and then the fun was over:

"From the lofty rostrum of the Supreme Soviet, we warn those countries that make their territory available for launching planes with anti-Soviet intentions: *Do not play with fire, gentlemen!* The governments of Turkey, Pakistan and Norway must be clearly aware that they are accomplices in this flight. . . . If these governments did not know—and I allow in this case they were not informed—they *should* have known what the American military was doing in their territory against the Soviet Union."

Khrushchev noted the indignation of American congressmen and journalists that the Soviet Union should have downed an American plane: "How would *they* react if *our* plane intruded into the United States and flew about two thousand kilometers over American territory? Perhaps these outraged people would rather seek the answer from Allen Dulles. . . . The whole world knows that Allen Dulles is no great weatherman!"

As for Powers, "I think it will be proper to prosecute this flier so that world opinion can see what actions the Americans are taking to provoke the Soviet Union and heat up the atmosphere, thus reversing those successes which have been achieved in relieving international tensions.

"I remember the talks I had with Americans. They impressed me very much. I still believe that those who met me want peace and friendly relations with the Soviet Union. But apparently the Pentagon militarists and their monopolist allies cannot halt their war efforts."

Once again Khrushchev divorced this military clique from Eisenhower: "I am quite willing to grant that the President knew nothing about the fact that such a plane was sent into the Soviet Union. . . . But this should put us even more on guard.

"When the military starts bossing the show, the results can be disastrous. Such a pirate, prone to dizziness, may in fact drop a hydrogen bomb on foreign soil. And this means that the peoples of the land where this pirate was born will unavoidably and immediately get a more destructive hydrogen bomb in return."

As the deputies stood and pounded their benches with fists, Priscilla Johnson felt "emotionally spent and years older than when I had entered the hall."

•

The AP's London bureau flashed the astonishing news:

PREMIER NIKITA KHRUSHCHEV TOLD THE SOVIET
PEOPLE IN MOSCOW TODAY THAT THE PILOT OF THE
AMERICAN AIRCRAFT SHOT DOWN OVER SOVIET TERRITORY IS
ALIVE. MOSCOW RADIO, REPORTING KHRUSHCHEV'S
ANNOUNCEMENT, DID NOT IMMEDIATELY GIVE THE PILOT'S
CONDITION.

The bulletin rattled out in newsrooms on the Eastern Seaboard after dawn on Saturday—too late for almost all but Western papers to remake their front pages. The *Los Angeles Times* yanked its headline and ran a huge new banner across the top of its final edition: "DOWNED PILOT ALIVE, NIKITA TELLS SOVIET." Forty hours before deadline, *Time*'s editors junked the cover story already printed for next week.

In Pound, Virginia, Oliver Powers and his family were told the news and they wept. When a reporter asked about Khrushchev's charge that Francis was a spy, the father said, "Absolutely ridiculous."

In Paris, Charles de Gaulle found the whole story "a bad comedy in questionable taste."

In London, when brought the news, Harold Macmillan was brooding about the Commonwealth. In his diary, he wrote, "The Russians have got the machine, the cameras, a lot of the photographs—and the pilot. The President, State Department and Pentagon have all told separate and conflicting stories and are clearly in a state of panic.

"Khrushchev has made two very amusing and effective speeches attacking the Americans for spying incompetently and lying incompetently too. He may declare the Summit off. Quite a pleasant Saturday—the Commonwealth in pieces and the Summit doomed!" He found it "hard to avoid a feeling almost of despair."

Cancellation of the Summit was not Macmillan's only anxiety. Perhaps the best-guarded secret of all was that the U-2 incursions had actually been jointly waged by the British and American intelligence services. The previous weekend at Chequers, Macmillan's official country residence, his intelligence briefer, Sir Patrick Dean of the Foreign Office, had reported that the U-2 pilot was waiting to fly from Peshawar.

The Prime Minister often mused that only eight hydrogen bombs were required to remove the British people from civilization. Despite his threats to the Turks and Pakistanis, Khrushchev was unlikely to take military retaliation for the U-2. But what might he do if and when he discovered that the British had been partners in the violations of Soviet airspace?

•

From Moscow, Llewellyn Thompson cabled Washington:

Watching Khrushchev on television deliver his speech to the Supreme Soviet today, it was evident he was thoroughly enjoying his performance and frequently departed from his written text to underscore points. . . . From shots of the Presidium and audience, I received the impression of anxiety in contrast to his speech at the opening, where there was clear expression of nationalistic feeling.

From such information as we have received, the general reaction of the ordinary Soviet citizen is one of deep resentment—particularly the fact that the event occurred on May Day. The Soviet people are deeply concerned about the possibility of war and their frequent demonstra-

tions of pro-American sentiment are probably directly related to the realization that friendship and understanding with the U.S. is the surest
way to prevent the recurrence of war. . . .

It is difficult to assess Khrushchev's motives in playing this so hard. I
believe he was really offended and angry, that he attaches great importance to stopping this kind of activity, and that he believes this will put
him in an advantageous position at the Summit. There is no doubt that
we have suffered a major loss in Soviet public opinion and probably
throughout the world. . . .

A more menacing interpretation is that Khrushchev realizes . . . that
he cannot make progress at the Summit and . . . therefore could be exploiting this incident to prepare public opinion for an eventual crisis. . . .
I also cannot help but think, although evidence is very slight, that
Khrushchev is having some internal difficulties and this incident affords
him a convenient diversion.

Judging by the display which Khrushchev made of evidence in the
Supreme Soviet today, I would doubt that we can continue to deny
charges of deliberate overflight. Khrushchev has himself stated the dilemma with which we are faced: should we deny that the President
himself had actual knowledge of this action?

●

From Denver, John Eisenhower returned to the former Pitzer
Schoolhouse in Gettysburg, where he and his family lived a mile from
the President's house. The President's son was a self-effacing presence
in the White House entourage, viewing the events and personalities
around him with the keen eye of the historian he later became.

Born in 1922 at the Denver home of his maternal grandparents
after the death of the Eisenhowers' firstborn son, John was a fierce de-
fender of the President and his works, a loyal aide and a strong-willed
man striving to win a "degree of independence" from a strong-willed
father. Son of an obscure Army officer for his first twenty years, John's
change of fate made him perhaps more impatient with the demands of
paternal celebrity than other sons who grew up accustomed to them.
He loathed "big-time publicity" and the memory of his West Point
graduation on D-Day 1944, of all moments, when photographers had
chased him and his mother to the superintendent's great black car, in
which they were driven away "like royalty."

From the European theater, the General wrote Mamie of their son,

"I'm so tied up in him it hurts." After VE-Day, the senior Eisenhower was feeling lonely in Germany. Posted half an hour away, John and his father spent what John later considered the most amiable time of their lives, listening to Gershwin records and playing with the General's dogs. Then the father went to Washington and the son to Vienna, where he met his future wife, Barbara Thompson, a beautiful and extroverted Army daughter who made up for John's shyness and impatience with small talk.

He taught English at West Point, took a master's degree in English literature at Columbia University, and served at Fort Knox before entering combat in Korea. Returning to America in 1953, he resisted the White House "as best I could, fighting to retain the identity of myself and my family." Still he had to lead a double existence, enduring harassment by his superior at Fort Benning before boarding the Presidential airplane with his family to spend Thanksgiving with the President and First Lady.

Like Franklin Roosevelt and his son James, Dwight Eisenhower saw no reason why the fact that he was President should deny him the pleasure of his son's companionship and help. In 1954, John was briefly posted to the Presidential staff. In 1957, his father told him, "Goodpaster's going on leave. You're *it* for the time he's gone." In 1958, when John was serving at the Pentagon, the President asked him to join the White House full-time as Goodpaster's deputy.

During the week, John lived on the third floor of the Mansion. In the early evening, he was often summoned for cocktails with "the Boss," as he fastidiously called his father around the West Wing. Sitting in overstuffed chairs in the upstairs Oval Room with its war trophies and decorations, father and son spoke of baseball, the stock market, almost anything but the day at work. Ann Whitman soon noticed that John was with his father "practically all the President's free time—and a good thing, I am sure."

●

The telephone rang in the Pitzer Schoolhouse: it was Goodpaster, calling with "tough news." John asked, "Just how tough *are* things, General?"

"About as tough as they can get. They've got the pilot alive."

John bitterly recalled Allen Dulles's "absolutely categorical" assurances that a U-2 pilot would not survive a crash. Many years later, he said that the memory still put him "into a war dance," and insisted that "Allen Dulles lied to Dad."

Some at the White House thought staff members had a tendency to arrange for John to be the one to bring his father bad tidings: the President's temper was notorious and he was one aide assured of job security. On weekends at Gettysburg, he was (in his own words) the President's "principal link with the outside world."

He climbed into his car, drove down Waterworks Road and turned right, past the Secret Service guardpost, down the driveway to the rambling white house his parents had built over the frame of an old red farmhouse in the mid-1950s. He found his father standing in the glassed-in porch in the rear, looking out on the lime-green Civil War battlegrounds he cherished. On this porch eight months ago, Khrushchev had sat John's children on his knee. That day seemed a lifetime ago as John broke the news.

The President's reaction: *"Unbelievable."* He had seen Thompson's cable that the pilot might be alive, but that had been only a rumor. Now he knew that Khrushchev had irrefutable evidence that his administration had deliberately violated Soviet airspace, spied on the Soviet Union and several times lied about it to the world.

There must be some response to Khrushchev's speech—especially Khrushchev's "willingness to grant" that the CIA and Pentagon had sent the U-2 into Russia without the President's knowledge. Evidently Khrushchev was offering him an escape hatch. If Eisenhower used it, maintaining this fiction, then the Paris Summit might proceed.

But this would create other problems. What would the world think if the American President had so little control over his own government that minions could, without his knowledge, send planes into Russia that might conceivably start a war? And what if Khrushchev had already decided to scuttle the Summit anyway? The escape hatch might turn out to be a trap: if Eisenhower shirked responsibility for the U-2, Khrushchev might then reveal new evidence revealing the President personally to have lied.

Thus he had the choice of presenting himself as a leader whose government was capable of accidental provocation—or declaring in public that he was the man behind the U-2, the first time in history that an American President confessed that his government practiced espionage.

Repeatedly assured that he would never face such a dilemma, Eisenhower could fairly wonder how "this goddamned plane" had fallen in Russia and the pilot survived. Just a week ago, he had sat with his family in the cinema room at Camp David, looking forward to a "splendid exit" from office. Now he faced leaving the White House in the wake of perhaps the bitterest disappointment of his life, as if the gods who had always looked so kindly on him had suddenly decided to exact a price for their gifts of the past.

Tomorrow was the fifteenth anniversary of victory in Europe.

★

3

The Espionage Assignment

IN AUGUST 1945 and the afterglow of the Grand Alliance, Dwight Eisenhower and Marshal Georgi Zhukov boarded the General of the Army's personal plane, the *Sunflower,* for the journey from Berlin to Moscow. Over the drone of the engines, the two generals traded stories about the war they had just won together—Zhukov unhooking the stiff collar of his tunic plastered with decorations, Eisenhower laughing and slapping his knees.

As viceroys over Germany since VE-Day, they had passed many hours comparing their countries' political philosophies, reliving the war, thinking aloud about their families and hopes for the future. At a banquet, Eisenhower had declared that what he and Zhukov wanted was peace, and they wanted it so badly that "we are going to have peace if we have to fight for it."

Soon after the *Sunflower* landed in Moscow, Eisenhower was taken to see the leader of the Soviet Union, resplendent in white uniform. Stalin noted that the American was not coarse and brusque like most generals he knew and pronounced him "a very great man—not only because of his military accomplishments, but because of his human, friendly and frank nature."

The Generalissimo gave him the signal honor of standing at his side atop the Lenin Tomb as a hundred thousand Mongols, Russians,

Georgians and other national groups observed victory by marching through Red Square performing chants, dances, stunts and acrobatics. When the crowd saw Eisenhower, arms crossed, wearing his famous green waist-length jacket, it roared. Before the parade was over, Stalin introduced the guest of honor to the leader of the Ukraine, whose eldest son had been killed in the war. For the first time, Eisenhower shook hands with Nikita Khrushchev.

The rest of the five days was a triumph of Soviet-American amity. Eisenhower toured collective farms and factories; at a soccer game, when his presence was announced, he slipped an arm around Zhukov's brawny shoulders and tens of thousands of Russians raised the skies with applause. Zhukov kept joking with John Eisenhower that he intended to marry him off to one of the girls from the parade—"a terrifying prospect," thought John, "since any one of those powerful women could have broken me in half with no effort."

At the end of the trip, Eisenhower invited Zhukov to America and offered John as his escort. He told American reporters, "I see nothing in the future that would prevent Russia and the United States from being the closest possible friends."

•

For his first fifty-one years, the Soviet Union had seldom crossed Eisenhower's mind, with the exception of the anti-Communist pronunciamentos he heard from his superior Douglas MacArthur in Washington and Manila, and of which he generally approved. Throughout the war, he had, like Franklin Roosevelt, concentrated on victory and postponed detailed thinking about the postwar world. Not until May 1945 did the Soviet Union move to the cynosure of Eisenhower's concerns, where it remained for the rest of his life.

General George Patton and Field Marshal Bernard Montgomery were independently pondering how the Wehrmacht might be rearmed for war between the Soviet Union and the West. Such notions did not pass Eisenhower's lips. He angrily dismissed a reporter's question about war against Russia and told the U.S. House Military Affairs Committee that "Russia has not the slightest thing to gain by a struggle with the United States. There is no thing, I believe, that guides the policy of Russia more today than to keep friendship with the United States."

Churchill, de Gaulle and other Old World statesmen feigned no such roseate expectations about what might emerge from the ashes of war: the theme of the final volume of Churchill's war memoirs was "How the Great Democracies Triumphed, and So Were Able to Resume the Follies Which Had So Nearly Cost Them Their Life."

But as a representative man of the country Woodrow Wilson called the only idealistic nation in the world, Eisenhower believed that the tens of thousands who had died by his orders had to have perished for something nobler than the resumption of the ancient power politics that Americans had always scorned. If East and West showed patience, restraint, flexibility, they might shape a fresh world without hostile alliances or arms races, in which nuclear weapons were controlled by a vigorous United Nations. Building mutual trust was the first step: this was one of the reasons he thought the Soviets deserved the honor of capturing Prague and Berlin.

That soldiers hate war because they know its cost is scarcely a universal truth (consider George Patton). But Eisenhower's well-informed disgust at war's irrationality and waste and his experience in Europe and North Africa disposed him more emotionally than the average Western political leader against solving problems on the battlefield. He had "seen bodies rotting on the ground and smelled the stench of decaying human flesh." As he wrote Mamie during the war, he had formed "a veneer of callousness" but could not forget "how many youngsters are gone forever." When the atom bomb was detonated at Los Alamos, unlike other American leaders exhilarated at the prospect of ending the Pacific war, Eisenhower had only "a feeling of depression."

Having seen the U.S. Army almost starved to death during the isolationist 1920s and 1930s, he wondered how long the American people—especially fellow Kansans and other Midwesterners—would tolerate the expense of huge peacetime armies and weapons. As a fiscal conservative, he feared that bankrupting the country to build a military leviathan would destroy the society it was meant to defend. With his skeptical mind and thirty years of strategic training, Eisenhower was not quick on the trigger. At a White House meeting in 1946 to gauge the chances of a Soviet attack on Western Europe, he said, "I don't believe the Reds want a war. What can they gain now by armed conflict? They've gained about all they can assimilate."

But by 1947, the freedoms for which the West had fought were being extinguished in Eastern Europe. The avatar of Soviet-American friendship, Marshal Zhukov, was banished by Stalin to Odessa. Eisenhower deplored Soviet "political pressure and subversive tactics" in Greece, Iran, Turkey, but still resisted what he called "the smouldering doubts and fears that are plaguing this country." He reminded American leaders that the Russians were not supermen: when Army intelligence estimated that the Red Army could seize Western Europe within two weeks, he said, "My God! We needed two months just to overrun Sicily." But in September 1947, he sadly concluded in his diary that "Russia is definitely out to communize the world. . . . We face a battle to extinction between the two systems."

By 1952, Eisenhower was a thoroughgoing Cold Warrior. From SHAPE in Paris, his warnings against the Soviet threat were almost indistinguishable from those of the Truman State Department. Still, unlike many other Cold Warriors, he kept alive the hope that the cycle of hostilities could one day be broken.

During the Presidential primary campaign, militant Republicans acidly recalled Eisenhower's friendship with Zhukov, his failure to take Berlin, his glowing postwar talk about the Russians. When John Wayne saw an ex-GI waving an Eisenhower banner, he bellowed, "Why don't you get a red flag?"

Eisenhower tried to recast history by stressing his warnings to Western politicians during and after the war about the danger from Moscow. He tried to outbid the Democrats by declaring that if he became President, the United States would never recognize Soviet domination of Eastern Europe. Still he put a damper on the most robust anti-Communists in his party by affirming that the Iron Curtain would be rolled back only by peaceful means.

•

On March 4, 1953, shortly after midnight, the CIA's all-night monitors roused Allen Dulles from bed: Stalin had suffered a stroke and was thought to be dying. At 7:40 A.M., the President walked into his office, looked at Dulles, Jim Hagerty and other aides, and tartly said, "Well, what do we do about *this?*"

A day later, Radio Moscow announced that the heart of the "inspired continuer of Lenin's will" had ceased to beat. Secret police sealed off the center of the Soviet capital. Loudspeakers warned against "panic and disarray," but people were trampled to death. In the Hall of Columns, the old Noblemen's Club where the Czar's court had performed quadrilles and Stalin thrown old Bolsheviks on show trial, stunned workers filed past the Great Father's remains, an old woman sobbing here and there.

On March 9, as the Red Army band played Chopin, the coffin was carried into Lenin's mausoleum by the new leaders of Russia—Georgi Malenkov, the heir apparent; Vyacheslav Molotov, the Foreign Minister; Lavrenti Beria, head of the secret police. Nikita Khrushchev, chairman of the funeral commission, could not forget the words of the dead leader: "You'll see! When I'm gone, the imperialist powers will wring your necks like chickens!" They set down the casket near the chalk-white body of Lenin. Factory bells and whistles sounded. Then there was silence all over the Soviet Union.

The hallmarks of American-Soviet relations in 1953 were the truculent accusations cabled back and forth between Washington and Moscow and the armies at war in Korea. The *New York Times* said on Stalin's death, "Our children's children will still be paying the price for the evil which he brought into the world."

What would happen now? Some optimists in Washington allowed themselves to hope that Russia's revolutionary traditions might incite the people to throw off the bonds of the Soviet state. Pessimists feared a Kremlin power struggle that might encourage the new leaders to try something reckless like a surprise nuclear attack against the West. At the White House, Eisenhower considered a CIA warning that the new regime might not enjoy Stalin's skill in avoiding world war: "A struggle for power could develop within the Soviet hierarchy at any time."

But to almost everyone's surprise, Malenkov called for warmer relations with the United States: "There is not one disputed or undecided question that cannot be decided by peaceful means."

John Foster Dulles warned the President against the Russians' "phony peace campaign." Eisenhower did not question this judgment, but he worried about the enthusiastic world reaction to Malenkov's speech and wondered whether this might be a time to begin rebuilding mutual trust: "Look, I am tired—and I think everyone is tired—of just plain indictments of the Soviet regime. I think it would be wrong—in fact, asinine—for me to get up before the world now to make another one of those indictments."

Dulles opposed a Presidential speech: relaxation of tensions now might harm American efforts to bargain on Korea and coax Western Europeans into a supranational army. But in no mood to antagonize a

President he had scarcely known before January, he contented himself with hardening the speech with demands including the "full independence" of Eastern Europe.

On April 16, before the American Society of Newspaper Editors, Eisenhower gave the best speech of his life. He recalled that after World War Two, while America disarmed, the Soviet Union had maintained a war footing. Despite Soviet provocations, the United States was still ready to seek peace. He welcomed Malenkov's offer and said that when it was backed by deeds, he would be willing to join the Soviets to limit arms and place atomic energy under international control. But what gave the address its power was Eisenhower's evocation of the price of an eternal arms race:

"Every gun that is fired, every warship launched, every rocket fired signifies, in the final sense, a *theft* from those who hunger and are not fed, those who are cold and not clothed. This world in arms is not spending money alone. It is spending the sweat of its laborers, the genius of its scientists, the hopes of its children. . . . We pay for a single fighter plane with a half million bushels of wheat. We pay for a single destroyer with new homes that could have housed more than eight thousand people. . . . This is not a way of life at all, in any true sense. Under the cloud of threatening war, it is humanity hanging from a cross of iron."

The Cross of Iron speech confided Eisenhower's second greatest anxiety about the arms race. It did not confide his worst—that some American or Soviet leader, confronted with the paralyzing cost of an endless arms race, might try to destroy the source of the threat with a surprise nuclear attack. To Eisenhower, this was the most urgent reason for disarmament. In his diary, he wrote, "As of now, the world is racing toward catastrophe."

In December 1953, he went to the United Nations and proposed Atoms for Peace: "Today, the United States stockpile of atomic weapons, which, of course, increases daily, exceeds by many times the explosive equivalent of the total of all bombs and all shells that came from every plane and every gun in every theater of war in all the years of World War Two." Unless the arms race was curbed, the "two atomic colossi" would be doomed to "eye each other indefinitely across a trembling world." He suggested joint American-Soviet-British contributions from their nuclear stockpiles to a UN atomic agency for peaceful uses.

This would curb the arms race at an early stage without requiring the on-site inspections that the Soviets had always refused. Eisenhower knew that the United States could afford to reduce its stockpile by several times the Soviet rate and still remain ahead: in his speech, he allowed that the ratio of American to Soviet contributions could be five to one or more. Privately he believed that all one superpower needed to deter the other was a few hundred bombs: the Russians wanted nothing badly enough to risk losing the Kremlin.

But the Soviets feared permitting an eternal American lead; they did not even issue a prompt response to Eisenhower's offer. The frustration of Atoms for Peace made the President more sensitive to the problem of protecting the United States against surprise attack.

•

Several levels down from what Lenin would have called the "commanding heights" of the American government was a blunt, decisive, impatient, profane Welshman named Trevor Gardner, assistant to the Secretary of the Air Force for research and development. Born in Cardiff in 1915, trained as an engineer, he worked on the Manhattan Project at the California Institute of Technology, became vice president of General Tire and Rubber by age thirty and managed his own R-and-D firm, Hycon, before Eisenhower personally invited him to join the new administration.

Pearl Harbor had burned the danger of surprise attack into the national soul. Gardner joined a national security establishment that had been newly alarmed. Albert Wohlstetter and other strategic thinkers at the Rand Corporation in California had lately issued a top-secret warning that a Soviet strike might destroy as much as eighty-five percent of the Strategic Air Command's bomber force. After a disturbing visit with General Curtis LeMay at SAC headquarters in Omaha, Gardner flew to Pasadena, where he saw Lee DuBridge, president of Cal Tech and chairman of the Science Advisory Committee established under Harry Truman to advise Presidents on scientific aspects of national security.

Cocktail in hand, as an aide recalled, Gardner told DuBridge that his panel wasn't worth "a good goddamn. . . . You're abnegating your responsibility to science and the country, sitting on your dead asses in fancy offices in Washington, wasting your time and the taxpayers' money going through a lot of goddamn motions on a lot of low-level, shitty exercises—all in the name of science." The Committee should do a study on surprise attack and American "ability, or inability, to meet it. The *true* story, not that shit Washington is feeding the American people."

Gardner made his appeal to the Committee, which went to see the President on Saturday, March 27, 1954. Eisenhower told them that he too was "haunted" by the problem of surprise attack. Among those present was James Killian, president of the Massachusetts Institute of Technology. On the recommendation of DuBridge, the President had him to breakfast at the White House and asked him to chair a secret commission on potential new military and intelligence weapons to protect the nation against surprise attack.

Born in 1904 in North Carolina, Killian had spent his entire adult life at MIT—as an undergraduate in business and engineering, editor of the *Technology Review* and then while climbing the bureaucratic ladder until he became president in 1949. A skillful manager of scientists with their egos and idiosyncrasies, he believed that universities like MIT should muster "the democratic ranks of American scientists into invincible battalions" in the Cold War.

Killian had voted for Eisenhower in 1952 and twice attended the President's intimate stag dinners at the White House, but this had not prevented him from opposing some aspects of Eisenhower's defense program on Capitol Hill or sharing the outrage of many American scientists at the excommunication of J. Robert Oppenheimer. He accepted the President's offer and won a leave of absence from the MIT Corporation.

Killian was concerned that it might not be easy to attract scientists angry at Oppenheimer's treatment to work for the President who had done the deed, but he found that most "could not fail to respond to a call for help." By September 1954, he had assembled forty-six experts and staff in the gray nineteenth-century splendor of the Executive Office Building next to the White House.

The Technological Capabilities Panel (or Killian Commission, as members soon called themselves) worked fast and hard, for the President wanted a report on his desk by February. Except for field trips to the CIA, Pentagon, SAC and elsewhere, members worked behind locked doors manned by Air Force guards. During coffee breaks, like children told to look and not touch, secretaries gazed out the windows at the distant figure of the President greeting foreign leaders and knocking out golf balls on the South Lawn.

●

The most secret unit of Killian's group was the intelligence panel chaired by Edwin Land. The world knew Din Land best as inventor of the Polaroid Land camera, but he had long been working on classified government projects, including guided missiles, infrared searchlights, anti-aircraft training devices and 3-D film for aerial photography. Dark, reclusive, sensitive, abrupt, Land had always exalted "the art of the fresh, clean look at the old, old knowledge."

Born in Bridgeport, Connecticut, in 1909, he dropped out of Harvard as a freshman to work on a filter to cut glare in cameras, sunglasses, telescopes. He founded the Polaroid Corporation to sell the filters, hoping that it would prosper enough to support his scientific curiosity. On a wartime trip to the Southwest, Land's three-year-old daughter Jennifer asked him why snapshots could not be produced right away. He went for a stroll and worked out the basic design of an instant camera in his head. In 1948, his first cameras went on sale at the Jordan Marsh department store in Boston. Twenty-five years later, Land's interest in Polaroid was worth half a billion dollars.

But money remained only a means. By 1954, working in his nondescript office and laboratory near Polaroid headquarters in Cambridge, he held 164 patents, including detection devices for atomic exposure and cancer and a process for 3-D movies: theatergoers donned Polaroid glasses for the illusion of watching tribesmen in *Bwana Devil* hurling spears, or so it seemed, into the audience. Land was an MIT lecturer and Cambridge friend of Killian, who thought him "an authentic genius."

His panel knew that the first line of defense against surprise attack was intelligence on the enemy's military capabilities and intentions. The Soviets held a clear advantage. In any five-and-dime, they could buy maps of American bridges, factories, highways, ports, air bases, missile sites, atomic testing grounds. Soviet agents and diplomats gathered all sorts of American secrets. Some of this espionage was sophisticated, such as the Americans paid to steal classified papers; some was crude, such as the aerial photographer paid seven hundred dollars by a Soviet air attaché to fly over military sites around New York City. The FBI was on the trail, but how much could be concealed in a free society?

In the Soviet Union, even the Moscow telephone book was classified. If American generals did not know the location of vital Soviet installations, how establish bombing targets if war broke out? If they did not know the shape and rate of Soviet military development, the Russians could trick the United States into building the wrong kinds of weapons and bleeding itself white on defense. If they had no early warning of a Soviet strike, the West would continue to be vulnerable to surprise attack.

The brightest possibility was to gather such intelligence from the air. At the MIT Beacon Hill Summer Study on aerial reconnaissance in 1951, Land had listened to the air ace General James Doolittle lecture on the "importance and near-impossibility" of flying cameras and electronic equipment deep into the Soviet Union. By Land's recollection, self-confident Air Force men declared that such planes and equipment could not be perfected in much less than ten years. Land did not believe it. He exhorted his panel to take a fresh, clean look at the old, old knowledge.

•

The earliest recorded aerial reconnaissance mission was staged in 1794 by a French army captain, J. M. J. Coutrelle, who flew tethered manned balloons above enemy positions during the Battle of Fleuries. American aerial intelligence-gathering began with the Civil War. In 1861, Thaddeus Lowe, balloonist and magician, went to the White House and offered President Abraham Lincoln his balloon, the *Enterprise*, to provide Union commanders with battlefield reports. Lincoln accepted and later formed the Army Aeronautic Corps, but the swaying of the balloons, the cameras' slow speed and Rebel fire made clear photography difficult.

In 1911, an Italian captain flew his monoplane over Ottoman positions near Tripoli, the first time an airplane was used for wartime reconnaissance. During the First World War, all of the major rivals used reconnaissance planes: the Royal Flying Corps considered them "routine insurance against surprise." By the end of the war, at least one fourth of all aircraft involved were used for photography.

During the late 1930s, pilots of British and French commercial airliners used hidden cameras to photograph Hitler's military buildup, the first known instance of covert aerial reconnaissance. After Pearl Harbor, aerial intelligence-gathering came of age, providing the Allies with over ninety percent of their intelligence.

Then the Cold War began. American and British intelligence

needed hard information on the Soviet order of battle; atomic weapons developments; movement of tanks, ships, planes and men; installations such as military bases, communications centers, factories, highways, airfields. The CIA, MI-6 and military intelligence used secret agents and other old intelligence methods to pierce Soviet secrecy, but the take was fragmentary and ambiguous.

Western pilots were ordered to fly along the Iron Curtain for photographic and electronic reconnaissance. Occasionally they dashed across the border to test radar, radio traffic and air defenses on the other side. Some of this espionage was done by the U.S. Air Force's new snub-nosed jet fighter, the F-86 Sabre. Strapped to the belly of a B-29, the plane was flown to a predetermined point along the frontier from which it streaked to its target and then darted back to safety.

Findings of the border flights were augmented by human intelligence. In September 1949, shortly after the West learned that the Russians had detonated their first atomic explosion, an unmarked American plane flew southeast over the Ukraine. By parachute, it dropped two Ukrainians trained to spy and send information back to the West.

To photograph the Soviet Union's innermost territory, the Navy and Air Force tried balloons. With the CIA's help, beginning in the late 1940s, an estimated hundred balloons per year were floated from Western Europe over Russia bearing high-altitude cameras. With luck, when they reached Japan, a ground radio signal caused the instrument packages to detach and float safely by parachute to earth. But too often they dropped into the hands of the Russians, who gleefully displayed them in Moscow. Before hundreds of journalists, Soviet Foreign Ministry officials ridiculed stories handed out in Washington that the balloons were merely collecting weather information. Something had to be done.

In the fall of 1950, General Nathan Twining, Air Force Vice Chief of Staff, sat down at a meeting of the Joint Chiefs, filling in for his boss, General Hoyt Vandenberg. As Twining later told the story, the chairman, General Omar Bradley, told him he was "elected" to "tell Harry Truman about our overflight plan." The plan: make deeper penetrations of Russian airspace than anything tried before. Twining took the papers and maps to the Oval Office, where Truman studied them: "Chiefs all buy this?"

"Yes, sir. We're very anxious to start on this program right away.

We realize the seriousness of it, but we feel this is the only way we're going to get this information."

By Twining's account, the President signed the authorization and said, "Listen, when you get back there, you tell General Vandenberg from me: *Why in the devil hasn't he been doing this before?*"

Like bees buzzing about the head of a frustrated giant, Western airmen flew into the outer reaches of the Soviet Union. As Twining later said, "One day, I had forty-seven airplanes flying all over Russia and we never heard a word out of them. Nobody complained."

But these planes were not invulnerable. In November 1951, a Navy bomber flown by ten crewmen disappeared off Siberia in a burst of Russian fire. In June 1952, an Air Force B-29 with thirteen crewmen aboard perished in the Sea of Japan. October 1952: eight airmen on a B-29 crashed near Japan. The State Department conceded that the plane "may have glided into Soviet territory." July 1953: a B-50 with sixteen men aboard fell over the Sea of Japan.

Before his death, Stalin was said to be irate that Soviet airspace could be violated at all. According to the Soviet historian Roy Medvedev, Soviet military experts told the Great Leader that the best way to stop the invasions was to build special ground-to-air missiles that could knock the pirate planes out of the sky.

For the British and Americans, these shallow penetrations were not enough: much of the Soviet land mass remained unseen by Western eyes. In 1953, Robert Amory, chief of the CIA directorate that gathered and weighed intelligence, was alarmed by reports of Soviet missile testing at Kapustin Yar, said to be seventy-five miles east of Stalingrad. He told colleagues, "We just can't ignore it. This is going to be a major new thing, this whole missile development, and we've got to get on top of it in the beginning and judge it."

But Kapustin Yar was out of easy reach by the shallow overflights. Twining said it couldn't be photographed. General Philip Strong, a retired Marine advising Amory on the intelligence applications of science, persuaded British intelligence in London to do the job. The Royal Air Force took a B-57 (fittingly called the Night Intruder), stripped off all but vital equipment and installed cameras and extra fuel tanks. From West Germany, the pilot flew down over southwestern Russia and took pictures of the site, but the Soviets nearly downed him. The plane reached Iran full of holes.

Someone had evidently tipped off the Soviets that the spy plane was coming. Perhaps it was Kim Philby, the MI-6 man not yet un-masked as a Soviet agent. As Amory later recalled, "The whole of Russia had been alerted to this thing and it damn near created a major international incident. But it never made the papers." The British told the Americans, "Never, never, never again."

Amory: "Then we went to Twining and said, 'You've just *got* to devise a plane that will do this, that will be high enough so it will go over their radar.' And the damned Air Force insisted that every plane be an all-purpose plane. It had to have some fighter ability, it had to have some maneuverability and so on."

Undeterred, Philip Strong told Amory, "We've just got to get up-stairs." On his own hook, he flew out to California and saw his friend Kelly Johnson, the legendary Lockheed designer who, during the war, had put America's first tactical jet fighter in the air in just 141 days: "Kelly, what could you do if all you were trying to do was get as high as you could—get moderate speed but not too great speed and just sit above their air defense?"

"Jesus, I've got just the thing for you," said Johnson. "I'd take the Lockheed F-104. I'd give it wings like a tent. It's a cinch!"

Johnson worked with four Lockheed engineers on a plan for a new spy plane that would fly over seventy thousand feet for as much as four thousand miles. In April 1954, he took his plan and a construction timetable for thirty planes to Washington, where he briefed a Pentagon group including Trevor Gardner. Nine months before, the Air Force had let study contracts to Bell, Martin and Fairchild Aircraft for work on a high-flying plane. Johnson's design was examined, but some of the Air Force men doubted that it would work. They gave a tentative go-ahead to Bell.

Johnson told his men to keep on working while he tried other ave-nues in Washington, including the CIA. Allen Dulles warmed to the notion of allowing Lockheed to build a high-flying spy plane for the Agency while the Air Force's Bell project diverted attention from it. Trevor Gardner showed Johnson's proposal to Edwin Land and in-vited the designer back to Washington "to see whether I could make any sense," as Johnson later recalled. Land and his colleagues thought Johnson made a mountain of sense. They resolved to recommend the plane's development for deep flights into Russia using new precision cameras and other intelligence equipment.

Land and Killian thought the project so vital that it must not wait until the full Commission made its formal recommendations in February. They made an appointment to see the President.

•

November 1954 was a crowded month for Eisenhower. He dedicated the Eisenhower Museum in Abilene, met with the Indian Vice President, and threw stag luncheons for the Austrian Chancellor and Prime Ministers of Denmark, Norway, Sweden, France. For the benefit of photographers in the Oval Office, he purchased the season's first sheet of Christmas Seals and accepted a copy of *America's Spiritual Recovery* from the author, Reverend Edward Elson. By letter, he thanked the Japanese Prime Minister for a cloisonné vase and a congressman for fireplace tongs, and wished Senator John Kennedy a swift recovery from back surgery.

Pierre Mendès-France, the French Prime Minister, had sent advance word that he wished a few minutes alone with the President. Eisenhower saw no harm: he would "stick pretty much to generalities." He grumbled to Foster Dulles that everybody in the State Department was "obviously so afraid" to leave him alone with Mendès-France.

That month, the President also held one of his celebrated stag dinners. While Mamie saw a movie or retired early, ten or twenty men would dine and then go upstairs for cordials and cigars. The next morning, Eisenhower usually did a post-mortem with Ann Whitman, who recorded it in her diary: "Harry Bullis was pompous. President liked Jim Copley who has 29 papers. General Donovan gave a talk on Thailand. . . . A. D. Welch big man, completely bald." Another evening: "President said stag dinner was the most interesting he had had. Thinks partially due to reducing number to sixteen."

In the fall of 1954, Dwight Eisenhower did not plunge into the midterm Congressional campaign: Harry Truman's barnstorming while President had "shocked" his sense of "the fitting and the appropriate." But now he may have wished he had. He could not think of anything worse than working with a Democratic Congress.

"I really think a man can be classed as a politician only after he has spent his life in a political arena," he told Merriman Smith of UPI that November. "But I can say this and, I think, without egotism: in many, many ways, I will make smarter political decisions than a lot of guys who are pros because they have gotten too used to the narrow, quick advantage rather than taking a look at the longer range."

The President was more blunt in a letter to his brother Edgar: "The voteseeker rarely hesitates to appeal to all that is selfish in mankind." Politics? "A combination of gossip, innuendo, sly character assassination and outright lies" in which "the demagogue tries to develop a saleable list of items to hold before the public."

•

Before noon on Sunday, November 7, eleven Air Force men in a B-29 were taking pictures along a zigzag course which brought them close to a big Soviet air base near Japan. Two Soviet fighters appeared and someone cried, "They're firing!" Ten of the airmen bailed out safely; the eleventh was enmeshed in his parachute lines and drowned.

Foster Dulles called the President: "Whenever the boys go over there, it is a deliberate risk. We think the plane was over Japan, but the Soviets probably think it was over their territory."

In the wake of the Democratic victory, a bipartisan group of congressmen was coming to the White House to discuss foreign policy. Eisenhower told Dulles that he was "sure" the congressmen would ask about the plane incident. He assumed "we would not want to admit too much." He was "certainly" not going to admit that the United States made deliberate flights over the Soviet Union.

Soon thereafter, Killian and Land came to the Oval Office to recommend deep flights into Russia. As Killian recalled, Eisenhower asked "many tough questions." How much chance was there that the intelligence would be worth the provocations?

Land and Killian thought that even if the take was marginal, the flights might cause the Kremlin to shift precious rubles from offensive to defensive weapons. They might also demonstrate the futility of Moscow's obsessive secrecy: maybe then the Russians would sign disarmament agreements with adequate inspections.

The President himself had used the pictures taken by reconnaissance fliers during World War Two, especially on D-Day. He thought American intelligence overrelied on human sources and was impatient with the balloons and shallow penetrations.

Killian and Land had expected the President to say he would study their plan. But as Killian recalled, he gave tentative approval on the spot—with one proviso: the Air Force must not fly the missions. Eisenhower did not want the provocation of sending uniformed soldiers into Soviet airspace. He was also concerned that the project would be eviscerated by interservice rivalries. The Air Force should help, but the missions must be flown by the CIA.

"And essentially, the Air Force's eye was wiped in you-know-what," Robert Amory later said.

On Friday, November 19, Land's panel brought Kelly Johnson back to Washington. "They wanted to be reassured that our proposal was technically feasible," Johnson wrote in his diary. After "a grilling as I had not had since college exams," he lunched with Allen Dulles, Air Force Secretary Harold Talbott and General Donald Putt, Director of Air Force Research and Development. Someone said, "Let's stop talking about it and build the damn plane."

Monday, November 22: Allen Dulles ironed out details with the President in the Oval Office. In her diary, Ann Whitman wrote, "Discussion of advisability of going ahead with new photographic reconnaissance plane at some considerable cost."

At 8:15 on Wednesday morning, November 24, 1954, the key players filed into the Oval Office—Charles Wilson of Defense; Harold Talbott; Generals Twining and Putt; Allen Dulles and his deputy, General Pearre Cabell, who had been Air Force intelligence chief before joining the CIA. Foster Dulles took his customary place to the left of the President's desk chair.

It was the day before Thanksgiving. The Eisenhowers were scheduled that afternoon to drive to National Airport, where the First Lady was to smash a bottle of water from one of the President's favorite trout steams against the nose of the new Presidential plane, *Columbine III*, a Lockheed Superconstellation (also serviceable for aerial reconnaissance). Then they would take off for a long weekend of bridge and golf with friends at the Augusta National Golf Club in Georgia. Field Marshal—now Viscount—Montgomery, was coming along for the ride. The President privately groused that Monty had "invited himself."

The men formally asked the President to sanction development of thirty planes for about $35 million. Allen Dulles noted that the CIA could not bear the whole sum without drawing attention to it. Wilson agreed to have the Pentagon foot a "substantial part" of the bill.

Twining did not say it aloud, but he was disturbed that the CIA was getting this choice project. He was surprised that the Agency had been able to talk the President into it; earlier, when Land and Killian had raised the prospect of deep flights into Russia, Curtis LeMay had said, "You'll never get a President to agree to that sort of thing."

Twining privately thought the CIA men were getting "too big for their britches. They did not know how to handle this kind of an operation." He knew that this meeting with the President was not the time or place to voice his objections, but neither he nor LeMay intended to roll over and play dead.

Eisenhower told the group, "Go ahead and get the equipment, but before initiating operations, come in to let me have one last look at the plans."

It was all over in fifteen minutes. Before the meeting adjourned, Foster Dulles said, "Of course, difficulties might arise out of these operations. But we can live through them."

•

Two hours later, William Knowland, Republican leader of the Senate, was shown into the President's office. For two years, Knowland had made the President's life miserable by promulgating his own hard-shell foreign policy from the Senate floor. Eisenhower once wrote in his diary that in Knowland's case, there seemed to be no final answer to the question, "How stupid can you get?"

After the Russians downed the American plane in early November, Knowland had publicly demanded that the President break diplomatic relations with the Soviet Union: other "innocent" planes would be attacked if Eisenhower did "nothing more than merely send notes to Moscow." Foster Dulles warned the President that reporters would press him "on the Knowland foolishness." If the President wanted to "slap Knowland's ears back," that would be fine with him.

But Eisenhower had to coexist with his Senate leader, so he asked Knowland to the White House for today's heart-to-heart talk. As the Californian entered the room, the President threw the switch activating a secret tape recorder concealed in a large, ugly piece of furniture in the next room. (He once told his Cabinet, "It's a good thing when you're talking to someone you don't trust to get a record made of it. There are some guys I just don't trust in Washington and I want to have myself protected so they can't later report that I said something else.")

Eisenhower brought up the plane incident. He said he knew there were arguments for breaking relations with the Soviet Union. But that was a step toward war: "If you do that, then the next question is, 'Are you ready to attack?' Well, I am *not* ready to attack."

The President hinted that the plane downed in the Far East might not have been innocent: "In the conduct of foreign affairs, we do so many things we can't explain that, once in a while, something happens. . . . There is a very great aggressiveness on our side that you have not known about, and I guess this is on the theory of: why put burdens on people that they don't need to worry about and therefore make them fearful that they might give away something? I know so many things that I am almost afraid to speak to my wife.

"Now in the way of reconnaissance and a great many things, we are very active and there are a great many risky decisions on my part constantly so that, once in a while, something happens. And I just don't dare let it lead to a question in the United Nations. You apparently think we are just sitting supinely. . . . Here's the thing to remember: suppose one day, we get into a war. If too many people knew we had done something provocative—

"I just want to say that we *might* have to answer to charges of being too provocative rather than being too sweet."

●

At the CIA, Allen Dulles summoned Richard Bissell: "I have just come back from a meeting in the White House. There is a project for a high-flying reconnaissance aircraft. I want you in a meeting at four o'clock this afternoon at the Pentagon. . . . The President has approved this and it has a very high priority."

Through streets clogged with Thanksgiving traffic, Bissell was driven in a black Agency pool car over Memorial Bridge and past Arlington National Cemetery. At the Pentagon, in Room 4E964 overlooking the Potomac, he greeted Trevor Gardner and Air Force officers. Their voices rose in exhilaration: these were the men who would open secrets of the Soviet military complex to Western view for the first time.

More than anyone else, Trevor Gardner had championed the project and bulled it past nay-sayers in the Air Force and elsewhere. All agreed that he should have the honor of placing the long-distance call to California. He lifted the black receiver from its black cradle, muttered a few words to the operator and waited. Then he gave his triumphant command: "Kelly, begin cleaning out that hangar this afternoon!"

★

4

Building a Covert Operation

AFTER HE LEFT the Pentagon, Richard Bissell marveled that "nobody had really worked out how anything was to be done." The decision to build a plane to fly deep into Russia had been made at such a high level that "nobody knew where the money was coming from. Nobody knew how much it would cost. Nobody knew where it would develop, where flight testing could be done, where people could be trained or by whom, who could fly it or anything." Now these were his problems.

Bissell was a New Deal Democrat and prewar isolationist, urbane, lucid, informal, perfectionist, "a very naturally spookish guy," as Robert Amory said. In his CIA office, he always seemed in motion, tossing a ball into the air, twisting paper clips, brushing lint from his trousers, wiping his horn-rimmed glasses and springing from his chair to lope down the corridor. Sometimes he threw pencils at filibustering subordinates. When Cord Meyer sent a document for Bissell's last-minute consent once too often, he was called and told, "I'm going to tear it up! I'm going to tear it up!" And Meyer heard the sound of pages being shredded at the other end of the line.

The ferocious commitment with which Bissell attacked his job was leavened with throwaway humor. He once presented himself to a table of high government officials by saying, "I'm your man-eating shark."

Toward covert means of international behavior he was more than open-minded. "There are many times when my friends think that I am not devoted to democracy as a principle of government," he said years later. "And I will go this far in that direction: there are an awful lot of things that are much better done in private. You accomplish *nothing* by making them public, except to inflame people."

•

The man-eating shark was born in 1909 to the Connecticut patriciate that adored Theodore Roosevelt, ran insurance companies and banks in Hartford and sometimes worked in Washington, usually for Republican Presidents. His father was president of the Hartford Fire Insurance Company; the family lived in the eccentric gingerbread house designed by Mark Twain in which Twain spent the happiest years of his life.

At Yale, Bissell led what a classmate called "a brilliant coterie of iconoclasts, candid in speech, brutal in analysis, entirely uninhibited in their attack on the old tribal gods." Bissell's iconoclasm was probably less ideological than it was intolerance of orthodox thinking. As a professor of economics at Yale and MIT, he was said to irritate colleagues with his openness to innovation.

During World War Two, Bissell handled problems of American shipping. As Amory recalled, "He knew just where they could pick up one vessel in the South Atlantic, two in the Red Sea and so on. His mind could just tick off their names and do the mental arithmetic: at 11½ knots, you could be in Tunis and Carthage at such-and-such." After the war, Bissell served as deputy chief of the Marshall Plan, helping to persuade congressmen to spend billions of dollars and colliding with the civil service mind: once he became so "thoroughly fed up" with the French bureaucracy that he half-seriously threatened to "cut off all aid to France."

Bissell was disheartened by Eisenhower's election in 1952. He would almost certainly have been in line for a high post under President Adlai Stevenson. Like his friend and fellow economist John Kenneth Galbraith, he felt somewhat as if Washington had become a forbidden city: there was an incivility, "a real meanness" in the transition that offended him. At the close of the Truman Administration, he and Paul Nitze had worked on a long list of national security proposals signed by Dean Acheson and Robert Lovett, Secretaries of State and Defense. The paper was rebuffed by the new President. When Allen

Dulles asked Bissell to join the Eisenhower government as his special assistant, Bissell at first demurred.

Later controversy has sometimes obscured the fact that in 1953, the CIA was far from a haven for fanatics of the Right. Dulles believed in recruiting anti-Communist progressives like William Sloane Coffin, Thomas Braden, Tracey Barnes and Lyman Kirkpatrick. At the same time, he believed in the old-boy network. By the 1950s, with Wriston-ization, other reforms and more intense public interest in foreign policy, the homogeneous elite operating without close public scrutiny was no longer the State Department but the CIA. Men who would have been pillars of State a generation earlier now joined the Agency.

Bissell qualified on both counts. He knew the CIA as "a place where there was still intellectual ferment and challenge and things going on." In February 1954, he swallowed any doubts he may have had. His first assignment was to explore ways the Agency might stir up serious trouble in Eastern Europe and thereby help to implement Eisenhower's campaign pledge to liberate the captive nations by nonmilitary means.

Since the Second World War, American intelligence had recruited exiles, ex-Nazis and assorted anti-Communists and dropped them with supplies and weapons into Albania, Yugoslavia, Poland, Georgia, the Ukraine. Polish freedom-fighters sent back some of the most promising reports. What the Americans evidently did not know was how many of these agents were dropping into the hands of Soviet-bloc agents, who infiltrated the network and sent its members to prison, torture and death. In 1952, the Russians presumably feared that Eisenhower might actually believe his campaign rhetoric about liberating Eastern Europe: it was revealed that they had been secretly managing resistance agents of the Polish Home Army all along.

The new President phased down the project. But exiles approached the CIA all the time with information and contacts behind the Iron Curtain. Dulles hoped that the Agency might build a scaled-down network from which a resistance movement could be built when and if war began. Bissell looked at the secret records and found a plan for expanding Albanian guerrilla operations to the point where they could support an invasion. He found this a mild hallucination: How could you wage a secret assault on a country from halfway around the world? Soon he essentially agreed with Dean Acheson that liberation was "a check we cannot cash."

In May 1954, the White House and the CIA were preoccupied with

Guatemala. President Jacobo Arbenz Guzman had lately expropriated 225,000 acres owned by the United Fruit Company and worked closely with the Communist party. By now, with few illusions about rolling back Communism in Europe, Eisenhower and the Dulles brothers were doubly determined to head off new Communist regimes, especially in the Western Hemisphere and near the Panama Canal. They earmarked $20 million to throw Arbenz out.

Bissell planned the propaganda broadcasts, leaflet drops and strafing missions by CIA-trained rebels to panic the Guatemalan people and government. When two planes were lost and Allen Dulles asked for replacements, Eisenhower asked what were the chances for success if the rebels got the new planes. "About twenty percent," said Dulles. The President smiled: Dulles's conservative estimate showed that he had "thought this matter through carefully. If you had told me that the chances would be ninety percent, I would have had a more difficult decision."

Bissell "negotiated" the "sale" of more U.S. Air Force planes to the rebels. After more sorties, Arbenz fled to Switzerland and the hand-picked new leader arrived grandly in Guatemala City aboard the American Ambassador's plane. "Our job was simply to get rid of Arbenz," Bissell said much later. "It was a success at one point in history, but this does not assure a happy ultimate outcome."

In Latin America, the Guatemalan coup injected a new, long-lasting dose of antipathy toward Uncle Sam. Achieved just months after the Shah's restoration to power in Iran, the coup instilled a buoyant sense among high ranks of the American foreign policy government that the CIA could do almost anything. Bissell himself was exhilarated by the effectiveness of covert action, the "very direct kind of intervention," using power "just to get things done." He liked the elegance of the clandestine operation, the high proportion of results to effort, the freedom from scrutiny by press, bureaucracy and Congress, the flexibility and independence he had known during the war.

Bissell had never been a textbook organization man. Like Allen Dulles, he did not see himself as a bureaucrat, and Dulles had not hired him to be one. Richard Helms and other CIA men thought Bissell's methods somewhat "harum-scarum" but this did not bother him: "I've heard that label put on other Washington figures, and they've usually been the men who were so concerned with substance that they didn't spend all their time on organization charts and budgets."

Many years later, the intelligence historian Thomas Powers wrote that "a lot of CIA people distrusted Richard Bissell, thinking—especially in light of what happened later—that his extraordinary mind was fatally flawed, that his confident enthusiasm for ambitious projects crossed the threshold of recklessness." But this was in distant retrospect. In December 1954, Bissell was a rising star at CIA: many senior colleagues would have given their right arms for the chance to run the new spy flights into Russia.

The project seemed tailor-made for Bissell and his gift for improvisation, secrecy, bullheadedness, daring and genial cooperation with other creative, unconventional men like Land, Trevor Gardner and Kelly Johnson. The war, the Marshall Plan and Guatemala had taught him how to supervise logistics. His grandfather was a railroad president; captivated by trains since boyhood, Bissell was said to be able to cite the hours and miles between almost any two major cities and the railroad gauges of countries in Africa and Latin America. While walking, he often devised ways that other countries' train systems might be rebuilt.

Since his work on Eastern Europe, Bissell had complained that the CIA relied too much on the James Bonds and Mata Haris: human spies cost too much time, money and organizational energy for the result. Now he had the chance to guide the innovation of revolutionary pieces of technology and unite them in a way that would change the craft of intelligence forever. Years later, when it was all over, he said that he had never done anything more satisfying in his life.

•

Problem Number One was money. At the original Pentagon meeting with Trevor Gardner and the Air Force, someone brought up the "ugly question" of who would finance the program. Bissell looked expectantly across the table and the Air Force men looked expectantly back. He looked some more and they looked some more. Finally Bissell said, "All right, I get the point."

He persuaded Allen Dulles to channel money for the project through the CIA Director's Reserve Fund. Heeding Secretary Wilson's promise, the Air Force evidently transferred $22 million into the account. Air Force men declared that "with some clever footwork," they could shift about thirty Pratt & Whitney aircraft engines from other projects to this one without discovery. General Osmond Ritland made himself responsible for "stealing engines and stealing spare parts."

On December 14, 1954, Kelly Johnson returned to Washington to see Gardner, Bissell and other members of the "special agency," as Johnson discreetly called the CIA in his diary: "We discussed at length problems of security and method of dealing with each other. Large amount of time taken on the optimum cover story for the project." Bissell told Johnson that, unlike the Air Force, he didn't much care what the plane looked like, as long as it was built quickly. He simply wanted a plane that would fly a given height and distance and run large cameras and equipment smoothly over the surface of the earth.

Johnson said, "Good. That will save you a good deal of money. On the other hand, I'm going to put my top force on it, and that's going to cost you money." They settled on a price of roughly $22 million for twenty planes; Lockheed could return for more money if needed. Bissell hammered out an interim truce with the Air Force, which was "a moderately bloody affair." The Air Force was not used to having the CIA build planes.

Bissell set up shop near CIA headquarters in a rickety building said to be a house of ill fame during the First World War. Floors were so weak that he was told to bring no new furniture heavier than a typewriter. He appointed a steering group including Gardner, Pearre Cabell and Donald Putt. Finance and other officers were hired to help supervise the people from the CIA, Air Force, Lockheed and other contractors who would build cameras and other elements of the system.

Throughout the project, Bissell considered it his "private duchy": "It was completely compartmentalized in the interest of security and walled off. Allen Dulles knew less of what went on in that component of the Agency than he did about any of them. There were an awful lot of details that never came to anybody else's attention." The President had told Dulles that secrecy was essential: if there were any leaks about this project, he was perfectly ready to kill the whole thing.

•

In January 1955, the scene shifted to California. Lockheed Aircraft Corporation was quartered in the Los Angeles suburb of Burbank, a land of ranch houses, filling stations, palm trees, used car dealers and hamburger stands. The first McDonald's restaurant in the nation had opened nearby the previous year. When Bissell flew out to keep an eye on progress, as he often did that winter, he looked vaguely like a puritan in Babylon.

Lockheed was a city within a city enjoying the fruits of the postwar aircraft building boom. Hundreds of hangars, warehouses, office buildings—beige and gray boxes of every size—rose amid thousands of De Sotos, Fords, Packards, Plymouths, on a vast slab of asphalt under skies often gray with smog. In the middle of the complex, behind barbed wire fences and guardhouses, was the Skunk Works.

This high-security workshop for "black programs" was inspired by the spot in Al Capp's *Li'l Abner* where Hairless Joe brewed his Kickapoo Joy Juice. To Kelly Johnson, the Skunk Works was what Menlo Park was to Edison. From this cavernous edifice with its blacked-out windows rolled one engineering triumph after another—the first American tactical jet fighter (the F-80, 1943), the world's fastest plane (the F-104, 1953) and dozens of other aircraft that constituted a history of modern aviation. Years later Johnson was considered "probably the most brilliant aircraft designer alive," but he remained almost unknown to the general public.

He looked like a taller, sober version of W. C. Fields. Born in the mining town of Ishpeming, Michigan, in 1910, he was the seventh of nine children of a Swedish immigrant bricklayer. He watched pilots take off at the local airfield, read Tom Swift and books on aviation in the Carnegie Library and at twelve, vowed to become an aircraft designer. After five years working his way through the University of Michigan, he bought an old Chevrolet and drove to Burbank.

Kelly and Althea Johnson were childless, to their chagrin, and it took little insight to notice that he looked on his planes with the affectionate concern of a father. Driving a tractor on his ranch near Santa Barbara, he sometimes stopped to sketch new designs with a twig in the dirt. His irascibility earned him the nickname of "the Old Goat": his men were willing to endure the screaming and table-pounding because he also turned his temper on Lockheed and Air Force men who tried to interfere with their work.

Before Thanksgiving, as soon as Johnson received the telephone call from Trevor Gardner, "we went right to work because we promised to design and fly the plane in eight months," as he recalled. He put twenty-four engineers on hundred-hour weeks. "Talked to each man on the project to impress them with the need for speed and secrecy," he wrote in his diary. "Extremely difficult to pull these engineers from other projects at this time, particularly in that I cannot tell anyone why." The project was code-named AQUATONE. Secrecy was so strict that when Johnson submitted his first two vouchers to Washington for payment, two checks for $1,256,000 arrived in the mailbox of his Encino home.

Lockheed janitors had no security clearance for the Skunk Works, so Johnson's team worked among trash and cigarette butts on the problem that some had branded insoluble. In the thin air over seventy thousand feet, jet engines scarcely ran. Since the new plane could hardly touch down at Leningrad or Minsk for a friendly refueling, it had to be able to stay in the air for up to ten hours. The Catch-22 was that at such altitude and distance, the engine would probably burn so much fuel that no standard fuel tank would be large enough. Any tank large enough would weigh the plane down so badly that it could not stay so high in the air.

They solved the puzzle with a design that was less a jet airplane than a glider with a Pratt & Whitney turbojet engine attached. To conserve fuel, the engine would frequently idle: the plane would alternately fly and glide through the stratosphere for almost eleven hours and 4,750 miles on little more than a thousand gallons of fuel. The men pared every conceivable ounce from their design and built a craft of spectacular grace, which they named the Angel.

The Angel was made of titanium and other lightweight materials. Wingspan was roughly twice the length of the fuselage. The razorlike tail was joined to the rest of the plane by just three bolts. The aircraft was slung so low that on the runway its nose was only the height of a man. It was so light that later, at first glimpse, pilots wondered whether this was intended to be the world's first disposable plane, built for only one flight.

Other components were perfected. James Baker of Land's intelligence panel worked on a new telescopic lens. Eastman Kodak devised a new Mylar film thin enough to be carried aloft in large quantities. Under Land's oversight, Trevor Gardner's old firm Hycon built the massive cameras that swung from horizon to horizon, covering a swath of land literally 750 miles wide—about one tenth of this in three dimensions. With 12,000 feet of film, the cameras were considered able to photograph a path from Washington to Phoenix in one flight.

Some in the CIA and Air Force still doubted that "Dulles's Folly" or "Bissell's Bird" would ever fly, but in February 1955, eighty-eight days after the program's inception, Kelly Johnson called Bissell in Washington to say that the experimental model was ready. Final cost: $19 million.

The plane still needed a name. The Angel would not do (nor would Dulles's Folly, for that matter). Bissell and Johnson might have given the plane the prefix "X," which was used for other experimental aircraft like Chuck Yeager's fabled X-1, but that would draw too much attention: people might wonder just what barrier this plane was designed to smash, and why. Reconnaissance planes often had the prefix "R," but that would also give away the secret. So Johnson's plane was assigned to the catch-all category of "U"—utility planes—and named the U-2.

This choice was not as clever as it may have seemed. The name U-2 had already been taken by the Soviets, who had used it on a single-engine biplane before the Second World War.

•

Where could the new plane be tested in absolute secrecy? Edwards Air Force Base, where Yeager had broken the sound barrier, would not do: too many people there. Johnson wanted "a salt lake someplace with a nice hard, flat surface, and very remote." One of his best test pilots, Tony LeVier, spent two weeks flying over and photographing possible desert sites in California, Nevada and Arizona. First choice was a dry lake bed called Groom Lake, about a hundred miles northwest of Las Vegas. Johnson and Bissell flew out with him to investigate.

Near Groom Lake was a deserted Second World War airstrip. They decided not to land on the strip—wisely, it turned out, for it had reverted to deep sand. Bissell said, "If we had chosen to land on that strip, I think we probably would have been killed. That would have been the end of the program." Once on the ground, they found the lake bed "as flat as a billiard table." At Bissell's instance, Allen Dulles persuaded the President to bar unauthorized pilots from the land by annexing it to the federal government's vast atomic testing ground.

Construction crews volunteered by the Atomic Energy Commission worked around the clock in hundred-degree heat among tumbleweed and tarantulas. Soon there were roads, an airstrip, wells, two large hangars and a mess hall. By July 1955, Watertown Strip, as the new base was called, had a population of roughly 150 employees of the CIA, Air Force, Lockheed and other contractors. James Killian thought the speed with which Bissell and Johnson had worked "almost a miracle."

During the spring, aided by British and West German intelligence, the CIA had been secretly tunneling into East Berlin to eavesdrop on sensitive conversations between Moscow and the East German military command. With his air of whimsical self-confidence, Allen Dulles went to the Oval Office and reported on the U-2 and the Berlin Tunnel: "I've come to tell you about two acquisition projects—one very high and one very low." But that July the President was preoccupied with Geneva.

•

The last time an American President had sat in the same room as his Soviet counterpart had been Harry Truman's encounter with Stalin at Potsdam ten years earlier. Since 1953, Eisenhower and his Secretary of State had resisted Winston Churchill and other pleaders for an East-West meeting. Amiable talks might dissipate Western anxiety that was useful in building NATO. In the United States, Joseph McCarthy and the Right opposed another conference like Munich or Yalta at which Western leaders might practice appeasement behind closed doors; Eisenhower publicly forswore a summit until the Russians showed "sincere intentions" by accepting strict American demands such as those he had set down in his Cross of Iron speech.

But by November 1954, he changed his mind. The British and French wanted a summit. The post-Stalin leadership struggle in Moscow seemed to be ending. In the absence of progress on disarmament, the President was willing to meet with the Russians. At a press conference, he suggested that they meet only one demand as evidence of sincerity: one way was to sign a treaty removing occupation troops from Austria. Details of the arrangement had long been worked out.

The Soviets agreed. In May 1955, the treaty was signed in Vienna. When a jubilant throng called them onto a balcony of Belvedere Palace, Molotov joined his hands over his head and Foster Dulles waved his handkerchief.

Dulles had long viewed an East-West summit mainly in terms of its potential to throw the West off guard; he noted that the Russians were spending roughly one fifth of their Gross National Product to catch up in nuclear bomber and long-range missile development. The President later said, somewhat disingenuously, "I didn't think any more of them than he did, except I thought once in a while they couldn't hurt, and they might do something useful—particularly as far as public opinion was concerned." Ann Whitman wrote "Geneva" across Eisenhower's schedule for the third week of July.

On June 22, the Soviets shot down a U.S. Navy patrol plane over the Bering Strait. For the first time, the Kremlin sent regrets and offered to pay half the damages. This was especially magnanimous because the plane was evidently flying a reconnaissance mission into Soviet airspace. Publicly the President blamed the affair on "misunderstanding," bad weather and a trigger-happy Soviet pilot. To make sure that it did not happen again, he told his Chairman of the Joint Chiefs of Staff, Admiral Arthur Radford, to keep all planes and vessels "well outside the fifteen-mile limit during the period between now and the summit conference."

●

John Foster Dulles was troubled about Geneva. "What I am most worried about is the President," he told his friend C. D. Jackson, who had left the White House staff to return to Time-Life in New York. "He and I have a relationship—both personal and operating—that has rarely existed between a Secretary of State and his President. As you know, I have nothing but admiration and respect for him, both as a person and as a man aware of foreign policy and conference pitfalls.

"Yet he is so inclined to be humanly generous, to accept a superficial tactical smile as evidence of inner warmth, that he might in a personal visit with the Russians accept a promise or a proposition at face value and upset the apple cart. . . . The President likes things to be right and pleasant between people. . . . You know, I may have to be the Devil at Geneva, and I dread the prospect. . . .

"This is something that I have never breathed to a soul or even intimated. . . . I am afraid that something will go wrong in Geneva, some slip of the Allies, some slip of the President's, which will put me in the position of having to go along with a kind of foreign policy for the U.S. which could be described as appeasement—no, appeasement is too strong a word, but you know what I mean. On the other hand, I may have to behave in such a way at Geneva that my usefulness as Secretary of State, both domestically and abroad, will come to an end."

Despite his unremitting deference, Dulles sometimes could not keep himself from treating Eisenhower like an amiable innocent being tutored by a diplomatic virtuoso. He once told the President that it was Eisenhower's world stature combined with his own diplomatic experience that made them such a strong team. The President agreed, but John Eisenhower later joked that what Dulles had really meant was "With your contacts and my brains, we can't miss!"

Dulles gave off a sense of melancholy weightiness which reminded the President of an Old Testament prophet. He had a tic in one of his deep-welled eyes which strangers sometimes mistook for a wink. Once in a foreign hotel, with a twitch of the eye, he was said to have asked a room service waiter for some bottled water. The waiter returned with a tray of liquor. "No," said Dulles (another twitch), "I said I would like some *bottled water.*" More minutes passed. A call girl arrived. The Secretary of State's response was not recorded for history.

Born in 1888, son of a Presbyterian minister of Watertown, New York, the young man went on sundry diplomatic missions with his grandfather and uncle, John W. Foster and Robert Lansing, Secretaries of State under Benjamin Harrison and Woodrow Wilson. As a partner at Sullivan and Cromwell in New York, he became known as the world's best-paid international lawyer. During the Second World War and the Truman years, Dulles functioned essentially as the shadow Secretary of State.

After Eisenhower's election, Dulles's appointment to the State Department was almost inevitable, but Milton Eisenhower recalled that his older brother "was not tremendously enthusiastic." The new President had only known Dulles since April 1952, when they met in Paris. He valued his internationalism but regretted his sometimes bellicose rhetoric. As his deputy Eisenhower appointed his wartime chief of staff, General Walter Bedell Smith—"Beetle" Smith—who had been serving as Truman's Director of Central Intelligence. Smith later told a friend that Eisenhower had told him that he did not feel he knew Dulles "well enough" and would "feel much better" with him at the State Department.

Dulles recalled how Wilson had fired his uncle and how Roosevelt had bypassed Cordell Hull: no one must disturb his relationship with the President. Early on, when Sherman Adams, White House chief of staff, tried to act as middleman, Dulles told Eisenhower that there could be only one Secretary of State, and it worked. The two men spoke incessantly in person and on the telephone. In the fading afternoon, the President often invited Dulles for a drink upstairs in the Mansion, where they ruminated about the motives of the men in the Kremlin, the final outcome of the Cold War.

"Foster's a bit sticky at times, but he has a heart of gold when you know him," Eisenhower once told Harold Macmillan (who was unconvinced). The President told his son that Dulles had an "ego problem": "Old Foster takes such a beating that I have to keep bolstering him all the time with these lavish statements—'the greatest Secretary of State in history' and that sort of thing." Dulles's penchant for public attention did not annoy Eisenhower—quite the contrary, for it allowed him to shift blame for unpopular policies. Behind the scenes, there was never any question who was in charge.

Dulles did not share Eisenhower's optimism that the cycle of Soviet-American distrust might be broken. As Goodpaster recalled, "The whole set of his mind was that the Soviets were inescapably hostile to our values and that no real improvement was likely." This did not disturb the President, who exploited the difference to play good cop and bad cop, but it did others in the inner circle. "Dulles was so anti-Communist, it was almost pitiful," said Milton Eisenhower. "His mind exaggerated the danger and neglected the positive things we might do to improve the situation."

Dulles was ever anxious that bureaucratic duties might divert him from dominating the foreign policy process. He periodically spoke with Eisenhower about leaving State to become a sort of First Secretary for Foreign Affairs. This never happened, but the activism of Presidential aides in foreign policy alarmed him. Like a dowager whose husband was spending time with a pretty, young vamp, he worried about the extent to which the President was listening to Nelson Rockefeller.

●

With his broad shoulders, granite profile and Big Man on Campus personality, Rockefeller did not much resemble the Secretary of State. His enthusiasms ran from Jackson Pollock to Venezuelan development; he had what Henry Kissinger called "the most absolute, almost touching faith in the power of ideas." Rockefeller was the only member of the Eisenhower Administration whose birth (in 1908) was reported on the front page of the *New York Times.*

His activism in foreign affairs began in 1940, when Franklin Roosevelt hired him as a dollar-a-year man on Latin America. After Eisenhower's election, he worked on a study on streamlining the federal government and then served as Undersecretary of Health, Education and Welfare. In December 1954, he landed with both feet in foreign policy, succeeding C. D. Jackson in a post the Founders could never have dreamed of—Special Assistant to the President for Cold War Strategy.

"Being less than fully restrained in my approach to life," as he once

confessed, Rockefeller was a Presidential aide with no passion for ano-
nymity. In his White House office, at dinners and on the tennis court of
his twenty-seven acres on Foxhall Road, he used his formidable charm
to bulldoze opposition to pet projects. One of these was Geneva.
Dulles thought the President should use the conference mainly to establish a genial climate for later talks at the foreign ministers' level;
Rockefeller thought Eisenhower should not spend five days in the
global spotlight with nothing new to offer. In June 1955, with Presidential approval, he sequestered eleven experts at Quantico Marine Base
in Virginia to draft a set of proposals.

"He seems to be building up a large staff," Foster Dulles grumbled
to Sherman Adams. "He's got them down at Quantico and nobody
knows what they're doing."

•

The stumbling block to an arms control treaty was verification. In
May 1955, the Russians conceded for the first time that any arms treaty
must be monitored by on-site inspections. What this might have meant
was international inspection teams at crossroads and other key points
to watch movement of military units and hardware. Western experts
were unimpressed: in Korea, the Chinese had foiled such teams by
simply rerouting their forces away from the monitors.

Why not verification from the air? Western defense intellectuals
had discussed the idea for years, but in the arctic freeze of the early
1950s, few were optimistic that the Soviets would accept. Perhaps
things would be different at Geneva. At Quantico, Max Millikan of
MIT, a sometime CIA officer, suggested that Eisenhower call on
America and Russia to grant each other the right to fly over and photograph each other's military sites. The plan was soon tagged "Open
Skies." Hans Speier of Rand worried that it was dangerously akin to
the U-2 and might draw publicity to the program. Open Skies was included in the Quantico Group's final proposal to the President, but it
languished for weeks.

Meanwhile, the CIA got into the act. Given the choice, many in the
Agency preferred legal overflights to violating Soviet airspace. That
way, they could gain the information they needed without provoking
the Russians or risking an international incident that might embarrass
the U.S. government or the Agency. The United States was so open
that the Russians would have relatively little to gain from the plan, but

for the Americans, Open Skies would be an intelligence bonanza. Allen Dulles noted that the U-2 was "ideally suited" to make such flights.

General Lucian Truscott, an old Eisenhower friend and former CIA station chief in Germany, apparently commended the plan to the President and stirred up support elsewhere. He went to the CIA's Dino Brugioni, whose job it was to establish bombing targets in Soviet industry: "What information might you want besides photographs?"

"Hell, I'd want the blueprints." Brugioni showed him a boxful of industrial plans. Many Soviet factories had been built by the West. In the 1930s, when Ford phased out the Model A, it sold old tools and dies to the Russians. Walter Reuther and other auto workers had gone to the Soviet Union to show the Russians how to operate the machinery. Valuable factory blueprints and other information had made their way back to Western intelligence, but much of this was outdated. Brugioni and colleagues conferred with Nelson Rockefeller and put their needs on paper. As the CIA man recalled, "We had learned to put a memo into 'Ikolese.' Eisenhower liked his memos in military fashion: *Conclusion, Fact One, Fact Two, Fact Three.*"

In early July, Rockefeller implored the President to make Open Skies a focal point at Geneva. By Rockefeller's account, Eisenhower called Foster Dulles: "Nelson is here and he has got a tremendous idea." At the other end of the wire, Dulles's heart sank. He said that State had already thrown out that idea. The President shouldn't consider it.

Eisenhower brought Dulles and Rockefeller to the Oval Office like quarreling schoolboys. As Rockefeller recalled, Dulles advised the President to use Geneva merely to "identify the problem areas" for referral to foreign ministers. "You can't do that," said Rockefeller. "Nobody is going to take seriously that General Eisenhower, President Eisenhower, comes all the way to Geneva to a summit meeting and says, 'I am going to identify the problems.' "

"Nelson, you have heard Foster. This is not acceptable and this is the way it is going to be." Rockefeller later recalled that he persisted until the President exploded: "Goddamit, I have told you we are not going to do that. Now stop talking about it."

Divorced from intramural politics between Dulles and Rockefeller, Open Skies appealed to Eisenhower. It would burnish America's peaceful reputation without risking vital concessions to the Soviets and it might speed the way to arms control. If the Russians accepted, the plan would spare him from ordering U-2 planes to violate Soviet air frontiers. If they refused, illegal overflights would be more justifiable. Perhaps to calm the nerves of his Secretary of State, the President tabled the issue for now. But before leaving for Geneva, he asked Rockefeller to stand by in Paris.

•

On Friday, July 14, as the *Columbine III* sailed into the blue night over the North Atlantic, John Eisenhower played Scrabble with his mother to distract her from her dread of flying. In the pre-jet era, Presidential travel abroad was an event: this was Eisenhower's first trip beyond North America since taking office. Before departure, he had assured Congressional leaders that Geneva would not be another Yalta. Foster Dulles groaned when he heard the President tell Americans on television that he hoped to "change the spirit" of American-Soviet relations and groaned again when he asked them to go to church to pray for peace.

"Eleven years ago, I came to Europe with an army, a navy and an air force," Eisenhower declared on landing at Geneva Airport. "This time, I come with something more powerful ... the aspirations of Americans for peace." Helicopters hovered overhead. Secret Service men trotted alongside as the 1942 Cadillac that Eisenhower had used during the war bore him to his headquarters for the week, an eighteenth-century villa on Lake Geneva lent by a perfume magnate.

Newsmen, diplomats and international socialites roamed the city. Security men were everywhere—Americans in bright ties and tropical suits, Russians in dark suits with theatrically well-padded shoulders. "Reporters are interviewing the reporters," complained the columnist Drew Pearson. The President and John relaxed from their eighteen-hour flight by hitting out golf balls in the garden of what aides called the Geneva White House.

•

On Sunday, the Soviets arrived. Nikita Khrushchev wore a shapeless, shiny suit with flapping trousers, Nikolai Bulganin a summer overcoat that reached the ground; the Premier's goatee and courtly manner gave him the aspect of a Czarist governor. As Khrushchev later said, he and his colleagues considered Geneva, their first prolonged encounter with the West, a "crucial test" of whether they could "keep the other side from intimidating us." Khrushchev saw that the British, French and American planes at the airport were "more impressive than ours." The comparison was "embarrassing."

By July 1955, Soviet leadership had devolved upon Bulganin and Khrushchev—"B and K," as Eisenhower and Goodpaster called them. The journalist John Gunther thought they looked as "cozy as twin peanuts in the shell." Bulganin was head of government, Khrushchev head of party, a distinction made clear when a Swiss guard shoved Khrushchev aside at their airport welcoming ceremony. The best Western estimate was that Khrushchev had the upper hand, but the President was not certain. By week's end, he hoped to find out for himself.

•

Bikini-clad women ran up from Lake Geneva to wave at Eisenhower as he rode to the Monday opening session in the Palais des Nations. When Bulganin and Khrushchev entered the large, crowded chamber, they brought Marshal Zhukov, now rehabilitated as Soviet Defense Minister, who greeted the President with a bear hug.

At a break in the session, Khrushchev told Eisenhower, "I must let you in on a Zhukov family secret. His daughter is being married this week, and he would have been in Moscow for the wedding, but he wanted to see you so much that he came here." The President sent for a radio and desk set as wedding presents. That evening, before dinner with Russians at his villa, he asked John to stay close to Zhukov: memories of their time together in Moscow after VE-Day might prod the Marshal to some confidence that he might not offer the other Americans.

At dinner, the President ignored Dulles's counsel to keep an "austere countenance" when the Soviets were around. Khrushchev sat next to the Secretary of State, whom he elsewhere called the "chained cur of capitalism." Later Khrushchev said, "Just imagine! We not only greeted each other, but I was seated next to him.... I think we spent more time talking about the food than anything else."

Impatient with banalities, Eisenhower told the Russians over dessert that it was "essential" to "find some way of controlling the threat of the thermonuclear bomb. You know, we both have enough weapons to wipe out the entire northern hemisphere from fallout alone."

Khrushchev agreed: "We get your dust, you get our dust, the winds blow and nobody's safe."

John Eisenhower sadly noted that Zhukov was no longer "the cocky little rooster we had known in Germany at the end of the war." The Marshal seemed "alive but broken." John concluded that Zhukov had been brought to Geneva only to help cultivate his father. Before the evening ended, Zhukov told the President, "Things are not as they seem."

•

Monday and Tuesday were a disappointment. Eisenhower opened by challenging the Russians on the most intractable issues—free elections in a unified Germany, Eastern Europe, Communist expansionism. Khrushchev declared that the German people "have not yet had time to be educated to the great advantage of Communism." Bulganin said that Soviet "internal affairs" like Eastern Europe were not open for discussion.

The President raised the danger of surprise attack. As a first step toward arms control, perhaps they should seek "dependable ways to supervise and inspect military establishments so that there can be no frightful surprises." The Russians did not respond. Determined to avoid a stalemate, Eisenhower decided to get specific. He called Nelson Rockefeller to Geneva.

Wednesday evening: Foster Dulles, Admiral Radford, General Alfred Gruenther of NATO gathered with Rockefeller by the hearth in the President's villa. When Eisenhower brought up Open Skies, Radford and Gruenther endorsed the plan. Evidently overwhelmed by the military men, Dulles reversed himself. The next morning, Rockefeller found John Eisenhower: "You have *got* to be in the conference this afternoon. Your dad is going to throw a bombshell."

Between sessions, the President introduced Khrushchev to Rockefeller. For Khrushchev, this was like the puppet introducing his puppeteer. "So this is Mr. Rockefeller himself!" he said, punching the puppeteer in the ribs. Khrushchev was startled to find the "biggest capitalist in the world" dressed "fairly democratically"—no giant diamond stickpin, gold pistol or other such props as in Bolshevik cartoons of Morgans and Rockefellers.

Thursday afternoon, with a breathtaking view of Lake Geneva through the tall window behind him, Eisenhower picked up his typed pages. He looked at the British delegation led by Prime Minister Anthony Eden, the French led by Premier Edgar Faure, and then read aloud from a statement on disarmament. Rockefeller turned around and whispered to John Eisenhower, "Now listen, here it comes."

The President took off his glasses, looked Bulganin and Khrushchev in the eye and issued his plea for Open Skies: "I have been searching my heart and mind for something that I could say here that could convince everyone of the great sincerity of the United States——" Rockefeller grinned and slapped John Eisenhower on the knee. A crack of thunder knocked out the lights and sound system. Some of the Russians reputedly wondered how the Americans had arranged such a dramatic coda.

Caught unprepared, Bulganin said that the President's plan had "real merit" and was worth "further study." But during the cocktail hour, Khrushchev told Eisenhower, "I disagree with our chairman. The trouble is, this is just espionage. We do not question your motives in making this proposal, but who are you trying to fool? . . . This kind of plan would be fine for you because it would give your strategic forces the chance to gather target information and zero in on us."

Zhukov joined the group. Eisenhower said he was sure that during the war, Marshal Zhukov would have given "a great many rubles to have had good photography of the enemy's positions." Khrushchev and Zhukov replied that this may have been true, but that was wartime.

"Don't kick the idea out the window," said Eisenhower. What he was trying to do was to "outline one first concrete step" which would "dispel fear and suspicion and thus lighten international tension by reassuring people against the dangers of surprise attack." This would confirm for the world their "joint intention not to fight against each other."

But Khrushchev insisted that the plan would increase neither peace nor stability. It was nothing but a "bald espionage plot." The boldness of Khrushchev's response left no doubt in Eisenhower's mind who ruled Russia.

●

The rest of the week was anticlimax. "Khrushchev is a mystery," wrote Harold Macmillan in his diary. "How can this fat, vulgar man with his pig eyes and ceaseless flow of talk, really be the head—the as-

pirant Tsar—of all those millions of people of this vast country?" An-
toine Pinay, the French Foreign Minister, was equally appalled at the
"coarseness" of "this little man with his fat paws." Eisenhower found
Khrushchev "rotund and amiable, but with a will of iron only slightly
concealed."

Khrushchev later professed to be astonished by the sight of "Dulles
making notes with a pencil, tearing them out of a pad, folding them up
and sliding them under President Eisenhower's hand. Eisenhower
would then pick up these sheets of paper, unfold them and read them
. . . like a dutiful schoolboy taking his lead from his teacher." Khrushchev could not fathom how a chief of state would permit himself to
"lose face" that way. He thought the President sincere and good, "but
that vicious cur Dulles was always prowling around Eisenhower, snapping at him if he got out of line."

•

Years later Eisenhower said he "knew" that the Soviets would
never accept Open Skies: "We were sure of that." But Goodpaster's
later memory was that the President felt there was "at least a chance"
that the Russians might accept the plan.

At the end of the week, Bulganin told Eisenhower, "Don't worry.
This will come out all right." So strong was the President's will to persuade the Russians on Open Skies that after the final session adjourned
he swept up Charles Bohlen, Ambassador to Moscow, and rushed to
the Soviet delegation's office for one last try. But Khrushchev and Bulganin had already gone home.

It was raining when the *Columbine III* landed in Washington.
Richard Nixon banned umbrellas at the airport to avoid glib comparisons with Neville Chamberlain and Munich. Despite irreverent newsmen who joked about Madison Avenue's intercession in foreign affairs, Open Skies and Eisenhower's performance drew glowing reviews
in the West. "That man has an absolutely unique ability to convince
people that he has no talent for duplicity," wrote Richard Rovere in
The New Yorker.

Geneva failed to halt or slow the Cold War. The size of the meeting
room and the publicity impeded hard bargaining. But the conference
made it possible for future American Presidents to meet Soviet leaders
without condemnation as appeasers. The sight of Eisenhower and the
Russians agreeing to disagree soothed world opinion. Macmillan told
reporters in London, "There ain't gonna be no war."

At the White House, the President told Congressional leaders that the Russians genuinely wanted to make a fresh start. So did he. He told the congressmen a secret not to be "let out of this room": Khrushchev and Bulganin had asked to come to America. "They would come fast. They want to be more in the public eye." Eisenhower said that his first instinct had been to tell them, "Good, come on over." But Foster Dulles "thought I had been impulsive enough," so he had merely told Bulganin that he would study the matter.

●

During the Open Skies deliberations, Eisenhower said, "I'll give it one shot. Then if they don't accept it, we'll fly the U-2." Now Allen Dulles "redoubled" efforts to "get this plane quickly going." The first U-2 was dismantled, loaded into a C-124, flown to Watertown Strip and reassembled.

On August 8, 1955, the sand-swept plain, the slender aircraft and cluster of spectators recalled the Wright Brothers at Kitty Hawk. A few days earlier, Tony LeVier had taken the U-2 down the runway for a taxi test. The plane was so buoyant that it popped thirty-five feet into the air and the pilot could not bring it down. After four or five tries, Kelly Johnson cried into his radio, "Tony, cut the power and just put it on the ground!" He did; the plane slammed onto the runway. Excessive airworthiness was a problem they could handle. That night, the Lockheed men celebrated with traditional beer and arm-wrestling contests.

Now as Johnson and Bissell watched, the pilot took the U-2 into its elegant curve and quickly out of sight. As Johnson later said, "From then on, it was drive, drive, drive. Build the airplanes, get them in operation, train ground and flight crews, maintenance men, military pilots."

●

Curtis LeMay still had his eye on the U-2. At the time Eisenhower originally asked CIA to develop the plane, the SAC General had reputedly said, "We'll let those SOBs get in and then we'll take it away from them."

In the summer of 1955, Allen Dulles was relaxing in the mountain air of Colorado Springs, home of the Air Defense Command, when Bissell arrived for a briefing. As the two men left the room after a meeting, someone muttered into Dulles's ear, "Don't let LeMay get his cottonpicking fingers on the U-2!"

With his famous ever-present cigar and bulldog manner, LeMay had been the youngest major general in the Army during World War Two; he became a hero overseeing the bombing of Tokyo in 1945. After the war, operating from Omaha, he used the same pugnaciousness to win SAC funding from Presidents and congressmen. LeMay was unabashed about interservice conflict: once, when he set his sights on the Navy's Polaris submarine, he was said to have adorned his office with a model of the sub painted with SAC's insignia just to irk Navy visitors.

LeMay and other Air Force commanders looked at the CIA with the unease of an older brother watching a younger brother grow brawnier each day. Since collaboration on spy flights and other missions after the war, the Air Force and CIA had been much intertwined. CIA agents worked undercover as Air Force officers; Air Force men were "sheep-dipped" for tours with the CIA. Many left the CIA true believers, which helped the Agency when it needed men, bases, equipment and other support from the Air Force. By 1955, the CIA was a considerable rival with an enthusiastic patron in the White House.

At Colorado Springs, LeMay told Dulles and Bissell that it had been "unusual enough" for the CIA to develop the U-2. Once it was ready to fly, "of course" it would pass to SAC.

"No, it won't," said Bissell.

Dulles sided with Bissell but did not relish a fight with the Air Force. At lunch, Bissell found his boss "grumpy and quite silent" about the matter. As Bissell recalled, the question went back to the President, who said, "I want this whole thing to be a civilian operation. If uniformed personnel of the armed services of the United States fly over Russia, it is an act of war—*legally*—and I don't want any part of that."

LeMay was not used to being outgunned. As one CIA man observed, he had not reckoned with "the power of the Dulles brothers." Nathan Twining was indignant about CIA's victory: "They took it over lock, stock and barrel. We had nothing to say about it. Ike approved it too, which he shouldn't have done.... CIA just kind of talked him into these things."

At the President's behest, Bissell negotiated a lasting armistice with the Air Force. Dulles and Twining agreed in writing that SAC would recruit U-2 pilots and train them. LeMay reputedly said, "If I can't operate the aircraft, I goddamn well ought to have a lot to do with training the crews." The Air Force would also lend help on communications, maintenance, aeromedicine and other logistics around the world. In exchange, the Air Force gained the right to appoint a deputy to Bissell.

Soon SAC officers began flying to Watertown Strip, where Tony LeVier and other Lockheed test pilots showed them how to train the fliers who would take the U-2 over Russia.

•

In August 1955, the President and First Lady went to Denver for a long vacation. Relaxing with customary vengeance, Eisenhower played bridge, cooked, painted, rode, played golf and fished for trout in a stream high in the Rockies. He spent the third week of September in the crisp altitudes of Byar's Peak Ranch with his banker friend Aksel Nielsen and George Allen.

Early on Friday, September 23, he cooked eggs and bacon for his companions and was driven through gold-flecked forests down to the Summer White House at Lowry Air Force Base. Looking through mail, he handed Ann Whitman a letter from Milton—"See what a wonderful brother I have?"—and frowned at a dilatory message from Bulganin on Open Skies.

He changed into golf clothes and played eighteen holes at the Cherry Hills Country Club. After lunching on hamburger and raw onion, he played nine holes more, complaining of heartburn. Someone called him back to the clubhouse for a call from Foster Dulles, but by the time he picked up the telephone, he found that Dulles had gone somewhere else. Irritated, he returned to the course and was called back again. This time, something was wrong with the wire. On the third try, he finally spoke with Dulles and approved a State Department letter to Moscow on arms control.

Once he returned to his game, he was called back again: someone, unaware that Eisenhower and Dulles had already spoken, had placed the call again. The President's friend and doctor General Howard Snyder later said he had never seen Eisenhower so irate.

Before dawn the next morning, the President writhed in his bed. Mamie asked, "What's the matter, Ike? Are you having a nightmare?" Snyder pulled up to the house in an Air Force car, divined that Eisenhower had had a heart attack and gave him a shot of morphine, inducing eleven hours of sleep. Only later, after being rushed to Fitzsimons Army Hospital and zipped into an oxygen tent, was the President told the diagnosis. Snyder watched his patient's eyes fill with tears.

At Lowry, Ann Whitman was weeping. At Fort Belvoir, Virginia, John Eisenhower got the news from a Secret Service man. At his home in the Spring Valley section of Washington, Richard Nixon was called by Jim Hagerty and said, "My God!" Two weeks later, Nixon went to Denver and saw the President, who said, "I never told Mamie how much it hurt."

In the President's absence, Foster Dulles told his brother that the Vice President must be fully briefed on current CIA methods and operations. Allen took Nixon on a tour of CIA headquarters and Camp Peary, Virginia, which career men called "the Farm." Disguised as a Pentagon research site, the Farm had weapons ranges, jump towers and a simulated closed border of a mythical Communist land. Eisenhower had told Nixon that the CIA was planning deep flights into Russia, but not the details. Now the Vice President learned that U-2 pilots were being recruited at this very moment.

•

Some of the best fliers in the Strategic Air Command went to motels where they were asked to fly for the CIA. While his wife waited in their car outside the Radium Springs in Georgia, Sammy Snider had his encounter with "Bill Collins." As the pilot later recalled, "We didn't sleep at all that night. We did an awful lot of talking because it was a big decision. We had a five-month-old baby." The next day, he returned to the motel and told Collins yes.

The CIA gave Snider, Frank Powers and other recruits aliases and false addresses, which they did their best to memorize so they would not draw a blank when asked. As instructed, they checked into the Du Pont Plaza in Washington and waited in their rooms for a call. The caller told them to gather in another room, where a CIA man searched under beds and dresser drawers for bugging devices. A radio blared music to mask conversation. Collins lamented the border flights' failure to reach critical Russian targets and pulled a picture of the U-2 from his satchel.

"What do you call it?"

"No one calls it anything publicly yet. This project is so secret that, other than those involved in the operation, only top-level government people know about it. But for your information, it's been dubbed the—" Someone snapped off the radio to hear better. Collins glared at the offender and did not speak until it was turned back up.

All fliers were evidently cleared for top secret, but since they considered themselves not spies but pilots they chuckled at the cloak-and-dagger methods. All were subjected to the lie detector, which some of the men resented. Each meeting with Collins in Washington was held at a different hotel. Travel was also scheduled to avoid routine: the men moved in groups of one to four, sometimes with Collins, sometimes without.

They flew to the Lovelace Clinic in Albuquerque, which did aeromedical work for the Air Force. Lovelace was the clinic Tom Wolfe made notorious in *The Right Stuff.* For a week, doctors, nurses and orderlies strapped down, whirled, electroshocked, whirled, probed, inoculated and forced other indignities upon the men who would stray further from the surface of the earth than virtually anyone before. This was the forerunner of the regimen applied three years later to candidates for Project Mercury.

Once the pilots survived Lovelace and an FBI security check, they were in. Contracts tied them to the CIA for eighteen months—$1,500 a month while stateside, $2,500 a month abroad. Five hundred dollars a month would be kept in escrow until contracts were satisfactorily fulfilled. The CIA told the fliers that this was to ease the tax bite; some suspected that the real purpose was to keep them from defecting or selling secret information to the Russians. Pilots were promised reinstatement in the Air Force with no time lost toward promotion or retirement.

"All the pilots in this difficult enterprise were most carefully selected," Allen Dulles said later. "They were highly trained, highly motivated and, as seemed right, well compensated financially. But no one in his right mind would have accepted these risks for money alone."

●

In November 1955, the first newly-minted pilots landed at Watertown Strip. Kelly Johnson called the place Paradise Ranch to boost pilot morale: "It was kind of a dirty trick, since Paradise Ranch was a dry lake where quarter-inch rocks blew around every afternoon." Life at the Ranch was the nightly tedium of the pool table and poker hand and the daily excitement of shattering the world's known altitude record (65,889 feet) with flights to Canada, Texas, Wyoming, Tennessee, Baja California. "There was only one thing wrong with flying higher than any other man had ever flown," recalled Frank Powers. "You couldn't brag about it."

The CIA took the pilots to a safe house in the East for escape and evasion training. "We got a chance to fire all the Russian weapons in case we went down somewhere," Sammy Snider said years later. "We learned lock-picking and how to disarm a guard and kill him if you had to. You've evaded for quite a while, there's a gate in the fence, on the other side is freedom and there's a guard there. . . . To this day, I feel confident that if you were guarding me and you had a pistol stuck in my stomach, I could tell you, 'I feel sorry for you because I'm going to take your gun away from you and I'm going to kill you with it.' "

As with most planes, the U-2's shakedown period was not free of accident. One day, Richard Bissell was called at his Washington office: a U-2 over the Southwest had suffered a flameout. Bissell called the base commander in Albuquerque, who mustered his troops just in time to screen off the area. The pilot made a dead-stick landing. Bissell worked with Pratt & Whitney on a new engine to solve the problem. Without this change, he later said, "there was at least a fifty-fifty chance that we would have had a flameout and been shot down and what happened that ended the program would have happened right at the start."

Another pilot taking off from Paradise Ranch found that one of the pogo sticks on wheels supporting the wings through takeoff would not drop off. He flew back over the airstrip but still could not shake it away. Heavy with fuel, his U-2 stalled, crashed and killed him. Another flier at night was blinded by lights at the end of the airstrip and died when he cracked into a telephone pole.

•

In early 1956, Bissell paid his call on Hugh Dryden, then head of the National Advisory Committee on Aeronautics. Precursor to NASA (the name was changed in 1958), NACA was purely a domestic operation, furnishing information on air turbulence and other weather problems to military and commercial aircraft makers.

Bissell told Dryden about the U-2 and told him what he wanted. NACA would announce the existence of a plane called the U-2 to be used for a NACA weather program. The plane would indeed be used to gather weather information, and NACA would release progress reports to the public. Dryden would get weather information impossible to get from any other plane, but the main purpose would be to disguise Bissell's intelligence missions.

The proposal made Dryden nervous. In 1956, Congress was by no means resolved to spend vast sums to send men into space. If something went wrong with the U-2 and NACA was exposed as the CIA's servant, the space program might never get off the ground. Still he felt the "duty to cooperate with an agency that is getting information vital to our national defense." In the spring of 1956, NACA announced that "a new type of airplane, the Lockheed U-2," had been developed for use in a new "high-altitude meteorological program with U-2s borrowed from the Air Force." NACA said that the pilots were civilians borrowed from Lockheed.

•

Meanwhile American intelligence decided to take another chance at gathering information over Russia from balloons. The take would not only be useful in itself but would help U-2 mission planners to find high-priority targets. In January 1956, the Air Force announced that hundreds of large plastic balloons were being sent to carry "weather instruments" all over the world. The Soviet Union was not excluded.

Late that month, the Soviet Ambassador, Georgi Zaroubin, asked for a meeting with Eisenhower. Foster Dulles feared that the Russians were about to issue "a very strong protest" against the balloons, denounce Open Skies and launch "a worldwide propaganda campaign against the United States, picking up the old charges of warmongering and all the rest."

"I haven't thought too much of this balloon thing and I don't blame the Russians at all," said the President. "I've always thought it was sort of a dirty trick. But that was the gamble we took when we made the decision."

Zaroubin called on Eisenhower and Dulles in the Oval Office. Afterwards the President laughingly noted that the Russian had not even mentioned the balloons. "Maybe that's what you get for having somewhat of a guilty conscience," said Dulles. What the Ambassador wanted was a twenty-year friendship treaty with the United States, which Dulles thought "preposterous."

The Americans' luck did not hold. The Russians shot down many of the balloons. At a Moscow press conference, a Red Army colonel warned that the American government could use them to drop anything from Christmas presents to disease-bearing insects intended to start a Soviet epidemic. Reporters were invited to Molotov's official residence, where they were led around a driveway lined with balloon baskets, gas bags, parachutes, cameras, radio receivers and placards in several languages: "THIS BOX CAME FROM THE SKY. IT IS HARMLESS. IT HAS WEATHER INFORMATION IN IT. NOTIFY THE AUTHORITIES. YOU WILL RECEIVE A VALUABLE REWARD WHEN YOU TURN IT IN AS IT IS."

At the White House, Eisenhower reminded Dulles that he had been "rather allergic" to the balloon project and doubted that the results justified the risk. Dulles said, "I agree, but I think we should handle it so it would not look as though we had been caught with jam on our fingers." The President told him not to apologize or concede that the balloons had been sent for espionage. He should simply tell the Soviets that no more would be sent.

•

Richard Bissell searched for an overseas base from which the U-2 could pierce the Iron Curtain. Given the intimate Anglo-American intelligence partnership, a base in Britain would be most secure. Anthony Eden gave permission to use Lakenheath, a SAC base northeast of London. Bissell flew there with an air attaché from the American Embassy and found it perfect.

In Washington, he walked into another roomful of CIA and Air Force men at the Pentagon. It had been eighteen months since their first conclave. As cigarette smoke curled toward the lights on the ceiling, the training supervisor from Watertown Strip declared that the first detachment of U-2 pilots had been graduated: "This outfit can go anywhere, and it's all ready."

NACA announced that it was extending its weather program to Europe, where the "First Provisional Weather Reconnaissance Squadron" would study conditions in the area of the Baltic Sea. A half-dozen U-2 pilots flew to Britain and lodged in an inconspicuous corner at Lakenheath. All they needed now was the word from their Commander-in-Chief.

★

5

"The Most Soul-Searching Decision"

AFTER HIS HEART ATTACK, doctors warned Eisenhower to avoid "irritation, frustration, anxiety, fear and, above all, anger," but when they tried to lay down the law, he barked, "Just what do you think the Presidency *is?*"

Liberated from hospital in November 1955, he went to Gettysburg, where he stalked the frozen grounds with a nine-iron, telephoned commands to the West Wing and wondered "what the failing health of a President might do to the office and to the cause for which a whole administration might be working." He told Jim Hagerty, "I just hate to turn this country back into the hands of people like Stevenson, Harriman and Kefauver."

On Leap Day 1956, the President declared for re-election. "I really don't know the exact moment when he decided to run again," said Hagerty. "But I do know that history was made sometime in those weeks at Gettysburg. It was then that he really faced the sheer, God-awful boredom of not being President." Eisenhower's friend General Lucius Clay said, "I don't care what happens to the Republican party but if he quits, it'll kill him."

The lower half of the ticket remained unresolved. The President doubted that Richard Nixon could attract the "discerning Democrats" and independents required if the Republicans were ever to become a majority party. He knew that as sitting Vice President, Nixon might be the inescapable nominee in 1960. He told Nixon that perhaps he should take a Cabinet post during the second term: four years at the Pentagon might give him executive experience that would be useful if he ever wished to run for President. Nixon was noncommittal.

Another talk was pure Alphonse and Gaston. Nixon: "You tell me what you want me to do and I'll do it." Eisenhower: "No, I think we've got to do what's best for *you.*"

"Nixon will never be President," Eisenhower told the Republican national chairman, Leonard Hall. "People don't like him." Hall said it would be "the easiest thing to get Nixon out of the picture willingly. I have known Dick a long time." Recording their talk on his hidden machine, the President said, "All right. You see him and talk to him, but be very, very gentle." Hall failed; he later said, "I never saw a scowl come so fast over a man's face."

For months, as a friend recalled, Nixon went through "absolutely indescribable anguish." He refused to commit hara-kiri; Eisenhower refused to fire him. Perhaps the President feared that a scorned Nixon would mobilize the Right against him, perhaps that a public execution would harm his genial image. In March 1956, before reporters, he announced his view that the Vice President should "chart his own course." In April, Nixon went to the Oval Office and said he would be "honored" to run again: "The only reason I waited this long to tell you was that I didn't want to do anything that would make you think I was trying to force my way on the ticket if you didn't want me on it."

The President said he was glad and had only wondered why it had taken him so long to say so. He called Jim Hagerty: "Dick has just told me that he'll stay on the ticket. Why don't you take him out right now and let him tell the reporters himself?" In later years, Milton Eisenhower said that "a more sensitive man" than Nixon would have taken his brother's hint and left the ticket: "But he wanted to be there. He thought this was his chance to be President."

•

That month, for the first time in history, a major peacetime American spy operation was exposed to the world. Builders of the Berlin Tunnel had forecast that if it were ever uncovered, the Soviets "would probably suppress knowledge of the tunnel's existence." Like Foster Dulles's forecast about a U-2 downing, the CIA had felt that for the

Soviets "to admit that the U.S. had been reading their high-level communications circuits" would cause them to lose face.

In 1955, with Eisenhower's approval and British help, CIA men in West Berlin burrowed into the eastern zone and tapped the telephone lines from Berlin to Leipzig. Western agents sat inside the narrow passage far underground, listening in on conversations about the Soviet order of battle and location of Soviet troops. The tunnel brought in so much material that Richard Bissell considered limiting the amount sent to Washington.

In the winter of 1955, heaters inside the tunnel melted snow on the East Berlin farmer's field under which it ran. The CIA bought up Sears, Roebuck's East Coast inventory of plastic pipe and installed an air-cooling system. It has been said that the Soviets had learned of planning for the tunnel at the start from George Blake, an agent in the British Secret Service, but let the project proceed to protect him. Another version has it that the project was discovered during routine maintenance of the telephone line. Whatever the story, on the evening of April 15, 1956, Soviets and East Germans burst into the tunnel. Americans fled to the western side so hastily that when the enemy arrived, a percolator inside the tunnel was still brewing coffee.

The Kremlin denounced the "perfidy of the American and British aggressors." East Berliners were taken to view the "criminal conspiracy" of the "terrorists and warmongers." The Chinese tacked up pictures of the tunnel in shops and factories; Peking's press reported them as "aroused to lively discussion and indignation." But Western papers almost all lauded the project. The *New York Herald Tribune* called it "a venture of extraordinary audacity. . . . If it was dug by American intelligence forces—and that is a general assumption—it is a striking example of their capacity for daring undertakings." When the tunnel was exposed, Foster Dulles ribbed his sister Eleanor, a German expert in the State Department; she shot back that it was "all Allen's fault."

Soon the Berlin Tunnel was called "the most highly publicized peacetime espionage enterprise in modern times." But no American newspaper prominently suggested that Eisenhower had authorized the project or had even known about it. At his next press conference, reporters did not ask a single question about the tunnel.

Privately the President was sorry that its usefulness was done, "but you had to anticipate that it was coming to an end," Andrew Goodpaster recalled. "I think he felt that there had been carelessness that drew the attention of the East Germans." Eisenhower responded by tightening White House supervision of all CIA activities encroaching on foreign sovereignty.

•

Four days after revelation of the Berlin Tunnel, the West was once more thrown on the defensive by the exposure of another spy operation. Khrushchev and Bulganin had sailed to Great Britain aboard the Soviet cruiser *Ordzhonikidze,* for a goodwill visit. The trip, Khrushchev's first to the West, was widely considered an off-Broadway try-out for a later visit to the United States. Eager to preserve the cordial spirit of Geneva, Anthony Eden ordered British intelligence to refrain from operations against the Russian ship. But the Admiralty wished to learn the pitch of the cruiser's screws as it sat in Portsmouth harbor. A "free-lance" frogman, Commander Lionel Crabbe, "offered" to do the deed on his own.

One evening at dinner, one of the Russians asked the First Lord of the Admiralty, "What was the frogman doing off our bows this morning?" Crabbe was never seen again alive. Later his headless body was washed ashore; there was evidence that homicidal Soviet counterintelligence men had been waiting for him in a hidden compartment under the cruiser.

The Soviets publicized the affair. Eden's Labour opposition forced the issue in Parliament. The Prime Minister fired the Director General of the British Secret Service. Apprehensive about further humiliations that might damage his reputation and sour relations with the Russians, he remembered the U-2 and told Washington, "This isn't the moment to be making overflights from here."

Bissell and the Brothers Dulles thought of West Germany. Although the Federal Republic had joined NATO in 1955, Konrad Adenauer remained wary of abandonment by the United States. After Geneva, when Eisenhower sent Zhukov a friendly note by diplomatic pouch, West German intelligence informed Adenauer, who reputedly suspected a secret dialogue on how to sell West Germany down the river. Such evidence of American fidelity as the Berlin Tunnel and the large CIA station in Frankfurt made the Chancellor feel less insecure.

Bissell and Pearre Cabell flew to Bonn. In Adenauer's office, they showed him U-2 pictures and briefed him on the program. As Bissell recalled, the Chancellor was "delighted" by the technical achievement and the fact that the Americans were being "rather ingenious in the whole matter of the Cold War." The U-2 pilots, support people and planes were moved to Wiesbaden.

•

Khrushchev and Bulganin could not have expected that the West would hand them such propaganda gifts as the Berlin Tunnel and the Commander Crabbe affair during their British tour. Before they sailed for Russia, Jacob Malik, then Soviet Ambassador to London, threw the two leaders a boisterous farewell in the faded bourgeois grandeur of Claridge's.

"A very unusual party, to say the least," muttered a guest as four thousand politicians, earls, editors, dowagers, radicals and gate-crashers feasted on caviar and salmon, knocked over lamps and vases and stamped cigarettes into the rug. Some sagged to the floor, unused to vodka in Russian servings; they were trampled by others surging across the steamy room to have a look at the guests of honor. Introduced to Charlie Chaplin, Khrushchev said, "You are a genius." Blacklisted by Hollywood and the U.S. Passport Agency, the Little Tramp and Paul Robeson were cherished Soviet symbols of American political repression. Khrushchev declared, *"They repudiate* you—but *we honor* you."

Harold Stassen was serving in London as Eisenhower's delegate to disarmament talks. Andrei Gromyko found him in the crush and asked, "Have you met Khrushchev yet?" Stassen shook his head and was taken to an anteroom for an audience.

Khrushchev bellowed against Open Skies: "You treat the Soviet Union like a rich uncle treats a pauper nephew!" The Soviet Union didn't want pictures of anyone else's land. Why were Americans always so eager to peek into other people's bedrooms? Only the Soviet leadership's great respect for President Eisenhower had kept them from turning down Open Skies right away in Geneva.

Why did Americans always meddle in other people's business? Look at Guatemala! "We are not ignorant savages any more. You cannot frighten us as you could have done thirty years ago." Khrushchev said he was sure that Eisenhower wanted peace, but not John Foster Dulles. "Gromyko would not have said that, but he is a diplomat. I am an amateur."

Stassen hurried to the American Embassy and cabled Washington that Khrushchev had seemed to turn down Open Skies once and for all.

•

By now, Eisenhower was ready to resort to the U-2. Allen Dulles and Richard Bissell wished to begin flying into Russia by mid-June. By then, the spring rains would be done and the fliers could clearly view long-range bomber bases and other sites in the western Soviet Union. U-2 pictures of American cities from seventy thousand feet were unveiled in the Cabinet Room. The President marveled that he could "easily count the automobiles in the streets and even the lines marking the parking areas for individual cars."

Eisenhower asked Allen Dulles what would happen if a plane malfunctioned. As Goodpaster recalled, "Allen's approach was that we were unlikely to lose one. If we did lose one, the pilot would not survive. . . . We were told—and it was part of our understanding of the situation—that it was almost certain that the plane would disintegrate and that we could take it as a certainty that no pilot would survive . . . and that although they would know where the plane came from, it would be difficult to prove it in any convincing way."

Perhaps, but the President was still troubled by the risk of invading Soviet airspace in peacetime. Time and time again he said, "Such a decision is one of the most soul-searching questions to come before a President. We've got to think about what our reaction would be if *they* were to do this to *us.*" To Goodpaster, the answer was clear: "Our reaction would be to try to shoot them down, of course. . . . It would be approaching a provocation, a probable cause of war because it was a violation of their territory."

Eisenhower agreed in principle to a first set of flights into Russia: the pilots must cover vital targets quickly. He asked Dulles to "concentrate the operations on high-priority items" and suggested a "ten-day period of operations followed by a report."

•

Late at night on June 7, 1956, Mamie Eisenhower thought the President was suffering another coronary. Doubled up with pain, he was taken from his bed to Walter Reed Army Hospital, where physicians found a blocked intestine: immediate surgery was required to prevent gangrene. "If we don't move fast, we are going to lose our patient," said one doctor. Twenty-four hours after the attack, Goodpaster called

Sherman Adams from home and said, "I am leaving right now to go to Walter Reed."

"For what purpose?"

"To observe his competency should any military decisions become important." Goodpaster was joined by Adams and Hagerty in the operating room, where they had the "eerie and striking" experience of watching surgeons work on the motionless body of the President. Two days later, Eisenhower was out of sedation. He wrote his boyhood friend Swede Hazlett, "My 'innards' have been pictured, described and discussed in the papers, to say nothing of the television and radio, until you, along with many others, must be heartily sick of the whole business."

The President's brush with death did not postpone the U-2's maiden voyage into Russia. But there were clouds over the western Soviet Union and it took some time to put equipment in place in Wiesbaden. While waiting for the weather to clear, Bissell won permission "to do some preliminary overflights over the satellites in Eastern Europe"—an excellent opportunity to show Eisenhower what the U-2 could do.

On June 21, Bissell, James Killian and Edwin Land spoke with Goodpaster about the "yield to be expected" from U-2 flights and "thoughts and preparations regarding malfunctioning." Goodpaster told them that "the President must be contacted before deep operations into the Soviet Union are initiated."

●

Another delay. During the final week of June, Nathan Twining and nine other Air Force men went to Moscow. The U-2 could hardly begin violating Soviet airspace while Twining and his party were enjoying Soviet hospitality. The group had been invited by their Soviet counterparts to view Aviation Day, the annual rite in which Soviet pilots flew new aircraft over the capital in spectacular formations. Aviation Day was obviously designed to impress the West with Soviet air power: in 1955, Western attachés had been astonished by the number of long-range bombers on display.

In the spring of 1956, Twining, LeMay and other Air Force titans testified before Congress that Russia "has almost closed the air power gap. In airplane after airplane, they are approaching us in quality and surpassing us in quantity." Eisenhower was skeptical of the Bomber Gap but hoped that Twining's group would find out more about Soviet air power. Perhaps the mission might achieve a primitive form of Open Skies: "If they want to trade military visits and really see what the other country has in a military sense, they might invite our chiefs. . . . I am very anxious to see how far the Soviets are ready to go in making offers and working for relationships."

Twining's party viewed Soviet aerial acrobatics, aircraft factories and flying schools. Riding in the private plane of his opposite number, Marshal R. A. Rudenko, Twining noted that it was "quite ornate and furnished in mid-Victorian style, with Persian rugs on the floor and flowered china in racks along the wall."

On Aviation Day, Khrushchev unexpectedly joined foreign guests at an Army reception in Moscow and toasted Eisenhower, friendship and peace. When he toasted China, the Americans sat stock-still and did not raise their glasses. By the end of the affair, Khrushchev was reliably reported to be drunk. "You are probably interested in our rockets and our ballistic missiles!" he called across the room to Twining. "You would like to see them, wouldn't you?"

Twining nodded, wondering whether this might be a trap.

"Well, we want to see yours too! Show us your *planes* and we'll show you our *ballistic missiles!* But we won't show them to you today. Today is too early. We'll do it at some future date. Meanwhile, you keep yours and we'll keep ours. We'll show you what competition is!"

All laughed and applauded. Khrushchev shook hands with Twining, certain that he had had the last word. He did not know that Twining was involved in a plan to begin flying deep into the Soviet Union a few days hence, and that if it worked, the United States would begin to have a better idea how many planes and missiles the Russians really had.

On Monday, July 2, Soviet skies were clearing. Richard Bissell asked Goodpaster for permission to begin crossing the Soviet border. The mission was lent greater urgency by communications intelligence that suggested possible mobilization. Next morning, Goodpaster saw the President, recuperating at Gettysburg. Eisenhower granted ten days to fly. Then the CIA must return with a report. Goodpaster returned to Washington and told Bissell, "The President has authorized flights for a period of ten days."

"Of course, that's ten days of good weather."

"That is absolutely wrong. Ten days from *now*."

•

The U-2 project team of 1956 was housed in the CIA's K Building, one of the hideous wartime "temporary" office blocks on both sides of the Reflecting Pool near the Lincoln Memorial. Bissell found the place "unappetizing." One day a CIA man was working there alone, "plotting the downfall of the Soviet Union," when Allen Dulles walked in and said, "Good God, this is a damned pig sty!"

By Bissell's account, it was six o'clock on Tuesday evening, July 3, when he walked into the U-2 Operations Center. The base in West Germany had been notified that "we may be flying a mission, and this will be the flight plan and you'd better get pilots, navigational aids and everything else set up." Bissell found that "the boys had laid out a flight directly to Moscow, ninety-degree turn, then directly over Leningrad, then down the Baltic coast—all coastal, air, radar installations." Bissell's men told him, "Let's go for the big game the first time. We're safer the first time than we'll ever be again."

Six o'clock was "the major briefing and a full review of weather," Bissell later recalled. "If everything looked good, a single code word went to the field saying, 'The mission is on, the flight plan as transmitted is approved.' " Bissell told them to send the code word to West Germany. By 11:30, a summer moon glimmered on the Reflecting Pool. Bissell returned to the Ops Center: "The weather was still good, so I sent the 'go' message."

•

Next morning, as Bissell recalled, he went to CIA headquarters at 8:30. It was Wednesday, July 4, the 180th birthday of the United States. By his recollection, he walked into the Director's office and said, "Well, Allen, we're out and running."

"Where is it flying?"

"It's flying first over Moscow, then over Leningrad, then home."

Dulles turned pale: "Was it really wise to do that the first time?"

"The first time is the safest. We should hear within another hour."

•

As American planes began flying deep into his country, Khrushchev stood, of all places, in the garden of Spaso House, the American Ambassador's residence in Moscow. Charles Bohlen was presiding over the Embassy's annual Independence Day reception; in the spirit of Geneva, Khrushchev had decided to attend. The yellow 1914 mansion was built by a sugar baron for his mistress, confiscated after the Revolution and leased to the United States in 1933 when it opened diplomatic relations with the Soviets. Avis Bohlen showed Khrushchev the corn she was raising in her garden. Almost nothing was more likely to impress the leader known in the provinces as Nikita the Corn-Grower. He said, "I am glad to see American corn grows so well in Russia."

Khrushchev boasted to the American journalist Marvin Kalb that the Soviets had "the best, the tallest basketball players in the world." Kalb politely reminded him that this distinction belonged to the United States. Khrushchev ascertained that Kalb played basketball and asked how tall he was. "Only six centimeters shorter than Peter the Great," said Kalb. From then on, Khrushchev addressed him as Peter the Great.

A professor from Columbia University asked the Soviet leader about Soviet decision-making. "We disagree and we take a vote," said Khrushchev. He pointed at Molotov and said, "We have had differences between us."

"Not noticeably," said the American.

Khrushchev laughed: "Not noticeably."

Chip Bohlen knew about the U-2 project but not that the first plane was flying over Moscow: that way, if it were ever revealed, he could more honestly say that he did not know anything about the matter. Before Khrushchev left, newsreel men rolled their cameras as the Soviet leader congratulated Americans on their holiday and toasted the health of President Eisenhower.

•

President Eisenhower was at Gettysburg, chipping golf balls onto the putting green behind his house. The surgery had weakened his stomach muscles and he stooped as he walked.

"I am ready to put the whole nasty business behind me," he wrote Swede Hazlett. "The farm has never looked better and I have been happily renewing my acquaintance with my tiny Angus herd. Official business, a small amount of 'farming,' and a strict regime of treatment, mild exercise and rest more than occupy my days." A Secret Service man brought David and Anne Eisenhower from Fort Belvoir to spend the holiday with their grandparents, but by noon it was raining and the President moved the celebration indoors.

•

At the CIA, Richard Bissell shouted with pleasure. The weather over Russia had been perfect, the pilot had used all his film and it was on its way to the United States. As Bissell recalled, "It was a very exciting moment." He called Allen Dulles and told him that "our boy" was home safe. "A very relieved man he was," said Bissell later, "and so was I, for that matter." He scheduled another flight.

On Thursday, July 5, Nathan Twining went to Gettysburg to give the President an eighty-minute report on his Soviet trip. He told reporters that his tour had convinced him that Russia was "rapidly catching up" with the United States. During his visit, the door to Soviet military development had been opened "a little crack, but what lies in those rooms, we do not know." He did not tell the press that he soon expected the U-2 to show him.

More planes crossed the western Soviet Union. Bissell told Goodpaster that there was no further evidence of mobilization. Bissell and Dulles had hoped that the planes "would not be picked up at all" by Soviet radar. But Soviet radar turned out to be so strong that it was tracking every flight.

In West Germany, James Killian was inspecting a National Security Agency listening post as the first U-2s soared into Russia: "I found there this group of people who were listening in on what was happening in the Soviet Union, baffled and astonished at what they were hearing." It seemed to be an intruder plane, but the NSA people knew—or thought they knew—that no plane in the world could fly over seventy thousand feet. As Killian recalled, "I didn't tell them what it was."

In Moscow, Khrushchev knew exactly what it was, and he was angry. How could Twining be so arrogant as to send American planes to violate Soviet frontiers immediately after accepting Soviet hospitality? "We welcomed him as a guest and entertained him," Khrushchev complained in May 1960. "He left our country by air and next day sent a plane flying at great altitude into our country. . . . Only an animal like Twining would do its dirty business in the same place it eats. From such behavior, we drew one conclusion—*Improve rockets! Improve fighter planes!*"

•

Friday, July 6. Eisenhower and George Allen watched carpenters building a playhouse for the President's grandchildren on the Gettysburg lawn. Goodpaster called to say that he had talked to Bissell: "No operation was run today, and it appears that none will be run tomorrow."

More flights. Then Moscow lowered the boom. On Tuesday, July 10, the Soviet Ambassador marched into the State Department and handed Foster Dulles a formal protest against pirate flights by "a U.S. Air Force twin-engine plane" from West Germany. With specific times, dates and routes, the note complained that the violations were obviously "intentional and for purposes of reconnaissance." What was more, they were waged at a time "when relations between governments are improving and when mutual confidence is growing." Who must have sanctioned the violations? "Reactionary circles hostile to the cause of peace" who were "worried by the relaxation of mutual tensions."

Zaroubin turned on his heel and left the building. Copies of his note were passed out to reporters, who rushed to their atlases. Lincoln White declared, "We know absolutely nothing about this." Another State Department official: "If American planes penetrated that deep inside Russia and remained so long, why didn't Soviet fighters attempt to shoot them down?" Allen Dulles gave the bad news to Goodpaster, who found the President unstartled by the Soviet protest; he later said that Eisenhower had "anticipated something like this."

On Wednesday, July 11, Foster Dulles wrote a draft reply avowing that no *military* plane had violated Soviet airspace. He read it over the telephone to his brother, who said, "Fine—perfect—good luck!" Then he submitted the draft for Eisenhower's approval. The President asked him to "button it up" by adding that American flight plans "carefully exclude such overflights as the Soviet note alleges."

In Moscow, at the French Embassy's Bastille Day reception, Bulganin took Chip Bohlen aside and asked if he knew anything about the incursions. Bohlen said he had "no information whatsoever." Bulganin told him the Kremlin had "indisputable evidence" from radar that the Americans had violated Soviet airspace: "This is a very serious matter."

At an Egyptian Embassy fete, newsmen asked Marshal Rudenko

about the Soviet protest: How did they know that the planes were American? Rudenko said that the planes had flown too high to see their markings but the silhouettes looked American. Didn't many countries own American planes? Maybe so, but even then, Washington was responsible. Why hadn't the Soviets shot down the planes? The Kremlin did not wish to exacerbate world tensions, but if the flights continued, it would take "all necessary measures."

Eisenhower admired the CIA for doing what the Air Force probably could not have done—building new spy planes and sending them deep into Russia within nineteen months. But Moscow's instant, angry protest changed the terms of the U-2 program. It was one thing to dart in and out of Soviet airspace with the Russians dimly aware, quite another for them to track every flight and issue a public complaint. Zaroubin had made it clear that the Russians considered the flights an insult that would "aggravate relations between the Soviet Union and the United States."

As Goodpaster recalled, "There was a high level of provocation here, a considerable level of risk, and the President wanted tighter control, a great deal tighter control." Eisenhower called Allen Dulles to the White House.

•

With his signature bow tie, well-trimmed white mustache and tweed jacket fragrant of pipe tobacco, the CIA Director resembled the Free World's chief intelligence man less than he did a Princeton history professor who perhaps spent a few months each winter skiing in Switzerland. Little more than the quick movement of the intelligent eyes behind his rimless glasses suggested his past life as a spy.

Dulles's demeanor, his interest in food and wine and his sardonic sense of irony were all more European than American. He was more attuned than Eisenhower—or Foster Dulles—to the ambiguities and minor hypocrisies in people, foreign policy and political theory. A captivating storyteller and connoisseur of secrets and mysteries, he once noted, "There is something about intelligence that gets into the blood."

Richard Bissell found Allen Dulles a warmer man than the Secretary of State, "and I think he inspired more loyalty." Robert Amory said, "I loved Allen Dulles. A pain in the neck in many ways, but he was so sweet. He could bawl your ass out for something . . . and then about a quarter of five on a summer afternoon, he'd say, 'How about making a fourth for tennis on my courts on Q Street?' He meant more to me than any other man of his generation but my father."

"His charm was irresistible and his intensity of rage was occasionally overwhelming," said his sister Eleanor. "I know that there were months in our later years when I stayed out of his orbit to avoid the stress and furor that he stirred in me." The intensity was never far from the surface. At a State Department meeting on Egypt's Gamal Abdel Nasser, the CIA Director reputedly once said, "If that colonel of yours pushes us too far, we'll break him in half."

Dulles did little to discourage the notion that he was a commander on the front lines of the Cold War who could change hostile regimes, frustrate the KGB, pierce the Iron Curtain and do other minor miracles of daring and skill. He once counseled a reporter to think of the CIA as "the State Department for unfriendly countries." In the Soviet press, Ilya Ehrenburg called Dulles "the most dangerous man in the world, far more dangerous than John Foster Dulles." If the CIA chief ever managed to force his way into heaven, "he would be found mining the clouds, shooting up the stars and slaughtering the angels." Dulles sometimes read this encomium aloud before audiences, adding that he was pleased that the Russians put him a notch higher than his brother.

Although the majority of the CIA's work was intelligence analysis, covert operations were his undying love. "Boy, he loved to get into the exact details of 'Where are you going to meet this guy and what's the fallback position?' " said Amory. Colleagues called him "the Great White Case Officer." Dulles saw his task as that of devising ways to help the United States prevail in a hard world: "If you believe in a program, you may have to break a little crockery to put it into effect." He told his sister Eleanor, "Do you realize my responsibilities? I have to send people out to get killed! Who else in this country in peacetime has the right to do that?"

•

He was born in 1893 with a club foot, which his father reputedly believed to be the mark of Cain. When it was corrected, brothers and sisters were told never to mention the problem outside the family. At eight, he wrote a six-thousand-word history of the Boer War, which Foster pronounced "an infantile effort," but which their grandfather had privately published and sold to raise funds for Boer relief. Allen followed his older brother to Princeton and taught in missionary schools in India, China and Japan.

In 1916, his uncle Robert Lansing invited him to join the Foreign Service, but this was not his natural habitat. When the American minister in Vienna gave him his suit for cleaning, Dulles said, "I may be your third secretary, but I am not your valet."

During the First World War, he took charge of intelligence in Berne. Since boyhood, he had been entranced by the heroes who strode across the pages of British spy fiction. Intelligence was an inevitable channel for his curiosity about the difference between people's public and private selves and his British public school-type penchant for doing complex feats with seeming lack of effort. "I am one of the many cogs in the wheel and I cannot tell you much what I do," he wrote his family. "Except that it has to do with Intelligence!"

He gathered information from exiles of Russia, Germany and other lands who were moving through Switzerland. As he later told CIA recruits, once he was called by a Bolshevik who said he must speak with someone in the American legation in Berne. Dulles resisted because he had a tennis date with an appealing young woman; by the time the Russian arrived, his office would be closed. "Tomorrow will be too late," said the Russian, but Dulles would not stay to see the caller. As he later revealed, the Russian turned out to be Lenin, on his way to Petrograd to command the Russian Revolution and remove his country from the war.

After the war, when the United States reduced its intelligence service, Dulles returned to the State Department in Washington, where he became chief of Near Eastern affairs. No doubt stifled by the bureaucracy, he took night law courses to join his elder brother at Sullivan and Cromwell in 1926. Improbably he ran (without success) for Congress from Manhattan.

At the 1940 Republican convention, he saw William Donovan, onetime Republican candidate for governor of New York, who told him that Franklin Roosevelt had quietly asked him to lay the groundwork for a new American intelligence organization. Dulles asked, "When do you want me to start?" In an office at Rockefeller Center, he built a staff of European experts and renewed old links to European refugees. J. Edgar Hoover complained to the President that Dulles was "hiring a bunch of Bolsheviks."

During the war, working from a fifteenth-century house in Berne, he earned his name in Donovan's Office of Strategic Services by running espionage operations against Germany. He became romantically involved with Mary Bancroft, student of Jung, the Boston-born daughter of the publisher of the *Wall Street Journal*. She later recalled that one evening at Dulles's house they had begun to "thoroughly enjoy ourselves" when the doorbell rang. He put his hand over her mouth and scribbled, "DON'T MOVE. DON'T MAKE A SOUND." After more rings, he smiled and wrote, "PERSISTENT BASTARD, ISN'T HE?"

She asked, "How do you know it was a *he*?" and Dulles let out his Santa Claus laugh.

At the end of the war, the Swiss frontiers opened to a flood of Americans. Bancroft noticed that "much of the sparkle and charm went out of Allen's personality as I had known it. It was rather like the way an exuberant young person behaves when his parents show up." Harry Truman disbanded the OSS and Dulles returned to the law.

In 1947, Truman asked Congress for a permanent agency to give Presidents reliable, balanced information and forecasts of global events. Before Congress Dulles testified, "The Central Intelligence Agency should have nothing to do with policy. It should try to get at the hard facts on which others must determine policy." Congress also licensed the CIA to perform "other functions and duties related to intelligence affecting the national security." In time, these included deploying private armies and greasing the skids under foreign leaders.

The Agency's raison d'être was to warn the President against a Soviet surprise attack. "America's people expect you to be on a communing level with God and Joe Stalin," Director Walter Bedell Smith told his men in 1950. "They expect you to be able to say that a war will start next Tuesday at 5:32 P.M." In 1951, Smith made Dulles his deputy. He valued Dulles's experience and ties to the foreign policy establishment and was almost confounded by the breadth of his acquaintanceship: "Allen, can't I ever mention a name that you haven't played tennis with?"

After Eisenhower's election, Beetle Smith told a friend that he would have preferred to remain at CIA but his old boss wished him at State. Allen Dulles was the logical heir. One story had it that Dulles had accepted the deputy's post on condition that Smith would recommend him for the top job when he resigned. Smith doubted the wisdom of placing two brothers at State and CIA. He thought Dulles "a fair operator of clandestine operations, but a weak administrator for an organization as large and diverse as the CIA." Dulles was "too emotional to be in this critical job."

Eisenhower had known Dulles during the war. In 1949, they were fellow members of a study group at the Council on Foreign Relations. In 1952, Dulles briefed Eisenhower campaign advisers on Eastern Europe. But the new President also recalled that during the final winter of the war, Dulles had antagonized the Soviets while secretly bargaining for the surrender of German troops in Italy. Roosevelt had been compelled to send an apology to Stalin on the day he died. This episode was one reason for Eisenhower's insistence in 1945 on working to build mutual trust with the Russians.

Still, the President-elect could not ignore Dulles's thirty-five years in intelligence, his subtle mind and skill with journalists and congressmen. As Eisenhower said of the elder Dulles as Secretary of State, Allen seemed to have been in schooling for this job all of his life. He won the appointment, but the President evidently remained somewhat wary. Eisenhower's junior aide William Ewald (who later helped to write his memoirs) felt that "such trust as he usually reposed in his leading lieutenants he did not repose in Allen Dulles."

•

Late in life, Dulles told his sister Eleanor that 1953 and 1954 were the good years at the CIA. It was a time when the world seemed young, when intelligence people under a sympathetic President were helping to reshape the world for free and decent people. By the middle fifties, with more people and money than State, the CIA was acquiring its own training grounds, soldiers, bases, equipment, ships, planes and other tools to perform global operations with more self-reliance.

Dulles's relations with Capitol Hill were unexcelled. Before one private session with Richard Russell's Senate Armed Services Committee, he told an aide, "I'll tell the truth to Dick. I always do." Then, with a chuckle and twinkling eyes: "That is, if Dick wants to know!" Wayne Morse of Senate Foreign Relations once told him, "Once again your keen mind here this afternoon has provided us with another great seminar." Clarence Cannon of House Appropriations: "Mr. Dulles, I want to ask you one more question. Are you sure you have enough money?"

The "brother act," as Amory called it, was a crucial source of influence. Since childhood, Allen had looked at Foster with admiration, envy, affection and some unease. It was Foster who was shown off to visitors as a child and who received the largest share of the family inheritance. Foster was said to think that Allen's enthusiasms were sometimes faintly adolescent and that he sometimes needed guidance for his own good. Allen once said that he never regretted that his life had been freer and more adventurous than his brother's.

Running State and CIA put the iron into their relationship. One CIA man "always had strong feelings that their effective relationship was conducted over the telephone . . . or after or before dinner, or in brief meetings outside their office, with nobody else present." Another recalled that "a word from one to the other substituted for weeks of interagency debate." Even if the two brothers had primly refrained from dealing with business outside the office, the illusion of power would have conferred nearly the same influence as power. In the absence of the brother act, the U-2 might never have won the President's approval or been built and flown so swiftly.

•

Dwight Eisenhower did not quarrel with the notion that the Cold War must be waged by new rules. "I have come to the conclusion that some of our traditional ideas of international sportsmanship are scarcely applicable in the morass in which the world now founders," he wrote Lewis Douglas in 1955. "Truth, honesty, justice, consideration for others, liberty for all—the problem is how to preserve them, nurture them and keep the peace (if the last is possible) when we are opposed by people who scorn these values."

In the 1982 study that became a milestone of Eisenhower revisionism, the political scientist Fred Greenstein cast Eisenhower as a "hidden-hand President" who preferred to use behind-the-scenes methods to avoid expending mass political support. Eisenhower's interest in covert action was the international expression of this hidden-hand leadership. He was reluctant to send troops into combat or compromise his reputation for seeking peace and self-determination, but neither was he willing to be a passive contender in the Cold War. Between the State Department's persuasion and the Pentagon's open force, the CIA offered a middle route.

Covert action allowed Eisenhower to achieve foreign policy aims without alienating American or world public opinion (unless or until the operations were revealed). Preparing the nation for a military adventure, defense buildup or negotiation meant the expensive, exhausting work of educating congressmen and voters and seeking their approval. A clandestine solution needed almost no one's approval but his own. Covert action allowed the President to moderate the costs of conventional forces: a quiet threat uttered to a foreign leader, a briefcase full of cash handed to a rebel commander cost less than keeping great armies and navies girded for war.

Eisenhower was doubtless sensitive to the fact that the CIA had great power both to help and hurt him. If the cover were blown on a covert operation and the President's role was revealed, it would damage his reputation and moral authority. It was not accidental that Richard Bissell won final permission to fly the U-2 into Russia not from Eisenhower but Goodpaster. That way, in a mishap, the President could plausibly deny involvement in the adventure. But this caused other problems. Walling off the President too much from covert action deprived him of the chance to scrutinize operations which, if they failed, could wreak momentous damage on American foreign policy. Throughout his Presidency, Eisenhower groped for ways to tighten supervision of the CIA. This was not easy. As Goodpaster said, covert action remained "a very weakly controlled business."

In 1954, Senator Mike Mansfield and Congressman Stuyvesant Wainwright pressed for a House-Senate intelligence watchdog panel. Allen Dulles resisted: "In intelligence, you have to take certain things on faith. You have to look to the man who is directing the organization and the result he achieves. If you haven't got someone who can be trusted or who gets results, you'd better throw him out and get somebody else." Eisenhower told Wainwright that he would be damned if he would give Joe McCarthy the chance to get his foot in the CIA's door.

Instead the President asked James Doolittle to chair a secret panel to examine the Agency. The panel concluded, "We must develop effective sabotage and counterespionage services and must learn to subvert, sabotage and destroy our enemies by more clever, more sophisticated and more effective methods than those used against us."

But General Doolittle gave Eisenhower a mixed report on the Director: Dulles's main strength was "his unique knowledge of the subject. He has his whole heart in it. . . . He is a man of great honesty, integrity, loyally supported by his staff. His weakness, or the weakness of the CIA, is in the organization." Doolittle questioned the "family relationship" with the Secretary of State: "It leads to protection of one by the other or influence of one by the other." Dulles's "emotionalism" was evidently "far worse" than it appeared.

The President rose to Dulles's defense. He thought the family relationship might be "beneficial." As for emotionalism, "I have never seen him show the slightest disturbance. . . . Here is one of the most peculiar types of operation any government can have, and it probably takes a strange kind of genius to run it." Nevertheless Eisenhower called Dulles to the White House and asked him to hire "a top administrative man" to improve CIA management. Dulles simply replied that he had done "a good deal of tightening up" and would continue to do so.

In late 1954, the President formed a permanent panel to oversee covert activities. The 5412 Committee, or Special Group, included Dulles and representatives of the White House, State and Defense. They were asked to evaluate all covert projects large enough to cause political damage if exposed. The most potentially damaging operations must be referred to the President's office for consent. It was after the Berlin Tunnel's failure that Eisenhower ordered them to know in advance about every CIA project encroaching on foreign sovereignty. But this mandate did not include the U-2: he thought the spy flights too sensitive for consideration by even the Special Group.

In January 1956, Eisenhower formed the President's Board of Consultants on Foreign Intelligence Activities for periodic outside evaluation. The Board's chairman was James Killian; its bipartisan membership included such eminent citizens as Doolittle, Omar Bradley, David Bruce, Joseph P. Kennedy and Robert Lovett. By the end of its first year, the PBCFIA found "extraordinary blockages and delays" in CIA communications. Members complained that the Agency's covert action branch was "operating for the most part on an autonomous and free-wheeling basis in highly critical areas." Covert operations were "sometimes in direct conflict with the normal operations being carried out by the Department of State."

Killian and colleagues thought Allen Dulles an impressive intelligence man, "particularly in the dark parts of intelligence gathering," but "a bad administrator." Repeatedly they complained to the President. Each time, Eisenhower said, "Well, where can I find his equal as an intelligence expert?" The Board told the President he should either fire Dulles or force him to hire an administrative deputy.

Goodpaster later recalled that Eisenhower "raised it with Dulles and finally concluded that he had a choice to make. Dulles would not stay under those circumstances, and if he wanted Dulles to stay, he wasn't going to be able to force this on him. At that point, he decided it would be better to have Dulles stay and keep the pressure on him. . . . He thought Dulles was very, very capable and had great ideas, great understanding. He really was tied into the realities, country by country, so that he was a tremendous national asset and he didn't want to give him up."

•

At the White House, Dulles presented the first U-2 pictures of the Soviet Union. As Bissell recalled, these included aerial photos of the Kremlin and the Winter Palace—dazzling evidence of the fact that "we can take pictures of Moscow and Leningrad and they can't lay a mitt on us." The President praised their quality, but when Dulles asked for more flights, he refused. Troubled by the Soviet protest, he said, "We'd better stand down more or less indefinitely. Don't start again until you get permission."

Dulles was disappointed. Then Eisenhower told him that the CIA would never again get blanket permission to make unlimited U-2 flights during a given period. Each future flight plan must be brought to the Oval Office for approval. As Bissell later said, "It became pretty evident as the weeks passed that permission would be pretty hard to get." In August 1955, Pearre Cabell called Foster Dulles about "our favorite project." He wished to know "where we stand" and "where we might go."

"Not sure there is much place to go," came the reply. "This latest episode upset things quite a bit."

•

That month, Frank Powers and Sammy Snider flew commercially to London on the first leg of their trip to Turkey, where the CIA and Air Force had established the second major U-2 base. During a visit to Pound, Powers had told his parents that he was joining a NACA weather research program, but his father was skeptical. The pilot gave his wife a list of emergency telephone numbers and a mailing address:

Mr. Francis G. Powers
c/o Mr. Calvin E. Mundell
P.O. Box 4054
Valley Village Station
N. Hollywood, California

Barbara wondered why her husband's name was typed without military rank.

After their flight to London and another flight to Athens, Powers and Snider boarded an Air Force transport. As Snider recalled, "We were pretty well conscious of not talking shop in public—even on an Air Force plane." They landed in Turkey and gazed out at the desert on which they had pledged to spend at least the next year of their lives.

Powers knew that he had failed to deceive his canny mountain father about what he was really doing abroad. Before departure, when he called his parents to say good-bye, Oliver had said, "I've figured out what you're doing."

"What do you mean? I told you what I'm doing."

"No, I've figured it out. *You're working for the FBI.*"

★

6

"Every Blade of Grass"

ON THE TURKISH BASE after dawn, a naked American stumbled from his trailer, used a baseball bat to beat an empty metal washtub hanging from a rope and cried, "I hate this goddammed place!" For some of the U-2 personnel, the scene became a wake-up ritual. When a rare female visitor saw this spectacle, she shrieked and fled her trailer.

The Second Provisional Weather Squadron was housed ten miles outside Adana, Turkey's fourth largest city (population 231,548). Nearby was Tarsus, birthplace of St. Paul. Owned by the Turkish government, the Incirlik air base already housed a U.S. Air Force unit that serviced planes crossing the Mideast. NATO rules allowed one member country to ask another's permission to use its territory for "defense planning." Thus, as Bissell recalled, he had sent his assistant, James Cunningham, to win the consent of Premier Adnan Menderes to fly from Adana into the Soviet Union.

Menderes was evidently pleased by the prospect of an additional link to the United States and access to U-2 intelligence on Syria, Cyprus and other spots of interest to Turkey. When the U-2 squadron, Detachment 10-10, arrived in Adana, Turkish Air Force men noticed that the new American pilots were under awfully tight security for a weather operation.

Except for the onion domes and camels, the trailers, control tower, runways and desert looked much like Watertown Strip. Thirty miles south was the Mediterranean; sixty miles east was Syria. In the absence of women, "our appearances went to hell," a U-2 technician recalled. Food was indigestible; the pilots became gaunt. Sometimes they drove into town for dinner at a restaurant, but the CIA warned them of throat-slashers cowering in the shadows.

Weeks passed with no order to fly into Russia. From the grapevine, the pilots knew that colleagues in West Germany had already done so. They did not know that the ban on flying now had been personally imposed by the President. They did not know for certain that Eisenhower was aware of the U-2 program. "I didn't even know who Mr. Bissell was until the program was over," Sammy Snider said later. "It was always Mr. B. And what Mr. B. said, *happened.*"

Pilots played poker and toured mosques, bazaars and Roman ruins. They flew some actual weather missions and soared east along the southern Soviet border to pick up radio and radar signals but wondered whether they would ever get to cross the frontier. Sparse news from the world outside reinforced the sense of restlessness and disconnection. Like most of the world, the fliers were uninformed about the war about to explode in the Mideast.

•

Britain, France and Israel were on the verge of attacking Egypt. In 1956, the last great French colony, Algeria, was in rebellion: the French government suspected that guerrillas were supported by Egyptian arms and money. Israel was eager to strike its chief Arab enemy. The British were indignant about Nasser's seizure of the Suez Canal. To Anthony Eden, this was an obstruction of commerce and an affront to the dignity of the Empire: "The Egyptian has his thumb on our windpipe."

Eden and French Premier Guy Mollet presumably suspected that Eisenhower would not sanction their cabal so they concealed plans from their ally. British and French intelligence transmissions to Washington dried up. American codebreakers could not decipher all of the radio traffic between London and Paris but noted that it was ominously heavy. Foster Dulles told his brother, "I'm quite worried about what may be going on in the Near East. I don't think we have any clear picture as to what the British and French are up to there." The President asked Allen Dulles to send U-2s over the Mideast to find out what was going on.

On September 27, 1956, Francis Gary Powers got his first order to fly over the Mediterranean and watch for concentrations of two ships or more. He and fellow fliers photographed Egypt, Israel, Jordan, Saudi Arabia and Cyprus, where they looked for the gathering of an invasion fleet. As Bissell recalled, "We mapped most of the Middle East."

By mid-October, the U-2s showed that Israel was mobilizing for war. In his diary, Eisenhower wrote, "Our high-flying reconnaissance planes have shown that Israel has obtained some sixty of the French Mystère pursuit planes, where there had been reported the transfer of only twenty-four." The jets seemed to have "a rabbitlike capacity for multiplication." This evidence suggested that despite the British-French-American Tripartite Pact of 1950 to preserve the Mideast status quo, the French were arming Israel and lying about it to Washington.

During the next three weeks, the U-2 was accounted the President's most reliable source of information on the crisis. Eisenhower expected Israel to attack Jordan, after which Britain and France would exploit the confusion to seize the Canal. On October 26, Allen Dulles convened the CIA's Watch Committee. Bissell displayed U-2 pictures of French arms being loaded on ships at Toulon and Marseilles and British convoys gathering at Malta and Cyprus: "It doesn't look as if they're holding a regatta." The next day Robert Amory said, "I'm positive the Israelis will attack the Sinai shortly after midnight tomorrow."

Early on October 29, Israeli paratroopers screened by French fighter planes dropped into the Sinai. Israeli tank forces prepared to move west and south into Egypt. Eisenhower wanted an instant ceasefire: "All right, Foster, you tell 'em that, goddammit, we're going to do everything that there is so we can stop this thing."

U-2 flights were stepped up. On October 30, over Egypt, Frank Powers looked down and saw black puffs of smoke, probably the first shots of the first daytime battle in the Sinai. In Washington, Eisenhower said, "I just don't know what got into these people. It's the damnedest business I ever saw supposedly intelligent governments getting themselves into."

On Halloween, a U-2 pilot flew over the main Egyptian military field near Cairo, swung northwest and crossed the field again. This time, planes and hangars were burning fiercely. The CIA reputedly telephoned the incriminating pictures to the Royal Air Force in London, which suavely cabled a thank-you: "QUICKEST BOMB DAMAGE ASSESSMENT WE'VE EVER HAD." The U-2 revealed that a two-hundred-ship British-French armada was sailing toward Egypt. At one point, Foster and Allen Dulles crawled around the floor of the elder brother's office, looking at a mosaic of U-2 pictures of the Suez Canal.

These were the final, frantic days of the American Presidential campaign. Eisenhower had to make fast decisions not only on the Mideast but on Hungary's rebellion against Soviet domination. Combined with uprisings in Poland, the Kremlin's worst nightmare seemed to be coming true. Eisenhower wondered whether the Russians might use "extreme measures" to keep their satellites—"even global war." Hungarian rebels begged for Western aid. If the CIA was ever to mobilize its network in Eastern Europe, the time was probably now.

But the President would not challenge the Soviets so close to their borders. He denied permission to air-drop arms and supplies; as for troops, Eisenhower said that Hungary was "as inaccessible to us as Tibet." Two hundred thousand Hungarians fled the country as Soviet tanks crushed bodies in the streets. "Sick at heart," Robert and Mary Amory sponsored a Hungarian refugee "by way of expiation."

On November 5, British and French paratroopers landed on the Suez Canal, followed by amphibious landings. From Moscow, Bulganin invited the United States to join the Soviets to stop the invasion and threatened to rain nuclear bombs on London and Paris. Eisenhower presumed that the Soviets, fearing the dissolution of the Warsaw Pact, were hoping to use the Suez crisis to shatter NATO: "Those boys are both furious and scared. Just as with Hitler, that makes for the most dangerous possible state of mind. And we better be damn sure that every intelligence point and every outpost of our armed forces is absolutely right on their toes. . . . If those fellows start something, we may have to hit 'em—and, if necessary, with *everything* in the bucket."

November 6 was Election Day. At 8:37 A.M., Allen Dulles informed the President that the Kremlin had promised Nasser to "do something" in the Mideast: perhaps the Russians would send their air force into Syria. Eisenhower told Dulles to fly the U-2 over Syria and Israel, "avoiding however any flights into Russia." If the Soviets attacked the British and French, "we would be in war." Darkly Eisenhower asked whether American forces in the Mediterranean were equipped with atomic anti-submarine weapons.

At nine, the Eisenhowers went to Gettysburg to vote. By noon, they were back; Goodpaster reported that the U-2 had found no Soviet planes on Syrian airfields or moving into Egypt. World War Three was not imminent. That evening, Eisenhower paced the crowded Presidential Suite of the Sheraton Park Hotel, waiting for Adlai Stevenson to concede: "What in the name of God is that monkey waiting for? Polishing his prose?" Finally Stevenson appeared on television. The victor walked away and said, "I'm just looking for a drink."

•

Suez ended in cease-fire. The United States became the momentary hero of Third World leaders who would never have believed that Eisenhower would turn his back on his European allies. But in the aftermath of Bulganin's threat, American-Soviet relations were uneasy. At the White House, Dulles and Bissell asked the President to lift his ban against U-2 flights into Russia. "Why do we need to go in?" asked Eisenhower. "What good will it do? . . . Everyone in the world says that in the last six weeks, the U.S. has gained a place it hasn't held since World War Two. To make trips now would cost more than we would gain in solid information."

"If we lost a plane at this stage, it would be almost catastrophic," said Herbert Hoover, Jr., of the State Department.

Bissell noted that the new Turkish base was "a better way to get at most of the targets in Russia." He wished to send the U-2 over Soviet bomber fields, Kapustin Yar, the Ukraine and Caucasus, the cities on the Volga. Apprehensive about Russian moves after Hungary and Suez, the President approved only two shallow flights: "Stay as close to the border as possible and still cover the fields."

In Turkey, the U-2 commander stopped one of his pilots and said, *"You're it, Powers."* In late November, Frank Powers took the spy plane for the first time from Adana into Soviet airspace. There were evidently also flights over Eastern Europe.

The Russians privately protested. On December 18, Eisenhower told Foster Dulles he was "going to order complete stoppage of the entire business." Dulles agreed that "our relations with Russia are pretty tense at the moment." This was no time to be provocative.

●

Flights resumed in 1957. By now the President and Allen Dulles had fashioned a process for making decisions about the U-2 which served the intelligence community's need for flights and Eisenhower's will to supervise. Assisted by an Ad Hoc Requirements Committee, Bissell consulted people in the CIA and other intelligence agencies about targets. Someone might say, "If you could go here, maybe you could just tip the plane a little this way. We just want a look at the next pasture without changing course."

Then Bissell appealed to Pearre Cabell, a champion of the U-2, and Allen Dulles: "What do you think the chances are?" Either Dulles said there was no chance of approval or, "I'll speak to my brother about it." If Dulles came back and reported that "Foster is strongly opposed," Bissell gave up: the President would never approve a mission without the Secretary of State's consent. If Foster approved, Allen Dulles called Goodpaster and said, "We are going to recommend an activity on this project and we would like to have a meeting with the President."

Then one version or another of the standard group assembled in the Oval Office—Eisenhower, the Secretaries of State and Defense, the Chairman of the Joint Chiefs, Allen Dulles, Cabell and Bissell. Goodpaster ordinarily stood over the President's shoulder as Bissell laid out his maps on the desk, lecturing on expected risks and rewards. Eisenhower sometimes said, "I want you to leave out that leg and go straight *that* way. I want you to go from B to D, because it looks to me like you might be getting a little exposed over here."

Bissell later explained: "I don't think he intended to be profound. I think he thought, 'Maybe they're getting into a heavily inhabited area and they really don't need that target. Let's go from B to D and we'll shorten it a little bit and we'll avoid a rocket.' ... Remember, the woods are always full of the stories of the unauthorized things that intelligence people do. And he never caught us, because we never did do anything unauthorized." A few days after the meeting, if the President approved, Goodpaster called Bissell with the go-ahead. Then the coded message was sent overseas.

●

What happened in Turkey? On the night before a mission, after dinner with his backup, the chosen pilot usually took sleeping pills from an Air Force doctor. Like a best man, the understudy took him back to his trailer and, next morning, woke him up. The pilot showered, shaved, dressed, donned his flight suit and helmet and breathed oxygen through a hose to avoid getting the bends. He could smell nothing but the blast of oxygen mixed with sweat, see nothing but the view through his faceplate, hear nothing but the voices piped into his helmet by radio.

Then he was briefed by a navigator and weather officer. Approval to penetrate Russia was hard to get: if there were clouds over his primary targets, he must take an alternate route. Outside, the backup walked around the U-2 and looked inside the cockpit at switches, levers, knobs, gauges, dials. The pilot's hose was yanked out and he was attached to a walk-around oxygen bottle. He was driven to the runway and helped into the cockpit. Through his headset he heard his backup reading aloud from a checklist.

The backup jumped into a truck and yelled into his radio, "Taxi into place!" Looking at his wristwatch, he began counting: "Five . . . four . . . three . . . two . . ." Inside the cockpit, the pilot heard the banshee cry of the engine and the pounding of his heart as the Turkish landscape fell beneath him like a trap door. Then the strange pogo sticks on wheels which supported the wings fell off—with the exception of the day one pogo stayed on and then dropped through the roof of a mosque. Worshippers thought it had fallen from paradise.

Once across the Soviet air frontier, the pilot knew that the Soviet military was more than likely tracking his plane and scrambling to shoot him down. There were other reasons for tension. Despite engine improvements, the U-2 was still vulnerable to flameouts. In the thin air around seventy thousand feet, the engine would go sometimes go *WHUMP* and all would be silent, the plane dropping and the pilot praying his engine would restart at lower altitude. Once one pilot fell to five hundred feet before his engine revived. Mercifully this was outside Soviet territory.

U-2 fliers rarely conceded the possibility of a fatal crash. This was the ethic of the fighter pilot: *his* plane would not go down, and if by some fluke it did, he would nonetheless survive. When he flew into Russia, Sammy Snider took pleasure in reminding himself that without the U-2 information, the U.S. Air Force would be groping in the dark if it came to a Third World War: "I could see someone pushing that red button and here go the B-36s driving across Russia to their target and the navigator looking at his maps and saying, 'Okay, bombardier, we're three minutes from target.' And the bombardier looking out and saying, 'Hey, there ain't no target out there! Where in hell *are* we?'"

Other compensation was the experience of sailing through the midnight blue stratosphere; of looking down on mysterious regions like the Ukraine, the Urals, Siberia; discovering cities and airfields and missile sites that no American had known of before; photographing night launchings of Soviet rockets whose fire lit the black skies for hundreds of miles in all directions.

Once on the ground, the pilot limped from his plane, his head and inner ears splitting from hours on oxygen, his bladder and bowels distended. A tow bar was fastened to the tail wheel, the wings propped up, the plane towed into the hangar. Film, tape and other product were sent to America. Under glaring lights, the pilot answered dozens of questions: *Did you get off course? How did the cameras work? Were the maps accurate?* All over the U-2 section of the base, the waiting was over; life returned to normal.

Later when the Mercury astronauts were presented to the world, the U-2 pilots could not help but dwell on the comparisons. The astronauts were instant heroes before a single man had climbed a gantry at Cape Canaveral. If Project Mercury succeeded, they would be deluged with offers from business, politics and Hollywood and decorated by the President in the Rose Garden.

Like the spacemen, the U-2 pilots were soldiers in the American-Soviet competition. But they were to the astronauts as mistresses were to wives. If the program succeeded, they might return to the Air Force with more money than they had dreamed of. They might win medals from the CIA, but if so, they probably would be barred from showing them to anyone. Perhaps only on some distant day might they have the satisfaction of telling their grandchildren about the elation and perils of flying far into the Soviet Union during the bleak years of the Cold War.

●

On the day after a U-2 flight, Richard Bissell usually gave a report at Allen Dulles's morning briefing. As Bissell recalled, the negatives were guarded "as a crown jewel." CIA quickly searched the film for crucial targets. The National Security Agency and other agencies studied the tape and other material.

"From the time the film was recovered, the responsibility was all mine," said Robert Amory. He recalled that in 1952, when he became Deputy Director for Intelligence, CIA photointerpretation consisted largely of "a guy named Brown, who'd come in half a week and look at old German photos." Amory wished to build up his operation; he recruited Arthur Lundahl, a University of Chicago geology graduate whose photointerpretation skills were well regarded by his Navy superiors. "If you're going to parachute me into Salerno or something, forget it," Lundahl said. "I'm a scientist." But Lundahl finally agreed and, as Amory recalled, "he mobilized a splendid team."

In December 1954, Lundahl was called to the Director's office. With Bissell standing nearby, Allen Dulles gave him the disconcerting news that he was being relieved of all of his duties. Then the two men showed him plans for the U-2 and told him that he must swiftly build an organization to analyze the expected photographs.

Lundahl leased fifty thousand feet of office space on the upper floors of a Ford repair shop at Fifth and K Streets, northwest of the U.S. Capitol. The neighborhood was so ramshackle that Lundahl thought it an excellent cover: who would imagine that the U.S. government would house a vital national security operation among winos and muggers?

The operation was code-named HTAUTOMAT. Years later, Lundahl chuckled at the memory of Richard Nixon, Foster Dulles and other high officials rolling up in limousines for briefings on U-2 findings and having to step across rats and garbage to make it into the building. Lundahl's downstairs neighbors apparently never knew what was going on: when they saw U-2 couriers rushing in guarded by men with machine guns, they figured that the government must be using the offices to print money.

Lundahl's growing number of analysts used the U-2 photography in conjunction with previous intelligence about the areas under study—maps, statistics, reports from tourists and secret agents, old pictures from ground and air. "It was a whole new ball game," said Amory. "I remember Art telling me that the raw film that came in each time to Westover Air Force Base, if laid down, would cover all four lanes of the Baltimore-Washington Turnpike from beginning to end." During the Second World War, British intelligence had scored a secret triumph by breaking German codes. Now, as the CIA's Ray Cline said, "Photography became to the fifties what codebreaking was to the forties."

Richard Helms found the U-2 material "mindboggling in that it was so much larger and fuller and more accurate than anything we'd been able to come up with." But Helms was distressed by Bissell's low opinion of the value of running secret agents into foreign countries. He worried that the "gadgeteers" would so dazzle the Agency that "everyone would forget the historic side of it." He told colleagues, "You just can't do away with the human side."

After the U-2 material was digested, Allen Dulles, Bissell, Lundahl and other analysts briefed the President. To the West Wing, Lundahl brought magnifying glasses and huge boards—"as big as your couch, forty by sixty inches. You could see the guys walking around down there and all the small details." Usually the President was briefed in the Oval Office. For larger groups, Lundahl stood the enlargements on an easel at the end of the Cabinet table. Sometimes Goodpaster asked for a quick once-over in the West Wing basement with its deep leather sofas, maps and war-room atmosphere.

Asking his usual volley of questions, Eisenhower put on and snatched off his reading glasses as his eyes darted up and down the pictures of factories, railroads, highways, bomber fields and submarine pens. Once the President slapped an analyst on the back and said what a mistake it had been to staff Army intelligence with castoffs before Pearl Harbor: "Thank God for you careerists who came in during the war!"

•

In 1957, the U-2 operation in West Germany was phased down. Bissell had moved the first squadron from Wiesbaden to Giebelstadt, closer to the East German border. Soon some thought the new base compromised: pilots noticed a car parked near a runway that was later traced to an Eastern bloc government. Bissell moved the squadron to Adana. But from Turkey, it was hard to reach the critical eastern regions of the Soviet Union.

That year, a third U-2 detachment was sent to the U.S. Marine base in Atsugi, Japan. Japan was still emerging from postwar occupation. As Bissell recalled, the 1951 peace treaty did not require the American government to ask permission of the Japanese Prime Minister, Nobusuke Kishi, to fly the U-2 from a U.S. base, but Kishi was informed. Marines were puzzled by the strange-looking plane and its distinctive scream: "Some of us would run out of the hut just to watch it take off."

Adana and Atsugi became the workhorses of the program. From

these bases Bissell also staged U-2 missions that took off or landed in Pakistan, Iran, Norway and elsewhere. Offering air bases to serve American violations of Soviet airspace put the host governments at grave risk. As Charles Bohlen privately told the Senate Foreign Relations Committee in 1957, "The Soviets believe that great powers have a certain dispensation to behave badly. This is not for little powers." With little powers, Moscow need not worry about picking on someone its own size. "The Pakistanis were always worrywarts," said Robert Amory. "The Norwegians were firm, but they damned well didn't like the Bodö field."

By Bissell's recollection, the Shah said yes during private talks with a CIA man in Tehran—"I think maybe the station chief, who was very intimate with the Shah." Norway "was done, I am pretty sure, through Norwegian intelligence and the Norwegian air force."

Washington promised host governments that if use of their soil for U-2 flights was ever revealed, the United States would declare it had waged the incursions without their approval. Allen Dulles: "One thing that we never reveal at any time is any association or possible association of our allies with us." These countries were not simply tugging their forelocks and bowing to the wishes of Uncle Sam. As in diplomacy, America's intelligence partnerships with smaller powers were based on mutual need and obligation. The Shah had only lately been rescued by the CIA, which was now training his intelligence service, SAVAK. The Pentagon was grooming his armed forces to make Iran an island of stability in the Middle East.

The American government wanted a base in Pakistan, but Pakistani leaders were less pliable. When the CIA asked to fly the U-2 from Pakistan into Russia, they evidently complained about the current rate of American military aid. In January 1957, Eisenhower approved a three-year increase. One month later, facilities for housing personnel, planes and equipment were under construction on a corner of the Peshawar airfield.

By Bissell's recollection, James Cunningham made arrangements with Pakistan's military leader, General Mohammed Ayub Khan, for flying the U-2 from Lahore and Peshawar. Ayub Khan was said to be proud of his hard bargaining. He probably did not know that the CIA expected the U-2 flights into Russia to end after just a few years: if permission to fly the U-2 from Pakistan was part of the quid pro quo, then his power to demand renewed aid would be diminished.

The General shared power with his fellow Sandhurst man, President Iskander Mirza. Eager to end the chaos that had long rent Pakistan and to win dominance for himself, Ayub Khan flew to Washington in May 1958, where he golfed at Burning Tree and lunched with Allen Dulles. That October in Karachi, Mirza was sleeping in the Presidential mansion when three generals arrived, drew pistols and said his services were no longer needed. He called the American Embassy and was told that the Ambassador was unavailable. This he took to be the handwriting on the wall. He flew to exile in London.

In his exile, Mirza told his son that he had had no objection to U-2 flights from Pakistan: the main thing that had turned the Americans against him was his refusal to countenance a long-term American base. Indeed in 1959, Ayub Khan signed a ten-year lease for an American base at Peshawar, but more likely, the United States felt that Ayub Khan had the better chance of curbing instability in Pakistan and ensuring American interests. Asked years later about Mirza's version of his ouster, Bissell said, "Broadly and generally, it strikes me as a lot of nonsense. I can't believe that the U.S. government would be so stupid as to base their whole attitude to a foreign political leader on whether he'll lease a base or not. . . . Mirza was taking much more of a risk in letting the U-2 fly out of there than in leasing some ground on a base." Bissell did not go further and deny any American involvement in the coup.

Perhaps the most sensitive partnership of all was between Washington and London, which in 1957 was recovering from the rupture of Suez. Since the start of the Second World War, it had been a close-knit union of Romans and Greeks: the Americans drew on Britain's old knowledge of intelligence tradecraft, the British on the superior military and technological resources of the United States. Gluttons for secrecy, the British lamented what they saw as inadequate security-consciousness in Washington, the Americans what they saw as British condescension. But both sides needed each other.

In 1957, frustrated by Eisenhower's reluctance to sanction U-2 flights, Richard Bissell suggested converting the program into a joint project with the British. Since the start of the program, British agents had been briefed on U-2 flights and provided with much of the product. Bissell proposed that both the President and Harold Macmillan, who had succeeded Eden in January, be designated to order a mission. He told colleagues that he wanted a situation where either the President or the Prime Minister could say yes: the one thing he did *not* want was a situation where *both* of them had to say yes.

Eisenhower and Macmillan approved the plan. The Royal Air Force sent pilots for training at Watertown Strip. RAF officers were dispatched to Washington and Adana. The British sent timing, route and target requirements to the CIA, which laid out several flights into Russia made by British pilots flying American U-2s. These missions were flown by Macmillan's permission and, at least theoretically, were not an American enterprise.

By now, CIA men called the U-2 fleet "R.B.A.F."—Richard Bissell's Air Force. Bissell was presented with an "R.B.A.F." coffee mug emblazoned "OUR LEADER." He later said, "With a week's warning, I could take a photograph of any spot on the earth. For anything that was within reach of one of our detachments—most of European Russia, most of Siberia, all of China, the whole Middle East, the whole Mediterranean Basin, the whole of Southeast Asia—I could fly anywhere in the world with about forty-eight hours' notice."

He was especially proud of the minuet by which he staged flights from Pakistan: "A C-130 would fly in there with all kinds of stuff and people on it with the mission pilot. . . . Then the U-2 would fly in and be refueled and the mission pilot put in place and take off. . . . At least on the first mission, the recovery base was a little airstrip in eastern Iran—nothing but a strip in the desert south of Meshed, near the Baluchistan border. He came in, landed, got into the C-130, the ferry pilot got into the U-2, and they all went back to Adana. It was a very neat, precision operation. Everything had to go on schedule and did go on schedule."

From Peshawar, the U-2 searched for targets including atomic energy installations along the Trans-Siberian Railway and a large downrange radar array that was a terminal site for missile firings from Kapustin Yar. Pilots gathered information that helped the CIA to learn of Soviet nuclear test explosions, their location, force and fallout. Bissell said, "We ran sort of a milk run for a number of months where one U-2 would fly a true weather mission daily to the North Pole and another would fly a daily mission to the South Pole and back." From Alaska, the plane soared over the Kamchatka Peninsula, which was the down-range end of long-range missile tests launched from Tyuratam. These flights were, by Bissell's recollection, the only U-2 penetrations of the Soviet Union from American soil.

Espionage in China had always been a problem for the West. It was hard to slip a white man into a sea of Asians, especially in a police state. After the 1949 revolution, the CIA sent Nationalist volunteers onto the mainland by parachute and rubber boat to hide among old friends and family while seeking information. Ray Cline, Taipei station chief, sometimes sat in the radio shack above the city waiting for signals from his agents: "It was heartbreaking when, after a time, they came through with the prearranged coded signal that indicated that the radio operator had been captured."

The U-2 was a safer method. From Taiwan, Bissell sent pilots over the Chinese missile range in Kansu province and the nuclear test site at Lop Nor. One mission reputedly produced a photo of what looked like a long-range missile aimed directly at Taipei. On closer inspection, it turned out to be a twelfth-century watchtower.

•

On October 4, 1957, the Soviet Union launched the first man-made satellite into orbit. Americans ran to their lawns and saw *Sputnik's* distant light soaring through the dark. An NBC announcer said, "Listen now for the sound which forevermore separates the old from the new," and millions heard the eerie *beep—beep—beep* from outer space. The President asked his staff and Cabinet to greet *Sputnik* with calm poise. "We never thought of our program as one which was in a race with the Soviets," said Jim Hagerty. Sherman Adams said the U.S. wasn't interested in "an outer-space basketball game."

Eisenhower had been braced for *Sputnik*. That summer, a U-2 had photographed a rocket on the launching pad at Tyuratam. But he had not fully anticipated how the Russian achievement would shatter the self-confidence of the nation which, until now, had thought of itself as the mightiest, best-educated and most advanced society in the world. Senator Henry Jackson demanded a "National Week of Shame and Danger."

Many Americans did not realize that launching an earth satellite was not the same thing as dropping a bomb on a target; some presumed that Khrushchev now had the technology and missiles in hand to launch a pre-emptive attack on the United States. On November 3, the Russians sent up a second *Sputnik* with a dog aboard. Eisenhower's Gallup Poll rating dropped twenty-two points.

The White House scheduled a Presidential television speech. Foster Dulles asked Eisenhower to consider disclosing that "the United States has the capability of photographing the Soviet Union from a very high altitude without interference," but the President refused: it might calm the public, but why compromise the program after only sixteen months? Besides, it would aggravate the Soviets at a moment of tension. Instead Eisenhower accelerated the American missile program and hired James Killian as the first Presidential assistant for science and technology.

This did not satisfy critics. For six years, some had searched vainly for Eisenhower's Achilles heel. Now they charged him with complacency. "It is not very reassuring to be told that next year, we will put a better satellite in the air," said Lyndon Johnson. "Perhaps it will even have chrome trim—and automatic windshield wipers."

On November 25, the President suffered a stroke. Richard Nixon and Foster Dulles told each other that the unprecedented criticism may have been the cause. Eisenhower quickly recovered; within three weeks, he flew to Paris for a NATO meeting. Still the First Lady worried about his health: "I'm not so sure we're ever going to be able to live in Gettysburg."

December was not much better. At Cape Canaveral, a rocket designed to launch the first American satellite exploded on the launch pad. The *Washington Post* leaked the findings of a Presidential commission on civil defense: "The still top-secret Gaither Report portrays a United States in the gravest danger in its history. . . . It shows an America exposed to an almost immediate threat from the missile-bristling Soviet Union." In fact, Eisenhower had privately shelved many of the panel's conclusions on grounds that they lacked "certain vital information" like the U-2 material. But the public did not know this and the clamor grew.

Sputnik and the Gaither Report threw into partisan politics an issue that had heretofore been principally debated behind closed doors by American intelligence and the Pentagon. It all began with the Bomber Gap. By 1954, the Russians had developed a long-range bomber that Americans dubbed the Bison. In April 1954, American air attachés saw twelve to twenty Bisons in the distance. From this and other intelligence, the Air Force reasoned that the Soviets might have as many as forty of the planes off the production line. This was only months after Albert Wohlstetter's warning about the vulnerability of SAC bases to a Soviet strike. If the Soviets had enough bombers, they might well be able to wage a successful surprise attack on the United States.

July 1955 brought a worse scare. On Soviet Aviation Day, Western attachés reported seeing ten Bisons flying by, then nine more and nine more again. The Air Force concluded that the Russians must have built twice that number. Combining this with a host of other data, Generals Twining, LeMay and their cohorts warned Congress in the spring of 1956 that Russia's long-range bomber fleet might be twice the size of SAC's by 1959. Their concern was sincere; they also knew that evidence of a massive Soviet bomber program would inspire a budget large enough for an American counterpart.

Then came the U-2. Early flights over bomber bases in the western Soviet Union and the Moscow plant that produced the Bison found no hard evidence of a massive effort to build long-range bombers. Nor did other sources. Some in Washington wondered whether the Bisons on Aviation Day might actually have been the same planes flying twice across the reviewing stand. *Sputnik* altered anxieties over a Bomber Gap: American analysts still assumed that the Russians wished to build a mammoth nuclear force aimed at North America, but now they assumed it would be done with missiles.

Nineteen fifty-eight was the year of the Missile Gap. "At the Pentagon, they shudder when they speak of the Gap, which means the years 1960, 1961, 1962 and 1963," wrote Stewart and Joseph Alsop in their column. "They shudder because in those years, the American government will flaccidly permit the Kremlin to open an almost unchallenged superiority in the nuclear striking power that was once our superiority." Many Americans feared that if the Russians were first to deploy an ICBM, they would gain a decisive military edge over the United States. The President thought that American deterrence would be sound until the Russians gained the power to destroy virtually all of America's bomber bases at once. But a National Intelligence Estimate in 1958 warned that the Russians could have a hundred ICBMs by 1959 or 1960—enough to do the job.

Anxiety over a Missile Gap made intelligence more urgent, but by 1958, Eisenhower was less willing to authorize U-2 flights into Russia. As Bissell recalled, the reason was "fear of being shot down and simply fear of provocation." Andrew Goodpaster said, "It always distressed Eisenhower that he was doing this, and it was only out of necessity . . . an ugly necessity." Three weeks after *Sputnik,* Bissell had asked for more flights but the President refused, saying, "It might be best to 'lie low' for a while in the present tense international circumstances."

In January 1958, when Foster Dulles and General Twining appealed for more missions, Eisenhower warned that they might trigger "a Soviet reaction which, superficially at least, might seem justified." Perhaps Khrushchev would strike West Berlin. Twining voiced his doubts: flights into Russia had been "a rather regular practice for the last ten years." Why should the Russians retaliate now?

On March 6, the Soviet Embassy gave the State Department a note protesting a violation of Soviet airspace in the Far East. In the Oval Office, the President told Dulles, "Such infractions must be discontinued. We should reply to the Soviets by saying that we were not aware of the matter referred to, but that strong measures are being taken to prevent any reoccurrence." Weren't American generals always talking about retaliation if Soviet bombers ever neared the United States? "The Soviets might have the same attitude and might misinterpret the overflight as being designed to start a nuclear war."

Goodpaster called Allen Dulles and asked him to stop "further operations contemplated in the plan for special reconnaissance activities." Later, flights resumed. The Russians issued another protest on April 21.

•

During the lull, Bissell used the U-2 to monitor the Indonesian rebellion. By the spring of 1958, President Sukarno had expropriated Dutch private holdings, brought Communists into his government and asked Moscow for military aid. The President asked Allen Dulles to launch a $10 million effort to topple him. Rebels got CIA money and arms. To stir the people into panic, Guatemala-style, bomber pilots secretly employed by the CIA roared over the islands. When Sukarno charged American involvement and warned the United States not to "play with fire," Eisenhower told a press conference that "our policy is one of careful neutrality."

On May 18, one of the bomber pilots, Allen Pope, was shot down. As with the U-2, the CIA had told fliers to strip themselves of anything that might tie them to the American government, but Pope had disobeyed. Sukarno's forces threw him into jail, showed off the pilot's documents and planned a lavish trial castigating the United States. Much of the Western press described Pope as an American "soldier of fortune," but the President could hardly keep on claiming that the United States was neutral. Allen Dulles ordered his men to disengage. The revolt collapsed, Sukarno tightened his grip on Indonesia and Eisen-

hower was presented with an example of insubordination that undermined his foreign policy and nearly caused him grave embarrassment.

There were more to come. In July, an RB-47 reconnaissance plane
flew into Soviet airspace over the Caspian and narrowly escaped. Foster Dulles told the President he didn't know why it happened but
thought it was a "permissible" mistake. "I am of the opinion it is *not*
permissible," barked Eisenhower. "I am getting weary of orders being
disobeyed—and someone should be fired." That same month, the Soviets protested incursions by U.S. Air Force balloons that the President
had earlier ordered the Air Force to stop.

Eisenhower blew his top. He told an aide that if he had done
"some of the things that have been done in the last few days," he
would have shot himself. "People in the service either ought to obey
orders or get the hell out of the service!" He told Defense Secretary
Neil McElroy that "there is disturbing evidence of a deterioration in
the processes of discipline and responsibility within the Armed Forces."
He wanted action at once: "The harm done by this type of thing to
the conduct of our international affairs and to our national security
is obvious."

Although the President did not know it, the U-2 program was not
exempt from this lack of discipline. One reason for this was that the
men who flew the planes had not cut their teeth as CIA agents but as
daredevil pilots. Like Allen Pope, some U-2 fliers carried identification
over Russia; one, by his own account, managed to smoke cigarettes
while flying his plane. This was outside the Soviet Union and presumably at low altitude, yet one need only imagine Eisenhower's reaction
had this been reported to him.

•

In Moscow, Khrushchev claimed that the Soviet Union was cranking out missiles "like sausages." But the U-2 found no hard evidence of
crash Soviet long-range missile production. Instead the black planes
and other sources discovered failures and delays: by August 1958, the
Russians had evidently launched only six ICBMs, a trivial number if
they were to deploy a hundred by 1959 or 1960. James Killian showed
the President U-2 pictures "which showed how far behind they were."
By now, Killian and other scientists realized how complex it was to
build long-range missiles, launchers and other apparatus: even if the
Russians had secretly managed to build dozens of missiles, it was
doubtful that they could have many ready to fire.

The first model of Soviet ICBM, dubbed the SS-6 by Americans, was so large and heavy that it had to be moved along railroad tracks and heavy roads that were not difficult for the U-2 to survey. Air Force officers argued that the Russians could be hiding the missiles in barns, silos, monasteries and strange-looking buildings in Siberia. One CIA man later recalled that "to the Air Force, every flyspeck on film was a missile." In August 1958, Stuart Symington came to the Oval Office and told Eisenhower that he was being too complacent. The President replied that whatever Symington's sources in Air Force intelligence, he could not possibly know everything that a President knew. He did not mention the U-2.

Eisenhower had long been horrified by the prospect of spending "unconscionable sums" for defense far into the future. He believed that the high taxes and deficits required would sap productivity, fuel inflation and ruin the American system: "Any person who doesn't clearly understand that national security and national solvency are mutually dependent and that permanent maintenance of a crushing weight of military power would eventually produce dictatorship should not be entrusted with any kind of responsibility in our country."

The notion of a military-industrial establishment and Cold War psychosis feeding off of each other disturbed him. He was disgusted by advertisements placed by defense contractors in *Aviation Week* and the "selfish" demands especially of Air Force generals. When Neil McElroy once warned him that further budget cuts might harm American security, he replied, "If you go to any military installation in the world where the American flag is flying and tell the commander that Ike says he'll give him an extra star for his shoulder if he cuts his budget, there'll be such a rush to cut costs that you'll have to get out of the way." And: "God help the nation when it has a President who doesn't know as much about the military as I do."

The President believed that the greatest threat to national security was being frightened into an eternal arms race that would induce wild inflation and ultimate national bankruptcy. He was as skeptical of the Missile Gap as he had been of the much-feared invasion of Western Europe a decade before. He sent Goodpaster to look through old intelligence warnings of a Bomber Gap and list the false assumptions that had underlain them. Eisenhower was determined to keep a tight rein on the Pentagon: he reduced conventional forces and increased American reliance on nuclear defense in order to hold military spending to roughly $40 billion per year. Average annual inflation was held down to just over one percent throughout his Presidency.

Eisenhower's caution about Soviet missiles and American defense inspired public caricature as a doddering Micawber. In public, Richard Nixon stood by the President. In private, he let it be known among influential journalists that he opposed Eisenhower's parsimony on defense. He confidentially told the Alsop brothers that the President "regards me as a political expert only. If I try to speak up on defense matters, say, from a strict military point of view, he says, 'What does this guy know about it?' So I put the case on a political basis. . . . Well, Eisenhower said the greatest danger was national bankruptcy, and he had the final decision. . . . You've got to realize that a Vice President is in a very special position, a difficult position."

Nixon suggested that McElroy was "a fine man, a very charming guy," but not a tough Secretary of Defense: "There just aren't enough sons-of-bitches about now. You know what I mean? That's an impossible job anyway, but you need a son-of-a-bitch in it." He complained about the President's aversion to public conflict: "You know, there is this myth now, that a man has to be noncontroversial, that everybody's got to like, that he never gets into fights—this 'togetherness' bullshit. I don't believe in that. I think the time will come when we'll look back at this era and ask ourselves whether we were crazy or something."

Joseph Alsop wrote to Isaiah Berlin, "One prays—how odd it seems!—for the course of nature to transfer the burden to Nixon (who exactly resembles an heir to a very rich family . . . now utterly distraught because Papa has grown a little senile and spends his time throwing the family fortune out the window—really he is like that, I lunched with him the other day, and he all but asked me how it was possible to argue with a ramolli papa without getting disinherited yourself!)"

In the Oval Office, the President excoriated the "sanctimonious, hypocritical bastards" making hay from the false issue of the Missile Gap. But he could not fully rebut them without revealing classified intelligence: revealing the U-2 evidence would compromise the program. As Thomas Gates said, "We had the dope, but we couldn't say we were flying the U-2." Eisenhower was agonized by his inability to meet the public attack with full force.

•

In the fall of 1958, Allen Dulles asked Bissell to take over the CIA's covert action department as Deputy Director for Plans. As Robert Amory said, "Once Bissell had the U-2 behind him, he could do no wrong." Unsure he wanted to seal his career so permanently in secrecy, Bissell took ten days to think it over before saying yes. When he moved into his new office, he asked young aides to handle overnight cable traffic and somewhat circumvented Richard Helms, his inherited deputy. Helms bore this with characteristic stoicism, but this sometimes lapsed: once he reputedly told a colleague, "Why don't you take it up with Wonder Boy next door?"

From his new post, Bissell continued to manage the U-2 program. Through 1958, the black planes informed CIA on Soviet sites including the weapons plant near Alma-Ata, the defensive missile test site at Sary-Shagan, the nuclear test ranges at Novaya Zemlya and Semipalatinsk. Combined with information from other sources like the American listening post at Samsun, Turkey, Washington was often able to announce Soviet missile and nuclear tests before Moscow did.

Allen Dulles later said, "We would get some indication, for example, that there was some nuclear development in Tomsk. We wouldn't know much about it, but we targeted the flights on the basis of all the intelligence that we had and then, of course, we picked up a good many things that had not been covered by intelligence."

The CIA had known about Kapustin Yar since 1947 but not about the newer missile testing site at Tyuratam until early 1957, when it was located by radar and the U-2. A U-2 pilot flew from Peshawar to Bodö, roughly the same route as that assigned Frank Powers on May Day 1960. "I remember about a week after that flight when Tyuratam was sighted and we had a session in Allen's office," said Bissell. "Art Lundahl came in and he had a complete scale model of Tyuratam—everything in it."

Before the U-2, the Joint Chiefs had been myopic in choosing Soviet targets. Operational and target planners had often been forced to depend on maps of Czarist vintage, captured German aerial photographs from the early Second War, even the 1912 edition of Baedeker's. They had known precious little about the large new cities and installations beyond the Urals. After the flights into Russia began, Lawrence Houston of the CIA went to Omaha and asked a colonel in SAC's targeting section, "What has been the impact on your work of the U-2 project?"

"As far as Russia and Siberia are concerned, we've had to start over from scratch."

Houston said, "That's just what I wanted to hear." During the years in which the U-2 flew across the Soviet Union, the American list of potential Soviet targets rose from roughly three to twenty thousand.

The U-2 brought a measure of stability to the nervous relations between the United States and Soviet Union. By providing intelligence that helped to reassure Eisenhower that Moscow was planning neither a surprise attack nor a crash missile program, the U-2 allowed him to resist enormous post-*Sputnik* pressures from the Pentagon, Congress and the public to escalate the arms race. By exposing large portions of the Soviet military complex, it enabled him to allocate American defense resources more effectively. A few American generals thought that knowing the United States could fly over their territory at will was making the Russians a bit less cocky.

"One thing that's always amused me is that after the first week of flights, when they tracked two or three of them, when you stop and think of it, the Russians knew almost everything significant about the U-2," Bissell said years later. "They could estimate its range. They knew its altitude pretty well. They obviously knew its speed. Pretty clearly they could infer, at least, that it was a reconnaissance aircraft. And so what else is there that is really important to know?

"Yet for three and a half years, this remained one of the most highly classified programs that the U.S. operated. And for those three and a half years, aside from three diplomatic protests, the Russians never said anything about it. . . . The Russians were not about to admit to the whole world, or especially their own people, that the U.S. could overfly them at will and with impunity. . . . You can almost say that the U.S. and U.S.S.R. governments collaborated in keeping this program secret from the U.S. and Russian publics. . . . It seems to me that with quite a lot of intelligence activities, each side tacitly better preserve the other side's secrets. . . . This thing went on for three years or more and, aside from a dozen people in Moscow, nobody got inflamed."

•

What about the dozen people in Moscow?

In the nuclear age, when both sides could destroy each other, American policy-makers were sometimes inclined to presume that Soviet anxieties were largely a mirror image of their own. This was not altogether sensible. For most of its history, the United States had been protected by two oceans. Its northern border was undefended; millions of Latin Americans crossed the Texas border without arousing a war scare among the American people.

This luxurious sense of geographical security was alien to Russia with its ancient history of invasion by Scythians, Khazars, Visigoths, Avars, Varangians, Huns, Mongols, Tatars, Swedes, Poles, Turks, Teutons and Napoleonic hordes. In 1918, the fledgling Soviet Union struggled against Allied intervention and in 1941 against invasion by Hitler's armies. No matter that the Czars and their heirs had expansionist ambitions themselves. What Soviets drummed into their populace in schools, the press, by billboards and lectures was how often they had been injured by foreign invasion. This was used to justify the obsessive secrecy and brutal will of the Soviet government.

In the Bolshevik parlance, the Soviet Union was faced with "capitalist encirclement." In the 1950s, this meant Western bases in Britain, West Germany, Turkey, Iran, Japan and other states, eavesdropping gear on land and sea, spy planes that played cat-and-mouse with Soviet fighters along the Soviet perimeter. Added to this was Soviet sensitivity about foreign subversion and espionage—CIA agents dropped into the Ukraine, British businessmen "caught red-handed," other incidents that propagandists inflated and endlessly repeated to increase national vigilance.

What made the Russians feel most insecure, of course, was their military inferiority. Soviet secrecy was not only an expression of national character but a deliberate instrument of national defense. Concealing the Soviet military complex made Western targeting more difficult and allowed Khrushchev to panic Western governments and citizens with false claims of military buildups and awesome new weapons.

The U-2 was capable of arousing virtually every major Soviet anxiety: it took off from Turkey, Japan and other Western bases (encirclement) to violate Soviet frontiers (invasion) for espionage (espionage) in the course of which it photographed and eavesdropped on the Soviet military (lack of secrecy) and confirmed Soviet weakness (military inferiority). The black plane had the potential to undermine the authority of the regime: What might the Soviet people say if they learned that their government was unable to perform the most fundamental task of protecting them from foreign invaders?

As Eisenhower noted, the worst risk was that the Russians would mistake the U-2 for a nuclear bomber. The U-2's size and shape did not suggest a bomber, but given imperfect Soviet radar and rumored American developments in lightweight nuclear weapons, some Soviet general might interpret the blip on his screen as the spearhead of a surprise nuclear attack and launch World War Three.

Anyone in Washington who convinced himself that the Soviets had grown resigned to the U-2 had only to listen in 1958, when Andrei Gromyko publicly complained about SAC atomic bombers that routinely flew to the edge of the Soviet Union and turned back: "Mankind has several times been on the brink of war, which could have flared up instantly through irresponsible or provocative actions of the U.S. Air Force." The State Department replied that American proposals to protect against surprise attack like Open Skies were designed not only to defend one side against the other, but also "to give each side knowledge of the activity of the other so as to reduce fears and misjudgments."

Khrushchev himself gave the Soviet rebuttal: "Aircraft flights of one country over another's territory, which the Open Skies plan provides for, do not further the solution of the disarmament problem. The peoples of our countries will hardly feel very safe and have peace and tranquility if American planes started flying up and down our land while Soviet planes plowed the American skies at a time of tension and distrust between us. Wouldn't it be more correct to expect the opposite?"

•

Since the start of the U-2 program, the National Security Agency had continued to load intelligence gear onto planes that flew along the Soviet border, recording emissions from Soviet radar, microwave and ground communications. Some of the most important radar could only be set off by actual border violation. Pilots played "fox-and-hounds," storming the border and then pulling away at the last moment. Sometimes they did not pull away.

In June 1958, nine CIA men under Air Force cover were flying a courier mission from Adana to Tehran in one of the two C-118s used by Allen Dulles as his personal plane. Highly secret papers were in the tail compartment; some evidently described U-2 missions in the Mideast and other governments' participation in the program. The plane strayed into Soviet Armenia. Two Russian MiG pilots rose into the air and fired.

Five of the men jumped; the other four rode the burning plane to the ground. Some who survived were badly beaten by their Russian captors. One was reportedly about to be lynched from a telephone pole when police broke up the screaming mob. Nine days later, the Americans were released to the State Department on the Soviet-Iranian border. Pearre Cabell had departed the plane in Wiesbaden just hours before it was shot down. The Soviets apparently did not know how close they had come to capturing the Deputy Director of Central Intelligence.

On September 2, an EC-130 spy plane with electronics experts aboard crossed into Armenia. NSA technicians in Turkey heard and recorded the radio transmission of a Russian MiG pilot firing on the American plane: "There's a hit. . . . The tail assembly is falling off. . . . That will finish him, boys." The Russians protested the violation and brought six badly mutilated bodies to the Turkish border. The State Department asked why the Soviets had fired on an unarmed plane—and where were the other eleven passengers? The Soviets said they had not fired on the plane—it had crashed on its own. They had no further information.

Eisenhower wanted his eleven crewmen back. NSA had its taped evidence that Russia had fired on the plane. Revealing it publicly would constitute the first time the United States conceded publicly that it eavesdropped on the Soviet Union. The President did not care; he thought it might shame the Soviets into releasing the men. Mikhail Menshikov, the new Soviet Ambassador, was called to the State Department, where the American diplomat Robert Murphy told him that he was about to play the tape. Menshikov said that he was no technician and walked out.

The damning transcript was leaked to the *New York Times* and published on page one, but the eleven Americans were never heard from again. There was speculation that some had survived the crash and been beaten to death by the Russians, and that the Kremlin was too embarrassed to release their remains to Washington.

•

"The significance of these incidents wasn't lost on us," recalled Frank Powers. "At our altitude, we weren't too worried about MiGs, but we were beginning to be concerned about surface-to-air missiles." Before 1958, Soviet SAM strength consisted of SA-ls mainly concentrated in rings around Moscow, but these could not soar high enough to strike the U-2. Then the Russians deployed the SA-2. "Some were uncomfortably close to our altitude. But we knew too that the Russians had a control problem in their guidance system. Because of the speed of the missile and the extremely thin atmosphere, it was almost impossible to make a correction. This did not eliminate the possibility of a lucky hit."

At the outset of the U-2 program, Allen Dulles and Richard Bissell had told Eisenhower that with advances in Soviet fighter planes and ground-to-air missiles, the U-2 would probably be able to fly safely over Russia for only two or three years. By September 1958, the program was two years and two months old. The President was thinking of halting the flights into the Soviet Union. As Goodpaster said, "They were unlikely to be used very much, if at all, during their remaining useful life. There was more risk of interception."

Eisenhower did not order Allen Dulles to shut down the program. Instead, in his oblique manner, he raised the idea of shifting the program to the Air Force to save the CIA money. He did not say aloud what both he and Dulles knew: if the Air Force got the U-2, it would probably never fly into Russia again because the President would not send military planes over Soviet territory in peacetime.

Dulles did not wish to surrender his prize. The CIA estimated that the Russians did not yet have the capacity to shoot down a U-2, so why give it up now? Disinclined to pick a fight, he had Bissell bring the CIA's answer to Goodpaster: "The capability should be kept active for as long as there is little chance of interception. . . . The aircraft should be kept in a small, autonomous organization so as to provide secrecy, direct control and extremely close supervision." Giving the U-2 to the Air Force would save little money, and "the extremely high standards of maintenance on which the operation is utterly dependent would be lost."

Eisenhower did not relent. Perhaps more than anyone else in his government, he knew much how the U-2 provoked the Kremlin. And what if there should be a mishap? The Berlin Tunnel, Allen Pope, the unauthorized plane and balloon flights were all cautionary lessons. Still the President would not simply tell Allen Dulles to fold the program. In the same way he tried to force Richard Nixon to leave the

Republican ticket and Dulles to hire an administrator, he continued to use indirection.

In December 1958, Eisenhower saw his Board of Consultants on Foreign Intelligence Activities and suggested a "re-evaluation of the U-2 program." Both he and the Board had been "highly enthusiastic" about the U-2, but by now, "we have located adequate targets." Now he wondered "whether the intelligence which we receive from this source is worth the exacerbation of international tension that results." Members did not take what Goodpaster later called the President's "hint." They said that the U-2 was "highly worthwhile." The President did not press the matter.

"Dad used to say that he did better when he followed his hunches than when he listened to his advisers," recalled John Eisenhower. "We knew we were going to run out of luck sometime. It was like a bomber pilot bombing Germany: how many missions is that rabbit's foot going to last?"

7

Khrushchev's Ultimatum

T HURSDAY, NOVEMBER 27, 1958. At one minute after four, Nikita Khrushchev stepped into the oval mahogany chamber of the Council of Ministers for what was billed as the first formal press conference ever held in the Kremlin. Reporters had been called at the last moment; Americans had raced here from Thanksgiving tables. They noticed that in the lapel of his dark blue suit Khrushchev was wearing a new emblem—a gold dove of peace.

"West Berlin," he declared, "has become a sort of malignant tumor. If the tumor is not removed, the situation is fraught with such danger that there might be quite undesirable consequences. Therefore we have decided to do some surgery." He noted that thirteen years after the war, there was still no German peace treaty. If the West did not leave Berlin and sign one within six months, he would sign a separate peace allowing the East Germans to govern access routes to West Berlin. Khrushchev had just set down perhaps the gravest challenge to the West since the Berlin Blockade of 1948.

Eisenhower received the news at Augusta, Georgia, where he and his family were spending Thanksgiving. He told his son that he would never bargain under such an ultimatum. If the United States abandoned West Berlin, "then no one in the world could have confidence in any pledge we made." If the West were compelled to crash through an East German blockade, it could escalate to nuclear war. "In this gamble, we are not going to be betting white chips, building up gradually and gradually. Khrushchev should know that when we decide to act, our whole stack will be in the pot."

•

Why had Khrushchev chosen this moment to push the world toward the brink? Western leaders were hard-pressed to know; most thought the Soviet leader a bizarre, dangerous, mercurial figure risen far beyond his cultural and intellectual limits, pledging world destruction one moment and peace talks the next. From their week's encounter in Geneva, Eisenhower recalled Khrushchev as the Russian version of a "drunken railway hand."

Psychological profiles of Khrushchev by Western intelligence could not have provided much reassurance. Khrushchev's behavior at diplomatic gatherings did not reinforce his image as a leader of *gravitas.* Khrushchev was said to have once barreled across a crowded room to an aloof foreign woman, nuzzled her bare neck and said, "My little white pigeon!" When someone praised the large number of Soviet working women, he said, "Not like the women in France, who are all whores!" During Suez, Khrushchev announced, "I've just heard a good joke. Eden is sick. Do you know what he's suffering from? *Inflammation of the canal!"*

At a Kremlin fete, he denounced the Third World as "unimportant." And why were the French still pretending to be a great power? The British (waving his glass) had nothing to offer but "diplomatic cleverness." As Khrushchev blustered on, one of his minions muttered, "It's about time we closed this and got Nikita Sergeyevich out of here." Marshal Zhukov flicked his hand and told Chip Bohlen to ignore the scene: "It's the way things are done around here."

Khrushchev did not resemble the other Soviet leaders to whom the West had tried to accustom itself. Waddling as he walked, the oversize suit coat flapping over the medicine ball stomach, he looked like a Botero come to life, with darting bullet eyes that gave him the aspect of a naughty child. Whether dancing with Ukrainians, presenting a tiger cub to the Queen of England, exhorting farmers to hasten production or shouting of his ability to drop nuclear weapons on London and Paris, he was an unforgettable walking demonstration of the triumph of the Russian underclass.

Richard Nixon later recalled that "few foreigners had been invited to meet Khrushchev, and those who did were often deeply disturbed by him. At times, he was almost seductively charming. At other times, he was boorish and obtuse. Some visitors came away swearing that he was the devil incarnate. Others came away swearing that he was just a drunk. All thought he was a bully."

●

Born in 1894 in Kalinovka, a Russian village near the Ukrainian border, Khrushchev was one of the hundred million Dark People who constituted eighty percent of imperial Russia. The Khrushchevs were lords of great estates who served the Czarist court—but not these Khrushchevs. The Soviet leader's grandfather was probably a serf owned by the Khrushchevs who took his owner's surname. There were rare and slanderous rumors that Khrushchev's ancestors were landowners, but perceptive observers noted that peasant characteristics like Khrushchev's took more than two generations to learn.

In a wooden hut with icons and the fumes of oil lamps, the boy grew up poor and often hungry. He herded sheep and won prizes as an altar boy in the Russian Orthodox Church. Until the end of his life, he always felt most at home among farmers and embodied their stubbornness, crudeness, cunning, stoicism, exuberance, hostility to officialdom and love of talk. But Khrushchev's father never managed to scrape a living from the land. In 1908, he moved his family south to a workers' colony and consigned himself to work the coal pits in the Donbas region of the Ukraine.

Nikita found a job fixing machinery. He later said, "I worked at a factory owned by Germans, at pits owned by Frenchmen, at a chemical plant owned by Belgians. . . . All they wanted from me was the most work for the least money that would keep me alive. . . . If Gorky's university was his life among the people, mine was those pits. They were a working man's Cambridge, the university of the dispossessed people of Russia."

The dispossessed were in upheaval. Accounts vary on Khrushchev's role. The Soviet historian Roy Medvedev has written that Khrushchev joined illegal Bolshevik units in the coalfields and showed off the agitative skills that came from the cradle. In March 1917, workers at the local railway station intercepted telegrams announcing the fall of the Czar. Khrushchev was said to have overseen the arrest of the local police and founded a workers' militia. But none of this appeared in Khrushchev's official biographies while he was in power; one might presume that if it were true, it would have been printed in boldface type.

After revolution was civil war. Leading a metalworkers' battalion, Khrushchev helped to defeat a Cossack army; when Germans occupied the Ukraine, he reputedly crawled for miles through a mine tunnel and barely escaped alive.

The cannons fell silent in 1920. Trains, mills and factories were destroyed. The people of the Donbas, the nation's key source of coal, were freezing and starving to death. Khrushchev's young wife apparently died of scarlet fever, leaving their children Leonid and Julia. Political leader of sixteen mines, the illiterate Khrushchev entered a school for miners. Like other ambitious Bolshevik activists, he was backed and monitored by Cheka, the internal police created by Lenin to extrude subversives and counterrevolutionaries by search, arrest and execution. Among the students, Khrushchev evidently served as local commissar, police informer, interpreter of the news and whip, shouting, "All you demand you must get with your own hands. No manna from heaven is going to fall on you. So beat on your picks with all your might!"

By 1925, Khrushchev was said to be wholly literate and adept in discerning the distinctions between loyal Leninists and the Social Revolutionaries, Mensheviks, anarchists and others branded enemies of the people. He married a young party lecturer called Nina Petrovna Kukharchuk, and caught the attention of the Ukraine's boss, Lazar Kaganovich. In 1929, he followed Kaganovich to the national capital, enrolled at the Moscow Industrial Academy and then thrust himself into Moscow city politics.

In the late 1920s, impatient with lagging farm and factory production, Stalin declared war on his own people, forcing whole villages into collectives at gunpoint: all but the ablest were deported, starved or murdered. By the time Khrushchev arrived in Moscow, Stalin's methods were on display. He did not turn back. By 1935, Khrushchev was first secretary of the Moscow Party, effectively the Mayor of Moscow: "I was literally spellbound by Stalin, by his attentiveness, his concern. . . . I was absolutely overwhelmed by his charm."

Stalin's rivals had been largely vanquished, but opposition remained. In 1934, he used the assassination of the Leningrad Party chief

Sergei Kirov as a pretext to finish off real and imagined enemies. Grigory Zinoviev and Lev Kamenev, colleagues in the post-Lenin troika, were tried and put to death on well-fabricated charges. In 1937 and 1938, supporters of Leon Trotsky, Nikolai Bukharin and other public nuisances were put on show trial and executed. Stalin ordered the murder of nearly anyone who had ever opposed him—and tens of thousands more. Almost the entire Party establishment over thirty-five and much of the Red Army were arrested, charged with espionage and sabotage and liquidated.

Where was Khrushchev during the Great Purge? As a minor member of Stalin's band, he was lashing crowds of Muscovites into frenzy: "We will uncover and annihilate them and reduce to dust every one of them and scatter them to the four winds!" He was aiding the show trials: "They raised their villainous heads against Comrade Stalin. . . . Stalin is our will! Stalin is our victory!" And inside the Kremlin, he mutely watched as hundreds of top Party leaders were put to death. Unlike Kaganovich, Khrushchev apparently refrained from drafting death lists and argued to save some Party colleagues' lives, but in public he was a cheerleader against hundreds of thousands of innocent Russians. "I don't know where these people were sent," he later said, "I never asked."

Khrushchev was handsomely rewarded. In 1938, he went to Kiev as Stalin's viceroy over 44 million Ukrainians. Over two thirds of the Ukrainian Central Committee elected in 1937 had been eliminated. Khrushchev's job was to purge remaining allies of the purged. On arrival he declared, "For every drop of the honest blood of workers that has been shed, we shall draw a bucketful of the black blood of our enemies." Stalin made him a full member of the Politburo.

In September 1939, the Second World War began. After the Nazis crushed Poland, Hitler and Stalin divided the spoils. When Red Army tanks rumbled into eastern Poland, Khrushchev was close behind to accept the submission of local officials; he saw to it that businesses were nationalized, new Communist leaders anointed, a puppet regime established and oversaw the region's incorporation into the Soviet Union. A million fresh enemies of the people were deported to Siberia. Fifteen thousand Polish soldiers vanished, many into mass graves.

In June 1941, Germany invaded the Soviet Union. Hundreds of thousands of Soviets were captured and killed. The Ukraine was in retreat. Khrushchev went to Stalin's command post in a Metro station in

Moscow. By Khrushchev's account, the leader complained, "They used to talk of Russian gumption. Where is it now, that Russian gumption?" By November, the Nazis had fought their way to the outskirts of Moscow and Leningrad and beyond the western Ukraine. Khrushchev moved Ukrainian industry to the East to keep building Soviet mines, tanks, artillery, munitions, rifles and planes. With Lend-Lease help from Britain and the United States, these new plants helped to turn the tide. Appointed a Red Army lieutenant general, Khrushchev went on radio to exhort Ukrainian resisters: "We are straining every nerve to liberate you."

In 1942, he helped plan the disastrous assault on Kharkov, in which a hundred and fifty thousand Soviets were captured; he was political adviser and man-on-the-spot when the Soviets defeated the Germans at Stalingrad and when they won the largest tank battle in history at Kursk. In November 1943, in his military greatcoat and fur collar, he marched with Soviet troops into Kiev and, by his own account, later told Stalin, "Kiev is like a city of the dead."

More than anyone near the top of the Soviet leadership, Khrushchev had seen war at first hand. Unlike comrades who had stayed in Moscow, he must have known how many soldiers had fought not for Stalin but Mother Russia, how able commanders were hamstrung by irrelevant Kremlin orders, the bravery of Kursk and Stalingrad, where his flier son Leonid was killed. After the German surrender, he called Stalin with congratulations: "He acted as though he weren't in the least surprised by our victory. . . . But I knew better."

The war had killed twenty million Soviets. The Ukraine, breadbasket of the Soviet Union, had been largely destroyed. Khrushchev's mandate was to rebuild the Ukraine and restore Party dominance. In 1949, Stalin restored him to his old post as Moscow Party leader and made him secretary of the Central Committee, one of the half dozen most powerful men in the Soviet Union.

Life was lonely at the top. As Khrushchev recalled, the Great Father said in his last years, "I trust no one, not even myself." Khrushchev shuddered when the old man peered at him and asked, "Why don't you look me in the eye today?" By Khrushchev's account, Stalin often gathered his courtiers for a late-night cowboys-and-Indians film in the Kremlin, cursing the ideology between reels. Then the motorcade left the Kremlin for Stalin's dacha; routes were varied to avoid assassins. In the wee hours, they dined and drank themselves under the table at the leader's vehement bidding. Stalin asked "Mikita" to dance the *gopak,* and Khrushchev somehow squatted and kicked out his heels, Ukrainian-style.

When the merriment was over, Stalin fired off orders until daybreak. Heads swimming, the men ran from the room and called waiting bureaucrats. As Khrushchev recalled, Bulganin once told him, "You come to Stalin's table a friend. But you never know if you'll go home by yourself, or you'll be given a ride—to prison!"

Stalin's paranoia grew. In 1952, alleged conspirators in the so-called "Doctors' Plot" against Kremlin officials were arrested. There were rumors of an imminent purge at the Kremlin's highest level. During a meeting in February 1953, Stalin used a red pencil to draw pictures of bloodthirsty wolves. The peasants knew how to deal with wolves, he said. They killed them.

As Khrushchev later told the story, on Sunday evening, the first of March, he went to bed, surprised not to be called for dinner with Stalin. Then Malenkov called him to the dacha, where the old man was lying half-paralyzed and speechless. Khrushchev was less worried about Stalin than about Beria, the internal police chief who once said he could take an innocent man for one night and "have him confessing he's the King of England." When Stalin regained consciousness, Beria threw himself on his knees and kissed his hand; when the coma resumed, Beria stood up and spat. Later, when Stalin's breathing finally stopped, a hulking Russian pounded on the leader's heart. "Can't you see the man is dead?" cried Khrushchev. According to him, a smiling Beria got into his car and drove away.

"I wasn't just weeping for Stalin," Khrushchev said later. "I was terribly worried about the future of the Party and the future of the country." Leadership fell to the troika consisting of Premier Malenkov, Beria and Molotov. But not even a week after Stalin's funeral, Malenkov was forced out of the Secretariat; in all but title, Khrushchev became head of the Party. In July, the Kremlin announced Beria's arrest and charged him with sowing discord among Soviet allies and—of all things—links with foreign agents. By one account, the police chief flung himself about and begged for mercy before being shot to death. Later Khrushchev told a Kremlin visitor that he was sitting on the exact spot on which Beria had been executed.

Khrushchev's popularity in the Moscow Party and his years touring the provinces while others stayed at Stalin's side in Moscow paid off. In September 1953, he formally became First Secretary of the

Central Committee. In speeches, he revealed details of the sorry state of Soviet agriculture and urged cultivation of virgin lands in Siberia and Kazakhstan. Was the military concerned about overtures to the West and resources being shifted from arms to consumer goods? Khrushchev bid for support by castigating Malenkov's "consumerism" and his un-Stalinist warnings that nuclear war would spell the end of civilization.

In February 1955, Malenkov was demoted to Minister of Electric Power. The West did not fully know it yet, but Khrushchev had become the supreme leader of the Soviet Union.

•

In February 1956, at a secret session of the Twentieth Party Congress, Khrushchev turned Stalin's picture to the wall and gave the most important speech of his career: "It is impermissible and foreign to the spirit of Marxism-Leninism to elevate one person and transform him into a superman with supernatural characteristics akin to those of a god."

Astonished delegates broke down and cried as Khrushchev used secret documents to expose the transgressions of the father-god—the disloyalty during Lenin's last months, "intolerance, brutality and abuse of power," paranoia, mistakes in farming and foreign policy. Stalin's cult had caused "grave perversions" of Party principles: "Lenin often stressed that modesty is an absolutely integral part of a real Bolshevik."

Twenty-five years later, Roy Medvedev called Khrushchev's Secret Speech "the principal feat of his life, overshadowing all of his mistakes, both before and after." With this speech, Khrushchev exposed himself to grave risk: the Soviet people might well have cut off the feet of the bearer of bad tidings. Why did he go through with it?

The Secret Speech was the culmination of reforms that had been carried out almost from the moment of Stalin's death. As early as the spring of 1953, many of the tyrant's favorite witch hunts, notably that of the "Doctors' Plot," had been shut down; political prisoners had begun to be released from labor camps. Beria's Ministry of Internal Security had been divided into a unit for internal affairs and one for state security, the KGB. By calling for liberalization, Khrushchev could not have been too far ahead of his colleagues: the speech must have been approved by a Presidium majority.

Tarring Stalin allowed him to tar rivals like Molotov and Malenkov more closely tied to Stalin than he was. By presenting the case against Stalin, he was able to minimize his own complicity in Stalin's crimes. The speech established Khrushchev and Party leadership as the central alternative to the personality cult. He gave every sign of genuinely believing that Communist ideology would work once freed from Stalinist dogmatism. He had seen how state terror had paralyzed the bureaucracy. He must have wished the Soviet people to begin living like human beings again—as long as it did not threaten the regime.

The speech was read aloud at closed meetings of shocked Party members throughout the Soviet Union and Eastern Europe. Allen Dulles got word and cabled CIA station chiefs to obtain a copy. Six weeks later, they did, apparently from a Polish official in contact with the Israeli Secret Service. For Dulles, the speech confirmed what the West had charged for years—that Stalin's rule had been as arbitrary and bloody as Hitler's. The full text was conveyed to the *New York Times* and published on the first page. Western reporters asked Khrushchev whether it was authentic. He told them to go ask Allen Dulles.

●

Alongside his indictment of Stalin, Khrushchev had declared that there could be more than one road to socialism and even included the independent-minded regime of Yugoslavia on the approved list. Satellite governments were encouraged to liberalize. Eastern Europeans exploited the new mood with a burst of nationalism.

June 1956 brought the rebellion of the Poles. By fall, the danger of revolution was spreading so fast that Krushchev was nearly ousted. He evidently saved himself only by flying to Warsaw, demanding a crackdown, and sending the troops into Hungary, for which the world reviled him. By January 1957, Khrushchev was a straitened man. He declared, "When it is a question of fighting against imperialism, we can state with conviction that we are all Stalinists."

With Khrushchev's blood on the water, Molotov, Malenkov, Kaganovich and Bulganin saw their opportunity. In June 1957, while their leader was in Finland, they convened the Presidium and demanded his resignation: rapid liberalization had harmed the world Communist movement. Arrest was not ruled out. But Khrushchev refused to quit until the verdict was ratified by hundreds of members of the Central Committee. This was a Khrushchev stronghold: party officials were grateful for his efforts against centralization and the arbitrary terrors of Stalin's day. With Zhukov's help, Army planes ferried Khrushchev supporters to Moscow from every corner of the Soviet Union.

The second echelon overturned the will of the first. The men whom Khrushchev now branded the "Anti-Party Group" had tried to kill the king and failed. Khrushchev exiled Malenkov to a Siberian power plant, Molotov to Ulan Bator. Zhukov's decisive aid during the Anti-Party Coup had shown Khrushchev the potential danger of his national influence: Khrushchev cried "Bonapartism" and fired him. He replaced Ivan Serov, the secret police chief, with a loyalist and Bulganin with himself.

Hence by 1958, as only Lenin and Stalin had been before, Khrushchev was head of Party and government. Men he treated as handservants stood at the helm of the Army and KGB. Khrushchev knew that the illusion of absolute authority conferred power: asked during a foreign trip who was minding the Kremlin store, he said, "My grandsons!" But privately he knew there might be further threats to his political life. The majority of Presidium and Central Committee leaders retained reservations about the shape and tempo of his reforms. They were willing to go along with Khrushchev—as long as his programs remained a success.

•

During the years spent consolidating power, Khrushchev had lacked the breathing space and self-confidence for a dramatic new initiative that would recast relations with the West. The ultimatum on Berlin was issued only months after dislodging his rivals. Like the Secret Speech, this was presumably a calculated gamble designed to win several aims at once.

Since 1945, the Western presence in Berlin had been a "malignant tumor" on the Soviet domination of Eastern Europe. The Western sector harbored what was often called the world's greatest concentration of Western espionage and propaganda agents. The postwar miracle of West Berlin's revival was a shining capitalist monument in the bleak heart of Eastern Europe. Hundreds of thousands of doctors, engineers, scientists, teachers and other East Germans each year were escaping to the West.

If Khrushchev succeeded in driving the Americans from Berlin, he might shatter faith in American protective power and divide the Western alliance. By demanding talks on a German peace treaty, he hoped to force the West to approach and tacitly recognize his East German client regime. He could not forget that the 1956 rebellions had almost toppled him. Llewellyn Thompson thought he was determined to "nail down the eastern frontiers of Germany and of Poland, and thus remove these sources of future trouble."

Perhaps most of all, Khrushchev feared the prospect that Eisenhower and his allies might arm the West Germans with nuclear weapons. Centuries of Russians had been animated by fear of Germany. Now West Germany was being rearmed as a keystone of NATO. Despite his public braggadocio, Khrushchev presumably knew that U-2 and other intelligence had shown Eisenhower that he had no need to quake before the Soviet military machine. If Khrushchev could not use strategic strength to compel serious bargaining on a German peace treaty and a pledge to keep Bonn from gaining nuclear weapons, he would therefore have to do it by threatening the West with nuclear war over one of its most vulnerable protectorates. "Berlin," he once said, "is the testicles of the West. Each time I give them a yank, they holler."

Eisenhower met Khrushchev's bluff, knowing that he might be "risking the very fate of civilization." He reinforced American troops in Europe, but only enough so that Soviet intelligence would know the United States meant business. For the event that someone tried to stop a Western convoy moving toward West Berlin after Khrushchev's deadline of May 27, 1959, the President considered plans to stage a new Berlin airlift, break diplomatic relations with Moscow and prepare the American people for possible world war.

Congressmen demanded mobilization of American armed forces and a surge in defense spending, but Eisenhower refused to alarm the public. He thought that one purpose of "Khrushchev's manufactured crisis" was to "frighten free populations and governments into unnecessary and debilitating spending sprees." With his gift for defusing crises, the President calmly proceeded with a planned reduction of thirty thousand Army men.

•

Public tremors over Berlin gave new life to the Missile Gap debate. Neil McElroy was defending Eisenhower that winter against congressmen who charged the President with accepting faulty intelligence that underrated Soviet missile strength. After an NSC meeting on February 12, 1959, the Defense Secretary stayed behind with his deputy, Donald Quarles, and General Nathan Twining to ask the President for more U-2 flights. Now that war seemed closer than ever, the Pentagon must know whether the Russians had built any first-strike ICBMs. McElroy said that the Joint Chiefs felt "our planes will not be shot down."

Eisenhower demurred. He wanted U-2 flights "held to a minimum" until reconnaissance satellites were ready. Besides, he doubted that the Russians could build a first-strike ICBM force any time soon. The President reminded McElroy that the CIA had warned him four years before that by 1959, the Russians would build a huge bomber force. Where was it? U-2 flights now would be an "undue provocation." Nothing would make him ask Congress to declare war "more quickly than violation of our airspace by Soviet aircraft."

Twining said, "The Soviets have never fired a missile at one of our reconnaissance aircraft." McElroy and Quarles repeated that more flights were critically necessary. Eisenhower backed down: one or two flights "might possibly be permissible" but not "an extensive program." He reminded the three men of "the close relationship between these reconnaissance programs and the crisis which is impending over Berlin."

The Berlin crisis did not abate. Several weeks later, Andrew Goodpaster called Twining to say that "the President has decided to disapprove any additional special flights by the U-2 unit in the present abnormally tense circumstances."

•

In London, Harold Macmillan feared that the crisis was sliding into war. On February 21, with Eisenhower's lukewarm consent, he flew to Moscow. As he stepped off of the Queen's Flight and shook hands with Khrushchev, the Prime Minister wore the black coat and white astrakhan hat he had worn as a junior minister in Finland during the Winter War of 1940.

Even when he laughed, Macmillan gave off an aura of sadness. The drooping, hooded eyes, walrus mustache, graying pompadour and rumpled suits from the 1920s added to his air of languor and diffidence, but close advisers knew his capacity for shrewd maneuver. They chuckled about the time the P.M. shuffled down a railroad platform with his normal semi-elderly gait. The whistle blew and the train pulled out. Macmillan broke into a sprint and hopped aboard.

Born sixty-six days before Khrushchev in 1894, he was the great-grandson of a Scottish tenant farmer whose son founded the Macmillan publishing house in 1843. Like Churchill, his mother was an American and he too cherished the Anglo-American relationship. Macmillan was an Edwardian figure, a Trollope addict who punned in Latin, hated television, loved club gossip and, even while Prime Minister, sat down at the common table at the Beefsteak or Buck's.

After Eton and Oxford, he had fought in France; his pelvis was shattered by gunfire and he lay abed in excruciating pain for twenty months. For years, he could not bear to return to Oxford because it aroused memories of so many classmates who had been killed. In 1920, he married the daughter of the Duke of Devonshire with Macmillan authors Rudyard Kipling and Thomas Hardy in attendance. As a Tory member of Parliament, he was rarely one of the boys. Hidebound colleagues were outraged by his extended essay *The Middle Way* (1938), which espoused a synthesis of British capitalism and British socialism. Appalled by Munich, he did not join the Cabinet until the rise of Churchill in 1940.

Churchill sent him to Algiers as resident minister, where he worked alongside de Gaulle and Eisenhower. He found the American General "openhearted and generous," an "American Duke of Wellington," and was amused by Eisenhower's visible relaxation after he told him that his mother was American. In 1943, Macmillan was badly burned and almost killed in a North African airplane crash. After the war, he went to the Ministries for Housing and Defense, the Foreign Office, the Exchequer and then to Number Ten.

Khrushchev knew that of all the chief Western leaders, Macmillan was the most eager for a summit and some compromise on Berlin. The Prime Minister was greeted warmly. Outside Moscow, he rode through snow in a troika and huddled with Khrushchev in a wicker basket spinning down an icy slope as startled Russians and Britons looked on. In his diary, Macmillan wrote that Khrushchev was "a curious study. Impulsive, sensitive of his own dignity and insensitive to anyone else's feelings, quick in argument ... vulgar, and yet capable of a certain dignity when he is simple and forgets to 'show off.' Ruthless but sentimental—Khrushchev is a kind of mixture between Peter the Great and Lord Beaverbrook."

Sunday, May 1, 1960. Two weeks before the Eisenhower-Khrushchev summit meeting in Paris, the CIA's Francis Gary Powers took off for a 3,788-mile spy flight across the Soviet Union (1956 photograph). Why the plane crashed at Sverdlovsk has remained a mystery.

Khrushchev learned of the downing while reviewing the annual May Day parade from atop the Lenin Tomb.

Eisenhower was told at Camp David. Assured that the pilot and spy equipment could not have survived the crash, he ordered that a false cover story be issued concealing the fact that the plane's mission had been espionage.

May 5, 1960. NASA spokesman Walter Bonney announced that the downed U-2 had been a NASA "weather research plane" that must have strayed accidentally into Russia.

May 7, 1960. Khrushchev revealed that the American government had lied: "We have remnants of the plane, and we also have the pilot, who is quite alive and kicking!"

November 1954. CIA Director Allen Dulles won Eisenhower's consent to spend $35 million on a high-flying plane that could spy on the Soviet Union without being shot down.

Kelly Johnson and colleagues at the Skunk Works of Lockheed Aircraft built a prototype in eighty-eight days.

The CIA's Richard Bissell, father of the U-2 project, during a visit to West Berlin.

British Prime Minister Harold Macmillan had the same authority as Eisenhower to order U-2 flights into the Soviet Union. That the U-2 was an Anglo-American partnership has been a closely guarded secret.

July 4, 1956, Moscow. Ambassador Charles Bohlen (right) greeted Khrushchev and Premier Nikolai Bulganin at the annual Independence Day reception at the American Embassy. On that day, the first U-2 was flying over Moscow and Leningrad.

Among the tens of thousands of pictures the U-2 took of the Soviet military-industrial complex are these views of a Soviet bomber base (above) and Tyura-tam, the Soviet Cape Canaveral.

July 1959. At the start of a Soviet tour, Vice President Richard Nixon and Khrushchev toasted the opening of an American exhibition in Moscow. Later Milton Eisenhower (second from right) told the President of Nixon's private misbehavior on the final night of the trip.

September 1959. Khrushchev's arrival at Andrews Air Force Base, Maryland, for a ten-day American tour. Standing in back row, left to right, are Andrei Gromyko, Soviet Foreign Minister, Henry Cabot Lodge, Ambassador to the UN, Mikhail Menshikov, Soviet envoy to Washington, and Secretary of State Christian Herter.

Eisenhower and Khrushchev boarded the Presidential helicopter for an aerial view of Washington. Until told that the President would accompany him, Khrushchev evidently suspected that the flight was an attempt to assassinate him.

Nina Petrovna Khrushcheva and Mamie Eisenhower joined their husbands at a White House state dinner.

In Hollywood, Khrushchev met Louis Jourdan, Shirley MacLaine and Frank Sinatra during filming of *Can Can*. At left is his son Sergei.

On the Coon Rapids farm of hybrid corn grower Roswell Garst, Khrushchev and his host celebrated the Iowa harvest.

Khrushchev went to Camp David for two private days with Eisenhower. They agreed on the Paris Summit and a Presidential trip to Russia in the spring of 1960. The world welcomed the "Spirit of Camp David." Eisenhower hoped to sign a nuclear test ban treaty with the Soviet Union as the crowning achievement of his career.

Eisenhower at his press conference on the same day.

May 11, 1960. Khrushchev denounced the U-2 as an American effort to "sabotage" the Paris Summit.

May 15, 1960, Paris. On the day before the Summit, Khrushchev went to the Elysée Palace and told French President Charles de Gaulle that he would not remain at the table unless Eisenhower apologized for the U-2 and punished those guilty.

That night, Defense Secretary Thomas Gates threw American forces on worldwide alert.

May 16, 1960. Khrushchev stormed out of the Elysée after Eisenhower refused to apologize.

As Eisenhower departed, he shook hands with French Premier Michel Debré. At left, with satchel, is his aide Andrew Goodpaster. At center rear is de Gaulle.

May 17, 1960. "Unless President Eisenhower apologizes . . . I will return home."

Eisenhower took Macmillan for a tour of his old home at Marnes-la-Coquette as they waited, hoping that Khrushchev would change his mind.

That evening, the Summit collapsed.

May 18, 1960. "We caught the American spy—like a thief, red-handed! We told the Americans that they act like thieves...." Marshal Rodion Malinovsky, Soviet Defense Minister, at right.

When Eisenhower returned to Andrews Air Force Base, he blinked back tears.

John Eisenhower watched off-camera as his father told the nation of the "re-markable events in Paris" and displayed a U-2 picture of San Diego.

ED STATES

Henry Cabot Lodge rebutted Soviet complaints about the U-2 by showing UN Security Council members a seal from the American Embassy in Moscow that had been bugged by the Russians.

Christian Herter testified on the U-2 in a secret session of the Senate Foreign Relations Committee. Richard Helms censored Herter's testimony on behalf of the CIA. Years later, he said, "If that's not perjury, then I don't know the meaning of the word."

August 1960. The Soviets subjected Powers to their most flamboyant show trial of the Cold War.

Behind the scenes of the trial, according to the FBI, his wife Barbara confided that she actually "hated" her husband and that he was a "no-good bum."

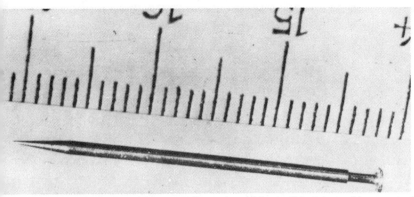

Among the Soviet evidence was Powers's suicide pin, "the latest achievement of American technology for killing their own people."

Powers declared himself "deeply repentant and profoundly sorry" for flying into the Soviet Union. He was sentenced to ten years in Soviet captivity. Through months of interrogation, he had actually withheld vital information from the Russians, but his courtroom plea would haunt him for the rest of his life.

September 1960. In the wake of the U-2 affair, Khrushchev went to the UN, where he denounced Eisenhower and pounded his fists and shoe on his desk. At left is Andrei Gromyko.

In the 1960 Presidential campaign, John Kennedy attacked Nixon on Eisenhower's handling of the U-2. Later Nixon cited the U-2 affair as a primary reason for his defeat.

February 1962. To the disgust of FBI Director J. Edgar Hoover, the Kennedy Administration freed the Soviet spy Rudolf Abel in exchange for Powers's release from prison.

After debriefing by the CIA, Powers testified before the Senate but left many questions unanswered.

Hired and then fired by Lockheed, where the CIA secretly paid his salary, Powers was unemployed for years. Finally he worked as a broadcast pilot in Los Angeles. In August 1977, his helicopter crashed and he was killed.

Khrushchev was shocked when (as agreed with Eisenhower beforehand) Macmillan offered nothing more than a Big Four foreign ministers meeting to discuss Berlin and other issues. What could foreign ministers achieve? If he asked Gromyko to take down his pants and sit on a block of ice, Gromyko would have to obey. Khrushchev revoked his public invitation to escort Macmillan to Kiev and Leningrad, explaining that a filling had fallen out of his tooth. Teeth didn't grow back at his age, and what good was a premier without teeth? British papers decried "THE TOOTHACHE INSULT."

Macmillan thought of going home "in a mood of affronted dignity," but decided instead to "enjoy ourselves, see the sights and wait upon events." Returned to Moscow, he improved his offer and told Khrushchev he would not object if the foreign ministers meeting led to a full-fledged summit. For his part, Khrushchev replied that his ultimatum had not been intended to "put pressure on anyone." May 27 had no special significance. It could be June 27 or August 27 or any date Macmillan wanted, but the West had better hurry!

"Mr. Khrushchev is *absolute* ruler of Russia and completely controls the situation," Macmillan wrote in his diary. "The uneasy period after the death of Stalin is now over. . . . He is the boss, and no meeting will ever do business except a Summit meeting."

•

On March 20, Macmillan went to Camp David for a weekend with Eisenhower. "We had a film called *The Great Country* or some such name," he wrote in his diary. "It was a 'Western.' It lasted three hours! It was inconceivably banal."

The President was angry when he learned that Macmillan had told Khrushchev he would support a full-fledged summit. Privately he was worried that his old friend's "desperation" to end the Berlin crisis would cause him to go his own way—especially because Macmillan faced elections in the fall. With tears in his eyes, Macmillan told Eisenhower that the British people must not be subjected to nuclear attack for the sake of two million of their former enemies in West Berlin. Eight nuclear bombs could kill thirty million Englishmen. "World War One, the war which nobody wanted, came because of the failure of the leaders at that time to meet at the summit."

The President tartly replied that in a nuclear war, more Americans would die than Englishmen. He would not be "dragooned" into a summit by Khrushchev's ultimatum. After further talks, he and Mac-millan reached a compromise: a summit with Khrushchev might be scheduled, but only after serious progress at a Big Four foreign minis-ters meeting at Geneva. On March 30, Khrushchev agreed to the meeting.

●

On April 6, the President approved more U-2 flights into Russia, but the next day, he called McElroy and Bissell to the Oval Office to say he had changed his mind: "As the world is going now, there seems no hope for the future unless we can make some progress in negotia-tion. It is already four years since the Geneva meeting." He was con-cerned about the "terrible propaganda impact" if a plane crashed. "We cannot in the present circumstance afford the revulsion of world opin-ion against the United States that might occur."

Eisenhower agreed that new intelligence was needed, especially given the "distortions several senators are making of our military posi-tion relative to the Soviets," but did not think the information "worth the political costs" of U-2 flights now.

McElroy said it was "far easier for Cabinet officers to recommend this activity than for the President to authorize it" and that he accepted the decision "very willingly." But a few days later, the CIA, Pentagon and Joint Chiefs were back to ask for more U-2 missions.

●

In the spring of 1959, John Foster Dulles was dying of cancer. Ann Whitman wrote, "Mostly the President does not dwell on death and indeed I have seen him rarely shaken by the death, or thought of death of any of his close friends." Not so with Dulles. After Eisenhower re-turned from a visit with the Secretary of State at Walter Reed, she wrote, "The President was in a queer mood, seemed to want only to be left alone, said he was 'talked out,' that he wanted to 'mope' around alone."

Between radiation treatments, calls to Foggy Bottom and hours spent reading and sending cables on the Berlin crisis, Dulles dictated memos on American foreign policy for his successor. In April, he re-signed and recommended his deputy, Christian Herter, for his job. The President complied, although he worried about Herter's crippling arthritis and metal crutches. Before Dulles sank into a coma, his aide

William Macomber came to his bedside, and Dulles said, "Bill, just remember this: if the United States is willing to go to war over Berlin, there won't be a war over Berlin."

The state funeral was attended by Churchill, Macmillan, Adenauer and the French, British and Soviet foreign ministers, who flew in with Herter from their initial sessions in Geneva. As fate would have it, the date was May 27, 1959—Khrushchev's deadline on Berlin. There was no Third World War, but Khrushchev's ultimatum remained. Eisenhower asked the Big Four foreign ministers to lunch at the White House and told them not to land in Geneva until they reached an agreement: "I will provide the services of an American tanker airplane to extend your flight time indefinitely."

But they remained in deadlock. Khrushchev was obviously resolved to avoid hard bargaining at anything less than a summit meeting, Eisenhower to eschew a summit until the foreign ministers made progress. Here the story might have ended but for a fateful accident of history.

•

In July 1959, Khrushchev was relaxing in Czarist splendor at his dacha on the Moscow River when he received a call from his Deputy Premier, Frol Kozlov: "I have a special message for you from President Eisenhower." The message was an invitation to visit the United States.

"I couldn't believe my eyes," Khrushchev later said. "We had no reason to expect such an invitation—not then, or ever, for that matter. Our relations had been extremely strained . . . and now, suddenly this invitation. What did it mean? A shift of some kind?. . . It occurred to us that part of the reason may have been that public opinion in the United States had begun more and more to favor an improvement in relations with the Soviet Union."

Khrushchev accepted at once. What he did not know was that the blanket invitation was almost as much of a surprise to the host as it was to the guest. All year Eisenhower had been dodging a summit until progress was made at a lower level. In the Oval Office, told that an unqualified invitation had been issued in his name, he blew up: now he must personally "pay the penalty" of going through with a meeting which would be "a most unpleasant experience" and "subject to serious misinterpretation." What had gone wrong?

Through the spring of 1959, despite the Berlin crisis, the American and Soviet governments had proceeded with plans for art and technology exhibitions in each other's largest cities. Khrushchev asked Kozlov to open the New York show; Eisenhower asked Nixon to go to Moscow. At the same time, Khrushchev dropped numerous public hints that he wished to come to the United States; he told visiting American governors in Moscow that he was "ready for travel."

Christian Herter and Douglas Dillon suggested to the President that he meet with Khrushchev "in a fairly secluded spot" to break the Geneva stalemate. Eisenhower wished it the other way around: a qualified invitation might lead Khrushchev to break the stalemate. He assigned Robert Murphy of State to meet Kozlov at Idlewild Airport before he returned to Moscow on July 12. Murphy should say that if the foreign ministers made progress, the President and Khrushchev could hold informal talks in the United States. If Khrushchev wished to tour the country, the President would make arrangements.

On July 21, Eisenhower received Khrushchev's note that he would be delighted to come for a ten-day visit; there was much he wished to see. He called in Dillon and Murphy and said, "Someone has failed." Murphy said he hadn't understood the linkage between the invitation and progress at Geneva. The President said he was "staggered": when Foster Dulles was alive, he would put such things on paper and send them to the White House to correct or confirm! As John Eisenhower later recalled, "Dad felt he was left holding the bag."

●

The accidental invitation transformed Richard Nixon's Russian journey from a goodwill gesture into the prelude to the talks between Eisenhower and Khrushchev. The President kept the strings in his own hands: he told a press conference that constitutionally the Vice President was not a part of the negotiating machinery and he was simply going to Moscow as the President's envoy.

Nixon plunged into briefing books on more than a hundred topics in Soviet-American relations. He went to HTAUTOMAT to be briefed by Lundahl's men on intelligence targets to watch for in the Soviet Union. When the State Department sent him drafts of speeches for use in Russia, he thought the language sounded suspiciously like that of his old nemesis Dean Acheson. By memo he told his military aide, Major Robert Cushman, that the speechwriters "are never again to use, 'We endorse the principle of peaceful coexistence.' ... I realize that this is the Acheson line in the State Department and I will not put it out!!!!!!! Cushman, tell all of them—it is never to be used again ... or whoever does it will be shipped back from Russia on the next plane."

H. R. Haldeman, not yet a Watergate conspirator but an advertising man doing advance work on Nixon's unannounced Presidential campaign, wrote the staff that "if RN is looking for a thoroughly-experienced non-professional staff man for the Moscow journey, give me shout." No one gave him shout, but Nixon's party did include Admiral Hyman Rickover, father of the American nuclear navy, Professor William Yandell Elliott of Harvard, other officials and businessmen interested in Soviet trade.

At the President's request, Nixon was also accompanied by Milton Eisenhower. President of Johns Hopkins University, Milton was the President's most confidential adviser: the President perennially called him "the smartest one in the family" and touted him for a future Presidential nomination. Vice Presidential aides (wrongly) suspected Milton of abetting the "Dump Nixon" movement in 1956 and (perhaps rightly) that the President had assigned him to keep an eye on their boss in Russia.

At Wednesday noon, July 22, Nixon went to the Oval Office for final instructions. Eisenhower gave him a letter from Macmillan which noted that Soviet leaders "want to be accepted as members of the club." The President recommended "a cordial, almost light atmosphere, on the basis that once the Soviets get us worried, they act tough." Nixon said that he intended to debate with Khrushchev and try to cause some "blurting out" of his "real feelings." He hoped to "lay to rest some of Khrushchev's misconceptions about America," especially "the familiar line that the American people want peace but their leaders do not."

The President had received Khrushchev's shocking letter just the night before. "So that you will not be astonished or feel let down by your own government," he told Nixon that Khrushchev was coming and would arrive in September. He intended to write Khrushchev suggesting a return trip to Russia later in the fall. Nixon should not raise the matter; if Khrushchev did, he should simply say that the President intended their American talks to hasten progress at Geneva.

That evening, the Nixons and their party took off in an Air Force jet. As the Vice President said later, he was "keyed up and ready for battle as the flight neared Moscow." Reporters in a backup plane sang,

Moscow Kremlin, here I come.
What a place to campaign from!

After they arrived, as Jane Thompson recalled, Mrs. Nixon asked, "Why were there no people on the streets? Why was no one waving? Where was the advance party?" The Ambassador's wife was astonished that her guest had not been better briefed. Later Mrs. Nixon won her over when, after making sure she was out of reporters' eyesight, she borrowed a cigarette and told her, "You don't know what it's like to be a politician's wife. I'd only voted once in my life—and that was for Roosevelt!"

On their first night in Moscow, Nixon slept fitfully and awoke before dawn. With a Secret Service man, he strolled through Danilovsky Market. People recognized him and asked for tickets to the American exhibition. Having none, he offered them a hundred-ruble note with which to buy some. *Pravda, Izvestia* and *Trud* headlined Nixon's attempts to "bribe" and "degrade" Soviet citizens.

With his subtle sense of how to make a point, Khrushchev just happened to be examining a model of a Soviet rocket when Nixon walked into his Kremlin office later that morning. "I could sense that he was in a testy mood," Nixon recalled. "He kept looking me up and down from head to toe as a tailor might estimate a customer's size . . . or perhaps more as an undertaker might view a prospective corpse with a coffin in mind."

The U.S. Congress had lately passed its annual Captive Nations resolution exhorting Americans to work for the liberation of Eastern Europe. Despite Nixon's explanation that the bill was routine and that Presidents couldn't tell Congress what to do, Khrushchev took it as a personal insult timed for Nixon's arrival: "It appears that though Senator McCarthy is dead, his spirit still lives. For this reason, the Soviet Union has to keep its powder dry. . . . This resolution stinks. It stinks like fresh horse shit—and nothing smells worse than that."

Determined to match him point for point, as Nixon recalled, he looked Khrushchev in the eye: "I am afraid that the Chairman is mistaken. There is something that smells worse than horse shit—and that is pig shit." For a second, Khrushchev hovered on the edge of rage, then burst into a smile and changed the subject.

Soon they were off in a Zil limousine to the American Exhibition in Sokolniki Park. Housed mainly in a fan-shaped glass pavilion and geodesic dome by Buckminster Fuller were a seven-screen film by Charles Eames, a 360-degree American travelogue, a beauty salon, Edward Steichen's photographs of "The Family of Man," an IBM computer programmed to answer four thousand questions about America, a Pepsi-Cola stand, Singer sewing machines, Polaroid cameras, Fords, Chryslers and contemporary art which Khrushchev found "revolting" and "perverted." He was "especially upset" by the Gaston Lachaise sculpture "Standing Woman": "I'm simply not eloquent enough to express in words how disgusting it was."

Khrushchev and Nixon went to an RCA color television studio, where their twenty-minute exchange was videotaped for American broadcast. Lambasting the consumer gimmickry and "aggressive" foreign policy of the United States, Khrushchev caught Nixon off guard. William Safire, not yet a Nixon aide or *New York Times* columnist, was there to publicize the display of a fourteen-thousand-dollar American house with the latest appliances and furniture. As he later recalled, "Nixon came out of the TV studio sweating profusely, knowing he had 'lost' and anxious to find a way to make a comeback."

Safire saw his chance and cried, "This way to the typical American house!" Nixon led Khrushchev into the display and they stopped at the "Miracle Kitchen."

The Kitchen Debate soon entered American folklore. Photographs wired back to the United States showed Nixon calmly refuting Khrushchev's barbs as the two men leaned over a railing beside a washing machine crowned with a box of Dash detergent. *Time* found this Nixon "the personification of a kind of disciplined vigor that belied tales of the decadent and limp-wristed West." Adlai Stevenson told a friend that Nixon had indeed "scored heavily" and would doubtless be "a formidable candidate" in 1960—"all of which fills me with a feeling that must be nausea and wonder about the new image of the American hero to inspire our little boys."

Khrushchev surprised his guest by insisting that the Nixons spend the night at his dacha. (Jane Thompson understood that the house had once been Beria's.) The next morning, he took them with Milton Eisenhower in a speedboat up the Moscow River "so that you can see how the slaves live." Time after time, he stopped the boat and called out to bathers, "Are you captive people?"

"No! No! Peace and friendship!"

Finally Nixon said, "This is the eighth time you've stopped at the right place. You never miss a chance to make propaganda, do you?"

Khrushchev said, "I never make propaganda. I make only truth."

At three-thirty, he gave the Americans a whitefish lunch on his lawn under a magnificent stand of white birch planted at the time of Catherine the Great. Khrushchev noted that whitefish was "Stalin's favorite dish—he said it put steel in his backbone."

For nearly six hours, he bragged about Soviet power and willingness to use it. He demanded that the West get out of Berlin and lauded Soviet missiles: "Missiles are much more accurate and not subject to human failure and human emotions. Humans are frequently incapable of dropping bombs on assigned targets because of emotional revulsion."

Near the end of the long meal, Nixon told his host that he could assure a warm welcome in the United States by making progress at Geneva. Khrushchev was noncommittal. At midnight, Nixon cabled the President, "I met for eight hours with Khrushchev today in what can only be described as an extraordinary experience. . . . I repeatedly emphasized that the element of crisis, for which he was responsible, must be removed from the picture by Geneva if there were to be fruitful further negotiations."

Years later, Nixon said that of all the leaders he had met, none had a "more devastating sense of humor, agile intelligence, tenacious sense of purpose and brutal will to power" than Khrushchev.

The Vice President flew by Soviet jet to Leningrad, Novosibirsk and Sverdlovsk. Rickover presumably looked for information of use to American intelligence while touring the Soviet icebreaker *Lenin*. Nixon's party was equipped with dosimeters to measure atomic radioactivity. Rickover thought their readings indicated "some sort of an atomic explosion." Before leaving the United States, the Vice President had wired Ambassador Thompson to remind the Russians "we have offered to let Mr. Kozlov see our missile launch sites, etc., and the V.P. would like to see theirs. Emphasize that we offered this to them. Now I want to see theirs."

The Russians refused. But at Sverdlovsk, Nixon reportedly saw evidence of a new missile defense site near an industrial complex. The site was said to be unusual because it had hemispherical, domed launch points—not the herringbone pattern of old Soviet ground-to-air missiles. This information was transmitted to U-2 mission planners.

"Crowds along the city streets and in country villages were unboundedly enthusiastic," Nixon cabled the President. "At every opportunity, I have brought them your best wishes and presented Milton, with enormously enthusiastic response to the name Eisenhower.... Ambassador Thompson and the other senior officers with me are greatly encouraged by this favorable popular reaction. They consider it demonstrates the really fervent desire of the Soviet people for peace, the counterproductive effect of Moscow's constant pounding of the line that the U.S.A. is the target to emulate, to 'overtake and surpass.'"

Khrushchev had offered Nixon the chance to address the Soviet people on television and radio at the end of his trip. Thompson told Nixon that his first draft was too belligerent and oriented toward domestic American politics: "You are the first American Vice President to address the Soviet people. You've got to make sure that you are not the last." Thompson, Professor Elliott and Nixon worked late to revise the text. The next evening, after Nixon's speech, the Thompsons gave a small dinner at Spaso House for his party and senior people at the Embassy and their wives.

In 1983, shortly before his death, Milton Eisenhower recalled, "He made the speech. It was all right and he came back terribly upset, terribly nervous and high-strung from the nervous situation he'd been through. So he drank about six martinis before we sat down to dinner. ... As soon as we sat down, he started going around the table to see what everyone thinks about the speech. And he'd keep interrupting the person: '*Did you hear me say this? Did you hear this?*' And then he began using abusive—well, not abusive, but vulgar swear words and everything else in this mixed company. Well, I wasn't terribly surprised. He was a strange character and still is."

Vladimir Toumanoff of the Embassy later said, "The fact that he unwound, that he had a couple of extra drinks didn't bother me so much as the fact that ... he was vicious, he was foul-mouthed, he was coarse, he was riddled with anger and hostility and self-praise and arrogance. There wasn't an attractive aspect to him that whole evening."

When Milton returned to the United States, he reported to the President. He felt that Nixon had handled the public part of his trip with "distinction and loyalty," but not on that final evening at Spaso House. At a stag dinner, the President had once professed to recall having, as a younger officer, carried Franklin Roosevelt off to bed after an evening of excessive drinking—a memory that "appalled" him in the nuclear age. Milton's report may have provided Eisenhower with an additional reason for his ambivalence toward his Vice President and putative successor.

•

At a Washington press conference on August 3, the President revealed that he and Khrushchev had agreed to visit each other's countries. Many Americans praised Eisenhower's bold step to break the Cold War deadlock. Others remembered only that Khrushchev was the Butcher of Hungary, author of the threat "We will bury you" and the Berlin ultimatum. William F. Buckley, Jr., thought that the visit "profanes the nation" and proposed filling the Hudson with red dye to make it a "river of blood." Richard Cardinal Cushing implored Americans to "pray in the streets, pray anyplace" while Khrushchev was in their country.

Western European leaders were thrown off balance. Harold Macmillan recorded that Eisenhower's invitation to Khrushchev "has caused me great annoyance—alarm—and even anger. It is not (as some of my colleagues seem to feel) the result of American bad faith, but rather of their stupidity, naïveté and incompetence . . . . Everyone will assume that the two Great Powers—Russia and U.S.A.—are going to fix up a deal over our heads and behind our backs."

The President flew to London, Paris and Bonn to assure Macmillan, de Gaulle and Adenauer that no separate peace was in the offing. John Eisenhower later recalled, "I don't think he said, 'I've been had by my own people,' but he said, 'I'm not going to represent my views without representing yours too.' "

For the President, welcoming the Soviet leader to the White House had little appeal—especially since the world remained under the Damoclean sword of Khrushchev's ultimatum. Khrushchev stood for everything in government he found "abominable." Eisenhower worried that Americans' expectations might rise far beyond what the talks could possibly achieve. If Khrushchev spread "objectionable statements" about the land, he would go on television to correct them before he left the country.

But the President did not restrict himself to damage limitation. When reporters asked what he wished Khrushchev to see, he gave what Ann Whitman later called a "love song to America." He wanted Khrushchev to see his boyhood home in Abilene and understand how a small-town boy could become President; to fly in a helicopter over Washington and see the office buildings and homes and traffic at rush hour; to see workers on a picket line and parking lots, because Khrushchev had not believed it when Nixon told him there were sixty million cars in the United States. Most of all, "I want him to see a happy people . . . a free people, doing exactly as they choose within the limits that they must not transgress the rights of others."

For Khrushchev, the invitation was a personal triumph. No Russian chief of state—not even the czars—had ever been received in Washington. The trip allowed Khrushchev the chance to expand his domestic political technique to Soviet-American relations and gain a palpable sense of the mythical, mystifying land: "I'd been to England, Switzerland, France, India, Indonesia, Burma and so on . . . but they weren't America. America occupied a special position in our thinking and our view of the world."

He remembered meeting Eisenhower atop the Lenin Tomb in 1945: "I frequently heard Stalin speak about Eisenhower's noble characteristics. . . . Stalin always stressed Eisenhower's decency, generosity and chivalry in his dealings with his allies. Stalin said that if it hadn't been for Eisenhower, we wouldn't have succeeded in capturing Berlin."

At the same time, Khrushchev questioned whether Eisenhower had the audaciousness and grasp of world affairs to bargain seriously. He could not forget Eisenhower at Geneva reading notes from Foster Dulles "like a dutiful schoolboy taking his lead from his teacher." But he hoped to build a close relationship with the President and persuade the businessmen who (he thought) *really* ran America to trade with Moscow. He no doubt wished to show Americans his sincerity about peaceful coexistence and press them to force their leaders to make concessions at the bargaining table.

Americans who assumed that Khrushchev had absolute power did not know how much of a gamble his American visit might have been. If it brought concrete rewards, he would be celebrated as a statesman and hard-line rivals compelled to bite their tongues. If he somehow wound up appearing a lackey of the West, he would have dealt himself a blow. On Monday, September 14, Khrushchev, his wife, daughter, son-in-law and a large traveling party climbed aboard a Soviet plane for the flight to America. A Kremlin announcement said, "One can hardly overestimate the significance of the forthcoming meetings of the leaders of the U.S.S.R. and the U.S.A."

•

As the silver plane crossed Scandinavia and moved out over the Atlantic, Khrushchev dozed: "When I woke up, the sun had come up. All sorts of thoughts went through my head as I looked out the window at the ocean below. It made me proud to think that we were on our way to the United States in our new passenger plane. Not that we worshipped America. . . . I'd met some Americans during the first years after the Civil War when I came home from serving in the Red Army. . . . I'd heard from American workers themselves about the United States and I knew it was no paradise.

"No, the reason we were proud was that we had finally forced the United States to recognize the necessity of establishing closer contacts with us. . . . We'd come a long way from the time when the United States wouldn't even grant us diplomatic recognition."

Khrushchev pondered the meeting with Eisenhower that lay ahead: "It's not that I was frightened, but I must admit that I was worried. I felt as though I were about to undergo an important test. I didn't let myself get depressed—in fact, the opposite was true. The challenge of the situation helped me mobilize all my forces to prepare for the meeting. I was about to meet with the leader of the country which represented the biggest military threat in the world to discuss with him the major issues of our times."

After more hours of sleep and reverie, Khrushchev learned that the plane was about to land. It was Tuesday noon in Washington: "In a few minutes, we'd be face to face with America, the America which I'd read about in Ilf and Petrov and Gorky. Now I'd be able to see it with my own eyes, to touch it with my own fingers. All this put me on my guard and my nerves were strained with excitement."

★

8

Camp David

WEARING A GRAY-BLUE STETSON, the President squinted as he watched Khrushchev's plane soar into view. Cabinet members, diplomats, soldiers, reporters and thousands of spectators stood at his side on the hot white tarmac at Andrews Air Force Base, Maryland. Little girls held bouquets. WELCOME KHRUSHCHEV, said the placard of a college student who told newsmen, "Better to greet him with an open hand than with a sneer." Cameramen on a scaffold focused on the runway.

"Looking out the window as our plane came in for a landing, I could spot throngs of people all dressed in colorful summer clothes," Khrushchev later said. "I could see a podium and an honor guard and a red carpet." Remembering his embarrassment in 1955 landing in the smallest plane at Geneva, he had made this journey on the Soviet Union's new turbojet, the largest passenger plane in the world—so large that the landing had been moved from National Airport to the longer runway at Andrews.

Khrushchev's plane touched down and came to a stop. Then there was a problem: "It turned out that our plane was too high for American standards, so when the motorized stairs were brought up, they didn't reach up to the door. Our pilot said we'd have to leave the plane not in the formal, dignified way called for by protocol, but practically climbing down, using our hands and legs! We didn't let ourselves be embarrassed by our problem. Far from it. It was an embarrassment for the Americans. They hadn't known our plane was such a giant."

The Chairman of the Council of Ministers and First Party Secretary of the Soviet Union was beaming as he stepped onto American soil. The two gold stars of a Hero of Socialist Labor and a gold Lenin Peace Prize gleamed against Khrushchev's black suit coat. Khrushchev was startled that the President wore a business suit, not military regalia. As the two men shook hands, Eisenhower was taciturn: a cold contracted golfing in Scotland made his throat hurt and he did not want to raise Americans' hopes about this visit too high by smiling too much.

Ambassador Menshikov had insisted on being the first to greet Khrushchev when he arrived. Knowing his boss's terrible temper, he was probably anxious to avert some mishap that would cost him his scalp. His demand was bucked all the way up to the President, who had always considered Menshikov "evil and stupid." Eisenhower said, "Tell him he'll do it our way or he'll go home." Now Menshikov declared in his oiliest fashion, "Nikita Sergeyevich, I salute you on American soil."

The President introduced his guest and Madame Khrushcheva to Christian Herter, Henry Cabot Lodge, Ambassador to the UN, and other Cabinet members. Khrushchev shook hands with Nathan Twining and grinned, recalling the General's trip to Moscow in 1956. His eye strayed to other Americans beyond the receiving line: "These people were looking at us as if we were some kind of oddity."

Eisenhower led him to the platform. "It was decorated with a red carpet and equipped with microphones so that our speech could be heard not just all over the airfield, but perhaps broadcast outside the country as well," recalled Khrushchev. "I was terribly impressed. Everything was shining and glittering. We didn't do such things in our country. We always did them in a proletarian way which sometimes, I'm afraid, meant they were done a bit carelessly."

The President did not deliver the spontaneous greeting offered old friends like Harold Macmillan: he read out a conspicuously formal statement. Khrushchev's reply was not especially considerate of his host. Three days before, the Russians had fired a rocket to the moon to remind the world of Soviet space superiority on the eve of Khrushchev's trip. Now Khrushchev twisted Eisenhower's tail before millions on television:

"Shortly before this meeting with you, Mr. President, Soviet scientists, technicians, engineers and workers filled our hearts with joy by launching a rocket to the moon. . . . We have no doubt that the excellent scientists, engineers and workers of the U.S.A. will also carry the pennant to the moon. The Soviet pennant, as an old resident, will then welcome your pennant."

The President grimaced.

Four howitzers fired a twenty-one-gun salute. Khrushchev and Eisenhower reviewed an honor guard and heard a fifty-six-piece band play the Soviet and American anthems. "It was a very solemn moment. It even shook me up a bit," said Khrushchev later. "Here was the United States of America, the greatest capitalist power in the world, bestowing honor on the representative of our socialist homeland—a country which, in the eyes of capitalist America, had always been unworthy or, worse, infected with some sort of plague."

The President walked the Khrushchevs to his open black Lincoln and squeezed between them in the back seat. Amid an armada of motorcycles and black Secret Service Cadillacs, the limousine rolled down the fifteen-mile parkway to Washington. Riflemen scanned the route; police helicopters roared overhead. Reporters assayed the sparse crowds; one thought the scene looked "more like a funeral procession than a parade." This probably had little to do with the man who had driven down the motorcade route some time earlier with a sign: NO APPLAUSE. NO WELCOME TO KHRUSHCHEV. Goodpaster later asked the Secret Service to investigate whether the Russians had put the man up to it themselves to embarrass the United States.

Once the procession neared downtown Washington, there was more gaiety. Military bands played at streetside; Khrushchev waved his homburg to light applause. Few Soviet flags hung from the lampposts. People held up angry signs (GO HOME TYRANT); the Washington police chased salesmen of black skull-and-crossbones stickers away from Khrushchev's view. When the Khrushchevs disembarked at Blair House, the Presidential guest quarters, the bells of St. John's Church played "Nearer My God to Thee."

Khrushchev's arrival in the Capital may have been subdued, but this did nothing to dampen the ardor of *Pravda*'s word artists:

> All Washington was on the streets. . . . The local radio announced that there had not been such a sea of people in the streets of the city since the celebration of the end of World War Two. . . . "WELCOME!"

shouted the people of Washington. "FRIENDSHIP! PEACE!" Millions of Americans know and believe that the leader of the great Soviet power came here with an open heart and the most noble intentions to make a new contribution to the relaxation of world tensions and the strengthening of world peace.

•

Khrushchev had been warned of the Washington heat, and he was suffering. After changing his clothes and lunching on cold soup and roast beef, he and his delegation went to the West Wing for the first meeting with Eisenhower. They included Andrei Gromyko, Menshikov, Aleksandr Soldatov, the top American expert in the Soviet Foreign Ministry, and Oleg Troyanovsky, Khrushchev's translator.

At 3:30 P.M., they walked into the Oval Office and shook hands with the President, Nixon, Herter, Lodge, Llewellyn Thompson, Foy Kohler, Assistant Secretary of State for Europe and Soviet specialist, and the veteran translator Alexander Akalovsky. Khrushchev merrily handed Eisenhower a polished wooden box containing replicas of the spheres and pennants his rocket had just flown to the moon. Astonished that Khrushchev would taunt him twice in one day, the President accepted it with all of the grace he could command. "After all," he later told his son, "the fellow *might* have been sincere."

Had this meeting been staged in the Kremlin, Khrushchev would have seated the Americans across from his delegation at a long table draped in green baize. He was surprised when Eisenhower invited them to sit on chairs and sofas.

The two leaders had agreed to defer their most vital conversation until their two-day encounter at Camp David at the end of Khrushchev's tour of the United States. Now they discussed the agenda. Eisenhower said that he wished to explore the Berlin question and a Big Four summit. Perhaps they might also talk about Soviet-American trade and increased traffic of ideas and people between their countries. America had sent almost fifteen thousand tourists to Russia in 1958, the Soviets only sixty-six to the United States.

Khrushchev declared that his government wished to have normal relations with the United States: "We believe that you do not want war and we assume that you also believe this about us."

"I see no profit in mutual suicide."

"The main thing is to establish trust. Probably we can't take each other's word at this time, but we must try to bring about trust. There is no other way. Of course, there are differences in our political systems and the whole basis of our social systems is different.... If we approach each other in the expectation that the other's system will be overturned, then there will be no basis for understanding. Let us allow history to be the judge of which system is preferable, and meantime live in peace as good neighbors."

Eisenhower replied that the problem wasn't mutual suspicion, but national psychology: "Frankly, our people are aware of Communist ideology and read its doctrine starting all the way back to Marx on the destruction of our society—even by force. Our people become uneasy and say things which are irritating.... Sometimes this feeling becomes excessive and leads to witch hunts, as in the days of McCarthy." He wished to "increase confidence and improve the situation, perhaps step by step."

Therefore, with Chairman Khrushchev's permission, he would raise one subject right now—Berlin. Admittedly, the fact that the Allies still occupied Berlin fourteen years after the war was "abnormal." But America had assumed responsibilities in 1945: "Until the United States can discharge its obligation to the German people, there should be no unilateral action on the part of the Soviets embarrassing to us and making it impossible for us to discharge these responsibilities." Khrushchev's ultimatum had caused "a serious crisis."

"Believe me, we would like to come to terms on Germany and thereby on Berlin too," said Khrushchev. "We do not contemplate taking unilateral action—though on your side, you took unilateral action in Japan in which *we* were deprived of rights we should have had. We had to accept that.... We must find a way out which would not leave an unpleasant residue in our relationship."

Khrushchev said the problem was that basically Americans were afraid of Marxism. Look at Nixon: he knew nothing about Marxism but fear of it. Nixon had just given a tough speech to the American Dental Association. Khrushchev said the speech hadn't given *him* a toothache, but it certainly hadn't reduced tensions the day before his arrival in Washington.

Eisenhower seigneurially divorced himself from his Vice President by saying that he must read this speech that the Chairman was talking about. Defending himself, Nixon noted that Khrushchev had made some tough speeches before *his* visit to Moscow.

"*You* read the speeches. *You* be the judge," Khrushchev told the President, adding that he knew a thing or two about American freedom of the press: "Of course, the American government gets printed what it wants printed and is able to suppress what it does not want printed."

Eisenhower replied that if Khrushchev wished to investigate American press freedom for himself, he would gladly invite any journalists the Chairman wanted to meet with him alone.

"I believe you," said Khrushchev.

After ninety minutes, photographers were summoned to record the historic sight of Eisenhower standing in the Oval Office with the leader of world Communism. Then the President asked for a private word with his guest.

He told Khrushchev he had asked him to the United States because he was deeply convinced that the Chairman could "become the greatest political figure in history." Khrushchev had "tremendous power in a complex of states with great might." As for himself, he held power only in the United States. America's allies all did things their own way. He had only sixteen months left in the White House. After that, he would still love people—all people, including the Russian people—just as he loved them now. He wanted them to live in peace and happiness. But Khrushchev would have great power for a long time to come. If he used it wisely, he could be "the man to do a great deal to secure peace in the world."

It is difficult to imagine this remarkable statement being spoken deadpan by a later American President to a Soviet leader. It displayed Eisenhower's unfeigned yearning for peace and mutual trust. (He had earlier told Goodpaster that he had to make the appeal to satisfy his conscience.) But at the same time, it revealed the condescension with which the world's number-one power still often addressed the Soviet Union in 1959. It coyly underestimated Western unity as it overstated the slavishness of the Warsaw Pact and Khrushchev's own power in the Kremlin. It played to Khrushchev's ego but by the equivalent of telling an obstinate schoolboy that there would be a big prize if he stopped his misbehavior.

Determined to be treated as Eisenhower's equal, Khrushchev must have been infuriated. But he was equally resolved to get along with the President. Dryly he noted that one side could not make peace alone: they must both work to solve their differences. Eisenhower said that they should "pray" this would come true. Later he told Ann Whitman, "Those sweet words—but he won't change his mind about anything!"

•

The President walked Khrushchev out to the South Grounds, where *Marine One* was waiting. When a helicopter ride had first been suggested, Khrushchev seemed to be afraid that he might be blown up or hurled overboard. But when Eisenhower explained that he would go along, Khrushchev said, "If you are going to be in the same helicopter, of course I will go!"

The President had been a helicopter devotee since using one during a civil defense drill in 1957. He sat Khrushchev in the window seat and spread a map of Washington across his lap as the chopper moved along the Potomac, over the memorials, the Custis-Lee Mansion at Arlington and thousands of "decent, fine, comfortable homes." He asked the pilot to hover low so that Khrushchev could see the traffic at rush hour.

The Soviet leader may have been impressed, but he would not admit it. Of course, the Soviet Union did not have as many cars and houses as America: his country was only forty-two years old and had twice been devastated in world wars! When the chopper landed, Khrushchev walked up to a reporter on the White House lawn and said, "We're never going to have automobiles like you have in this country, jamming up the highways. Absolutely uneconomic."

Khrushchev evidently thought the President's use of the helicopter was one more effort to lord American superiority over him. Later when he returned to Moscow, he reputedly told Soviet aviation experts that the helicopter was a new symbol of state power and that they had better build one better than Eisenhower's—fast.

That evening, the Khrushchevs joined the Eisenhowers in the White House family quarters before going downstairs for the largest state dinner in years. The Soviets—even the normally resplendent Menshikov—refused to wear bourgeois white tie. "Did you know that they're going to wear business suits and street dresses to a full state dinner?" Mamie Eisenhower had asked the White House head usher. "My husband would just as soon dress that way too if I'd let him!"

The First Lady had decreed a "typically American" menu of roast turkey with cranberry sauce. Fred Waring and the Pennsylvanians played such American standards as "Zip-A-Dee-Doo-Dah," "Over the

Rainbow," and "The Battle Hymn of the Republic," the President's favorite, which he felt "our guest seemed to enjoy thoroughly."

In his formal toast, Khrushchev said, "What we should do now is strengthen our relations. We need nothing from the United States and you need nothing that we have. It is true that you are richer than we are at present. But then tomorrow we will be as rich as you are. The next day? Even richer! But is there anything wrong with this?"

Richard Nixon introduced Lyndon Johnson to Khrushchev as the leader of the President's Senate opposition. "Well, *I've* never been able to see any difference between your two parties," harrumphed the guest. Then—who ever would have believed it?—Khrushchev came face to face with Allen Dulles, who said, "You may have seen some of my intelligence reports from time to time."

"I believe we get the same reports," said Khrushchev, "and probably from the same people."

"Maybe we should pool our efforts." Dulles chuckled.

"Yes, we should buy our intelligence data together and save money. We'd have to pay the people only once!"

Nixon could not resist presenting Khrushchev to another member of the Kremlin's rogues gallery, J. Edgar Hoover. The FBI Director was uncharmed. Later he testified before Congress that Khrushchev's presence had created an "atmosphere favorable to Communism among Americans."

●

At 7:40 the next morning, Khrushchev in shirtsleeves stepped out onto the front steps of Blair House for a breath of air. He toured the Lincoln Memorial and addressed a nationally televised luncheon of the National Press Club.

The question period that followed was standard fare for most foreign leaders visiting Washington. Not so for Khrushchev. The first questioner asked him about a famous yarn: at a meeting after the Secret Speech, a Soviet official was said to have asked Khrushchev in writing what he had been doing while Stalin performed his heinous crimes. Khrushchev had supposedly asked the official to stand and show himself. No one did, and Khrushchev had said, "There's your answer."

The Press Club audience guffawed. Khrushchev's eyes narrowed, his cheeks flamed and he spat out a tirade of indignant Russian. His translator Troyanovsky barely succeeded in toning down the scathing language.

Someone else asked about Khrushchev's notorious pledge "We will bury you" and received a calmer reply: "My statement was deliberately misconstrued. It was never a question of anyone being buried at any time, but of how a social system changes. . . . In the historical sense, I meant that capitalism would be buried and that Communism would come to replace it."

At five o'clock, Khrushchev took tea with the Senate Foreign Relations Committee in its ceremonial chamber in the Capitol: "I feel that I have known practically all of you a long time but until now, you have been sort of ethereal beings to me. Now you appear in the flesh." He advised the senators to resign themselves to the fact of socialist states in the world, pointing to the wart on the bridge of his nose: "The wart is there and I can't do anything about it."

He complained about the CIA: "Subversion of other countries is hardly conducive to peaceful coexistence. . . . Speaking in businessman's terms, this is an enterprise which yields no profit." (Khrushchev did not offer to scrap the KGB.)

Senator Richard Russell, one of Allen Dulles's old reliables, replied with equal disingenuousness: "I know of no appropriations anywhere for any subversive work in Russia—and I have been a member of the Appropriations Committee for twenty-five years." Perhaps probing Khrushchev for useful information, Russell asked him whether the Russians had had trouble launching their moon rocket, as Richard Nixon had suggested in his speech the other day.

"You had better ask Nixon. He answered your question when he said that the launching of our moon rocket miscarried three times. He knows how things are with us better than we do. Nixon said he was using information from a secret source. But of course, he didn't specify the source."

Arriving late was John Kennedy, already campaigning for President. "I was impressed with Kennedy," Khrushchev recalled. "I remember liking his face, which was sometimes stern but which often broke into a good-natured smile." After the tea, Khrushchev asked the Soviet Embassy staff what they knew about the young Senator. The most favorable report was that "while Kennedy was not yet another Roosevelt, he was independent and could be counted upon for new departures." Khrushchev filed this away for the future.

That evening, he gave a return banquet for the Eisenhowers at the Embassy. Huge portraits of Lenin and Stalin were removed from the reception room so that Khrushchev would not have to greet guests under the gaze of his personal Lucifer. Ann Whitman wrote that "security restrictions along Sixteenth Street were so rigid that I, a small individual trying to get home, wondered just who was living in a police state."

After the meal of borscht and shashlik, Khrushchev delivered his toast: "My friends and I have had a fine day today. You are real exploiters, I must say, and have done a good job of exploiting us!" All laughed. "I feel sure—perhaps because I want it very badly—that our coming at your invitation, Mr. President, and your forthcoming visit to our country will help to thaw international relations. The ice of the Cold War has not only cracked, but has indeed begun to crumble."

The next morning, Khrushchev and a hundred Russians boarded a special Pennsylvania Railroad train for New York.

•

Nixon had counseled the President to give Khrushchev "a subtle feeling of the power and the will of America." Eisenhower asked his 1952 campaign handlers to advance the tour and told them to make sure the schedule was not dominated by "the Henry Fords" and other tycoons. He asked Cabot Lodge to serve as Khrushchev's escort. Political columnists speculated that the President was trying to build up Lodge as an alternative to Nixon in 1960. Actually, Nixon's quarrels with Khrushchev had convinced Eisenhower that Lodge would be a more compatible choice. And Lodge's debating skills, honed through years in the Senate and UN, would enable him to rebut any "misleading statements" Khrushchev gave out during his trip.

Lodge was a major general in the U.S. Army Reserves. By Khrushchev's recollection, at the start of the trip, he reminded his escort that he was a lieutenant general: "Therefore you're my subordinate and I'll expect you to behave as a junior officer." As Khrushchev recalled, the Bostonian saluted and snapped, "Major General Lodge reporting for duty, sir!" Twice a day he reported to Eisenhower in code through the Signal Corps on the Soviet leader's doings and sayings.

As Khrushchev gazed out of his club car at factories, shopping centers and housing projects in Baltimore, Wilmington, Philadelphia, Newark, Secret Service men on a pilot train ahead scanned the tracks for mines and bombs. In Manhattan, Khrushchev rode in a closed limousine up an avenue swept clear of traffic. Overhead was no ticker tape—just a billowy cross, a skywriter's talisman against the godless visitor. A Polish reporter cabled Warsaw that one of Khrushchev's American admirers had painted a great "K" in the sky.

Khrushchev found New York a "huge noisy city" with "vast quantities of exhaust fumes that were choking people." He lunched with Mayor Robert Wagner and a thousand civic leaders, and paid a call on Averell Harriman, America's wartime envoy to Moscow and an old soldier for détente. Harriman had asked men who had owned or controlled assets roughly worth a hundred million dollars each to gather in the library of his East Side brownstone before dusk.

Harry Truman publicly refused Harriman's invitation. John Kenneth Galbraith flunked the admission test but, by his own account, got in as Harriman's friend and token member of the proletariat. Other guests included Dean Rusk of the Rockefeller Foundation, David Sarnoff of RCA, John D. Rockefeller and Herbert Lehman, former New York Governor and Senator and wartime head of the UN Recovery Agency. Khrushchev had run the agency's Ukraine office; he embraced Lehman as "my boss." Galbraith later recalled the peculiar sight of "the very shapeless man in a rather shapeless suit with a very large pink head and very short legs beneath the Picasso."

Khrushchev was almost smothered by the tobacco smoke: "One thing I couldn't help noticing about Harriman's guests was that they smoked a lot. . . . Through this cloud people kept coming up to me to exchange a few words, obviously trying to sound me out and see what kind of man I was." The guests looked to him "like typical capitalists, right out of the posters painted during our civil war—only they didn't have the pigs' snouts our artists always gave them." Khrushchev had hoped that the group would pledge to work for trade with the Soviet Union. He was provoked by their needling about Hungary and Soviet slave labor.

That evening, Khrushchev spoke to a banquet of the New York Economic Club at the Waldorf-Astoria. During the question period, someone asked why the Soviet people could not see American newspapers or hear the Voice of America. "I am here at President Eisenhower's invitation," replied Khrushchev. "We agreed that our talks would not concern third countries and that there would be no interference in the internal affairs of each other's nations—"

"Answer the question!" someone shouted.

"If you don't want to listen, all right!" Khrushchev shouted back. "I am an old sparrow and you cannot muddle me with your cries. You should show enough hospitality not to interrupt. If there is no desire to listen to me, I can go." A tomblike silence filled the room. "No cries can make the world forget the great achievements of the Soviet people. What our people hear on the radio is of no concern to other nations. . . . Your great Negro singer Paul Robeson was denied the right to go abroad for some five to seven years. Why was *his* voice jammed?"

Outside on Park Avenue, men and women called out slogans and walked with signboards: KHRUSHCHEV, THE BUTCHER OF THE UKRAINE. . . . SIX MILLION STARVED BY KHRUSHCHEV IN FAMINE HE PLANNED AND SUPERVISED. . . . FREEDOM FOR HUNGARY.

The rest of Khrushchev's New York visit was more sedate. He spoke on disarmament at the UN, rode to the top of the Empire State Building and insisted on touring Harlem's slums. At Hyde Park, he laid a wreath on the grave of Franklin Roosevelt, patron saint of Soviet-American amity. Eleanor Roosevelt laid out refreshments at her cottage, but Khrushchev ate and ran: as he left, he held up a seed roll and cried, "One for the road!"

He renewed acquaintance with Nelson Rockefeller, newly elected Governor of New York. In 1957, a Moscow publisher had issued a book on the Rockefeller brothers called *Ever Knee-Deep in Blood, Ever Trampling Corpses.* Someone had told the Governor that psychiatrists in Khrushchev's party were watching possible Presidential candidates for signs of weakness, so when Khrushchev proposed a toast to coexistence, the Governor refused and toasted cooperation instead. Rockefeller reminded Khrushchev that a half million Russians had come to America for freedom and opportunity.

"Don't give me that stuff," said the visitor. "They only came to get higher wages. I was almost one of them."

Rockefeller said, "If you had come, you would have been the head of one of our biggest unions by now."

•

Next stop: Los Angeles. Flying west on an Air Force Boeing 707, Khrushchev extended his boasts about Soviet superiority in the arms race and space race to the race for intelligence. "You Americans are wasting money on intelligence," he told Lodge. "You might as well send it direct to us instead of middlemen, because we get most of it anyway. Your agents give us the codebooks and then we send false information back to you through your code. Then we send cables asking for money and you send it to us."

Khrushchev bragged about sending American defectors back to the United States, where they filched secret information and sent it to Moscow. He said he had recently seen letters from the Shah of Iran to Eisenhower, and from Eisenhower to Jawaharlal Nehru of India. He told Lodge that he read "most of the stuff Allen Dulles puts out" but would "rather read good novels."

Khrushchev went to Hollywood, which seemed to him "like a special republic within the larger republic of the U.S.A." Twentieth Century–Fox threw a luncheon with Bob Hope, Henry Fonda, Elizabeth Taylor and four hundred other stars. Ronald Reagan boycotted the affair. Marilyn Monroe was reputedly asked to wear her "tightest, sexiest dress" and to leave her husband, Arthur Miller, home: a meeting between the leftist playwright and Khrushchev might besmirch the name of Hollywood.

According to her maid, she later said, "I could tell Khrushchev liked me. He smiled more when he was introduced to me than for anybody else. . . . He squeezed my hand so long and so hard that I thought he would break it. I guess it was better than having to kiss him." She could not see how someone "fat and ugly" with "warts on his face" could become the leader of so many people: "Who would want to be a Communist with a president like that? . . . I guess there's not much sex in Russia!"

At the dais, Khrushchev complained that he had been barred from seeing Disneyland: "What do you have there? Rocket-launching pads? Your American security says it cannot guarantee my safety if I go there. Is there an epidemic of cholera there? Have gangsters taken control of the place? . . . What must I do now—commit suicide?" Madame Khrushcheva murmured her disappointment to David Niven. Frank Sinatra leaned over to Niven and said, "Screw the cops! Tell the old broad you and I'll take 'em down there this afternoon."

The Khrushchevs toured the set where Sinatra, Shirley MacLaine, Maurice Chevalier and Louis Jourdan were filming *Can Can*. Sinatra sang the tune "Live and Let Live," and told the Russian guests, "It's a marvelous idea." A show girl came forward to pose with the Khrushchevs; cameramen shouted, "Raise your dress higher, higher!" She refused. Later when Lodge gave his report to Eisenhower, the President said he wished he had the woman's name so that he could send her a thank-you letter.

Khrushchev later used the incident to score another debating point. He startled reporters by turning his back, bending over, flipping up his coat and doing the can can: "This is what you call freedom—freedom for the girls to show their backsides. To us, it's pornography. . . . It's capitalism that makes the girls that way."

Everything seemed to be going wrong. Riding through Los Angeles, Khrushchev exploded at the sight of a woman in mourning dress with a sign: DEATH TO KHRUSHCHEV, BUTCHER OF HUNGARY. At a banquet that evening, despite Lodge's pleas, Mayor Norris Poulson used Khrushchev as a stage prop for an anti-Soviet harangue: "You shall not bury us and we shall not bury you!"

Khrushchev thundered, "I can go, and I don't know when—*if ever*—another Soviet premier will visit your country. . . . The unpleasant thought sometimes creeps up on me as to whether Khrushchev was not invited here to enable you to sort of rub him in your sauce and show the might of the United States to make him shake at the knees. If that is so, then if it took me about twelve hours to get here, I guess it will take no more than ten and a half hours to fly back!"

Khrushchev thought he saw Llewellyn Thompson's wife burst into tears: "She was afraid there would be a war or something." The President later heard from his friend Freeman Gosden, of radio's *Amos 'n' Andy,* that Khrushchev must have just replaced Washington with Los Angeles as the number-one Soviet bombing target.

At two o'clock the next morning, Khrushchev was still angry. By his account, he called Gromyko to his hotel room and cried, "How dare this man attack the President's guest like that?" He complained about the aborted tour of Disneyland, the sealed cars that walled him off from the American people, protesters at every stop—obviously stationed by the American government. Maybe they should pack up and go back to Moscow.

As Khrushchev later recalled, Lidiya Gromyko turned to find him a tranquilizer. He gave her a look to show that he was only venting his spleen for the benefit of Lodge who, he was certain, was listening through an eavesdropping device. He ranted on about how he would not tolerate such treatment.

Gromyko officially complained to Lodge. The next morning,

Lodge told Khrushchev, "We have decided to manage the trip as though you were a Presidential candidate." They boarded a Southern Pacific train for the journey north to San Francisco. At Santa Barbara and San Luis Obispo, Khrushchev orated, kissed babies and pinned hammer-and-sickle badges on children before climbing back on the train as the whistle blew. This time, when he spied hostile placards, he told Lodge, "Poor Eisenhower! I am just beginning to understand what his problems are." Later: "The plain people of America like me. It's just those bastards around Eisenhower that don't."

•

Khrushchev's American adventures were a media event. Chalmers Roberts, White House correspondent for the *Washington Post,* found them "undoubtedly the most fascinating story that I covered" in forty years. "It had everything—a fabulous personality, conflict, human interest, the unexpected ... more than any of us could possibly write, even though we filed thousands and thousands of words daily."

Madame Khrushcheva won American hearts with her grandmotherly ways. Khrushchev thought official travel with wives and families a "petty-bourgeois luxury," but as another sop to the West, he brought his son Sergei, daughters Rada and Julia and his son-in-law Adzhubei, who covered the tour for *Izvestia.* American reporters largely ignored the scientists, writers and artists Khrushchev had brought along to meet their American counterparts. The few who noticed Mikhail Sholokhov badgered the novelist about Boris Pasternak, whose *Doctor Zhivago* had lately won him the Nobel Prize and expulsion from the Soviet Writers' Union at Khrushchev's behest.

The Soviet press was literally compelled to write paeans to Khrushchev's trip. Each stop was more triumphant than the last. American workers were learning how misled they were about Khrushchev and Communism. The whole United States agreed that such an impressive statesman had never graced its shores.

Izvestia: "There has been and can be nothing nobler than this mission! ... The Soviet people are greeting the news from across the sea with enormous enthusiasm. This news testifies to how the international prestige of our homeland, worthily represented by that outstanding fighter for peace, Nikita Sergeyevich Khrushchev, has risen."

Pravda: "It is hard to convey how intently the luncheon guests hung on every word uttered by the head of the Soviet government. . . .

202 : M A Y D A Y

Even the recently selected twenty-year-old Miss America has taken the first step in her imposing role by informing reporters of her fervent dream—to talk with Khrushchev."

Literaturnaya Gazeta: "Even the malicious Harry Truman, who has already been impolite, had to admit that Khrushchev was welcomed cordially."

Khrushchev's tour made its way into Soviet humor, one of the last forms of political expression left to the average citizen. Ukrainians joked that during his talks with Eisenhower at the White House, Khrushchev had lamented the rampant American alcoholism that *Pravda* always talked about. The President had replied that there were no drunks in America: to prove it, Khrushchev was welcome to gun down any drunks he could find. As the story went, the next day, the *New York Times* reported that a fat, bald man had gunned down twelve Soviet diplomats on the streets of Washington.

•

"You have charmed me," Khrushchev told San Francisco. "But you have charmed my heart, not my mind. I still think our system is a good system." He met Walter Reuther, now chief of United Auto Workers, whom he disliked because he now struggled for the "extra nickel or dime," not the "victory of the working class." Khrushchev found Harry Bridges more satisfactory: the longshoremen's boss was a "true progressive" who backed the policies of the Soviet Union.

In Coon Rapids, Iowa, Khrushchev visited Roswell Garst, the noted hybrid-corn grower who had corresponded with him about corn and livestock and had called on him at his summer home on the Black Sea. Khrushchev considered Garst a "class enemy," but liked his willingness to "trade secrets with others—even with us." Having planned a relatively private day with Khrushchev, farmer to farmer, Garst was outraged by the arrival of hundreds of newsmen. When photographers blocked Khrushchev's view of the Iowan's corn silage loading operation, he threw corn cobs at them and kicked reporters in the shins. Another guest was Adlai Stevenson, who had met Khrushchev in the Kremlin in 1958. Arms around shoulders, he and Garst and Khrushchev posed for pictures. Khrushchev took Stevenson's consent to pose with him as a "sign of tolerance toward the Soviet Union."

A strike had closed union steel mills in Pittsburgh. The guest toured a non-union machine works. The mayor of Pittsburgh presented the Soviet leader with the key to his city. Khrushchev said he accepted as a symbol of trust: "And you can rest assured—I *promise* you—that this key will never be used without the hosts' permission."

•

Americans did not quite treat Khrushchev as he viewed himself—a man of the people who led a great state and world movement and deserved awe. It was obvious to Khrushchev that many who turned out to see him "came more out of curiosity than friendship. They had paid their fifty kopecks to have a look at this Russian bear. What does he look like? Does he know how to sit at a table in polite society and properly hold a knife and fork, or will he lap up his food off his plate?"

Newsmen baited him. What about Stalin? What about the purges? Citizens killed him with kindness. See how friendly we are? Why would you want to bury us or make us all Communists? "I have no intention of calling you into the Communist realm," Khrushchev declared. "You may not agree just now, but the time will come when you will agree that Communists have the noblest of thoughts and aspirations." Despite the constant hostile demonstrations and the boorishness of local show-offs like Mayor Poulson, Khrushchev's tour had its effect on Americans. "We now know that he is no buffoon reeling drunkenly through the Kremlin," said *Newsweek,* "but a shrewd, tough and able adversary."

The trip showed Khrushchev that the United States was not on the verge of falling to Communism. Ambassador Menshikov, known to White House aides as "Smiling Mike," was notorious for sending Khrushchev information about the United States that was just what he wanted to hear—mass unemployment, racial tension, incipient revolution among the proletariat.

At the end of the trip, Lodge told the President that although Khrushchev claimed he had learned nothing that he did not already know, it was obvious that he now viewed the United States "quite differently." Khrushchev had refused to look at American missile sites (perhaps so that he need not show Russian sites to Eisenhower). But he had gained an unforgettable sense of America's productive might:

"He is deeply impressed by . . . the conditions and attitudes of our people, our roads, our automobiles, our factories. He was struck by the vitality of our people. He probably does not now really think the Soviets are likely to surpass us—at least anytime soon. . . . It is clear that he wants peace and thinks that Russia needs peace in order to do what he wants the nation to do."

•

In August 1959, when Khrushchev was informed that his final weekend in the United States had been reserved for private talks with Eisenhower at Camp David, he "couldn't for the life of me find out what this Camp David was." He recalled that in the years after the Russian Revolution, a Soviet delegation was invited to a meeting held "someplace called the Prince's Islands," where stray dogs were sent to die. Was Camp David a similar place of quarantine?

Research revealed that a weekend at the President's hideaway was an honor. "We never told anyone at the time about not knowing what Camp David was," Khrushchev said years later. "I can laugh about it now, but I'm a little bit ashamed. It shows how ignorant we were in some respects."

Pravda told its readers that "Camp David, named for President Eisenhower's grandson, would seem to have been created for fruitful reflection by nature itself. A canopy of red, green and orange foliage, touched with the breath of autumn, conceals small cabins made of rough, unfinished boards. . . . During the war, this was the secret residence of President Roosevelt, who called it Shangri-La—the valley where people don't grow old."

On Friday, September 25, Khrushchev was back in Washington. Ann Whitman wrote in her diary, "This was the day of the beginning of the conference with Mr. K. and approached not with great anticipation but, I think, with some dread."

•

The President had scheduled the private talks at the end of Khrushchev's trip (on Milton Eisenhower's suggestion) to keep him on good behavior while he was in the United States. "It will be very difficult to adhere to an agenda," he told aides gathered in the Oval Office. "Some say that Khrushchev is a master debater. In fact, he seems to be a skillful evader of tough questions."

Eisenhower had promised de Gaulle and Macmillan that he would not negotiate with Khrushchev: serious talks must only take place with the leaders of France and Britain in the room. What the President wished to learn was whether such a Big Four summit would be fruitful.

He would focus on Berlin: "The key point is that Khrushchev precipitated a crisis when he should have called for negotiations." He would probably approve a summit if Khrushchev lifted his Berlin ultimatum: "This would then give us the opportunity to pursue other questions without a pistol at our head."

By Friday afternoon, Eisenhower was still feeling "lousy" from his cold. After a nap in the Mansion, he returned to the West Wing, where he greeted Khrushchev at five o'clock and walked him outdoors to the helicopter. "We flew over a big green field where he told me he played golf," the guest recalled. "He asked me whether I liked this sport. I didn't have the slightest idea what it was all about. He told me it was a very healthy sport."

When the chopper set down in Maryland, the two leaders were driven a quarter mile in a tail-finned black Cadillac to the Presidential cottage, Aspen Lodge. They posed for pictures, walked through the front door under the handcarved sign, ASPEN, and paused inside before the picture window overlooking the Catoctin Valley. "I see that all seems to be quiet along this front," said the President.

"I notice that all the soldiers are peacefully inclined here," said Khrushchev.

The two leaders and Herter and Gromyko took adjoining rooms in the south wing of the house. On her first visit in 1953, Mamie Eisenhower had found the place a bit down at the heels and refurbished it in a fifties-modern scheme of greens, yellows and beiges. Khrushchev thought the outside looked "like a barracks," but found the inside "luxuriously decorated" and "very businesslike—typically American." He was delighted to find the mountain air of Camp David cooler than Washington.

After dining on roast beef and red snapper, the two leaders and their aides watched movies of the North Pole taken by U.S. Navy officers aboard the nuclear submarine *Nautilus.* As Khrushchev later recalled, the President said, "Personally, I like Westerns. I know they don't have any substance to them and don't require any thought to appreciate, but they always have a lot of fancy tricks. Also I like the horses."

Khrushchev said, "You know, when Stalin was alive, we used to watch Westerns all the time. When the movie ended, Stalin always denounced it for its ideological content, but the very next day, we'd be back in the movie theater watching another Western."

Khrushchev had slept poorly during his travels; Eisenhower had his cold. They retired at midnight. In the Gettysburg High School gymnasium, where hundreds of newsmen were camped out, Harrison Salisbury wrote his dispatch for the *New York Times:* "On the pleasant mountain peak in the northwest Maryland wilderness, the man who had started life as an Abilene farm boy and the man who began as a Kalinovka shepherd lad were settling down for a little more than forty-eight hours of talk on which humanity's fate may depend."

●

The next morning, Camp David was enveloped in fog so dense that helicopters were banned from landing. State Department and White House aides were driven up from Washington at ninety miles per hour to reach meetings on time. Khrushchev woke up early and pulled on a collarless embroidered white shirt and trousers. In the morning chill, he walked with Gromyko down a wooded path to discuss strategy away from American bugging devices.

At 8:15 A.M., they returned to Aspen for breakfast with the President, Herter and a small group. Over grits, hotcakes, eggs and minute steaks, Khrushchev spoke of World War Two. Sitting across from his host, he leaned forward, elbows on the table, waggling his index finger, working hard to build an old-soldier rapport. So engrossed in his words that he hardly ate, Khrushchev chattered about life as a commissar, the battle of Stalingrad and Stalin's flaws as a military commander.

Khrushchev noted that the President had been close to Zhukov. Zhukov was one general who stood up to Stalin: "He was a very strong-minded man and could not be swayed from what he thought was right, which is a fine thing in a military man"—then, with a leer— "so long as this is limited to *military* things. . . . Your friend Zhukov is all right. Don't worry about him. He's down in the Ukraine fishing and, like all generals, he's probably writing his memoirs."

Standing around the table, Khrushchev complained to John Eisenhower about his kidneys and other ailments. This was of more than passing interest, for American intelligence had gleaned hints that the Soviet leader had a serious illness. After his Russian trip, Nixon had reported that Khrushchev was "not a sick man" but that he "drives himself unmercifully" and "lacks the stamina he once had." Intelligence services routinely gathered information about the health of visiting leaders, even to the point of taking surreptitious bathroom samples. Khrushchev's time in the United States was no exception.

●

The President, Khrushchev and aides moved to the Aspen terrace for their first full working session. Conversation skated over many subjects but kept returning to Berlin. The State Department had written a talking paper for Eisenhower that attacked Khrushchev's ultimatum:

> This is as direct a threat of aggression as if a bandit kept us out of our own house at gunpoint. The Soviet position is phony and all the world knows it. The Soviets should not underestimate our determination to maintain our position in Berlin, at whatever cost, against this aggressive Soviet challenge.

The President paraphrased this and called negotiations on Berlin impossible until Khrushchev removed his ultimatum. Khrushchev cited his UN speech of the previous week proposing the abolition of all weapons by 1963 (without any inspection or supervision). All they had to do was agree on total disarmament. That would solve Berlin automatically! Eisenhower was not amused. At 10:45 A.M., he took his guest for a stroll, hoping that Khrushchev might get more serious in private. They reached the new Camp David recreation hall, where a Navy yeoman, bowling, had the shock of his life. Eisenhower asked the yeoman to continue and his Secret Service man to bowl on the next lane.

Khrushchev was intrigued: bowling was unknown in the Soviet Union. The two leaders autographed the yeoman's scorecard, returned to Aspen Lodge and sat down at a bridge table on the terrace. With the valley shining beneath them, they spoke privately for hours but could make no headway on Berlin. At two o'clock, hours behind schedule, they joined their aides in the dining room for lunch. The President whispered to Goodpaster, who scrawled the word "Impasse" in his notes.

The atmosphere at lunch was supercharged. Khrushchev made a Herculean effort to keep himself from erupting at his host. Perhaps he had expected that Eisenhower had invited him to the United States with a dramatic proposal in mind and now he was angry to learn that there was none. Khrushchev was clearly looking for substitute targets; his fellow diner Richard Nixon served nicely. He attacked the exhibition that Nixon had opened in Moscow. The Soviet people were not impressed by such things as a "Miracle Kitchen." They already had a high living standard. Any further efforts to lure them to capitalism would fail.

The President tried to change the subject: how hard it was to be President. The telephones were always ringing—even during vacations. To Khrushchev, in his surly mood, this was an insult to Soviet technology. Almost violently he exclaimed that the Soviets would soon have better telephones, so much better that the Americans would cut off telephone service to the Soviet Union to avoid embarrassing comparisons. George Kistiakowsky later wrote in his diary, "I could see by the President's expression that he was intensely angry and just managed to control himself."

After lunch, Eisenhower took a nap while Khrushchev went for another walk with Gromyko. On the terrace, Nixon explained to Herter and other colleagues that Khrushchev's performance at lunch was the result of an "extreme inferiority complex" which took the form of arrogance.

By four, the President was awake. He found Khrushchev on a path near Aspen Lodge and invited him for a visit to his Gettysburg farm. Khrushchev accepted. As their helicopter took off, "everybody was very much depressed," wrote Kistiakowsky. "There was a general feeling that the meeting will end in a nearly complete failure and hence may actually worsen rather than improve relations."

•

Khrushchev thought the President's farm reflected Eisenhower's "reasonable and modest" character: "Not that his own house on the farm was a poor man's house. Of course not. It was a rich man's house, but not a millionaire's." As the master of a dacha near Moscow, a hunting lodge in the Ukraine, a summer place in the Crimea and other estates, Khrushchev knew the difference.

He admired the "dark brown color" and "sturdy torsos" of Eisenhower's Black Angus herd and described his own work to improve Soviet cattle breeding. With a smile, the President promised to send Khrushchev one of his heifers. Khrushchev thought Eisenhower's face "was always very pleasant when he smiled."

Inside the house, the President picked up the telephone and asked John and Barbara Eisenhower to scrub their children and bring them to meet the guest. Over tea on the glassed-in porch, every inch the doting grandfather, Khrushchev asked the four children their names and strained to come up with the Russian versions. He grandly invited the President to bring his whole family to the Soviet Union and gave the children red-star badges. When John found his son David wearing one to school a few days later, he explained "in no uncertain terms" what it stood for: "If Khrushchev could take us over, guess which family would be the first to be shot?"

By 6:30 P.M., the two leaders were back at Camp David for cocktails and dinner. Goodpaster noted that Khrushchev was "considerably more relaxed" and showed "none of the ill manners" of lunch.

●

On Sunday morning, Eisenhower went to the Presbyterian church in Gettysburg. He had asked Khrushchev to come along, but the guest had said it would be a "shock" to the Soviet people.

While the President was gone, Herter and Douglas Dillon spoke with Khrushchev about trade. When Dillon suggested exporting American shoes to Russia, Khrushchev blew up: "*Shoes?* Look at my shoes! We make the best shoes in the world! We don't need any shoes!" Dillon asked when the Soviets might repay the $2.6 billion owed the United States for wartime Lend-Lease aid, and Khrushchev blew up again: the Soviet people had already paid with the blood shed during the struggle against the Nazis!

At 10:30 A.M., Eisenhower was back. Khrushchev said he found it strange that, although a military man, the President had such an obvious interest in peace. Eisenhower replied that he may have had moments of exhilaration during the last war, "but now war has become nothing more than a struggle for survival." He was unashamed to say that he was afraid of nuclear war. Everyone should be.

Now Khrushchev asked what the United States intended to do about China.

●

Eisenhower did not fully know it yet, but the most momentous change in the world balance of power since 1945 was taking place. The Sino-Soviet alliance was breaking apart. Mao Tse-tung was determined to build nuclear weapons and challenge Soviet leadership in this generation.

By now, Khrushchev privately considered the Chinese leader a "lunatic on a throne." He recalled that in 1957, Mao had told him not to fear a war with the West: "No matter what kind of war breaks out— conventional or thermonuclear—we'll win. As for China, if the imperialists unleash war on us, we may lose more than three hundred million people. So what? War is war. The years will pass and we'll get to work producing more babies than ever before." As the leader of 230 million, Khrushchev had not found this comforting.

In June 1959, Khrushchev evidently reneged on a Soviet pledge to give Peking a sample atomic bomb and other nuclear assistance. When a frontier dispute erupted between India and China in September, the Kremlin's official position was far from unreserved support for Peking. Khrushchev threw more sand in Mao's face by accepting Eisenhower's invitation to the United States. Mao almost certainly suspected a potential conspiracy of the white Europeans to dictate world politics, based not least on fear of China. He presumably agreed not to denounce the journey only because Khrushchev pledged to visit Peking immediately on his return.

Khrushchev's fear of a nuclear China was probably matched by his fear of a nuclear West Germany and Japan. One reason that he was so eager for a Big Four summit may have been that he planned to ask the West to ban nuclear arms from the two countries as part of some kind of formula that might include a Soviet pledge to throw a damper—if it could—on Chinese nuclear development. At the Twenty-first Party Congress in January, he had proposed a nuclear-free zone in the Far East "and the whole Pacific Ocean." Now Khrushchev had a decided interest in sounding out Eisenhower about collaboration to contain China while pretending that the "unshakable unity" of the Sino-Soviet alliance remained intact.

The President was not ignorant of tensions between Peking and Moscow. Since 1957, the two governments had differed publicly over Mao's Great Leap Forward, Quemoy and Matsu, and the Chinese-Indian dispute. Eisenhower privately suspected that the Russians were "becoming worried about Communist China as a possible threat to them in the future." He knew that a Sino-Soviet schism could best be exploited by playing one power off against the other and would have been delighted to foil China's nuclear ambitions. Peking preached— and as a nuclear, industrialized power, could practice—a far more aggressive, anti-Western brand of Communism than Moscow.

The President had once told friends at a stag dinner that it was "foolish" to "pretend" that such a large country as China did not exist. The day before he went to Camp David, he asked Herter "how we could negotiate on controls in light of our rigid policy against any recognition of Red China."

Herter replied in State Department boilerplate: "We do not wish to change our stand on Red China. They will not renounce the use of force on Taiwan, nor will they release our prisoners."

Now that Khrushchev had himself brought up China, Eisenhower had a magnificent opportunity to explore the depth of the Sino-Soviet divide and the possibility of joining the Soviet Union to keep China out of the nuclear club. But for whatever reason, he did not take advantage of it. He told Khrushchev that there was "little use" discussing Red China because she had "put herself beyond the pale" as far as the United States was concerned. Five Americans were still prisoners in China. The Red Chinese had not renounced their pledge to take Taiwan by force. They were generating trouble in Southeast Asia.

Especially without prodding by Eisenhower, Khrushchev was not about to weaken his bargaining position by revealing the extent of his anxieties about Mao. He responded by reciting the Kremlin's official line: Why didn't Washington abandon Chiang Kai-shek? You couldn't have two governments in one country. Dealing with Chiang was like dealing with Kerensky. On second thought, he had lately heard that Kerensky had "married a rich American lady, so maybe Kerensky would not be interested." Did the President prefer Chiang? Fine. That was a matter of taste. He preferred Mao Tse-tung and Chou En-lai.

Eisenhower declared that their views on China were obviously so far apart that there was "really no point in discussing the question in detail."

•

The President later noted that "when Khrushchev and I were alone together at Camp David, he was very convivial with me, especially eager to be friendly. He kept belittling most of our differences and gave every indication of wanting to find ways to straighten them out." But when Gromyko appeared, Khrushchev "kept reminding me that he would have to take up these matters with his government before making a decision on them."

They had made no progress on the German issue. Time was running out, for Khrushchev soon had to be in Washington for a press conference and television speech to the American people. Eisenhower decided that one more private walk in the woods would offer the last, best chance for Khrushchev to lift his ultimatum on Berlin.

It worked. The Soviet leader removed his threat but declared that someday the German issue had to be settled. The President quickly pledged to seek a solution acceptable to all parties as soon as possible. By his lights, this betokened "a general improvement of the atmosphere." Hence he could, in good conscience, recommend a Big Four summit meeting. This was music to Khrushchev's ears. He suggested a summit in November or December 1959, to be followed by the President's trip to the Soviet Union in May or June 1960. The "beautiful scenery and wonderful scent of blooming trees" would inspire them during their talks.

At 12:15 P.M., Eisenhower walked happily into Herter's bedroom; they worked on the draft of a joint statement for him to issue with Khrushchev. They would say that there had been no agreements of substance at Camp David. Disarmament was the main problem. Both sides pledged to seek a Berlin solution palatable to all. The Berlin talks would be free of any threat. The President would tour the Soviet Union in the spring.

Sunday's lunch was to Saturday's like day to night. Khrushchev pulled out a box of chocolates from Van Cliburn; the pianist had asked him to share them with Eisenhower. As the box was passed around the table, Menshikov tried to score points with his boss by muttering that Soviet chocolates were better. "Don't translate that remark!" said Khrushchev.

After lunch, the Soviets and Americans examined the proposed joint statement. Khrushchev astonished the President by asking that his concession on Berlin be omitted. Eisenhower exploded: "This ends the whole affair—and I will go neither to a summit nor to Russia."

Khrushchev quickly explained that he could not publicize his concession before explaining it privately to his colleagues in Moscow. If the President would wait until then to announce the concession, he would confirm it instantly from Moscow.

Eisenhower agreed. He and his aides later concluded that Khrushchev had exceeded his negotiating instructions and dared not reveal his concession until safely back in the Kremlin.

At 2:10 P.M., behind schedule, Khrushchev and Eisenhower

climbed into the President's Lincoln to race back to Washington with sirens screaming and state troopers blocking every intersection on Route 240. Jim Hagerty solemnly assured reporters at Gettysburg that no nation's freedom had been surrendered.

The two leaders shook hands on the front steps of Blair House. Khrushchev said he looked forward to Eisenhower's visit in the spring. "I'll bring the whole family," said the President. "You'll have more Eisenhowers there than you'll know what to do with."

At six o'clock Eastern Daylight Time, American television viewers not watching *Gunsmoke* or *Have Gun, Will Travel* saw the leader of the Soviet Union on NBC: "Good evening, American friends. I am glad of this opportunity to speak to you before my departure for home. We liked your beautiful cities and wonderful roads, but most of all, your amiable and kindhearted people."

As she watched, Ann Whitman thought Khrushchev seemed to have "mellowed" since Friday.

Khrushchev said it was impossible for anyone to expect a "sudden change in the world situation" but he and the President had enjoyed "very pleasant talks" at Camp David: "I have no doubts whatever that the President sincerely desires an improvement of relations between our countries." After sixty minutes (one of his shorter efforts), he closed with a few words of English: "*Goot-bye! Goot-lock! Friends!*"

Late that evening, the Nixons went to Andrews to see the Russians off. "I thank you from the bottom of my heart for your kind hospitality, for your bread and salt," Khrushchev told the crowd, his pink face glowing under the television lights. "I would like to wish that we more and more frequently use in the relations between our countries that short and good American word—*Okay!*"

•

Camp David had achieved few dazzling results. Khrushchev had suspended his Berlin threat and Eisenhower approved a Big Four summit. But even these concessions probably would not have been reached at a lower level. Without them, the two superpowers might have remained in a state of near-war over Berlin.

Khrushchev's trip elevated his Kremlin standing. Years later, he called it "a colossal moral victory. I still remember how delighted I was the first time my interpreter told me that Eisenhower had called me, in English, 'my friend.' " The Soviet press reminded the Soviet nation again and again that it was Khrushchev whom the President had entertained as an equal, Khrushchev who knew how to handle the Americans, Khrushchev who, if things got out of hand, could retrieve a miscalculation or overcommitment. Khrushchev must have presumed that in the nuclear age, this was a vital resource which might make conspiratorial colleagues think twice before plotting against him.

By receiving Khrushchev, Eisenhower made visits between American and Soviet leaders more of a commonplace and American-Soviet relations more normal. Perhaps only a President as popular as Eisenhower could have had the Antichrist to the White House and Camp David in 1959 without at least some political harm. Stuart Symington observed that if Harry Truman had tried to bring Stalin to Washington, he probably would have been impeached.

Their private talks enabled Khrushchev and Eisenhower to gauge each other's motives, weaknesses and sensitivities more acutely than by simply reading the KGB or CIA profile of the adversary. For the two men who could obliterate the world, this reduced the chance of nuclear conflict hastened by ill-chosen rhetoric or tactical blunder. Walking alone at Camp David and Gettysburg gave them the opportunity to communicate directly without colleagues, allies and the rest of the world breathing down their necks. This afforded greater candor than the usual superpower dialogue of speeches, diplomatic notes and other pronouncements via the Voice of America, Radio Moscow, *Pravda* and the *New York Times*.

If Eisenhower were Talleyrand, he might have used the opportunity to explore an American-Soviet alliance against China. As it was, the two leaders acquired a sense of what bound them together. Both were among the most moderate members of their governments. Both wished to devote money spent on arms and soldiers to a better living standard for their people. By Khrushchev's account, Eisenhower told him, "My military leaders come to me and say, 'Mr. President, we need such and such a sum. . . . If we don't get the funds we need, we'll fall behind the Soviet Union.' "

Much affected, Khrushchev replied that it was just the same in Moscow: "Some people from our military department come and say, 'Comrade Khrushchev, look at this! The Americans are developing such-and-such a system, but it would cost such and such.' I tell them there's no money. It's all been allotted already. So they say, 'If we don't get the money we need and if there's a war, then the enemy will have superiority over us.' "

The President had said, "We really should come to some sort of agreement to stop this fruitless, really wasteful rivalry," and Khrushchev had nodded. Camp David convinced Eisenhower for perhaps the first time that Khrushchev might be a responsible leader with whom he could do business. Soon he would be leaving office. The Summit meeting would be his last chance.

•

Through all of their private talks, Khrushchev never raised the subject of the U-2. Probably he did not wish to place himself at an embarrassing disadvantage by pleading with Eisenhower to stop overflying his country. To Khrushchev, the best defense was always a good offense. Was the Soviet military behind America's? Boast that the Russians had more and better missiles and bombers! Were the Soviets unable to down American spy planes? Boast to Lodge and Allen Dulles that the KGB was so effective that it had penetrated the CIA!

Years later, Douglas Dillon observed that if Khrushchev had told Eisenhower, "These flights are very upsetting to us and we hope that you'll stop them," the President would probably have complied. But Khrushchev said nothing. Richard Bissell and the CIA began mapping out more penetrations of the airspace of the Soviet Union.

★

9

"The Great Thaw"

KHRUSHCHEV STEPPED onto the starlit Moscow airfield, where ten thousand Russians cheered in the dark. His first word was in English: *"Okay!"*

A hundred thousand Muscovites roared as Khrushchev's motorcade moved toward a homecoming rally suitable for a sports hero or rock star. The KGB and Party workers had packed seventeen thousand of the faithful into the Lenin Sports Palace to hail the outstanding fighter for peace on his American triumph. Seated in a place of honor, the only foreigner on the platform, was Edward Freers, the American chargé d'affaires whose career had been devoted to avoiding such attention. The Russians would have preferred Tommy Thompson, but the Ambassador had stayed behind for consultations in Washington.

"Dear Comrades!" Khrushchev began, his voice resounding in the hall and on radio and television sets throughout the Soviet Union. "We have just left the plane which completed a nonstop flight from Washington to Moscow." Applause and ovation.

"I must say from this high platform to the Muscovites and to all of our people, the government and the party, that President Dwight Eisenhower has displayed wise statesmanship in assessing the present international situation. He has shown courage and valor." Stormy applause (as *Pravda* always called it).

Khrushchev gave a rambling travelogue on his visit to Washington,

New York, Los Angeles, San Francisco, Coon Rapids, Pittsburgh. "Comrades, on September twenty-fifth, we again met with the President at the White House and left with him by helicopter for his country residence, which is called Camp David. . . . We could not, of course, clear out with the President at one go all the Cold War rubble that has piled up during many years. . . . But I will tell you frankly, dear Comrades, that I got the impression that the President sincerely wanted to liquidate the Cold War and improve relations between our two countries." Stormy applause.

"The President was kind enough to invite me to his farm. He showed me his cornfields. Of course, I could not miss the chance of seeing the President's corn!" The audience laughed. "I made friends with the President's grandchildren. I asked them whether they wanted to come to Russia. Big and small, they all declared they wanted to go to Russia and see Moscow. . . .

"We Muscovites like Moscow at all times. But for us, as for all people, spring is the most pleasant time of year because it is the time of joy, of the lush flourishing and awakening of life. So I told the President that, to my mind, it was best to come here at the end of May or early in June." Stormy applause.

"I do not doubt the President's intention to exert all of his will to reach agreement between our two countries. . . . Nevertheless I got the impression that some people in America do not act in the same way as the President. These forces want to continue the Cold War and the arms race. . . . I would not be in a hurry to say whether these forces are large or small, powerful or weak, and whether the forces supporting the President can win. . . .

"Let it be known to those who want to continue the Cold War . . . that in our time, only a madman can start a war and he himself will perish in its flames. . . . The peoples must straitjacket these madmen. We believe that sound statesmanship and human genius will triumph. As Pushkin said, 'Hail reason! Down with obscurity!' "

As the hall rocked in thunderous ovation, Khrushchev walked over to a startled Freers, grabbed his hand and thrust it into the air: "Long live Soviet-American friendship! Long live friendship among all the peoples of the world!"

•

Soon cinemas all over Russia were packing them in for epics starring the leader of the Soviet Union. The first told the story of the "barefooted miner boy" who had risen to be one of the two most powerful men in the world. The second covered the American tour in which Eisenhower and Lodge were mere extras in the gripping drama of Khrushchev's progress across "the chaotic panorama called U.S.A."

Alexei Adzhubei and eleven other writers were pressed into service for a seven-hundred-page adulation called *Face to Face with America*, studded with spontaneous tributes from "simple Soviet men and women" to the "maker of peace." *Pravda* ran an American-style editorial cartoon—Khrushchev attacking the snowman of the Cold War with an ice pick.

Enthusiasm among the Soviet people for Khrushchev's trip was amplified by the Kremlin propaganda machine, but it was genuine. A *Newsweek* correspondent cabled New York, "Wherever I went in Russia, the ordinary folk have been filled with great expectations by the Eisenhower-Khrushchev talks. And they give the credit for what they believe is a great change in the Cold War to Nikita Khrushchev. Make no mistake about it. Khrushchev has never been so popular in the U.S.S.R. . . . His journey across America is the topic on all lips. References to 'Eowa' and 'Peetsburg' are as common as mention of Moscow."

In Washington, a delighted President read Khrushchev's homecoming speech and learned that Khrushchev had kept a promise to stop jamming Voice of America broadcasts to the Soviet Union. Eisenhower asked Christian Herter to "keep the ball rolling" on trade, student exchanges and other possible collaboration. Communications between the two governments should be handled by Thompson, not Menshikov: "The reason for this should be obvious." Gordon Gray noted these developments in a slightly skeptical memo to Allen Dulles called "The Great Thaw."

"It would be an overstatement to say that we fell into a state of euphoria," John Eisenhower said later. "But we were relieved that Khrushchev, still glowing from the visit, was . . . obviously trying to ease tensions."

•

Not even a day after landing in Moscow, a weary Khrushchev flew to Peking for a fraternal celebration of the tenth anniversary of the Chinese Revolution. He had some explaining to do. A perceptive cartoonist for the London *Evening Standard* portrayed Khrushchev with his I LIKE IKE button emerging from a Cadillac to shake hands with

Mao Tse-tung in front of a portrait of the "bloodstained capitalist" Eisenhower.

When Khrushchev arrived in Peking, he noted that Mao and his colleagues were "seething with resentment against the Soviet Union and against me." Hanging everywhere were great portraits of Marx, Lenin, Stalin and Mao. Khrushchev's image was nowhere to be seen. In a speech atop the Gate of Heavenly Peace, Khrushchev extolled Eisenhower and peaceful coexistence, and warned against testing the capitalists by force. In private talks, he evidently failed to convince Mao that negotiating with the West was not a betrayal of world Communism.

The intensity of the Sino-Soviet conflict remained a secret, but Khrushchev never saw Mao again. The Chinese leader longed for Khrushchev to be taught a lesson that would show him once and for all the folly of truckling before the imperialists.

•

In Moscow during the fall of 1959, a Russian with close ties to the Kremlin warned the British journalist Alexander Werth that the West had better hurry and improve relations: "If you are too slow about it, Khrushchev himself may throw up the sponge and perhaps adopt a different policy. He may seem to be the supreme, unchallenged boss now, but conditions may change. If his Western policy is sabotaged by the West, he may—or somebody else may—switch over to a different policy."

Since his accession to power, Khrushchev had pursued contradictory aims. He wished to consolidate his position without Stalinist purges, relax the police state without domestic rebellion or alienating the KGB, reduce military spending without angering the Army, ease the grip on the satellite regimes without allowing them to slip from Moscow's orbit. He wished to improve relations with the West, but also to exploit the liberation of the Third World from colonialism, undermine NATO and uphold Lenin's doctrine that capitalism would ultimately be vanquished by Communism.

By the fall of 1959, Khrushchev had perhaps already antagonized Soviet power blocs vital to his political survival—the KGB and Moscow bureaucrats whose wings he clipped, others indignant about his failure to feed the Soviet people and tame Yugoslavia and his capriciousness and crude behavior in front of the world. Even before Khrushchev's American trip, some Party leaders had complained about the leader of world Communism going to Washington like a traveling salesman.

By now a host of powerful Russians may have been aroused against détente. Ideologues presumably complained that peaceful coexistence was anti-Marxist, Foreign Ministry officials that the new line would alienate Soviet allies—especially China. As in the United States, leaders of the Soviet military-industrial complex doubtless feared that they would suffer from a relaxation of tensions.

By advertising his ability to deal with Eisenhower and his faith in détente, Khrushchev was almost surely taking a calculated risk. No doubt he hoped to arouse the people of the West to pressure their leaders to make large concessions at the Summit. And in speeches, he always left himself a way out by reminding the Soviet people that Cold Warriors like the "unholy Rockefeller-Truman-Acheson trinity" might be too powerful for even Eisenhower to overcome. Nevertheless he was tying his fortunes to events largely beyond his control. Failure of "the Great Thaw" would very likely be a severe setback to a leader who could ill afford one.

In public, Khrushchev's two days with Eisenhower at Camp David grew warmer with each retelling. Glossing over the conflicts that had almost ruined the talks, he built up the President as the Western champion of détente, almost as if the two men had built a tacit alliance against Cold War forces in both of their countries. In private, Khrushchev still worried about Eisenhower's determination to take risks for peace. "There was something soft about his character," he said much later. "He was a good man, but he wasn't very tough."

Khrushchev was determined to hold the Big Four summit as soon as possible. His UN envoy, Valerian Zorin, sent word to the White House that Khrushchev "definitely would like a summit before the end of the year." Delay would grant Khrushchev's Kremlin enemies, Mao and others additional months in which to undermine him. And who could tell what else might go wrong? Better to act while the bloom was still on the rose.

Khrushchev had failed to reckon with the stubborn will of Charles André Joseph Marie de Gaulle.

●

Towering, aloof, melancholy, sardonic, with an unrelenting instinct for grandeur, the legendary President of France had long modeled himself on the leaders of the classical age. As the historian Louis Halle wrote, de Gaulle distinguished between the French people, for whom he had no great respect, and France, which he identified with himself.

Born in 1890, son of an intensely Catholic and monarchist philosophy professor in Lille, he matured in a France obsessed by the Franco-Prussian War and the Siege of Paris. He later wrote that "nothing saddened me more profoundly in my youth than our weakness and our mistakes."

He spent the early years of the Second World War waiting with the Free French armies in Algeria as head of a provisional government. In 1946, when quarreling parties hamstrung the Fourth Republic, he retired to his house at Colombey-les-Deux-Eglises and wrote memoirs that were among the best of the century. In 1958, when the Algerian revolt cast his country on the verge of civil war, he consented to save his nation for the second time with authority not notably less than that granted Louis XIV.

Determined to restore France to its ancient status as world power, de Gaulle dislodged the French fleet from NATO and called for a new Western federation under French leadership. He was not especially eager for a Big Four summit. Memories of wartime humiliations by Roosevelt and Churchill induced wariness against a conspiracy of the Anglo-Saxons to rob France of its destiny. He worried that Eisenhower and Macmillan would cave in to Khrushchev and let Germany make trouble for all of Europe.

Despite wartime clashes over Darlan and Giraud in North Africa, de Gaulle had a remotely amiable relationship with Eisenhower, who was thirty-nine days his senior. "I like Eisenhower," he once told a reporter. The President was "honest and good." Then, with a deep sigh: "Men can have friends. Statesmen cannot." He declared in 1957 that the age of giants was over. What was this? The epoch of Eisenhower, Khrushchev and Macmillan! Asked his confidential view of the three leaders, he said of the first two, *"Ce sont des cons"* ["They are idiots"]. The third he dismissed with a flick of the hand.

"Roosevelt didn't like him," Eisenhower once said. "A lot of people don't like him. But I can't help but feel that he is truly and sincerely devoted to his country and restoring its self-respect, and you can't really fault him for that."

Harold Macmillan, who had supported de Gaulle in wartime North Africa, had a different view: "He talks like a king. There really isn't any way of explaining anything to him in terms of practical politics. He's above that. What he needs is a couple of question periods in the House of Commons. But no one questions *him.*"

De Gaulle was clearly maneuvering to delay the Summit until well into 1960. This would give him more time to assuage right-wing Frenchmen angry about retreat from Algeria. And by then, he could attend the meeting as a more genuine equal of the other three powers, for by then France would have tested its own atomic bomb. When Eisenhower visited Paris in September 1959, de Gaulle had told him that France had to have its own Bomb. Who could assure that a future American President would start a nuclear war just to save Europe? When he suggested that the Americans should help, Eisenhower replied that the McMahon Act prevented him from sending nuclear information abroad.

"McMahon Act indeed!" said de Gaulle. "I changed the constitution of France when I found it was not practical. You tell me it is dangerous for me to know something that a thousand Soviet corporals already know? This I cannot accept. France retains the desire to be great. . . . Unlike the British, we have not lost our taste for excellence."

The French Bomb would not be ready for testing until February 1960. In late October 1959, the Elysée Palace announced its considered view that a Big Four summit should not be held before the spring of 1960. From Washington, an exasperated Eisenhower suggested an immediate American-British-French meeting to speed up the process, but de Gaulle replied that he would not be ready for such a meeting until mid-December. By that time, it would be impossible to arrange a summit with Khrushchev before the spring.

At the White House, Eisenhower told Christian Herter that he was "getting a little weary of the other heads of Western governments setting times of meeting at their convenience." By cable, he asked Llewellyn Thompson to see Khrushchev and explain that he was "trying to get the top people together on the Western side to work out something constructive, but that this takes time." Khrushchev should know that "we are just as interested as he is in pushing forward to resolve causes of tension, and the fact that he may not see anything happening on occasion does not mean that we have lost interest—rather that there are great difficulties involved."

De Gaulle had won. In December 1959, the Western leaders formally invited Khrushchev to a Big Four summit to start on Monday, May 16, 1960. They agreed to meet at de Gaulle's palace in Paris—acknowledgment that France was a power of highest rank. By then, eight months would have passed since Camp David.

•

On New Year's Eve 1960, Jane and Llewellyn Thompson went to the annual reception at the Kremlin. At two in the morning, during the ballroom dancing, Khrushchev invited them and the French envoy and his wife to an antechamber, newly furnished in Soviet Modern: the fountain was complete with colored plastic rocks. Khrushchev's Deputy Premiers, Mikoyan and Kozlov, slipped in before the doors closed.

Khrushchev told the Thompsons that he had hoped to have them and their children to his dacha the next day, but Nina Petrovna had a fever. He hoped that they could come next weekend. For the umpteenth time, he recalled how President Eisenhower had "simply overwhelmed" him with his personality at Camp David. If only the President could serve another term, he was sure that all of their problems could be solved. As usual, he interspersed professions of peace with bellicose remarks, noting that the Soviet Union had fifty nuclear bombs earmarked for Britain, thirty each for France and West Germany.

"How many do you have for us?" asked Jane Thompson.

"That is a secret," said Khrushchev. Ambassador Thompson proposed a toast to the Paris Summit. Khrushchev said an agreement was "essential"—especially if the West did not want him to sign a peace treaty with East Germany and halt Western access to Berlin.

Thompson did not regard this as a revival of Khrushchev's Berlin ultimatum. With Kozlov and Mikoyan as witnesses, Khrushchev was more likely showing that he could still talk tough to the Americans and that he meant business at Paris. Progress on Germany and Berlin was probably vital to his standing with fellow members of the Presidium, for he was about to take another severe political risk.

•

In January 1960, Khrushchev told the Supreme Soviet of his intention to cut the Soviet military by 1.2 million men. As a result of his "historic" visit to the United States, "the clouds of war have begun to disperse." In the nuclear age, large standing armies, surface navies and bomber fleets were growing obsolete. Soviet missiles were so accurate that they could hit a "fly in outer space." Missiles were cheaper than financing millions of soldiers. The savings derived from armed forces reductions would give Soviet workers a better chance to own apartments and television sets. Khrushchev joked that the Red Army would be the first in history to "voluntarily liquidate itself."

Khrushchev's sense of humor did not appeal to the Red Army. Over a million soldiers, including a quarter million officers, were slated for retirement from their posts. In Leningrad, naval officers reputedly wept as nearly built cruisers and destroyers were cut up for scrap on Khrushchev's orders. Officers who had come to Khrushchev's aid during the Anti-Party Coup warned that Khrushchev's "recklessness" would harm Soviet security. Others charged that by reducing conventional forces, Khrushchev was undercutting the chief means of aiding pro-Moscow liberation movements and Soviet allies in the Third World.

Khrushchev had almost certainly known that once he announced his military reduction plan, his political position and perhaps his ability to make concessions at a Big Four summit would be weakened. This was probably why he had been so eager to hold the meeting before the end of 1959.

In Washington, Allen Dulles told a private session of the Senate Foreign Relations Committee that Khrushchev was "undoubtedly stepping on many toes" and had "probably disgruntled many of the military by his recent reductions." Christian Herter said that Khrushchev had certainly "changed his tune," but they would not know until the Paris Summit "whether he is still the same intransigent individual with whom we have had to deal in the past."

Ambassador Thompson sent his interpretation by diplomatic pouch to the Secretary of State:

> Khrushchev has committed himself to a course where retreat becomes increasingly costly and where the changes already introduced, if successful, tend to encourage additional changes leading in time to a more normal society within the U.S.S.R. The pace of this evolution is difficult to gauge, but I believe it is developing rapidly—due in part to the fact that Khrushchev is 65 and a man in a hurry.
>
> I believe it to be sound American policy to facilitate this evolution in every way practicable.

•

That winter, Eisenhower traveled the world with the ambition of proving that many nations regarded the United States as something other than a wicked imperialist power: "Such prestige and standing as I have on the earth, I want to use it." In December, he boarded *Air Force One,* the new Presidential jet, for a three-week goodwill journey to Rome, Ankara, Karachi, Kabul and New Delhi, where six million Indians cried, "Long live the King of America!" In Tehran, he privately told the Shah that his thinking had "matured." Then to Athens, Tunis, Paris, Madrid, Casablanca. Two months later, he was off again for South America.

The trips affirmed that Eisenhower was the world's most respected and beloved leader. At their start, Khrushchev had sent the President a good-luck message, but he was reportedly made nervous by the warmth of Eisenhower's reception—especially in the Third World and nations along the Soviet border that had yet to be educated to the advantages of Communism.

●

Khrushchev was keeping an eye on the American Presidential campaign of 1960. He was convinced that Nixon's election would be a disaster. On New Year's Eve and other occasions, Thompson had tried and failed to persuade him otherwise. Rockefeller seemed little more promising, although Khrushchev would have enjoyed having a President who was such an obvious symbol of America's domination by Rockefellers, du Ponts and Morgans. Kennedy was a question mark.

Khrushchev's nominee was Adlai Stevenson. In January 1960, Ambassador Menshikov invited the former Illinois Governor to the Soviet Embassy in Washington and told him that Khrushchev thought him "more likely to understand Soviet anxieties and purposes" than others. How might the Soviets aid Stevenson's election? Should their press criticize him and, if so, for what?

As Stevenson later told a friend, Menshikov seemed "quite aware" that a successful Paris Summit and Eisenhower's Russian visit would help Nixon, "which seems to leave them in some dilemma." He refused the offer. "As I think about it, I get more and more indignant about being 'propositioned' that way, and at the same time more and more perplexed, if that's the word, by the *confidence* they have in me."

●

In February 1960, with Eisenhower's encouragement, Henry Cabot Lodge went to the Soviet Union on a private visit. Calling on Khrushchev at the Kremlin, he tried to reassure his old traveling partner about Nixon: "Don't pay any attention to the campaign speeches."

Khrushchev brought up the Paris Summit. The "most burning question" was Berlin. If the U.S. came in good faith and "not in the wake of Adenauer," it could reach solutions without loss of face to either side. But if no agreement was reached on Germany, Soviet-American relations would deteriorate.

Lodge replied that there ought to be many things "in the pot." No one at the Summit should adopt an attitude of "this—or else." The world expected that Paris would be the first in a regular series of meetings. There must not be a break, which would destroy this possibility. He asked the translator to translate very carefully as he said, "There is always a minimum of flexibility in foreign relations in the United States in an election year. What is hard or impossible to do in 1952 or 1956 or 1960 is often quite susceptible of achievement in 1953 or 1957 or 1961."

•

During the winter of 1960, Khrushchev had been working on preparations for Eisenhower's trip to the Soviet Union. In January, he smilingly told Thompson that the President was welcome to go "anyplace in the Soviet Union"—even denied areas like Vladivostok and the naval base at Sevastopol, "despite the fact that as a military man, the President is an especially dangerous person." The reception would be "friendly in the extreme" and there would be no need for security precautions. He hoped that Eisenhower would spend twice the time in the Soviet Union that he had spent in the United States—it was a larger country—and he must be sure to bring his grandchildren.

At Gettysburg, when Khrushchev had invited the grandchildren to Russia, they were thrilled but their father was horrified. John Eisenhower told the President that "our battle to avoid spoiling the children by excessive publicity and attention" was "difficult enough without this exercise." The President asked him to change his mind and was piqued when he refused.

The President thus wrote Khrushchev that "it will probably be impossible to bring the grandchildren along." If he brought some and not others, there might be "a real family upheaval." But he would be joined by his wife, son and daughter-in-law. He would have liked to stay for more than ten days, but in June, Congress would still be in session. He hoped that formalities could be minimized "so that we can have more opportunity to become acquainted with your country, its people and each other."

Soon the schedule was fixed. On Friday, June 10, the Eisenhowers would arrive in Moscow, where they would attend a state dinner at the Kremlin, visit the Pushkin Gallery, the Exhibition of Economic Achievements, the Baptist Church and the Bolshoi Ballet, and lunch with the Khrushchevs at their dacha. Then to Leningrad for a tour of the Hermitage, dinner at City Hall and a fifteen-minute speech to the Soviet people on radio and television.

In Kiev, the President would lay a wreath at the Tomb of the Unknown Soldier, deliver another broadcast speech and go to a concert. Back in Moscow, he would receive an honorary degree from Moscow University, view Soviet paintings on American themes, hold a dinner in Khrushchev's honor at Spaso House and speak for thirty minutes on radio and television. Then he would fly to Irkutsk for a boat trip down the Angara River to a hydroelectric station. On Sunday, June 19, he would fly to Tokyo for the first visit of an American President to Japan.

Khrushchev supervised the plans like a Soviet Ziegfeld. Had he been barred from Disneyland? He was improbably said to be building his own version outside Moscow—a Khrushchevland, depicting great events in Russian history. Eisenhower would be emphatically invited to attend. The Soviet Union had no golf course. Thompson told Khrushchev that this hurt Soviet prestige; he did not need to remind him of the President's favorite game. Soviet engineers graded land for an eighteen-hole course. Khrushchev was said to be taking lessons so that he could play a few holes with Eisenhower. On a magnificent pine bluff over Lake Baikal, the Russians were building a grand house for the President's use that years later was still called the Eisenhower Dacha.

Jim Hagerty led an American advance party. At Moscow, an airport guard accosted him for snapping pictures as he walked down the ramp from his plane. But when Hagerty revealed that it was Khrushchev who had given him the camera, the guard begged his apology. From that moment on, Hagerty was allowed to photograph whatever he wished. On a visit to the studios of Radio Moscow, his escorts were mortified when they realized that they had brought him into the room where Voice of America broadcasts had been jammed before Camp David.

Hagerty arranged for a press plane to precede the President to Moscow so that reporters could stand on the airfield at the start of the first peacetime visit of an American President to the Soviet Union.* Among the hundreds on the White House list were James Reston and Harrison Salisbury of the *New York Times,* Walter Cronkite and Marvin Kalb of CBS, David Brinkley and John Chancellor of NBC.

In Washington, the State Department compiled a list of Presidential gifts: luggage for Madame Khrushcheva, traveling cosmetic cases for the Khrushchev daughters, a Flexible Flyer sled for Khrushchev's grandson Nikita Adzhubei, a Steuben vase for President Leonid Brezhnev. Other Russians would receive recordings of *Porgy and Bess, Kiss Me Kate* and *Showboat.* The best gift of all would go to the host—an American hydrofoil, which Khrushchev might use for cruises on the Moscow River.

Eisenhower wrote to Khrushchev asking for permission to use his own plane within the Soviet Union. Khrushchev told Thompson that this put him in "difficulty" with the Soviet military: they were afraid that the plane would use "secret means of photographing Soviet territory." He might have noted that he had not used his own plane to fly within the United States.

Thompson replied that no one should worry: the pilot would be accompanied by a Soviet navigator. Khrushchev later wrote Eisenhower that he had "finally succeeded" in winning his military's consent to use the plane. The President replied, "This must have presented some problems for you, and I am grateful for your efforts to accommodate my request."

Khrushchev's generals were sensitive to the threat of spying from passenger planes because they had been doing the same thing for years. Aircraft flying Soviet officials to the UN in New York had long been said to carry reconnaissance cameras. So was the plane that brought Khrushchev to Washington. After nearly four years of U-2 flights, the Soviets knew that the Americans had more than a passing interest in aerial photography.

They were right to be concerned. In September 1959, when a group of congressmen flew from Moscow to Warsaw in an American plane, Air Force pilots evidently distracted the two Russian escorts in the cockpit while Air Force men in the rear surreptitiously photographed Soviet territory.

And now at Andrews Air Force Base, with Eisenhower's approval,

* Franklin Roosevelt had, of course, gone to Yalta in February 1945.

Air Force One was secretly being turned into a spy plane. In a tightly guarded hangar, riveting guns and blowtorches were used to weld high-resolution cameras into the belly of the aircraft. The Air Force and CIA knew that the President and his party would fly over Soviet bridges, highways, railroads and other points of interest at half the U-2's altitude. Photographs taken during test flights at thirty thousand feet put even the U-2 photos to shame. The Soviet navigator would be no problem. Cameras were designed to be turned on with a switch disguised as an air valve. Tiny lights visible only to the pilot would show that the cameras were working.

Richard Bissell later said, "I think Ike would have taken the position, 'All right, if you can put some equipment on my aircraft unobtrusively and take what you get, that's all right.' But I think he would have drawn the line at not altering the flight path in any shape or manner. . . . It would have been very unwise to let it be thought that his trip was being made in any sense or conditioned by intelligence."

•

For many of the Soviet people, the spring of 1960 was "the American Spring." Thompson noted that Russians were "extremely excited" about Eisenhower's visit. An official of a tiny Russian village told an American diplomat passing through that the town was being face-lifted for the President's arrival. The diplomat said he hadn't known that the village was on the itinerary. He was told, "We don't know either, but we're sprucing everything up because he just might come here. You know, when that President of yours gets here, we will give him a welcome the likes of which no Soviet leader has ever had."

In Moscow, Soviet citizens had always been cautious about telephoning the U.S. Embassy out of suspicion that the lines were tapped. But now Russians called up Americans they had met and said, "There's a jazz band in from Leningrad—let's go take it in" or "I've just flown in from Kiev and I'll only be here for three days—let's have a party." Soviet diplomats developed the astonishing habit of telephoning acceptances for receptions at the American Embassy several hours in advance. Muscovites asked American reporters why "Ike," America's "peaceloving President," could not run for another term.

Khrushchev almost certainly looked forward to basking in the acclaim shown his American partner when he toured the Soviet Union, but he may have wondered whether things were going too far. What if

Eisenhower got *too* warm a reception, with its implied criticism of the Soviet regime? Who could tell what kind of anti-Soviet propaganda he might pour out during all of those television speeches the White House had insisted on?

Far more worrisome was that Khrushchev's rapprochement with the United States may have been starting to have the same effect on the Soviet police state as the Secret Speech had had on Soviet domination of Eastern Europe. The burning hunger for information about the United States and the outside world, the fear of another war, enthusiasm for Eisenhower and détente were all powerful forces which, if unleashed, might threaten the regime. Vladimir Toumanoff of the American Embassy felt that the Soviet people were already showing signs of "stampeding out of the corral."

Like the Red Army, the KGB thrived by exploiting the perception of an imminent American threat. The secret police might well have reported to Khrushchev that if the opening to the West grew too wide, they could not guarantee the security of the regime.

•

In Washington, cherry blossoms were beginning to line the banks of the Potomac as the President and State Department prepared for the Paris Summit.

At press conferences that spring, Eisenhower gave the sense of near-intransigence on Berlin. But in the privacy of the Oval Office, he reminded aides that he had promised Khrushchev at Camp David that he would bargain seriously over the issue. When Christian Herter suggested that they try to "buy time," the President shook his head: the Russians would not be so generous. "The East Germans can stop all economic connection with West Berlin. They could make West Berlin a dead weight on us. . . . The Western world made a mistake in 1944 and 1945 and must now find a way to pay for it."

Eisenhower suggested reintroducing Open Skies at Paris, as well as other proposals to curb mutual "secrecy and suspicions." To knit Moscow and Washington closer together, he planned to suggest annual East-West summits, ministerial meetings, technical and cultural accords.

But his main aspiration was arms control. For seven years, he had hoped to move the world toward disarmament and had failed. This was his final chance. He knew that audacious diplomacy in an election year could become a political lightning rod, but was convinced that he would have a better chance than Nixon or a Democratic President of negotiating a treaty and pushing it through the Senate.

By the middle 1950s, for many politicians, disarmament had become a minor branch of rhetoric. The President sought a new approach—a treaty that would ban all nuclear testing and thereby curb the increasing size and sophistication of nuclear stockpiles. Such a ban might prevent the acquisition of nuclear weapons by China and less responsible governments who might one day trigger Armageddon. It might lead to other accords that would help to slow the arms race at an early stage and generate mutual trust. World opinion was driven toward a ban by reports of radioactive fallout sweeping over innocent peoples and of strontium 90 in children's milk.

In 1957, the Gaither Commission told Eisenhower, "This could be the best time to negotiate from strength since the U.S. military position vis-à-vis Russia might never be as strong again." The President wrote in his diary, "We now enjoy certain advantages in the nuclear world over the Russians. . . . The most important of these gaps can be closed only by continuous testing on the part of the Russians." He disagreed with those in his own government who held that "should we discontinue our tests, the Soviets would, by stealing all of our secrets, equal and eventually surpass us."

That December, he asked some of his science advisers, "Why don't you fellows help me with this nuclear test ban? Everybody in the Pentagon is against it."

In October 1958, East and West met for test ban talks at Geneva. To improve the climate, both sides voluntarily agreed to suspend nuclear testing. Despite agreement on many issues, within twelve months the talks were deadlocked. Khrushchev suspected that control posts and inspection teams proposed by the West would act as espionage brigades on Soviet soil, where they might learn new truths about Soviet military weakness. Eisenhower and his allies suspected that testing far below ground or at high altitude could not be monitored by current methods.

But the President wanted a treaty, followed—he hoped—by some actual disarmament. In October 1959, Llewellyn Thompson advised him that Khrushchev too was eager for an accord because "his main objective is to keep China and Germany from getting these weapons." Thompson believed that the Soviet leader was "far out in advance of many of his people on this issue. . . . Khrushchev really means and wants to make some progress in the reduction of armaments. He will have great opposition from some of his colleagues, and it is by no means sure that he can carry this out."

Eisenhower agreed that "Khrushchev cannot be as confident of his position as Stalin was."

He was ready to try a new approach: ban only those tests that were detectable and then broaden the treaty as detection methods improved. Ban all tests in the atmosphere, all underwater, as high in space as they could be discovered, and underground if they exceeded the force detectable by current means. Both sides should permit about twenty on-site inspections per year on each nation's territory.

The Soviets agreed—with two stipulations. Khrushchev wanted a voluntary moratorium on small underground tests for at least four years. And something must be done about that outrageous number of on-site inspections.

The President was ready to bargain. In March 1960, he told aides, "We must get an agreement. . . . We cannot continue to refuse to go a part of the way. . . . It is in our vital interest to get an agreement." If they did not succeed, then there was "no hope whatsoever for disarmament." He was ready "to give Khrushchev every chance to prove that he will do what he says."

He told reporters, "All the signs are that the Soviets do want a degree of disarmament, and they want to stop testing. That looks to me to be more or less proved."

On March 28 at Camp David, the President confided to Harold Macmillan that to reach some kind of test ban at Paris, he planned to "capitalize" on Khrushchev's fear that the Chinese would develop nuclear weapons. He would warn Khrushchev that "action against our rights in Berlin" would "bring a rapid end to the détente, in general, and to any prospect for early disarmament, in particular." They could negotiate over the length of the moratorium and the number of on-site inspections.

In his diary, Macmillan wrote, "All the omens are good. He is *really* keen on this and—although he hasn't said much about it yet— would accept further concessions in the course of negotiation to get it."

So Eisenhower and Khrushchev each stood on the verge of taking the risk each leader had vowed never to take—a partially unsupervised test ban and inspection teams on Soviet soil. A treaty could be signed at Paris or during the President's tour of the Soviet Union. Khrushchev felt that the months since Camp David had shown that the Americans had "recognized the failure of their past efforts to discredit us, to humiliate us and to eliminate us."

•

The CIA had yet to discover a single operational Soviet ICBM. On August 18, 1959, Allen Dulles told the President that the consensus within the intelligence community was that the Soviets would probably have ten such missiles ready "either in 1959 or in 1960."

Reports from American agents in Russia and signals intelligence revealed much about Soviet missile development, but Dulles wished to fly more U-2 missions. Eisenhower was hardly willing to fly while Khrushchev was in the United States. Thus on October 26, 1959, Dulles came to the Oval Office with another request.

The President agreed that "there may be substantial intelligence value involved," but he was "pretty unhappy about the suggestion." As Bissell recalled, Eisenhower was apprehensive about the chance of a downing and determined to fly as few missions as possible until an American spy satellite came on line, as they hoped, in 1960. In the past, the President had banned U-2 flights during periods of Soviet-American tension. Now he banned them during the months of relative calm.

During the winter, while snow covered much of the Soviet Union, the U-2 was evidently sent to gather intelligence on French nuclear test sites in the Sahara—a risky venture, since close allies professed not to spy on close allies. The plane was also flown over Castro's Cuba: at the White House, Allen Dulles showed Eisenhower aerial pictures of a sugar refinery that the Agency wished to sabotage.

In February 1960, the President met with his PBCFIA. Perhaps spurred on by Dulles, James Doolittle urged Eisenhower to use the U-2 over Russia "to the maximum degree possible." But the President demurred: when he went to Paris in May, he would have "one tremendous asset." That was his reputation for honesty. "If one of these aircraft were lost when we were engaged in apparently sincere deliberations, it could be put on display in Moscow and ruin my effectiveness."

Eisenhower said that authorizing U-2 missions was "always an agonizing question." It was essential not to "dissipate" his reputation for "a different mode of behavior from that of Khrushchev" in international affairs—especially since "the embarrassment will be so great if one crashes."

•

That month, the President exploded when the *New York Times* ran a story, based on leaks from unnamed sources, implying that the United States had an excellent means of intelligence-gathering on Soviet missile development. As Kistiakowsky noted, Eisenhower was "exceedingly angry and talked at length about lack of loyalty to the U.S. of these people."

The President apparently did not know how much the U-2 program had begun to stretch the limits of the word "covert."

In the summer of 1958, Hanson Baldwin of the *Times* called Robert Amory and said, "I hope you can break any lunch date so that I can lunch with you at noon." At the Hay-Adams, where Walter Lippmann was lunching two tables away with Ambassador Menshikov, Baldwin told Amory that despite a crude effort to distract him, he had seen the black plane with the long wings in West Germany: "I know what's going on. I'm afraid I've got to publish it because I was in an unclassified position and it's a great story."

"*Jesus, Hanson, no!*" Amory asked him to let Allen Dulles appeal to his publisher, Arthur Hays Sulzberger. Sulzberger agreed to kill the story but told Dulles, "This thing is set in cold type and ready to go if we hear that a Drew Pearson or anybody is about to publish it."

The *Times*'s James Reston and Arthur Krock also discovered the U-2 story and remained silent. So did John Leacocos of the *Cleveland Plain Dealer* and Chalmers Roberts of the *Washington Post,* who consulted his editors and decided not to run the story "because we knew the United States very much needed to discover the secrets of Soviet missilery." Later, to have been in on the secret of the U-2 became a minor status symbol at Washington cocktail parties.

The voluntary silence of the press was not absolute. In 1958, *Model Airplane News* reported an "unconfirmed rumor" that "U-2s are flying across the Iron Curtain taking aerial photographs." Two Oxford students who had been in the Royal Navy wrote in a student monthly that it was not uncommon for Western planes to "lose their way" beyond Soviet frontiers to "provide accurate estimates of the size and type of Russian armaments and troops and the nature of their tactical methods." They were arrested and sentenced to three months in jail under Britain's Official Secrets Act.

In September 1959, a pilot testing a U-2 near Atsugi ran out of fuel and made an emergency landing at a glider club's airstrip. The plane was Number 360, the same aircraft provided Francis Gary Powers for his flight from Peshawar seven months later. For fifteen minutes the pilot waited, mired in mud, radioing the base for help, while club members rushed to the side of the plane and clicked their shutters furiously. American military police landed by helicopter and ordered the Japanese away at gunpoint. The Japanese journal *Air Review* suspected that the plane was being used for something other than weather reconnaissance: "Otherwise why was it necessary to threaten Japanese with guns to get them away from the crippled plane?"

The restraint of the American press was emblematic of the age. Had the *New York Times* or *Washington Post* discovered the U-2 at the time of the Pentagon Papers and Watergate, they would have been more likely (although by no means certain) to go ahead and publish.* Had Baldwin and his colleagues revealed the U-2 flights to the world, they would have probably killed the program and a crucial means of intelligence. On the other hand, these leaks gave clear warning that after four years, with hundreds of people and a half dozen foreign governments involved, it was growing harder and harder to keep the U-2 covert.

If details of the U-2 had reached the ears of reporters not in the business of sleuthing for American state secrets, it might only be imagined what information had reached agents of the KGB, who were. The longer the program went on, the greater the chance for the Soviets to learn about it and stop it in a manner of maximum embarrassment to the United States—by hiring one of the pilots as a double agent, sabotaging equipment, developing anti-aircraft weapons to stop the black plane from crossing the Russian skies.

•

The CIA knew that the U-2 program was a top Soviet intelligence target. In Adana, members of the unit were suspicious of the Turks who swept the hangar floors. Frank Powers's commanding officer told him that the Soviets were mounting a major effort against the bases in Turkey and Japan: they probably had dossiers on him and his fellow pilots.

Bissell later said, "I'm sure there were intelligence agents at all the

---

* National American media acceded to the CIA's request not to publish details about the *Glomar Explorer* in 1974. (See Notes.)

bases from which we operated. They would have been fairly easy to recruit and the U.S.S.R. had a high priority, I'm sure, on the U-2 as an intelligence target for them. After all, when your chief rival has shown that he can overfly your country with impunity, your reasoning may well be, 'Well, today it's cameras but tomorrow it's bombs.' "

In early 1959, the CIA learned from Pyotr Popov, one of its prize moles in Soviet military intelligence, that the Russians had amassed much information about the U-2. "It brought me right out of my seat," Richard Helms recalled. "Bissell and I wondered where they could be getting their information from." Before Popov could tell them, he was captured while passing notes to an American on a Moscow bus and executed.

In October 1959, a surly twenty-year-old ex-Marine who had worked on radar in Atsugi walked into the American Embassy in Moscow, slapped his passport on the counter and renounced his citizenship. Lee Harvey Oswald was only the third American enlisted man to defect since the Second World War. He boasted that he had offered to tell the Russians about his radar work and that he might have something "of special interest" for them.

Oswald had had a knockabout childhood in New Orleans, Fort Worth, the Bronx and Dallas. At fifteen, after quitting high school, he discovered Marx and told a friend that he would like to "kill President Eisenhower" because he was "exploiting the working class." At seventeen, he joined the Marines and was trained as a radar controller. Assigned to Atsugi, he was told that the U-2 was a secret reconnaissance project not to be discussed with anyone outside his unit. The unit was sent to the Philippines, where U-2 planes were housed at Subic Bay. One night, a Marine guard was mysteriously shot to death beside one of the hangars. Speculation later had it that Oswald had shot the guard while looking for information about the U-2 for presentation to the Russians.

When he first applied for asylum, the Soviets refused. He slashed his left wrist and languished in Moscow hotels for two months until employed as a factory hand in Minsk. Oswald undoubtedly revealed information about the U-2, but his security clearance had been low. From gossip and his own observations, he might have known details about the plane, its rate of climb, cruising altitude and payload, the radar, the pilots, base security and how it might be circumvented. Had the Russians found Oswald valuable, they probably would not have left him within reach of Western reporters for two months, and he might have gotten something better than a factory job. Bissell later said, "I don't think Oswald could have told them much they didn't already know. . . . Now what that has to do with the Kennedy assassination God only knows."

•

Through the early months of 1960, the public clamor over a Missile Gap had not abated. With the added stimulus of a Presidential campaign, it grew louder.

In Congress, Thomas Gates defended the President against accusations that Soviet missiles were being deliberately underestimated in order to balance the budget. The President invited him to the White House family quarters for a Scotch: "I know you're having a tough time. . . . I'm trying to help you in my press conferences."

Gates reported that the "roughest of all" would be Lyndon Johnson's Preparedness Committee: "What's more, that's under oath. That's an investigation."

Eisenhower said, "You took an oath of office, the same as I did. Just stand up there and tell 'em you won't take their oath."

"Well, some nights it's easy to be President," said Gates, unconvinced. "I think I'll have another Scotch."

In fact, the American intelligence community was growing somewhat more relaxed about Soviet missiles. In January 1960, Allen Dulles told Eisenhower that while U-2 coverage was incomplete, a crash Soviet missile effort could not have escaped detection. He and his colleagues had found no such crash program: the Russians still had no operational ICBMs. They would probably have thirty-five or so by mid-1960, perhaps 140 to 200 by mid-1961.

In his diary, Kistiakowsky wrote that "mid-1961 is the point of maximum threat because as of then we still won't have hardened missile bases and SAC will be vulnerable too, but the threat is not catastrophic. In fact, the missile gap doesn't look to be very serious."

•

Late that winter, Dulles and Bissell asked the President to resume U-2 flights into the Soviet Union. By Bissell's later recollection, they had not been allowed to fly deep into Russia since Camp David. He and Dulles wished to look at ICBM launch sites in the northern Urals and westward near the White Sea, bomber fields, factories and other targets.

By 1960, the Russians were installing their new SA-2 Guidelines throughout the Soviet Union. The CIA felt these missiles could strike a target as high as seventy thousand feet but, as Bissell later said, "what you were counting on was that when they got above, say, sixty thousand feet, they couldn't effectively maneuver." Bissell believed that if one reached a U-2, "it would be a near-miss rather than a hit."

He had taken precautions. In 1958, U-2s were equipped with granger boxes to foil Soviet radar. In 1959, more powerful engines were installed to increase altitude, especially under the weight of new, heavier espionage equipment. Missions were routed away from known SA-2 sites.

Whenever the CIA asked for a U-2 flight, Goodpaster or the President generally asked, "Do we have anything to indicate that they've improved the air defense capability against the aircraft?" As Goodpaster recalled, they were once again assured in 1960 that Soviet anti-aircraft was no grave threat; even if it was, they relied on the Agency's assurances that no pilot or equipment would survive a downing intact.

Eisenhower viewed his role in the U-2 program chiefly in terms of weighing intelligence needs against diplomatic needs. As Goodpaster later said, Eisenhower knew that resumption of the flights might be "prejudicial to the kind of improvement we were working toward with the Soviets."

But perhaps Khrushchev had indeed decided to accept the flights as a fact of life until he could stop them. The Russians had not complained for many months. Khrushchev had not uttered a word of protest at Camp David. And the first American spy satellite might not be working until the end of 1960 or later. Without U-2 flights, the CIA would have to go largely blind on Russia. They would almost surely lose the chance to photograph the first operational Soviet ICBMs under construction.

The President set aside any objections he may have had. On April 9, 1960, a U-2 took off from Peshawar and shot into Soviet airspace.

•

Khrushchev was flabbergasted. The Americans "knew they were causing us terrible headaches whenever one of these planes took off on a mission." So the terrible headaches were not over, after all! "As far as we were concerned, this sort of espionage was war—war waged by other means." In October 1959, he had publicly asked the West to "take no action" before the Summit conference that would "worsen the atmosphere" and "sow the seeds of suspicion." How much more direct did he have to be?

Soviet air defense tracked the U-2 and failed to shoot it down. Andrei Gromyko suggested a diplomatic protest. As Khrushchev recalled, "A public protest could be registered in our press, but we weren't going to resort to public protest and diplomatic channels any more. What good did it do? The Americans knew perfectly well that they were in the wrong. . . . We are sick and tired of these unpleasant surprises—sick and tired of being subjected to these indignities. They were making these flights to show up our impotence. Well, we weren't impotent any longer."

•

In the inner reaches of the Kremlin, the incursion may have turned Khrushchev into something of a laughingstock. Was *this* the work of the President Eisenhower who had displayed such "wise statesmanship" and "desire for peace" at Camp David? Was *this* Khrushchev's thanks for his opening to the West? Was *this* what the Soviet Union could anticipate from peaceful coexistence?

Charles Bohlen years later felt that Khrushchev took the resumption of U-2 flights as "almost a personal insult. More than that, I think it made him out a fool. He'd been telling obviously all the other leaders that Eisenhower was a good, solid guy and you could trust him, and then—*whambo*—this plane comes over, and this shook a lot of Khrushchev's authority in the Soviet Union."

Khrushchev's foes could chortle that just five weeks before the Paris Summit, the United States was returning to its old tricks. Either the Americans were giving up on détente or they had never been serious in the first place. Perhaps *that* was why Eisenhower had allowed the Summit to be delayed and delayed.

For eleven days after the U-2 incursion, Khrushchev vanished from public view. He was said to be relaxing in the Caucasus, but for Khrushchev, this was an unusually long period of silence. Another omen was his failure to resurface in Moscow for Lenin's ninetieth birthday celebration on April 22, a command performance for Communist leaders around the world.

Through the winter and early spring, Khrushchev had been making tough speeches on what the West had better do about Berlin, largely to strengthen his bargaining position at the Summit. In April, Richard Nixon, Christian Herter and Douglas Dillon reciprocated. Dillon demanded Soviet concessions on Eastern Europe, Korea and elsewhere: by threatening Berlin, Khrushchev was "skating on very thin ice." Herter and Dillon were presumably trying to lower public expectations and strengthen American leverage before Paris, but the timing of the speeches made them ripe for citation by Khrushchev's rivals as more evidence that the United States was reverting to Cold War.

That month, Eisenhower wrote Khrushchev that if the Summit lasted longer than a week, he would have to depart for a planned state visit to Portugal and leave Nixon in his place. To Khrushchev, sending Nixon to a peace conference was "like putting the goat in charge of the cabbage patch": was *this* the deed of a President who was serious about bargaining at Paris?

The Soviet press responded with attacks on Herter, Dillon, Allen Dulles and other "Cold War circles" in the United States. The President was excluded from criticism, but *Pravda* notably reprinted a statement by Adlai Stevenson rebuking the Eisenhower Administration for its "fruitless anti-Communism and self-deception."

From Peking, Mao Tse-tung was delighted to pour oil on troubled waters. A diatribe called "Long Live Leninism!" (evidently written by Mao) denounced Khrushchev's campaign for détente as a betrayal of the founding father. The *People's Daily* informed its readers of thirty-seven "aggressive" acts committed by the United States since Camp David: "We see no substantive change in the imperialists' war policy or of Eisenhower himself."

Khrushchev suffered other blows. Two pillars of the Soviet military were replaced by men whom Western intelligence considered more hard-line. Mikoyan, a Khrushchev ally and proponent of détente, was said to be in sudden decline. Khrushchev may have felt that he had been through all of this before—in 1956, when Eastern Europe flared up after his Secret Speech and he had ended similar weeks of seclusion by chanting, "We are all Stalinists." Now was he under pressure to toughen his American policy before the Paris Summit?

•

On Monday morning, April 25, Soviet Party workers hung red hammer-and-sickle banners in the main square of Baku for the fortieth anniversary of the Bolshevik liberation of Azerbaidzhan. Khrushchev had chosen this moment to re-emerge into public view with a speech on nationwide radio and television. It was three weeks before the start of the Paris Summit.

Standing under a large portrait of himself, he said, "I presume that you would like to know what the Soviet government thinks of the present international situation. We consider it to be good. . . . We trust that common sense will prevail—that when the Summit closes and the leaders leave Paris, relations between the countries at the talks will be better than before."

But recent events had put him on guard. "Take the recent speech by the American Undersecretary of State, Douglas Dillon. . . . That speech just reeks of the spirit of the Cold War. . . . Why did Dillon have to make a statement so clearly out of keeping with relations between the Soviet Union and the United States since my talks with President Eisenhower at Camp David?"

Other things made him "sit up with a start." Disarmament—the West seemed to be dragging its feet. And the German problem? "Some people seem to hope to reduce this meeting to an ineffectual exchange of opinions and pleasant—*they may be*—talks." If the talks did not ultimately lead to a German peace treaty, he would sign his separate peace to bar the West from Berlin. The crowd clapped and cheered. "Comrades, the Soviet Union is now stronger than ever before! Our might is indomitable!"

●

After the April 9 U-2 flight, Eisenhower was impressed by the fact that Khrushchev, "for his own reasons," did not protest. As Kistiakowsky later said, "This was virtually inviting us to repeat the sortie."

Dulles and Bissell appealed for another mission. Importance: "well above average." They wished to get a fresh look at Tyuratam and other Soviet military-industrial landmarks such as Sverdlovsk. But according to Bissell, the most vital target was six hundred miles north of Moscow at Plesetsk. As Arthur Lundahl recalled, the April 9 flight and other sources had found evidence that the first operational ICBMs were being deployed there, but they had not obtained the kind of photography they would have wished. Another run would reveal Soviet progress.

Bissell argued that if they waited, they might miss the chance to see the missiles under construction. And by then, the missiles might be camouflaged. In the northern latitudes, the sun's angle was judged critical for U-2 photography. It was argued that a mission over Plesetsk could only be flown effectively from April through July.

Christian Herter later said, "The summit meeting was very much on my mind, as it was on everybody's mind at that time. The real issue was: How urgent was the information, and is there any one time that is more favorable than another? From a technical point of view, the time was more favorable at that time than another. From a diplomatic point of view, it seemed to me that with the President scheduled to go to Russia later, there would have been the same difficulty."

If they waited until July and weather was poor, the U-2 might be barred from taking clear pictures of Plesetsk until April 1961. In the meantime they might obtain other forms of intelligence, but these would probably be inconclusive. They might photograph the target from a satellite, but so far the United States had been unable to launch one.

Allen Dulles later noted that in times of tension, people said that "flights should be stopped because they increase tension. In times of sweetness and light, they should not be run because it would disturb any 'honeymoon' in our relations with the Soviet Union." By that logic, he said, one would never fly at all.

"There is always some international conference or something," said Thomas Gates.

More than Herter, Dulles or Gates, the President was eager to build a lasting détente and knew how each incursion provoked the Russians. Still Khrushchev had not complained of the April flight and had not been able to knock it down. Perhaps it was caution enough to close down the program for the weeks immediately before the Paris conference. Thus Eisenhower sent the U-2 into the Soviet Union one more time.

★

10

"I Would Like to Resign"

Now it was Saturday, the seventh of May. The President stood on his glassed-in veranda at Gettysburg staring out at the battlefield of General Robert E. Lee's defeat and digesting the news that Francis Gary Powers had been captured by the Russians alive.

A Rome newspaper cried, "*Dio mio!* What next?" At the State Department, reporters closed in on Lincoln White, demanding answers to Khrushchev's latest charges. In West Virginia, Lyndon Johnson told the press, "There is no doubt that a serious international crisis is in the making."

At ten in the morning, Allen Dulles assembled an action group at CIA headquarters—Richard Bissell and Pearre Cabell from the CIA; Hugh Cumming, Charles Bohlen and Livingston Merchant from State; Andrew Goodpaster from the White House. Dulles offered his resignation: the President could tell the world that his CIA Director had been fired for exceeding his authority by sending a U-2 into Soviet airspace.

"That's the last thing the President would want," said Goodpaster. "The President isn't in the business of using scapegoats."

Someone suggested a scapegoat at a lower level: perhaps the U-2 commander in Turkey could be fired with great fanfare and later be quietly rehabilitated in another job. This was also rejected. Most of those present felt they should continue to stonewall it. A draft statement was written:

As previously announced, it was known that a U-2 plane was missing. However it has already been established that, insofar as the authorities in Washington are concerned, there was no authorization for a flight of the kind described by Mr. Khrushchev.

It should be noted that his report is based on the purported statements of a pilot who is a prisoner in Soviet hands. It would appear either that Mr. Khrushchev is exaggerating what actually happened with regard to this U-2 plane for his own purposes or that somehow standing instructions to avoid incursions over Soviet territory were, in this instance, not observed.

This statement allowed for the possibility that Khrushchev was able to prove that Powers had deliberately flown deep into the Soviet Union. In that case, they could keep the blame away from the President by saying the flight was unauthorized. Public release of this further deception required the consent of the Secretary of State.

Christian Herter had just returned from his trip to Iran, Turkey and Greece. At two o'clock Saturday afternoon, he convened State Department men in his fifth-floor office—Douglas Dillon, Merchant, Bohlen, Foy Kohler and deputy Richard Davis. Goodpaster sat in for the White House.

Herter had learned of the downed U-2 from a note passed to him during a NATO meeting in Athens. He had been disturbed by the cover stories handed out in Washington on May 3 and May 5: far better to have said nothing than tell tales that Khrushchev could easily disprove. Now that they knew the espionage equipment and U-2 pilot had survived the crash, "we had to make a decision," as Herter later said. "Were we going to keep on lying about this or were we going to tell the truth?"

•

Six-foot-five, gaunt, soft-spoken, with kindly eyes under fierce, thick brows, Herter was "everyone's picture of a Boston Brahmin," as John Eisenhower recalled. Crippled by osteoarthritis, he moved slowly, always smiling, it was said, through some unspeakable pain. When Herter entered this job, Richard Nixon had asked White House cameramen to honor their old practice under Franklin Roosevelt and avoid photographing Herter's crutches.

Born in 1895, the fifty-third Secretary of State spent the first decade of his life in Paris, where his parents were painters. After a Harvard degree in fine arts, he dropped out of architecture school at Columbia to join the Foreign Service. Along with other promising young men like Walter Lippmann and John Foster Dulles, he served as an aide to the American delegation at Versailles and then as Herbert Hoover's assistant in European food relief and at the Commerce Department.

Hoover advised him to get some experience outside of government, so in 1924 Herter returned to Boston, where he edited a small journal, *The Independent,* and lectured on international relations at Harvard. In 1930, his silk-stocking Boston district sent him to the Massachusetts House of Representatives, which he later served as Speaker. Elected to Congress, he was a postwar national spokesman for collective security and the Marshall Plan. In 1952, he joined the Eastern Republicans who followed Henry Cabot Lodge to Paris and urged Eisenhower to run for President. To aid the Republican ticket, he gave up his seat to make a seemingly hopeless race for Governor of Massachusetts, and won.

In July 1956, Harold Stassen publicly declared his conviction that Richard Nixon would cost the President too many votes and should be dumped in favor of Herter—an idiosyncratic choice, given Herter's physical condition, his diffident campaign style and identification with the Eastern elite. Eisenhower did not mind waiting to see whether Stassen's announcement started a movement away from Nixon. It did not, so he asked Sherman Adams to lower the boom. In his frostiest voice, Adams told Herter that if he supported Nixon for Vice President, he might get an important post in foreign policy during the second term. If not, that would be impossible.

Herter did not need the warning. Always the Harvard man, he made Nixon's nominating speech at San Francisco. After the election, Foster Dulles, wary of promoting a potential rival, offered him Assistant Secretary of State for Europe. Herter thought this an insult and protested. Dulles gave in and made him his deputy. But once in Washington, Herter found himself the "number-two man in a one-man Department." He told a friend, "I have left this office many nights thinking quite clearly that I should do only one thing—and that was to go home and pack my bags."

When Dulles resigned in April 1959, Herter was the natural successor, but there was an embarrassing interval while Eisenhower publicly required him to take a physical to show that he could tolerate the

rigors of the new job. James Hagerty later said that Herter had "an easier working relationship" with the President than Dulles because he
was "a little less arbitrary in his beliefs." The State Department's Loy
Henderson thought Eisenhower would have preferred "a stronger man
as his Secretary." When Herter came to the Oval Office, Goodpaster
and John Eisenhower sat in and took notes, which they never would
have dared to do with Dulles.

At a time when the President was making his last great exertion toward a Soviet-American détente, he was satisfied to use Herter less as a
tactician in the Dulles manner than as a spokesman and liaison with
Congress. Eisenhower once said, "When you just look at him, you
know you are looking at an honest man."

•

At the meeting in Herter's office, Douglas Dillon argued that Allen
Dulles should resign. As he later recalled, "I liked Allen Dulles. We all
did. But, I mean, this was the United States. It was a great big problem.... We wouldn't have changed our feeling for him. We would
have thought he was a greater hero—and a lot of people would have
known underneath that he was just taking the rap for somebody higher
and would have admired him for it.... Dulles would have gone on
and done other things and would have been fine. But our feeling was
that if that had happened, the Summit conference would have gone on
and Khrushchev would have made some remarks, but whatever was
possible would still be possible."

Kohler disagreed. At this point, he felt it "essential" to issue an
honest statement. Reporters were downstairs besieging the press office,
ready to punch holes in any further cover-up; the prime witness was in
Soviet hands. Someone insisted on informing the public that Soviet secrecy gave them "not only a right but a duty" to spy on the Soviet
Union. This angered Bohlen, who said it "might appeal to American
prejudices" but would "damage our case with other nations." He recommended simply telling the press, "No comment."

Herter overruled him: the time for silence was long past. It was a
"very difficult time in our form of society" to say nothing. He had read
the statement Cumming had brought over from the CIA and thought it
wouldn't work. They couldn't "just go on lying forever." There must
be some form of admission that the United States had waged deliberate espionage against the Soviets.

This pleased Goodpaster, who thought that Khrushchev was angling for some sort of confession from Washington: if he did not get it, he might issue shriller and shriller indictments that would poison American-Soviet relations and embarrass the President. Goodpaster thought if they gave Khrushchev a "certain degree of satisfaction," he might be willing to "cut this thing off."

Herter decreed a statement that was half-true, half-false. It would admit that the United States had flown espionage missions for four years along the Soviet border and that a U-2 had "probably" flown into Soviet airspace, but deny that the incursion had been authorized in Washington. This might give Khrushchev the satisfaction he was asking for and still protect the President. Perhaps Khrushchev would have an easier time coming to Paris if the U-2 incursion were judged an accident rather than a deliberate insult by Washington.

By telephone, Herter informed Allen Dulles of his decision: he was trying to "get the President off the hook." Dulles promised to do "anything" to help, but when he put down the receiver, he was very upset. Since 1776, the United States had maintained that it did not spy on other nations. Now Herter was about to expose the border flights—if not the deep penetrations—and claim that the U-2 had flown into Russia without high-level permission. Ultimately this would turn unwanted attention on the CIA and provoke a Senate investigation that might result in the increased oversight that, Dulles believed, could wreck American intelligence.

•

While Eisenhower golfed with George Allen at Gettysburg, reporters waiting in the lounge of the Gettysburg Hotel were indignant: twelve hours had passed since Khrushchev's revelation that the pilot was alive, and still no response from the U.S. government. Where was the President? Out on the golf course, fiddling as Rome burned!

In fact, the President was waiting for Herter's recommendation. The Signal Corps could connect him to Herter as easily on the fairway as in the Oval Office. Amid the gathering storm, Eisenhower did not want to alarm the nation by rushing back to Washington: that would only aggravate the crisis. Late in the afternoon, on the glassed-in porch, Hagerty was warning the President of the public relations damage of his conspicuous sangfroid when the red telephone rang in the den. A Filipino houseboy stepped out: "Mr. President, the Secretary of State is calling."

Herter outlined the statement he had in mind. Goodpaster got on

248 : M A Y D A Y

the line. Eisenhower asked whether another statement was "really necessary." Goodpaster told him that it had been "very carefully considered" by Herter. They wished to see whether the Russians were willing
to cut off the escalation of the controversy. The President thought it
"might prove to be a mistake" but agreed that it was "worth a try."

•

During the long afternoon, overwhelmed by reporters, Lincoln
White had several times burst into the Secretary of State's office and
cried, "I've got to have a statement!" All the men in the room turned
silent until he departed: White must not know which way their deliberations were heading. Shortly after six, he was summoned and handed
the freshly typed announcement.

"W-wait a minute," he said. "I've got to read this." He asked Bohlen to help him answer questions from the press, but Bohlen said,
"You'd better just stick to what's on the paper."

Crestfallen, the spokesman walked into the press room. Twenty-
nine hours earlier, he had told reporters that there was "absolutely
no—N,O—deliberate attempt to violate Soviet airspace." Now he read
aloud:

The Department has received the text of Mr. Khrushchev's further
remarks about the unarmed plane which is reported to have been shot
down in the Soviet Union. As previously announced, it was known that
a U-2 plane was missing. As a result of the inquiry ordered by the President, it has been established that insofar as the authorities in Washington are concerned, there was no authorization for any such flight as
described by Mr. Khrushchev.

Nevertheless, it appears that in endeavoring to obtain information
now concealed behind the Iron Curtain, a flight over Soviet territory
was probably taken by an unarmed civilian U-2 plane.

It is certainly no secret that, given the state of the world today, intelligence collection activities are practiced by all countries, and postwar
history certainly reveals that the Soviet Union has not been lagging behind in this field. The necessity for such activities as measures for legitimate national defense is enhanced by the excessive secrecy practiced by
the Soviet Union in contrast to the Free World.

One of the things creating tension in the world today is apprehension over surprise attack with weapons of mass destruction. To reduce

mutual suspicion and to give a measure of protection against surprise attack, the United States in 1955 offered its Open Skies proposal—a proposal which was rejected out of hand by the Soviet Union. It is in relation to the danger of surprise attack that planes of the type of unarmed civilian U-2 aircraft have made flights along the frontiers of the Free World for the past four years.

Electricity surged through the room. "Linc, why do you say 'probably'? Is the information about the operation unsure or is Washington not fully informed on what happened?"

"I can't answer that."

"Was the suggestion that the pilot *himself* made this decision?"

"Again, I can't answer that."

"Linc, there are two things in that statement that bother me. One is either that this pilot or his local superior went off on his own, misinformed NASA about the true nature of his mission—or that the NASA flights mentioned are being used as cover by someone else. Is that the impression you want to leave us with?"

"I have to leave you with what is stated in the statement."

For the first time since Independence, the United States government had publicly admitted that it had committed espionage in peacetime and deceived the world about it. "Almost instantly you could feel the anger harden," wrote Richard Strout under his pseudonym as "T.R.B." in the *New Republic.* "Newsmen discovered, to their horror, that they had participated in a lie."

•

At the National Press Club, the news rattled out of tickers at 6:18 P.M. Valentin Ivanov of the Soviet Embassy, who spent much time there playing chess and gleaning information, dashed out of the building shouting, "Admitted! Admitted! Admitted!" Dean Acheson was lecturing at the National War College, he later recalled, "and a madder, more disgusted group of officers I never saw."

From Independence, Missouri, Harry Truman wrote him, "It seems to me that the President of the United States ought not to admit that he doesn't know what is going on. It looks as if we are in a very ridiculous position with our friends. We have always been known for honesty and fair dealing as a nation and I really don't know how we are going to recover."

On the West Virginia campaign trail, Hubert Humphrey said, "Mr. Khrushchev has us on the run in a propaganda battle now, making us look sick." Senator Hugh Scott of Pennsylvania: "We have violated the Eleventh Commandment—Thou Shalt Not Get Caught." Senator Homer Capehart reported that fellow citizens of Indiana were "beginning to wonder if we in Washington know what is going on in the world. It is about time that the administration . . . took the Senate and House into their confidence. God knows they need it!"

•

Sunday, the eighth of May. The new statement dominated front pages from New York to New Delhi. "U.S. CONCEDES FLIGHT OVER SOVIET, DEFENDS SEARCH FOR INTELLIGENCE," said the *New York Times*. "KHRUSHCHEV'S STORY PARTLY CONCEDED," said the *Washington Star*. "MORAL LEADERSHIP OF U.S. HARMED," said the *San Francisco Chronicle*.

The *Washington Post* declared, "This country was caught with jam on its hands." The *St. Louis Post-Dispatch* asked, "Do our intelligence operatives enjoy so much freewheeling authority that they can touch off an incident of grave international import by low-level decisions unchecked by responsible policy-making power? There must be an investigation of the circles which placed our country before the world in the light of a barefaced liar."

"The Americans have made fools of themselves," said the *News Chronicle*, London. The *Daily Telegraph* said, "A secret service must have some secrets from its own government. What it must never do is have more secrets from its own government than from the enemy." The *Daily Mail:* "Both America and Russia have been playing this game. Khrushchev is better at it. He can make rings round the honest, likeable but slower-witted soldier in the White House."

The *Sunday Express* condemned the "utterly unnecessary and stupidly provocative flight." *The Times* warned against the "trigger-happy fingers of a handful of American generals." The *Daily Mirror* demanded that Eisenhower punish the "idiots who were responsible." The *Paris Presse* found the affair "at once dramatic and farcical." *La Fuistizia*, Rome, said, "Every time things appear to be improving, *zac!* Something happens that spoils everything."

At an outdoor rally in Peking, a million Chinese were reminded that the United States was "the most vicious enemy of the people of the world." In Moscow, someone asked an American reporter, "How can such things happen without the knowledge of your President? We did not think your system was so irresponsible." A Soviet schoolteacher said, "Americans just aren't fanatics. A German or Japanese pilot—now, *he'd* have committed suicide." Another Russian said, "You Americans are bloody fools. Fools to do it, and fools to get caught!"

Max Frankel of the *New York Times* reported that the U-2 was almost the only topic of conversation in Moscow: "The Soviets have grown accustomed to the freer contacts with the West, cultural interchanges and tourist exchanges and explain that the relaxation of tensions has meant a better standard of life here. It is the reversal of this trend that they appear to fear most."

Llewellyn Thompson reported to Washington that telegrams received by his embassy noted that the American people "must be as disturbed by the incident as are the Soviet people" and called on Eisenhower "to put a stop to the activities of warmongers, thus drawing the distinction between them and the President."

American political columnists attacked the man in the White House. In the *New York Times,* James Reston said, "The heart of the problem here is that the Presidency has been parcelled out, first to Sherman Adams, then to John Foster Dulles, and in this case to somebody else—probably to Allen Dulles, but we still don't know." Eisenhower's "institutionalized Presidency" removed him from key decisions and left "the nation, the world and sometimes even the President himself in a state of uncertainty about who is doing what."

In the *New York Herald Tribune,* Walter Lippmann wrote that if some command outside Washington could send a plane into Russia, it must also be able to send a hydrogen bomb: "In denying that it authorized the flight, the Administration has entered a plea of incompetence." Why had Eisenhower allowed this to happen just before the Paris Summit? "It seems as if the country has been humiliated by absentmindedness in the highest quarters of the government."

●

Reading the Sunday papers, Thomas Gates was infuriated by the suggestion that low-level officers under his watch could send spy planes into the Soviet Union without permission. He called Herter and said that somebody had to take responsibility for the U-2: "While the President can say he didn't know about this one flight, he *did* approve the policy." Herter replied that for the moment they didn't want to say anything, "and we have been trying to keep the President clear on this."

At Gettysburg, wearing a Mother's Day carnation, Eisenhower went to Sunday church. Like Gates, he was inwardly rebelling against last night's statement on the U-2. It galled him to keep silent while Khrushchev hypnotized the world with a "passionate but highly distorted presentation of one particular phase of international espionage"—especially when the KGB was so much more active than American intelligence. He disliked having to lie to the world and say he had not approved the U-2 flight.

He was not priggish about lying for his country. During the CIA's adventures in Iran, Guatemala, Indonesia and elsewhere, he had dissembled and said that the United States did not meddle in other countries' affairs. As his son put it, "I'll lie as much as the next guy when my country's interests are involved—*if* I have a chance of being believed." But Khrushchev might go on television again to raise irrefutable evidence that the President had indeed authorized the May Day mission. Some reporter might exploit a leak from someone who knew that the President had approved every single U-2 flight. Then Eisenhower's credibility would be lost forever: as he once told a friend, when a President lost his credibility, "he has lost his greatest strength."

His entire training suggested that the man at the top should take full responsibility. When the Allies landed at Salerno, he had noted that a Supreme Commander must "take the blame for anything that goes wrong," whether the result of his mistake or a subordinate's. In the famous contingency note for defeat scrawled before D-Day, he declared that "if any blame or fault attaches to the attempt, it is mine alone." As Douglas Dillon said later, "He didn't like to blame other people.... He felt that more strongly than a civilian leader might have. He had this thing about honesty and that was the military tradition."

Milton Eisenhower told his brother that he must not take the rap for the U-2. The President barked back that if he blamed a subordinate, he would have to fire him and he would not "be guilty of such hypocrisy." Not only would this be a "glaring and permanent injustice," but it would confirm that the President was not in control of his own government. How then could he negotiate with Khrushchev or any other leader? People around the world would fear that a low-level U.S. officer could start World War Three.

After returning from church, the President called Herter and said he had changed his mind: they must issue a new statement admitting that for four years, the U-2 had been deliberately sent into Russia under a broad Presidential order to get "adequate knowledge" of the Soviet military-industrial complex and protect the nation from surprise attack.

He was still not ready to tell the full truth: the statement should say that while the President knew that sometimes "unusual and unorthodox" means were required to do this, he had not been given the details of reconnaissance missions. He wanted "no specific tie" of the May Day flight to him.

By this statement the President hoped to end world concern that a low-level American could start a world war and yet evade specific responsibility for the insult of sending the U-2 into Russia on May Day. Back at the White House, at six that evening, he gave Herter, Goodpaster and Hagerty their orders. All knew that this would be the first time an American President had taken explicit public responsibility for a major act of peacetime espionage.

•

In London, Harold Macmillan had "no direct news" about the U-2, but thought it a "very queer story." He advised Robert Murphy of the State Department to have the President follow the British formula and say, "We do not discuss in public our intelligence activities." But Eisenhower had already made his decision.

At Pound, Virginia, Oliver Powers wrote to Khrushchev as "one coal miner to another," asking him to "be fair to my boy." He sent a telegram to the President: "I WANT TO KNOW WHAT ALL THIS IS ABOUT MY SON FRANCIS G. POWERS THAT IS GOING ON AND I WANT TO KNOW NOW. ANSWER."

In Burbank, Kelly Johnson had been hard at work since the moment Richard Bissell called him from Washington and said, "Three-sixty is missing." After Khrushchev's first speech on the U-2, the Soviet trade union paper *Trud* published a photograph identified as the American "pirate plane," showing men and women picking over a heap of wreckage. Shards of metal were so twisted that no pilot could have survived the crash: the picture had been clearly intended to trick the Americans into concluding that Powers had been killed.

When Johnson saw the photo, he said, "That's no damned U-2. I don't recognize any parts and, besides, the Russians would certainly not allow the U-2 to be handled like that." Then Khrushchev revealed that the pilot was alive, and Johnson said, "My God, did he just up and *land* it?" There were already rumors that Powers had been a double agent and been spotted in a Sverdlovsk nightclub.

Bissell and Johnson wanted to find out what had brought down their plane. The Lockheed designer agreed to publicly declare the *Trud* picture a fake: he would "insult the Russians to the point that they put the U-2 on display." Then with careful instructions from the CIA on what to look for, Americans in Moscow could discreetly inspect and photograph the wreckage.

•

Monday morning, May ninth. As Ann Whitman wrote, "The matter of the spy-in-the-sky was uppermost on everyone's minds." After breakfast with Republican congressmen, the President arrived at the Oval Office "very depressed." He said, "I would like to resign."

At the State Department, Herter, Dillon, Kohler, Bohlen, Gates and his deputy James Douglas worked on a new statement on the U-2 reflecting the President's change of heart. Chip Bohlen stubbornly opposed implicating the President, but was quickly silenced. This was merely a drafting session.

In Burbank, Kelly Johnson told reporters that he had examined the Soviet photo of the U-2: "I am convinced that the Russians, for some reason, have released the photo of some other airplane crash. . . . It would be very interesting to know why they have hidden the U-2."

At noon in Washington, Eisenhower went to the Army and Navy Club for a long-scheduled luncheon with fellow members of the West Point Class of 1915. After one such reunion, Ann Whitman had noted that her boss "was all wound up and very happy—appointments with individual classmates were to be made, he wanted a stag dinner for all of them, etc." Today by the time the President returned to the Oval Office, she found that he had "bounced back with his characteristic ability to accept the bad news, not dwell on it and so go ahead."

Goodpaster was waiting with a draft of the new statement on the U-2. Eisenhower changed wording that seemed defensive. He was feeling "anything but defensive."

Meanwhile Richard Nixon called Herter and said they must "get away from this little-boy-in-the-cookie-jar posture." They must not be apologetic. "We just can't say no flights before an international conference because there just wouldn't be any flights." Herter told him about the new statement.

At 2:35 P.M., the President convened the National Security Council in the Cabinet Room: "Well, we're just going to have to take a lot of beating on this—and I'm the one, rightly, who's going to have to take it." He ran over the history of the U-2 and explained why he was going to take general public responsibility: "Of course, one had to expect that the thing would fail at one time or another. But that it had to be such a boo-boo and that we would be caught with our pants down was rather painful." Eisenhower said that from now on, no one but the State Department must comment. "We will now just have to endure the storm."

As the meeting broke up, several officials stayed behind to ponder whether Francis Gary Powers had been "in cahoots with the Soviets" before May Day.

•

In the Capitol chamber where Khrushchev had drunk tea with senators the previous fall, Herter and Allen Dulles briefed eighteen bipartisan leaders of Congress on the U-2. The President had asked them to speak "fully but without apology." Dulles had won Eisenhower's permission to reveal a few U-2 pictures and demonstrate what had been achieved: "If I can't show the photos, I would rather not do it at all."

"Any statement?" newsmen asked Dulles when he arrived. "About the usual," he said, and they laughed. Once the room was sealed, Herter announced that the President would take public responsibility for the U-2 later that day. Dulles denied rumors that Powers had been a double agent and pronounced the pilot's record "exemplary." Turning to Arthur Lundahl, he said, "Mr. Lundahl will now give you a briefing on what we've accomplished," and whispered in his ear, "You've got to be good."

Using one briefing board after another, Lundahl gave one of his best performances as Dulles smoked his pipe approvingly. At the end of the show, there was a standing ovation. Rising from his chair, Dulles dropped his pipe into the lap of his suit. As an aide recalled, Lundahl was torn between accepting the ovation and saving his boss, smiling at his audience as he helped Dulles bat out the embers.

As they left the room, Dulles muttered to Herter, "That was a rough one."

•

That evening in Moscow, Khrushchev attended a celebration of the fifteenth anniversary of the liberation of Czechoslovakia at that nation's embassy. In no time, he started on the U-2 and the State Department's Saturday-night statement: "Here is how they explain the spy plane affair—it is impossible to admit but impossible to deny. It's like the famous anecdote about the spinster who isn't a spinster because she has a baby!" All laughed.

"It is said that the U.S. military did this. Was it *only* the military? What kind of a state is it where the military can do what the government opposes? . . . If one of *our* military took such an act upon himself, we would grab him by the ear immediately. . . . What about Allen Dulles? He certainly knew about everything. He is a member of the U.S. government—and this was Allen Dulles's airline!"

Khrushchev thought the State Department story "a bit transparent": "Furthermore it blames *us* for preventing people from flying over our country, studying our defenses and learning our secrets. . . . It seems to say that such flights are possible in the future too because the Soviet Union does not reveal its secrets to countries that pursue unfriendly policies toward us."

He did not want to "heat up passions" against the United States: "Today I declare once again that we want to live in peace and friendship with the American people." He swung his open hand in the direction of Tommy Thompson: "I respect the U.S. Ambassador and am sure that he had nothing to do with this incursion. . . . I am convinced of the moral qualities of this man. . . . I suppose he is feeling very badly about this incident both for himself and for his country."

Khrushchev raised his glass: "To the end of wars, to the end of provocations, to peace and friendship among peoples!"

Then he cornered the two envoys whose countries had lent bases for the "pirate flight." To Salman Ali of Pakistan: "Peshawar has been marked on our map. In the future, if any American plane is allowed to use Peshawar as a base of operations against the Soviet Union, we will retaliate immediately." To Oskar Gundersen of Norway: "You knew about these flights. I can see it in your eyes."

Watching this scene, someone asked the Turkish chargé, Hamit Batu, "Shouldn't you be up there?" Batu shook his head: "I feel safer here with you."

Throughout the evening, Soviet officers had walked up to Ambassador Thompson saying that they wished to smooth things over: they didn't want a war with the U.S.A. Before Khrushchev left the party, he told Thompson, "I must talk with you," and took him into a side room for their first private meeting since May Day.

When the door closed, as Thompson recalled, Khrushchev said, *"This U-2 thing has put me in a terrible spot. You have to get me off it."*

Thompson pledged to do everything he could. But in Washington, the State Department was about to announce that Eisenhower had personally authorized the flights.

•

In Washington, it was 3:55 P.M. Lincoln White walked into the press room to read the State Department's fourth utterance on the U-2 in five days, this time a two-page statement signed by Christian Herter:

> Ever since Marshal Stalin shifted the policy of the Soviet Union from wartime cooperation to postwar conflict in 1946 . . . the world has lived in a state of apprehension with respect to Soviet intentions. . . . With the development of modern weapons carrying tremendously destructive nuclear warheads, the threat of surprise attack and aggression presents a constant danger. . . .
>
> I will say frankly that it is unacceptable that the Soviet political system should be given an opportunity to make secret preparations to face the Free World with the choice of abject surrender or nuclear destruction. The Government of the United States would be derelict . . . if it did not . . . take such measures as are possible unilaterally to lessen and to overcome this danger of surprise attack. In fact, the United States has not and does not shirk this responsibility.
>
> In accordance with the National Security Act of 1947, the President has put into effect . . . directives to gather by every possible means the information required to protect . . . against surprise attack. . . . Programs have been developed and put into operation which have included extensive aerial surveillance by unarmed civilian aircraft, normally of a peripheral character but on occasion by penetration. Specific missions . . . have not been subject to Presidential authorization.
>
> The fact that such surveillance was taking place has apparently not been a secret to the Soviet leadership, and the question indeed arises as to why at this particular juncture they should seek to exploit the present

incident as a propaganda battle in the Cold War.... Far from being
damaging to the forthcoming meeting in Paris, this incident should
serve to underline the importance to the world of an earnest attempt
there to achieve agreed and effective safeguards against surprise attack
and aggression.

The statement implied that there might be future U-2 flights into
Russia. Privately the President thought this unlikely, because the program had been compromised. But leaving it open gave him a useful
bargaining chip: if it later became vital to make a concession to
Khrushchev to save the Summit, Eisenhower could formally pledge
not to send the U-2 into Soviet airspace again.

•

The Associated Press ran a bulletin:

THE UNITED STATES ACKNOWLEDGED TODAY THAT
IT HAS SENT SPY FLIGHTS INTO RUSSIA UNDER PRESI-
DENT EISENHOWER'S GENERAL ORDERS. THE STATE DE-
PARTMENT DID NOT DISCOURAGE A DEDUCTION THAT
SUCH FLIGHTS MAY CONTINUE UNTIL SOVIET LEADERS
OPEN THEIR BORDERS TO INSPECTION.

From Washington, James Reston wrote in the *New York Times,*
"This was a sad and perplexed capital tonight, caught in a swirl of
charges of clumsy administration, bad judgment and bad faith. It was
depressed and humiliated by the United States having been caught
spying over the Soviet Union and trying to cover up its activities in a
series of misleading official statements."

In the *Herald Tribune,* Walter Lippmann noted that "what is unprecedented about the avowal is not the spying as such, but the claim
that spying when we do it should be accepted by the world as righ-
teous.... Spying between nations is, of course, the universal practice.... The spying is never avowed and therefore the government
never acknowledges responsibility for its own clandestine activities....
We should have abided by that rule."

Joseph Alsop was delighted to learn that the CIA had been keeping
more closely abreast of Soviet ICBMs than he had thought; he entitled
his column, "The Wonderful News." The *Wall Street Journal* surveyed
national reaction to the revelation that the U.S. had sent spy planes

into Russia for four years. Findings were summarized in one sentence: "It's just too bad we got caught."

Some were less enchanted. The *Nation* asked how Americans would have reacted had "Sergei Popoff" been shot down while spying over New York and the Russians pleaded their old fear of attack and insisted that they would keep on invading American airspace. A cartoonist for the *Daily Sketch,* London, showed Eisenhower addressing pilots of the "U.S. Unintelligence Service," each equipped with a suicide pin. *Stockholm Tidningen* complained that Washington's original denials had turned into "an eagerness to confess which knows no limit."

Harold Macmillan, who had thought Khrushchev might accept either silence or some formal disclaimer, was horrified. At a dinner party in Washington, Allen Dulles said, "We should have kept quiet." In Peking, Mao Tse-tung declared his hope that the U-2 would wake up "certain people" who had lauded Eisenhower as a "lover of peace."

●

Given the news in Moscow, Khrushchev was apoplectic. He had gone out of his way not to accuse the President of sending the U-2. Now this latest statement seemed "as though Eisenhower was boasting arrogantly about what the United States could do and would do. . . . Here was the President of the United States defending outrageous, inadmissible actions!" To Khrushchev, once again the Americans were showing that "they didn't give a damn about anyone else, that they would pursue only their selfish goals. They wanted to dictate to us their conditions from a position of power."

●

Tuesday, May tenth. At the White House, a CIA man arrived with the latest information on what might have afflicted the U-2 on May Day. As Kistiakowsky wrote in his diary, "It is pretty clear that it couldn't have been flameout of the engine, but what did happen is difficult to say. The picture of the crashed plane which Khrushchev passed around is not that of a U-2, so it begins to look as if the pilot might have landed it undamaged.

"On the other hand, our information about his maneuvers is strongly against the idea that he was a double agent. At most, he decided to turn 'state's evidence' when under pressure and, at least, he just chickened out. Very depressing."

•

In the Oval Office, the President told Herter that he might call on Khrushchev in Paris before the Summit to try to clear the air. But Herter convinced him that Khrushchev might take this as "a gesture of weakness."

Eisenhower predicted that Khrushchev would "probably try by his deportment to force the conference along the lines he wants." Perhaps he should "throw" back "clear evidence" of the extreme volume of Soviet spying in the United States. If Khrushchev raised the U-2, the best course might be "to chuckle about it and turn the subject off." Or perhaps he would let Khrushchev talk as much as he wanted to about the plane "and then quietly suggest that he should come around and talk privately to the President about it."

Eisenhower asked Herter to try to arrange for Khrushchev to "come around to the American Embassy residence after the first day's meeting—say, at about four P.M."

•

When Herter returned to the State Department, he cabled the Embassy in Moscow to ask Gromyko for an interview with the pilot. If granted, they should "pass on the love and prayers of Powers's entire family. Tell him that his wife Barbara is waiting and praying for him, that she brought Eck von Heinberg (their German shepherd dog) with her to Georgia, and that his little niece, Tamie Gay, is healthy and well (Mr. Powers's favorite 9-month-old niece)." They must look for "signs of fatigue, nervousness, pallor or glassy stare." They should "try to find out what had happened to his plane—particularly whether or not he was shot down (at what altitude?) and the altitude at which the parachute was used."

Old bureaucratic foes in Washington were savoring the spectacle of egg on the faces of Allen Dulles and the CIA. General Twining felt that the Air Force had been vindicated: "*We* might have got caught, but we wouldn't have got caught *that* way—a disgraceful way."

An FBI field agent in San Francisco informed J. Edgar Hoover that local people were convinced that the U-2 mess "came about because of the stupidity of CIA and that when the matter has settled down some, there should and will be a big inquiry as to the operations, efficiency and cloak of secrecy of CIA." The *New York Mirror* opined that Eisenhower should have given the U-2 program to the FBI.

In Milledgeville, Barbara Powers held a press conference from a lawn chair in front of her mother's house. Reporters were told that she had broken her leg waterskiing. With red-rimmed eyes, she said, "My husband is not a spy and I fully believe that. . . . In view of Mr. Khrushchev's actions in the past in reuniting separated families, I have hopes Gary will be returned to me."

In Moscow, Khrushchev and the Party Presidium met to decide on Khrushchev's response to the State Department's latest announcement on the U-2.

•

Wednesday, May eleventh. For days, Soviet workmen had been hauling metal debris into the Chess Pavilion of Gorky Park in Moscow. Just as Eisenhower had predicted for years, the Russians were putting the U-2's remains on display in a carnival of agitprop.

Ten months earlier, Nixon and Khrushchev had opened the American Exhibition in Sokolniki Park. Now Muscovites referred to this display as "the *second* American Exhibition." American military attachés in Moscow planned discreet attendance at the show to try and learn what had happened to the U-2. Inside the pavilion, light streamed through tiny windows onto the U-2's wings and tailpiece at the center of the room. Glass cases bore relics of the *Amerikanski samelot* (American airplane); one was labeled THIS IS WHAT THE AMERICAN SPY WAS EQUIPPED WITH.

"His genuine documents!" barked a guide. "Everything, comrades, everything! Stop your conversations and move on!" Russians filed past the huge aerial cameras, the infamous ejection seat, the orange-and-white parachute, the package of Kents, the rubles (MONEY FOR GRAFTING RUSSIANS), the notorious suicide pin. A young man ogled a snapshot of Barbara Powers and said, "It must have been hard leaving *her!*"

The crowds were angry—not at the aggressive United States but the aggressive guards, who cried, "Hurry up, comrades! Three thousand people are waiting to get in!" Near the exit was a guest book called *The Book of Wrath.* Visitors scrawled their indignation: "Shame, shame, Eisenhower! . . . Death to Imperialism. . . . What kind of a friend are you? ... Wolf in sheep's clothing. ... We students are glad that the American pirate has been shot down. ... Punish the spy with all severity. ... We believe that Nikita Sergeyevich Khrushchev will do everything he can in Paris to see that this will not happen again."

The hall was cleared at four o'clock. A black Chaika limousine pulled up. Khrushchev bounced out and moved quickly through the front door. Trailed by hundreds of newsmen, he bustled about the hall like a child in a candy store, examining the gold Napoleon francs, a receipt for Powers's Mercedes, the gold watches and noiseless pistol, collapsible rubber boat, flight maps, pressure suit, ejection seat and destructor unit. A guide played the U-2 pilot's tape of Soviet radar stations: "*Bleep—bleep—bleep ...*"

"An exchange of technical knowledge!" cried Khrushchev. He stood atop a wicker chair so that all could see him. A Soviet spokesman rounded up straggling newsmen. Someone shouted, "Will this plane incident affect Soviet public opinion when Mr. Eisenhower comes to Moscow?"

"I would not like to be in Mr. Eisenhower's place. I would not like to be asked the questions which might be put to him when he comes to the Soviet Union. I can only say that the Soviet people are very polite, so there will be no excesses. But questions will be asked, of course."

Had the State Department's newest statement changed Khrushchev's opinion of the President? "It has, of course. I was not aware that this plan was not the caprice of an irresponsible officer. I was horrified to learn that the President had endorsed the acts." He continued to maintain that Eisenhower had not really approved the U-2 flights beforehand: probably Allen Dulles had blackmailed the President into taking responsibility. "The American militarists have placed me in a very difficult position."

Khrushchev spared Eisenhower but denounced Herter. Shaking his fist, he cried, "Far from feeling guilty and ashamed of aggressive actions, he *justifies* them and says they will continue in the future! Only countries which are at war with each other can act this way. ... *Impudence,* sheer *impudence!*" The Soviet Union would *never* send a plane over another country's territory.

"Our country is a strong and mighty state. ... If the U.S.A. has not yet suffered a real war on its territory and wants to start a war, we will fire rockets and hit their territory a few minutes later. ... We do not live under American laws. We have our own laws . . . and violators be thrashed!"

"Do you still want President Eisenhower to come to the Soviet Union?"

Khrushchev knitted his brow for fifteen seconds: "What do you want me to say? Come up here and say it for me. . . . You know my attitude toward the President. I have often spoken about it. I am a human being and I have human feelings. I had hopes and they were betrayed. . . . You must understand that we Russians always go the whole hog: when we play, we play and when we fight, we fight. So how can I now ask our people to turn out and welcome the dear guest who is coming to us. They will say, 'Are you *nuts?* What kind of a dear guest allows a plane to fly over us to spy?' "

"Wouldn't you prefer President Eisenhower's visit to be postponed?"

"I do not want to answer this question in front of you journalists. I will discuss this with the President in Paris. We still want to find ways to improve relations with the U.S.A." Khrushchev announced that he planned to go to Paris two days early. "I like Paris. It's a nice city. . . . And if the conference does not take place? We have lived without it for many years and will live for another hundred!"

Khrushchev evidently had second thoughts about his loose tongue. Correspondents telephoning his comments to the West were cut off in mid-sentence by Moscow censors, who did not lift the embargo for twenty hours. When they did, the official transcript omitted his remark that he had been "horrified" by Eisenhower's endorsement of the U-2 and that this had changed his opinion of the President.

After Khrushchev's press conference, a Soviet journalist said, "They'll make it up in Paris. He'll come. We want him to come. He could not have easily known about the plane." At an outdoor Moscow café, a Soviet professor said, "Eisenhower will come, but it won't be the same as before."

The professor's wife said, "Ah, what a welcome we'd have given him before *this* happened."

•

It was Wednesday morning in Washington. No one at the White House had yet seen Khrushchev's comments at Gorky Park. Goodpaster arrived early to draft a statement for the President to read at his press conference, the first Presidential remarks on the U-2. Eisenhower had told him to include the fact that espionage was an "ugly but vital necessity." Goodpaster changed "ugly" to "distasteful."

As Goodpaster toiled, the President told Senators at breakfast that he still hoped for "some useful progress" at the Summit: "Khrushchev is much too smart to believe this was the first time such a flight has occurred." At 9:10 A.M., he joined Goodpaster and Hagerty to work on his statement. Hagerty had told the rest of the staff that the President didn't need "any advice on how to answer questions on the U-2."

Before 1950, press conferences had been held at the President's desk until the crowd grew too large and Harry Truman moved them across the street to the fourth floor of the Executive Office Building. Since 1953, Hagerty had allowed reporters to quote his boss directly, but only after he vetted the transcript for errors and garbled syntax: "It's not that we want to censor any of his remarks. What we are actually trying to do is to prevent a human fluff that the Communist propagandists can use to good advantage."

In 1955, angry at charges that Eisenhower had been soft on Joseph McCarthy, Hagerty began allowing press conferences to be filmed for delayed broadcast. "To hell with slanted reporters," he wrote in his diary. "We'll go directly to the American people who can hear exactly what the Pres said without reading warped and slanted stories."

Eisenhower held about two sessions a month, fewer than Roosevelt and Truman. His sometimes awkward usage was an easy target for parodies like the famous Eisenhoverian version of the Gettysburg Address: "I haven't checked these figures, but eighty-seven years ago, I think it was, a number of individuals organized a governmental set-up here in this country . . ." So were what seemed like astonishing admissions: "You're telling me something about my own administration I never heard of." Often he unshyly leaned over and whispered to Hagerty for guidance.

Sometimes Eisenhower's syntax was genuinely garbled, especially after his stroke. Sometimes he genuinely did not know about the subject raised. "I'm supposed to set the tone," he once told his son. "Let the other fellows give the details." But other times, it was pure subterfuge. In 1953, he prefaced a comment on his Iranian countercoup by saying, "I believe I read in the paper this morning . . ." as if he knew no more than any other reader. At another famous instant, he gave Hagerty one of his wicked grins and said, "Don't worry, Jim. If that question comes up, I'll just confuse 'em."

•

At 10:29 A.M., the President strode into the Indian Treaty Room—less briskly than normal, someone thought. He stood behind the carved wooden desk with its double stand of microphones. Hagerty took his usual place behind him, against the windows. Reporters knocked back folding chairs to stand up.

"Good morning," said the President. "Please sit down. I have made some notes from which I want to talk to you about this U-2 incident." He pulled out typed pages and donned reading glasses. "No one wants another Pearl Harbor. This means we must have knowledge of military forces and preparations around the world." Intelligence gathering was "special and secret," divorced from the visible agencies of government and supervised under broad directives.

"It is a distasteful but vital necessity. We prefer and work for a different kind of world and a different way of obtaining the information essential to confidence and effective deterrence. . . . This was the reason for my Open Skies proposal in 1955. . . . I shall bring up the Open Skies proposal again at Paris, since it is a means of ending concealment and suspicion. . . .

"We must not be distracted from the real issues of the day by what is an incident or a symptom of the world situation today. This incident has been given great propaganda exploitation. The emphasis given to a flight of an unarmed, nonmilitary plane can only reflect a fetish of secrecy. The *real* issues are the ones we will be working on at the Summit—disarmament, search for solutions affecting Germany and Berlin and the whole range of East-West relations."

As during the tense months of Khrushchev's Berlin ultimatum, Eisenhower was trying to muffle the crisis by publicly denying Khrushchev's complaints. He would not lose his composure, endanger Western unity and thereby give Khrushchev what he apparently wanted on the eve of the Summit. Privately he predicted that Khrushchev's "recent theatrical behavior" would not set the tone of the meeting; nor would the United States be "encumbered" by the U-2 at Paris.

For four years, more than any of his aides, the President had been the one to warn that sending the U-2 into Russia was a provocation that was nearly an act of war. But today, at this press conference, he would not concede Khrushchev an inch: "I'll tell you *this:* the United States and all of its allies that I know of have engaged in nothing that could be considered honestly provocative. We are looking to our own security and our defense and we have no idea of promoting any kind of conflict or war. This is just—it's absolutely *ridiculous* and they *know* it is."

●

Thursday, May twelfth. At a White House breakfast, Eisenhower told Republican congressmen that he would not cancel his Soviet trip unless Khrushchev revoked the invitation. In that case, his time could "easily be utilized elsewhere." After a Cabinet meeting later that morning, he asked Herter and Gates to "call off all activities that might be taken by the Soviets as provocative." Goodpaster gave the same order to Allen Dulles.

The CIA's Office of Current Intelligence gave the President an interpretation of Khrushchev's comments at Gorky Park: in view of Khrushchev's "deep personal commitment" to the Summit, high-level exchanges and peaceful coexistence, the remarks were probably not intended to cause the President to withdraw from the Summit and his trip to the Soviet Union. "While he certainly intends to extract the maximum political advantage, he does not wish to slam any doors or to upset at the last minute his long campaign to bring the Western leaders to a meeting under what he considers highly favorable conditions."

The report said that in Khrushchev's "present mood of arrogant confidence mixed with resentment toward the United States, it probably was difficult for a man of Khrushchev's temperament and flair for histrionics to suppress an off-the-cuff reaction of this kind."

Llewellyn Thompson sent a cable to Washington that said almost the opposite. He was convinced that Khrushchev's comments at Gorky Park were "another indication that the Cold War is on again. I have little doubt that Khrushchev hopes that the President will cancel his trip." He said the Soviets knew how to organize professional heckling but might not be able to prevent an embarrassing show of friendship if Eisenhower came. "All signs now appear to point to Khrushchev's intention of trying to extort maximum propaganda advantage from the Summit rather than attempt a serious negotiation."

Goodpaster brought this message to the Oval Office in the afternoon. The President read it, put on spiked shoes and whacked out golf balls on the South Lawn for an hour. At five o'clock, as Ann Whitman recorded, he went home to the Mansion, "nervous, tense, said his blood pressure was high."

•

At his farm in Libertyville, Illinois, Adlai Stevenson was feeling "explosive, barely controllable rage" at how Eisenhower was handling the U-2 affair. For months, he had refused to throw his hat into the Presidential ring. Now he was telling friends that he might have to reconsider. Two days before, John Kennedy had won the West Virginia primary. Stevenson punched a newspaper filled with foreign news and said, "Can he deal with this?"

That evening, at the University of Chicago, Stevenson scrapped a speech on Latin America to speak on the U-2: "Could it serve the purpose of peace and mutual trust to send intelligence missions over the heart of the Soviet Union on the very eve of the long-awaited Summit conference? . . . Our government has blundered and admitted it. And the blunder has made the President's task at the Summit meeting more difficult."

A White House staff member told colleagues that the President's old rival was trying to "make an issue of the U-2 incident" and had "got himself into the position of the candidate of the Kremlin."

•

Friday, the thirteenth of May. For years, Khrushchev had rattled Soviet missiles to scare nations along his border away from collaboration with the United States. "Don't make me laugh with your pacts!" he once told the Shah of Iran. "You know perfectly well that we could flatten England with seven atom bombs and Turkey with twelve!" This morning, Andrei Gromyko formally summoned the envoys of Pakistan, Norway and Turkey and threatened military attack in revenge for their complicity in the U-2 flights.

Since Khrushchev's revelation of the U-2 downing, the United States had kept its pledge to conceal its allies' collaboration. After Khrushchev's threats at the Czechoslovak Embassy, Lincoln White had declared that it was "typical that the Soviet Union singles out as the objective of its threats those smaller countries of the Free World who bear no responsibility for the recent incident." He claimed that the United States had used these nations' territory to launch U-2 missions into Russia without their knowledge or permission.

Armed with this contention, the governments concerned responded suavely to the Soviet threats. A Pakistani spokesman noted that the Russians seemed to have a "pathological conviction" that his country housed secret foreign bases: "We have categorically told them that no such bases exist in Pakistan." Ayub Khan told reporters, "The Americans are our friends. These planes come and visit our country. How do we know where they go after they leave our country?"

After consulting Washington, the Turks claimed that they too had never given the Americans approval to fly from their soil into the Soviet Union. Norway made the same assertion: for the record, Ambassador Paul Koht lodged an official protest at the State Department. Herter privately assured him that Washington would stick by its promise and claim that Oslo "knew nothing about this flight and was in no way involved." The Shah denied all knowledge of the U-2, announcing that he was "certain the flight did not originate in Iran" (which no one had ever suggested).

Afghanistan in 1960 was a prime target of opportunity for the Soviet Union. The U-2 affair offered Moscow an excellent chance to spoil Kabul's good relations with the United States and its troubled relations with Pakistan. To Sardar Mohammed Naim, Deputy Premier of Afghanistan, the Russians gave maps, pictures and other evidence to show that Pakistan and America had conspired to violate Afghan airspace on the U-2's way from Peshawar into the Soviet Union. Naim was informed that "after arriving in Peshawar from Adana, the pilot remained long enough to be entertained socially by his Pakistani opposite numbers, who knew all about the mission."

Naim told the Pakistani Ambassador that this violation was "extremely serious." The Pakistani denied that the U-2 had been launched from Peshawar: even if it had, "the government of Pakistan had no control over what it might have done after takeoff."

Naim summoned Norman Hannah of the American Embassy and said he had thought that Washington was "fully aware of Afghanistan's policy of neutrality." Hannah replied that this "isolated event" must not be allowed to harm their relations: America's "friendship and desire to help Afghanistan" were as strong as ever. Hannah wired Washington that he was "somewhat relieved" by the moderation of Naim's protest.

Japan was a different story. The chilly, intense Premier Kishi had been a protégé of the wartime leader Hideki Tojo: after the war, he sat cross-legged, writing poetry, in a prison cell for three years. With the twin menaces of the Soviet Union and China looming to the West,

Kishi was determined to keep his nation under the American nuclear umbrella but to rid it of the demeaning constitution of 1951.

The United States was eager to maintain Japan as the Asian bastion of the Free World. A new security treaty was drawn up that would remove American ground forces from Japan: U.S. military bases like Atsugi could remain, but the Tokyo government would have to be consulted on their use. In January 1960, Kishi signed the treaty in Washington. After ratification by the Japanese Diet, Eisenhower was scheduled to stop in Tokyo in June on his way home from the Soviet Union.

But for months, ratification had been in danger. Business leaders disliked being kept from dealing with China; intellectuals, religious groups, labor unions and Socialists feared that the treaty would drag Japan into war.

The U-2 gave them perfect ammunition. Word was put out—perhaps with Soviet help—that U-2s had been flown on provocative missions into Russia and China from Japanese soil. Snake-dancing crowds surrounded the Diet bearing pictures of the U-2 and the legend PATRON OF THE BLACK JETS—THE BLACK-HEARTED KISHI.

Herter cabled the American Embassy in Tokyo: "Should you desire, you may tell Kishi these planes are based in Japan for weather reconnaissance purposes. If Kishi considers a public statement to that effect necessary, the U.S. government will support his statement as feasible and advisable." At the State Department, Lincoln White told the press, "There is no truth to reports that a U-2 aircraft conducted intelligence missions from Japan. Period."

But Japan was a problem that would not go away.

•

At Lubyanka Prison, Moscow, the KGB and military men continued to grill the pilot. As Powers later recalled, he demanded that the American government be informed that he was alive. Finally they showed him the May 8 *New York Times,* which included the full text of Khrushchev's speech the day before. Powers read aloud: "We have parts of the plane and we also have the pilot, who is quite alive and kicking!" He said, "You could have had that paper printed right here in Moscow." Then they read him articles about his wife's flight to Georgia and his father's plea to "be fair to my boy," and he wept.

Day after day, his routine was the same. At six, he was up for hot tea, a trip to the lavatory, breakfast, a doctor's examination. Before the morning interrogation, he was forced to initial the transcript from the day before, although he could not understand a word of the Russian text. After lunch, he exercised on the Lubyanka roof, watched by guards with machine guns. Then afternoon interrogation, supper, lavatory, evening interrogation, lavatory and back to his cell to read Agatha Christie and Ellery Queen while the Kremlin clock tolled and tolled and tolled.

As he later recalled, at one point he cried, "Why should I bother answering your questions when as soon as you have everything you want, you're going to take me out and shoot me?" One of the jailers said, "There may be another way." Realizing that he had been invited to defect, he did not raise the matter again.

One morning, his captors shouted, "You lied to us!" Contrary to his claims, the *New York Times* had reported that all CIA men took polygraph tests. Powers replied, "That may be true of the agents, but we were pilots." The Russians believed him, but now that his case was being covered so intensively by the world press, he was convinced that he could not deceive them about certain matters forever.

•

Saturday, May fourteenth, the day of Eisenhower's departure for Paris. In the morning, he had a haircut in the Oval Office, saw aides, signed letters and received a telegram from Francis Gary Powers's sister: "PRAY FOR SUCCESS OF MEETING. PLEASE DO EVERYTHING POSSIBLE FOR SAFETY AND RETURN OF BROTHER. CONSIDER HIM YOUR SON." In the afternoon, he went to Burning Tree to watch a golf match.

His helicopter landed at Andrews Air Force Base before dusk. He walked onto the runway where he had greeted Khrushchev eight months before. Microphones had been set up for a pre-Summit statement to the American people, but he ignored them. It was starting to drizzle. He climbed the aircraft steps, faced the crowd of officers, children and spouses, saluted and ducked into the forward hatch of *Air Force One.*

His trip to Europe on this plane in September had been the first Presidential journey by jet. Eisenhower had found it exhilarating. "Seats far more comfortable than the old *Columbine,*" wrote Ann Whitman in her diary. "There are four washrooms, and I must say I was impressed by flush toilets!" When the jet passed over Manhattan, she thought the island had never looked more beautiful: "From 29,000 feet, it looked like a tiny jeweled pin set with emeralds and rubies. In another few minutes, we were over Boston, sprawled out and mostly green. Then on to almost deserted Maine and the ocean."

The President's plane was equipped with oxygen tanks that had never left his side since his heart attack. (Hagerty concealed this from the press to foreclose rumors.) His cabin was supplied with the latest paperback Westerns. Sometimes he dozed, sometimes he read, sometimes he stared at the stars as the aircraft moved into night over the North Atlantic.

It had been seven days since he stood on his Gettysburg veranda and learned that the Russians had captured the U-2 pilot alive. As James Reston had written in the *Times,* he had brought about "almost all the things he feared the most. He wanted to reduce international tension and he has increased it. . . . He glorified teamwork and morality and got lies and administrative chaos. Everything he was noted for—caution, patience, leadership, military skill and even good luck—suddenly eluded him precisely at the moment he needed them most."

Throughout this excruciating week, the President had kept an almost supernatural composure, except for an epithet or two spoken through clenched teeth and the momentary depression that Ann Whitman noticed. He did not want to alarm Americans or let Khrushchev know he had gotten his goat. In private, he betrayed no sense of mortification to his aides or, it appeared, even to himself: if the U-2 hadn't gone down, Khrushchev probably would have used something else to embarrass the United States. But on this flight, there was a break in his stoicism.

John Eisenhower came to the Presidential cabin. He loved his father and had been stung by the criticism of the past seven days. His anger focused on Allen Dulles. John rarely gave his father unsolicited advice, but now he told him that Dulles had let him down: Dulles had promised that a pilot would never be captured alive. John said, "You ought to *fire* him."

This provoked a Vesuvian explosion. The President cried, "I am *not* going to shift the blame to my underlings!" As John later said, "He let me know that I was a kid in short pants in no uncertain terms." The outburst suggested to him that "Dad was fighting a hard battle himself internally about Dulles" and "would like to have canned him."

This was not far from the mark. The President told Goodpaster and Gordon Gray that he never wanted to see Dulles alone again.

•

The sun rose over the ocean. Eisenhower awoke, reworked his arrival statement and read over his briefing books. A red carpet and welcoming party awaited at Orly Airport. "There is a dreadful clatter and shaking of the plane every time the landing gear is lowered," Ann Whitman noted.

Khrushchev had already arrived in Paris. The curtain was lifting on the next act of the drama.

11

Debacle at Paris

P ARIS HAS FILLED UP with diplomats, statesmen and journalists for the dramatic Big Four Summit meeting that may, because of the U-2, be a bust," wrote C. L. Sulzberger of the *New York Times* in his diary. "Every chief of mission in Europe is here," wrote his wife Marina in hers. "So a series of garden, cocktail and other parties—all rather nice, if you don't have to give them yourself and only stay half an hour to see old friends."

At Orly Airport, beneath a leaden Sunday morning sky, the President read a statement for the television cameras: "The hopes of humanity call on the four of us to purge our minds of prejudice and our hearts of rancor. Far too much is at stake to indulge in profitless bickering. The issues that divide the Free World from the Soviet bloc are grave and not subject to easy solution. But if goodwill exists on both sides, at least a beginning can be made. The West, I am sure, will meet Mr. Khrushchev halfway in every honest effort in this direction. America will go every foot that pride and honor permit. It will be a pleasure to meet again with my old friends President de Gaulle and Prime Minister Macmillan."

Reporters noted whose name was missing from the last sentence. Eisenhower and Amory Houghton, his Ambassador to Paris, climbed into an open French limousine and rode to Houghton's official residence on the Avenue d'Iéna. When the President arrived, he reminded Herter that if Khrushchev brought up the U-2 at the Summit, he intended to suggest that they "talk privately about this."

•

Khrushchev had walked down the same red airport carpet the day before, waved his gray fedora and pledged his delegation to "exert all effort to make the conference a success" in spite of the "influential circles trying to revive the Cold War."

As with Eisenhower, the past two weeks had been among the most difficult he had spent as head of government: "My visit to the United States . . . had seemed to herald a promising shift in U.S. policy toward our country. But now, thanks to the U-2, the honeymoon was over." Twice in the past fortnight, he had felt deliberately abused by the Americans. On May Day, they had violated Soviet airspace at a time of good relations. He probably had to overrride opposition from more belligerent colleagues to declare that he was "willing to accept" that the President had not known of the incursion.

Then Eisenhower not only avowed that he had authorized the flight but suggested that he might do it again because Soviet secrecy gave America the right to violate Soviet airspace in peacetime. After this, the Presidium barred Marshal Vershinin's trip to Washington. Khrushchev's blood enemy Mao Tse-tung was invited to Moscow for the first time in three years. (He refused.) The Soviet press launched a fierce campaign against "American aggression." At Gorky Park, Khrushchev had confessed that the Americans had placed him in a "very difficult position." Stalin would never have made such a reference to internal Kremlin politics—or pleaded with the American Ambassador to help him get out of his ordeal.

What to do about the Summit? Khrushchev had won colleagues' approval to go ahead to Paris and to go early, presumably to meet privately with Eisenhower and establish whether the conference and the President's trip to Russia might still be saved. But a price was imposed: for the Summit and Eisenhower's trip to proceed, Khrushchev must first win the President's public apology for sending the U-2 and a confession that America had no right to violate Soviet borders.

"With our relations falling to pieces, we couldn't possibly offer our hospitality to someone who had already, so to speak, made a mess at his host's table," Khrushchev said later. "To receive Eisenhower without first hearing him apologize would be an intolerable insult to the leadership of our country."

•

Khrushchev spent Saturday night at the former royal hunting lodge at Brunoy that served as the Soviet Ambassador's country retreat. While he slept, his government gave itself one more propaganda victory in space by launching *Sputnik IV* with a four-ton dummy aboard. Keith Glennan of NASA wrote in his diary, "Here we are again—the Russians are successful in launching something for Ike's benefit as he steps out of his plane in Paris."

On Sunday morning, Khrushchev ate a large breakfast, strolled down the lane and used a scythe to help a Frenchman cut hay. The farmer told reporters, "Monsieur Khrushchev has a fair cutting motion, but as he is a stout gentleman, his stomach interfered with his swing." Then Khrushchev rode into Paris to call on de Gaulle, accompanied by his Defense Minister, Marshal Rodion Malinovsky.

Fat, diabetic, with heavy black eyebrows and a resounding voice, the Marshal had been added to the Soviet delegation just a day before Khrushchev left Moscow. Diplomats and newsmen noticed that he stuck to Khrushchev "like a leech." They guessed that he had been sent by the Presidium to report on Khrushchev's behavior and make sure that Khrushchev was not taken in by Eisenhower and the West. Perhaps just as likely, Khrushchev was happy to have Malinovsky at his side as a witness who could affirm for Kremlin colleagues Khrushchev's wise statesmanship in Paris.

Born in 1898 in Odessa, Malinovsky joined the Czarist Army at sixteen and fought in France. As a commander in the Ukraine during the Second World War, he became friends with Khrushchev, who in 1957 chose him to replace Marshal Zhukov, perhaps because he appeared to lack Zhukov's threatening magnetism and ambition.

Malinovsky was nonetheless the leader and spokesman of a military that was unenthusiastic about Khrushchev's overtures to the West, seething over his defense cuts and outraged by the U-2—especially the humiliating public revelation that they had been unable to stop the planes for four years. It was not for nothing that his presence in Paris might have made Khrushchev nervous.

•

At the Elysée Palace, a band played a salute. Cavalrymen of the Garde Republicaine raised sabers to helmets when Khrushchev's car pulled up. In March, conferring with Khrushchev in Paris and Rambouillet, de Gaulle had found him "friendly, alert and nimble." When together they learned of the second French atomic test, Khrushchev said, "I understand your joy . . . but, you know, it's very expensive!" At the end of the trip, Khrushchev pledged his "enthusiastic presence" at the Summit in May.

Now as they met in the Presidential chamber, de Gaulle found Khrushchev "a character so changed in identity and meaning as to belong to the realm of Russian fiction." De Gaulle looked on espionage, as on most matters, with an air of worldly indifference. French intelligence had exploited some of the harvest from U-2 missions, and when de Gaulle was shown U-2 photographs of Russia in 1959, he had had the good manners not to ask how they had been taken.

The previous day, Arthur Lundahl had come to the Palace to brief de Gaulle on the U-2. Briefings by CIA men were not a novel experience for Western European leaders: when an agent named Smith once introduced himself to Adenauer, the Chancellor sighed, *"Immer Schmidt"* ["Always Smith"]. Lundahl tailored his seventy-minute briefing to what the CIA knew of de Gaulle's values and interests; knowing the old General's eyesight was poor, he brought along a magnifying glass. De Gaulle was "deeply impressed and very grateful."

Today the French President listened as Khrushchev ranted and raved. Why did Eisenhower have to admit he knew about the flights? This showed not American honesty but contempt for the Soviet Union! He handed de Gaulle a six-page statement of his terms for the Summit to proceed. All four leaders must pledge not to violate other nations' sovereignty. The United States must condemn its past acts of "inadmissible provocation," punish those guilty and renounce further such provocations. If these conditions were met, Khrushchev would do "everything" to aid the meeting's success. If not, he could not sit down with the leader of a country "which has made perfidy the basis of its policy toward the Soviet Union."

Khrushchev did not ordinarily express himself to foreign leaders by handing them a typed document. Had the statement been drafted in the Kremlin beforehand and Khrushchev sworn to present it to de Gaulle? That way, he would not have the chance for impulsive concessions. Or perhaps, if he intended to bargain with Eisenhower over his terms for attending the Summit, he might have thought that written demands might strengthen his position.

De Gaulle took off his thick spectacles and laid down the paper. He told Khrushchev that he "could not seriously expect" that Eisenhower would apologize to him. That sort of thing was just not done by responsible heads of government.

•

In his bedroom upstairs at the Ambassador's residence, Eisenhower awoke from a nap. At one o'clock, he went downstairs for lunch with the Houghtons, the Herters, Goodpaster and John Eisenhower. Theodore Achilles of the State Department reported that Khrushchev had put on "quite a demonstration" with de Gaulle: if the United States didn't apologize for sending the U-2, he wouldn't remain in Paris. This alarmed most of the diners, but not the President, who declared, "This is no time to be bulldozed."

Now he evinced little but anger at Khrushchev. It was Khrushchev who had tricked his administration into public deception and embarrassing uncoordination, renewing the old slander that Eisenhower could not control his own government. Serious leaders did not play such juvenile games. For years, America had flown the U-2 into Russia. Then at the moment before the Summit, Khrushchev had inflated the matter into a cause célèbre.

Eisenhower later reasoned that Khrushchev had probably deduced that he would not get his way on Berlin. Perhaps his military or the Chinese had exerted great pressure to renounce détente. Perhaps he had grown nervous that his own people might welcome the American President too warmly. The ultimatum given de Gaulle suggested to Eisenhower that, whatever his motive, Khrushchev was using the U-2 as a pretext to ruin the Summit and convince the world that the Americans were at fault.

The previous evening, Livingston Merchant had dined at the Palais d'Orsay with Selwyn Lloyd, the British Foreign Minister. Lloyd had said, "A détente suits us," and urged that Eisenhower have a "long, confessional talk" with Khrushchev: "Confession is good for the soul." Merchant had replied that he "could not imagine the President being in a confessional frame of mind."

Merchant was right. Eisenhower had by now come to look on the Summit as a duty: "It might prove unpleasant, but I had no intention of evading it. Indeed I welcomed the opportunity to uncover more Soviet hypocrisy."

•

After lunch, the President went to the Elysée for a formal meeting with de Gaulle, Macmillan and Adenauer. The Chancellor was in Paris to ride herd on his allies as they bargained over Germany. Eisenhower noted that he and his Summit partners had gone back a long way together: "I don't know about anybody else, but I myself am getting older."

"You don't look it," said a smiling de Gaulle.

"I hope that no one is under the illusion that I'm going to crawl on my knees to Khrushchev."

"No one is under that illusion." De Gaulle noted Khrushchev's threat to attack U-2 bases in Turkey, Japan and elsewhere. Eisenhower grimly replied, "Rockets can travel in two directions." Before the meeting's end, the Frenchman told him, "With us it is easy. You and I are tied together by history."

•

Back at the residence, Eisenhower assembled Herter, Bohlen, Tommy Thompson, Merchant, Foy Kohler and Goodpaster to assay Khrushchev's threat: "We must consider whether it would be better to break the conference off ourselves."

Thompson said that if that was to be the decision, they had better do it over something other than spy flights: "Khrushchev may be taking a reading with our allies to test our resolution on this." He noted that Khrushchev was "vulnerable at home over his impulsiveness." The United States could say it "could not negotiate with a man who uses language of this kind in a serious conference."

Eisenhower wondered aloud why Khrushchev had not issued his threat five days ago, before everyone had taken the trouble of coming to Paris. If Khrushchev simply wanted a four-power statement deploring espionage, that was acceptable. "We will not go beyond that to forswear specific activities unilaterally, however."

Merchant: "All things considered, it would be better to have Mr. Khrushchev walk out of the conference than the President."

Bohlen proposed informing the Russians at once that they had learned about Khrushchev's demarche and that if it was presented, the United States would have to stand firm: "The Russians are trying to get us to grovel—or to assert a legal right to overfly, which they will challenge as untenable."

"Espionage is simply a practice that has been carried on throughout history," said the President. "It is up to the affronted country to defeat spies attempting to operate against them." Still he complained that the CIA had failed to recognize the "emotional, even pathological reaction of the Russians" to violations of their frontiers.

He wished to make a statement at the opening of the Summit tomorrow: "It could be quite simple. Everybody knows there has been espionage throughout history. For the Russians to demand that we forswear espionage while knowing that we are the victim of their espionage is completely unacceptable." Under the "right circumstances," he would be willing to renounce sending the U-2 into Russia again. Its use was over anyway.

•

At 4:30 P.M., Khrushchev called on Macmillan at the British Ambassador's residence. As Macmillan wrote in his diary, "He made a speech in violent terms, attacked the U.S.A., President Eisenhower, the Pentagon, reactionary and imperialist forces generally. . . . He said that his *friend* (bitterly repeated again and again), his friend Eisenhower had betrayed him."

•

At six, Eisenhower returned to the Elysée to meet with de Gaulle, Macmillan and their aides. Macmillan later recorded, "The French view was cynical but logical: the Conference was over. The Americans were more hopeful and thought it was largely bluster. The British thought the Conference might be saved if the President would take a reasonable line—especially undertake to make no more U-2 flights."

Eisenhower complained that Khrushchev had given his protest and ultimatum to the other two leaders, but not to him. The U-2 business was "distasteful and disagreeable, but our relative intelligence position was so dangerous that I decided there was no recourse." He would not forswear espionage and "permanently tie the hands of the United States government for the single purpose of saving a conference."

Macmillan said that the whole affair showed "the necessity for doing something to relieve tensions." Perhaps Khrushchev was being so adamant because he had gotten into "something of a spot at the Kremlin."

De Gaulle told Eisenhower that if Khrushchev opened the meeting with a violent blast, the President should declare that everyone committed espionage—even the Soviets: "Obviously you cannot apologize, but you must decide how you wish to handle this. I will do everything I can to be helpful without being openly partisan." He resolved to open the Summit by calling on Eisenhower, who could then respond to the written protests Khrushchev had presented to his two allies.

•

At 8:20 P.M., the President joined the Houghtons and other houseguests for cocktails and dinner. Following his preference, the men all wore black tie. John Eisenhower kept hopping up from the table to arrange a private meeting between his father and Macmillan, but dinner was not served until nine. The President told John that it was getting too late and went upstairs to bed at 10:15.

Macmillan wrote in his diary, "Dinner quietly at Embassy. I went to bed with rather a heavy heart, but not without hope."

At the Soviet Embassy on the Left Bank, Khrushchev was furious. He had flown to Paris two days early. He had said at Gorky Park that he expected to have a private meeting with Eisenhower in Paris before the Summit. As the aggrieved party, he felt he should not be the one to have to call on Eisenhower. He could not understand why the President had not made a single attempt to see him.

•

At a studio on Times Square, New York, Richard Nixon sat down for a four-hour late-night television interview with David Susskind. He explained how essential the U-2 flights had been to American security: "Now that is why these flights were made in the first place. That is why an indication has been made that such activities may have to continue in the future. Let's suppose that as a result of what happened here, that we say that since this flight was discovered, the United States will announce to Mr. Khrushchev, 'Well, since this plane has been knocked down, we're going to discontinue activities of this sort.' Look at the position this puts the United States in—and our allies."

But renouncing the flights was exactly what Eisenhower was planning to do on Monday morning in Paris. Americans later cited Nixon's remarks as further proof of uncoordination in the Eisenhower government. In Moscow, a Soviet spokesman called them "brazen and shameless"—evidence that President Eisenhower intended to wreck the Summit.

●

In Paris, Thomas Gates concluded that the Summit was about to collapse and fracture relations with the Soviet Union. Especially with the President, the Secretary of State, himself and other top officials in Paris, he thought it vital to increase American military readiness for such a crisis. After clearing his decision with Eisenhower and Herter, he moved from his suite in the Ritz Hotel to a command post in the Houghton residence, where he stayed for most of the night.

Shortly after midnight, word was flashed from Paris to put U.S. forces on alert. Such alerts were ranked from one to five—from a practice drill to the brink of war: in Washington, the Joint Chiefs decreed a Code Three. Around the world, soldiers, sailors and airmen manned their battle stations. A civilian radio announcer near Lowry Air Force Base in Denver terrified citizens: "All fighter pilots F-101 and fighter pilots F-102: Code Three Alert! Hotcake One and Hotcake Six scramble at Lowry immediately!"

In Washington, reporters demanded to know whether some general had tried to seize power while civilian leaders were in Paris—or whether some secret conflict between Eisenhower and Khrushchev had thrown the world on the precipice of war. Unprepared, the Pentagon press office could not tell them. Only later did it explain that a military exercise had been staged.

"The timing of the exercise was just a shade worse than sending off the U-2 on its perilous mission two weeks before the Summit," wrote Walter Lippmann. "If the alert was concerned with possible surprise attack, when in the name of common sense would there be less danger of a surprise attack on the Western world than when Mr. Khrushchev in person was in Paris?"

"An extraordinarily reckless act," said Senator Stephen Young, Democrat of Ohio. "What seems to be the Eisenhower concept of the Presidency . . . frequently by remote control from Augusta and Gettysburg, and frequently altogether at the direction of subordinates, is not sufficient for 1960 and this grim period of international anarchy."

●

In Paris, the rising sun shone on the windshields of Citroëns and Dauphines moving down the Champs-Elysées and Avenue d'Iéna.

"One of the things I had forgotten about Paris is the amount of noise caused by the traffic in the streets," John Eisenhower wrote in his diary. "At times during the day, this seems rather a pleasant sound— but not at 5:15 in the morning with the grinding of gears from the trucks."

It was Monday, May 16, 1960. The day of the long-awaited Summit conference was here.

At 7:30 A.M., Khrushchev emerged from his embassy. Trailed by his Paris Ambassador, Sergei Vinogradov, and nervous gendarmes, he strolled into a specialty food store and boomed, "Good morning, ladies and gentlemen!" After looking over the produce and wine, he walked outside, patted a female student on the head and cross-examined a worker sitting atop a cement mixer, just as he had during the building of Moscow in the 1930s.

Harold Macmillan had scarcely slept all night. Deploring the un-civilized hour, he went to the American residence at eight o'clock. As he later wrote in his diary, he ate breakfast with the President in an upstairs sitting room "with the door open and two French footmen in cotton gloves serving a series of rather improbable dishes. The Presi-dent, after consuming some 'cereals' and (I think) some figs, was given a steak and some jelly. I was fortunate enough to get a boiled egg.

"I thought Ike depressed and uncertain. The conversation was rather strained. I made it clear that we stood absolutely together ... and it was just bad luck that the Americans, after a great run of suc-cesses, had suffered this set-back. Anyway, the only thing was to make the best of things together. Ike seemed to cheer up at this, but still didn't know what to do."

More bad news: Khrushchev had sent word that he wanted the first session of the Summit to begin at eleven, not ten. The four leaders should not meet alone with translators, as planned, but with two ad-visers each. This suggested that Khrushchev expected to issue another *Diktat* that might be reported back to Moscow to show that he had been adequately belligerent.

Goodpaster and Herter brought in their draft of Eisenhower's opening Summit statement. Macmillan thought it "much too trucu-lent." It did not clarify whether the United States still claimed the right to fly into the Soviet Union or not. The President said, "One thing is very clear in my mind: until we get to satellites, we will not do this kind of overflying any more." Macmillan noted that Khrushchev's main grievance was the American threat to keep up the flights. Removing it would be of great value.

As Macmillan later recalled, "A lot of people began to crowd into the room and argue"—his confidential aide Philip de Zulueta, Selwyn Lloyd, John Eisenhower, Bohlen, Merchant, Kohler, Gates and Hagerty. They pitched in on the President's draft. "The President was drawing upon the ideas of all, regardless of station," John Eisenhower wrote in his diary. "The spirit of all was unmistakable and the President never lost his sense of humor about the thing. Indeed, at times of crisis such as this, the President would be at his best, always seeming to keep matters in their perspective and with a little surprised detachment."

The Prime Minister, with his nineteenth-century conception of proper statecraft, was less impressed: "There was great confusion, and some bitterness. Actually, I felt that the Americans were in considerable disarray. However, the phrase was finally agreed 'in point of fact, these flights were suspended after the recent incident *and are not* to be resumed.' " Macmillan and his aides departed.

Followed by Herter and Gates, the President went downstairs. His son noted that "after this grueling couple of hours, he walked with amazing bounce." Before the limousines departed for the Elysée Palace, Christian Herter cabled Douglas Dillon in Washington:

MOUNTING EVIDENCE SUGGESTS SOVIETS INTEND WRECK CONFERENCE AT OPENING SESSION ON U-2 ISSUE. PLEASE INFORM VICE PRESIDENT. THIS MORNING'S MEETING WHICH AT KHRUSHCHEV'S REQUEST HAS BEEN TRANSFORMED INTO THREE A SIDE AND NOT FOUR HEADS ALONE WITH INTERPRETERS AS PLANNED SHOULD BE DECISIVE.

•

At the Palace, Khrushchev and his colleagues were first to arrive. De Gaulle took them up the grand stairway to the small green and gold chamber once used by Louis XV and his mistress, the Marquise de Pompadour, for intimate dining. Khrushchev sat down with Gromyko, Malinovsky and de Gaulle's aides at the green-draped round table. He felt anger "building up inside me like an electric force which could be discharged in a great flash at any moment."

Three minutes later, de Gaulle brought in the British: Macmillan and Khrushchev shook hands. Three minutes after that, the Americans: Eisenhower and his party greeted their British and French allies. They merely nodded to Khrushchev and the Russians, who by now were muttering among themselves like the opposite side in a divorce hearing.

The twenty-four men took their places. Sitting with his back to French windows overlooking the garden, Eisenhower was flanked by Gates, Herter and Colonel Vernon Walters, the diplomatic man-of-all-work who often translated for the President. Behind them sat Bohlen and Alexander Akalovsky. A senior American had asked Walters to bring a bugging device into the conference room. Walters had irked him by refusing: the French were skilled in detecting such devices. De Gaulle would be furious if he learned that the room had been bugged without his knowledge.

At the Americans' right, with their backs to more windows, were the Russians. Malinovsky wore his uniform with fifty-four decorations, including the American Legion of Merit. Next to the Russians were the French, including Premier Michel Debré and Foreign Minister Maurice Couve de Murville. Next to the French were the British, including Selwyn Lloyd and Sir Frederick Hoyer-Millar, the Defense Minister.

At 11:01 A.M., the doors behind the French President swung closed. He said, "We are gathered here for the Summit Conference. Yesterday I received a statement from one of the participants, Mr. Khrushchev, which I conveyed verbally to the other participants, President Eisenhower and Mr. Macmillan. Does anyone therefore wish to say anything?"

"*Da!*" cried Khrushchev, springing to his feet. "I would like the floor."

"I would also like to make a short statement," said Eisenhower.

De Gaulle ruled that as a chief of state as well as government, Eisenhower should be first to be heard, but Khrushchev objected: "I was the first to ask for the floor and I would like my request to be granted. Permit me to address you with the following statement—" De Gaulle raised his eyebrows and turned to Eisenhower, who nodded with faint disgust.

Khrushchev put on his rimless glasses. His left eyebrow twitched. The hand holding his papers trembled as Malinovsky glowered (Bohlen's phrase) "like a picture of dominating evility." For forty-five minutes, Khrushchev read angrily aloud, pausing for translation and gulps of water. He inveighed against the "aggressive" flight, the earlier incursions, the "ridiculous" cover stories and Eisenhower's avowal that "American flights over Soviet territory have been and remain the calculated policy of the United States."

Eisenhower ground his teeth; his bald head and neck turned an angry shade of pink and he scrawled a note to Herter: "I am going to take up smoking again."* Bohlen hissed, "We can't sit still for this." De Gaulle affected polite boredom: when Khrushchev bellowed too loudly, he said, "The acoustics in this room are excellent. We can all hear the Chairman." Khrushchev glared back over his spectacles and pressed on:

"How is it possible to productively negotiate and examine the questions facing the Conference when the U.S. government and the President himself have not only failed to condemn this provocative act ... but declared that such acts will *continue?*" Malinovsky grimaced and nodded furiously.

"We want to participate in the talks on an equal footing—and that is only possible if the United States declares that it will not violate Soviet borders, that it deplores the acts undertaken in the past and will punish those directly guilty of such actions." Evidently the current American government did not understand "that there is no other way but peaceful coexistence." Thus they should "postpone this conference for about six to eight months." By then, Eisenhower would no longer be President. Unless Eisenhower apologized for his provocations, Khrushchev was going to shun him until he left office.

"I wish to address the people of the United States of America. I am deeply convinced that all levels of American society do not want war. The exception is just a small, frantic group in the Pentagon and militarist circles who benefit from the arms race and reap huge profits."

He thanked de Gaulle and Macmillan for helping to arrange the Summit. "We regret that this meeting has been torpedoed by the reactionary circles of the United States. ... We regret that it has not achieved the results expected by all nations of the world. Let the disgrace and blame for this rest with those who have proclaimed a bandit policy toward the Soviet Union! ...

"As everybody knows, President Eisenhower and I agreed to exchange visits. ... We were preparing to give a good welcome to this

* He had given up the habit in 1949.

honored guest." But now the Soviet people could not receive him with "proper cordiality." So the visit should be postponed. "I believe that both President Eisenhower and the American people will understand me correctly. On its part, the Soviet government will continue to do its utmost to relax international tension and resolve problems that still divide us today."

The only sound in the room was the ticking of the gold clock at the center of the table.

•

As Eisenhower prepared to speak, Herter passed him a note: "Do not let K interrupt, as he will try to." Containing his anger, the President said, "I had been previously informed of the sense of the statement just read by Premier Khrushchev." The Premier had been misinformed. The American government had not threatened more overflights. "The actual statements go no further than to say that the United States will not shirk its responsibility to safeguard against surprise attack. In point of fact, these flights were suspended after the recent incident and are not to be resumed. . . .

"I have come to Paris to seek agreements with the Soviet Union which would eliminate the necessity for *all* forms of espionage, including overflights. I see no reason to use this incident to disrupt the Conference." He would propose a new Open Skies plan under which mutual surveillance missions would be flown by the UN.

"We of the United States are here to consider in good faith the important problems before this Conference. We are prepared either to carry this point no further, or to undertake bilateral conversations between the United States and the U.S.S.R. while the main conference proceeds."

•

Looking stricken, Macmillan said, "I naturally deplore that after the long and painful ascent to the Summit, we now find this dark cloud upon us. I quite understand the feelings that have been aroused by this incident. But I would like to appeal to you and make two points. First, what has happened, has happened. Second, we all know that espionage . . . is a disagreeable fact of life, and also that most forms of espionage involve violation of national sovereignty."

Macmillan noted that Khrushchev's main concern had been that aerial incursions were the calculated policy of the United States. Now the President had made clear that overflights would not be resumed. "I am glad Mr. Khrushchev did not propose abandonment, but postponement only. However I would suggest to him, as the French proverb goes, *ce qui est déféré est perdu* [what is postponed is lost]. A long delay after all our efforts ... will itself bring great harm to the cause for which we have worked so hard."

•

By now, de Gaulle was angry. He told Khrushchev, "Before you left Moscow and after the U-2 was shot down, I sent my ambassador to see you to ask whether this meeting should be held or should be postponed. You knew everything then that you know now. You told my ambassador that this conference should be held and that it would be fruitful.... You have brought Mr. Macmillan here from London, General Eisenhower from the United States and have put me to serious inconvenience to organize and attend a meeting which your intransigence will make impossible....

"Overflights, whether by aircraft, missile or satellite are, of course, a serious matter and they increase tensions. But the concept of these overflights is bound to change and they are bound to become a natural phenomenon. At this moment, a Soviet satellite is going around the world and it crosses French skies eighteen times a day.... These satellites can take photographs, and tomorrow they may be in a position to launch terrible destruction.

"We should examine this question in its proper framework, that of disarmament and international tension.... It would not serve humanity to break up on the basis of a parochial incident." He proposed a day's recess.

•

Khrushchev shook his head. Eisenhower had not apologized for his "aggressive act." In fact, "he spoke of its necessity and then tried to justify it. Naturally we cannot agree to this. The President referred to Open Skies. I heard about Open Skies in Geneva in 1955. We declared then that we were opposed to it, and I can repeat it now: we will allow no one—but *no one*—to violate our sovereignty. A government must be master in its own house."

De Gaulle: "Yesterday that satellite you launched just before you left Moscow to impress us overflew the sky of France eighteen times without my permission. How do I know that you do not have cameras aboard which are taking pictures of my country?"

"Our latest *Sputnik* has no cameras."

"Well, how did you take those pictures of the far side of the moon which you showed us with such justifiable pride?"

"In that one I had cameras."

"Ah, in *that* one you had cameras! Pray continue."

"The United States has put one up that is photographing our country. We did not protest. Let them take as many pictures as they want."

"France has nothing to fear from photography."

Khrushchev said, "The idea of a recess is all right, but for how long? It is hard to say. We could take time for reflection and we might cool off. Paris has many wonderful shady chestnut groves where we can sit and think and perhaps something good will come out."

For the first time in eight months, he spoke directly to Eisenhower: "We don't understand what devil pushed you into doing this provocative act to us just before the Conference. If there had been no incident, we would have come here in friendship and the best possible atmosphere. I recall that at Camp David, the President and I said to call each other 'my friend.' And now these two friends have collided in the skies. Our rocket shot the plane down. Is this *good friendship?*" He raised his hands above his head: "As God is my witness, I come with clean hands and a pure soul."

(Eisenhower later said that when he heard Khrushchev say that, he almost choked.)

De Gaulle: "There are many devils in the world and it is the job of this Conference to exorcise them."

Eisenhower: "I cannot speak for my successor—"

Khrushchev: "Nor am I eternal."

"—and I do not know what decision the next President will make. However the flights will not be resumed not only for the duration of the Conference but for the entire duration of my term."

"For us that is not enough," said Khrushchev. "There is no reference to condemnation or regret for the insult made to us." Despite de Gaulle's request to the contrary, Khrushchev said he intended to publish his opening statement: "Otherwise the Soviet people will think the United States has forced the Soviet Union to its knees by our coming to Paris and engaging in talks in the face of a threat.

"We don't want to aggravate relations. They require a great deal of improvement anyhow. But please understand that our internal politics requires this. It is a matter of honor." (Bohlen was astonished by Khrushchev's reference to internal politics and thought it showed the severe pressure on him inside the Kremlin.)

"Please understand: how can I invite as a dear guest the leader of a country which has committed an aggressive act against us? ... Even my small grandson would ask his grandpa, 'How could we welcome as an honored guest one who represents a country that sends planes to overfly us?' ... We are not prepared to come as poor relatives to beg NATO members for mercy and beg your leader not to violate our frontiers.... We will defend ourselves and our honor with force, if necessary—and we have the necessary force.... As to bilateral talks, we would agree if any other party would want them."

Any other party did not exclude the United States.

Macmillan said, "It would be desirable to fix a time for the meeting tomorrow because the press might think the Conference has broken down, which it may." Khrushchev corrected him: "This is not the beginning of the Conference. That has not started yet. We regard this meeting as preliminary."

•

It was 2:06 P.M. Escorted by de Gaulle, Khrushchev and his entourage marched downstairs to his limousine in the palace courtyard. Khrushchev slapped his driver on the back and said, "Mine is the only ruddy face. Eisenhower's is white, and Macmillan's has no color."

Upstairs Eisenhower exclaimed, "What kind of apology does that man *want?*" Paternally de Gaulle took him by the arm: "I do not know what Khrushchev is going to do or what is going to happen. But ... I want you to know that I am with you to the end." Eisenhower was moved: it had taken this crisis to move his ally from his usual icy assertions of independence. As he left the Palace, he told Walters, "That de Gaulle is really quite a guy."

Back at the residence, John Eisenhower waited for news. As the hours passed, he had been thankful that the conference had not broken up. When the President's open car pulled up the driveway, he looked out the window: "Andy Goodpaster was riding in the back seat with the Boss, and Andy's grim look told the story that things had not been a success."

The President marched into the house and cried, "You might have thought *we'd* done a Hungary!" The bland facade maintained for three hours by superhuman effort now fell away. He stomped about the living room: "I'm just fed up! I'm just fed up!" He stormed against the impudence and hypocrisy: Khrushchev was nothing but a "son-of-a-bitch" putting on an act to impress the Kremlin—"completely intransigent and insulting to the United States." Had Khrushchev revoked the invitation to Russia? Fine. That only saved *him* the bother of turning it down himself!

Bohlen declared, "It was the coldest gathering of human beings I believe I've ever seen." He reminded the President that the Russians were going to publish Khrushchev's declamations. Eisenhower asked him to work with Hagerty on an American reply: the United States must not be drowned out in the propaganda battle to come.

"Luncheon itself was animated, since the group was still recovering from the drama of the morning's activities," John Eisenhower wrote in his diary. "Under the surface, we all felt the impact of the insults, all harboring strong resentment and bewilderment at Khrushchev's violent conduct." After lunch, the President approved the statement written by Bohlen and Hagerty. Then he went upstairs and slept.

•

Across the Seine at the Palais de Chaillot, a Soviet spokesman mopped his brow and read out the text of Khrushchev's morning statement for two thousand newsmen. At 4:30 P.M., Hagerty arrived to read the statement he and Bohlen had written in Eisenhower's name: "Mr. Khrushchev was left in no doubt by me that his ultimatum would never be acceptable to the United States. The only conclusion that can be drawn from his behavior this morning was that he came all the way from Moscow with the sole intention of sabotaging this meeting on which so much of the hopes of the world have rested."

"Well, Jim, is the Conference over?"

"I think it was left wide open when the meeting broke up."

"Has the machinery been set up to arrange a bilateral meeting between Mr. Khrushchev and Mr. Eisenhower?"

"The President made the offer. We have heard nothing from the Soviets."

•

The *New York Times:* "U.S.-SOVIET CLASH DISRUPTS SUMMIT TALKS/KHRUSHCHEV CANCELS EISENHOWER'S VISIT/U-2 SPY FLIGHTS ENDED, PRESIDENT REVEALS." The *Rochester* (New York) *Times-Union:* "America will not bow and scrape in appeasement of the rage, real or feigned, of a Communist tyrant." Senator Thomas Dodd: "A new all-time low has been hit in the world when a man of Khrushchev's record, having the blood of millions on his hand, can lecture a man like Dwight Eisenhower about morality."

John Kennedy called Khrushchev's threat to deal only with Eisenhower's successor a "clumsy attempt to divide us along partisan lines in an election year." Richard Nixon declared that whatever happened in Paris, the struggle between the Soviet and American ways of life would go on "for our lifetime, probably for this century."

Radio Moscow broadcast highlights of Khrushchev's Summit statement every half hour. *Izvestia* ran a cartoon showing the Statue of Liberty being replaced by a "Statue of Liberty of Espionage"—a figure of Francis Gary Powers. Soviet workers' meetings were staged to resolve that Eisenhower could not be welcomed to the Soviet Union. *Literaturnaya Gazeta* published an "open letter" from Sholokhov and other Soviet writers against American espionage. A film on American "atrocities" in Korea was run on the evening television news. The Voice of America was jammed for perhaps the first time since Camp David.

•

In Paris, at 5:15 Monday afternoon, Eisenhower awoke from his nap. John brought him a draft of a letter on the "events, or lack of them, at the Paris Summit" to be sent to allied leaders. The President invited de Gaulle and Macmillan for a drink that evening. Couve de Murville feared this would look too much like an anti-Khrushchev cabal, but Macmillan accepted.

At 6:30 P.M., Eisenhower donned his black tie and dinner jacket and walked downstairs. For a time he meditated alone in the living room, then strolled through the gardens, chatting with secretaries when Macmillan arrived. The Prime Minister had just seen de Gaulle, who was "charming but not amused." De Gaulle had told him that the Russians had decided in Moscow to wreck the Summit and there was no hope of saving it now.

In his diary, Macmillan wrote, "Eisenhower was relaxed but he talked very strongly against Khrushchev. He was a real S.O.B. He did not see what more he could do. He had gone a long way in his offer. He could not 'condemn' the action which he had authorized. . . . The demand for punishment was absurd. What more could he do? I said I supposed he could 'say he was sorry'—or, preferably, a formal diplomatic apology. But I really could not press Ike much further. His staff (including Herter) obviously thought he should have reacted more strongly or left the room himself. It was a terrible thing for their President to be insulted in this way."

After Macmillan departed, the President and his party dined and talked until near midnight. Someone suggested that Eisenhower play golf tomorrow to show the world that he had not been unnerved by Khrushchev. But golf was ruled out: there had been too many stories about the President on the links while vital decisions were being made.

That evening, Macmillan went to the Soviet Embassy: "Khrushchev was polite, but quite immovable. The Marshal (silent, immovable, hardly even blinking) and Gromyko (also silent) as well as others were also present." Macmillan presumed that a nearby lamp contained a bugging device. As he left the Embassy, he muttered, "The Soviets may know how to make *Sputniks* but they certainly don't know how to make trousers!"

●

Tuesday morning, May seventeenth. John Eisenhower had resolved to have breakfast with his father, "but I didn't realize what I was in for." When he walked into the President's sitting room just after eight, he found him with Herter, Goodpaster and Hagerty discussing tactics for the day. His father had not slept soundly but looked "very much refreshed."

The President, de Gaulle and Macmillan were to meet at the Elysée at ten. There Eisenhower would ask that a full-scale session of the Summit be held. If Khrushchev stayed away, he would have to bear the stigma of wrecking the Conference. The President's aides had heard that some of the Russians were "peddling the idea around town" that suspending U-2 flights had largely solved the problem and that perhaps just a telephone call from Eisenhower to express regret would keep the Summit going. Another report had it that Khrushchev's flight crew had checked out of their quarters. John recorded, "All of this foment by the Soviets is an effort to create a war of nerves and force us into acceding to their demands."

Outside the Soviet Embassy at 9:25 A.M., Khrushchev told reporters, "Unless President Eisenhower apologizes and admits America made an aggressive action against the Soviet Union, I will return home."

At the Palace at ten, the three Western leaders resolved that de Gaulle should send Khrushchev a written invitation to a three o'clock session and ask for a written reply. After their meeting, Eisenhower returned with Macmillan to the British Embassy, where they drank coffee under the chestnut trees. The President suggested a drive in the country. In his diary, Macmillan wrote, "Ike's object was clear—ingeniously clear. If Khrushchev must break up the Summit Conference, there is no reason to let him break up the Anglo-American alliance."

Soon Eisenhower's Presidency would be over. This morning, he wished to show Macmillan where it had all begun. A call was made to the office of General Lauris Norstad, current laird of the château in Marnes-la-Coquette where the Eisenhowers had lived when he was Supreme Commander of SHAPE. Twenty-five minutes later, the open car drove up the carriageway. Eisenhower took Macmillan into the backyard and through the rooms of the house.

In 1951, Cabot Lodge and other American leaders had trooped here asking him to run for President. Eisenhower had said that he would respond to a "genuine" draft but would not otherwise lift a finger. That December, Lodge told him that he had better come home and run or else Senator Robert Taft would lock up the nomination: Isolationism would be alive and well. Again the General refused. He privately told his friend William Robinson of the *New York Herald Tribune,* "The seeker is never so popular as the sought. People want what they can't get."

In February 1952, in the living room of this house, the aviator Jacqueline Cochran had shown the Eisenhowers film of a midnight rally at Madison Square Garden where fifteen thousand had stamped their feet and cried, "We want Ike!" Mamie wept. When the lights were turned up, Cochran raised her glass and said, "To the President." Eisenhower later said that the film brought home to him the depth of the American longing for a change. With his self-possession cracked and tears streaming down his cheeks, he spoke of his father and mother and said, "You can go tell Bill Robinson that I'm going to run."

Now Eisenhower and Macmillan drove to the town hall. A messenger was sent to find his old friend, the rotund Mayor Jean Minot, who came running into the square with a two-day growth of beard: "My dear President! How are you, and how is Madame?" Entertained by the Mayor's surprise, Eisenhower explained that his wife had stayed behind in America: "I would like you to meet the Prime Minister of Great Britain."

In halting Etonian French, Macmillan said that the President would like to see the chamber in which he had been made an honorary citizen of Marnes-la-Coquette. The Mayor took them there and then to his office, which was adorned with pictures of de Gaulle, Eisenhower and Louis Pasteur, a son of the region. He declared that the town's two most distinguished citizens were the President and Maurice Chevalier, but declined to state a preference. Eisenhower and Macmillan shook hands with children gathered around their car. The Mayor said, "I regret you cannot come back and see us."

Eisenhower replied, "After January, maybe I'll come back to Paris and stay awhile."

While Eisenhower and Macmillan toured the countryside, Selwyn Lloyd asked Christian Herter why the President could not say he was sorry for the U-2. Herter replied that he could not because he was not.

•

Meanwhile Khrushchev had also decided to take a country drive. Malinovsky said, "Let's go visit the place where our unit was quartered during World War One." Khrushchev liked the idea. Malinovsky had shed his blood to defend Paris from the Germans. Perhaps this gesture would arouse French sympathy for the Soviet position on Germany.

While Paris drivers pounded their horns, Soviet limousines roared eastward toward the battlefield of the Marne. They were stopped by a linden tree that had fallen across the highway. Khrushchev borrowed an axe from the road crew and chopped away, knowing that it "wouldn't do our delegation's image any harm" for people to see that the Soviet government was composed of workers.

At Pleur-sur-Marne, Malinovsky found his old landlady, whom he still called "young Marie Louise." His old roommate and she had been lovers. Her son brought wine and cheese and she listened uneasily as Malinovsky told war stories. Khrushchev and Malinovsky walked outside, where villagers had joined the cows and chickens. Someone cried,

"Of course we remember you! You had a Russian bear in your outfit, didn't you?" The Marshal laughed and told Khrushchev that his unit had picked up a bear cub on the way to France.

Malinovsky asked about a beautiful young woman who had worked in the local tavern. Someone said, "He remembers!" But the woman was long gone. Khrushchev observed that she had "obviously left a mark" on Malinovsky. During the Second World War, the Marshal had used to tell him stories about her and said, "I've loved some beautiful girls in my time."

Two motorcycle messengers from the Elysée thundered into the barnyard and broke the idyll. Khrushchev tore open the envelope and read the three o'clock invitation. He and Malinovsky broke all speed limits to get back to Paris.

•

At three, Eisenhower, Macmillan, de Gaulle and their aides sat down at the conference table in the Palace. De Gaulle said that no reply had been received from Khrushchev, who at last report was "kissing babies on the street and generally electioneering for the French Communist Party."

In fact, Khrushchev was evidently relaxing in a hot bath at the Soviet Ambassador's residence. At 3:20, one of his aides called the Elysée: Was this session to be an actual Summit meeting or another preliminary session to clarify the discussion on Monday? If the former, Khrushchev could not attend, because Eisenhower had not yet apologized for the U-2.

When Couve de Murville brought back this message, de Gaulle barked that Khrushchev had been invited in writing and must reply in writing. That way, there would be written evidence to show the world who had killed the Summit. This was conveyed to Khrushchev, who presumably sent his reply from the bathtub: he wanted an answer to his question and would not respond in writing.

De Gaulle: "Tell him that it is the custom between *civilized* nations to respond to written communications by written communications."

De Gaulle and Eisenhower wished to notify the world that it was all over. But with tears in his eyes, Macmillan asked to let him appeal once more to Khrushchev to return to the table. Two years of work for peace were about to collapse in "the worst crisis my country has experienced since the war." All over the British Isles, trusting people were praying in their churches. Failure of the Summit would devastate their hopes and aspirations. As leaders, they three owed it to their people's passionate yearning for peace to make one final effort.

Eisenhower whispered to Herter, "You know, poor old Hal is very upset about this, and I think we might go as far as to meet him on this one point." Bohlen scribbled Herter a fierce note that emotional appeals were the wrong approach to use with Soviet leaders. De Gaulle said that he could not agree with Macmillan: the proposal was "too Byzantine." They must never forget that the Byzantine Empire caved in under similar intrigues and roundabout methods.

At 4:15 P.M., a written message arrived from Khrushchev: the Soviet delegation would join them only if the Americans opted "to condemn the treacherous intrusion of American military aircraft into Soviet airspace, publicly to express their regrets for this intrusion, to punish those responsible and to give assurances that in future, there will be no further intrusions."

De Gaulle, Macmillan and Eisenhower wrote out a communiqué: "The absence of Premier Khrushchev was noted. President de Gaulle noted that in these circumstances, the planned discussions could not take place."

At the Soviet Embassy, Khrushchev learned that his terms had been definitely refused. He later said that he had hoped de Gaulle and Macmillan would press Eisenhower to apologize for the U-2: "De Gaulle always unswervingly guarded the honor of France and the French people, so we suspected that, secretly at least, he was sympathetic to our defense of our honor." And he had known how eager Macmillan had been for this Summit. Now he knew that the British and French were standing firm beside their American ally.

•

Back at the Houghton residence, Eisenhower was "more interested in Khrushchev's leaving town than anything else." Mamie called from the White House, concerned about his morale. She believed that Khrushchev had canceled his invitation to Russia out of exasperation that John had banned the grandchildren from going on the trip. John Hay Whitney asked the President if he had been concerned about Macmillan's emotional pleas to press on after the Summit had obviously failed. "Not at all," said Eisenhower. "I know Harold well and that's just an act he puts on."

John Eisenhower, Ann Whitman and Vernon Walters set out for

dinner. After learning that the Eiffel Tower restaurant was closed, they found a spot in the Bois de Boulogne. It did not open until 8:30 P.M., but, as John recorded, the Colonel's excellent French convinced the maître d'hôtel that he was "not involved with a bunch of rubes" and should bend the rules. At nine, Walters went back to work. His dining partners repaired to the Crillon Hotel for B-and-B's, which tasted to John like "straight benedictine."

At the Elysée, de Gaulle, Eisenhower and Macmillan met and issued a declaration that outstanding world questions must not be settled by force: they were ready to resume talks with the Russians "at any suitable time in the future." Macmillan returned to his embassy and wrote, "So ended—before it had ever begun—the Summit Conference."

At the Houghton residence, Eisenhower's doctor examined him before he retired, fearing that the turbulent two days had strained his patient's cardiac reserves.

•

In Moscow, tomorrow's *Izvestia* rumbled off the presses: "U.S.A. WRECKS SUMMIT MEETING." Macmillan and de Gaulle were ridiculed as puppets in Eisenhower's "clumsy" attempt to get Khrushchev to the Summit table without an apology. Millions of Soviets went to rallies and shouted epithets against the United States.

On the other side of the world, the *New York Times* proclaimed, "SUMMIT CONFERENCE BREAKS UP IN DISPUTE/WEST BLAMES KHRUSHCHEV'S RIGID STAND/HE INSISTS ON EISENHOWER SPYING APOLOGY." James Reston wrote, "What troubled Paris tonight was not primarily what President Eisenhower and Premier Khrushchev would do now, which nobody knows, but the realization that the two most powerful nations in the world are also the least experienced of the great powers—both subject to the element of accident, to the ingrained habits of the past and to the whims of personal pride and caprice." This was "the conference that everyone lost."

•

Wednesday morning, May eighteenth. While the President had breakfast, his aides debated how long he should remain in Paris. A week had been blocked out for the Summit, after which he was scheduled to fly to Lisbon for the state visit whose timing had so bothered Khrushchev. Now that the Conference had failed, he could not cool his heels in Paris for five days. A hasty series of calls between Paris, Lisbon and Washington moved up the Portuguese visit: he would leave tomorrow.

What to do today? Golf was out. A helicopter journey to Chartres had been planned, but the skies were dark with rain. Looking out the window, John Eisenhower could see the tip of the Eiffel Tower and hence saw "no reason why the chopper couldn't fly," but more prudent aides said no.

Instead the bubble top was attached to the President's limousine and he rode with Amory Houghton to Notre Dame. He stood in the soaring darkness of Sainte Chapelle and studied a picture of a gilded crown displayed only during Lent: "Well, by Lent next year, maybe I will be free to come." With the Summit in ruins, he was speaking more and more of retirement.

•

Khrushchev called on Macmillan at the British Embassy. The Prime Minister had hoped that Khrushchev would come alone, but he arrived "with all his followers or his 'tail,' as a Highland chief would have said." Khrushchev said that he maintained his desire for peaceful coexistence and another summit. He told Macmillan that he should have pressured Eisenhower to accept all of his terms.

Macmillan replied, "Do you really think that?"

Khrushchev thought he could tell "from the expression on his face" that Macmillan understood the Soviet position and merely defended his ally "to register his general solidarity with the United States." During a farewell visit with de Gaulle, Khrushchev bitterly denounced Eisenhower as "a second-rate fellow, a pawn in the hands of his services, incapable of commanding." De Gaulle sensed that he was "worried about what might ensue."

After Khrushchev left the Elysée, Eisenhower arrived with his son and Amory Houghton for lunch with de Gaulle. John wrote in his diary, "I had expressed a desire to go to this luncheon since I had not seen Le Grand Charlie yet on this trip. . . . The entire group went out to sit in the beautiful gardens of the Elysée Palace for coffee and brandy. . . . From the door of the Palace to the street could not be more than a five-iron shot. However, the foliage is such that . . . one has the impression of being ten miles out of town."

John noted that de Gaulle "seemed completely unperturbed by all these turns of events. Perhaps he had never put much stock in the Summit anyway."

•

In a packed, sweltering hall at the Palais de Chaillot, Khrushchev walked on stage and clasped his hands over his head. This provoked boos, applause and catcalls from the thousands in the audience: the *New Yorker*'s Janet Flanner called it "the noise and violence of a quasi-riot." Flanked by Gromyko and Malinovsky, Khrushchev stood behind a table and pounded it so hard that he toppled a bottle of mineral water:

"I have already been informed that Chancellor Adenauer sent here some of those Fascist bastards we didn't finish off at Stalingrad. We hit them so hard that we put them ten feet underground right away. If you boo us and attack us again, *look out!* We will hit you so hard that there won't be a squeal out of you!"

The crowd leapt from seats, shrieked and shook fists. Khrushchev reddened and veins coursed on the side of his head: "I am a representative of the great Soviet people, who under the leadership of Lenin and the Communist Party, accomplished the Great October Socialist Revolution, and—" He was drowned out, then: "I will not conceal my pleasure. I like coming to grips with the enemies of the working class and it is gratifying for me to hear the frenzy of these lackeys of imperialism."

Someone managed to shout a question: Why hadn't Khrushchev asked Eisenhower at Camp David to halt the U-2 flights? "I will answer that question with pleasure. When I was talking at Camp David with President Eisenhower, I almost opened my mouth to make that statement. The atmosphere was so convivial, with the President telling me to call him 'my friend' in English and calling me *'moi drug'* in Russian. Like a brother he was. It was then that I wanted to tell my friend that it was not nice to fly over a friend's territory without his permission.

"But then I thought better of it and decided, 'No, I am not going to tell him. There is something stinky about this friend of mine.' I did not broach the subject. And it turned out that I was right in my doubts, because we caught the American spy—like a thief, red-handed! We told the Americans that they act like thieves and they say, 'No, this is our policy. We have flown and will keep on flying over your territory.'

It's their *thief-like policy,* that's all! How could a summit conference be started under these conditions?"

Waving his fists, he cried, "To hear President Eisenhower, it would seem that the question of whether U.S. military planes will or will not fly over the U.S.S.R. depends on him and him alone. Just think—*what presumption!* Now he says they will not overfly—*what magnanimity!* This to be decided by us and us alone. We shall shoot such planes down. We shall deal shattering blows to the bases where they came from—and at those who set up the bases!"

At the American residence, Eisenhower read the text of Khrushchev's harangue as it came over the ticker and cried, "Incredible! Unbelievable!" At his embassy, Macmillan did the same and thought it "reminiscent of Hitler at his worst."

Western peoples were shocked, for modern leaders did not usually shout that way. Khrushchev himself had not orated in public with such raw passion almost since his days as Stalin's cheerleader in the thirties. But what was more important was what he did not say. He did not threaten to sign an immediate German peace treaty. Test ban talks in Geneva would proceed. Another summit should be held after Eisenhower was gone from power.

He declared, "This spy flight has affected relations between the U.S.S.R. and the United States. But in the end, it will be necessary to overcome its consequences and digest all of this. Relations must be normalized so the American and Soviet peoples can live not only in peace but friendship." Exhausted by the end of the two and a half hours, Khrushchev raised a glass of mineral water and cried, *"Vive la paix!"*

•

"It's a tragedy, a real tragedy," said a Soviet diplomat, adjourning with a British reporter to a café. "I was in Moscow just a few days ago. Everybody was rushing to Gorky Park to see the 'new American exhibition,' the remnants of the spy plane. People were furious and rather worried.

"Khrushchev had been telling them that there were warmongers and Cold War maniacs in America, but he trusted Eisenhower. A few, I don't mind telling you, whispered that this was un-Marxist, that Eisenhower was a class enemy like the rest of them. But Khrushchev kept on stretching points.

"Now everything has changed. He has come to the conclusion that Eisenhower may be a good man, for all he knows, but hopelessly weak and helpless and dominated by the CIA. . . . What the Americans proclaimed by refusing to make even the most routine apologies to us was that the Soviet Union was a totalitarian country *whose sovereignty it was not necessary to respect.* . . .

"And to think that only a fortnight ago, they were preparing to give Eisenhower a more tremendous reception—and a perfectly genuine one—than our country had ever given to *any* foreign statesman from either West or East. It was *that* which those Pentagon and Allen Dulles bastards were afraid of. . . .

"Eisenhower could have ended his Presidential career as the Man of Peace. Now, thanks to what he did these last few days, he will go down in history as one of the most absurd and feeble Presidents the United States has had. A General with no guts. One who allowed himself to be engineered into this mess by Allen Dulles, his CIA with its thirty thousand agents, the Pentagon and all that."

•

At four, Macmillan received Eisenhower at the British Embassy. He found the President "very upset at the turn of events, so I tried my best to comfort him." Then they went to the palace for a final session with de Gaulle. Later Macmillan wrote the Queen, "I shall not conceal from Your Majesty the shock and disappointment which I have sustained."

Back at the residence, Eisenhower read a telegram from his staff in Washington: "ALL REPORTS HERE BEAR OUT THE FACT THAT AMERICA IS SOLIDLY BEHIND YOU AND HOLDS HIGH PRAISE FOR YOUR MAGNIFICENT HANDLING OF A MOST DIFFICULT SITUATION."

By 7:45 P.M., he was in his white apron, broiling steaks in the little backyard for the guests of the household, the Jock Whitneys, the Thomas Gateses, the Llewellyn Thompsons and others. Laura Houghton had found barbecue equipment after much effort and apprehension. Cooking was therapy for Eisenhower: on hearing about Pearl Harbor, he went straight to the kitchen and made vegetable soup.

While the President fretted over the grill, Amory Houghton took pictures of the guests with his new Polaroid. When the steaks were ready, the President commanded the guests "to drop what they were doing and head for the dining room," as his son recorded. "The initiated knew this was not an idle utterance. Everyone had to be at his place so that the steaks, when served, would be perfection. So it was this evening."

After dinner, the men separated from the ladies and drank brandy in the living room. Earlier in the day, Eisenhower had received a message from Lyndon Johnson, Adlai Stevenson, House Speaker Sam Rayburn and Senator J. William Fulbright asking him to convey to Khrushchev their view that he should reconsider postponing the Summit until after the Presidential election. (They had not consulted John Kennedy.) The President thought this brazen interference with his conduct of foreign affairs and had them notified that the Summit had already collapsed.

Now Johnson's office called from Washington insisting that the message go to Khrushchev anyway. The President and his fellow diners suggested that Herter call the Majority Leader. Herter did, but Johnson irascibly maintained his demand: he had already announced on the Senate floor that Khrushchev would receive the telegram. Herter consulted Eisenhower, who gave in on condition that the message be delivered with a covering note that it represented the "unity of America." As John Eisenhower noted, "This useless exercise occupied enough time so that it was settled only by midnight."

For other Americans in Paris, the heat of the past four days was off. Arthur Lundahl had spent the week confined to a CIA safe house; only through the open window did he encounter the smells and sounds of Paris. After the Summit collapsed, he was finally allowed to emerge for a bowl of steaming French onion soup with Bissell's aide Jim Cunningham. Lundahl never learned why he was ordered to stand by in Paris: perhaps Eisenhower had wished to retain the option of presenting the U-2 photos at the Summit table.

"We never went to bed at all and had the wildest week in years," wrote Marina Sulzberger. "Chip [Bohlen] and the [Llewellyn] Thompsons some nights ending up at the LIDO (yes) and then at several places for 'just one more drink' and Chip at his wildest best and thriving as he usually does on action and crisis.... Joe [Alsop] too was wonderful and strangely he the prophet of doom when doom was more or less upon us optimistic as never before and glorying in the company of what Diana Cooper calls his camp followers. All those beautiful women he always has up his sleeve."

●

Thursday morning, May nineteenth. At seven, the President flew by helicopter to Orly Airport, where the French Air Force Band played "The Star Spangled Banner." John Eisenhower had long thought that the French played the anthem better than the Americans: "This time, the rendition was unusually meaningful. De Gaulle had stood by the Boss and had made it clear that he would continue to do so." They boarded *Air Force One,* where John was chagrined to be served a large steak at the early hour.

At Lisbon, the affection of airport crowds was a tonic for the President after Paris. He said, "I'm sure glad to be *here* and away from *there.*" For a day, he met with the Portuguese dictator Antonio Salazar and strolled the lush gardens of Queluz Palace, telling Ambassador Burke Elbrick how "disgusted and fed up" he was with Khrushchev. At home, polls showed his popularity stronger than ever. (One year later, when the same happened after the Bay of Pigs, John Kennedy said, "It's just like Eisenhower. The worse I do, the more popular I get.")

Not all rallied behind the President. Adlai Stevenson told Mayor Richard Daley of Chicago that he was "damned sore" about the Summit and wished to address a scheduled banquet for Cook County Democrats. He asked the diners to consider the spectacle— the U.S. government had flown into Russia just before the Summit, denied and then admitted it. When Khrushchev said he assumed Eisenhower was not responsible, the President "proudly" asserted that he was:

"To compound the incredible, we postponed the announcement that the flights were terminated just long enough to make it seem we were yielding to pressure, but too long to prevent Mr. Khrushchev from reaching the boiling point. And as if that weren't enough . . . we ordered a worldwide alert of our combat forces! . . . We handed Khrushchev the crowbar and sledgehammer to wreck the meeting."

The Republican National Committee issued a press release saying that Stevenson had fallen "like a ton of bricks" for the Kremlin line. James Farley, former Democratic national chairman, declared that Stevenson was using the Paris failure to "sledgehammer and crowbar another disastrous nomination for himself as the Apostle of Appeasement."

•

Friday afternoon, the twentieth of May. In the now-remote past, the President had anticipated the pleasure of returning this day from Paris. Now as he walked down the ramp from *Air Force One* at Andrews, he saw Mamie with tears in her eyes. He averted his glance and blinked hard, himself on the verge of tears. *Newsweek* said, "This had been the biggest disappointment of his life and he made no attempt to hide it."

The band played, the crowd cheered. Eisenhower declared, "After a trip of this kind, you can well understand what it means to me to have this kind of welcome." Fireboats sprayed greeting as the open black car crossed the Potomac. Two hundred thousand Americans lined the route. On Pennsylvania Avenue, he passed under a great banner which said, THANK YOU, MR. PRESIDENT.

The car rolled to a stop beneath the North Portico of the White House. The President and First Lady stepped out. Eisenhower turned toward the throngs pressing against the black iron fence and thrust both arms into the air as he had done long ago while riding down Broadway after victory in Europe. Then he disappeared into the Mansion.

★

12

Cold War

Parisians jeered and shook their fists at Khrushchev as he left their city, but when he landed in East Berlin, there was a tumultuous ovation. On radio, East German leaders had heard his philippic at the Palais de Chaillot: maybe now he would finally sign a separate peace and call them to arms against West Berlin. Ten thousand Party members jammed into Seelenbinder Hall in high anticipation. A huge banner exclaimed, END THE PROVOCATIONS OF EISENHOWER AND ADENAUER.

On stage, Khrushchev put on an angry face and cried, "The American President committed *perfidy!* I repeat the word—*perfidy!*" But that was as far as he went. As in Paris, he declared that the "best thing to do" was to reconvene the Summit in six or eight months. In the meantime, he pledged not to "aggravate the international situation and bring it back to the worst times of the Cold War." Premier Otto Grotewohl was so disgusted by Khrushchev's timidity that he refused to see him off at the airport.

When Khrushchev greeted airport crowds in Moscow, he drew two frenzied circles in the air, then swung his fist down. Party officials laughed and applauded: at Paris, their leader had yanked the lion's tail. Khrushchev apparently wished to cast the Summit as a victory over the West and the U-2 as a bad storm which would blow over.

Once the Americans had elected a new President and passions had cooled on both sides, East and West could resume progress toward détente.

But not everyone in Moscow seemed eager to forgive and forget. *Pravda* said, "Yes, we wanted to believe Eisenhower. We wanted to believe him for the sake of peace on earth. . . . But unlike certain simple-minded persons, we were not exactly moved to enthusiasm by the President's foggy, evasive statements." That such an outright condemnation of Khrushchev could be published in the official newspaper did not bode well for his future.

Reporting on the Summit at a nationally televised workers meeting in the Great Kremlin Palace, he issued an extraordinary denial that he was in political trouble: "American propaganda has been spreading the most . . . silly allegations that the situation within our Party and government is unstable, and that this besets Khrushchev with problems, and that he is being opposed by officers released from the Army in connection with its reduction. . . . Obviously Allen Dulles's intelligence service, on which the U.S.A. spends so much of its taxpayers' money, is not worth a damn if you base your policy on such absurd and primitive fabrications."

Khrushchev reminded the audience that after Camp David he had warned that no one could know whether Americans favoring an end to the arms race would defeat the Cold Warriors. With its two aerial provocations, the U.S. had given its answer. After May Day, he had "even declared that the President hardly knew or approved of such actions and that evidently the Pentagon hotheads and Allen Dulles were to blame. But Eisenhower did not take advantage of the opportunity granted him and declared that he had approved the spy flights."

Khrushchev reported that at Paris, he had expected the President to come to see him privately and work out a formula to preserve the Summit: "And yet Eisenhower did not even avail himself of *this* opportunity! Who should have taken the initiative? It is clear to all that it should have been the person who *broke* the good relations growing between our two countries. But you see, he expected *me* to ask for an audience!" Yes, Eisenhower had stopped the U-2 flights, but only as a favor. The Soviet Union no longer took handouts from imperialists.

"I still believe that the President himself wants peace, but evidently the President's good intentions are one thing and his government's foreign policy quite another. The road to hell is paved with good intentions, and that is where Eisenhower will land! ... The Americans themselves say their President has two jobs—golfing and being President. Which is the main one? Playing golf!"

Khrushchev professed to have seen Eisenhower's "weak character" all along: "At Camp David, I gritted my teeth and did not complain about the flights because I knew whom I was dealing with—*not* because I thought they were any less important than I do now."

He continued to maintain that Eisenhower had not really approved the flights: better for Khrushchev to have misplaced his trust in a political weakling than a wolf in sheep's clothing. This transparent contention drew a stinging rebuke from *Pravda* of the Ukraine: "Everything, absolutely everything was known to the President."

•

In the West Wing of the White House, Ann Whitman recorded that since the Summit, Eisenhower "has been almost without exception in a bad humor—with me, that is—but on the surface has managed to hold his temper and control emotions far better than I thought even he could." At a National Security Council meeting, someone raised the need to "regain our leadership" in world opinion. The President exploded: "We did not lose the leadership." No one must ever use that expression again: "All failures happen at the wrong time, and the failure of the U-2 on May first was no exception."

But in his diary, Keith Glennan wrote, "We have been turned up to the rest of the world as just another ordinary nation mouthing platitudes and moralities but indulging in a variety of activities of doubtful character. It is clear on reflection that we might have been taking much more of a chance in sending U-2s over Russia than we were willing to admit. If a Soviet plane were to come over our part of the world, I doubt not that we would have alerted our SAC force and started them on their way. Because they can be recalled this would have been a sensible thing to do. If the Russians had wanted to look at the U-2 as an invader, could they not have been justified in launching missiles toward this country?"

Congressional leaders asked Eisenhower to explain the Summit failure in a speech to a joint session of Congress. The President feared that this would inflate the event. Instead he asked his speechwriter Malcolm Moos to work with Goodpaster on a television address.

Eisenhower often said he could think of "nothing more boring for the American public than to sit in their living rooms for a whole half hour looking at my face." The actor-producer Robert Montgomery was hired to coach him, but the President never discarded his belief that wearing makeup in front of cameras and hot lights was a sad fate for an old soldier.

Asked for visual aids, the CIA made up boards showing Soviet nuclear, missile and long-range bomber sites. Pictures of Leningrad were set side by side with pictures of San Diego. Montgomery saw them and said, "Spectacular." But Eisenhower wanted "something the American people will understand." Montgomery and Hagerty chose a photo of the naval air station at San Diego. At eight o'clock Wednesday evening, May 25, the President sat down at his desk in front of cameras in the Oval Office:

"Tonight I want to talk with you about the remarkable events last week in Paris and their meaning to our future." He said he had gone to the Summit because a "small improvement" in relations with the Russians had been discernible. Since taking office, preventing surprise attack had been one of his "most serious preoccupations." In the course of this, "the widely-publicized U-2 incident occurred."

Why send the flight so close to the Summit? Halting the program might have prevented gathering "important information that was essential and likely to be unavailable at a later date." Why the false initial cover story? "To protect the pilot, his mission and our intelligence processes at a time when the true facts were still undetermined." The story had been based on "assumptions that were later proved incorrect."

At Paris, he had told Khrushchev that he had stopped the flights and offered to "discuss the matter with him in personal meeting" while the Summit proceeded. "Obviously I would not respond to his extreme demands. . . . In torpedoing the Conference, Mr. Khrushchev claimed that he acted as the result of his own high moral indignation over alleged American acts of aggression." But Khrushchev had long known of the U-2 flights and had not complained at Camp David.

The U-2's success had been "nothing short of remarkable." Eisenhower gestured at the easel at his side: "This is a photograph of the North Island Naval Station in San Diego, California. It was taken from an altitude of more than seventy thousand feet. You may not perhaps be able to see them on your television screens, but the white lines on the parking strips around the field are clearly discernible from thirteen miles up."

Now what of the future? "In a nuclear war, there can be no victors—only losers. Even despots understand this." (He would not have called Khrushchev a despot in public four weeks ago.) "Despite the hostility of the men in the Kremlin, I remain convinced that the basic longings of the Soviet people are much like our own." Americans must not be dismayed by the "zigs and zags" of Moscow.

The Soviet press agency Tass called Eisenhower's address "the same old bankrupt position." The Voice of America broadcast the speech in Georgian, Armenian, Ukrainian, Estonian, Russian, Lithuanian and Latvian, but the Soviets jammed it.

•

The next morning, the President reminded bipartisan leaders of Congress over breakfast that there was "no glory" in espionage: "If it's successful, it can't be told." Mike Mansfield asked him whether he now endorsed creation of Congressional committees to oversee the CIA. The President said that he wouldn't mind "some bipartisan group going down occasionally and receiving reports from the CIA" but would "hate to see it formalized."

William Fulbright lamented that the Summit collapse had revived the old contest between Democrats and Republicans over which party was softer on Communism: "In the end, both parties might find themselves in the position where it would be impossible to renew contacts with the Soviets." The President agreed. Fulbright went on to say that he did not think Eisenhower should have taken responsibility for sending the U-2 into Russia.

This raised the President's dander: "Look, Senator, this is modern-day espionage. In the old days, I could send you out or send a spy out and, if he was caught, disavow him. But what do you do when you strap an American-made plane on his back?" No President would want to "put the CIA on the spot" or "disown" its Director. "If anyone were punished, they should impeach me first."

Sam Rayburn said, "You haven't got enough time to go for that," and everyone laughed.

That afternoon, the President told his Cabinet that perhaps the lesson of the U-2 was to "count to ten before saying anything at all." If critics wanted to say he had committed a blunder, that was their privilege. Caving in to Khrushchev at Paris would have been "unthinkable." That would have led to more "vilification" and "no accomplishment whatsoever." He reported de Gaulle's and Macmillan's surmise that Khrushchev had "seized upon the U-2" as a means of getting out of his trip to the Soviet Union for fear that the Soviet people might receive him too warmly. Keith Glennan thought Eisenhower looked "tired" and "somewhat haggard."

Chip Bohlen gave his view that Khrushchev had concluded in March and April that he "would not get at the Summit what he wanted regarding Berlin." Thus he had used the U-2 to sabotage the conference.

•

In London, Macmillan told the House of Commons that seldom since the Second World War had Britain been "so united in the face of crisis." The Royal Air Force was being placed on full readiness. Extension of the military draft was being considered. An Army reduction of fifty-five thousand men was being abandoned.

Hugh Gaitskell, leader of Macmillan's Labour opposition, rose to ask Selwyn Lloyd if the Americans had consulted Whitehall after the U-2 went down. Could he assure that no British bases would be used for future overflights without Britain's consent? Had the British been consulted about the U.S. military alert? To the first and third questions Lloyd said no; he refused to answer the second.

In Paris, de Gaulle told his people on television that France accepted the Summit failure with composure: "Yes, international life, like life in general, is a battle.... The purpose is great. The task is hard. But in the midst of world alarms, you can see, women and men of France, what influence French determination can have again."

•

Now the scene shifted to the world's greatest debating society. Since Khrushchev's first harangue on the U-2, the Russians had vowed to bring the case to the UN for acrimonious debate. An hour after returning from Paris, Eisenhower had asked Henry Cabot Lodge to confer with him upstairs at the White House.

Born in 1902, Lodge was the namesake grandson of the Massachusetts Senator who had almost single-handedly kept the United States out of the League of Nations; he had been raised by the old Senator after his father's early death. Like his fellow Bostonian Christian Herter, Lodge was not given to the bloviation of electoral politics. After Harvard, he wrote editorials for the *New York Herald Tribune* and won election to the Massachusetts House. In 1936, he defied James Michael Curley and the Roosevelt landslide to follow his grandfather into the U.S. Senate.

During the Second World War, Lodge left to join the Army and was re-elected on his return. His preoccupation with Eisenhower's campaign in 1952 had much to do with his defeat by John Kennedy. The new President asked Lodge to be chief UN delegate and raised the post to Cabinet rank. Robert Amory thought that Lodge was "very disappointed" and had "hoped for Secretary of State or Defense," but Lodge later averred, "Eisenhower told me I could have any Cabinet office. I didn't take the Secretaryship of State because I couldn't get along with Senator Taft."

At the UN, Lodge told friends that he had the "best job in the federal government." Like almost all foreign policy players under Eisenhower, Lodge had early skirmishes with Foster Dulles: he had known the President longer and, though technically subordinate, held equal status as a Cabinet member. Douglas Dillon complained to Dulles that Lodge was getting "a bit big for his britches," Robert Murphy that he was turning the New York mission into a "second foreign office."

In his diary, Eisenhower ranked Lodge just below his brother Milton as an able public servant, although Lodge had "long been in politics and is therefore apt to form judgments somewhat more colored by political considerations" than Milton. After Lodge's graceful performance in televised UN debates on Suez, Hungary and Lebanon, and his management of Khrushchev's American tour, he was the front runner to run for Vice President with Richard Nixon.

Upstairs at the White House, the President and Lodge war-gamed the impending debate in the UN Security Council. Lodge should stress that U-2 flights into Russia had been stopped and that Washington was ready to negotiate an Open Skies plan. Eisenhower said he did not want the U-2 flights to be adjudged "aggressive" but was willing to concede that they were "illegal and, in fact, immoral."

The two men might well have even argued that they were legal. The upper boundaries of a nation's airspace had never been firmly established by international law. Some defined air sovereignty as the altitude to which human beings could survive without special equipment, others as the height to which an aggrieved nation could shoot an invader down. The Russians had never signed the Chicago Convention of 1944, the most generally accepted air agreement. They had not claimed that satellites violated national sovereignty: when *Sputnik* was launched in 1957, Eisenhower had applauded the Russians for affirming the "freedom of international space."

Others rejoined that spy planes were a different case from satellites because they could be used to drop bombs. It was Allen Dulles's contention that high-level reconnaissance "in no way disturbs the life of the people, does not harm their property. They do not even notice it." The President and Lodge did not wish to be mired in legal argument: Lodge later said, "If there ever was a case where we didn't have the law on our side, it was the U-2 case."

To underscore the importance Moscow attached to the UN debate, Gromyko himself flew to New York and laid out the Soviet argument in the blue and gold chamber of the Security Council: the U-2 must be condemned as aggression. It only took one plane to drop a nuclear weapon. At Paris, Khrushchev had done "everything possible" to save the Summit, but Eisenhower had merely advocated once again the "espionage and sabotage which is allegedly necessary for American security." Eisenhower's "perfidy" in planning U-2 flights while Khrushchev was at Camp David was like the Japanese diplomats "smiling in Washington before Pearl Harbor."

France's Armand Bernard: "Is there not a flagrant lack of proportion between the May first incident and Soviet actions causing the failure of the Summit and ruining the hopes of all humanity to see the beginning of détente?" Britain's Sir Pierson Dixon reminded Gromyko that they were no longer in the eighteenth century: the U-2 must be treated as a "symptom of the fear of surprise attack." They must remove the root cause.

Lodge explained to delegates that Washington had sent the spy planes to defend the Free World against surprise attack by a nation that often boasted of its power to devastate other nations with nuclear missiles. Open Skies would "obviate forever the necessity of such measures of self-protection." Apparently Khrushchev hadn't thought the U-2 flights were serious enough in 1959 to complain about them to President Eisenhower at Camp David. Why were the Russians creating tension by raising them at the UN today? Where was the Soviet concern for international law when they "forcibly and brutally snuffed out" Hungarian independence in 1956?

Lodge saved his best volley for last. In 1952, a British radio expert in Moscow had been startled to pick up the sound of Ambassador

George Kennan dictating letters in Spaso House. American counterintelligence splintered Kennan's desk before finding an eavesdropping device inside a U.S. seal on the wall. Lodge reported that his government had found over a hundred such devices in its embassies in recent years, and held up his trophy: "Now here is the seal. I would like to just show it to the Council. . . . You can see the antenna and the aerial and it was right under the beak of the eagle."

Delegates guffawed. Gromyko charged that the seal had been fabricated by the CIA. The Soviet motion was defeated seven to two (the Soviet Union and Poland), with two abstentions. Lodge asked Anatoly Dobrynin of the Soviet Foreign Ministry why Moscow had charged the United States with aggression: accusation of trespassing would have "caught us where we were clearly in the wrong." As Lodge later recalled, Dobrynin replied that the Russian word for aggression was the same as for trespassing.

•

On May 27, the Turkish government was overthrown. Premier Adnan Menderes, who had secretly approved the U-2 base and many other forms of Turkish-American cooperation, was arrested and later hanged. Thomas Gates called Herter: "It looks like we are about to lose all our communications in Turkey." The listening posts were all the more vital now that Washington could no longer spy on Russia from the U-2. Herter asked the Ambassador in Ankara to "make strong representations" to the new regime not to interfere with the installation. The new regime agreed.

•

Even while the President was still in Paris, senators had demanded an investigation of the U-2 and the failed Summit. Mike Mansfield wished to "trace the chain of command, or lack of it" that had set in motion the May Day flight and the "confusing zigzags of official pronouncements." Barry Goldwater opposed him: "What the CIA has done was something that had to be done." Eisenhower wished to put the episode behind him, but when the committee unanimously called for secret hearings, he said that he "heartily approved" and would "of course, fully cooperate."

Fulbright modeled the probe after the hearings on Truman's firing of MacArthur in 1951. Rhodes Scholar and elegant skeptic, the Arkansan would have been a likely future Democratic Secretary of State but for his orthodox Southern views on race and his Arabist sympathies. After gaveling the first session to order on Friday morning, May 27, he reminded senators that great nations had always been involved in "lying, cheating, murder, stealing, seduction and suicide" for self-preservation: "This is one of the ugly facts of life in this world."

Christian Herter testified for six hours, with several interjections by Douglas Dillon. What was the lesson of the U-2? "Not to have accidents." Had the government weighed the risk that the May Day flight would jeopardize the Summit? "That was a risk that we were running in connection with every one of them.... Call it bad luck, if you will. It *was* bad luck. But if we had tried to adjust these things to particular meetings, it would have been almost impossible for the program to succeed."

Even at this late date, Herter was still trying to conceal the President's role in authorizing the ill-fated flight and the false cover stories. When Fulbright asked if there was "ever a time" that Eisenhower approved each U-2 flight, Herter untruthfully replied, "It has never come up to the President." Fulbright asked if there had been flights between April 9 and May Day. "I can't tell you, quite honestly." What was the route of the April 9 flight? "I am ashamed to say I can't remember."

Many years later, Dillon conceded that these replies were "just gobbledy-gook": "That was one of the most embarrassing things I ever went through because we didn't want to tell a falsehood. On the other hand ... our testimony was not totally frank because we were defending—we were trying to hide the White House responsibility for this."

Richard Helms sat in the hearing room as a censor for the CIA. In 1977, as a former CIA Director, he pleaded nolo contendere to a charge of failing to testify fully and completely before Fulbright's committee about CIA efforts for a Chilean military coup in 1970. In 1983, he expressed his belief that Herter and others who deceived the committee during the U-2 hearings could have been subject to similar charges: "They were all sworn. So if you don't come to the same conclusion, then my recollection is bad....Knowing what they knew and what actually went on, if it isn't perjury, I don't understand the meaning of the word. And I'm not against it. I'm simply saying that it's not the first time officials have perjured themselves in the interest of protecting a President."

This was another measure of the greater ease with which American intelligence and foreign policy were conducted in the age before public faith in the credibility of the Executive Branch broke down over Vietnam, Watergate and public revelations about the CIA. Had the U-2 testimony been subjected to the standards of the later time, Eisenhower might have ended his Presidency as his Secretary of State and other high officials were indicted for perjury.

Allen Dulles appeared for six hours, occasionally aided by Pearre Cabell. Pictures of Soviet bases, airfields and Navy yards were used to show that the U-2 was "one of the most valuable intelligence collection operations that any country has ever mounted at any time." The U-2 had revealed that the Soviets had sharply reduced long-range bomber production and recently developed a new supersonic medium-range bomber. It had made the Russians "far less cocky."

Fulbright asked him why the President had taken responsibility. Although he had privately opposed the decision. Dulles defended his boss: "The fact that I was going ahead on my own authority to do something of this magnitude may not have been widely believed, even if I had asserted and stuck to it." Why the flight on May Day? "I don't discuss what the President says to me or I say to the President."

What were they looking for? "Certain targets that we were afraid we would not be able easily to get at a later time and which we thought were of great value to our national security." Might Powers have actually landed his plane and defected? "He loved flying, was making good money and was very happy. . . . If you are going to defect, you don't fly into the heart of Russia, where you may be shot down anywhere before you get there." No Senator asked whether CIA malfeasance might have contributed to the May Day downing or the embarrassments that followed. Later CIA directors did not enjoy such kid-glove treatment.

After Dulles's appearance, Fulbright met reporters and publicly absolved the CIA of "questionable decisions" in the U-2 affair: "political officers" were to blame. Dulles called Herter to say that he was "very disturbed": "Fulbright is just trying to bolster his own theory that we should have kept our mouths shut."

Hugh Dryden testified that the U-2 had gone on 199 actual weather flights since 1956. He noted his fear that if the world learned of NASA's full involvement in the U-2 program, foreign governments would halt cooperation on Project Mercury: "We are regarded in one popular story as a piano player who didn't know what was going on upstairs. We would like to remain in the position of the stupid—well, of a stupid person."

Thomas Gates said, "Everyone should be terribly proud of the dignity and character of the President in this Paris meeting. I happened to be sitting next to him and it was the most remarkable performance of strength of character and dignity of any man I have ever seen." He defended his military alert: "Primarily a measure of checking command and checking communications." Asked if the CIA or Air Force had flown over China, he dissembled: "I don't know to my own knowledge that we have."

Each day, Richard Helms and Chip Bohlen pored over the transcript for information that might damage U.S. interests and censored it before issuance to the press. The complete testimony was locked in a Senate vault for twenty-two years. As the senators argued over the final report, Frank Lausche said that attacking the President aided Khrushchev: "We are serving the Soviet Union and not our country." Fulbright replied that he resented the insinuation: "We don't happen to have Mr. Khrushchev here to question him." George Aiken cried, "Let's subpoena him!"

Fulbright declared that the "real issue" was Eisenhower's decision to take responsibility for the U-2. Alexander Wiley said that by telling the truth, the President had "taught the world a lesson" which would "echo down through the years." Fulbright carped, "It is echoing down through the years already."

They debated the timing of the ill-fated flight. Homer Capehart said it made his blood boil: "They had been doing it for four years and they had all the information they possibly needed." George Aiken said it reminded him of the bum arrested for throwing a brick through a window: "It seemed like a good thing to do at the time." Fulbright supposed that there had been no good reason for flying so close to the Summit: otherwise Dulles and Herter "would have told us." Aiken wondered who had really made the decision to fly on May Day. Fulbright challenged Eisenhower's contention that U-2 flights were warranted because the Soviet Union was a closed society: if a man was starving to death, he was justified in breaking into a grocery store, "but we just don't accept it legally."

The final report did not fault the U-2 pilot or CIA preparations for the May Day mission: what befell the U-2 had been "just plain bad luck." But the senators felt that too little heed had been paid to the flight's possible effect on the Paris Summit. The cover stories should have been more careful and the government better coordinated. All members signed, except Capehart. Lausche and Wiley added their own appendix denouncing Khrushchev for wrecking the Summit and praising the U-2 program and Eisenhower's performance.

Fulbright was never convinced that he and his colleagues had reached the heart of the matter. In 1960, suggesting that the American government may have intentionally permitted the U-2 to be downed and thereby to wreck the Summit would have been political suicide. But years later, Fulbright said, "I have often wondered why, in the midst of these efforts by President Eisenhower and Khrushchev to come to some understanding, the U-2 incident was allowed to take place. No one will ever know whether it was accidental or intentional."

•

In Lubyanka Prison, Powers was "shaken" by the news that the Paris Summit had collapsed and that his mishap was the reason. His captors told him that he would be tried for espionage; he was still certain that he would be shot.

On May 17, they took him to see the U-2 wreckage at Gorky Park; technicians asked for details about the equipment. On May 26, for the first time, he was allowed to write his parents and wife. The letters were edited by the Russians and he was told to copy the revisions:

My dearest Barbara,

I want you to know that I love you and miss you very much. I did not realize how much until I found myself in this situation. Not knowing when, if ever, I will see you again has made me realize how much you mean to me. I have had plenty of time to think since I have been here and plenty of time to regret past mistakes. . . .

I have been told that there is a lot of publicity in the U.S. papers about me. I was also told that you had returned to the States and that you are presently with your mother. Barbara, tell me how my mother and father are taking this. Is my mother all right? I was afraid that it might be too much of a shock to her.

Well, to get back to me, I am getting along as good as can be expected. . . . I have been treated much better than I expected. For the first week or so I had no appetite at all but I am doing fine now. When I had to bail out of the plane I skinned my right shin a little and carried a black eye for two weeks. A lady doctor treated them both and they are well now.

That was my first experience with a parachute and I hope I will

318 : M A Y D A Y

never have another. I could not use the ejection seat because of the G forces and had to climb out. My chute opened immediately—how I don't know. . . . The people here tell me that I am lucky to be alive, but only time will tell me whether or not I was lucky.

Things happened pretty fast after that. Before dark that night I was in Moscow. . . . It gets pretty lonely here by myself but they have given me books to read and it helps to pass the time. I also get to walk in the fresh air every day that it doesn't rain. One day I even took a sun bath. It has been a little too cold to do that every day.

On May 2nd I was taken for a tour of Moscow which I enjoyed very much. These people are real proud of their capital city. . . . Just now a guard asked me if I wanted to walk but I prefer to finish this letter so I said no.

Barbara, I don't know what is going to happen to me. The investigation and the interrogation is still going on. When that is over there will be a trial. . . . I was told that if the U.S. government would let any of you come that *you* would be allowed to see me. I would rather you waited until the trial or after so that I could tell you what the results were. . . .

I did take a walk after all. . . . It was getting pretty smoky in here and I needed the fresh air. By the way these cigarettes here are pretty good.

You are on your own now and I don't know for how long. Just be careful and maybe we can still buy a house some day. . . . Well, Darling, it is dark outside now and I guess I had better go to bed. Barbara, once again I say I am very sorry for everything. I am sending you, with this letter,

All my love,
Gary

Barbara received the letter in Milledgeville. She read it, wept and, as instructed, sent it to the home address of a CIA man.

•

The U-2 and the Summit collapse handed Democrats an irresistible campaign issue. Stuart Symington accused Eisenhower of subjecting the nation to a "humiliating disaster." The Democratic Advisory Council called it more proof of the "lack of competence of the present administration." Campaigning in the Oregon primary in May, John

Kennedy charged that the President had let "the risk of war hang on the possibility of an engine failure": Eisenhower might have "expressed regret" for the U-2 flight, if that would have saved the Summit.

Kennedy's Senate office was deluged with angry telegrams: "When one apologizes to Khrushchev, it's the same as apologizing to the Devil. . . . Saying or implying Eisenhower goofed at the Summit will breed disgust for you and your party. . . . YOU'RE UNFIT TO BE PRESIDENT. They need your kind of double-dealers in Russia. Go to Russia."

Campaigning in the West, Lyndon Johnson told audiences, "I'm not prepared to apologize to Mr. Khrushchev—*are you?*" Richard Nixon publicly denounced Kennedy's comments as "naïve." Kennedy replied, "If Vice President Nixon feels the conduct of this administration at the time the U-2 flights were discovered was commendable, that is his prerogative."

After winning Oregon, Kennedy called on Adlai Stevenson at his Illinois farm. Afterwards Stevenson wrote their mutual friend Arthur Schlesinger, Jr., "He *seemed* to feel that my reaction to the Summit was correct and that we shouldn't, either for the country or the party, let this one be buried in maudlin mush. But I will wait to see what he *does* with interest. He felt that Nixon would take the tough guy with Khrushchev line now, that he *had* to, and his strategy would be to put us on the defensive as the soft-on-Communism party."

•

The President had been scheduled to arrive in Tokyo on June 19 as the coda to his triumphal tour of the Soviet Union. Now that the Soviet tour had been canceled, the White House replaced it with goodwill stops in the Philippines, Taiwan, Okinawa and Korea. A resounding welcome in the Western Pacific might redeem the travesty of Paris.

But Premier Kishi was in grave trouble. When the American security treaty was brought to the floor of the Diet, Socialists staged a sit-in and were removed from the chamber. Liberal Democrats who remained unanimously approved the treaty, unleashing national demonstrations against Kishi's naked bid for one-party rule, the treaty and America's presence in Japan. In Tokyo, rioters shouting, "Ike don't come!" tore open the gates of Kishi's residence and put up signs: WE DON'T WELCOME IKE! U-2 OUT OF JAPAN!

From Moscow, *Izvestia* warned that Eisenhower's goal was to heat up world tensions so that "Kishi and other favorites who have sold their souls to the American devil may be exploited even more fully in their aggressive policy against the Asian peoples." Someone crudely forged and disseminated a message from the American air attaché in Tokyo advising that "we trick the Japanese by temporarily removing planes from Japan to Okinawa and return them secretly after the hullabaloo over U-2s and the anti-Kishi demonstrations die down."

Ambassador Douglas MacArthur II, nephew of the President's old boss, cabled Washington from Tokyo that Kishi was "fighting for his political life." In early June, when he met Jim Hagerty's advance party at Haneda Airport, hundreds stormed their Cadillac with signs: WE DISLIKE IKE. . . . REMEMBER HIROSHIMA. . . . EISENHOWER CAN'T SAVE KISHI. . . . TAKE BACK YOUR BASES. . . . GO TO HELL IKE. Rioters pounded the roof and broke windows. Hagerty lit up a cigarette and pretended to photograph the crowds. Only after eighty minutes were they rescued by a U.S. Marine helicopter. *Pravda* warned that this was "only a dress rehearsal" of what lay in store for Eisenhower. Allen Dulles feared a kamikaze attack.

Kishi promised to clear the entire city and send 27,000 policemen to guard the streets if the President would still consent to come. A vast crowd organized by the left-wing Zengakuren forced their way into the Diet and trampled a woman to death. While Eisenhower toured Manila, Merriman Smith recorded, "The people around Ike remain on pins and needles about Tokyo. More rioting tonight." Japanese leaders feared for Emperor Hirohito, who was scheduled to ride with Eisenhower through Tokyo. As John Eisenhower recalled, Goodpaster called MacArthur from Manila and said, "Are you so sure that there's going to be no trouble that you're willing to put your career on the line?"

Kishi decided to cancel his invitation and resign. Before he relinquished office, he was stabbed five times in the thigh by a right-wing nationalist. In July, Herter informed the President that "we have withdrawn all the U.S. U-2 aircraft from Japan and the Japanese government is very much relieved."

As Eisenhower's party sailed for Taiwan, the Mainland Chinese shelled Quemoy and Matsu: Radio Peking reported that as soldiers jerked the lanyards of their cannons, they shouted, "Eisenhower go back!" and "Get out of Asia!" In Okinawa, leftists marched and cried, "Ike go home!" *Pravda* exulted, "ONE FIASCO AFTER ANOTHER." As Harrison Salisbury recalled, the Presidential tour of

Russia and Japan had turned into a "macabre" journey, a "pretty miserable sort of windup for what had been planned as the great visit of the late twentieth century."

Returned to Washington, Eisenhower gave a television speech from the Oval Office, blaming the Communists for using "every possible method" to stop his trips to the Soviet Union and Japan: "These disorders were not occasioned by America. We in the United States must not fall into the error of blaming ourselves for what the Communists do. After all, Communists will act like Communists."

The *Washington Post* observed that the undertones of disappointment in the President's speech were especially pointed because he was so near leaving office: "It is tragic for the country as well as himself that the termination has been marked by the collapse of the Summit Conference, the outburst of violence in Japan and a general resumption of the Cold War."

On June 27, the Soviets walked out of the test ban talks at Geneva.

•

On July 1, an American RB-47 spy plane took off from its British base and flew along the northern coast of the Soviet Union. Over the Barents Sea, it vanished. John Eisenhower brought the President the grim news at Gettysburg, where he and Mamie were celebrating their forty-fourth anniversary. Might Khrushchev now fulfill his threat to destroy Western bases in the event of another incursion? John thought his father looked as if he had had the wind knocked out of him.

In Moscow, Khrushchev announced that the Soviets had shot down the plane to halt another "gross violation" of their airspace. Two survivors had been rescued. The "new act of American perfidy" showed that Eisenhower's pledge to stop the spy flights was "not worth a busted penny." The British should know that lending their bases for "aggressive actions" would bring their people great danger.

American intelligence showed that the RB-47 had been more than thirty miles outside the Soviet frontier: still smarting from the revelation that it had allowed U-2s for years to fly deep into Soviet territory, the Soviet military had probably shot down the plane to enhance its image. When the Russians ascertained that the plane had been downed over international waters, Khrushchev had probably tried to forestall embarrassment by trying to turn the matter into another U-2 case.

At the White House, Eisenhower told Herter that he had gotten to the point where he didn't trust the Russians "to the slightest degree": if the United States could prove that the plane was over international waters when downed, it should break relations with the Soviet Union. But revealing this evidence would compromise American tracking stations. Allen Dulles told the President that the Soviets were trying to scare American allies into denying use of their bases. The UN Security Council refused to condemn what the Russians called the "American provocation."

Western planes flew in international airspace along the Iron Curtain every day. The President told aides that if the Russians kept shooting at them, he would retaliate, and it might start a world war. With spectacularly bad timing, during the UN debate, an American C-47 strayed over the Kurile Islands. The Soviets tried to shoot it down and missed. This proved to be the last major aerial incident during the Eisenhower Presidency.

In August, Gordon Gray secretly suggested to Eisenhower that the Pentagon lure a Soviet plane, submarine or trawler toward American waters. The craft would be forced down, up or boarded without a fire-fight: "We would then claim a violation of territorial waters, whether absolutely technically true or not." The President could regain the world propaganda offensive by publicizing a Soviet spy case—and demonstrate that Washington dealt with intruders more humanely than Moscow. But Eisenhower declined.

●

That summer, the CIA and Pentagon were concerned about the loss of U-2 information on Russia. The President's pledge not to fly into Soviet airspace again had returned Western intelligence to an earlier age. Satellite reconnaissance would not be in full operation for months. Thomas Gates called a secret meeting of the Joint Chiefs and top intelligence officials at Quantico. Some demanded that the U-2 fly into Russia again, no matter what Eisenhower had pledged to Khrushchev.

In *U.S. News & World Report,* an anonymous American official warned that the Soviets were relocating and camouflaging ICBM sites and building new ones: "The next President will probably wake up to discover that his military commanders cannot guarantee that they know the sites of Soviet missiles and can knock them out. If you don't know where to strike, your military power is limited."

Bissell sent a petition to the White House, "disowned by the Director" and "to be destroyed after reading," proposing a much-reduced and redeployed U-2 operation. It allowed that the President had made a "firm decision" not to fly again into the Soviet Union. But what if the world situation should crumble? Then Eisenhower or the next President might want to change his mind. Hence why not keep the planes flying to complete coverage of vital areas like China?

The President was reserved. He told aides he wished they would pay more attention to world opinion. All his advisers had "missed badly" on the U-2. They had given him no idea what the world reaction to a downing would be. He didn't want to say, "I told you so," but recalled that he was "the one and only one" who had ever put much weight on this. When Goodpaster raised a Pentagon-CIA proposal to use RB-47s in the Far East, Eisenhower said they must wait for the "political picture to develop more stability." Another failure would hand the Presidential election to the Democrats.

•

The CIA and Pentagon were racing to perfect successors to the U-2. In 1956, Richard Bissell had already begun working with Kelly Johnson on a new plane—ultimately called the SR-71 Blackbird—that would fly much higher and at speeds over Mach 3. In June 1960, the President ordered work to proceed, but "on low priority, as a high-performance reconnaissance plane for the Air Force in time of war." He thought that there was little chance of using the plane in peacetime.

In 1958, Bissell and Allen Dulles had persuaded Congressional leaders to approve secret funding for the first American spy satellite, code-named CORONA. In February 1959, Eisenhower told the CIA that U-2 flights should be "held to a minimum pending the availability of this new equipment."

By May Day 1960, the CIA and Air Force had made eleven attempts to launch a satellite, but each time, the rocket, camera or other equipment had failed. In August 1960, one finally made it into orbit, photographing the Soviet Union with a regularity and comprehensiveness that the U-2 could never achieve. These and later pictures would almost certainly reveal once and for all whether there really was a Missile Gap.

•

The U-2 affair had provided Khrushchev's enemies in the Soviet Union with an excellent opportunity to tame him. Some demanded to know why he had embraced the American President as a "lover of peace" when all clear-minded Soviet leaders knew that he was merely a captive of the Pentagon and monopolistic aggressive capitalism. In May 1960, on its front page, *Pravda* ominously reprinted a Walter Lippmann column referring to Khrushchev's "critics within the Soviet Union."

In public, Khrushchev distanced himself from Eisenhower, but not with such vigor as to confess that he had been duped. In early June, at a Kremlin press conference, he declared that Eisenhower was "completely lacking in will power" to curb the Cold Warriors: "I think that when the President is no longer in office, we could give him a job as a kindergarten director. I am sure he would not hurt the children. But it is dangerous for a man like that to run a nation. . . . I say this because I know him.

"I watched him in 1955 at the Geneva Conference and I felt sorry for him. . . . Whenever the President had to speak, John Foster Dulles handed him notes. In decency, he ought to at least have turned his back while reading the note, but he would take the note, read it and lay it aside. . . . Well, Comrades, at that point, I was tempted to wonder just who was running the state. . . . It is just dreadful that such awesome power should be in such hands. . . . The world situation is strained and yet the President leaves to play golf! . . . Eisenhower's Presidency is a time of troubles for the United States and all the world."

In mid-June, the Kremlin held a large conference on farming. Western analysts noted that Khrushchev was not invited to speak on his favorite topic and that his agriculture minister used the occasion to challenge Khrushchev's policies. On June 18, he went to Bucharest for a meeting of world socialist leaders. Since May Day, Mao Tse-tung had exploited the U-2 episode to undermine Khrushchev's dominance of the Kremlin and the socialist camp. Behind closed doors at Bucharest, the Chinese proposed a resolution condemning Khrushchev's opening to the West. Khrushchev reportedly vilified them as "children" who "mechanically parroted" Lenin's views on imperialism and wished to start another world war. Khrushchev withdrew twelve thousand technical advisers from China and tore up contracts for further aid.

In mid-July, Western analysts were intrigued anew when Khrushchev did not give the main report to the Central Committee on the Bucharest meeting. Instead it was delivered by Kozlov, who had not even been there. As members went on to discuss the Soviet economy, Khrushchev maintained his uncharacteristic silence. His contributions were reportedly confined to hectoring some of the speakers from his seat.

Domestic problems loomed. Soviet industrial growth was sagging, as was agriculture: Khrushchev's fabled Virgin Lands idea had by now been proven a failure. It was later said that he might have been thrown out at this moment but for the fact that the world might have taken his firing as capitulation to the Chinese and admission of the failure of Soviet foreign policy. By now, it was probably incumbent upon Khrushchev to show the Kremlin and the world that he was a tough and able leader, that he knew how to stand up to the West and seize opportunities in Cuba, the Congo and the rest of the Third World. Within a year, he scrapped his vaunted plan to reduce the size of the Soviet armed forces.

Years later, just before his death, Khrushchev dated the beginning of his decline in power to the day that the U-2 was shot down: after May Day 1960, he was "never again" able to regain full control of his government. He said that from that day on, he had to share power with those who believed that "only military force" enabled Moscow to deal with Washington.

This contained more than a hint of retrospective self-justification: it was easier for Khrushchev to blame his decline on American "betrayal" and "treachery" than on the failure of his own policies. But to the extent that the U-2 affair undermined his exhortations for closer relations with the West and military reductions, it doubtless served potential rivals.

●

Eisenhower had expected to be a commanding figure this summer, back from Paris and Moscow with agreements that formed the basis for détente. Perhaps he and Khrushchev would educate the American and Soviet peoples to the benefits of shifting government spending from the arms race to social and consumer needs. In the United States, enthusiasm for détente would run so high that the fall campaign would be largely a referendum on who could best continue Eisenhower's steps toward peace.

Instead his dreams were turning to sand. Khrushchev's "vituperation and false charges" now reminded him of Stalin. Americans of all stripes were demanding an increased defense budget. Democrats and Republicans challenged each other on who could best stand up to Khrushchev. Joseph Alsop marveled to a friend that even Chip Bohlen thought that Khrushchev was moving toward a major showdown: "The change of tone in men like Chip impresses and disturbs me almost as much as the change in the Soviet tone. Meanwhile Eisenhower remains the same, like a dead whale on a beach or, rather, like a nice old gentleman in a golf cart."

One day that summer, Eisenhower told George Kistiakowsky of how he had concentrated his efforts the past few years on ending the Cold War and felt that he had been making big progress. Then the "stupid U-2 mess" came and ruined all of his efforts. He sadly concluded that there was "nothing worthwhile" left for him to do before the end of his Presidency.

★

13

Final Reckoning

I N JULY 1960, at the Democratic National Convention in Los Angeles, speaker after speaker decried the beatings American diplomacy had taken in Moscow, Paris, Ankara, Tokyo and Havana. Sam Rayburn boomed, "Would you have thought that Truman or Roosevelt or Woodrow Wilson would have had the debacle that Eisenhower had at Paris?" Accepting the nomination, John Kennedy reminded delegates that the President "who began his career by going to Korea ends it by staying away from Japan."

As Eisenhower took a summer's rest at the naval air station in Newport, Rhode Island, he did not find his own party much more satisfactory. Since the failure of the Summit, Nelson Rockefeller had publicly demanded $3 billion more per year for defense, deplored the Missile Gap, announced that he would accept a Presidential draft, and threatened a floor fight against a Republican platform rubber-stamping the President's policies.

Richard Nixon feared that a floor fight would harm prospects for victory in the fall. Three days before the Republican convention opened, he secretly went to Rockefeller's Fifth Avenue apartment. He vainly pressed the Governor to join his ticket; then the two men bargained over the platform until 3:20 A.M. Two hours later, the press received copies of the proclamation instantly known as the "Compact of

Fifth Avenue," suggesting that Nixon had come to endorse key elements of Rockefeller's critique of the Eisenhower policies.

Barry Goldwater called it the "Munich of the Republican Party." From Newport, an angry President called Nixon and said it would be difficult for him to support a platform which did not show "respect for the record of the Republican administration." Platform language was found to appease all sides, but after addressing the delegates in Chicago, Eisenhower left town without waiting to witness Nixon's nomination as his successor.

•

By July, Powers's sixty-one days of interrogation were over. He was paid a call in Lubyanka by his newly appointed defense counsel, Mikhail Griniev, a balding, goateed expert in losing important Soviet state cases. Ironically, the U-2 pilot was a beneficiary of the Khrushchev reforms. Under Stalin, he would not have been granted defense counsel at such an early stage; he might have been physically or psychologically compelled to denounce his own government before an almost certain execution.

The criminal indictment charged Powers with breaking a Soviet law barring outsiders from gathering state secrets for foreign governments. It charged the U.S. with sending aggressive spy planes into Russia, lying about the provocation until proof was irrefutable, breaking international law on air sovereignty, espionage and using other nations' bases and airspace without permission. Evidently the only matter for the judges to decide was the pilot's sentence—a maximum of fifteen years in prison or death by shooting.

By Powers's account, Griniev told him that the sentence might depend on whether he was sorry for his crime. As the prisoner later said, he thought about it and decided that he *was* sorry—sorry he had made the May Day flight, sorry he had been shot down, sorry he was a prisoner, sorry that the Summit had collapsed. If his life depended on it, he could say he was sorry, as long as he did not have to define exactly what he meant.

•

From Washington, the State Department still badgered the Soviets to allow someone from the Embassy to see the prisoner. But the Russians argued that during an interview, the pilot might give away some of the intelligence he had been sent to obtain. Thus the CIA secretly hired two Virginia lawyers, Alexander Parker and Frank Rogers, to "aid" Griniev and discreetly try to get some information from the prisoner. Officially they were being sent to Moscow by the Virginia Bar Association. If the Russians learned that the CIA was actually behind them, they would almost surely deny them visas.

In Washington hotel rooms and restaurants, CIA and State Department operatives briefed the two lawyers on what they wished to know from Powers. What had he seen while flying across the southern Soviet Union? What had brought down his plane? Why hadn't he destroyed it?

•

In Milledgeville, it had been a bad summer for Barbara Powers. She later recorded that when the press revealed her husband's handsome salary, her mother ran up large bills and demanded that her daughter pay. Barbara was eager to go to Moscow. The CIA was not delighted to have the irrepressible woman in the city while her husband was tried but, bowing to the inevitable, the Agency secretly footed the bill. Parker and his wife were appointed as chaperones.

The CIA also offered to fly Oliver and Ida Powers to Moscow, but the parents declined. Preferring independence, Oliver accepted *Life*'s offer of five thousand dollars plus expenses in exchange for the exclusive story of their adventures in Moscow. Before May Day, relations between daughter and parents-in-law had been chilly; since then, they had been glacial. The two camps refused to fly to Moscow aboard the same plane.

•

In New York, a CBS assignment editor called in one of his reporters, Sam Jaffe, and said, "You're going to the Powers trial."

Slight, electric, with russet hair and a russet mustache, Jaffe had been a young radio newswriter at the UN in 1952 when the FBI first asked him for confidential reports on Russians he encountered. Jaffe agreed: his namesake uncle, star of *Gunga Din,* had lately been blacklisted for refusal to cooperate with the government as a member of the Hollywood Ten. In 1955, Jaffe applied for a job with CBS. By his account, a CIA man told him that he could go to Moscow for CBS if he would also work for the Agency. Jaffe refused; CBS hired him anyway and based him in New York.

Assignment to the Powers trial was a prize: the Russians were issuing few visas to the American press. Jaffe notified the FBI office in New York that he was going. Over lunch, Jay Reeves, who was evidently the CIA's New York station chief, and a CIA psychologist asked him to watch Powers closely to see whether he had been brainwashed. If Jaffe managed to interview Khrushchev, he should try to get the Soviet leader to "make some comment, no matter how much in passing, on China or Mao." He should also "study Khrushchev carefully for any physical changes since his 1959 visit to the United States." He was given data on Soviet espionage for rebuttal if Khrushchev denounced the U-2. In his reportage, Jaffe should refer to Powers not as a spy pilot but as a reconnaissance pilot.

On August 12, at Idlewild Airport, New York, Jaffe boarded a Sabena flight to Brussels that would connect with Aeroflot to Moscow. He was delighted to find that he had been assigned to the same flight and compartment as Barbara Powers, her mother, her doctor, the Parkers and the Rogerses. He sat down next to Barbara; the two hit it off and drank together as they flew east.

At Brussels, Jaffe was unnerved when the Aeroflot people treated him as a member of Barbara's party and Barbara asked him for advice on dealing with the press. He was further puzzled when in Moscow, he was given a room in the Sovietskaya Hotel four doors down from Barbara. Other reporters had second-class lodgings. "How the hell can I stay away from her?" he said later. "I'm not in the role of reporter—I am but I'm not. And I know I can get stories from her."

Jaffe later informed the FBI that he spent "almost every night in the company of Barbara Powers in her room drinking." Barbara's suite had been occupied by the Nixons a year before. Jaffe recalled the scene: "She's drinking like hell. I'm carrying her bottles out at three, four o'clock in the morning. She wouldn't go to bed." He begged her to speak to other reporters to avoid suspicion that he was a CIA pet, but the access was irresistible.

As he later recalled, Barbara told him that she actually "hated" her husband and was only putting up with him: he was a "no-good bum" who had run around with women "all over Turkey." She said that she had never really wanted to go to Moscow for the trial. Jaffe later told the FBI that Barbara's lawyers were "disgusted with her" and thought she was "sex-crazy."

Oliver and Ida Powers arrived in Moscow with their daughter Jessica, their family lawyer, a doctor and a friend from Pound. Oliver told his daughter-in-law, "I don't know why *you* even bothered to come."

The two sides mended their differences long enough to call on Griniev. Parker and Rogers gave him material to use in the prisoner's defense, but the counsel gave no sign that he intended to use it.

Tuesday, August 16, was the day before the trial. Barbara sent her husband a desperate telegram at Lubyanka but received no reply. She and Jaffe drank late into the night. Before dawn, she bade him take her to the prison. A taxi was found. Standing in front of Lubyanka, she wept. Then they returned to Barbara's hotel room. The FBI later recorded,

> There she told the informant that she was not in love with her husband and did not have any intention of staying in the Soviet Union. Barbara Powers grabbed the informant and started kissing him, but he repelled her. He told her that she could not talk that way and could not divorce her husband at this time. He told her that she would be accused of "deserting a sinking ship" and that she should not even mention this.
>
> The informant said that on this occasion, he could have been intimate with Barbara Powers, but he was not. He said that on many occasions when he was in Barbara Powers's company, she was in her pajamas, and he could probably have been intimate with her if he so desired, but at no time was he intimate with her.

•

Wednesday was cold and rainy. Crowds pushed against police barricades as the limousines arrived at the Hall of Trade Unions. Twenty-two hundred guests were ushered inside to the red plush seats of the Hall of Columns, the old white chamber where Tchaikovsky had played, victims of the Great Purge had been tried and Lenin and Stalin had lain in state. They included Khrushchev's daughter Yelena, the British defector Guy Burgess, newsmen and diplomats including Richard Snyder and Vladimir Toumanoff of the American Embassy. Once again, Llewellyn Thompson had elected to deprive the Russians of the propoganda value of his presence.

Television lights shone upon a gleaming red-and-gold hammer and sickle, which hung above the stage. Relics of the U-2 were on display. A theater bell rang. The room hushed as the prisoner was brought in. Powers blinked and looked out into the audience for his family. Sitting with her in-laws in a box far back in the hall, Barbara covered her eyes and wept.

The presiding judge asked, "Accused Powers, do you plead guilty of the charge?" He did. The chief prosecutor, Roman Rudenko, ran through the essentials of the prison interrogation. He showed the pilot his flight maps and logbook. When had he been first assigned to fly into the Soviet Union? Powers lied and said on May Day morning: this removed a degree of premeditation.

As in Lubyanka, he posed as an airplane jockey who had barely known what he was doing. What missions had he flown before May Day 1960? "Several flights—I cannot remember how many—along the southern border of the Soviet Union." What had he photographed? "I don't know. I just turned on the switches."

Throughout the cross-examination, Powers appeared so calm that Toumanoff realized that the U-2 pilots had been chosen as much as anything for their iron nerves. But as Powers recalled, by the end of those first four hours, he felt more distraught than at any time since May Day: several times he had been on the verge of screaming, "Sentence me to death and end this farce!"

That afternoon, Griniev portrayed Powers as a classic capitalist victim, driven by economic need to spy for political reasons of which he knew little and cared less. The defense counsel displayed photos of the Powers family's modest home, supplied by Oliver's lawyer. He asked the pilot if he had ever been interested in the Soviet Union. "No, political questions did not interest me." Why did he take the job with the CIA? "It enabled me to pay my debts . . . and save money for the future in the hope of buying a house and setting up my own business to be independent of my parents." Why had he once hesitated to renew his contract? "I had a feeling—I don't know what it was—I just didn't like what I was doing."

Griniev prompted: "Why are you sorry now?"

"Well, the situation I'm in now is not too good. I haven't heard much about the news of the world since I have been here, but I understand that as a direct result of my flight, the Summit Conference did not take place and President Eisenhower's visit was called off. There was, I suppose, a great increase in tension in the world and I'm sincerely sorry that I had anything to do with this."

When he first announced the U-2 downing in May, Khrushchev had declared that the plane had been stopped by a single rocket at over 20,000 meters (65,600 feet). This claim was at least partly inspired by the need to suggest Soviet military might at a moment the world was learning that Soviet territory had been successfully overflown for four years; it may also have been made to discourage Washington from trying to send thc U-2 into Russia again.

Years later, Powers said that during his first interrogation at Lubyanka, he was asked his altitude before he was downed: having given the matter "a great deal of thought," he replied, "At maximum altitude for the plane, 68,000 feet." By Powers's later account, 68,000 feet was neither the U-2's maximum altitude nor his actual altitude. It was an "arbitrary figure"—close enough to his real altitude to be credible but far enough away, he hoped, that if future U-2 pilots entered Russia and the Soviets used it to aim their rockets, they would miss. According to Powers, the Russians had believed him.

Under questioning on the first day of his trial, Powers reiterated that he had been downed at the plane's "maximum altitude" of 68,000 feet. He silently hoped that this would alert the CIA to his concealment of some vital information and that his bosses would not undermine him by releasing contradictory facts.

On Thursday morning, the second day of the trial, Griniev asked him if he had been struck by a *rocket* at 68,000 feet. Powers said, "At that altitude I was struck down by *something*. . . . I have no idea what it was. I didn't see it." Rudenko quickly produced a report from the Sverdlovsk anti-aircraft unit insisting that the U-2 had been struck at over 20,000 meters by a single rocket.

The presiding judge asked Powers if he had done his own country a good or bad service. "I would say a very bad service." Had it occurred to him that he might wreck the Summit conference? "When I got my instructions, the Summit was furthest from my mind."

After Thursday's adjournment (by Powers's later account), Griniev asked him why, despite ample opportunities, he had failed to disassociate himself from the reactionary militarists who had sent him into the Soviet Union. If he wished to avoid death, he had better tell the court that he was "deeply repentant and profoundly sorry" for his act and that he renounced the "aggressive, warmaking designs of the United States."

•

Friday was the day of judgment. Rudenko declared that the trial had exposed not only Powers's crimes but the "criminal, aggressive activities of the U.S. ruling circles and the actual inspirers and organizers of monstrous crimes directed against the peace and security of the peoples." The U-2 program? "A graphic example of criminal collusion between a big American capitalist company, an espionage center and the U.S. military."

Powers must not be allowed to plead that he had only followed orders: "Having voluntarily sold his honor and his conscience, the whole of himself, for dollars, he carried out criminal acts ... by a method fraught with danger for millions and millions of people. . . . And had his masters tried to start a new world war, it is precisely these Powerses, reared and bred by them in the conditions of the so-called Free World, who would have been ready to be the first to drop atom and hydrogen bombs on the peaceful earth. . . . But taking into account Defendant Powers's sincere repentance . . . I do not insist on the death sentence . . . and ask the court to sentence him to fifteen years' imprisonment."

Far back in the hall, Oliver Powers sprang to his feet and shouted, "Give *me* fifteen years here! I'd rather get *death!*" (Barbara later said that she felt like saying, "Sit down and shut up.")

Griniev replied that Powers was nothing but a "tool of the aggressive policy of the Eisenhower-Nixon-Herter administration." Mass unemployment had driven him to join the Air Force. Like all Americans, he had been taught to worship the Almighty Dollar. He had not realized that his $2,500 per month had a "most foul stench." When he signed his contract, Powers had not known what the CIA had planned for him. By testifying candidly, he had risked antagonizing his American masters. He deserved "a more lenient punishment."

Now the U-2 pilot rose: "I realize that I have committed a grave crime and I realize that I must be punished for it." He asked the court to consider that no secret information had reached its destination. "I realize the Russian people think of me as an enemy. . . . I plead to the court to judge me not as an enemy, but as a human being who is not a personal enemy of the Russian people, who has never had any charges brought against him in any court, and who is deeply repentant and profoundly sorry for what he has done."

•

At 5:30 P.M., the three judges returned to the stage after almost five hours of deliberation. Powers stood and gripped the wooden rail of the prisoner's dock. The presiding judge noted that Powers had been a long-time CIA agent performing spy missions against the Soviet

Union. The May Day flight had been a "grave crime." But the court was impressed by his confession and "sincere repentance." In the interest of "socialist humaneness," his sentence would be ten years' "deprivation of liberty," the first three to be served in prison.

The hall rocked with applause—thanks to the harshness or lenience of the sentence, no one could tell. Powers was taken to a room set out with sandwiches, caviar and tea. His family rushed into his arms; all wept together and spoke at once. Barbara proposed moving to Moscow and working at the American Embassy, but Powers explained that he might not be allowed visitors. Soon he would go to another prison outside the capital; after three years, he would probably be sent to a remote labor camp. Before his family left, Powers asked them to tell the press that he renounced Griniev's attack on the American government.

●

In Washington, Jim Hagerty told reporters that the President regretted the severity of the sentence. Radio Moscow called this "monstrous hypocrisy": "The U.S. leaders have begun to masquerade as humanitarians, shedding tears over the fate of the man who carried out their sordid wish." Powers was merely the "bondsman of the Rockefellers and Morgans who turn the tears of the mothers of the world into gold."

Many Americans denounced the bondsman for what they considered his "cooperation" with the Russians and his repentance. "A traitor to his country," one New Yorker told the *New York Times.* The military historian S. L. A. Marshall could not tell whether Powers was "a man, a mouse or a long-tailed rat." Robert Maynard Hutchins was alarmed by "the difference between the behavior of Airman Powers and of Nathan Hale." William Faulkner thought the Russians might free him at once "in contemptuous implication that a nation so deeply reduced is not worth anyone's respect or fear."

After speaking with Allen Dulles, C. L. Sulzberger recorded that "Dulles left me with the impression that Powers should somehow have knocked himself off. He said Powers had been brainwashed or brain-conditioned prior to the trial. . . . I gather Dulles is unhappy with Powers's behavior, but doesn't like to say so."

Others noted that Powers had refused to denounce his country. A country-and-western singer named Red River Dave borrowed the tune of "The Battle Hymn of the Republic" and recorded "The Trial of Francis Gary Powers":

> In the stately Hall of Columns, 1960 was the year
> When young Francis Gary Powers stood before the Russian bear.
> They were trying him for spying, o'er the Soviets he flew
> In the famous plane, U-2.
>
> Glory, glory, he's a hero! Glory, glory, he's a hero!
> Glory, glory, he's a hero who flew for Uncle Sam.

•

Four days after the trial, Powers saw his sister and parents one more time; he wondered whether he would ever see Oliver and Ida again. After they left, Barbara walked in with a news bulletin: the State Department had declared in Washington that Powers had obeyed his instructions and would receive full salary while in prison. Parker and Rogers helped her draft a clemency appeal to President Brezhnev and Khrushchev.

Before Barbara left town, Powers was asked if he wished to see his wife once more, without guards. He said, "You know the answer to that!" He was taken to a cell in another Moscow prison furnished with an easy chair, sofa, sheets and blankets. When Barbara walked in, he noted the "strong smell of alcohol on her breath." She later recorded what happened next:

> Gary and I began to make mad love. In nothing flat ... we were bouncing up and down on Gary's cot, enjoying the true union of man and wife. We had intercourse three times in those three hours. Gary hadn't been able to bathe for twelve days and he smelled like a billy goat! But I didn't mind. I was swallowed up by our passion. . . .

•

Sam Jaffe never discovered who had placed him in Barbara Powers's entourage or given him a seat among Soviet dignitaries at the front of the Hall of Columns during the trial. His royal treatment had fueled colleagues' suspicions that he was working for the CIA, the KGB or both.

In 1961, he opened ABC's first bureau in Moscow. The next year, after a late evening of drinking, he was driving with a Russian woman when the car ran into a ditch. She left for help. When she returned, she told him that she had been interrogated and beaten as a prostitute who consorted with Americans. By Jaffe's account, he later lunched with a Russian "editor" who reported that he had kept the story out of the papers and could help Jaffe in other ways if the help were reciprocal. Jaffe later said that he informed the American Embassy, which told him to disengage gradually and report all conversations.

In 1964, the KGB defector Yuri Nosenko told the CIA that Jaffe had "collaborated" with the Soviet secret police. The Agency branded Jaffe "disapproved" and ordained that he "should not be used in any capacity." In 1969, after a stint in Hong Kong, he was called to the FBI, where agents hammered him about his years abroad and accused him of being a sleeper agent. As he recalled, "They didn't believe a word I told them. I left there crying." ABC demoted him and he quit, unable to find another job in journalism.

In 1974, after an internal investigation, CIA Director William Colby conceded that Jaffe had not been a CIA agent, but the FBI refused to clear him of serving the Russians. Before his death of lung cancer in 1985, Jaffe called hundreds of friends and acquaintances trying to clear his name. One was Barbara Powers, but she told him that she did not wish to "rehash" the past.

•

Vacationing at the Black Sea, Khrushchev had watched the Powers trial on television. He decided to extend the Soviet propaganda offensive by going to New York to head the Soviet delegation at the opening session of the UN General Assembly. There he could hurl firecrackers and stink bombs at Western governments, woo the Third World and try to influence the American Presidential campaign.

From Washington, Richard Nixon wrote Llewellyn Thompson, "We shall be looking forward to Khrushchev's visit with interest. I was wondering if he might decide to take the trip in one of their rockets. He isn't, of course, a dog, but most people think he is a son of a ———!" At a Moscow reception before departure, Khrushchev encountered Thompson and loudly berated him for the U-2. He stamped on Thompson's foot and cried, "If you do that, you should say, 'Excuse me!' "

Only a year had passed since Khrushchev's first trip to the United States. The great plane he had taken to Washington in 1959 was in disrepair. Rather than use a smaller one, he boarded a Soviet passenger ship abruptly renamed after the Anti-Party Coup from the *Molotov* to the *Baltika*. When the liner pulled in at the Port of New York, long-shoremen shouted, "Drop dead, you scum!" and refused to moor it. Russian diplomats reputedly had to tug on the ropes with their own hands. Apprised of possible assassination plots, Eisenhower restricted Khrushchev, Castro and Hungary's Janos Kadar to Manhattan Island.

Khrushchev gave shirtsleeve interviews from the Park Avenue balcony of the Soviet mission, called on Castro at the Hotel Theresa in Harlem, and dined at the Plaza, where dowagers booed him and he booed back. On September 22, the General Assembly session opened with the most glittering array of world leaders since 1945—Macmillan, Nehru, Nasser, Tito, Sukarno, Nkrumah. Fourteen new nations sat in the chamber for the first time. Eisenhower spoke on opening day. The *Economist* reported that he "let himself be whisked on and off the podium, like a piece of property on a revolving stage, lest he come into physical contact with Mr. Khrushchev."

The next day, Khrushchev delivered a searing three-hour attack on Western governments, demanding that UN Secretary-General Dag Hammarskjold be ousted in favor of an East-West-neutral troika. Third World leaders proposed a new summit meeting between Eisenhower and Khrushchev. Chip Bohlen advised the President to say no unless Khrushchev gave some sign of good faith like releasing the RB-47 fliers: otherwise the world would think that the Soviets were so powerful that they could treat the U.S. with contempt and then return to the Spirit of Camp David at the drop of a hat.

Khrushchev announced that he would see Eisenhower only if he apologized for the U-2 and the RB-47; he vainly demanded a General Assembly debate on the U-2 and immediate independence for all colonial territories. From the rostrum, he denounced the Security Council as a "spittoon," castigated Eisenhower for "lying" about spy flights and charged that a U.S. submarine had trailed the *Baltika* in hopes of sinking it. America was a "disgrace to civilization."

In Washington, the President told Herter, "Khrushchev is trying to promote chaos and bewilderment in the world to find out which nations are weakening under this attack and to pick what he can by fishing in troubled waters." He said he was a "long sufferer," but if he were a dictator, he would "launch an attack on Russia" while Khrushchev was in New York.

During his formal UN speech, Macmillan mentioned Khrushchev's destruction of the Paris Summit. From the audience, Khrushchev wagged his finger and shouted, "Yes, let us talk about Powers. Don't send your spy planes to our country!" Macmillan said, "I should like it translated, if you would." Later, in an imperishable gesture, Khrushchev beat his fist and his shoe on his desk. The presiding officer pounded his gavel so hard that it broke. *Pravda* called Macmillan the prisoner of obsolete views which filled the air "with the musty odor of the Victorian Age."

•

On the campaign trail, John Kennedy noted that the Khrushchev confined to Manhattan was the same man who had been asked to Camp David: "The Spirit of Camp David is gone. . . . The Soviets have made a spectacle before the world of the U-2 flight and the trial of our pilot and have treated this nation with hostility and contempt." Citing the Missile Gap, the U-2 affair, Cuba, the Congo, space and other setbacks, Kennedy cast Eisenhower's and Nixon's America as a nation whose political and military might was eroding.

Eisenhower wanted Kennedy to tone down his criticism of American defense policies. In August, before Allen Dulles flew to Hyannis Port to brief the Democrat on intelligence aspects of America's world position, the President asked him to stress America's commanding military strength. Given the lack of more conclusive evidence like satellite photography and the intelligence he had hoped to gain on May Day, Dulles would not affirm without reservation that there was no Missile Gap. Hence when Kennedy asked him how America stood in the missile race, Dulles cautiously replied that only the Pentagon could properly answer the question.

Late that month, Kennedy flew to SAC headquarters in Omaha for another briefing. As his aide Theodore Sorensen recalled, it soon became obvious that the candidate was not to be given a full-scale top-secret fill-in on American-Soviet bomber and missile strength. Kennedy carped that he had had more access to information as a member of the Senate Foreign Relations Committee: if the Air Force was that complacent, he would remember next year at budget time. In September, General Earle Wheeler briefed Kennedy in Washington on behalf of the Joint Chiefs. After the slide projector was turned off, Kennedy questioned Wheeler's assurances about the Missile Gap: "General, don't you have any doubting Thomases in the Pentagon?"

The failure of Dulles, Wheeler and SAC to foreclose any possibility of a Missile Gap allowed Kennedy to use the issue in the fall campaign. For the most part, he referred to the Soviet missile "advantage," avoiding dates and numbers, citing nonpartisan experts: "I say only that the evidence is strong . . . that we cannot be certain of our security in the future any more than we can be certain of disaster." More than once he branded his opponents as "the party which gave us the Missile Gap."

Before May Day, Richard Nixon had expected to be able to exploit Eisenhower's foreign policy record. Now he had to fend off Kennedy's attacks. He warned voters that Kennedy was "the kind of man Mr. Khrushchev will make mincemeat of." Asked again and again to defend the President's handling of the U-2 episode, he said, "Any of us as Sunday morning quarterbacks might have done things differently."

Had Kennedy asked the President to "express regrets" to Khrushchev? "That shows such a naïve attitude. . . . An apology or expressing regrets without getting something in return wouldn't have satisfied him. It wouldn't have saved the Conference. It would only have whetted his appetite. There was another reason too why the President of the United States could not and should not have done that. I say that that reason is that no President of this country must *ever* apologize or express regrets for attempting to defend the security of the United States against attack by somebody else!"

Kennedy replied by noting that the Eisenhower Administration had expressed regrets for the plane that had strayed across southern Russia in 1958: "That is the accepted practice between nations. . . . If that would have kept the Summit going, in my judgment, it was a proper action. It's not appeasement. It's not soft. . . . It would have been far better for us to follow the common diplomatic procedure of expressing regrets and then try to move on."

•

Khrushchev watched the first Kennedy-Nixon debate on television before going back to Moscow. As always, he saw the American campaign as a "circus wrestling match." He told reporters that the candidates were a pair of boots: "Which is better, the right boot or the left boot?" Pressed on his choice, he said, "Roosevelt!"

Privately he was less indifferent. He told aides that Nixon was "a typical product of McCarthyism, a puppet of the most reactionary circles in the United States. We'll never be able to find a common language with him." John Kennedy seemed less problematic. But mixing in American politics, as he had vainly tried with Stevenson in January, was a risky game. Embracing candidates too warmly was poison; fierce denunciations scared American voters seeking a President who could deal with the Kremlin.

The Eisenhower government was pressing for the release of Powers and the RB-47 fliers. As Khrushchev later said, "We had nothing against doing this. There was no need for us to keep Powers in prison. But the question was, when?" He told colleagues, "If we release Powers now, it will be to Nixon's advantage. Judging from the press, I think the two candidates are at a stalemate. If we give the slightest boost to Nixon, it will be interpreted as an expression of our willingness to see him in the White House." Khrushchev kept Powers in prison and, as he later boasted, cast the "deciding ballot" in Kennedy's election "over that son-of-a-bitch Richard Nixon."

●

To Eisenhower, the 1960 election was "the biggest defeat of my life, a repudiation of everything I've done for eight years." More than once, Nixon blamed his defeat in part on the CIA. Not only was the Agency responsible for the U-2 failure, but he suspected that CIA "liberals" (perhaps led by Allen Dulles at Hyannis Port) had deliberately withheld evidence disproving the Missile Gap in order to give Kennedy a powerful campaign issue.

Almost anything could have tipped the scales in a contest decided by one-tenth of one percent of the vote. Had the U-2 not plunged on May Day, had Eisenhower gone without incident to Paris, Moscow and Tokyo, had Powers not been tried and Khrushchev not made his angry trip to the UN, Nixon might have campaigned as the heir to a triumphant diplomacy. Kennedy would have had a difficult time persuading Americans that their world position was in decline.

●

Shortly after the election, the first satellite photos of the Soviet Union were studied in Washington. They showed that had Francis Gary Powers reached Plesetsk on May Day, he might have seen the first four operational Soviet ICBMs. These and later pictures showed no evidence of other long-range missiles deployed anywhere in the

Soviet Union. The public did not know it yet, but the myth of the Missile Gap was being shattered.

•

During the fall of 1960, NBC News completed a documentary called *The U-2 Affair*. Airing was delayed until late November to avoid charges of influencing the election. The program began with the scream of an aircraft engine and Chet Huntley's introduction: "You are listening to the sound of a jet. It is not an ordinary jet. This is a U-2. This is the incredible plane that projected our country into a crisis that shook the world."

Using newsreel film and interviews with Kelly Johnson, Ida Powers, Jim Hagerty and others, the program reconstructed what was publicly known about the project, the May Day flight and its aftermath. Asked by Ray Scherer about what could be learned from the episode, Hagerty snapped, "Don't get caught." In his benediction, Huntley recalled that when asked the same question, Christian Herter had said, "Not to have accidents":

"We leave it to the American public to decide whether 'Don't get caught' and 'Not to have accidents' are the only lessons to be learned from the U-2. . . . This is not a matter for the history books but vitally affects our ability to survive as a nation. . . . In the world as it is today, we cannot afford another U-2 affair. Good night."

Watching in the family quarters of the White House, Eisenhower was so angry about the show that he complained to his friend David Sarnoff, founder and chairman of NBC. Sarnoff explained that he had not known about the program until its airing: his son, the network's president, would be called on the carpet. He would do all in his power "to correct any unpleasantness or embarrassment." In fact, he would order NBC News to run a televised tribute to the President in January before he left office.

When Nixon was asked to participate in the tribute, he replied that he did not wish to be in the public eye now and was "furious about the U-2 show." He told his staff that the "only way" to change the press was "not to cooperate with them." Leonard Hall found Nixon "completely irrational" about the program, but when the Republican chairman explained that absence from the tribute would be an insult to the President, Nixon said he would "do anything."

On New Year's 1961, the Soviet government and guests gathered in the Great Hall of the Kremlin for the annual celebration. With Orwellian rhetoric, Khrushchev raised his glass and declared, "No matter how good the old year has been, the new year 1961 will be better still." He said it was "well known" that relations with America had been damaged—especially by the spy plane incident and President Eisenhower's declaration that such flights were his deliberate policy toward the Soviet Union. "We would like our bad relations with the U.S.A. to become a thing of the past with the departure of the old year and the old President."

On January 20, 1961, John Kennedy took the oath of office. The old President and First Lady drove through the snow to Gettysburg, "where we expected to spend the remainder of our lives," as Eisenhower later wrote. "I had to admit to little success in making progress in global disarmament or in reducing the bitterness of the East-West struggle. . . . It seems incomprehensible that the men in the Kremlin can be ready to risk the destruction of their entire industrial fabric, their cities, their society and their ambitions rather than to enter into practical treaties, including systems of mutual inspection, that would immeasurably enrich their lives and those of all nations in the world.

"But though, in this, I suffered my greatest disappointment, it has not destroyed my faith that in the next generation, the next century, the next millennium, these things will come to pass."

●

On the day after the Kennedy inauguration, Khrushchev summoned Ambassador Thompson to the Kremlin and told him that he was releasing the RB-47 fliers as a step toward warmer relations with the United States. The new President greeted the airmen at Andrews Air Force Base. He declared that flights into Soviet airspace had been suspended since May 1960 and, as he had pledged during the campaign, would not be renewed.

Powers learned of the release while listening to Radio Moscow in his cell: he was "happy for the RB-47 boys," but could not help thinking that if they had not been downed, he might have been the one freed. In September 1960, he had been brought to Vladimir Prison, 150 miles east of Moscow. Lonely after months of solitude in Lubyanka, he had asked for a cellmate. Zigurd Kruminsh was a young Latvian who had been working in Latvia for the British Secret Service when the Soviets caught him, tried and failed to force him to name names, then sent him to Vladimir, where he taught Powers to weave Latvian carpets and speak some Russian.

As the months passed, Powers was deeply depressed by the paucity and diffidence of letters from Barbara. In February 1961, he wrote in his diary, "I can never have a future with her, because the past will always be between us. There seems no other way than a divorce when I return to the States. It should have been done in 1957. . . . I thought at the time I loved her too much to let her go, that I wouldn't admit failure, but now I don't know. . . . I am at my wit's end as to what to do."

•

That month in Washington, Ambassador Menshikov appealed to Chester Bowles, the new Under Secretary of State, for the release of Igor Melekh, a Russian in the UN Secretariat arrested for espionage in October 1960. Bowles said the request might be granted if the Soviets released Powers. Menshikov argued that Melekh should be freed without condition, like the RB-47 fliers.

Melekh was released; the State Department suspected that Powers's liberation might be the next step toward better relations. But when Tommy Thompson brought up the matter in Moscow, Andrei Gromyko merely said he was "glad" Thompson understood that the Melekh and Powers cases were "entirely different."

In June 1961, John Kennedy met Khrushchev at Vienna. Secretary of State Dean Rusk had advised him to let a member of his party raise the Powers case with a member of Khrushchev's party: it had been the American understanding that the Soviets would not have pressed for Melekh's release without a similar gesture in mind.

Over lunch with Kennedy at the American Embassy, Khrushchev recalled the last Soviet-American summit: he had respected Eisenhower and regretted the unhappy culmination of their relations. He was still "almost certain" that Eisenhower hadn't known about the May Day flight and had chivalrously taken responsibility for it. He was sorry to have missed receiving Eisenhower in the Soviet Union and hoped to welcome Kennedy when the time was ripe. Nixon had hoped to convert the Soviet people to capitalism with a dream kitchen that did not exist and would never exist. He apologized for mentioning Nixon, but "only Nixon could have thought of such nonsense."

Khrushchev told the President that he had "voted" for him in 1960 by postponing the RB-47 release, and Kennedy agreed. But the two-day talks in Vienna did not advance the U-2 pilot's freedom. Asked by newsmen about the Powers case, Kennedy said, "The matter wasn't even discussed." When Powers heard of this, he wrote in his diary, "I don't expect him to go out of his way to help me, but I feel that I would have been released long before now if he had made the slightest effort when he met with Khrushchev."

●

In Milledgeville, Barbara Powers took a job as a bookkeeper at the Log Cabin restaurant: "I didn't know that a vicious gossip network already was weaving a scarlet robe around my shoulders. Some of the wicked tongues had even renamed the Log Cabin 'the U-2'! It was darkly rumored that . . . one night, during a wild bash, I was supposed to have performed a 'naughty strip tease' in the party room upstairs."

In September 1961, Barbara's mother, brother and sister had her legally declared incompetent and committed to a psychiatric clinic in Atlanta, where she was assigned to Dr. Corbett Thigpen, author of *The Three Faces of Eve,* the famous account of split personality whose film version starred Joanne Woodward. Barbara's mother and sister wrote Powers in Vladimir that it "pained" them to report the bad news.

He wrote in his diary, "I am becoming more and more afraid of what the future holds for me."

●

Unbeknownst to Powers, the CIA was now trying to win his release in exchange for one of the highest-ranking Soviet agents ever captured in the United States. Rudolf Ivanovich Abel was a hawkfaced, pop-eyed, ascetic KGB colonel who had a weakness for Panama hats with hatbands in dazzling colors. He spoke Russian, German, Polish, Yiddish and English, the last in Scottish, Irish, Oxford and Brooklyn accents.

Abel claimed that he was born to a prominent family in Moscow in 1902. As far as the CIA knew, he was slipped into a German displaced persons camp after the Second World War and sent to North America. In 1950, he settled in Brooklyn and posed as a painter and photographer under the alias of Emil Goldfus. He relaxed by reading Einstein, working out mathematical problems and writing a pamphlet called *You Cannot Mix Art and Politics.* At the same time, he performed minor operational chores for the KGB, receiving instructions from Moscow on codes and ciphers evidently while waiting for the recruitment of an American spy of sufficient stature for assignment to him.

In 1957, his assistant, Reino Hayhayen, defected and exposed him. At the detention center in McAllen, Texas, federal agents could not break him: Abel refused even to admit that he was a Soviet citizen. As defense counsel, he was assigned James Donovan, a snow-haired Harvard Law graduate who had been an OSS general counsel and planner of the Nuremberg trials. Ordinarily condescending, Abel treated Donovan "like an understanding colleague" after learning of his OSS background.

The lawyer argued in court that Abel's room had been searched unconstitutionally. Stoical as ever, Abel did not utter a word in his own defense and got thirty years in federal prison in Atlanta. Donovan vainly fought the case all the way to the Supreme Court.

In June 1960, Oliver Powers wrote Abel in prison, offering to ask the American government to trade him for his son. Abel contacted Donovan: having consistently claimed to be an East German, he asked the lawyer to correspond with his "wife" in Leipzig. In the summer of 1961, she wrote him that she had gone to the Soviet Embassy in East Berlin and found the Soviets sympathetic to a Powers-for-Abel exchange. Donovan and the CIA's Lawrence Houston suspected that "Hellen Abel" was actually a KGB agent: the Russians probably were worried that, faced with prison until 1987, Abel might break down and tell all. Snatching back a captured agent would lift KGB morale all over the world. And Abel might be useful working on the American desk in Moscow.

Donovan wrote Mrs. Abel that the Soviets should release Powers unilaterally, as with the Melekh case. Then she could appeal to President Kennedy for her husband's clemency. She replied that the Embassy in East Berlin felt there must be a simultaneous exchange.

In November 1961, the CIA cleared the way. Pearre Cabell wrote Dean Rusk that while the Russians may have felt that they had learned everything from Powers worth knowing, the CIA believed that he had not revealed information that could embarrass the United States, such as details of U-2 flights without permission over nations in Europe, the Middle East and Asia. The CIA wished to know the "precise events" leading to his capture, and about his treatment and interrogation. Powers's letters from prison suggested that he was worried about his wife and Washington's failure to get him freed. Soon he might give away the secrets he had been holding back. Returned to Moscow, Abel would never be fully trusted again. Any American secrets he brought back would be at least five years out of date.

J. Edgar Hoover angrily opposed an exchange. He reminded Attorney General Robert Kennedy that Abel was a far more valuable agent than Powers—and that "it would be catastrophic if the United States arranged for Powers's release and he then refused to come home."

But in January 1962, Donovan was called to Washington and told that an exchange had been approved at the "highest level." Donovan wrote Mrs. Abel of "significant developments" and proposed a meeting at the Soviet Embassy in East Berlin at noon on February third. As requested, she cabled back the affirmative signal, "HAPPY NEW YEAR."

The CIA informed Donovan that the East Germans were also holding a Yale graduate student named Frederic Pryor, who had been arrested for espionage while researching a dissertation, and Marvin Makinen, a Fulbright scholar sentenced to eight years in prison for photographing Soviet military installations. Donovan should try to free all three Americans, but his principal objective should be Powers.

At the Embassy in East Berlin, he was greeted by a woman who introduced herself as Mrs. Abel. Donovan thought she looked more like a German character actress. Sobbing, she asked for details about Abel's prison life.

Then Ivan Schischkin walked into the room. Officially he was the Embassy's second secretary, but the CIA knew him as chief of Soviet espionage in Western Europe. He told Donovan, "Over a year ago, these Abel people came to my office ... because they are East Germans. I heard their story and told them I would intercede with the Soviet government to see whether Powers might be exchanged for Abel. I later received a favorable reply from Moscow because certain fascist factions in the United States have sought to link this East German Abel with the Soviet Union."

Mrs. Abel's attorney, Wolfgang Vogel, had told the American mission in West Berlin that she was "confident" Pryor and Makinen would be freed if the U.S. exchanged Abel for Powers. But now when Donovan mentioned the other two prisoners, Schischkin claimed that he had never heard of them. Donovan said that if Schischkin wouldn't discuss them, he would have returned home. On the other hand, President Kennedy had already signed a commutation of Abel's sentence for the event of an exchange. If they made a deal, Abel could be in East Berlin within forty-eight hours.

The talks lasted four days. Each evening, Donovan went back to West Berlin, dialed a special number, said, "Jim D. is back," and met his CIA contact at the bar of the Berlin Hilton. Reports were cabled directly to the White House. On Thursday, February 9, Donovan and Schischkin cut their deal: Powers would be traded for Abel. The East Germans would release Pryor at the same moment at a separate place. If Soviet-American relations improved, there was "every expectation" that Makinen would be freed. Adamant against confessing that the Soviets practiced espionage, Schischkin demanded that Abel not be publicly connected to the Soviet government.

At the White House, John Kennedy was concerned about Hoover's obstinacy. He asked aides to make sure that the FBI Director was "fully informed and in agreement with what is going on."

•

Saturday, February 10, 1962. Over the Havel River, spanning East Germany and West Berlin, the Glienicker Bridge had been prematurely named in 1945 "the bridge of unity."

It was altogether fitting for the old veteran of human intelligence to be surrendered for the most famous symbol of the new age of technology. Abel had been flown to West Berlin and housed in a maximum-security cell in the U.S. military compound. Powers was being kept in a luxurious, well-guarded safe house in East Berlin. Schischkin told him that if anything went wrong at the bridge, he must return to the East, but Powers later said that he had silently resolved to run for it—even if it meant dodging bullets.

At 8:20 A.M., the quadrille began. Through a chilly mist, Donovan walked to the center of the green bridge, escorted by an American diplomat and a U-2 alumnus named Joseph Murphy. Schischkin and two colleagues arrived from the opposite end. The principals shook hands and beckoned. From the West came Abel in sunglasses, carrying overstuffed bags, manacled to a guard. Powers arrived in fur hat and heavy coat, shackled to two Russian Goliaths. Abel was identified by a KGB man, Powers by his old friend Murphy.

As they waited for the Americans to confirm Pryor's release at

Friedrichstrasse, Schischkin told Powers, "Next time you come to see us, come as a friend." Powers pledged to come as a tourist. Schischkin replied, "I didn't say as a tourist. I said as a *friend.*"

Someone shouted, "Pryor's been released!" Schischkin cried, "The document! The document!" Kennedy's official pardon was countersigned and handed to Abel.

At the instant the two prisoners passed each other at the center line, the sun came out. Murphy slapped his U-2 colleague on the back: "You know who that was, don't you?" Powers shook his head: he had not been told that his liberation was part of a trade.

Abel returned to Moscow. The KGB would not trust him and few in the West really believed he was an East German, so the Russians turned necessity into virtue by making him a hero. He was reportedly granted the Order of Lenin, a chauffeured car and dacha, and enough Lucky Strikes to support his three-pack-a-day habit. In the mid-1960s, the Soviet press claimed that he had been a far more vital cog than the Americans had ever known and that he had destroyed crucial evidence in front of his FBI captors.

In 1971, after his death of lung cancer, the KGB stuck a finger in the CIA's eye one more time by revealing that Abel had actually been born in Britain to Russian emigré parents in 1903. Western newsmen were taken to his grave, where they discovered that his actual name had never even been Rudolf Abel but William Fischer.

•

While the Americans and Russians went through their paces at the Glienicker Bridge, the John Kennedys were holding a White House dinner for the Stephen Smiths: the President's brother-in-law was leaving his post in the State Department. At 11:30 P.M., Kennedy crossed the dance floor and ascertained from his friend Benjamin Bradlee of *Newsweek* that it was too late to change the magazine's next cover.

An hour later, he told him about Powers and Abel. Bradlee called the news in to *Newsweek*'s sister publication, the *Washington Post,* and later marveled, "Imagine a reporter dictating an exclusive story from the best of all possible sources to the strains of a dance orchestra playing inside the White House!"

At two in the morning, on an open telephone line from Berlin, the President learned that the exchange had taken place. At three, his press secretary, Pierre Salinger, made the public announcement. By Brad-lee's recollection, Salinger was flustered to find that the *Post* had had the story for two hours.

•

Flying from West Berlin, a doctor examined Powers and drew blood samples to establish that the Russians had not drugged him. At Wiesbaden, Powers, Donovan and Murphy boarded the plush Super-constellation assigned to the U.S. Air Force's commanding general in Europe. Powers said, "You know, a couple of weeks ago in my cell, I dreamed one night about a martini." As they dined on steak and pota-toes, Donovan related the events that had led to his freedom.

In 1960, Donovan had publicly criticized Powers for cooperation with the Russians during the Moscow trial. Now as they spoke, he concluded that the pilot was just the kind of man CIA would want to sail a shaky espionage glider over the heart of Russia: "Powers was a man who, for adequate pay, would do it and as he passed over Minsk, would calmly reach for a salami sandwich."

The plane landed secretly in Delaware. Powers was rushed to a fourteen-room Georgian house owned by the CIA on a hundred snowy acres in Oxford, Maryland. After a large breakfast and a session with a CIA psychiatrist, he was jubilantly reunited with Ida and Oliver. Then Barbara arrived, three months out of the Atlanta clinic and thirty pounds heavier than when he had last seen her. She burst into tears and he said, "Barbara honey, I swore in prison that the first tree I saw after I was released I would name after you."

Reporters discovered the safe house. The Powerses ducked down as a convoy sped them to a new location, of all places, near the Eisen-hower farm in Gettysburg. Kelly Johnson arrived by helicopter in a snowstorm: "Before we start, I want to tell Mr. Powers something. No matter what happens as a result of this investigation, I want you to know that if you ever need a job, you have one at Lockheed." Then: "What happened to my plane?"

After Johnson had his turn, CIA men debriefed Powers for eight days. The press once again learned their whereabouts and they moved to another safe house near the Agency's new headquarters in Langley. Powers was dissatisfied with the questions. Years later, he said, "I couldn't help discerning an obvious pattern behind them—that the Agency was not really interested in what I had to tell them. Their pri-mary concern was to get the CIA off the hook."

•

The U-2 pilot's return renewed the national controversy over his performance on May Day and during the Moscow trial. "A HERO OR A MAN WHO FAILED HIS MISSION?" asked the *New York Herald Tribune*. John Wickers of the American Legion told reporters that Powers was "a cowardly American who evidently valued his own skin far more than the welfare of the nation that was paying him so handsomely." Senator Stephen Young said, "I wish that this pilot who was being paid thirty thousand dollars a year had shown only ten percent of the spirit and courage of Nathan Hale." *Newsday* said that he should be denied his $52,500 in back pay: "He was hired to do a job and he flopped."

Unexposed to the original public attack in 1960, Powers was stunned by what he now heard and read. Americans did not seem to grasp that he had not been required to kill himself if his plane went down. They did not know that he had withheld information from the Russians about earlier intrusions, flights over other nations without permission, CIA personnel, American missiles in Turkey, the U-2's actual ceiling and British involvement in the U-2 operation. He had resisted pressure to denounce the United States at his trial and confirm absolutely that his plane had been downed by a Soviet rocket. He had resisted the charge that the flight had been sent to sabotage the Paris Summit.

During and after the trial, Powers had been lampooned in the West as merely "an airplane driver—simple, half-educated, nonpolitical, deliberately chosen for his lumpish lack of curiosity," as James Morris described the conventional wisdom in the *Manchester Guardian*. In fact, the pilot had worked hard to create this image to justify his professed ignorance about huge areas of the U-2 program. Especially given the fact that he had had minimal instruction on behavior if captured, Powers had displayed subtlety, shrewdness and boldness throughout his ordeal.

But what Americans would always remember was his confession that he was "deeply repentant and profoundly sorry" for what he had done—words that would haunt him for the rest of his life.

•

At the end of his debriefing, Powers was taken to Washington to be introduced to Allen Dulles. After the failed Cuban invasion at the Bay of Pigs, President Kennedy had decided to ease out Dulles and Bissell. At the old CIA headquarters in Foggy Bottom, Dulles was packing up his belongings. Bemused by the irony of their meeting, he shook the pilot's hand and told him that he had heard quite a bit about him. He said he had been reading Powers's debriefing reports: "We are proud of what you have done."

Dulles's successor, John McCone, was not so sure. As Lawrence Houston recalled, during the course of the investigation, they "were getting slightly different stories."

On Houston's suggestion, McCone set up a Board of Inquiry: members included retired Federal Judge E. Barrett Prettyman, John Bross, a lawyer and veteran CIA covert operator and Lieutenant General Harold Roe "Pinky" Bull of the CIA's Office of National Estimates, who had been General Eisenhower's wartime operations chief in Europe. They watched a Soviet film of the Moscow trial and questioned U-2 fliers and technicians, a National Security Agency analyst, a CIA counterintelligence man and Powers himself.

Powers disliked the whole process. The formal hearings reminded him of his interrogation and trial by the Soviets. At one point, he was so annoyed by Prettyman's "accusatory" manner that he cried, "If you don't believe me, I'll be glad to take a lie detector test!" The offer was accepted so quickly that he suspected he had been goaded to make it so that the CIA could tell the press that he had "volunteered" for a polygraph test.

The Board was under the gun to end the public controversy over Powers's performance in Russia with a prompt report. On March 3, after a twelve-day inquiry, McCone gave it to the President. Cautiously worded, the fourteen pages said that the Board's findings on what had really happened between Powers's takeoff from Peshawar and his Moscow trial had to be based mainly on his own testimony: "If his account is correct, the Board is of the opinion that in light of the circumstances, he acted in accordance with the terms of his employment and his instructions and briefings . . . and complied with his obligations as an American citizen during this period."

The report found Powers "inherently and by practice a truthful man." He had not been brainwashed. He had made "reasonable" efforts to destroy his plane and equipment when downed. He had complied with orders to tell the full truth about his mission, if captured, except for certain specifics of the plane. His public repentance in Moscow must be considered "trial tactics." He was entitled to back pay.

An expurgated version of the report was issued to the press. Powers thought it equivocal and evasive. Why couldn't the Board have told the country that he had withheld information from the Russians that was vital to national security?

•

After noon on March 6, 1962, spectators crammed into the Senate Caucus Room, where Joseph McCarthy had once pursued Communists and where John Glenn had been feted as the first American to orbit the earth two weeks before. The doors burst open. Shouting cameramen backed into the room. "One of the finest pieces of theater we've ever seen," wrote Richard Strout in the *New Republic.* "Center of the commotion was a calm, young man fresh from Soviet prison and CIA hideaway who wrecked a Summit, colored a campaign and shook the world."

The press had noted that the President had welcomed the RB-47 fliers at Andrews Air Force Base but snubbed Powers. The U-2 pilot himself had heard that Robert Kennedy thought he should be tried for treason. The morning of his trip to the Senate, by Powers's account, he was told that Kennedy wished to see him but, as he waited for his limousine, the White House called and canceled the appointment.

William Fulbright had bid to reopen the Foreign Relations Committee's U-2 hearings, but CIA officials recalled what they considered Fulbright's harsh treatment in 1960: Richard Russell's Armed Services Committee was a warmer ally of American intelligence. Now as Powers sat down at the witness table, someone thrust a U-2 model into his hands. Flashbulbs went off, and every paper in the United States had its page one photo.

For nearly two years, the world had speculated on what had brought down the U-2 on May Day. Soviet missile fire? Malfunction? Pilot error? Pilot defection? Sabotage? The Board of Inquiry had not provided an official explanation; that had not been its assignment. Presumably certain that it would leak, John McCone privately told congressmen that CIA experts had concluded that the U-2 was disabled at 68,000 feet by the near-miss of a Soviet missile. Soon this hit the newspapers.

Now the Caucus Room was silent as Powers told the senators of the dull noise, the bright orange light and the plane spinning out of control: "My first reaction was to reach for the destruct switches ... but I thought that I had better see if I can get out of here before using this. ... I was being thrown forward, and if I had used the ejection seat at that time, I would have probably lost both legs. ...

"I kept glancing at the altimeter as the aircraft was falling and it was going around very fast. ... I tried to get back into the aircraft so that I could activate these destructor switches. ... I couldn't get back in the airplane. I didn't know whether I could get those oxygen hoses loose or not. I couldn't activate the destruct switches, so then I decided just to try and get out. ..."

He described the poison pin, his capture, incarceration and apology in Moscow: "I made this statement on the advice of my defense counsel. ... My main sorrow was that the mission failed."

Leverett Saltonstall of Massachusetts asked about the parachute and survival kit, and praised him as a "courageous, fine, young American citizen." Powers choked up: except for his talk with Allen Dulles, this was his first commendation by a high government official. John Stennis of Mississippi noted that Powers had been "exonerated by the men who must know how to judge what you did. ... I know it makes you feel mighty good."

Powers replied, "There was one thing that I always remembered while I was there—and that was that I am an American."

"And proud of it?"

"Right." The room resounded. One reporter noted that at that instant, Powers seemed almost as beloved as Colonel Glenn. Other senators praised the witness, but Barry Goldwater was uncommonly silent: during the hearing, he sent Powers a penciled note ("You did a good job for your country—Thanks"), but he did not believe that the pilot's version of his downing was the way it had happened at all.

After ninety minutes, the star witness left the chamber. Reporters asked Powers what he planned to do with his back pay, and he cried, *"Spend* it!"

How?

"Slowly!"

Then, as *Time* reported, the U-2 pilot "disappeared into a waiting government car, leaving behind a persistent feeling that some of his story remained untold."

★

14

Who Shattered Détente?

ESPECIALLY SINCE THE DAY IN MAY 1960 when their government confessed that it had lied about the true mission of the U-2, Americans have been inclined to distrust official explanations. Serious people have pondered whether the Kennedy assassination, the Gulf of Tonkin incident, Watergate and other pivotal episodes were not secretly instigated by some individual or group to alter the course of history. Such suspicions have come full circle to the U-2. What caused Francis Gary Powers's plane to fall has never been finally resolved.

In May 1960, CIA officials quietly suggested to reporters that Khrushchev had lied when he claimed that Powers had been downed by a Soviet missile at over 65,000 feet. Instead, they said, a flameout or other malfunction had probably forced the pilot to a lower altitude, where he was a sitting duck for Soviet fighter planes and missiles.

The American government of 1960 had a powerful motive to sell this theory to the public: at the time, the principal delivery system for American nuclear weapons was the manned bomber, which could not reach anywhere near 65,000 feet. If the American people were told that the Russians could down planes at that altitude, they might conclude that the Soviet Union could now defend itself against nuclear attack. In the middle of a campaign, the national hysteria might have exceeded that after *Sputnik*. A Democratic landslide that November would have almost been assured.

The CIA may have had an additional motive: at a time when senators were scrutinizing its role in the U-2 affair and threatening tighter supervision, it might have been safer to blame the fiasco on bad luck than on the Agency's failure to forecast that the Soviets had missiles that could strike the U-2. In June 1960, Allen Dulles advised the Senate Foreign Relations Committee that when sending a U-2 deep into a hostile land, there was "no cushion against malfunction." Later that month in Paris, he spoke with C. L. Sulzberger of the *New York Times,* who wrote in his diary:

> Dulles is sure Gary Powers was not shot down at normal altitude (about 70,000 feet). The U-2, when it reaches rarefied altitudes, tends to get a flameout. We think Powers glided down to try and restart his motor. He was then shot down around 30,000–40,000 feet. Present Soviet defenses don't go above 60,000 feet. We think Powers parachuted.

In the summer of 1960, Khrushchev was obviously determined to convince the world that his armed forces had downed the U-2 at over 65,000 feet. He had already been under fire for his military reductions. Many Russians were furious to learn that their nation had not been able to keep earlier American aircraft from invading: if the Powers plane had been stopped only by the sheer bad luck of engine failure, that meant Khrushchev could not prevent future incursions. This was almost certainly why Powers was pressured to testify at his Moscow trial that a Soviet missile had struck him at what he had told them was the U-2's "maximum" altitude of 68,000 feet.

In February 1962, Powers was back in the United States. After simulating the May Day flight and studying *Life*'s pictures of the U-2 at Gorky Park, Powers's recollections and other evidence, Kelly Johnson proposed to the Board of Inquiry that the plane had indeed been downed by a Soviet missile at high altitude: "When the SA-2 went off, it blew off the right-hand stabilizer. . . . it wasn't a direct hit." He knew that the SA-2 was not supposed to be able to hit precise targets over 60,000 feet but speculated that the U-2's granger box, designed to throw off Soviet radar, may have allowed the Russians to get a fix on the plane at high altitude.

The National Security Agency protested: Powers may have been hit by a missile, but not at high altitude. Communications intelligence showed the U-2 slowly gliding down to 30,000 or 40,000 feet before dropping to earth. The NSA evidence made John McCone suspect that Powers had deliberately flown his plane to lower altitude and defected by parachute. John Bross argued against NSA's findings. Judge Prettyman told McCone that he would never have let such unverifiable hearsay into his courtroom.

The Board of Inquiry had been asked to approach the matter of Powers's downing chiefly in terms of how it bore on his fulfillment of his obligations. The Board's secret report argued that the NSA material must not invalidate the fact that Powers's testimony had showed "no substantial deviations" from most of the other evidence. The public version of the report tried to scotch the story that Powers had been downed at a lower altitude:

> Some information from confidential sources was available. Some of it corroborated Powers and some of it was inconsistent in parts with Powers's story, but that which was inconsistent was in part contradictory with itself and subject to various interpretations. Some of this information was the basis for considerable speculation ... that Powers's plane had descended gradually from its extreme altitude and been shot down by a Russian fighter at medium altitude.
>
> On careful analysis, it appears that the information on which these stories were based was erroneous or susceptible of varying interpretations. The Board ... could not accept a doubtful interpretation in this regard which was inconsistent with all the other known facts and consequently rejected these newspaper stories as not founded in fact.

After the press revealed John McCone's suggestion that Powers had been downed by an SA-2 near-miss at 68,000 feet, this became the semi-official verdict on the U-2. No comprehensive, impartial investigation of the downing was ever held, leaving a fog of doubt about how the black plane really fell on May Day.

•

In 1975, at the time the Senate Select Committee on Intelligence and the American people were listening to revelations about CIA assassination plots and other "family jewels," James Nathan of the University of Delaware published an article in *Military Affairs* suggesting that someone in the American government—perhaps the CIA—may have used the U-2 as a "device deliberately chosen to destroy an emerging détente":

> The anomalies in the Powers case suggest that the U-2 incident may have been staged. There was the timing of his trip, the unusually long route chosen to overfly the Soviet Union, his undisguised Ameri-

can origins, his retrieval by and continued association with the CIA, the reluctance of Congressional committees charged with the oversight of such matters to ask any searching questions, and other indications that Powers had done essentially what he had been told. . . .

The cover story was preposterous and unserious. . . . There was the unwillingness to affix responsibility for the flight below the level of the White House . . . the loudly-repeated claim that the violation of Soviet airspace was necessary for American security and might be resumed . . . and the last-minute nuclear alert. . . . All these "administrative failures" indicate that even if the weird flight and strange behavior of Powers was fortuitous, the U-2 presented an opportunity which may not have been unwelcomed.

This was a variation on Khrushchev's original contention that the CIA, Pentagon and other Cold War circles had sent the U-2 into Russia without the President's approval, hoping to cause an incident that would wreck détente. Even had Allen Dulles wished to thwart Eisenhower's policies, it is doubtful that he would have sought to do so in a fashion that would humiliate the CIA and provoke Congressional oversight. Had the President wished to get out of the Paris Summit, he could have done so in many ways that were less self-damaging than staging a U-2 affair.

In a 1975 television documentary, a Norwegian fisherman and convicted Soviet spy named Selmer Nilsen declared that the U-2 had been downed by a bomb planted by a Soviet agent in its tail before takeoff from Peshawar. Nilsen said that he had covered the Bodö base for Soviet intelligence and been told about the bomb by a KGB officer in Moscow at a party held in May 1960 to celebrate the downing of the U-2.

Throughout the U-2 program, American counterintelligence had evidently questioned Turkish broomsweepers and other base personnel on suspicion of spying or trying to sabotage the planes. The KGB and GRU may have contributed to Powers's downing by their years of gathering information on the pilots, planes, bases and ground arrangements. They may have been aided by lapses in American security: on May Day 1960, coded radio transmissions to Adana reputedly broke down, causing a CIA man in Germany to break the rules and send approval for the U-2 flight over an open telephone that might have been tapped by the Russians. Moscow may have known when Powers was flying into Russia before he did. But how much that would have helped the Russians to down the plane is questionable.

There is a large difference between espionage and sabotage. At a time when Khrushchev was throwing laurels on his military for downing the U-2, it is not implausible that someone in the KGB should have tried to divert some of the credit. Informed of Nilsen's charge, Powers said that he did not think his plane was sabotaged: the U-2s were so heavily inspected before each flight that it "would have had to be an inside job." Richard Bissell thought the charge was "nonsense."

•

One must return to the most official judgment the American government ever rendered on the U-2: Was the plane downed by the near-miss of an SA-2 at 68,000 feet?

The Gorky Park photographs suggest almost at once that the U-2 was brought down by a large explosion at or near the rear of the plane. It is more difficult to accept that the explosion happened at 68,000 feet. Powers's plane was able to fly at least five thousand feet higher. The CIA knew that the SA-2 could hit precise targets up to 60,000 feet and was capable of reaching 70,000. Sverdlovsk was known to be defended by SA-2s. Prudence would have commanded the CIA to assign the pilot to an altitude over 70,000 feet before reaching the city to avoid trouble.*

A secret State Department report concluded in June 1960 that the U-2 debris at Gorky Park was in strangely good condition for a plane that had been struck at 68,000 feet and plunged to the ground: "Large undamaged sections would hardly have survived, and the fact that they did survive is inconsistent with the report by personnel of the missile battery of 'fragments of the foreign-spy aircraft falling in the rays of the May sun' and with statements that the wreckage was scattered over a 15-kilometer area."

If the U-2 was struck at lower altitude, why would the American government in 1962 have tacitly confirmed the official Soviet version (as presented at the trial) that Powers had been downed at 68,000 feet? One explanation could be that among the terms for Powers's release

---

* Powers, of course, maintained that 68,000 feet was merely a figure he had chosen to throw off the Russians. (See Chapter Thirteen.)

was a tacit American pledge, never to be revealed, that the U-2 pilot would not be allowed to recant his Moscow testimony about the circumstances of his downing once he returned to the United States. Khrushchev would have been ill-disposed to release Powers only to have him reveal that the Soviet government had lied to its own people and the world about the U-2.

For the Kennedy Administration to avoid gratuitously antagonizing Khrushchev, such a pledge would have been a small price to pay. Conceding that the Soviets had missiles that could reach 68,000 feet was not the political risk that it might have been in 1960: by now, large numbers of American bombers were being equipped with air-to-ground missiles that allowed them to launch nuclear warheads into the Soviet Union from well outside Soviet airspace.

Two days after Powers's debriefing began, President Kennedy told his friend Ben Bradlee that he did not know how high Powers was flying when he was hit. When Bradlee said he was convinced that Time-Life had "sewn up" the pilot's memoirs, Kennedy replied that his government would have "a hell of a lot to say" about what Powers wrote for anybody: he had no intention of giving Powers his back pay unless the government cleared what he said and wrote. This at least suggested Presidential eagerness to assure that the pilot said nothing that would damage the national interest.

If the U-2 was struck at lower altitude, how might this have happened? Despite John McCone's fears, there is almost no evidence that Powers deliberately guided his plane down and defected. The Russians knew that back in the United States, Powers would be under suspicion and hence of little use as a double agent. As a defector, his greatest value would have probably been in denouncing the American government at his Moscow trial. This he had refused to do.

As Allen Dulles told the Senate Foreign Relations Committee in 1960, the U-2 was subject to flameout at high altitudes. The Board of Inquiry's report did not mention the trouble with Powers's fuel tank and autopilot: either or both would have made the plane more vulnerable to malfunction.

The pilot's old U-2 friend Sammy Snider went fishing with him shortly after his release from the Soviet Union. Many years later, Snider recalled being told that as Powers's plane was brought to Peshawar for the May Day flight, the autopilot had stopped working: "Before Frank's flight, the autopilot people said they had it all fixed, but there was no test flight made." Snider's understanding was that as Powers neared Sverdlovsk, the engine had flamed out. Powers was downed by the Soviet missile when he came down low for an airstart: "Why would he have had a flameout? The only reason, based on the past history of the airplane, was a bad autopilot which had been repaired without a test flight."

Others threw the blame not on the plane but the pilot. Allen Dulles told a reporter in early 1961 that he had studied psychological tests measuring Powers's faith in himself, his plane and equipment before the May Day flight: if *he* had been the CIA agent in Peshawar that morning, he would never have sent Powers into Russia.

As an old Army Air Corps pilot, friend of CIA and member of Senate Armed Services, Barry Goldwater had the chance to fly the U-2 and study its characteristics. Later he wrote, "The aircraft was fragile. It was stressed to withstand a load of three G's—nothing more. A forgetful pilot, or one whose attention was distracted momentarily, could easily permit the aircraft to enter into a dive. Unless the pullout was slow and deliberate, the wings would come off. The other U-2s we had lost were the result of structural failure.

"I asked Gary Powers about this after his return to the United States. He gave an evasive answer, forcing me to conclude it was pilot error . . . which caused the U-2 to crash."

Daniel Williams, a photointerpreter in Adana during the early U-2 program, revealed years afterward that old colleagues who were with Powers in Peshawar on May Day told him that there had been parties during the wait for good weather. These plus the pilot's irregular sleep through four days of false starts had helped cause him to nod off while nearing Sverdlovsk. Then he dropped into the range of Soviet missiles.

In his memoirs, *Operation Overflight,* published in 1970, Powers confirmed that his plane had had fuel tank problems and that his autopilot had stopped working before nearing Sverdlovsk. But he maintained that he suffered "neither engine trouble nor flameout. . . . Nor had I descended to thirty thousand feet. Whatever happened to my plane had occurred at my assigned altitude." Like Kelly Johnson, he argued that "the plane must have been disabled by the shock waves from a near-miss." Although he noted his nervousness and fitful sleep in Peshawar, he gave no hint that he might have nodded off in midflight: by his account, he was writing in his logbook when the trouble came.

Despite his apparent success in deceiving Soviet interrogators about the U-2's maximum altitude and other issues, there is no reason to doubt the Board of Inquiry's finding that Powers was inherently a truthful man. If the American government had quietly pledged not to refute the Soviet version of his downing, however, he would have almost certainly concurred out of patriotism and gratitude for his release.

In 1985, Richard Bissell declared that no one would ever be able to establish beyond the shadow of a doubt what happened to the U-2 near Sverdlovsk: "They're *not*. Let's put it frankly: they're *not* going to be able to resolve it."

Bissell resigned from the CIA in the wake of the Bay of Pigs failure on February 16, 1962—just after the start of Powers's debriefing and before the Board of Inquiry hearings. Hence he was not privy to the full range of the Agency's secret evidence on the U-2 downing. Asked in 1985 how the U-2 was downed, Bissell first suggested the semi-official theory of a near-miss by an SA-2 at high altitude as the likeliest explanation. But he refused to abide by the story that Powers had been flying at an assigned altitude of 68,000 feet when struck. Bissell argued that while nearing Sverdlovsk, the pilot should have been at about 72,000 feet—two thousand feet above the SA-2's ceiling.

Unlike CIA colleagues, Bissell refused to discount the possibility that something else might have caused the crash. A flameout? Bissell believed that a near-miss by an SA-2 might have caused a flameout "by disturbing the inlet flow of air, sending a very strong shock wave." A spontaneous flameout? "Conceivable." He noted that the Pratt & Whitney engine aboard Powers's plane had a small statistical chance of spontaneous flameout at high altitude, but "if you had a flameout, prescribed course of conduct—what you had to do was to go into a slow dive in the hope of restarting the engine, and that's exactly what Powers or anybody else would have done."

Perhaps most striking was that Bissell would not rule out the possibility of pilot error, although he thought it unlikely: Powers had been "an experienced pilot. They had all flown that aircraft thousands and thousands of hours. They all knew perfectly well that maintaining altitude was essential for every purpose, including fuel economy as well as the threat."

Nevertheless, informed of hearsay evidence that with a failed autopilot, Powers might have nodded off or otherwise caused his plane to go into an accidental dive, Bissell said, "That could be. I must say I think keeping awake for those long missions must have been quite a problem. . . . I think I still attach a low probability to pilot error, but you can't rule out getting sleepy or inattentive. You can't—God knows, we all drive the highways and we all know that threat. . . . And if you put that together with a failed autopilot so that he was on manual, there's a possibility."

The mystery will probably linger even after the distant day that American and Soviet intelligence archives are fully opened to scholars. But the downing of the black plane was not in itself what shattered détente in May 1960. Comprehension of how the Cold War was reinvigorated requires a look at the larger forces that led to the U-2 affair and the actions and passions it loosed.

•

For the United States, sending spy planes into the Soviet Union was a rational response to Soviet secrecy, especially since Soviet agents had long fanned out through the free societies of the West. The forerunning incursions by American border pilots and balloons, the perfection of new planes and equipment, the election of an intelligence-minded President in 1952 almost predestined spy flights into the heart of the Soviet Union.

The American government might well have argued that the U-2 did not break established international law. And like human espionage, aerial spying was committed by both sides: the CIA had evidence of Soviet flights without permission over Syria, Iran, Turkey, Pakistan and other countries. The Soviets waged border flights and pinprick incursions along the frontiers of the United States, Japan and other nations. Had the Soviets built a plane that could soar untouched over American territory, they would almost certainly have used it.

The U-2 was never able to provide the United States full warning against surprise attack: occasional flights over Soviet terrain did not achieve the more comprehensive coverage offered by satellites, listening posts and later methods. But the CIA knew that it could send the black planes over targets if other intelligence sources suggested preparations for such an attack. Unlike early satellites, a U-2 could be flown on short notice over specific targets with precisely the right equipment aboard. This had at least some effect in reducing Western nervousness about surprise attack.

The sporadic flights did not open the entire Soviet military-industrial complex to Western eyes: instruments and factories of war could always be hidden. But the U-2 intelligence allowed the United States to make informed decisions in choosing Soviet bombing targets and allocating American political and military resources to meet the Soviet threat. As Eisenhower later wrote, "Armed with U-2 knowledge, which supplemented the strength of our armed forces, we were better able to plan our political-military course."

As its founders had hoped, the U-2 may have spurred the Russians to divert resources from offensive to defensive weapons. By showing Moscow that it could not maintain absolute secrecy forever, it may have hastened receptivity to arms control agreements requiring verification.

The U-2 provided information about the Soviet economy and other areas of Soviet life. "You could see the life of a whole people spread out," Bissell later said. "You see them going to beaches, you see the whole road network . . . the density of traffic . . . the use of farm machinery versus animals." It allowed the U.S. government to announce Soviet nuclear tests, space shots and other Soviet military developments, reassuring the American people—especially after *Sputnik*—that their leaders were not ignorant or diffident about the growing danger behind the Iron Curtain.

●

The U-2's high accomplishment was always balanced against high risk.

The worst peril was always that one of the flights would somehow provoke the Soviets to retaliate. Eisenhower himself said that nothing would make him ask Congress for a war declaration more quickly than Russian penetration of American airspace. This may have been overstatement, but it reflected the gravity with which the President took what he was doing. The U-2 lacked the profile of aircraft that normally carried nuclear weapons, but the Kremlin had no assurance that every one of the black planes was unarmed. By devising a bomb rack for the U-2, Kelly Johnson demonstrated that the aircraft was serviceable for at least a small conventional attack upon the Soviet Union.

John Kennedy once marveled at the inclination of American and Soviet leaders to give wholly different meanings to the same word. Nowhere was this more evident than in American and Soviet perceptions of the U-2 flights. Among those who managed the U-2 from

Washington, the majority view was that while the Russians found the incursions galling and provocative, they understood (and had largely started) the back-alley struggle of East-West espionage. The Soviets would keep trying to down the planes but in the meantime, Moscow and Washington would tacitly conspire to conceal the flights—Moscow to avoid humiliating revelation of its impotence to stop them, Washington to hide the fact that even the United States committed peacetime espionage and aerial violations.

The Russians gave wholly different meaning to the U-2. As Khrushchev later said, he considered the United States to be committing not espionage but war. Even if the U-2 was not technically a military operation (which Khrushchev did not necessarily know), that was of little comfort: the U-2 could drop bombs. Far from being inured to the invasions, as Khrushchev recalled, "We were more infuriated and disgusted every time a violation occurred." He had stopped the official protests, or so he said, because it had proved useless and embarrassing to beg the Americans to stop. Another reason may have been that further protests might have generated more demands by the Kremlin's inner circle that Khrushchev have the planes downed—demands that he could not meet.

The flights almost surely excited anxieties about American military bases along the Soviet perimeter and memories of the German overflights that had launched the invasion of June 1941. In the same way the Soviets had used *Sputnik* to frighten the West, Khrushchev evidently presumed that the U-2 flights were meant to rub the Kremlin's nose in its own military inferiority and force it to strike its best deal with the West before it was too late.

Each time the black plane crossed Soviet territory, it presumably inflamed and strengthened those in the Kremlin most inclined to distrust the Americans. As Khrushchev said later, the Americans "knew they were causing us terrible headaches whenever one of these planes took off on a mission." But the fact was that the Americans did *not* know: Soviet secrecy was so great that the President, State Department and CIA could not precisely gauge the impact of the flights on internal Kremlin politics.

•

Before May 1960, the U-2 was one of the greatest intelligence achievements in history and a secret triumph for the CIA—the construction of the prototype in eighty-eight days, collaboration with academics and technicians like Killian, Land and Kelly Johnson, the lightning development of esoteric equipment, the founding of a photointerpretation center, the rapid, elegant assembly of a global covert operation. The CIA staged nearly four years of flights over antiaircraft fire from bases around the world under changing weather conditions and exacting requirements.

This might have been hard to do with someone else in the Oval Office. A President without Eisenhower's background in military and foreign affairs might not have had the instinctive knowledge of the gaps in American intelligence that led him to found the Killian Commission. Throughout the U-2 program, he showed a becoming sensitivity to the hazards of flying over Russia. Preferring to fly under international law, he had proposed Open Skies at Geneva. When the Russians said no, he proceeded with caution and was warier than almost anyone about the danger of Soviet fears of encirclement and invasion.

Eisenhower knew that keeping the U-2 pilots from wearing military uniforms was a contrivance, but he knew that one day, the program would be revealed: that the fliers were civilians would carry weight with world opinion. A nonmilitary President might not have been so sensitive to the distinction. As supreme commander of the program, he was almost always deliberate—holding the first set of flights to ten days, demanding a halt when Moscow complained, then tightening his grip to approve the missions almost flight by flight. The crises of Suez, *Sputnik* and Berlin caused him to cancel flights that might overheat the East-West climate. Almost always he weighed "whether the intelligence which we receive from this source is worth the exacerbation of international tension that results."

Eisenhower was at his best in evaluating the U-2 evidence. Another President might not have been so skeptical about so-called Bomber and Missile Gaps. He kept his cool after *Sputnik* and the Gaither Report. To preserve the U-2's secrecy, he performed the supreme self-abnegation of not fighting back hard against those who charged that he was depleting American defense.

James Killian later said, "The President had enough intelligence to be assured that there was no Missile Gap. The U-2 had a very important role in keeping down the Air Force budget as Ike was so anxious to do. There were billions of dollars that the U-2 saved."

Still it was not the U-2 itself but Eisenhower's shrewd use of its findings, along with other intelligence, that defeated Khrushchev's efforts to deceive the West about a massive Soviet buildup. For years, the President resisted unnecessary defense spending almost single-handedly against immense pressure. This was perhaps the principal achievement of the U-2 program and of his Presidency.

•

The U-2 success increased Eisenhower's regard for the CIA. The President agreed with others that the Air Force could not have built and run a U-2 program so quickly and effectively. Allen Dulles, Cabell and Bissell were less prone than Air Force generals to inform reporters, off the record, that the President was tolerating military inferiority—or to appeal to Congress over his head for more money. In Iran, Guatemala, the Soviet Union and dozens of other countries, the Agency had proven itself a vital handservant of his foreign policy.

Still Eisenhower always knew that the CIA had the capacity to damage his diplomacy and his reputation. The PBCFIA kept him abreast of the Agency's flaws, including what it insisted were Allen Dulles's weaknesses as an administrator. The President thought that carelessness had partly caused the exposure of the Berlin Tunnel. He was irate when spy balloons and more than one low-flying plane crossed the Soviet border against his specific command. In 1958, it was only the self-restraint (or gullibility) of the press that kept him from being publicly branded a liar when the downed Allen Pope was exposed as a CIA pilot in Indonesia after Eisenhower had claimed in public that Americans were not involved.

The President's wariness of the CIA did not stem from fear that the Agency would conspire to undermine his foreign policy, but from knowledge that the benefits of covert action—speed, flexibility, no need to plead for mass public support—were purchased at the cost of using a decision-making process that made mishaps more likely. Secrecy demanded that managers of a project like the U-2 be limited mainly to those directly involved in its conception, planning and execution. Without the scrutiny of the press, Congress and others who traditionally spot false assumptions and other flaws, this left evaluation largely to insiders who often had a bureaucratic interest in seeing programs go forward.

The President tried to correct this built-in problem by supervising the Agency through such devices as the 5412 Group and PBCFIA. But the U-2 program was judged too secret for formal divulgence even to the 5412 Group. The PBCFIA examined the U-2 from time to time, but there was only so much that a part-time body of eminent private citizens could do.

This was why in July 1956, after the first series of flights, Eisenhower took a role essentially as U-2 project manager, making critical choices on when and sometimes where the planes should fly. But he had to do this without the aid of a disinterested group of expert outside advisers who could help him to challenge faulty assumptions by dint of the same knowledge and authority that the CIA men had themselves.

How could a President—especially one like Eisenhower, who preferred to deal with the big picture—keep himself fully abreast of technical matters that, if he knew of them, might have caused him to shut down the flights? He relied on the CIA's assumptions that equipment and pilot would perish in a crash, that Soviet counterintelligence posed no critical threat, that the danger of malfunction or pilot error was low enough to be tolerable, that the Russians could not down a U-2 in the spring of 1960.

The most basic assumption on which Eisenhower approved the program was that if a U-2 were downed, it would be plausibly deniable. By the National Security Council's definition in 1954, plausibly deniable operations were those in which American government involvement was "not evident to authorized persons and if uncovered, the government can plausibly disclaim any responsibility for them." The CIA and Joint Chiefs assured the President that if a plane were downed, the Russians would acquire no live pilot or equipment with which they could prove beyond doubt that the United States had deliberately invaded the Soviet Union for espionage.

Why was the President given such an assurance? The planes were indeed equipped with the famous destruct mechanism. Although four or five pounds of cyclonite might not obliterate all traces of espionage, the CIA hoped that enough of the plane and equipment would be destroyed that the American government could denounce the remnants as a Soviet fabrication. But, according to the CIA, this device was not automatic: it depended on the pilot's obedience in setting it off.

Richard Bissell considered the U-2 so fragile that it would "pretty much break up" in a mishap, as the plane over West Germany had in 1956: there was not "one chance in a million" that a pilot would survive—especially if he tried to parachute at 70,000 feet. But other U-2s had crashed outside Russia without killing their pilots. The fliers carried poison, but taking it was optional. And the planes were equipped with ejection seats that, at least officially, permitted escape.

One way to further reduce the possibility of a live pilot would have been to connect the destruct device directly to the ejection seat. Khrushchev, hardly a dispassionate observer, claimed that there was "an explosive charge in the aircraft which was to blow up the plane as soon as the pilot catapulted." Harold Macmillan, who had been heavily briefed on the U-2, was under the impression in May 1960 that using the seat would "automatically set off a mechanism to destroy the aeroplane"—not the same thing as a pilot setting off the destruct device by the voluntary action of flicking two switches.

Some of the U-2 pilots suspected that the CIA had rigged the destruct device so that it would not give the flier his full promised seventy seconds before it exploded. David Wise, journalist and student of the CIA, who with Thomas Ross in 1962 published *The U-2 Affair,* the first extended treatment of the episode, had the same suspicion. In a novel called *Spectrum* (1981), Wise fictionally described a CIA meeting of the mid-1950s at which the U-2 project was being planned:

> "The problem, gentlemen," Trilby Gates had purred, "is to decide just how long a time lag there should be, if any, once the destruct button is pushed. . . . From a technical and legal point of view, we will not be responsible for their deaths. They will push the button themselves. . . . The timing device will simply fail to function as the pilots were told it would. . . ."
>
> It was Towny Black who had come up with the perfect solution to the moral dilemma. "Since we're telling the pilots there will be a time lag," he said, "there should be one. But let it be about two seconds."

Even if the destruct device was automatically triggered by the ejection seat or if it lacked the full seventy-second delay, the pilot might still have survived if, like Powers, he did not use the seat or the explosive. The CIA presumed that between the plane's fragility, the suicide pins and destruct system, a pilot would not make it through a crash. But this was not the same as what Eisenhower considered to be the Agency's blanket assurance.

As James Killian later suggested, the President should have demanded a precise probability estimate of a pilot's survival. Had he done this or, better yet, established an expert independent group to scrutinize the assumptions behind the U-2 operation at each stage on his behalf, the course of history might have been different.

•

After it was all over, some thought it curious that Eisenhower should approve two U-2 flights in the spring of 1960 when he was ostensibly seeking détente with the Soviet Union. At earlier times of international volatility, he had canceled flights to avoid antagonizing the Russians. Why did he not do so now?

The Secretaries of State and Defense, the CIA Director and the Chairman of the Joint Chiefs all argued that the flights were important: information on a first Soviet ICBM and other targets might be impossible to get until months after May 1960. But Pearre Cabell later told Senate Foreign Relations members that the two missions were not considered supremely urgent—only "well above average."

The President later confessed that he had become "a bit careless with success." Perhaps he had been "lulled into overconfidence." The Soviets had not complained of the intrusions for over two years and he did not feel he could "oppose the combined opinion" of his associates that the U-2 should be sent back into Russia.

This reasoning illuminates the fatal weakness in the system Eisenhower had created to manage the U-2 program. Since 1956, he had seized for himself the main burden of estimating the damage that a flight—or a downing—might cause to his foreign policy. With the possible exception of Herter, the principals who came to the Oval Office to debate new U-2 missions all had a stake in pressing for flights. And there were those who evidently feared that if Eisenhower and Khrushchev achieved accord at Paris, the President might not approve a flight into the Soviet Union again, causing an intelligence blackout until spy satellites were in full operation.

The priorities of Herter, Gates, Allen Dulles and Twining in the spring of 1960 were not the same as Eisenhower's. None of them fully shared the President's optimism that a détente would or should be established—or his conviction that if a U-2 was downed, the backlash against the United States would "sweep the world." Only Eisenhower could weigh the diplomatic, military and intelligence impact of two more flights on his own larger aims. The recommendation of subordinates should not have done so much to decide the question.

The more basic problem was the difference between Washington and Moscow over what the flights represented. As the President later said, he saw them mainly as two more missions "within an intelligence policy already adopted." Certainly Khrushchev would not like them, but his silence at Camp David had suggested resignation to the intrusions. Eisenhower knew from FBI reports that the Russians had not stopped spying since Camp David. Why should he? Furthermore, he took the precaution of forbidding U-2 flights for the fortnight before the Summit to avoid provocation: two more missions should not have "any possible bearing upon the Summit meeting or my forthcoming trip to Moscow."

But the President was dealing with a leader with an extraordinary sense of vulnerability (which was not unwarranted, given Soviet military weakness and the tricks and threats Khrushchev had to use to gain treatment as an equal of the United States). In the fall of 1959, Khrushchev's anxieties might have been aroused when Eisenhower did not reciprocate his exuberant oratory about détente and the American President and people. Despite Khrushchev's plea for a prompt Summit, Eisenhower seemed to allow the conference to ·be postponed for eight months: from Khrushchev's point of view, this could not have augured great eagerness to negotiate. April 1960 brought the speeches from Herter, Dillon and Nixon suggesting that the West might not move at all on Germany. Against this backdrop came the resumption of U-2 flights.

During his American trip, Khrushchev had repeatedly ignored the pox against national leaders mentioning espionage to complain about the CIA and claim that he was cutting back Soviet operations against the United States. Perhaps this was his (characteristically opaque) means of suggesting that he regarded espionage as a notable element in American relations: thus stop the flights. During the period after Camp David when the violations ceased, he may have presumed that his message had been heard.

Then in April 1960, a new American intrusion, "a unilateral, unprovoked demonstration of their supposed superiority and outrageous treachery." Even a less suspicious leader than Khrushchev might have thought the plane had been sent "to return the state of American-Soviet relations to the worst times of the Cold War." Khrushchev had always warned of insubordinate Western officers touching off World War Three: he may have managed to convince himself and his colleagues that an American general had sent the U-2 on April 9 without Eisenhower's approval.

The May Day flight suggested that the April intrusion had been no mistake. To Khrushchev, it showed that "America had been following a two-faced policy. On the one hand, the U.S. had been approaching us with outstretched arms and all sorts of assurances about their peaceful and friendly intentions. On the other hand, they were stabbing us in the back."

Had Eisenhower systematically consulted a range of specialists in Soviet affairs, he might have encountered the view that resuming the U-2 flights in the spring of 1960 might send Moscow a hostile signal he did not mean. But the U-2 program was so closely held that this was almost impossible. Hence the President unwittingly poisoned the atmosphere of mutual trust he had been working to build.

Foreign policy is difficult enough to manage when a President hears diverse advice, understands the adversary's weltanschauung and sends the signals he means to send. Eisenhower prided himself on institutional decision-making, understanding his rivals' point of view and relating tactics to strategy. All of this failed him in his decision to resume the U-2 flights.

•

After the U-2 fell, Eisenhower continued to suffer from the exclusive, ad hoc procedure he had fashioned to run the U-2 program. The morning after May Day, he hastily approved the false cover story. There was no system to show him the full range of options and contingencies, including the chance that the Soviets had captured the pilot alive and could thus reveal the Americans as liars.

Had the cover story not been issued, Eisenhower could have coped with the U-2 problem without the additional albatross of also justifying an official lie. Khrushchev would not have had his opportunity to embarrass the United States by revealing the deception. "I didn't realize how high a price we were going to have to pay for that lie," Eisenhower said years later. "And if I had to do it all over again, we would have kept our mouths shut."

On May 5, 1960, when Khrushchev announced the U-2 downing and concealed the pilot's survival, the President's first, excellent instinct was to keep his government's mouth shut, but he allowed subordinates to change his mind. Permitting State and NASA to release more elaborate versions of the cover story further mired the government in deception and established the public expectation that Washington would respond to every charge by Moscow. The bungling when reporters rushed to NASA looking for a statement was another hazard of the kind of impromptu management that Eisenhower had always scorned.

The supposition of some of Eisenhower's aides that Khrushchev would never disclose a U-2 downing if it happened had already been destroyed. Still no one questioned the CIA's assurance that the pilot was dead. The President approved continuance of the cover-up because he thought it would work. Had he suspected that the Russians could ultimately prove that the plane had actually been sent for espionage, he might, as an old military commander, have cut his losses and told the world the truth then and there.

May 7: when Khrushchev revealed that Powers was alive and said he was "willing to believe" that Eisenhower had not approved the flight, the President was once again inclined to say nothing. He might have been well advised to announce that Khrushchev's charges were being investigated and that the government would have no comment. But some of his aides presumed that Khrushchev was demanding some kind of American confession. Torn between trying to "satisfy" Khrushchev with such a confession and keeping the President at arm's length from a covert operation, they drafted a partly false statement that suffered the weaknesses of both: A U.S. pilot had "probably" invaded Soviet airspace but the flight had not been authorized by Washington.

Eisenhower was virtually isolated at Gettysburg when read the statement by telephone. Although he rightly thought it "might prove to be a mistake," he approved it. This ignited the international scare that some American officer could start a war without the President's knowledge. Once that began, Eisenhower had almost no choice but to take clear responsibility for the May Day flight, whatever the impact on Soviet-American relations.

But the May 9 announcement that Eisenhower had authorized the flight, tacitly asserting the right to violate Soviet sovereignty in the future, seemed almost calculated to offend the Soviets. Khrushchev thought that this sounded "as though Eisenhower were boasting arrogantly about what the United States could do and would do." And, Khrushchev wondered, why had Eisenhower refuted his magnanimous statement that the President had not really known about the flight? Khrushchev did not seem to comprehend Eisenhower's anger at being tricked into affirming a public lie or that no American President could ever imply that he did not control his own government.

Few world leaders would sit down with a counterpart who had

publicly asserted the right to violate their airspace. Khrushchev was already under fire in Moscow for armed forces reductions, "softness" toward the Americans and tolerating previous U-2 violations. For him to have done so might have been politically fatal. By the second week of May, he may have concluded that the Summit was doomed anyway and that the best strategy was to posture as the aggrieved party who was making every effort to save the situation. But other evidence suggests that he genuinely wished to save the Summit and his opening to the West—the assertion that the President's invitation to Russia still stood and the blatant hints that he and Eisenhower should iron out their problems in Paris before the Summit convened.

Harold Macmillan felt that Khrushchev might have been mollified by a formal American disclaimer or diplomatic white lie. The Americans could have at least felt out the Russians to see if language acceptable to both sides could be found, perhaps by lower-level diplomatic back channel: during the Cuban Missile Crisis of 1962, vital messages passed between the two governments through Georgi Bolshakov of the Soviet Embassy in Washington.

Eisenhower knew that it was not ignominious to apologize to the Soviets for a border violation: his own administration had done so in 1958. But by now, he had largely concluded that the Summit was going to collapse anyway. If Khrushchev was going to scuttle the Summit, blame the Americans and try to split the Western alliance, Eisenhower wished to keep his head held high. By now Khrushchev was linked in his mind with the fact that his administration had embarrassed itself by lying and seeming out of his control, and that his career was ending not in triumph but black comedy.

●

In the spring of 1960, both Khrushchev and Eisenhower had a considerable stake in a Paris success—Khrushchev to justify his policies toward the United States, China and Germany, Eisenhower to close his term with a crowning American-Soviet accord. But the two leaders were like a Victorian couple, each not quite able to express what was deepest in his mind and dreading abandonment at the altar.

Whatever his private optimism about bargaining with Khrushchev, the President publicly scoffed at use of the term "the Spirit of Camp David." With his Lippmannesque distrust of public opinion, he did not want an American groundswell for peace to weaken American resolve at Paris. If détente failed, he did not want to appear to have been taken in by the Russians. This demonstrated one of the flaws of hidden-hand leadership. Involving the public can strengthen the conduct of American foreign policy. Had Eisenhower used his bully pulpit and immense popularity to show that a period of détente was possible and desirable, the disappointments of May 1960 might not have swung the nation so deeply into a Cold War mood and reduced his successor's flexibility in 1961.

Throughout his term, Eisenhower had shown himself willing to bargain with the Russians: there had been two summits, five foreign ministers' meetings, dozens of technical and cultural talks. But he was always restrained by his confidence that his was—and would for some time remain—the superior military power, his suspicions of the Russians and summit meetings and his conviction that a democratic alliance usually bargained with totalitarians at a disadvantage.

During the spring, the President displayed his customary composure through Khrushchev's shrill demands, notably at Baku, that the German issue be settled at Paris. His suspicions were perhaps first badly aroused by Khrushchev's first public complaint about the U-2: if Khrushchev was really serious about détente, then why choose this moment to inflate the U-2 into a major issue? The President's wariness may have kept him from fully considering Llewellyn Thompson's hypothesis that Khrushchev might be actually trying to *save* détente from Kremlin militants who were seizing the opportunity offered by the U-2 downing. Had Eisenhower taken this explanation more seriously, he might have calibrated American responses in light of the need to keep Khrushchev and his American policy from being fatally undermined.

As with the Sino-Soviet schism, Eisenhower was more aware of Khrushchev's internal problems than later given credit for, but as late as five days before the Summit, he was capable of advising senators that Khrushchev was "as close to an absolute dictator as current conditions in Russia will permit."

There is no evidence that during the fortnight after May Day, he asked for or received a briefing on the specific thesis that it was in the American interest to strengthen Khrushchev's internal position, if possible, that the U-2 had endangered that position, that Khrushchev was struggling to save it and that by taking responsibility for the U-2 and asserting the right to violate Soviet airspace, Eisenhower was dealing Khrushchev a devastating blow. As with Berlin in early 1959, the President did an admirable job of trying to muffle the U-2 confrontation—largely by denying that there was a crisis. But the ease with which he allowed himself to be diverted from serious bargaining suggests that in May 1960, he was still inclined to favor other elements of his strategy of containment of the Soviet Union.

By the time the Summit convened, Eisenhower and Khrushchev had each managed to convince the other that before May Day he had soured on détente and decided to use the U-2 as an excuse to wreck the conference and blame the other. By this moment, each was unwilling to flinch. Their confrontation had generated such antipathy to détente within both of their governments that it was almost impossible to turn back now.

•

What might have happened at Paris had the U-2 not fallen on May Day? In the absence of information from the Soviet side, we shall never know for certain.

The Summit might well have been a failure. It could be that by the spring of 1960, Khrushchev's bargaining ability was restricted by Soviet generals irate about reductions, KGB leaders warning that relaxation of world tensions might loosen the Kremlin's grip on Eastern Europe and the Soviet people, anti-American ideologues and others concerned about the Chinese and a host of Khrushchev's other policies. Khrushchev may have been so beleaguered by now that he needed concessions that he knew Eisenhower would never offer.

Perhaps Khrushchev had lost all hope of collaborating with Eisenhower to keep nuclear weapons out of the hands of China and West Germany. In April 1960, Peking announced that it would not obey any accord reached in talks in which it did not participate. The tough language from Washington about Berlin may have convinced Khrushchev that the West would be intransigent. His scientists may have told him what Eisenhower's scientists had told him—that a test ban would favor the United States—and that it had better be quashed.

Even assuming that Khrushchev decided in April 1960 that the Paris Summit would be fruitless, however, it is difficult to accept the argument that he "manufactured" or "welcomed" the U-2 episode as a means of scrapping the conference and Eisenhower's trip to Russia. It is not as if Khrushchev chose to down his first U-2 on May Day. His military leaders had been frantically trying to bag almost every one of its predecessors; it was only by antic fate that this turned out to be the first one to fall. Had Khrushchev tried to keep the debris and live pilot a secret, word would almost surely have diffused through the KGB and military that he was covering up for the Americans.

Had Khrushchev not loudly and publicly complained, his domestic rivals could have argued that he did not take his nation's defense with due gravity. For Khrushchev, the downing was far less a golden opportunity than a mortal threat to his leadership, handing rivals a flamboyant piece of evidence for their concerns about his defense policies and rapprochement with Washington. Had he wished to avoid the Summit, he could have done it in literally hundreds of ways that would have been potentially less dangerous to his domestic position.

Were he intent on scuttling the conference, he would almost certainly not have offered Eisenhower the opportunity to avow that he had not been the one to send the plane into Russia—an offer that embarrassed Khrushchev when it was refused. His decision to fly early to Paris in hopes of meeting with Eisenhower suggests that he may have hoped to find some compromise that would allow his long-called-for summit to go forward. Especially in light of the American assertion of its right to fly into Soviet territory, Khrushchev's conditions for attendance were probably among the lightest he could have set without causing himself grave domestic political trouble as one who had caved in to the Americans.

We know from the American side that before May Day, Eisenhower had no intention of humiliating Khrushchev by forcing him to leave Paris empty-handed. The President was determined to bridge the small gap that remained between the two leaders on a partial test ban. Preparatory documents and Goodpaster's recollection suggest that Eisenhower was willing to offer concessions and a negotiation process on the German issue that might have allowed Khrushchev to claim that his tough stand was showing results. Even if all of this failed, Eisenhower was ready to submit proposals on regular East-West meetings, culture and technology that Khrushchev was likely to accept. Even at worst, it is unlikely that the Summit would have reinflamed the Cold War as it finally did.

What about the best case—a conference that culminated in a limited test ban treaty and agreement by both sides not to exacerbate the German issue until agreement was reached in a reasonable period of time? If Khrushchev's chief goals included halting or delaying Chinese nuclear development and reaching a settlement that kept Bonn from having nuclear weapons, such an outcome might have gone a long way toward satisfying them.

We know that at Paris Eisenhower planned to "capitalize" on Khrushchev's fear of China's emergence as a nuclear power. In May 1960, the President had the same concern. It is not too difficult to imagine that once the subject was privately broached, the two leaders might have come to some sort of understanding to impede the Chinese—whether by Soviet economic or political incentives to bring them under a test ban, a Western pledge to keep Bonn from going nuclear (which, though Khrushchev apparently did not know it, was not an Eisenhower priority), a combination of both, or even a joint preemptive strike, if necessary, against Chinese nuclear facilities (which John Kennedy at least considered in 1963 and the Russians tacitly proposed in 1969).

As for Germany, the evidence suggests that while Khrushchev would have dearly wished to gain prompt Western recognition of the East German regime, he was more eager to keep nuclear weapons out of the hands of "revanchist" West German generals. In March 1958, he endorsed the Rapacki Plan, formally proposed by the Polish foreign minister but almost certainly drafted in Moscow. The plan called for a nuclear-free zone in Poland, Czechoslovakia and the two Germanys. The West said no. This was probably a mistake, for it could have meant the installation of some form of international control in Eastern Europe and reassured those West Germans who opposed building a sizable Bundeswehr because they feared that in war, West Germany would be decimated by nuclear weapons. What the Rapacki Plan showed was how much Khrushchev was willing to give up to prevent Bonn's emergence as a nuclear power. It was only after its rejection that he issued his Berlin ultimatum of November 1958.

Given Eisenhower's own disinclination to arm the West Germans with long-range nuclear weapons, it would not have been unthinkable for him to entertain such a prohibition either during the Summit or later negotiation. It has been cogently argued that Khrushchev's chief aim in renewing his Berlin ultimatum in 1961 and secretly sending nuclear-tipped missiles to Cuba in 1962 was to pressure the West for agreements that would reduce his anxieties about China and West Germany. Had he left Paris in May 1960 with these problems on the road toward solution, the world might have been spared the Berlin and Cuban confrontations that took it to the precipice of nuclear war.

Had Eisenhower and Khrushchev signed a limited test ban treaty in 1960, it would have done little to curb the arms race: the signers would have simply moved their testing underground (as they did after a more limited treaty was reached in 1963). But combined with progress on China and Germany, Khrushchev could have used it to show Kremlin rivals that Soviet-American diplomacy produced major results. His political position might have been strengthened instead of weakened, as it ultimately was, by the U-2 embarrassment and the failure of his Cuban gambit.

In an atmosphere of growing trust, there is at least the possibility that, as Eisenhower had hoped, the two nations might have enlarged the treaty into an absolute ban on nuclear testing. If signed in the early 1960s, this might have genuinely curbed the arms race at an early stage and allowed the two powers to work together to prevent the danger of the acquisition of nuclear weapons by governments all over the world.

In 1969, Anatoly Dobrynin, by then Soviet envoy to Washington, told Henry Kissinger during their first meeting that great opportunities had been lost in Soviet-American affairs—"especially between 1959 and 1963." He had been head of the American department of the Soviet Foreign Ministry during those years and said he knew that "Khrushchev seriously wanted an accommodation with the United States."

It is impossible to know whether he meant it. A pause in the Cold War would hardly have brought a lasting peace. The Soviets would still have pressed at least for military parity. The two nations would still have faced off against each other in the Third World and on scores of exacerbating issues. But a limited period of relaxation might have started to draw the two governments into a web of mutual needs and ambitions. Without the diplomatic smashup of May 1960, the American public and some of its leaders might not have shifted back to such a Cold War mood.

Without the humiliation of the U-2 affair, Khrushchev might not have been so desperate to convince rivals of his toughness and diplomatic mastery. George Kennan believed that the U-2 episode led to "the shattering of the political career of the only Soviet statesman of the post-Stalin period with whom we might conceivably have worked out a firmer sort of coexistence."

Of a similar watershed in Soviet-American relations Adam Ulam has written, "It can be argued that such a détente would have achieved nothing. But, it may be retorted, long-range solutions can be reached

in this sinful world only through short-range and partial accommoda-
tions. The tragedy . . . was that no such negotiations took place."

•

To the extent that the U-2 was responsible, it is difficult to escape
the conclusion that both the American and Soviet governments participated in the shattering of détente.

The Americans evidently failed to comprehend the full message
they were sending Moscow by resuming the flights. The CIA failed to
keep the plane from being downed and erroneously convinced the
President that no plane or pilot would survive a crash, clearing the way
for the ruinous cover story. Eisenhower's distrust of Khrushchev, fear
of betrayal, sense of military superiority and doubts about bargaining
with totalitarian leaders at the Summit may have colored his understanding of Khrushchev's motives in complaining about the intrusion,
concealing and then revealing the pilot's survival, professing that Eisenhower had not known about the flight and arriving early in Paris.

This might have led the President to give up too early on the Summit. Had he persisted in the notion that it might still be profitably
saved, he might have been less eager to issue statements affirming
American steadfastness at the possible cost of keeping Khrushchev
from the bargaining table. Eisenhower might also be fairly faulted with
failing to mobilize his entire foreign policy establishment behind his
Soviet policy. The evidence suggests that few top American officials
fully shared his vision: not even a President can pull off such an initiative single-handedly.

For their part, the Soviets evidently did not perceive that Washington viewed the U-2 flights simply in terms of the espionage that all nations practiced—not as provocations, belligerent displays of American
military superiority or efforts to undermine Kremlin leaders interested
in accommodation with the West. Khrushchev did not seem to understand that by refraining from major complaint after 1958—especially
at Camp David—he gave the Americans the impression that he had
grown resigned to the intrusions and would remain so until one could
be intercepted. Eternally incensed about American failure to heed Soviet sensitivities, Khrushchev never publicly conceded how difficult it
was for even the most telepathic Western government to comprehend
the motives of the leaders of a closed society.

Kremlin secrecy only deepened the problems inherent in Khru-

shchev's Jekyll-and-Hyde manner of statecraft. Threats of thermonuclear war alternated with demands for a virtual American-Soviet alliance were a clever way of diverting world attention from Soviet
military weakness and keeping the world's mightiest power off balance. But Khrushchev did not seem to understand the degree to which
his crisis diplomacy induced Western distrust, or that the boorish ha-
rangues that endeared him to the Soviet proletariat did not strengthen
his world reputation as a responsible leader.

Khrushchev aggravated the U-2 episode with his bluster and penchant for scoring propaganda points. Part of this was to protect his domestic political position; part of this was second nature. His
interpretation of American actions and responses seems to have been
distorted by his eternal hypersensitivity to signs that Washington was
treating his country as a second-rate power. His final verdict on the
U-2 affair: "We showed the whole world that while other Western
powers might crawl on their bellies in front of America's mighty finan-
cial and industrial capital, we wouldn't bow down—not for one second. Our goal was peace and friendship, but we wouldn't let ourselves
be abused and degraded."

The U-2 was a flaming javelin unwittingly thrown into the dry for-
est of suspicions and misperceptions that surrounded American-Soviet
relations in May 1960. The U-2 affair illustrates perhaps more than
anything the need for both governments to precisely understand each
other's motives and behavior. Throughout the Cold War, rivalry has
grown and opportunity been lost by miscalculation. In 1950, North
Koreans moved against the South largely because the Soviet Union
presumed that the United States would not defend it. In 1962,
Khrushchev put missiles in Cuba because he underestimated John
Kennedy's will to respond. Such misjudgments may one day lead to a
Third World War.

Henry Kissinger has described the behavior of the superpowers as
"like two heavily armed men feeling their way around a room, each
believing himself in mortal peril from the other, whom he assumes to
have perfect vision. Each tends to ascribe to the other a consistency,
foresight and coherence that its own experience belies." One of Eisenhower's paramount goals was to bring the two governments into closer
contact to reduce the chance of such misperceptions.

The tragedy of May Day was not of necessity but possibility. Had
the two sides been in closer communication during the spring of 1960,

382 : M A Y D A Y

each might have held fewer misperceptions about the other's intention to seek some curtailment of the Cold War. Instead, as Churchill might have said with only some hyperbole, the two great powers resumed the follies that could one day cost them their lives.

★

Epilogue: After the Storm

I N JULY 1961, Khrushchev summoned the old diplomat John McCloy from talks in Moscow to his summer place on the Black Sea. He spoke of Eisenhower, praising the General's command at Normandy and his understanding of the Red Army's role in the German defeat. He regretted that the U-2 had prevented the President from visiting the Soviet Union. Perhaps it was not too late: if Eisenhower cared to come, the Soviet people would ensure a warm welcome.

Why, after all of their angry history, should Khrushchev wish to reinvite Eisenhower to Russia? The Vienna talks with Kennedy had been somber and Khrushchev had revived his Berlin ultimatum. Perhaps he was trying to outflank Kennedy by renewing ties with the other most popular leader in the United States. Khrushchev was a sentimentalist: welcoming Eisenhower after all would mend the lamentable break in their relations and heal the nasty business of 1960.

McCloy conveyed the invitation to Eisenhower, who told his son after golf at Gettysburg, "Maybe you won't believe it, but this fellow Khrushchev has had the temerity to hint that he would like to reinstate the invitation to go to Moscow. . . . Of course, I'd never do it, but why Khrushchev would bring up such a thing sort of beats me." Later Eisenhower thought better of the idea, but worried that Americans might interpret the mission as an effort to inject himself back into public life.

He sent word to Khrushchev that "should the invitation be renewed through my government, I would accept."

But it never was. By the fall of 1961, the United States and Soviet Union were in bitter conflict. The Berlin Wall had been erected; Khrushchev had broken his pledge not to be the first to resume atmospheric nuclear tests by ordering the mightiest detonations ever. President Kennedy had called up American reservists and ordered a national effort to build fallout shelters. Eisenhower and Khrushchev never communicated again.

•

Khrushchev's final years in power were like the frenzied last movement of a Mozart symphony. The diplomatic analysts William Hyland and Richard Shyrock have written that "from roughly the time of the U-2 incident onward, Khrushchev seems to have been confronted with an increasingly effective opposition." Wolves were at the door—generals and KGB men angry about reduced budgets, bureaucrats threatened by endless reorganizations, intellectuals under attack, workers suffering from scarcity and rising prices.

Khrushchev's drive to build the Soviet economy by shifting money to consumer production was faltering. Agriculture and industry were stagnant. Renewed tension with the West commanded increased military spending. The scourge of Stalin and the personality cult now seemed to thumb his nose at collective leadership. Khrushchev's genius for manipulating allies and rivals seemed to be in atrophy: relatives and sycophants sat in high government positions.

Still Khrushchev searched for the gambit that would demonstrate his diplomatic brilliance and silence his foes. In 1962, he may, after secretly putting missiles in Cuba, have planned to reveal them to the world and thereby push Washington to the bargaining table. There he might have pledged removal in exchange for a Soviet-American agreement to keep China and Germany out of the nuclear club and settle other sources of world tension. Instead he suffered one more humiliation and inconquerable Kremlin demands for escalation of the arms race.

The end of the Cuban Missile Crisis brought a modest improvement in American relations. Khrushchev relaxed pressure for a German peace treaty. A "hot line," first discussed with Eisenhower, was installed between Moscow and Washington for instant communication during future crises.* The United States sold surplus wheat to the Soviet Union. And in August 1963, the two governments finally signed a partial test ban treaty that was less ambitious than what Eisenhower and Khrushchev had nearly reached in the spring of 1960.

But by now, Khrushchev's power was less than it was in early 1960. He had lost on Cuba and Germany. Inflamed by the test ban treaty, China formally announced its divorce from the Soviet Union and denounced it as an "imperialist state." Unbeknownst to Khrushchev, inside the Kremlin a coalition was building against his own personality cult, his defiance of the military and KGB, his public vulgarity and capriciousness, the sagging economy, the split with China, unrest in Eastern Europe. Khrushchev's rivals told each other that, necessary as it was, he had given away too much for the sake of an understanding with the United States.

●

In October 1964, Khrushchev was resting at Sochi when Leonid Brezhnev called from Moscow: The Presidium was debating Khrushchev's ideas on agriculture and he should be present. Khrushchev reputedly said, 'I'm on holiday and I need time to relax." But Brezhnev persisted. At the Moscow airport, Khrushchev was evidently met only by the chief of the KGB.

Presidium members battered him with charges of the kind he had not heard out loud since the Anti-Party Coup of 1957. As in 1957, he demanded a full meeting of the Central Committee. But this time, it was held the next morning to keep him from mobilizing support. Brezhnev and Alexei Kosygin were installed in Khrushchev's party and government posts. A fifteen-count indictment was read. From a side bench, flushed, clenching fists, Khrushchev shouted epithets and the others shouted back. He reputedly asked for appointment as Minister of Agriculture and they laughed.

Khrushchev's immense portrait was removed from a wall in Red Square. *Pravda* denounced "harebrained scheming," "phrase-mongering," "bragging" and "armchair methods" as it announced Khrushchev's retirement for reasons of health. The Chinese startled most of the world by testing their first nuclear device.

---

* This was encouraged by Llewellyn Thompson, who noted the dangers of the faulty communication between the two governments during the U-2 and Cuban episodes.

After his ouster, Khrushchev reputedly went home, threw down his briefcase and said, "Well, that's it. I'm retired now. Perhaps the most important thing I did was just this—that they were able to get rid of me simply by voting, whereas Stalin would have had them all executed." He was placed under house arrest and moved to Ozymandian exile in a small, well-guarded compound west of Moscow with a garden and ancient car. For months, he sat motionless in a chair. Asked about the "special pensioner," one of Khrushchev's grandsons said, "Granddad cries all the time."

Slowly he rallied, wandering to the banks of the Moscow River, posing for pictures with workers, riding to Moscow to view an art exhibition and vote in his old neighborhood. In 1967, after giving a brief television interview to a Western reporter, he was dressed down by Alexander Kirilenko of the Presidium, one of his old protégés. Khrushchev reputedly said, "You can take away my dacha and my pension. I shall be able to wander through this country with my hand outstretched and people will give me whatever I need. If *you* were destitute, no one would give you anything."

Khrushchev's family bought him a West German tape recorder and urged him to dictate his memoirs. He randomly recounted his youth in Kalinovka and the mines, the Revolution, his rise under Stalin and years at the helm. He said that Eisenhower was "not an unintelligent man, and I think he was speaking honestly . . . when he told me he was frightened of a big war. . . . He could concretely imagine what a war fought with missiles and nuclear weapons would be like. . . . I think he was sincere—and I don't care if some people sneer at me for praising the President."

On the Paris Summit, Khrushchev had the same historical amnesia that afflicts other autobiographers: he and his comrades "didn't have much hope" of reaching a "meaningful agreement among countries with different political systems." In Khrushchev's retelling, the U-2 episode was not a humiliation but a "landmark event in our struggle against the American imperialists who were waging the Cold War."

With his family's help, the tapes, documents and photographs were conveyed to the West. In the fall of 1970, a first volume was excerpted in *Life* and published as *Khrushchev Remembers*. Called once again to the Kremlin, Khrushchev reputedly said that any effort to silence him would cast him as Alexander I, who, according to legend, rose from the grave to travel Russia, staff in hand, telling the people his fate. Under pressure, he signed a formal denial that he had "passed on" memoirs to the West. Soon he entered a hospital with a failing heart.

In September 1971, Khrushchev summoned Yevgeny Yevtushenko, a target of his attacks on artists and writers in the early 1960s: "You are very lucky. You are a poet. You can tell the truth. But I was a politician. I had to shout to hold my job." A week later, he died. *Pravda* reported the news in a single sentence.

John Eisenhower was serving as President Richard Nixon's Ambassador to Brussels. He wished to sign a condolence book at the Soviet Embassy, but political counselors warned against it. He said, "The Russians know I had a special relationship with Khrushchev. . . . If the Russians want to treat their former heads of government like dogs, let them admit it."

Barred from a hero's place in the Kremlin wall, Khrushchev was buried in a Moscow cemetery for the elite. In the rain, his son Sergei stood before the open coffin and said, "There are people who love him and people who hate him, but no one can pass by without turning to look."

In the twelve years after his burial, the national Soviet press mentioned Khrushchev only once—a passing mention on the fortieth anniversary of the Battle of Stalingrad. A generation of Soviets who matured after 1964 scarcely recognized his name. But parents and grandparents remembered: so many pilgrims came to Khrushchev's grave that the cemetery was closed to the public.

•

In April 1961, after the Bay of Pigs, Eisenhower assured friends that it would not have happened under his watch. He recalled the upheaval over the U-2 and laughed: "Considering all the information we got out of the many, many U-2 flights, what happened at Paris fades into insignificance. But here we gained nothing, and it made us look childish and ridiculous." When some in Washington argued that the Cuban plan had been devised during the previous administration, John Eisenhower urged his father to issue a statement saying, "I don't run no bad invasions," but the father thought it "smallminded."

John was still angry about Allen Dulles's role in the U-2 affair and thought his father did John Kennedy "a disservice by not firing Dulles." The former President became convinced in retirement that Dulles had "fallen short" on the U-2, but would not say so in his Presidential memoirs.* The two volumes must show that he had known what was going on in his own government: blaming Dulles for withholding information would not help. John persisted. Eisenhower slammed the desk and cried, "Dammit, John, I'm writing this book!" The son replied, "You sure are. Do it your way."

Eisenhower's second volume of memoirs, *Waging Peace*, was published in 1965. In it, he wrote, "I think the Paris Summit, had it been held, would have proved to be a failure and thus would have brought the Free World only further disillusionment. Khrushchev could have used the failure as an excuse for revoking the invitation for me to visit Moscow. The U-2 incident made this easier." He understated the chances for a test ban and other agreements and stressed the possibility that deadlock over Berlin might have caused an angry breakup at Paris anyway.

Eisenhower's account did much to shape the diplomatic historiography for more than twenty years. Only after previously classified documents were released could scholars learn that in April 1960, the President was anything but convinced that the Summit would fail. Like most human beings, Eisenhower sometimes held disappointments at bay by denying them, such as when he said in 1965 that he had been "sure" at Geneva that the Russians "would never accept" Open Skies.

During his final days, Eisenhower rightly perceived that his greatest contribution as President had been to hold the line for eight years against bone-crushing demands to escalate world crises and the arms race: "We kept the peace. People ask how it happened—by God, it didn't just happen, I'll tell you that." But he also knew that historians reserve highest admiration not for leaders who preserve the status quo but for those who transform it. Not long before his death in March 1969, he told an old friend, "I had longed to give the United States and the world a lasting peace. I was able only to contribute to a stalemate."

Eisenhower was always his own severest judge. The lengths to which he went to deny what might have happened in the spring of 1960 suggest the degree to which he may have been wounded by his failure.

●

Allen Dulles and Richard Bissell survived the U-2 affair, but not the Bay of Pigs. For two men so closely linked with Eisenhower, they

* See Appendix.

had made a smooth transition to the Kennedy government. Dulles had sometimes golfed with the Massachusetts Senator in Palm Beach; with J. Edgar Hoover, he became one of Kennedy's first two Presidential appointments. A Democrat of Kennedy's generation, Bissell shared the new President's curiosity and aversion to bureaucratic decision-making. Some New Frontiersmen wondered how he had ever survived under Eisenhower. Kennedy privately said that he had Bissell in mind to serve as Dulles's successor.

Like the U-2, the Cuban operation was so large that it could hardly be called plausibly deniable. Newspaper leaks should have shown the government that the project was no longer secret, but the CIA and White House once again tried to plug the leaks by asking publishers not to publish. Once again, the White House was ill-equipped to evaluate the CIA's and Joint Chiefs' fundamental assumptions about the plan—that the invasion might trigger a Cuban uprising, that "failure was almost impossible," as Robert Kennedy recalled Bissell's assurance.

As with the U-2, the CIA erred in predicting the President's behavior in event of failure. On the U-2, Dulles and Bissell had expected that Eisenhower would stick to the cover story. On Cuba, they evidently presumed that, unwilling to brook defeat, Kennedy might escalate the operation with air strikes, open military force and perhaps even assassination, if necessary. When these assumptions proved wrong, once again the President was embarrassed and the CIA exposed.

There were also notable differences between the two operations. The U-2 occurred near the end of a popular President's term. The Cuban failure struck Kennedy as he was gaining momentum after a narrow election, suggesting to Khrushchev that his new counterpart was weak. As Eisenhower noted, the U-2 affair was one plane downed after four years of success. The Bay of Pigs was the failure of the world's mightiest state to invade an island ninety miles away. The U-2 gave Khrushchev one hostage; the Bay of Pigs gave Castro eleven hundred.

When the invasion failed, Allen Dulles told Richard Nixon, "This is the worst day of my life." Kennedy called Dulles in and reputedly said, "Under a parliamentary system, it is I who would be leaving office. But under our system, it is you who must go." The CIA Director was willing to quit but not to take the blame. A frequent visitor to his office that summer was his journalist friend Charles Murphy, who re-

vealed what Dulles thought were the Kennedy government's fatal hesi-
tations about Cuba in an article in *Fortune*.

That fall, Nixon wrote Dulles, "You can certainly take pride in the
fact that there were a few of us who were acquainted with all of your
actions and who knew how extraordinarily high your batting average
was. (And while this may sound partisan, I am among those who believe that the part that you and Dick Bissell played in the U-2 incident
was magnificent and, after reading Charlie Murphy's story in *Fortune*,
that you did everything possible to avert the failure in Cuba.)"

Dulles retired to Georgetown, where he wrote a lay handbook
called *The Craft of Intelligence* and a memoir of his efforts for a separate German surrender in 1945. He was appointed to the Warren
Commission and explored racial conditions in Mississippi for Lyndon
Johnson. But intelligence had been his life. He told Nixon that leaving
the CIA was "quite a wrench." He died in 1969, his old colleague
Howard Hunt recalled, "a very tragic, sad and unfulfilled figure of a
man."

Any bitterness Eisenhower felt toward Dulles may have been reciprocated. Shortly before his death, when Mary Bancroft asked Dulles
which of his Presidential superiors had been his favorite, he said, "I'll
tell you this: Harry Truman always did his homework, and he was awfully nice to me."

In the fall of 1961, Bissell told a friend that he was leaving the government: Kennedy had advised him that after the Bay of Pigs, any future mishap would be blamed on him. He would be better off out of the
CIA. After a spell as a Washington consultant, Bissell went home to
Connecticut and worked for a time at United Aircraft. The Kennedy
Administration gave him the nation's highest intelligence decoration,
the National Security Medal, in secret.

After being out of touch for years, he wrote Kelly Johnson, "I have
kept myself busy a good deal of the time with a variety of odd jobs that
bring in a little income but could scarcely be dignified by the term
'consulting.' For the most part, they are interesting and, in some cases
quite stimulating. I sometimes think it is totally irrational to go to work
fairly regularly and earn as little money as I do . . . ."

In the late 1960s, Robert Kennedy asked Robert Amory how Bissell was doing. Amory said, "I don't see him very much, but when I do,
he seems to be obviously unhappy not to be at the center of things. A
guy like that's built that way. . . . If you don't mind my saying, the one

thing I think was graceless about your brother's administration was giving him the National Security Medal *in camera.*" As Amory recalled, Kennedy scowled, leaned forward and said, "I didn't ask you to insult my brother." Then he paused and said, "You're absolutely right."

•

After May 1960, the U-2 continued to fly along the Iron Curtain but, as far as we know, never again deliberately penetrated Soviet airspace. In August 1962, a U-2 pilot "strayed" over the vital intelligence target of Sakhalin Island. The Soviets did not down the plane but they did protest. Washington apologized and reaffirmed its pledge to avoid Soviet airspace.

In September 1962, U-2 pilots brought back the first concrete evidence of Soviet missiles in Cuba. Stepping up the flights, Defense Secretary Robert McNamara had the fliers formally transferred from CIA back to the Air Force. Eisenhower may have worried about military overflights into Russia, but McNamara feared that if a CIA pilot fell in Cuba, the Soviets would inflate the incident into an "aerial Bay of Pigs."

At the peak of the crisis, on October 27, a U-2 flown by Major Rudolph Anderson was downed by a Soviet missile in Cuba, increasing Pentagon demands for an immediate attack on Cuba. These John Kennedy resisted. The next day, a U-2 flying toward the North Pole to spot Soviet nuclear tests veered deep into Soviet airspace over the Chukot Peninsula before turning back. As Eisenhower had always dreaded, Khrushchev may have wondered whether this was really the forerunner of a nuclear attack.

Brought the news, Kennedy laughed sardonically: "There is always some son-of-a-bitch who doesn't get the word." Khrushchev complained and Kennedy apologized. Later the U-2 helped to end the Cuban confrontation by assuring that the Russians were indeed removing their missiles.

In September 1970, U-2 photos suggested that a Soviet nuclear submarine base was being built at the Cuban port of Cienfuegos. This would have violated Khrushchev's pledge to keep nuclear weapons out of Cuba in exchange for Kennedy's forswearance of military action against the Castro regime. Washington raised the evidence with the Kremlin, which reaffirmed that the 1962 agreement was still on.

Even before May Day 1960, the CIA had planned to let Nationalist Chinese pilots carry the burden of U-2 flights over Mainland China. At least four U-2s flown by Nationalist pilots were shot down over the Mainland from 1961 to 1964. Ray Cline, CIA chief in Taipei, recalled that when trouble came, the fliers "destroyed their airplanes and themselves rather than let the Communists learn anything from their capture."

Debris was displayed in Peking, where workers were told that the planes had been downed by the power of Chairman Mao's thought. Mao's government vainly offered eight thousand ounces of gold to any Taiwanese pilot who would defect with U-2 intact. The planes evidently kept such close watch on Chinese nuclear development that Western intelligence was not astonished when the first device was exploded in 1964.

For such a fragile plane, the U-2 proved to be surprisingly durable. It surveyed Viet Cong activity and bomb damage in Vietnam. The original model had been followed by a U-2B and U-2C, a two-seater U-2D and a U-2R, a much larger version with more range and altitude. In 1981, Lockheed delivered another variant, the ER-1, to NASA's Ames Research Center near San Francisco. Gleaming white, with NASA's red logotype on its tail, it gathered comet dust to probe the origins of the solar system, did aerial mapping and assessed land-use. The TR-1, a modified U-2R designed for tactical reconnaissance, was based in southern England. Its electronic sensors were designed to relay information on enemy units by data link to air and ground commanders.

The U-2 and its descendants retained the same split personality as in the 1950s: they searched for marijuana fields and citrus blight in California and Florida and spied on poorly defended trouble spots like Nicaragua and El Salvador.

The spy satellite became the mainstay of American and Soviet intelligence. In August 1960, Eisenhower had secretly founded the National Reconnaissance Office to gather intelligence from outer space: by 1975, it was reputed to have the largest budget of any American intelligence agency. Not until 1978 did the American government officially concede that it spied from satellites. This was partly a legacy of the thinking of the U-2's original managers: announcing that the United States sent spy satellites into Soviet skies might gratuitously antagonize the Russians and increase their temptation to knock them out.

Before *Sputnik*, the Russians had argued that a nation's vertical sovereignty was virtually unlimited. But this stand was difficult to maintain after they launched a satellite over the United States and other countries without permission. One of Eisenhower's advisers told him after *Sputnik* that the Soviets had "done us a good turn unintentionally" by establishing the freedom of space.

But Khrushchev also feared the prospect of American spy satellites that would penetrate Soviet secrecy far more effectively than the U-2. At the Paris summit table, Khrushchev had told de Gaulle that the Soviet Union did not fear American photography of its territory. Nonetheless in the fall of 1960, Moscow announced that any foreign spy satellite would be "paralyzed and rebuffed" as the U-2 had been. Although the Soviets knew that the United States had vastly more to gain from such mutual reconnaissance, they accelerated their own spy satellite program and in 1963 accepted a UN resolution that national sovereignty did not extend into space.

By the early 1970s, at the Strategic Arms Limitation Talks in Geneva, the Russians were insisting that "national means of verification"— notably satellites—be used to ensure compliance with a SALT agreement. The chief American delegate, Gerard Smith, who had prepared Christian Herter for the Senate U-2 hearings in 1960, mused that the black plane had proved to be "the forerunner of the technology that has made SALT possible." American and Soviet satellites monitored each other's territory around the clock. Open Skies was, at least to some extent, a reality.

By the mid-1960s, Kelly Johnson had perfected the plane that Richard Bissell had commissioned in 1959 to fly into the Soviet Union after the Soviets became able to down the U-2. Called "perhaps the most enigmatic aircraft in service," the SR-71 Blackbird began flying intelligence missions too short-notice or low-altitude for satellites and too dangerous for other spy planes. Blue-black, the length of a Boeing 727, the SR-71 was at its creation the fastest plane on earth, zooming three times the speed of sound at heights far above eighty thousand feet.

Like the U-2 and other spy planes, the Blackbird flew along Soviet borders. Almost untraceable on radar, by the early 1980s it reportedly eluded a thousand attempts by the Soviet and other air forces to knock it out of the skies. Stripped of identifying markings, the plane was rumored to fly into Soviet airspace. If so, American-Soviet relations were once again being influenced by a secret undercurrent, arousing the same ancient anxieties as the U-2 about encirclement, invasion and weakness—especially since the SR-71 was said to be able to drop lightweight nuclear weapons on Soviet territory.*

The Kremlin's frustration at its inability to shoot down a U-2 had incited the Soviet Air Force to extreme vigilance against aerial incursion, demonstrated by the ferocity of the attacks on the two low-flying American planes that entered Soviet airspace in 1958. Frustration at the inability to down the SR-71 or other planes may have played a part in the trigger-happiness that led to the downing of a civilian Korean Airlines plane in Soviet airspace near Sakhalin Island in September 1983.

Soviet psychology has almost always been interwoven with self-justification. In November 1985, before Ronald Reagan met Mikhail Gorbachev at Geneva, Americans and Russians on U.S. television debated the merits of a "Star Wars" defense system. The American political analyst George Will noted that, unlike the Soviet Union, the United States had "virtually no defense" against invasion by bombers: "Why is it legitimate and good for the Soviet Union to defend against bomber-borne nuclear threats, but illegitimate and dangerous to defend against ballistic missiles?"

"Air defense has very important historic roots," said Roald Sagdeev of Moscow's Institute of Space Research. "Soviet aircraft have never crossed U.S. territory. We Russians witnessed how U-2 planes flew repeatedly over our country."

"Forgive me, but are you saying that you have ten thousand surface-to-air launchers and 2,200 interceptor aircraft because the United States once flew U-2s over your territory?"

"I simply started with the historical and psychological reasons. They are very important."

•

The U-2 affair resounded through other areas of American life. It was the first time many Americans discovered that their government was not always candid.

During the Eisenhower Presidency, it was said that if Diogenes were

* By 1985, the Skunk Works developed a new version of the Blackbird that flew higher, faster and farther. This was an unmanned drone steered by remote control, ending the problem of an American plane being downed on Soviet territory with a live pilot aboard.

still searching for an honest man, he should be taken to the Oval Office. It was ironic that Eisenhower should be the first American President to confess his administration had lied to the public, but his reputation for integrity was so strong that Americans continued to absolve the President. Most in 1960 would have been startled to learn that Eisenhower had personally approved the false U-2 cover story, or that his Secretaries of State and Defense had flirted with perjury to keep the depth of the President's involvement in the U-2 affair away from the Senate Foreign Relations Committee.

The U-2 did not immediately induce great public skepticism about government pronouncements: when the RB-47 was shot down two months later, Americans generally accepted official statements at face value. But repeated dissembling produced the credibility gap from which the American government never fully recovered. Evidence of how much public faith had shrunk since May 1960 was the fact that when the Korean Airlines plane was downed in 1983, the American press and public routinely speculated that the CIA or another Western intelligence agency had placed 269 civilian lives in jeopardy to spy on Russia.

The U-2 alerted many Americans for the first time to the existence of the CIA and American espionage. Iowans in 1960 joked that what CIA really stood for was "Caught in the Act." *Aviation Week* argued that the U-2 demonstrated American incompetence in the Cold War: "The bungling, naïveté and innocence our various government agencies have displayed in the U-2 episode show clearly that we are not yet organized for this type of conflict, nor do we really understand its scope and strategy." Despite Mike Mansfield's efforts, the U-2 did not start a public clamor for Congressional oversight of the CIA. Only in the mid-1970s, after damaging revelations about CIA activities, did the House and Senate form Select Committees on Intelligence.

The U-2 hastened the golden age of espionage in American popular culture. Spying was clearly enshrined as part of the American experience; secret agents no longer seemed so foreign and abstract. Television programs like *I Spy* and the literary and cinematic adventures of Ian Fleming's James Bond attracted a vast American following.

In 1982, William F. Buckley, Jr., published *Marco Polo, If You Can,* in which a drunken Khrushchev reveals to Eisenhower at Camp David that the CIA has a mole. To find it and also exacerbate Sino-

396 : M A Y D A Y

Soviet tensions, the President orders passed to Moscow a phony proto-
col for a Sino-American rapprochement to be launched by the gift of
four U-2s to Peking and an American test flight over Russia to show
Mao what the planes can do. The mission is flown in April 1960 by
Buckley's hero, Blackford Oakes, who deliberately flames out near
Alma-Ata.

•

Shortly after Francis Gary Powers returned from the Soviet Union,
someone wrote, "All's well that ends well. With Powers vindicated and
in clover and everybody all around smiling, this complex, confusing
and, at times, so recklessly played spy drama concludes with rather a
happy ending after all—a rare thing indeed in the grim underworld of
intelligence."

The U-2 pilot was welcomed home by eight hundred neighbors and
more relatives than he had ever known he had at a rally at Big Stone
Gap, Virginia. At the CIA's new quarters in Langley, he advised
trainees on how to cope with captivity as he pondered his future.

His marriage was over: when his divorce from Barbara was tried in
Milledgeville in January 1963, a CIA man sat in the courtroom signal-
ing questions he should decline to answer. With a ghostwriter, Barbara
wrote a fifty-cent paperback that she had wished to call *Fly Away, My
Love*. Before publication, one of J. Edgar Hoover's moles informed the
FBI that "emphasis will be placed on sex and drinking." The book was
issued as *Spy Wife*. David Cort wrote in the *Nation* that "a good deal of
Spy Wife is given to repleading her case at the divorce, and in a few
years, these passages will bore even Barbara."

One morning in May 1962, Powers walked around a corner at CIA
headquarters into a female colleague and spilled his cup of coffee.
Much later she recalled, "I fell in love with him the first time I laid eyes
on him." A handsome, well-poised Virginian, Sue Downey was a CIA
psychometrist who had bad-mouthed Powers in 1960; she had not
known that he had not been ordered to kill himself when captured. A
week after their meeting, the famous pilot asked her to dinner.

Restless in the only desk job he had ever had, Powers ascertained
from Kelly Johnson that his Lockheed job offer still stood, quit the
CIA and drove to California in the gray Mercedes he had bought while
in Turkey. In October 1963, he and Sue married and began what he
later called "the happiest part of my life." He adopted his seven-year-

old stepdaughter; in 1965, his wife bore him a son, Francis Gary Powers II.

For Lockheed, Powers test-flew U-2s that had been returned for maintenance or modification. He bought a house overlooking Burbank Airport so that Sue could watch his takeoffs and landings—before learning that Lockheed was moving flight testing to Van Nuys. In 1965, researching a piece for *Esquire,* Ovid Demaris found that reaching Powers was "like trying to reach Garbo." Calls to Lockheed's public relations office were fruitless: "Yes, he works here. . . . Sorry, an interview is out of the question. . . . Frankly, I think the CIA has the old hex on Gary. . . . Those guys think they're James Bond."

Demaris finally turned up on the Powers doorstep and was let in. Sitting in a gold velour chair, a glass of gin in his hand, the U-2 pilot described his experiences and said, "It seems more like something I've read in a book—a good book where you identify with all the characters." Past the Latvian rugs he had woven in prison, he walked to a picture window and gazed at the lights of the San Fernando Valley shimmering below: "This is what I used to dream about. A home and family. I'm very grateful."

For years after 1960, Thomas Gates had nightmares about the U-2. What Powers lost sleep over were the charges that he had performed ignobly in Russia: the public version of the Board of Inquiry report, with its "evasive wording," had "raised almost as many doubts as it had laid to rest." In April 1963, when the CIA gave Intelligence Stars to U-2 pilots, Powers was not invited. In 1965, he was finally asked to receive the medal, but was irked to find himself commended for courage and valor only before 1960: the Agency seemed to have felt "the Virginia hillbilly" wouldn't notice.

Book publishers had besieged him for his memoirs, but the CIA told him that a book would help neither him nor the Agency. In 1968, reapproached by Holt, Rinehart & Winston, he wrote the Agency again for permission to write his story and heard nothing: "Since they had helped to perpetuate the Francis Gary Powers mercenary label, I'd play the part. Sarcastically I wrote to them that I was going to write the book and . . . since they had been so anxious to suppress it, I'd be glad to consider their best offer."

As a contract employee, Powers had evidently signed no pledge to submit his writings to CIA censorship. The Agency told him it would not stand in his way. Wary of obligation, he refused its offer to help.

His publisher found him a ghostwriter, Curt Gentry; they taped and edited his reminiscences. In deference to the Agency, he omitted information on his altitude near Sverdlovsk, British collaboration on the program, the number of overflights, violation of certain other nations' airspace, some CIA methods and other sensitive details.

But he let stand his indictment of the CIA for failing to prepare the U-2 pilots for capture, the faulty cover story, the failure to rebut the public impression that he had violated orders by not killing himself and by talking to the Russians: "A scapegoat, by dictionary definition, is one made to bear the blame for others or to suffer in their place." He wrote, "It would be tragic if, in the process of trying to protect our government, we forgot that it was founded on the concept of the worth of the individual."

Published criticism of the CIA was far less common in 1969 than it was in the 1970s. Books by Victor Marchetti and Philip Agee, the Church and Rockefeller investigations were still years away. In October 1969, after giving his manuscript to the Agency for a courtesy reading, Powers was summoned by Kelly Johnson, who told him that U-2 testing was winding down. Powers asked how long he had. Johnson said, "Yesterday," and revealed that the CIA, not Lockheed, had been paying his salary.

When NASA hired pilots for its own U-2 program, Powers complained that he had not been asked. In a private memo, Johnson wrote, "I am very unhappy with Powers . . . and consider him extremely ungrateful for what Lockheed and I personally have done with him. . . . These pilots had to be acceptable to NASA, who would not wish to employ pilots who had had any publicity from the U-2 flights." Johnson noted that the NASA program would "undoubtedly involve flying over friendly countries who would be very upset should we have the U-2 piloted by Powers."

Operation Overflight was published on May Day 1970. On *The Dick Cavett Show,* the host mentioned the "terrific sentiment" that Powers should have killed himself. Powers said, "Yes, I ran across something like that today. My answer is, if they ask me why didn't you kill yourself, 'Why don't you kill *your*-self?' " The audience guffawed. Cavett asked whether his firing by Lockheed had any connection with his book's publication.

"They didn't *say* it did."

He hired an agent and overcame his shyness to give lectures. Near

Los Angeles, he told the North American Rockwell Management Club, "It's a great pleasure for me to talk tonight to a group of aerospace people who arc still *employed.*" He showed films of the U-2: "It's going down the runway now—you notice the pogos on both of the wings. . . . There go the pogos." He described the fateful day: "It was my duty to fly the U-2 from Peshawar, Pakistan, to Bodö, Norway. Unfortunately this was the one that didn't make it."

He scored the government's failure to clear his name: "The President of the United States, the CIA, the Senate Armed Services Committee *knew* the full story. They *knew* how much information I had withheld from the Soviets. . . . All they wanted to do, it seems, was to get the CIA out of the news, because an organization like that can't take too much news."

Powers was rapidly going through his savings. His wife later recalled going "several places in the aerospace industry where Frank had sent out resumes and they would fly us down and wine and dine us— first-class treatment all the way, but never a job forthcoming." He dreamt about his plane crashing in the Soviet Union and asked a hypnotist to return him to Vladimir to see whether he might have revealed something unconsciously to the Russians.

In 1972, he asked his friend Gregory Anderson to help him persuade Congress to reopen its U-2 investigation and clear his name. In 1968, Powers had campaigned door-to-door for Richard Nixon (which would have amused the candidate who had partly blamed the U-2 for his 1960 defeat). They contacted Republican friends in Congress and elsewhere without avail. In November 1972, Powers and his wife sold their house and planned to return to the East. As she recalled, "Frank said he would sit on the Agency's doorstep until somebody gave him a job."

KGIL Radio in Los Angeles hired him to fly a Cessna and report on traffic. Anderson recalled, "He was sitting there with his flight book on his lap and he's got another book here that's full of commercials— what he's going to do for Coast Federal Savings or Vons Markets. And he's flying the airplane and looking for traffic so that he doesn't run into someone, and he's also looking at the damn freeways. And in addition, he's talking to them at the station—and to the air controller. . . . It was a tremendous pressure-cooker up there and it was as if he was sitting in a warm bath, just totally relaxed and totally happy."

Grayer and stockier than during the days flying over Russia,

Powers bought a new house in Sherman Oaks and exploited his staccato workday to spend much time with his son. Fascinated by the Soviet Union, he hankered to return for a visit but feared that the Russians might kidnap him and announce his defection. He had never blamed Kelly Johnson for firing him; in 1975, he hung a picture in his study inscribed by the U-2's designer: "With thanks for doing a wonderful job with the U-Birds. I know!!"

His memoirs were made into an NBC television film starring Lee Majors. (Powers would have preferred Martin Sheen.) At his father's request, young Gary Powers played a Russian boy who picked up the notorious poison pin. In November 1976, Powers was hired by KNBC Television in Los Angeles. He went to Texas to learn how to fly a Bell Jet Ranger helicopter. Soon he was back in the sky covering weather, fires and police chases.

On the morning of August 1, 1977, the station asked him to cover a brushfire in Santa Barbara. He drove to Van Nuys Airport and climbed into the chopper with his cameraman. At 12:25 P.M., after photographing the fire, he called in for another assignment. Fifteen minutes later, they hovered over a field where boys were playing softball. Powers was only three miles from the Skunk Works where it had all begun.

One of the softball players heard a popping noise: "I looked up and saw the helicopter swaying in the air and making all sorts of dips, and then it kind of conked out. Then he looked as if he got it going again. Then it just conked out again and dipped down and hit the ground really hard and everything flew everywhere." Some of the boys were sure that the pilot—whoever he was—had swerved the chopper to avoid crushing them.

Seventeen years before, Francis Gary Powers had confounded the President of the United States and the highest ranks of his government by eluding death. This time, he did not.

A police sergeant said, "We found no evidence of fuel on board and the craft didn't burn, so from all appearances, it would seem he ran out of gas. That's the unforgivable pilot error." Gregory Anderson recalled that a few days before, Powers had filmed a moving train on fire. The gauge had said he was low on fuel: "When he got back and checked his fuel, he had enough left for another thirty minutes, so it really bothered him that he'd missed some great footage." By Anderson's account, Powers was never told that the gauge was repaired on the evening of July 31.

Sue Powers found this explanation hard to believe: "Frank was just too good a pilot to run out of fuel." Undeterred by the lack of concrete evidence, conspiracy theorists noted the presence of the CIA and Lockheed at Van Nuys Airport and charged that Powers's craft had been sabotaged to keep him from revealing damaging secret information or in retaliation for criticizing the CIA.

Powers had suspected that if he preceded his wife in death, she would try to have him buried at Arlington National Cemetery. He had told Anderson, "There isn't a chance. Don't even let her try." But now the widow said, "We've got to get Frank to Arlington." Anderson reminded her that the cemetery had long been closed to almost all but the highest military echelons.

"There is no alternative," she said. If crooked politicians and the rest of the types running around the country could be buried there, then the one hero this country had had in twenty-five years would be buried there.

Anderson called everyone he could think of in Washington. The matter was referred to President Jimmy Carter. Plains, Georgia, was forty-two miles from the Radium Springs Motel where Powers was recruited by the CIA. The future President had been working the peanut fields in May 1960 when he learned of the U-2 downing: he had thought Eisenhower an "honest and good man" and regretted that his administration had been tarnished by "telling the tale" about the weather plane. Upon the CIA's strong recommendation, Carter approved the pilot's burial in Arlington.

After the service, the Powers family met reporters. An uncle threw an arm around one of his nephew's old friends and said, "I want you to meet Sammy Snider. He flew the U-2 in the program with Frank. They were great buddies." Snider's face lost its color: this was the first time any other U-2 pilot had been publicly revealed to have violated the airspace of the Soviet Union. He had not even told his children.

Appendix: *Telephone Conversation Between Former President Eisenhower and Director of Central Intelligence John McCone, August 13, 1964, 10:10 A.M.*

In August 1964, Dwight Eisenhower was nearing the end of work on *Waging Peace,* his second volume of Presidential memoirs, when he turned to the U-2 affair. After perusing his own files, enough ambiguities remained in his mind to telephone CIA Director John McCone, who had once been Chairman of his Atomic Energy Commission. The CIA taped or otherwise transcribed their conversation:

Eisenhower: Say, John, I['ve] got a question to ask you. How much of the [Francis Gary] Powers report—what's happening, just telling my side of the U-2—that is, what I understood and what's happened now. Now, the Powers report was, of course, made to you people, and I don't know if it was ever published or not. Or I don't know whether I'd be justified in using any information out of it.

McCone: Yes. Well, his report was pretty well made public.

Eisenhower: That's what I remembered.

McCone: Yes.

Eisenhower: Could you send me—matter of fact, did he say that he was shot down?

McCone: That was the impression he had. He couldn't say positively. He felt a burst astern of him, a flare, and lost control of his plane.

Eisenhower: How far did he glide before he ejected?

McCone: He—as I remember it, he didn't glide. He nosed over and a wing came off, and then he went into a spiral and apparently ejected at twenty or twenty-five thousand feet.

Eisenhower: Now, the plane was pretty well destroyed.

McCone: Well, strangely enough, it was not pretty well destroyed. Apparently leveled off and made something of a soft landing so that—

Eisenhower: I thought the plane—maybe I['ll] go back and ask you a couple of other questions.

McCone: —rather large pieces.

Eisenhower: Yes, I remember that now. Now, let me ask you this, John. As I understood it, I mean, as was told me all those years by both [Richard] Bissell and by Allen [Dulles], this thing that the plane could never be recovered—it had self-destruction built in it and also they were—they assured me there was really no fear of ever getting back a live pilot if it was knocked down by a hostile action in Russia. Even if damaged, they figured that at that height, if he tried to parachute at seventy thousand feet, he'd never survive.

Now, the trouble is we've got records after the event—as late as May 20th [1960], or something like that—we've got conversation between [Thomas] Gates and Dulles. And Gates says, "Well, what was the pilot supposed to say if he landed?" And Dulles said, "He's to say he's a CIA man and that's it—and give his name."

McCone: That's correct.

Eisenhower: Well, now, the point of it is I was told it would be almost impossible for the man if he came down just . . . of his own and just glided down and no hostile action of any type—well, that might be a remote possibility, but otherwise they discounted. And the whole cover story was built on the basis that the man would never survive.

McCone: I realize that and I realized it at the time, but it was absolutely wrong. Now, there have been three pilots whose planes have performed just as his did in test flights and so forth where they lost control at seventy thousand feet. The wings came off and spiraled down and the pilots ejected and lived. Now, in interrogating Powers as to exactly what happened to him, the same interrogators interrogated the other pilots—and these events happened in Louisiana and Nevada and so forth, and the planes performed and the pilots performed in just identical manners.

Now, as far as the destruct mechanism is concerned, there was a destruct mechanism that presumably would destroy the camera and the film—not the plane, but that was—the destruct switch was not pushed, and the experts felt that Powers was in such a posture with his plane in a spin that he could not reach the destruct button prior to ejecting.

Eisenhower: Would you have any records of your own to show what these people—what the presentations they were making to people like [John] Foster Dulles and me about what would probably happen? You see, I don't want to be accusing people of having fooled me. But I do know that they told me that the possibility of anyone surviving—matter of fact, that's the reason I argued against putting out the cover story, and they said, "You just don't have to worry, General. It is perfectly all right because there's nobody there." That's all. . . .

McCone: Now, I['ll] tell you what I will do. Let me go into this thing and let me get something—I'd do it myself, but I'm going to go West for two or three days.

Eisenhower: O.K. If you'll just have some of your staff look up the sequence of events from the time we designed this blasted thing until the present—I mean, until it was finally ended with the Powers thing, that can be told—that is, where I could tell it without violating secrecy. If you could do that and then just tell them to send me something like that, I'd be much obliged to you.

McCone: I'll either send it to you or I'll have somebody come up and go over it with you.

Eisenhower: Fine.

(*Source:* Richard Bissell Private Papers)

If Allen Dulles had indeed told Gates that, on landing, Powers was to say nothing but his name and the fact that he was a CIA man, he was misinformed. U-2 pilots were told by their commanders that they were "perfectly free to tell the full truth about their mission," if downed, "with the exception of certain specifications of the aircraft."[1]

In *Waging Peace,* Eisenhower finally insisted that he "had been assured that if a plane were to go down, it would be destroyed either in the air or on impact, so that proof of espionage would be lacking."[2] On how the plane was downed, the former President was mute, but without further comment he quoted Andrew Goodpaster as telling him on May 2, 1960, that the pilot had "reported an engine flameout" before going down.[3] In his own memoirs, Powers found this "astonishing" and said, "I had neither an engine flameout nor did I radio back to the base."[4] The riddles remain.

1. Memorandum to Detachment Commanders, December 9, 1957, appended to CIA Board of Inquiry Report to John McCone, February 27, 1962, John F. Kennedy Library.

2. Dwight D. Eisenhower, *Waging Peace* (Garden City, N.Y.: Doubleday & Company, 1965), p. 547.

3. Ibid., p. 543.

4. Francis Gary Powers, *Operation Overflight* (New York: Holt, Rinehart and Winston, 1970), pp. 351–52.

Acknowledgments

One of the benefits of writing history is that of engagement with other scholars and their work, with diaries, letters, memoirs and other documents. An additional compensation of writing contemporary history is that of engagement with some of those who helped to shape the events under study.

I have benefited from many hours of formal and informal conversation with people who were active in the U-2 program and American-Soviet diplomacy during the days of Eisenhower and Khrushchev; they are listed in the General Sources and Notes. I wish especially to thank Richard M. Bissell, Jr., and General Andrew J. Goodpaster, who gracefully endured hour after hour of questions, argued fine points with the author, explained the context of declassified documents and otherwise helped to illuminate the subject and period.

Richard Bissell, John S. D. Eisenhower and Kelly Johnson allowed me to examine materials in their private papers. John Wickman, James Leyerzapf and others at the Eisenhower Library helped to provide access to the majority of documents consulted for this book and hastened the process of declassification. For assistance with other materials, I thank Benedict Zobrist and George Curtis of the Truman Library, Dan Fenn, William Johnson and Henry Gwiazda of the Kennedy Library, and the men and women of the Library of Congress, the National Archives, the Georgetown University Library and the Columbia Oral History Project.

Seven scholars interrupted overburdened lives and writing schedules to read and criticize the manuscript. Adam B. Ulam, Director of the Russian Research Center, Harvard University, brought to bear his singular understanding of Soviet history and Soviet-American relations. Stephen E. Ambrose of the University of New Orleans gave me the benefit of his close study of Eisenhower, American intelligence and the Cold War. My old teacher James MacGregor Burns of Williams College made comments that drew especially on his examinations of leadership and the American political system.

Thomas Powers read the manuscript against the background of his work on the history of the CIA and American security issues. Harrison E. Salisbury, formerly of the *New York Times,* made suggestions based on his long study of the Soviet Union and its leaders. Priscilla Johnson McMillan of the Russian Research Center, Harvard, reviewed the volume from the standpoint of a scholar and chronicler of Khrushchev and recent Soviet history. Arthur M. Schlesinger, Jr., made useful comments on the book's conclusions.

My brother Steven, to whom this volume is dedicated, used his journalistic skills to scrutinize the manuscript and helped the author in manifold ways.

My experience with Harper & Row has brought me to understand why it has traditionally been a congenial home for historians. Edward L. Burlingame, Vice President and Publisher, offered guidance throughout the project. M. S. Wyeth, Jr., Vice President and Executive Editor, treated the book and its author as if he had no other obligations. Daniel Bial, Sidney Feinberg, Florence Goldstein, Terry Karten, William Monroe and Greg Weber made vital contributions during the publication process.

Timothy Seldes of Russell & Volkening provided sound advice. My friends and family offered unfailing and indispensable support through the years of research and composition.

All of these people I thank. Final responsibility for the judgments expressed in this volume is, of course, my own.

Historiographical Note

Amassing primary sources for the study of recent history, American-Soviet relations and intelligence is triply difficult. For events two or three decades in the past, potentially vital documents may be unavailable. Western historians are virtually frozen out of Soviet archives. Even in the United States, whose Freedom of Information Act has been rightly called a tribute to American self-confidence, postwar intelligence records are generally inaccessible.

I would not have undertaken this book but for the happy confluence of two developments. In 1982, the United States Senate Foreign Relations Committee released the previously censored portions of its 1960 investigation of the U-2 program, the May Day flight and the Paris Summit. These 347 pages of transcript, combined with the 298 pages made public in 1960, are the basic source on the U-2. For few other recent intelligence operations do we have the contemporaneous testimony, under oath, of the Secretaries of State and Defense, the Director of Central Intelligence and other key figures.

At the same time, the White House, State and Defense Departments and other agencies were releasing documents essential to consideration of the U-2's impact on American-Soviet diplomacy—notably records of conversations among President Eisenhower, his staff, State Department, Pentagon and CIA officials on the genesis and progress of the U-2 missions, the May Day mission and its aftermath. These threw light on areas that had long remained murky.

Two other vital sets of primary sources were available, confirming my view that the program's place in diplomatic history could be studied with precision. This is one of the rare cases in which we have detailed memoirs from most of the principal figures in the story—Eisenhower, Khrushchev, Macmillan, de Gaulle, Francis Gary

Powers. Others involved in the U-2 program and East-West diplomacy were still alive and willing to be interviewed. Five years earlier, by their own account, some of these people would have refused to speak on the subject at all, or so candidly. Five years later, some would have died, their testimony lost to history.

We all know that original sources are only as rich as the degree to which they are regarded with critical scrutiny. Presidential and diplomatic documents, memoirs, diaries, letters, interviews and even sworn Congressional testimony can be distorted by self-justification, dishonesty, haste, hardness of hearing, bad memory, loyalty, anger, disloyalty, ideology, frustration, senility. The historian must carefully assess the motives, perspective and access to information of each writer and speaker. For the benefit of the reader and other scholars, I offer below a brief evaluation of the sources most essential to the writing of this book.

U.S. Senate Foreign Relations Committee Hearings, May and June 1960*

This source is lent authority by the fact that witnesses were questioned under oath less than a month after the May Day flight and Summit collapse, when memories were still fresh. They were encouraged to consult records. They were interrogated by senators who were especially eager to assess the U-2's relationship to the Summit collapse (although they did not ask some indelicate questions that would probably have been asked were an intelligence failure of similar magnitude being investigated fifteen or more years later).

The testimony must be read with the awareness that all witnesses were striving to defend themselves and their agencies against often-scathing charges of ineptitude. They dodged questions about some aspects of the U-2 program which, if leaked in 1960, might genuinely have damaged American diplomacy, such as collaboration with the British and other intelligence services. Perhaps most interesting of all, almost every witness took extraordinary pains to minimize the President's involvement with the program and with the ultimately ill-conceived actions in Washington after the May Day failure.† One may read the hearings and never learn, for instance, that Eisenhower sanctioned every single flight after July 1956 or that he read and personally approved the ruinous initial cover story. As noted in Chapter Twelve of the current book, these hearings are a cautionary lesson: not even in sworn testimony must the historian presume that the witness is being wholly truthful.

Declassified U.S. Government Documents

Of these, I have drawn most heavily on White House memoranda and records of conversations and diplomatic records and cables. Conversations in which Eisenhower took part were contemporaneously transcribed—on rare occasions by tape recorder, more usually by Andrew Goodpaster, John Eisenhower or Arthur Minnich. The records made by these men reveal their training to keep accurate notes even

* Complete citations for this and other materials appear in General Sources.
† Richard Helms later wondered whether they had been orchestrated to do so by the White House, although Douglas Dillon denied this. (Helms and Dillon interviews)

when it might cast the President in an unflattering light. Most vital of the diplomatic materials were Llewellyn Thompson's accounts and interpretations of conversations with Khrushchev. Like all diplomats, Thompson had his own bureaucratic and political viewpoint but, checked against other sources, his messages and memoranda indicate a superior sense of responsibility to provide the President and colleagues with undistorted information.*

The chief problem in using such recent sensitive documents is that some are partly or fully withheld because one or more agency fears harm to national security. This can be partially circumvented by careful use in conjunction with other sources. Several of those I interviewed, believing that the government had been too cautious, supplied phrases and paragraphs that had been deleted. With any work of history, of course, even the most energetic and careful research cannot preclude that future revelation of new materials might cause revision of interpretations based on the information available at the time of composition.

Access to some manuscript collections is conditional. Researchers approved for admission to the Allen Dulles Papers at Princeton, for instance, are required to provide a committee "for its approval" all quotations or citations "in the context of their intended publication." I have not applied for access to any such collection where there was even a remote chance of obligation to "clear" the manuscript of this book with an outside party.

Memoirs

Eisenhower wrote *Mandate for Change* and *Waging Peace* during the four years after he left office. This account is based on rough drafts written by William Ewald and John Eisenhower after examination of the President's papers and consultation with other members of the Eisenhower Administration. As with the Truman and Johnson Presidential memoirs, the two volumes lack the sound of Eisenhower's voice. They omit much information on sensitive issues like the U-2,† nuclear testing and CIA covert operations, but are generally a reliable starting point on the Eisenhower Presidency.

Except for the fact that they were edited and annotated by a careful scholar of Soviet affairs, the two volumes of *Khrushchev Remembers* belong more to the category of oral history than memoir. Khrushchev evidently lacked access to records and dictated his recollections a decade or more after the fact. This caused occasional obvious errors: while relating his American visit, Khrushchev placed his talk with Douglas Dillon just after arrival and a visit to a meat packing plant in Pittsburgh, rather than Des Moines. The reader must remember that these are the words of a depressed, massively frustrated man of vast ego who had been officially turned into a "non-person." This may have led Khrushchev to overstatement and exaggeration of his impact on history. For obvious reasons, he did not accuse incumbent Soviet lead-

---

* Thompson refused to write memoirs of his service in Moscow, believing that if he did, future Soviet leaders might not speak as freely with American ambassadors as Khrushchev did with him. (Jane Thompson interview)

† See Epilogue and Appendix.

ers or reveal state secrets. These memoirs are primarily useful not for documentation of names, dates and places but as a window on Khrushchev's retrospective attitudes and reactions to the monumental events in which he took part.*

Harold Macmillan completed his six-volume memoirs during the decade after which he left power in 1963. These were dictated from documents and notes and carefully revised by hand. One suspects that when the private diaries quoted therein are published in their entirety, they will be an essential source for the history of the mid-twentieth century. Charles de Gaulle was able to complete only one volume of Presidential memoirs between his resignation in 1969 and his death the following year. On the U-2 and the events culminating in the Paris Summit, they are accurate but incomplete.

Francis Gary Powers's *Operation Overflight* was ghostwritten by Curt Gentry, latterly author of *Helter Skelter,* a narrative of the Charles Manson murder case. By his own account, Powers refused the CIA's offer to help in order to avoid "unspoken obligation." He did allow the Agency a courtesy reading of a final draft and, according to him, deleted information said to be vital to national security. The book is based on Powers's taped reminiscences, fortified by letters, diary fragments, the transcript of the Moscow trial and Gentry's research. It is an extended argument on behalf of the thesis that he acquitted himself well through his flight and later ordeal. Given the lack of comprehensive documentation and whatever agreements Powers made not to reveal sensitive information, the book is primarily valuable as revelation of his response to his experiences.

Interviews

Andrei Gromyko, Vyacheslav Molotov, Nina Petrovna Khrushcheva and other key Soviet figures were alive at the time this book was researched but, as with unpublished documents, the Soviets generally refuse requests for interviews on the subject of an officially discredited Soviet leadership. I have been more fortunate in the West. As noted in the General Sources, I have interviewed principal figures of the Eisenhower White House, the CIA, State Department, Pentagon, Congress, the press, the British government, Lockheed, the U-2 squadrons, friends and family of Francis Gary Powers.

Interviews can be a fruitful source for the historian of an age in which business is often done in person, over telephone and without records. They are especially useful to the scholar of modern intelligence. The CIA's large archive of documents and internal histories is generally barred to outside historians. This problem is somewhat mitigated by the willingness of former Agency officials to speak with scholars. With the exception of one man still working with the CIA on sensitive projects, all with whom I asked to speak agreed.

---

* Technicians have persuasively verified the voice on the tapes from which *Khrushchev Remembers* was adapted as Khrushchev's. Some American counterintelligence officers are said to believe that the Soviet government compelled him to slip in deceptive facts and judgments as part of its disinformation campaign against the West (conversation with Jerrold Schecter, formerly of *Time,* who was involved in the memoirs' publication). Of this I have found no convincing evidence.

I came to most of these and other interviews armed with documents and other records to buttress the memories of the subjects. To ensure as much accuracy as possible, virtually all interviews were recorded on tape. I insisted that all be conducted without restriction and on the record. This may inhibit candor but has the more important effect of allowing the reader to assess every citation. When people speak not for attribution, they have the power to dispense misinformation without facing responsibility for it. This is sometimes acceptable for journalism but not for history.

I have also drawn on two other bodies of spoken reminiscence. During the course of conversations that were not formal interviews, I have obtained illuminating sidelights and cited them in the Notes simply as conversations. I have also exploited the oral histories compiled by the Eisenhower and Kennedy Libraries, the John Foster Dulles Collection at Princeton and the parent of them all, the Columbia Oral History Project. These interviews were conducted and tape-recorded under terms similar to mine, with the exception that subjects were usually allowed to revise and extend the transcripts of their remarks.

General Sources

Interviews

Robert Amory, Jr., May 21, 1983
Gregory Anderson, December 19, 1983
Richard M. Bissell, Jr., February 17 and 18, 1983, and September 18, 1985
Dino Brugioni, January 23, February 14 and July 2, 1984
Ray S. Cline, June 28, 1983
C. Douglas Dillon, June 15, 1984
John S. D. Eisenhower, May 4, 1983
Milton S. Eisenhower, March 10, 1983
Vincent Ford, May 17, 1985
J. William Fulbright, October 3, 1984
Andrew J. Goodpaster, January 3, 1983, March 15 and July 3, 1984
Karl G. Harr, August 8, 1984
Richard McG. Helms, April 25, 1983
Lawrence Houston, January 17, 1983
Sam Jaffe, November 27, 1984
Kelly Johnson, June 22, 1983
James R. Killian, Jr., February 22, 1983
Edwin H. Land, February 22, 1983
Arthur C. Lundahl, August 21 and October 1, 1985
Cord Meyer, Jr., May 27, 1983
Sue Powers, June 21, 1983
Ray Scherer, July 31, 1984
Herbert Scoville, Jr., April 11, 1985
Sammy V. C. Snider, May 5, 1983

Jane Thompson, October 9, 1985
Vladimir Toumanoff, August 27, 1984
Daniel Williams, May 11, 1984
Sir Philip de Zulueta, October 9, 1984

Manuscript and Oral History Collections

Joseph and Stewart Alsop Papers, Library of Congress, Washington, D.C., courtesy of Joseph Alsop.

Richard M. Bissell, Jr., Private Papers, Selected Material on the U-2, courtesy of Richard M. Bissell, Jr.

Central Intelligence Agency Files, Documents released under Freedom of Information Act, Central Intelligence Agency, Langley, Va.

Columbia University Oral History Project, Columbia University, New York, N.Y.

John Foster Dulles Oral History Collection, Princeton University, Princeton, N.J.

John Foster Dulles Papers, Dwight D. Eisenhower Library, Abilene, Kan.

Dwight D. Eisenhower Diary, Dwight D. Eisenhower Library.

Dwight D. Eisenhower Library Oral History Collection, Dwight D. Eisenhower Library.

Dwight D. Eisenhower Pre-Presidential Papers, Dwight D. Eisenhower Library.

Dwight D. Eisenhower Presidential Papers (Ann Whitman Administration Series, Ann Whitman File, Ann Whitman Name Series, DDE Confidential Staff Series, DDE Diary Series, Cabinet Notes, Legislative Leaders Meeting Notes, National Security Council Series, White House Central File, White House Memo File, White House Office of the Special Assistant for National Security Affairs, White House Office of the Staff Secretary), Dwight D. Eisenhower Library.

Dwight D. Eisenhower Post-Presidential Papers, Dwight D. Eisenhower Library.

John S. D. Eisenhower Private Papers, May 1960 Diary, courtesy of John S. D. Eisenhower.

Federal Bureau of Investigation Files, Documents released under Freedom of Information Act, Federal Bureau of Investigation, Washington, D.C.

T. Keith Glennan Diary, Dwight D. Eisenhower Library.

James A. Hagerty Diary, Dwight D. Eisenhower Library.

Christian A. Herter Papers, Dwight D. Eisenhower Library.

C. D. Jackson Diary, Dwight D. Eisenhower Library.

Kelly Johnson Private Papers, Selected Material on the U-2, courtesy of Kelly Johnson.

John F. Kennedy Library Oral History Collection, John F. Kennedy Library, Boston, Mass.

John F. Kennedy Pre-Presidential Papers, John F. Kennedy Library.

John F. Kennedy Presidential Papers, John F. Kennedy Library.

Richard Nixon Vice Presidential Papers, Federal Archives and Records Center, Laguna Niguel, Calif.

Sidney W. Souers Papers, Harry S. Truman Library, Independence, Mo.

Harry S. Truman Post-Presidential Papers, Harry S. Truman Library.

Harry S. Truman Presidential Papers, Harry S. Truman Library.
Ann C. Whitman Diary, Dwight D. Eisenhower Library.

Basic Book List

This list includes authors whose works are cited in more than one chapter. Each of these works is referred to in the Notes by the author's surname or other abbreviation as indicated below.

Adams, Sherman. *Firsthand Report: The Story of the Eisenhower Administration.* New York: Harper & Brothers, 1961.

Alexander, Charles C. *Holding the Line: The Eisenhower Era, 1952–1961.* Bloomington, Ind.: Indiana University Press, 1975.

Alsop, Stewart. *The Center: People and Power in Political Washington.* New York: Harper & Row, 1968.

Ambrose, Stephen E. *Eisenhower.* New York: Simon and Schuster. Volume One, *Soldier, General of the Army, President-Elect, 1890–1952* (1983): Ambrose (1). Volume Two, *The President* (1984): Ambrose (2).

———, with Richard H. Immerman, *Ike's Spies: Eisenhower and the Espionage Establishment.* Garden City, N.Y.: Doubleday & Company, 1981: Ambrose (3).

Bamford, James. *The Puzzle Palace: A Report on America's Most Secret Agency.* Boston: Houghton Mifflin Company, 1982.

Bancroft, Mary. *Autobiography of a Spy.* New York: William Morrow and Company, 1983.

Barnet, Richard J. *The Alliance: America, Europe, Japan: Makers of the Postwar World.* New York: Simon and Schuster, 1983.

Barron, John. *KGB Today: The Hidden Hand.* London: Coronet reprint, 1983.

Bohlen, Charles E. *Witness to History, 1929–1969.* New York: W. W. Norton & Company, 1973.

Bradlee, Benjamin C. *Conversations with Kennedy.* New York: W. W. Norton & Company, 1975.

Cline, Ray S. *The CIA Under Reagan, Bush & Casey: The Evolution of the Agency from Roosevelt to Reagan.* Washington, D.C.: Acropolis Books, 1981.

Corson, William R. *The Armies of Ignorance: The Rise of the American Intelligence Empire.* New York: The Dial Press, 1977.

Crankshaw, Edward. *Khrushchev: A Career.* New York: The Viking Press, 1966.

Dallin, Alexander. *Black Box: KAL 007 and the Superpowers.* Berkeley, Calif.: University of California Press, 1985.

Deakin, James. *Straight Stuff: The Reporters, the White House and the Truth.* New York: William Morrow and Company, 1984.

De Gaulle, Charles. *Memoirs of Hope: Renewal, 1958–1962.* Translated from the French by Terence Kilmartin. London: Weidenfeld and Nicholson, 1971.

De Gramont, Sanche (Ted Morgan). *The Secret War: The Story of International Espionage Since World War II.* New York: G. P. Putnam's Sons, 1962.

Dinerstein, Herbert S. *The Making of a Missile Crisis: October 1962.* Baltimore: The Johns Hopkins University Press, 1976.

Divine, Robert A. *Blowing on the Wind: The Nuclear Test Ban Debate, 1954–1960.* New York: Oxford University Press, 1978: Divine (1).

———. *Eisenhower and the Cold War.* New York: Oxford University Press, 1981: Divine (2).

Donovan, Robert J. *Eisenhower: The Inside Story.* New York: Harper & Brothers, 1956.

Dulles, Allen W. *The Craft of Intelligence.* New York: Harper & Row, 1963.

Eisenhower, Dwight D. *The White House Years.* Garden City, N.Y.: Doubleday & Company. Volume One, *Mandate for Change: 1953–1956* (1963): *Mandate.* Volume Two, *Waging Peace: 1956–1961* (1965): *Waging.*

Eisenhower, John S. D. *Strictly Personal.* Garden City, N.Y.: Doubleday & Company, 1974: JSDE.

Eisenhower, Milton S. *The President Is Calling.* Garden City, N.Y.: Doubleday & Company, 1974: Milton Eisenhower.

Epstein, Edward Jay. *Legend: The Secret World of Lee Harvey Oswald.* New York: The McGraw-Hill Book Company, 1978.

Ewald, William Bragg, Jr. *Eisenhower the President: Crucial Days: 1951–1960.* Englewood Cliffs, N.J.: Prentice-Hall, 1981.

Frankland, Mark. *Khrushchev.* London: Harmondsworth, Penguin, 1966.

Gaddis, John Lewis. *Russia, the Soviet Union, and the United States: An Interpretive History.* New York: Oxford University Press, 1978: Gaddis (1).

———. *Strategies of Containment: A Critical Appraisal of Postwar American Security Policy.* New York: Oxford University Press, 1982: Gaddis (2).

Goldwater, Barry M. *With No Apologies: The Personal and Political Memoirs of Senator Barry M. Goldwater.* New York: William Morrow and Company, 1979.

Gray, Robert Keith. *Eighteen Acres Under Glass.* Garden City, N.Y.: Doubleday & Company, 1962.

Grossman, Michael Baruch, and Kumar, Martha Joynt. *Portraying the President: The White House and the News Media.* Baltimore: The Johns Hopkins University Press, 1981.

Gunther, John. *Procession.* New York: Harper & Row, 1965.

Hearst, William Randolph, Jr., Conniff, Frank, and Considine, Bob. *Ask Me Anything: Our Adventures with Khrushchev.* New York: The McGraw-Hill Book Company, 1960: Hearst and Considine.

Helman, Grover. *Aerial Photography: The Story of Aerial Mapping Reconnaissance.* New York: The Macmillan Company, 1972.

Herken, Gregg. *Counsels of War.* New York: Alfred A. Knopf, 1985.

Hilsman, Roger. *To Move a Nation: The Politics of Foreign Policy in the Administration of John F. Kennedy.* Garden City, N.Y.: Doubleday & Company, 1967.

Hoopes, Townsend. *The Devil and John Foster Dulles.* Boston: Little, Brown and Company, 1973.

Hughes, Emmet John. *The Ordeal of Power: A Political Memoir of the Eisenhower Administration.* New York: Atheneum, 1963.

Hyland, William, and Richard Shyrock. *The Fall of Khrushchev.* New York: Funk & Wagnalls, 1968.

Infield, Glenn B. *Unarmed and Unafraid.* New York: The Macmillan Company, 1970.

Johnson, Kelly. *Kelly: More Than My Share of It All.* Washington, D.C.: Smithsonian Institution Press, 1985.

Kaiser, Robert G. *Russia: The People and the Power.* New York: Pocket Books reprint, 1976.

Kaplan, Fred. *The Wizards of Armageddon.* New York: Simon and Schuster, 1983.

Kennan, George F. *Memoirs: 1950-1963.* Boston: Little, Brown and Company, 1972.

Khrushchev, Nikita S. *Khrushchev Remembers.* Translated from the Russian and edited by Strobe Talbott. Boston: Little, Brown and Company, 1970: NSK I.

———. *Khrushchev Remembers: The Last Testament.* Translated from the Russian and edited by Strobe Talbott. New York: Bantam reprint, 1976: NSK II.

Killian, James R., Jr. *Sputnik, Scientists, and Eisenhower.* Cambridge, Mass.: The MIT Press, 1977.

Kirkpatrick, Lyman B., Jr. *The Real CIA.* New York: Macmillan, 1968.

Kissinger, Henry A. *White House Years.* Boston: Little, Brown and Company, 1979.

Kistiakowsky, George B. *A Scientist at the White House.* Cambridge, Mass.: Harvard University Press, 1976.

Klass, Phillip J. *Secret Sentries in Space.* New York: Random House, 1971.

Kohler, Foy D. *Understanding the Russians: A Citizen's Primer.* New York: Harper & Row, 1970.

LaFeber, Walter. *America, Russia, and the Cold War, 1945-1975.* New York: John Wiley, 1976.

Laqueur, Walter. *A World of Secrets: The Uses and Limits of Intelligence.* New York: Basic Books, 1985.

Linden, Carl A. *Khrushchev and the Soviet Leadership, 1957-1964.* Baltimore: The Johns Hopkins University Press, 1966.

Lodge, Henry Cabot: *The Storm Has Many Eyes.* New York: W. W. Norton & Company, 1973.

Lyon, Peter. *Eisenhower: Portrait of the Hero.* Boston: Little, Brown and Company, 1974.

Macmillan, Harold. *Tides of Fortune: 1945-1955.* New York: Harper & Row, 1969: Macmillan (1).

———. *Riding the Storm: 1956-1959.* New York: Harper & Row, 1971: Macmillan (2).

———. *Pointing the Way: 1959-1961.* New York: Harper & Row, 1972: Macmillan (3).

Martin, John Bartlow. *Adlai Stevenson and the World: The Life of Adlai E. Stevenson.* Garden City, N.Y.: Doubleday & Company, 1977.

McDougall, Walter A. *The Heavens and the Earth: A Political History of the Space Age.* New York: Basic Books, 1985.

McSherry, James E. *Khrushchev and Kennedy in Retrospect.* Palo Alto, Calif.: Open-Door Press, 1971.

Medvedev, Roy. *All Stalin's Men.* Translated from the Russian by Harold Shukman. Garden City, N.Y.: Anchor Press/Doubleday, 1984: Medvedev (1).

———. *Khrushchev.* Translated from the Russian by Brian Pearce. Garden City, N.Y.: Anchor Press/Doubleday, 1983: Medvedev (2).

Miller, Jay. *Lockheed U-2.* Austin, Tex.: Aerofax, Inc., 1983.

Mosley, Leonard. *Dulles: A Biography of Eleanor, Allen and John Foster Dulles and Their Family Network.* New York: The Dial Press/James Wade, 1978.

Murphy, Robert. *Diplomat Among Warriors.* London: Collins, 1964.

Neal, Steve. *The Eisenhowers: Reluctant Dynasty.* Garden City, N.Y.: Doubleday & Company, 1978.

Neff, Donald. *Warriors at Suez: Eisenhower Takes America into the Middle East.* New York: Simon and Schuster, 1981.

Nixon, Richard. *RN: The Memoirs of Richard Nixon.* New York: Grosset & Dunlap, 1978: Nixon (1).

———. *Six Crises.* Garden City, N.Y.: Doubleday & Company, 1962: Nixon (2).

Page, Martin. *The Day Khrushchev Fell.* New York: Hawthorn Books, 1965.

Parmet, Herbert S. *Eisenhower and the American Crusades.* New York: The Macmillan Company, 1972.

Penkovskiy, Oleg. *The Penkovskiy Papers.* Introduction and commentary by Frank Gibney. New York: Ballantine reprint, 1982.

Persico, Joseph E. *The Imperial Rockefeller: A Biography of Nelson A. Rockefeller.* New York: Simon and Schuster, 1982.

Pierpoint, Robert. *At the White House: Assignment to Six Presidents.* New York: G. P. Putnam's Sons, 1981.

Pinkley, Virgil. *Eisenhower Declassified.* Old Tappan, N.J.: Fleming H. Revell Company, 1979.

Powers, Barbara. *Spy Wife.* New York: Pyramid Books, 1965: Barbara Powers.

Powers, Francis Gary, with Curt Gentry. *Operation Overflight: The U-2 Spy Pilot Tells His Story for the First Time.* New York: Holt, Rinehart and Winston, 1970: FGP.

Powers, Thomas. *The Man Who Kept the Secrets: Richard Helms & the CIA.* New York: Alfred A. Knopf, 1979: Thomas Powers.

Prados, John. *The Soviet Estimate: U.S. Intelligence Analysis and Russian Military Strength.* New York: The Dial Press, 1982.

Prouty, L. Fletcher. *The Secret Team: The CIA and Its Allies in Control of the United States and the World.* Englewood Cliffs, N.J.: Prentice-Hall, 1973.

Reston, James B. *Artillery of the Press: Its Influence on American Foreign Policy.* New York: Harper & Row, 1967.

Richardson, Elmo. *The Presidency of Dwight D. Eisenhower.* Lawrence, Kan.: The Regents Press of Kansas, 1979.

Roberts, Chalmers M. *First Rough Draft: A Journalist's Journal of Our Times.* New York: Praeger Publishers, 1973.

Rostow, W. W. *Open Skies: Eisenhower's Proposal of July 21, 1955.* Austin, Tex.: University of Texas Press, 1982.

Salisbury, Harrison E. *A Journey for Our Times: A Memoir.* New York: Harper & Row, 1983.

Schlesinger, Arthur M., Jr. *Robert Kennedy and His Times.* Boston: Houghton Mifflin Company, 1978: Schlesinger (1).

———. *A Thousand Days: John F. Kennedy in the White House.* Boston: Houghton Mifflin Company, 1965: Schlesinger (2).

Seaborg, Glenn T. *Kennedy, Khrushchev, and the Test Ban.* Berkeley, Calif.: University of California Press, 1981.

Shevchenko, Arkady N. *Breaking with Moscow.* New York: Alfred A. Knopf, 1985.

Slater, Ellis D. *The Ike I Knew.* Privately published, 1980.

Smith, Gerard. *Doubletalk: The Story of the First Strategic Arms Limitation Talks.* Garden City, N.Y.: Doubleday & Company, 1980: Gerard Smith.

Smith, Merriman. *A President's Odyssey.* New York: Harper & Brothers, 1961: Merriman Smith.

Sorensen, Theodore C. *Kennedy.* New York: Harper & Row, 1965.

Sulzberger, C. L. *The Last of the Giants.* New York: The Macmillan Company, 1970: Sulzberger (1).

———. *A Long Row of Candles: Memoirs and Diaries, 1934–1954.* New York: The Macmillan Company, 1969: Sulzberger (2).

Tatu, Michel. *Power in the Kremlin: From Khrushchev's Decline to Collective Leadership.* Translated from the French by Helen Katel. New York: The Viking Press, 1969.

Taylor, Michael J. H.; and Taylor, John W. R. *Missiles of the World.* New York: Charles Scribner's Sons, 1976.

TerHorst, Jerald, and Albertazzie, Ralph. *The Flying White House: The Story of Air Force One.* New York: Newsweek Condensed Books edition, 1980.

Terrill, Ross. *Mao: A Biography.* New York: Harper & Row, 1980.

The Trial of the U-2: Exclusive Authorized Account of the Court Proceedings of the Case of Francis Gary Powers, Heard Before the Military Division of the Supreme Court of the U.S.S.R., Moscow, August 17–19, 1960, with introductory comment by Harold J. Berman. Chicago: Translation World Publishers, 1960: *Trial.*

Ulam, Adam B. *Expansion and Coexistence: Soviet Foreign Policy, 1917–73.* New York: Praeger Publishers, 1974: Ulam (1).

———. *The Rivals: America and Russia Since World War II.* New York: The Viking Press, 1971: Ulam (2).

United States Congress. Senate. Committee on Commerce. *The Joint Appearances of Senator John F. Kennedy and Vice President Richard M. Nixon and Other 1960 Campaign Presentations.* Washington, D.C.: U.S. Government Printing Office, 1961: *Joint Appearances.*

United States Congress. Senate. Committee on Foreign Relations. *Events Incident to the Summit Conference: Hearings Before the Committee on Foreign Relations: May 27, 31, June 1, 2, 1960.* Eighty-sixth Congress, Second Session [uncensored portions of hearings]. Washington, D.C.: U.S. Government Printing Office, 1960: S ᶠRC.

United States Congress. Senate. *Executive Sessions of the Senate Foreign Relations Committee (Historical Series), Volume XII.* Eighty-sixth Congress, Second Session [censored portions of hearings, declassified November 1982]. Washington, D.C.: U.S. Government Printing Office, 1982: DFR.

Walters, Vernon A. *Silent Missions.* Garden City, N.Y.: Doubleday & Company, 1978.

Werth, Alexander. *The Khrushchev Phase: The Soviet Union Enters the "Decisive" Sixties.* London: R. Hale, 1961.

West, J. B., with Mary Lynn Kotz. *Upstairs at the White House: My Life with the First Ladies.* New York: Warner reprint, 1974.

White, Ralph K. *Fearful Warriors: A Psychological Profile of U.S.–Soviet Relations.* New York: The Free Press, 1984: Ralph White.

White, Theodore H. *The Making of the President: 1960.* New York: Atheneum, 1961: Theodore White.

Whitney, Thomas P., ed. *Khrushchev Speaks: Selected Speeches, Articles and Press Conferences, 1949–1961.* Ann Arbor, Mich.: University of Michigan Press, 1963.

Wise, David, and Ross, Thomas B. *The Invisible Government: The CIA and U.S. Intelligence.* New York: Random House, 1964: Wise and Ross (1).

———. *The U-2 Affair.* New York: Random House, 1962: Wise and Ross (2).

Wolfe, Tom. *The Right Stuff.* New York: Farrar, Straus & Giroux, 1979.

Wyden, Peter. *Bay of Pigs: The Untold Story.* New York: Simon and Schuster, 1979.

Notes

The following abbreviations appear in Notes:

CAHP	Christian A. Herter Papers
CIA/FOI	Central Intelligence Agency Declassified Documents
COHP	Columbia University Oral History Project
CR	*Congressional Record*
DDEL	Dwight D. Eisenhower Library
DDEP	Dwight D. Eisenhower Presidential Papers
DOHC	John Foster Dulles Oral History Collection
FBI/FOI	Federal Bureau of Investigation Declassified Documents
HSTL	Harry S. Truman Library
JFDP	John Foster Dulles Papers
JFKL	John F. Kennedy Library
Memcon	Memorandum of Conversation
Memcon Pres	Memorandum of Conversation with the President
NA	National Archives, Washington, D.C.
NYHT	*New York Herald Tribune*
NYT	*New York Times*
SP	*The Current Digest of the Soviet Press*
Tel Call	Notes on Telephone Call
WP	*Washington Post*

Epigraph

Khrushchev quotation is from NSK II, pp. 472, 511. Slightly different versions of Eisenhower quotation appear in Merriman Smith, pp. 256–66, and Merriman Smith oral history, COHP, based on contemporaneous notes of a conversation with the President in the summer of 1960.

Preface

Adam Ulam on "irrational premises" is in Ulam (2), p. 382.

Prologue: April 30, 1960

Sources on Eisenhower's routine include Goodpaster interview; conversation with Mrs. Dolores Moaney; *Saturday Evening Post,* January 30, 1954; *Cosmopolitan,* July 1956; Jim Bishop, *A Bishop's Confession* (Little, Brown, 1981), pp. 284–85; Preston Bruce, *From the Door of the White House* (Lothrop, Lee & Shepard, 1984), pp. 18–69; and Gray, pp. 141–42. Eisenhower's weight and diet are described in *Today's Health,* April 1960. Henry Kissinger describes Eisenhower's eyes in Kissinger, p. 43. Eisenhower "just can't be bothered": *Time,* May 23, 1960. On Eisenhower's aversion to Presidential office seekers, see Sulzberger (1), p. 578.

Eisenhower's contemplation of a Nixon-Rockefeller accord is in Ewald, pp. 236–38. John Eisenhower on a third term: John Eisenhower interview and Neal, p. 412. Moaney and boxer shorts: West, p. 142. Eisenhower's daily activities referred to throughout the current volume are noted in President's Appointments Schedule, DDEL. John Eisenhower on his father's desk: interview. Oval Office description is based on photographs in DDEL and *National Geographic,* January 1961. Sources on Goodpaster include NYHT, July 21, 1958; his oral histories in COHP and DDEL and interviews; Ewald, pp. 91–92; Killian, pp. 50–51; Eugene Lyons oral history, DDEL. "I would ask for nothing more": Adams, p. 53. On Eisenhower's national security organization and Goodpaster's role therein, see I. M. Destler, Leslie H. Gelb and Anthony Lake, *Our Own Worst Enemy* (Simon and Schuster, 1984), pp. 171–81. Andrew Goodpaster described his intelligence briefing in interview and confirmed that only two other key staff members knew of the U-2 flights, as did John Eisenhower. On Soviet surveillance of the *George Washington,* see *Waging,* p. 571.

U-2 plane and program generally are covered in Chapters Four, Five and Six of the current book. Allen Dulles on "every blade of grass": conversation with Ernest Cuneo, president of the North American Newspaper Alliance. By this, he presumably meant the capability of seeing "every blade of grass," for the U-2 never achieved comprehensive coverage of Soviet territory. (Bissell interview, DFR, p. 308.) Bissell on "ninety percent of hard intelligence" is in Epstein, p. 119. Sources for scene as Eisenhower considered U-2 missions include John Eisenhower, Goodpaster and Brugioni interviews. More on U-2 and Missile Gap is in Chapter Six. Eisenhower's opinion of Alsop is in Kistiakowsky, pp. 250–52. Kelly Johnson described Soviet air defense action against U-2 in interview. On more powerful Soviet air defense and Eisenhower's increasing reluctance to sanction flights, see Chapter Six. On possible U-2 sabotage, see Chapter Fourteen.

Eisenhower's ambition is noted, with varying language, in John Eisenhower interview, *Waging,* p. 653; Pinkley, p. 373. One example of Eisenhower's use of the word "détente" is his undated letter to Macmillan and de Gaulle, May 1960, DDEP. Eisenhower on "haven't made a chip": *Waging,* p. 432. Khrushchev's visit to the United States is recounted in Chapter Eight of the current book. The period from Camp David to the Paris Summit is in Chapter Nine. Eisenhower to Macmillan on test ban, March 18, 1960, is in DDEP. Eisenhower to de Gaulle on "splendid exit" is in de Gaulle, pp. 243–44. Eisenhower on CIA–Joint Chiefs assurance on U-2: *Waging,* p. 546. Pilots' instructions on destruct device: FGP, pp. 34–35. Also see Chapter One of the current book. John Eisenhower on "complete given": interview. Goodpaster on "hard to say": interview. John Foster Dulles on probable Russian reaction to a U-2 downing is in *Waging,* p. 546. Eisenhower's conflicting view is noted in *Waging,* p. 546, and Goodpaster interview.

Protests and trailing off are in Bissell interview, Merriman Smith oral history. For contrasting American and Soviet perceptions of U-2 flights, see Chapters Six and Fourteen of the current volume. Eisenhower's approval of the April 9 and May 1 flights is noted in Chapters Nine and Fourteen. Eisenhower on "We don't want to have that thing flying up there" and attitude to May 1 flight is in Mosley, p. 454, and Goodpaster interview. Goodpaster's memo, April 25, 1960, is in DDEP. Eisenhower on wife's aversion to flying is in West, p. 165. His greeting to David is noted in WP, May 1, 1960. John Eisenhower's assessment of films for Khrushchev, May 10, 1960, is in DDEP. Eisenhower's filmgoing habits are noted in *Collier's,* June 20, 1953; West, pp. 156–57; and Donovan, p. 203.

1: *"I've Had It Now!"*

Powers rising in Peshawar is in FGP, p. 76. Departure from Adana is in FGP, pp. 74–75; Barbara Powers, pp. 66–67; and de Gramont, p. 255. Khyber Pass description is based on Sulzberger (2), pp. 534–38. Powers's days in Peshawar and preflight procedure: FGP, pp. 75–78. His nervousness about Number 360 and Soviet anti-aircraft fire: FGP, pp. 69, 72, 76. Number 360 has been reported to have had "a propensity for compressor section stalls and associated powerplant flameouts at altitude." This appears in Miller (p. 30), a mainly technical history of the U-2 plane based on extensive interviews with people involved with the plane's development who were all "given editing privileges" (p. 5). The Miller study was cited to the current author by Richard Bissell as a generally reliable account. CIA's development of shellfish toxin is noted in Thomas Powers, p. 328. Bissell on pilot instructions on suicide is in interview and his oral histories, COHP and DDEL. Dulles on nobility is in Sulzberger (1), p. 699. Powers's survival equipment is described in FGP, pp. 45–46. Slim Pickens's speech is from *Dr. Strangelove: or How I Learned to Stop Worrying and Love the Bomb,* directed by Stanley Kubrick, 1964.

Bissell on "one chance in a million": Ambrose (3), pp. 279–80, and Bissell interview. West German U-2 accident is noted in de Gramont, p. 250, and FGP, pp. 49–50. Pilot instructions on destruct device are noted in DFR, 287–88, 339, and CIA

Board of Inquiry Report to John McCone, February 27, 1962, in JFKL. Destruct device is described in FGP, pp. 34–35; DFR, pp. 287–88, 310–11; and Wise and Ross (1), pp. 123–24. Pilots' nervousness and suspicions about destruct device are in FGP, p. 52, and Wise and Ross (1), pp. 123–24. Pilot on "if my plane goes down": Williams interview. Pilots carrying identification despite orders is noted in Williams interview. Contents of Powers wallet are noted in FGP, p. 95, and photo section in *Trial.* Erotic literature is noted by the Soviet military journal *Red Star,* quoted in cable from Edward Freers to Christian Herter, May 10, 1960, in DDEP.

Powers on being a pilot, not a spy, is from *Counterpoint* (Villon Films, 1975), copy furnished author courtesy Peter Davis. Powers usually addressed as Frank is in Snider and Sue Powers interviews. His height and weight are on a military identification card reproduced in photo section in *Trial.* Description of Powers's voice is based on tapes of his appearances on *The Dick Cavett Show,* May 15, 1970, and before the North American Rockwell Management Club, May 17, 1971, courtesy of Sammy Snider and Sue Powers. Fliers knowing Bissell as "Mr. B." is from Snider interview. Sue Powers described her husband's political leanings. Powers on missing becoming a commercial pilot is in FGP, pp. 19–20. His envy of the astronauts is in Sue Powers interview and Ovid Demaris, "Going to See Gary," in *Esquire,* May 1966. Mrs. Sammy Snider called Powers "a dear, sweet man." Allen Dulles quoted the view of Powers as "outstanding among the pilots" in DFR, p. 289. The Air Force study is quoted in *U.S. News & World Report,* August 15, 1960.

Sources on Powers's early life include FGP, pp. 13–19; Wise and Ross (2), pp. 13–16, 20–21, 24–25; Sue Powers interview; Francis Gary Powers File, FBI/FOI. Powers on going to Korea: *Counterpoint.* Powers on "satisfaction of total responsibility": FGP, p. 18. His introduction to Barbara is in Barbara Powers, p. 14. Their courtship and wedding are in FGP, p. 19, and Barbara Powers, pp. 14–18. Barbara Powers on wedding night is in Barbara Powers, p. 18. Powers on not having proved himself is in FGP, p. 20. His recruitment by CIA is in FGP, pp. 3–8; Barbara Powers, pp. 22–23; and Snider interview. Powers on pride in country for developing U-2 is in *Counterpoint.*

Powers on "thrilling" early flights of U-2 is in *Counterpoint.* Barbara's arrival in Europe is in FGP, pp. 58–59, and Barbara Powers, pp. 26–28. Her love letter and their confrontation in Tripoli are noted in Barbara Powers, pp. 30–39, and FGP, pp. 273–75. Barbara on her husband's occupation is in Barbara Powers, p. 46. CIA invitation for families to come to Turkey is in FGP, pp. 63–64. Barbara's arrival and discovery of her husband's actual occupation is in Barbara Powers, pp. 46–61. Their life in Adana is described in FGP, pp. 64–65, 74, and Wise and Ross (2), p. 26. Barbara's broken leg and Powers's worries over her drinking are in FGP, p. 74, and Barbara Powers, pp. 65–66.

U-2 pilots' fear of overturning is in FGP, pp. 31–32. Sources on Powers's takeoff and entry into Soviet airspace include FGP, pp. 78–80, and Wise and Ross (2), pp. 9–11, 16. Powers on "no abrupt change" is in FGP, p. 80. May Day preparations are noted in NYT, May 1, 1960. Khrushchev's order to reduce military trappings is noted in NYT, May 1, 1960. *Pravda*'s list of May Day slogans is in SP, XII, 15, p. 15. Khrushchev's notification of the U-2 flight is in NSK II, p. 504.

"Every cell": William Bridgeman, *The Lonely Sky* (Bantam reprint, 1983), p.

270. Powers's flight through southern Russia is in FGP, pp. 80–81. Autopilot trouble is noted in FGP, p. 81. Nixon's shaking of Sverdlovsk policeman is in Nixon (2), pp. 276–77. Pat Nixon and Milton Eisenhower visit to Soviet family is in Milton Eisenhower, pp. 332–33. Sverdlovsk's defense by SA-2 Guidelines is noted in Prados, p. 97. Powers's arrival over Sverdlovsk is in FGP, pp. 81–82. Soviet alarms set off is noted in Bissell, Amory, Dillon interviews. *Pravda* on Soviet air defense unit's reaction is in SP, XII, 18, pp. 27–28. After his return to the United States, Powers gave two major public accounts of his downing—in sworn testimony before the Senate Armed Services Committee, March 6, 1962, and in memoirs, *Operation Overflight.* The account in Chapter One of the current book is based on those elements of both that have gone generally undisputed although, as the reader will note, much of the passage is explicitly qualified as being based on Powers's account. For the aspects of Powers's downing that remain disputed, see Chapter Fourteen. Striking of Powers's plane is in FGP, pp. 82–83. *Webster's New Twentieth Century Dictionary* (Simon and Schuster, 1983) notes the origin of the cry "Mayday!" Powers's escape from U-2 is in FGP, pp. 82–84. Pilots' fear of ejection seat is in FGP, p. 62, and Wolfe, p. 17. Powers's fall to earth is in FGP, pp. 87–89. Air defense unit's subsequent reaction is in *Pravda,* SP, XII, 18, pp. 27–28. Powers's capture is in FGP, pp. 89–93. Powers on being "completely unprepared" is in FGP, p. 91. Allen Dulles on pilot instructions is in DFR, p. 289. Powers described his exchange with his intelligence officer in FGP, pp. 70–71.

Description of Red Square May Day parade is based on newsreel footage viewed in NA; NYT, May 2, 1960; and NBC's *The U-2 Affair,* broadcast November 29, 1960, script provided the author by courtesy of Walter Pforzheimer, scholar of intelligence and Molière and former legislative counsel to the CIA. Khrushchev described the scene in NSK II, p. 505. Ehrenburg on May Day is in *Pravda,* SP, XII, 18, p. 28. Biryuzov's delivery of the news of Powers's downing is in NSK II, pp. 505–6. "As far as we were concerned": NSK II, p. 507. Powers's interrogation in Sverdlovsk is in FGP, pp. 93–97.

Allen Dulles's acceptance of the Golden Rule Award is in NYT, May 2, 1960. Robert Amory described the U-2 being tracked into the Soviet Union in interview. Word flashed from Bodö is in DFR, p. 287, and Wise and Ross (2), p. 29. Hugh Cumming's notification is in Wise and Ross (2), pp. 28–30. Gates's notification is in SFRC, p. 131. Dryden's notification is in DFR, p. 363, and Wise and Ross (2), pp. 33–34. Dryden's agreement to allow NASA to act as U-2 cover is described in Chapter Four of the current book. On history of Lubyanka, see Barron, pp. 95–96, and de Gramont, pp. 42–43. Powers's questioning and incarceration at Lubyanka is in FGP, pp. 98–104.

Allen Dulles's substitution for Bissell in sending go-ahead for U-2 mission is in Bissell interview, as is Bissell's notification of and reaction to the failure of the mission. U-2 project office as "Bissell Center" is in Helms interview. Bissell on "turmoil" and "quite prepared to say" is in interview. Description of May 1 meeting is based on Bissell interview and Wise and Ross (2), pp. 34–37. Wise and Ross write that Cumming acted after obtaining instruction from Dillion (pp. 30–32). Dillon in 1984 insisted that he did not learn about the U-2 problem until May 5 at High Point (Dillon interview). But an internal State Department account prepared soon after the event says that Cumming informed Dillon after the May 1 meeting of the group's decision and that Dillon concurred ("Chronological Account of Handling of U-2 incident," undated, DDEP).

Description of Eisenhower's activities on May 1 is based on NYT and WP, May 2, 1960, and John Eisenhower interview. Ann Whitman on previous rain-out is in her Diary of February 7, 1953. Goodpaster's notification and call to Eisenhower: Goodpaster interview and *Waging*, p. 543. In the latter, Eisenhower quotes Goodpaster as follows: "One of our reconnaissance planes on a scheduled flight *from its base in Adana, Turkey,* is overdue and possibly lost" (emphasis added). Goodpaster in 1984 suggested that the six words in question were probably an error of memory (Goodpaster interview). Eisenhower on "if one of these planes is shot down": Wise and Ross (2), p. 49.

2: *Eisenhower's Dilemma*

Goodpaster's West Wing office was described to the author by L. Arthur Minnich, who served as one of Goodpaster's assistants during the White House years. Sources on Goodpaster–John Eisenhower working relationship include interviews with both and JSDE, pp. 204–7. John Eisenhower on Goodpaster's reluctance to grant him independent authority: JSDE, p. 205. On New Year's 1959: John Eisenhower interview. John informed by father about atomic bomb and U-2: JSDE, p. 97, and interview. On the briefing by Bissell and Dulles's assurances of a dead pilot: John Eisenhower interview. Other sources on his May 2 meeting with Goodpaster include Goodpaster interview; JSDE, p. 270; Neal, p. 409. John's intention to commit suicide if captured in Korea is in JSDE, pp. 133–34. Also see Appendix of this book.

Eisenhower's dislike of tentative entrances is noted in Gray, p. 197. Goodpaster's face as an "etching of bad news" and Goodpaster's announcement about the U-2 are in *Waging*, p. 543. Eisenhower writes that Goodpaster added, "The pilot reported an engine flameout at a position about thirteen hundred miles inside Russia and has not been heard from since." Goodpaster in 1984 suggested that this recollection, like that of their talk on May 1, was probably an error of memory. But Bissell recalled that the U-2 may have been equipped with a device allowing the pilot to send a very brief "squirt" transmission to a friendly listening post in an emergency: the four or five messages might include "I am under attack," or "I am going down." As Bissell said, if the device was on the U-2, "that would increase the likelihood that Powers sent a message" (Bissell interview). Eisenhower on "eyes open": *Waging*, p. 546. "What the hell": Lyon, p. 809. Goodpaster's promise to "stay in touch" with CIA and Eisenhower's approval of the cover story: Goodpaster interview and memo, May 2, 1960, in DDEP.

Amory listening to CBS Radio, reading message on U-2 and hearing Bissell's indignation is in Amory interview. Bissell on live pilot being "impossible" is in Kirkpatrick, p. 207. Barbara Powers's notification of husband's disappearance and three-day party in Adana are in Wise and Ross (2), pp. 60–61; FGP, p. 297. Powers's May 2 activities in Moscow: FGP, pp. 105–8. Eisenhower's visit to Fort Benning: NYT and WP, May 4, 1960, and Ann Whitman Diary, May 3, 1960. May 3 cover story is reproduced in *Department of State Bulletin,* May 23, 1960. Oliver Powers's notification is in Wise and Ross (2), p. 67. WP on missing plane is dated May 4, 1960. Also see DFR, pp. 363–64. Eisenhower's May 4 activities are in Ann Whitman Diary of that date. Eisenhower's suspicion that Foster Dulles's prophecy might be correct is in *Waging*, p. 547. Vershinin announcement and test ban progress are noted in Tatu, pp. 54–56; NYT, May 5, 1960; Kistiakowsky, pp. 311–12; Seaborg, pp. 23–24; and *Waging*, p. 481. Khrushchev's meeting with Central Committee and building as "Little Kremlin" are noted in Tatu, pp. 41, 84–100; *Newsweek*, May 16, 1960. Khrushchev on his plan is in NSK II, p. 507. On "stupendous" announcement: *Los Angeles Times*, May 5, 1960.

Khrushchev's Moscow flat is described in *Time*, October 5, 1959, and WP, May 1, 1960. Sources for Khrushchev's May 5 speech include NYT, WP, *Washington Star*, May 6, 1960; *Pravda* in SP, IX, 11, pp. 4–19; Wise and Ross (2), pp. 72–75; newsreels in NA; and an unpublished article by Priscilla Johnson McMillan, courtesy of Mrs. McMillan. Thompson on May Day is in Jane Thompson interview. Sources on Thompson and relationship with Khrushchev include NYHT, February 26, 1958; Salisbury, pp. 489–90; Jane Thompson, Toumanoff interviews. Mikoyan's comment is in Jane Thompson interview. Thompson's puzzlement at prominent seat is in Wise and Ross (2), p. 73, Jane Thompson and Toumanoff interviews. Thompson's immediate reaction to the speech is in Jane Thompson interview. Sources on mass departure for High Point include Ann Whitman Diary, May 5, 1960; Goodpaster, Dillon, Harr, Scoville interviews; Kistiakowsky, p. 317; Wise and Ross (2), p. 76. Nixon's excuse is in Tel Call, May 4, 1960, DDEP.

UPI bulletin and Pentagon and Cumming reactions are in Wise and Ross (2), pp. 76–78. Snider's reaction is in Snider interview. Sources for High Point meetings include John S. Patterson oral history, COHP; Goodpaster, Dillon, Harr, Scoville interviews; Kistiakowsky, p. 317; *Waging*, pp. 548–49; Wise and Ross (2), pp. 77–80; Prados, pp. 98–99; DFR, pp. 394, 399–400. On Hagerty's anger: Dillon interview; Wise and Ross (2), p. 80; and Ann Whitman Diary, May 5, 1960. On Hagerty's background and character, see James C. Hagerty Diary, excerpts edited and published by Robert H. Ferrell as *The Diary of James C. Hagerty* (Indiana, 1983); Deakin, pp. 144–62; Grossman and Kumar; Pierpoint, pp. 122–28; Scherer, Dillon, Harr interviews; James Hagerty and Robert Donovan oral histories, COHP. Art Buchwald's parody is quoted in Deakin, p. 126. Hagerty's reaction is noted in the *Washingtonian*, January 1985. McCann on Hagerty is in his oral history, COHP. "Better you than me": R. Gordon Hoxie, *The White House* (Center for the Study of the Presidency, 1971), p. 4.

Eisenhower-Hagerty-Goodpaster May 5 meeting is noted in Goodpaster interview; Goodpaster memo, May 5, 1960, DDEP; and *Waging*, p. 549. John Eisenhower on myth about his father is in his oral history, DDEL. Sources on White House press in 1960 include Scherer interview; Donovan oral history, COHP; Pierpoint, pp. 27–32; Deakin, pp. 206–7; and conversation with Robert Pierpoint. Hagerty's announcement, May 5, 1960, is in DDEP. Eisenhower later told Goodpaster that when covert projects were "blown" in future, Hagerty "should be cut in at once and given information about them" before "people in government all over town" started talking (Memcon Pres, May 23, 1960, DDEP). Scherer's trip to NASA and NASA bafflement are in Scherer interview, DFR, p. 381, and Wise and Ross (2), pp. 80–81.

Goodpaster's explanation is in interview. Dillon and Allen Dulles drafting of statement is in Goodpaster memo, May 5, 1960, DDEP; Dillon, Goodpaster interviews. White's anger is in Dillon interview. State Department announcement and question-and-answer session is in transcript, May 5, 1960, DDEP.

Bissell's providing NASA with cover material is in Bissell interview and DFR, p. 364. Goodpaster's call to Glennan is in Goodpaster interview and memo, May 5, 1960, DDEP. Bonney's drafting of statement and announcement is in Wise and Ross (2), pp. 83–84, and NYT, May 6, 1960. Bonney in 1959 on astronauts: Wolfe, p. 91. Dillon's reaction to NASA statement is in Dillon interview, SFRC, pp. 75, 80–81. Priscilla Johnson McMillan's ordeal is described in her unpublished article. Jokes and information about Adzhubei are in Penkovskiy, p. 224, and Crankshaw, pp. 260–62.

Thompson's overhearing of Malik and cable to Washington: Thompson to Dillon, May 5, 1960, in DDEP. I have taken the liberty of restoring articles to the telegraphic language in cables in those cases where this can be done without any possibility of altering the sender's meaning. Thompson's inability to telephone Washington and interpretation of Malik's indiscretion are in Jane Thompson interview. Shevchenko on Malik's indiscretion is in Shevchenko, p. 94. Thompson on Khrushchev's moderation is in cable to Dillon, May 5, 1960, DDEP. John Eisenhower's conversation with his father is in JSDE, p. 270, and interview. U.S. note to Moscow of May 6, 1960, is in DDEP. May 6 Supreme Soviet debate is noted in NYT and WP, May 7, 1960, and Tatu, pp. 57–58. Thompson's interpretation is in cable to Herter, May 6, 1960, DDEP.

Congressional reactions to Khrushchev's speech are in CR and NYT, May 6, 1960. Dulles briefing of senior Congressional leaders: Bissell, Houston, Fulbright interviews; DFR, pp. 323, 511; Reston, p. 20; and Roberts, p. 171. Reston is in NYT, May 6, 1960. *Washington Post* editorial is in WP, May 6, 1960. On American press restraint on reporting U-2, see Chapter Nine of this book. Kistiakowsky on talk with Bissell is in Kistiakowsky, p. 318. Dillon on meeting with Eisenhower is in SFRC, p. 49, and Dillon interview. Eisenhower's refusal to confide in Congressional leaders is in Goodpaster, Dillon interviews; Kistiakowsky, pp. 318–19; and SFRC, p. 49. Eisenhower at trade show is in NYT, May 7, 1960; Scherer interview. Reporters run to telephones and Hagerty's "no comment": NBC, *The U-2 Affair,* and Wise and Ross (2), p. 94. Eisenhower's golf is noted in NYT, May 7, 1960. White's noon briefing transcript, May 6, 1960, is in DDEP.

Barbara Powers's departure for America is in Barbara Powers, p. 67. Powers's life in Lubyanka is in FGP, p. 110. Thompson's absence from Khrushchev's May 7 Supreme Soviet speech is noted in Toumanoff interview. Sources for Khrushchev's speech include NYT, WP, May 8, 1960; newsreels, in NA; Wise and Ross (2), pp. 95–99; K. P. S. Menon, *The Flying Troika* (Oxford, 1963), pp. 263–64; and McMillan article. AP bulletin appeared in *Los Angeles Times,* May 7, 1960, as did the headline. *Time*'s junking of cover story is noted in *Time,* May 16, 1960. Oliver Powers's denial that son is a spy is in NYT, *Los Angeles Times,* May 8, 1960. De Gaulle on "bad comedy" is in de Gaulle, p. 247. Macmillan's notification is in Macmillan (3), pp. 195–97. British-American collaboration on U-2 is noted in Bissell and de Zulueta interviews. Macmillan's briefing by Dean is in de Zulueta interview. Thompson's cable to Herter, May 7, 1960, is in DDEP.

John Eisenhower's return is based on interview. Sources on John Eisenhower include his oral history, DDEL, and JSDE, from which his observations on his background quoted in this section are taken. His father on being "so tied up in him" is in Dwight D. Eisenhower, *Letters to Mamie* (Doubleday, 1978), p. 36. John on resisting the White House is in JSDE, p. 169. President on Goodpaster's summer departure: Neal, p. 399. Ann Whitman on John's relationship with father is in her Diary, September 16, 1959. Goodpaster informing John of live pilot is in Goodpaster, John Eisenhower interviews, and JSDE, p. 270. John on Dulles's assurances is in interview. John's notification of his father is in John Eisenhower interview; *Waging,* p. 549.

3: *The Espionage Assignment*

Sources on Eisenhower's 1945 trip to Russia include Lyon, pp. 355–57; Dwight D. Eisenhower, *Crusade in Europe* (Doubleday, 1948), pp. 459–69; Ambrose (1), p. 429. Stalin on Eisenhower is in Ambrose (1), p. 430. John on Zhukov's proposition is in JSDE, p. 104. "I see nothing": Lyon, p. 356. Khrushchev notes his first meeting with Eisenhower in NSK I, pp. 220–22. On Eisenhower's pre-Presidential attitudes toward the Soviet Union, see Ambrose (1), pp. 399–404, 426–29, 447–52, 468–69; Gaddis (2), pp. 127–29; and Milton Eisenhower oral history, DDEL. "Russia has not the slightest": Lyon, 365. Churchill's final volume is *Triumph and Tragedy* (Houghton Mifflin, 1953).

Eisenhower on "bodies rotting on the ground" and "veneer of callousness" is in Ambrose (1), pp. 236, 293. On "feeling of depression": *Mandate,* p. 312. For the ideological context of Eisenhower's resistance to unlimited military spending, see Robert Griffith, "Dwight D. Eisenhower and the Corporate Commonwealth," *American Historical Review,* February 1982. "I don't believe" and "smouldering doubts": Ambrose (1), pp. 449, 468. "My God" and "Russia is definitely": Ambrose (1), p. 453, and Eisenhower Diary, September 16, 1947. Eisenhower and the Soviet issue in the 1952 campaign is discussed in Divine (2), pp. 12–19, and Ambrose (1), pp. 512–13, 547–48. John Wayne and red flag are noted in Parmet, p. 96.

On Eisenhower's response to Stalin's demise, see Donovan, pp. 40–42; Adams, pp. 95–96; and *Mandate,* pp. 143–44. On mourning and funeral in Moscow, see Salisbury, pp. 437–49; *Time* and *Newsweek,* March 16, 1953. Khrushchev's memory of Stalin's words is in NSK I, p. 392. *New York Times* on Stalin's death is dated March 6, 1953. Washington's reaction is in Divine (2), pp. 105–7; Ulam (2), p. 198; and Hughes, pp. 100–102. CIA's estimate on Stalin's death, March 10, 1953, is in DDEP. On Malenkov surprise and Eisenhower and Dulles reactions, see Divine (2), p. 107; Hughes, pp. 100–112; Ambrose (2), pp. 91–93. For Eisenhower government's consideration of new opportunities, see W. W. Rostow, *Europe After Stalin* (Texas, 1982). Background and text of Eisenhower's Cross of Iron speech are in Hughes, pp. 100–112; Ambrose (2), pp. 91–96; Herken, p. 104; NYT, April 17, 1953. Among contributors to the speech were Emmet John Hughes and Paul Nitze. Eisenhower's worry about pre-emptive surprise attack is noted in Ambrose (2), pp. 122–24. "As of now" is in Eisenhower Diary, October 10, 1953. Genesis and outcome of Atoms for Peace are in Ambrose (2), pp. 133–35, 147–51, 153; and Divine (2), pp. 112–14.

Sources on Trevor Gardner include Flint Du Pre, *U.S. Air Force Biographical Dictionary* (Franklin Watts, 1965), pp. 81–82; Ford, Bissell, Killian interviews.

Gardner to DuBridge is in Ford interview. Scientists' meeting with Eisenhower is noted in Ford and Killian interviews; Killian, pp. 67–69. On Killian: *Business Week,* November 16, 1957; NYT, November 8, 1957; Divine (1), p. 171; Killian and Ford interviews. Killian's worry about Oppenheimer problem is in Killian, pp. 223–24, and Killian interview. Arrangements and details of Killian Commission are noted in its report, "Meeting the Threat of Surprise Attack," February 12, 1955, in DDEP. Other sources on Killian Commission include Killian, Land, Goodpaster, Ford, Bissell interviews; Kaplan, pp. 127–54; Herken, pp. 106–9. Besides overflights of the Soviet Union, the Commission ultimately recommended many other ideas including acceleration of the American ICBM program and building of an anti-missile missile. Sources on Edwin Land include *Time,* June 26, 1972, and March 17, 1953; *Business Week,* June 12, 1954, and May 4, 1974; *Fortune,* March 23, 1981; *Forbes,* June 1, 1975. Killian on Land is in Killian interview. On need to pierce Soviet secrecy, see Allen Dulles in DFR, pp. 280–81; Eisenhower in *Waging,* pp. 254–55; Ambrose (3), pp. 160–61. Land on listening to Doolittle is in Land interview.

On history of aerial reconnaissance, border flights, balloons, see Infield; Helman; Klass; Rostow, pp. 189–92; Kirkpatrick, p. 10; Prados, pp. 29–30; Bamford, pp. 181–83; and Herken, pp. 106–7. September 1949 flight is noted in Thomas Powers, p. 39. Twining conversation with Truman and comment on forty-seven airplanes: Twining oral history, COHP. In 1960, Truman denied having ordered such flights, saying, "Espionage is a dirty deal. I didn't want to be part of it" (NYT, June 7, 1960). This must be regarded in context of the fact that by 1960, Truman's memory was beginning to falter. See, for instance, Merle Miller, *Plain Speaking* (Putnam, 1973). Full documentation on the border flights and Truman's role is not yet available among declassified papers in HSTL, but see Omar Bradley to Louis Johnson, May 5, 1950, HSTL. 1951–53 air incidents are noted in NYT, November 9, 1954.

Stalin's anger is noted in Medvedev (2), p. 151. Of the immediate postwar years, Khrushchev said, "I would even say that the Americans were invincible at that time, and they flaunted this fact by sending their planes all over Europe. . . . They violated the air space of the Soviet Union itself, mostly along the Baltic coast and in the north near Murmansk" (NSK II, p. 403). Amory and Strong arrangement of British overflight and Strong visit with Kelly Johnson are in Amory interview. Sources on Johnson's proposal, its initial rejection and ultimate acceptance are Johnson, Ford, Bissell, Killian, Land, Houston, Amory interviews; Miller, pp. 10–13; Killian, pp. 81–82; Johnson, pp. 120–21; Johnson's "Log for Project X," 1954, Kelly Johnson Private Papers. The Bell project, branded the X-16, proceeded until abruptly terminated in October 1955, after the Air Force ceded principal responsibility for high-altitude reconnaissance of the Soviet Union to the CIA (Miller, p. 18).

Eisenhower's November 1954 activities are noted in Ann Whitman Diary of that month. Eisenhower on Mendès-France visit and stag dinners is in Ann Whitman Diary, November 17, 1954, February 28, 1955, March 16, 1954. Eisenhower notes his "shock" at Truman's campaigning in a letter to Thomas Dewey, October 8, 1954, in DDEP. "I really think": Memcon Pres, November 23, 1954, DDEP. Eisenhower to Edgar, January 27, 1954, is in DDEP. Description of B-29 crash is based on *Newsweek,* November 12, 1954, and NYT, November 8 and 9, 1954. Foster Dulles to Eisenhower is in Tel Call, November 10, 1954, JFDP. Eisenhower to Dulles on meeting with Congressmen is in Tel Call, November 17, 1954, JFDP.

Killian–Land meeting with Eisenhower is noted in Killian, Land, Goodpaster interviews, Killian, pp. 82–83. Eisenhower and wartime photoreconnaissance is in Lundahl interview. Amory on Air Force's eye: Amory oral history, JFKL. Johnson's meetings in Washington are noted in his "Log for Project X," November 1954, Johnson and Houston interviews. Ann Whitman on Allen Dulles meeting with Eisenhower is in her Diary, November 22, 1954. November 24 meeting with Eisenhower is noted in Goodpaster, Memcon Pres, November 24, 1954, DDEP; Goodpaster, Killian, Bissell interviews; *Waging*, p. 544. Eisenhower on Montgomery's self-invitation is in memo, October 30, 1954, JFDP. "You'll never get a President": Killian and Land interviews. Twining's misgivings are noted in his oral history, COHP.

Eisenhower on Knowland is in Eisenhower Diary, January 10, 1955. Knowland on breaking Soviet relations is in NYT, November 8, 1954. Dulles on Knowland "foolishness" is in Tel Call, November 10, 1954, JFDP. Eisenhower to Cabinet on recording conversations is in Ewald, p. 89. On Eisenhower taping, see *Time*, November 5, 1979. Eisenhower–Knowland transcript is in DDEP. Allen Dulles to Bissell: Bissell interview. Pentagon meeting is described in Bissell, Killian, Ford interviews.

4: *Building a Covert Operation*

Bissell on work lying ahead is in his oral history, COHP. Amory on Bissell is in his oral history, JFKL. Bissell's activity and reprimand of Cord Meyer: Wyden, pp. 12–13. Bissell as "man-eating shark": Wyden, p. 95. "There are many times": Bissell interview. Sources on Bissell's background include Wyden, pp. 14–19; Alsop, p. 216; Bissell oral history, COHP; Bissell interview; Thomas Powers, pp. 93–94. "A brilliant coterie": Wyden, p. 16. Amory on Bissell in World War Two is in Amory interview. Bissell's run-in with the French is in Wyden, p. 13. His lamentation of Eisenhower's accession is in Bissell interview. On Bissell and NSC-141, see Kaplan, pp. 137–38. Much of the paper focused on the need for "measures to improve greatly our own defense against air and sea attack." Some of these overlapped with the Killian Commission's findings two years later. Bissell's work on Eastern Europe and CIA work on resistance after the war are noted in Thomas Powers, pp. 39–47. Acheson on liberation is in Sulzberger (1), p. 98.

CIA's 1954 operation in Guatemala and Bissell's role therein are in Richard Immerman, *The CIA in Guatemala* (Texas, 1982); Stephen Schlesinger and Stephen Kinzer, *Bitter Fruit* (Doubleday, 1981); Blanche Wiesen Cook, *The Declassified Eisenhower* (Doubleday, 1981), pp. 218–88; Thomas Powers, pp. 85–89; Bissell oral histories, COHP and DDEL. Eisenhower–Allen Dulles exchange is in Thomas Powers, p. 87. Bissell on "our job" is in Schlesinger and Kinzer, p. 225. Bissell on covert action is in Wyden, p. 13. "I've heard that label": Bissell oral history, DDEL. Thomas Powers on "a lot of CIA people" is in Thomas Powers, p. 95. Bissell's impatience with human intelligence is in Helms interview; Thomas Powers, pp. 100–101.

Pentagon discussion of program's financing is in Bissell interview. Financing through Reserve Fund and "stealing" engines and spare parts are noted in Bissell, Houston interviews. Johnson on meeting with CIA is in "Log on Project X," December 14, 1954, Johnson Private Papers. Bissell-Johnson exchange is in Bissell, Johnson, Houston interviews. Agreement on about $22 million is in Johnson, p. 121.

Bissell on "moderately bloody affair" and initial project organization are in Bissell interview. Bissell on "private duchy" is in Bissell oral history, DDEL; Wyden, p. 11; and Bissell interview. Eisenhower's willingness to kill project, if necessary, is noted in *Waging,* p. 544.

Inspiration for naming Skunk Works is in Don Moser, "Time of the Angel: The U-2, Cuba and the CIA," *American Heritage,* October 1977. Sources on Kelly Johnson's background include Johnson; Johnson interview; *Current Biography,* 1968; *Science 85,* September 1985. "We went right to work": Johnson interview. "Talked to each man": "Log for Project X," November 29–December 3, 1954, Johnson Private Papers. Checks sent to Johnson mailbox is in Johnson, p. 123. Johnson's design solution is noted in *American Heritage,* October 1977; Bissell, Johnson interviews. Other aspects of U-2's development are noted in Miller, p. 19; *American Heritage,* October 1977; *Aviation Week,* May 23, 1960; Jules Bergman, "The Amazing Saga of the U-2" in *Reader's Digest,* October 1960; Wise and Ross (2), pp. 45–47; Infield, pp. 166–67; Thomas Powers, pp. 95–96; Bissell, Johnson, Houston, Killian, Land, Ford interviews. Figures on U-2 range and fuel requirements are in Miller, p. 91. Photographic capability is noted in *American Heritage,* October 1977; Lundahl interview. CIA and Air Force skeptics are noted in Corson, p. 375. Final cost of $19 million is in Thomas Powers, p. 327. U-2 Soviet biplane is noted in Woodford Heflin, ed., *The U.S. Air Force Dictionary* (Air University Press, 1956), p. 542.

Finding Nevada lake bed and building of base are noted in Miller, pp. 19–20; *American Heritage,* October 1977; Ambrose (3), p. 269; Johnson, pp. 122–24; and Bissell and Johnson interviews. Bissell on "if we had chosen to land" and "flat as a billiard table" is in Bissell interview. Killian on "almost a miracle" is in interview. Dulles to Eisenhower on Berlin Tunnel is in Goodpaster interview. On the events leading to Geneva, see Rostow, pp. 14–25; Ambrose (2), pp. 247–49; Ulam (2), pp. 209–32; Ulam (1), pp. 564–71; Hoopes, pp. 284–95; Divine (2), pp. 116–18; Gaddis (1), pp. 213–16; Dillon Anderson and Goodpaster oral histories in DDEL. Eisenhower's professed skepticism about summits: Eisenhower oral history in DDEL. June 22, 1955, plane incident: Ambrose (2), p. 249, and *Mandate,* p. 508.

Foster Dulles on Eisenhower and Geneva: C. D. Jackson Diary, July 11, 1955. John Eisenhower on Dulles view of relationship with President is in Ewald, p. 9. Dulles encounter in a foreign hotel was told the author by one of Eisenhower's ambassadors, who wishes to remain anonymous. Sources on Dulles's background include Ronald Pruessen, *John Foster Dulles: The Road to Power* (Free Press, 1982), and Hoopes, pp. 3–133. Milton Eisenhower on brother's attitude on selecting Dulles is in interview.

Smith on appointment is in Sidney W. Souers to Ludwell Lee Montague, July 19, 1971, Souers Papers, HSTL. Souers served as the first Director of Central Intelligence in 1946. Montague was writing Smith's biography for CIA's internal archives. On Eisenhower-Dulles relationship, see Richard Immerman, "Eisenhower and Dulles: Who Made the Decisions?" in *Political Psychology,* 1979; Ambrose (2), pp. 20–22; Kistiakowsky, p. xx; *Waging,* pp. 367–69; Dwight D. Eisenhower, John W. Hanes oral histories, DOHC; Robert Bowie oral history, COHP. Eisenhower to Macmillan on Dulles: Macmillan (2), p. 608. To son on Dulles: John Eisenhower interview. Goodpaster and Milton Eisenhower views are from interviews.

Sources on Nelson Rockefeller include Persico; Michael Collier and David Horowitz, *The Rockefellers* (Holt, 1976); and James Desmond, *Nelson Rockefeller* (Macmillan, 1964). Kissinger on Rockefeller is in Kissinger, p. 4. Rockefeller on being "less than fully restrained" is in oral history quoted in Rostow, p. 49. Dulles's worry about Quantico is in Adams, p. 91. Sources on origins of Open Skies include the study by Rostow, a Quantico participant, as well as Ambrose (2), pp. 257-59, 263-64; Prados, p. 46; Herken, pp. 109-10; Brugioni, Bissell, Goodpaster interviews. U-2 "ideally suited": Allen Dulles in DFR, p. 357. Truscott's visit with Brugioni and CIA involvement with Open Skies: Brugioni interview. Eisenhower-Dulles-Rockefeller conflict on Open Skies: Rockefeller oral history, quoted in Rostow, pp. 46, 49-50. Eisenhower's attitude on Open Skies: Goodpaster interview and oral histories, COHP and DDEL.

Flight to Geneva is in JSDE, pp. 173-74, and Lyon, p. 660. Eisenhower departure speech and Dulles's reaction is in NYT, July 15, 1955, and Ambrose (2), p. 261. Eisenhower arrival and speech in Geneva: NYT, July 16, 1955. Atmospherics in Geneva are described in *Time* and *Newsweek,* July 25, 1955. Drew Pearson's lament was related to the author by Ernest Cuneo. Soviet arrival in Geneva is in *Time* and *Newsweek,* July 25, 1955. Khrushchev on Geneva as "test" and embarrassment at small plane: NSK I, pp. 393-95. "B and K" is noted in Goodpaster interview. Gunther on "twin peanuts" is in *Inside Russia Today* (Harper, 1958), p. 109.

Sources for analysis and description of Geneva conference include Ambrose (2), pp. 261-68; Ulam (2), pp. 232-36; Ulam (1), pp. 566-70; Gaddis (1), pp. 213-16; Lyon, pp. 660-65; *Mandate,* pp. 510-30; Divine (2), pp. 116-19; Bohlen, pp. 382-89; Rostow, pp. 3-13, 50-57; JSDE, pp. 174-79; NSK I, pp. 392-400; Anthony Eden, *Full Circle* (Houghton Mifflin, 1960), pp. 327-46; Donovan, pp. 343-51; Macmillan (1), pp. 611-28; Cline, pp. 181-84; Walters, pp. 285-89; Dillon Anderson oral history, COHP; Goodpaster oral histories, COHP and DDEL; John Eisenhower interview. Khrushchev on Zhukov "family secret": Hagerty press briefing transcript, July 18, 1955, DDEP; Bohlen memo, July 18, 1955, DDEP. On dinner with Dulles: NSK II, p. 410. Eisenhower-Khrushchev exchange at dinner: Hagerty oral history, COHP, and JDSE, p. 176. On Zhukov's reduced stature: JSDE, pp. 175-76. July 20 meeting is recorded in Memcon Pres, July 20, 1955, DDEP. Rockefeller to John: JSDE, p. 177. Khrushchev meets Rockefeller: NSK I, p. 399.

Text of Eisenhower Open Skies statement, July 21, 1955, is in DDEP. JSDE, p. 178, Vernon Walters oral history, DDEL, and other sources differ slightly on timing of thunder. Zhukov-Eisenhower exchange and Khrushchev rejection of Open Skies: Bohlen Memcon, July 21, 1955, DDEP; Robert Bowie oral history, COHP; Goodpaster interview; *Mandate,* pp. 521-22. Accounts of Khrushchev's exact reply vary because of translation. In 1957, at Geneva, the Russians accepted "in principle" a restricted version of Open Skies: the Soviets would overfly Western Europe and the American Eastern seaboard in exchange for legal American flights over the westernmost part of Russia. But the talks broke off (Herken, p. 122). Eisenhower certainty on ruler of Russia: *Mandate,* p. 521.

Macmillan on Khrushchev is in Macmillan (1), p. 622. Pinay on Khrushchev is in *Newsweek,* August 1, 1955. Eisenhower on Khrushchev: *Mandate,* p. 518. Khrushchev on Eisenhower's "domination" by Dulles: NSK I, pp. 397-98, and NSK II, pp. 409, 423, 567. Eisenhower "sure" of Soviet rejection: oral history in DOHC. Goodpaster's view: oral history, DDEL, and interview. "Don't worry": Adams, p. 179. Eisenhower's last try at acceptance is in Rostow, p. 63. Richard Rovere on Eisenhower is in his *Affairs of State* (Farrar Straus, 1956), p. 290. Macmillan on "no war" is in Neff, p. 148. Eisenhower to congressmen is in Memcon Pres, July 25, 1955, notes in DDEP.

Eisenhower on flying U-2 if Open Skies fails: Goodpaster, Bissell, Brugioni interviews. Allen Dulles on "redoubling" efforts is in DFR, pp. 281, 357. Account of U-2 taxi test and first formal flight is based on Johnson, Bissell interviews; *American Heritage,* October 1977; Johnson, pp. 124–25. Miller, pp. 19–22, differs somewhat from Johnson's version. I have relied primarily on the latter. LeMay's eye on U-2 and "Don't let LeMay" are in Bissell, Brugioni, Killian interviews. Sources on LeMay include his memoirs, *Mission with LeMay* (Macmillan, 1965), *Time,* August 13, 1945; Kaplan, pp. 42–45. LeMay and Polaris noted in Brugioni interview. Air Force–CIA relationship is noted in Thomas Powers, pp. 37–39; DFR, p. 283; *American Heritage,* October 1977; Bissell, Brugioni, Killian, Houston, Ford interviews. Dulles-Bissell-LeMay conflict and Eisenhower's verdict are noted in Bissell and Goodpaster interviews. "Power of the Dulles brothers": Brugioni interview. Twining's indignation is in his oral history, COHP. "If I can't operate": Brugioni interview. Air Force–CIA armistice is noted in Bissell interview.

Events leading to Eisenhower's heart attack are noted in Lyon, pp. 667–71; Parmet, pp. 408–13; Adams, pp. 180–89; Donovan, pp. 362–86; Deakin, pp. 16–25; *Time* and *Newsweek,* October 3 and 10, 1955. "See what a wonderful brother": Ann Whitman Diary, September 29, 1955. Eisenhower to Nixon on pain is in Nixon (1), p. 166. Nixon's tour of CIA and Camp Peary is noted in Mosley, pp. 394–96. Andrew Goodpaster shed light on Nixon's general briefing on intelligence matters, Cord Meyer on Nixon's attitude toward and relationship with the CIA.

Snider on CIA recruitment is in interview. CIA initial briefings are noted in Snider interview and FGP, pp. 3–9, 21–24. Lovelace regimen is described in Wolfe, pp. 72–78; FGP, pp. 24–25; Barbara Powers, pp. 48–52; and Snider interview. U-2 pilots' terms of employment are noted in FGP, pp. 25–27, and Snider interview. Dulles on pilot selection is in DFR, p. 288. Johnson on "dirty trick" is in Johnson, p. 123. Bissell confirms that early flights set altitude records (interview). The known record of the time was set in August 1955 by a British Canberra pilot in England (Miller, p. 23). Unclassified accounts of the U-2's maximum altitude have been generally imprecise. Performance of the U-2s that flew over Russia was affected by air temperature, humidity and especially weight: as the plane consumed fuel through a mission, it grew lighter and hence rose higher (Johnson interview). Bissell has estimated that by mission's end, a U-2 was capable of reaching roughly 74,000 feet (interview). Miller puts the plane's ceiling at 78,855 feet, although noting one case in which a pilot reached 81,000 feet over American territory (pp. 90–91). "There was only one thing": FGP, p. 33.

Snider on escape and evasion is in interview. Other accidents are noted in Bissell, Johnson, Snider interviews; de Gramont, p. 250; Miller, p. 116. Bissell–Dryden talks are in Bissell, Johnson, Killian interviews, DFR, pp. 361–78. Dryden on "duty" is in DFR, p. 371. NACA announcement is in Wise and Ross (2), pp. 51–52. Sources on

balloons include Rostow, pp. 189–94; Goodpaster interview. Air Force announcement, January 9, 1956, is in DDEP. Dulles and Eisenhower on Zaroubin request for
meeting and afterward is in James Hagerty Diary, January 24, and 25, 1956. Soviet
complaint on balloons and evidence displayed in Moscow are noted in WP, February 10, 1956. Dulles and Eisenhower on Soviet protest: Tel Call, February 6, 1956,
JFDP. Bissell's arrangements for British base and meeting with CIA and Air Force
at Pentagon: Bissell interview. First unit announced and sent to Britain: Bissell interview; Miller, p. 25.

5: *"The Most Soul-Searching Decision"*

Eisenhower's response to doctors' instructions is in letter to E. E. Hazlett, January
23, 1956, DDEP, as is his view on "failing health of a President." Sources on Eisenhower's decision to run include Ambrose (2), pp. 280–82, 288–91; Hagerty Diary,
December 14, 1955; Hughes, p. 176; Lyon, pp. 673–74; Ewald, pp. 179–84. Eisenhower's talk with Nixon on Cabinet post is in Nixon (1), p. 167. "Nixon will never be
President": Fawn Brodie, *Richard Nixon* (Norton, 1981), p. 350. Hall's failure to
nudge Nixon from the ticket is in Ewald, pp. 185–87. "Absolutely indescribable anguish": Bryce Harlow, quoted in *New Republic,* May 13, 1978. Eisenhower on chart-
ing own course is in NYT, March 8, 1956. Nixon talk with Eisenhower on decision to
run and Eisenhower's response: Nixon (1), pp. 172–73. Milton Eisenhower's view is
in interview.
   Sources on Berlin Tunnel include David Martin, *Wilderness of Mirrors* (Harper
& Row, 1980), pp. 72–90; Prados, p. 28; Cline, pp. 185–86; E. H. Cookridge, *George
Blake* (Ballantine reprint, 1982), p. 153; Dillon Anderson oral history, COHP;
Goodpaster, Bissell interviews. CIA forecast on Soviets suppressing knowledge is
quoted in David Martin, p. 87. Richard Bissell believes that the tunnel was not discovered until shortly before April 1956 and notes Allen Dulles's view that the project
brought "a highly valuable flow of raw intelligence" (interview). Kremlin on "perfidy" and "criminal conspiracy": Cookridge, p. 153. Chinese reaction is in WP, April
29, 1956. NYHT is quoted in David Martin, p. 87. Dulles to Eleanor is in Tel Call,
May 11, 1956, JFDP. Goodpaster on Eisenhower's reaction is in interview. Tightening of supervision is noted in Ewald, p. 266.
   Sources on Crabbe affair include Chapman Pincher, *Their Trade Is Treachery*
(Bantam reprint, 1982), pp. 65–67; Mosley, p. 367; Bissell interview. Eden's refusal of
overflights from Britain is in Bissell interview. Adenauer's nervousness about Eisen-
hower-Zhukov note is in Bohlen, p. 386. Adenauer's consent and U-2 shift to West
Germany are in Bissell interview. Another advantage of flying from Wiesbaden was
that the base was only fifteen miles from the CIA's Frankfurt facility (Miller, p. 26).
Sources on Claridge's reception and Khrushchev-Stassen talk include Adams, pp.
321–24; NYT, April 25, 1956; *Time,* April 30, 1956; and Janet Morgan, ed., *The
Backbench Diaries of Richard Crossman* (Holmes & Meier, 1981), pp. 492–94. Bissell
and Dulles eagerness to fly is in Goodpaster, Bissell, Brugioni interviews. Eisenhower examination of U-2 photos is in *Waging,* p. 545. Allen Dulles view on malfunction is in Goodpaster interview. Eisenhower on "soul-searching question" is in
Memcon Pres, February 2, 1960, DDEP; but he expressed the same view on other

occasions (Goodpaster interview). "Our reaction": Goodpaster interview. Eisenhower's instructions to Dulles are in Goodpaster memo, July 3, 1956, DDEP, and Goodpaster interview.
"If we don't move fast": JSDE, p. 186. Goodpaster-Adams talk and "eerie and striking": Adams, pp. 193–94. Eisenhower to E. E. Hazlett is dated July 3, 1956, DDEP. Bissell on preliminary overflights is in interview. June 21, 1956, meeting with Goodpaster is in Goodpaster memo of that date, DDEP. Soviet Aviation Day 1955 is noted in Dulles, p. 149; FGP, p. 57; Kaplan, p. 156. "Has almost closed the air power gap": General Thomas White, Air Force Vice Chief of Staff, in WP, February 10, 1956. Eisenhower on trading military visits: Memcon Pres, May 28, 1956, DDEP. Twining on Rudenko plane is from his trip report, June 23–July 1, 1956, in DDEP. Khrushchev appearance is in Twining trip report, *Time,* July 2, 1956, and Bohlen, p. 446.

The CIA has never officially confirmed the exact dates and routes of the first flights. Dates cited in text are based on recollections of Goodpaster and Bissell, checked against declassified documents that do exist. The Soviet protest note of July 10, 1956, in DDEP, gives July 4, 1956, as the date of the first deep penetration (as do *American Heritage,* October 1977; Miller, p. 26; and Neff, p. 451). In the 1960 Senate hearings, Allen Dulles says only that the first overflight was in July 1956 (DFR, p. 342). Sources on Goodpaster's transmittal of permission for first penetrations are Goodpster memo, July 10, 1956, DDEP; Bissell and Goodpaster interviews. Evidence of possible Soviet mobilization is noted in Goodpaster memorandum, July 10, 1956, DDEP, and Bissell and Goodpaster interviews. Bissell on "unappetizing" building is in Bissell to Osmond Ritland, November 29, 1965, Bissell Private Papers. Allen Dulles on "pig sty" is in David Atlee Phillips, *The Night Watch* (Ballantine reprint, 1982), p. 73. Bissell's meetings at Operations Center are in Bissell interview and Goodpaster memo, July 3, 1956, DDEP. Principal reasons to fly first over Moscow and Leningrad were the vital industry around both cities and the fact that since both were heavily defended, it might have been safer to fly over them first, exploiting the element of surprise (Miller, p. 26, Bissell interview). Dulles notification by Bissell of first penetration is in Bissell interview and Ambrose (3), p. 266.

Independence Day 1956 at Spaso House is noted in NYT, July 5, 1956; Marvin and Bernard Kalb, "Of Cannibals, Khrushchev and Kissinger," *TV Guide,* March 31, 1984; and conversation with Marvin Kalb. History of Spaso House is in *Washington Post Magazine,* May 26, 1985. Bohlen's knowledge of U-2 project is in Bohlen, p. 464. Eisenhower's appearance and activities on July 4 are in JSDE, p. 187, and NYT, July 5, 1956. Eisenhower to E. E. Hazlett, July 12, 1956, is in DDEP. Bissell and Dulles notification of first U-2 success is in Bissell interview. Twining to reporters is in NYT, July 6, 1956. Goodpaster notes that no evidence of surprise attack was found in interview and memorandum, July 10, 1956, DDEP. Bissell and Dulles expectation that Soviet radar could not track U-2 is in Bissell, Goodpaster and Killian interviews. Killian at NSA is in Killian interview. Khrushchev's anger at first U-2 flights is in *Aviation Week,* May 16, 1960, and NYT, May 10, 1960. Goodpaster July 6, 1956, report to Eisenhower is in Goodpaster memo of that date and Goodpaster interview.

Soviet protest, July 10, 1956, is in DDEL. Zaroubin's presentation thereof and

State Department response are noted in WP, July 11, 1956; INS dispatch, July 10, 1956, in DDEP. Folklore and the imprecision of much writing about intelligence have transformed Zaroubin's note into a "secret" protest (see, for example, Miller, p. 26), which it hardly was. Allen Dulles–Goodpaster call is noted in Foster–Allen Dulles Tel Call, July 10, 1956, JFDP. Goodpaster on Eisenhower's response to protest is in interview. Foster Dulles drafting of reply and reading to Allen: Tel Call, July 11, 1956, JFDP. Eisenhower on "buttoning it up": Eisenhower–Foster Dulles Tel Call, July 18, 1956, JFDP. Bulganin complaint is in Bohlen, p. 464. Rudenko's questioning is in Bohlen, pp. 464–65. Eisenhower's wish for tighter control of U-2 is noted in Bissell and Goodpaster interviews.

Sources on Allen Dulles include Mosley; Ambrose (3), pp. 173–77; Dulles, and his *The Secret Surrender* (Harper & Row, 1966). Dulles on intelligence in blood is in de Gramont, p. 172. Bissell on Dulles is in Ambrose (3), p. 173. Amory on Dulles is in interview. Eleanor Dulles on her brother is in Mosley, p. 15. "If that colonel": Thomas Powers, p. 85. Dulles on "State Department for unfriendly countries": Ambrose (3), p. 178. Moscow press on Dulles and his reaction are in Mosley, p. 5. Amory on Dulles and covert action is in interview. Dulles on "breaking crockery" and his responsibility: de Gramont, p. 16, and Mosley, p. 7.

Foster Dulles on Allen's story is in Mosley, pp. 15–17. Allen Dulles to minister in Vienna is in Mosley, pp. 39–40, as is his letter to family. His encounters with Lenin and Donovan are in Thomas Powers, pp. 83–84, and Mosley, pp. 107–10. Hoover's complaint is in Mosley, p. 114. Mary Bancroft describes her liaison with Dulles in Bancroft, pp. 129–74. Bancroft on Dulles at war's end is in Bancroft, pp. 138–39. Dulles on CIA's role in 1947 is in de Gramont, p. 28. Congressional sanction of other CIA functions is in U.S. Congress, Senate, *Final Report of the Select Committee to Study Governmental Operations with Respect to Intelligence Activities* (Church Committee Report), Book IV (U.S. Government Printing Office, 1976), pp. 6–9. Beetle Smith to CIA men is in de Gramont, p. 131. "Allen, can't I ever mention": Amory interview. Smith on Dulles and preference to stay at CIA is in Souers to Montague, July 19, 1971, Souers Papers. Eisenhower's attitude to Dulles's surrender efforts is in Lyon, pp. 10–11. Ewald on Eisenhower's attitude to Dulles is in Ewald, p. 265.

Dulles on good years at CIA is in Mosley, p. 323. On "telling truth" to Senator Russell: Church Committee Report, Book I, p. 547. Wayne Morse and Cannon to Dulles are in DFR, p. 16, and Mosley, p. 431. "Brother act": Amory interview. Mary Bancroft discusses the brothers' relationship in Bancroft, p. 139. Allen Dulles on life having been freer is in Mosley, p. 7. CIA men on the Dulleses' professional relationship are quoted in Schlesinger (1), p. 455. "I have come to the conclusion": Eisenhower to Lewis Douglas, March 29, 1955, DDEP. Greenstein's book is *The Hidden-Hand Presidency: Eisenhower as Leader* (Basic, 1982). Eisenhower's use of covert action is discussed in Gaddis (2), pp. 157–59. Ambrose (3) traces Eisenhower's use of intelligence and covert action throughout his military and political career. His effort to detach himself from covert operations is in Goodpaster interview. "A very weakly controlled business": Goodpaster quoted in Ewald, p. 270.

Dulles on taking things on faith is in an interview in *U.S. News & World Report*, March 19, 1954. His resistance to Congressional oversight is noted in Ambrose (3), p. 187. Doolittle Panel and Report are noted in Corson, pp. 347–48, and Ambrose (2), pp. 189, 226–27. Doolittle on Dulles is in Ann Whitman Diary, October 19, 1954, as is Eisenhower's response. Eisenhower's request to hire administrator and Dulles's reply are in Eisenhower Diary, October 22, 1954, and Goodpaster memo, February 3, 1955, DDEP. The 5412 Group is noted in Goodpaster interview; Ewald, p. 265; and Schlesinger (1), p. 456. U-2's failure to be considered by 5412 Group is noted in Gordon Gray memo, May 17, 1960, DDEP. Eisenhower appointment of PBCFIA and its initial findings are in Eisenhower Diary, January 24, 1956; Memcon Pres, October 24, 1957; Kirkpatrick, pp. 147–48; Schlesinger (1), p. 456. Board's complaint about Dulles's administration and Eisenhower's response are noted in Killian interview and Killian, p. 222. Goodpaster on Eisenhower's decision not to fire Dulles is in interview.

Presentation of first U-2 photos and "We'd better stand down": Bissell and Goodpaster interviews. "It became pretty evident": Bissell interview. Cabell–Foster Dulles Tel Call, August 28, 1956, is in JFDP. On July 24, 1956, Goodpaster asked Allen Dulles and Killian for an estimate of what had been gained from the U-2, what might be gained in future and how soon the Russians might down a plane (Goodpaster memo, July 24, 1956). Powers departure for Turkey is in Snider interview; Barbara Powers, pp. 23–24; and FGP, pp. 38–39. "We were pretty well conscious": Snider interview. "I've figured out": FGP, p. 39.

6: *"Every Blade of Grass"*

Wake-up ritual in Adana is noted in Williams interview. Negotiation on Turkish base is in Bissell interview; Ronald O. Seth, *Encyclopedia of Espionage* (Doubleday, 1974), p. 468–69; Hilsman, p. 70. The current author requested an interview with James Cunningham who, after considering the matter, replied that he still did some classified work and had been told by colleagues that they would prefer if he did not speak. For Turkish foreign policy of the period, see Kemal H. Karpat, ed., *Turkish Foreign Policy in Transition: 1950–1974* (Leiden: University of Leiden, 1975), Richard Robinson, *The First Turkish Republic* (Cambridge, Mass., 1963). Turks' awareness of tight security is in FGP, pp. 43–44. Appearances of U-2 group are noted in Williams interview. Life in Adana is described in FGP, pp. 43–51; de Gramont, pp. 251–54. Pilots' incomplete knowledge of U-2 activities, chain of command, "I didn't even know": Snider interview. The most comprehensive account of the Suez War is Neff. Eden on "the Egyptian" is in Lyon, p. 693. "I'm quite worried": Neff, p. 341. Powers's flights over Middle East are noted in FGP, pp. 308–9. "We mapped": Bissell interview.

Eisenhower on French Mystères is in Eisenhower Diary, October 15, 1956. U-2 as Eisenhower's most reliable source is in Ambrose (2), p. 341. "It doesn't look" and "I'm positive": Bissell, Amory interviews; Neff, pp. 353–54; Mosley, pp. 413–15. "All right, Foster": Kenneth Love, *Suez* (McGraw-Hill, 1969), p. 503. British cable on bomb damage is in Mosley, p. 518. Dulleses on floor is in Lundahl interview. Eisenhower's worry about Kremlin "extreme measures" is in *Waging*, pp. 67–68. Eisenhower's denial of arms and supplies to Hungary is in *Waging*, p. 89. Amory "sick at heart" is in Neff, p. 405, and Amory interview. Bulganin message is noted in *Waging*, p. 89. "Those boys are both furious": Hughes, p. 223. Allen Dulles on Kremlin promise and Eisenhower's order for U-2 flights are in Memcon Pres, November 6, 1956, DDEP. Goodpaster's noon report is in *Waging*, p. 91. "What in the name of God" and "I'm just looking": Hughes, p. 228. On the historical importance of Suez, see Neff, pp. 438–43; Ambrose (2), pp. 372–74; and Ulam (2), pp. 251–62.

Dulles-Bissell request for resumed U-2 flights and Eisenhower's response are in Memcon Pres, November 15, 1956, DDEP; Bissell and Goodpaster interviews. "You're it, Powers": FGP, p. 50. Eisenhower ordering stoppage is in Tel Call, December 18, 1956, JFDP. Sources on U-2 approval process include Bissell, Goodpaster, John Eisenhower interviews; Goodpaster oral history, DDEL; Bissell oral histories, COHP and DDEL; John Eisenhower oral history, DDEL; and Allen Dulles in DFR, pp. 283–84, 318–19. "I don't think he intended": Bissell interview. Sammy Snider carefully described U-2 takeoff, flight and landing procedures for the author, suplemented by FGP, pp. 52–56. The pilots were rumored to receive bonuses after penetrations of the Soviet Union. Daniel Williams recalled hearing fliers cry, "I'm rich now!" (interview) Bissell's recollection is that they were given "something like super-flight pay." (interview) Pogo through mosque is in Williams interview. Flameout, fighter pilot's ethic and "I could see someone pushing": Snider interview.

Aftermath of U-2 overflights is in Bissell, Amory, Lundahl interviews; Bissell oral history, DDEL: Amory oral history, JFKL. "From the time" and "a guy named Brown" are in Amory interview. Lundahl and Amory on establishment of photointerpretation group are in Lundahl interview, WP, November 28, 1982, and Amory interview. Also see *American Heritage,* October 1977, and Miller, p. 65. Ray Cline on photography is in Cline interview. Helms on U-2 is in Helms interview. His distress at Bissell's opinion of human agents: Helms interview and Thomas Powers, pp. 100–101. "As big as your couch": WP, November 28, 1982. On Presidential U-2 briefings and "Thank God": Bissell, Goodpaster, Killian, Scoville, Lundahl, Brugioni interviews.

Winding down of West German U-2 operation is in FGP, p. 61, Miller, p. 27, and Bissell interview. Although the squadron moved to Adana, overflights from West Germany evidently did not entirely cease in 1957. (Bissell interview and Miller, p. 27.) Bissell on U-2 arrangements for Japan is in interview. He notes that Japanese intelligence was of little aid because in 1957, it was "still a rudimentary service." "Some of us would run": Epstein, p. 54. Bissell's staging of missions from Adana, Atsugi and elsewhere is in Bissell interview. "The Soviets believe": Bohlen in U.S. Congress, Senate, *Executive Sessions of the Senate Foreign Relations Committee (Historical Series), Volume IX* (U.S. Government Printing Office, 1979), p. 516. Amory on the Pakistanis is in interview. Bissell on obtaining Iranian, Norwegian, Pakistani approval is in interview. Washington's promise to host governments is in Bissell interview. "One thing we never reveal": DFR, p. 303. On CIA and SAVAK, see Kermit Roosevelt, *Countercoup* (McGraw-Hill, 1979), pp. 9–10.

American-Pakistani negotiations on base are noted in M. S. Venkataramani, *The American Role in Pakistan, 1947–1958* (New Delhi: Radiant, 1982), pp. 329–42. On Mirza overthrow: Venkataramani, pp. 286–98, 391–98, and conversation with the deposed President's son, Homayun Mirza. Bissell on Pakistani coup is in interview. Bissell would have known why, how and whether the Americans were involved in Mirza's ouster because that was the fall he became Deputy Director for Plans. Ayub

Khan's signing of ten-year lease is in Chester Bowles, *Promises to Keep* (Harper & Row, 1971), pp. 481–84, Prados, p. 103. Bowles argues that the base allowed Pakistan to have a "political hammerlock" on American policy in Asia. On Peshawar base, see also Sulzberger (1), p. 374. Sources on Anglo-American partnership include de Zulueta interview; Miller, pp. 25–26; Mosley, pp. 369–70; and confidential source. In her May 8, 1958, Diary, Ann Whitman notes Harold Macmillan's "request for information on our flight plans. Andy Goodpaster tells me that the British Air Force has the information but they do not tell the Prime Minister! They have their troubles too." Bissell was still using his "R.B.A.F." coffee mug in 1985. "With a week's warning": Bissell interview. Bissell on Peshawar flights and targets, nuclear test information, "milk run" and Alaska flights is in interview and letter to author October 9, 1985. Espionage and U-2 in China are in Cline, pp. 200–201; Miller, pp. 32–33; Cline, Bissell interviews. U-2 photo of watchtower is noted in Alsop, pp. 231–32.

On *Sputnik* and its consequences, see Ambrose (2), pp. 423–35, Ulam (2), pp. 270–71, Cline, pp. 177–78, Lyon, pp. 753–58, *Waging*, pp. 205–26, McDougall, pp. 141–56. "Listen now" is quoted in William Manchester, *The Glory and Dream* (Little, Brown, 1974), p. 290. Hagerty and Adams reactions are in Hughes, p. 246, and Adams, p. 415. Dulles on possible disclosure of U-2 is in Memcon Pres, November 7, 1957, JFDP. It is not very reassuring: *Time,* October 28, 1957. Nixon and Dulles blame criticism for stroke: Lyon, pp. 760–61. "I'm not so sure": Slater, p. 171. WP on Gaither Report is dated December 20, 1957. Eisenhower on gaps in Gaither Report is in *Waging,* pp. 220–33, and Ambrose (2), pp. 434–35, Kaplan, pp. 127–54. Bomber Gap is discussed in Bissell, Goodpaster interviews, Prados, pp. 38–50, Kaplan, pp. 155–61. Alsop on "shuddering" at Pentagon: NYHT, August 1, 1958. Eisenhower's diffidence about first operational Soviet ICBM is noted in Ambrose (2), pp. 313, 397, 561–63. Robert Amory thought that the first "significant" Soviet capability would be one hundred ICBMs. (oral history, JFKL) Bissell on fewer U-2 flights in 1958 is in interview. "It always distressed Eisenhower": Goodpaster interview.

"It might be best": Memcon Pres, October 23, 1957, DDEP. Eisenhower and Twining on more flights: Memcon Pres, January 22, 1958, DDEP. "Such infractions" and Goodpaster call to Allen Dulles are in Memcon, March 7, 1958, DDEP. Soviet protest, April 21, 1958, is in DDEP. Sources on CIA, U-2, Allen Pope and Indonesian rebellion include Thomas Powers, pp. 88–92: Ambrose (3), p. 251; Cline, pp. 205–7; Mosley, pp. 436–38; Joseph B. Smith, *Portrait of a Cold Warrior* (Ballantine reprint, 1981), pp. 197–241; and Bissell interview. Eisenhower and Dulles on July 1958 air incident: Tel Call, July 30, 1958, DDEP. Also see NYT, July 31, 1958. Eisenhower on balloons and "disturbing evidence": Tel Call, July 31, 1958, and memo to Neil McElroy, July 31, 1958, DDEP. U-2 pilots carrying identification over Russia is noted in Snider, Williams interviews and FGP, p. 95. Smoking aboard U-2 is noted in Snider and Williams interviews.

Khrushchev on "sausages" is in Prados, p. 77. "To the Air Force": Wise and Ross (1), pp. 212–13, Adams, p. 220. Killian on showing U-2 pictures to Eisenhower is in interview. Other sources on Missile Gap include Laqueur, pp. 139–70, Edgar M. Bottome, *The Missile Gap* (Fairleigh Dickinson, 1971); James C. Dick, "The Strategic Arms Race, 1957–1962," *The Journal of Politics,* 1972, Killian, Kaplan, pp.

155-73, Prados, pp. 57-95, Ambrose (2), pp. 312-14, 397, 487; Herken, pp. 128-32; McDougall, pp. 250-62; Bissell and Goodpaster interviews and oral histories in COHP and DDEL. Goodpaster checking bomber estimates is in Kaplan, p. 169, as is Symington-Eisenhower talk. Eisenhower on "unconscionable sums" is in his Diary, January 22, 1952. "Any person who doesn't": Eisenhower to Charles Wilson, October 20, 1951, Eisenhower Pre-Presidential Papers. His disgust at defense advertisements and military selfishness: Killian, pp. 238-39, and Griffith in *American Historical Review,* February 1982.

"If you go to any military installation" and "God help": Robert Keith Gray lecture at Hofstra University, March 29, 1984, and conversation with the President's granddaughter, Susan Eisenhower. Eisenhower's views on arms race, inflation, bankruptcy are noted in Ambrose (2), pp. 149-50, 153, and Griffith, *American Historical Review,* February 1982. Nixon to Alsop is in transcript of undated interview, Alsop Papers. "One prays": Alsop to Isaiah Berlin, April 30, 1958, Alsop Papers. "Sanctimonious, hypocritical bastards": Goldwater, p. 78. "We had the dope": Thomas Gates oral history, COHP. Eisenhower frustration on his silence is in Goldwater, pp. 13, 78, 145, and Slater, p. 228.

"Once Bissell had the U-2": Amory interview. Bissell acceptance as Deputy Director for Plans and "Why don't you take it up": Thomas Powers, pp. 97-100. U-2 information in 1958 is noted in Bissell interview; Prados, p. 87; DFR, p. 332. Sources on what U-2 provided include DFR, pp. 284-85, Klass, pp. 30-31, 47-48, 50-51, 79; Gaddis (1), pp. 228-29, Gaddis (2), p. 186; Dinerstein, pp. 75-76; Prados, pp. 31-95; Kistiakowsky, p. 312; de Gramont, pp. 247-49; Dulles, p. 222; Peter Pringle and William Arkin, *SIOP* (Norton, 1983), pp. 76-81; Dick in *The Journal of Politics,* 1972, pp. 1073-74, 1089-90; Bissell interview, transcript of Bissell interview, February 22, 1966, in Bissell Private Papers. U-2 discovery of Tyuratam is in Bissell, Lundahl, Amory, Brugioni interviews and Laqueur, p. 146. Christian Herter told Senate Foreign Relations members in May 1960 that he had seen the Powers route "sketched out, and this is all coming off the record, two-and-a-half years ago." (DFR, p. 270) "What has been the impact": Houston interview.

The CIA has never declassified the exact number of U-2 flights over the Soviet Union. The number is no secret to the Kremlin—only to the American and Soviet peoples. The Agency's persistent silence may be explained partly by the desire to avoid gratuitously inflaming the Russians by announcing how many times their sovereignty was successfully violated; it may be also intended to avoid calling public attention to more recent overflights. In 1960, Allen Dulles told the Senate Foreign Relations Committee, "We consider the actual number so classified that I prefer not to give it here, but there were a considerable number." (DFR, p. 321) Andrew Goodpaster estimates that there may have been no more than a dozen or so penetrations (interview), but this seems low, especially if the CIA ran half a dozen missions during the program's first week. Richard Bissell estimates thirty to forty flights (interview), a more plausible figure. During the 1960 Foreign Relations Committee hearings, Hugh Dryden said that the U-2 made 199 weather flights for NASA in four years and that "perhaps eighty percent or more of the flights were NASA flights." (DFR, p. 371) An unnamed source suggested in *Foreign Intelligence Literary Scene,* October 1983, that this meant fifty U-2 flights into the Soviet Union. Bissell considers this figure too high and notes the number of U-2 flights that were not NASA flights and that did not penetrate the Soviet Union. (interview) Adding to the ambiguity is the fact that some flights over Russia evidently obtained only signals intelligence and no photography. (Lundahl interview)

Bissell on Soviet attitude to U-2 is in interview. On Soviet sense of geographical insecurity and encirclement, see Archie Brown and Jack Gray, eds., *Political Culture and Political Change in Communist States* (Macmillan, 1977); Stephen White, *Political Culture and Soviet Politics* (Macmillan, 1979); and Dallin, pp. 70–78. The U-2 may have also given Khrushchev trouble with satellite governments. An Eastern European leader is said to have reported that when his government detected high-flying spy planes, presumably American, above its territory, it asked Khrushchev for new ground-to-air missiles that might stop them. Such missiles were in too short supply in the Soviet Union to hand out freely to other states; Khrushchev reputedly replied, "Why worry over an occasional American spy plane? It's nothing to get excited about." (*Economist,* June 11, 1960) "Mankind has several times been on the brink" and State Department reply are in NYT, April 19, 1958. "Aircraft flights of one country": NYT, April 24, 1958. Kelly Johnson reports that Andrei Gromyko once quietly complained about the U-2 to Foster Dulles at the UN, saying, "We will shoot you down," and that Dulles replied, "Go ahead, if you think there is a problem" (Johnson interview).

On NSA border flights in late 1950s, see Bamford, pp. 178–86. On June 1958 air incident, see FGP, p. 66; NYT, June 29 and 30, 1958. On September 1958 incident, see Bamford, pp. 178–84; Murphy, pp. 512–13; Wise and Ross (2), pp. 29–30; Wise and Ross (1), pp. 210–11; DFR, p. 296; NYT, September 4, October 17 and 18, 1958; Prouty, pp. 328–37; Memcon Pres, September 4 and 9, 1958, DDEP. "There's a hit": NYT, February 6, 1959. At his February 10, 1959, press conference, Eisenhower told the nation that he had "personally" issued orders forbidding provocative flights over the Soviet Union. (NYT, February 11, 1959) Powers on these incidents: FGP, pp. 66–67. SA-2 deployment is noted in Prados, pp. 96–97, Miller, pp. 28–29. The U-2 intrusions also evidently prompted the Soviets to develop their own high-flying spy plane, the Yak-26 Mandrake, reportedly later used to fly over China, India, Pakistan and other states at roughly 56,000 to 65,000 feet. (Miller, p. 118)

Dulles-Bissell original prediction of life for U-2 over Russia is in DFR, p. 342. Eisenhower's suggestion of shifting U-2 to Air Force and the result are in Goodpaster interview, Memcon Pres, September 9, 1958, DDEP. Eisenhower's later suggestion of a U-2 re-evaluation is in Goodpaster interview and Memcon Pres, December 16, 1958, DDEP. "Dad used to say": John Eisenhower interview.

7: *Khrushchev's Ultimatum*

Sources on Khrushchev's Kremlin press conference are NYT, November 28, 1958; *Time* and *Newsweek,* December 8 and 15, 1958; and conversation with Priscilla McMillan. Eisenhower's reaction is in *Waging,* pp. 340–41, and JSDE, p. 212. "Drunken railway hand": Sulzberger (1), p. 321. Khrushchev on "my little white pigeon," French women and Eden's ailment are in a profile in Gunther, pp. 475–88. Khrushchev at Kremlin fete is noted in Bohlen, p. 497. Nixon on "few foreigners" is in Nixon (1), p. 203. On Khrushchev's character and personality, see James H. Billington, "Five Clues to the Khrushchev Riddle," *New York Times Magazine,* October 29, 1961.

Khrushchev's background and rise to power are described in NSK I, pp. 3–346; Crankshaw, pp. 3–213; Medvedev (2), pp. 3–103; Gunther, pp. 475–88. Crankshaw uses the term "Dark People" (p. 9) and notes the rumor of Khrushchev's descent from landowners (p. 4n). Eisenhower notes Khrushchev's prizes as altar boy in notes on Cabinet meeting, May 26, 1960, DDEP, and *Waging,* p. 625n. Unlike Medvedev (2) (pp. 4–8), Crankshaw (pp. 20–24) believes that Khrushchev did not actually join the Bolsheviks until their victory in the Donbas over rival revolutionary parties "was clear for all to see." "I worked at a factory": Medvedev (2), p. 4. Crankshaw describes him as "wholly literate" by mid-1920s (p. 32). "All you demand": Crankshaw, p. 30. "I was literally spellbound": Medvedev (2), p. 18. "We will uncover and annihilate": Crankshaw, p. 112. "They raised their villainous heads:": Crankshaw, pp. 107–8. "I don't know where these people were sent": NSK I, p. 79. "For every drop of the honest blood": Page, pp. 163–64. Stalin on "Russian gumption" is in Medvedev (2), p. 33. "We are straining every nerve": Medvedev (2), p. 35. "Kiev is like a city": Medvedev (2), p. 37. "He acted as though": NSK I, p. 219.

Stalin's last days are described in NSK I, pp. 276–320; Medvedev (2), pp. 51–55; Adam B. Ulam, *Stalin* (Viking, 1973), pp. 700–741. Stalin on trusting no one is in NSK I, p. 307. Stalin's pictures of wolves are noted in Salisbury, p. 430. Beria's boast about confessions is in NSK I, p. 104. "Can't you see": NSK I, p. 320. "I wasn't just weeping": NSK I, p. 323. On Beria's arrest and execution, see NSK I, pp. 322–41, and Medvedev (2), pp. 62–67, Crankshaw, p. 190, Adam B. Ulam, *A History of Soviet Russia* (Holt, Rinehart and Winston, 1976), p. 220. Khrushchev to visitor is in de Zulueta interview. Additional sources on the final stages of Khrushchev's rise to supreme power are Ulam (1), pp. 554–67; Ulam (2), pp. 220–25; Medvedev (1), pp. 158–61. The State Department's version of Khrushchev's speech, released June 4, 1956, is in NSK I, pp. 559–618. Additional sources on Secret Speech are Medvedev (2), pp. 83–103; NSK I, pp. 341–53; Crankshaw, pp. 227–30, Ulam, *A History,* pp. 225–29. "Principal feat of his life": Medvedev, p. 92. Crankshaw agrees with this assessment (Crankshaw, p. 233). CIA's acquisition of Secret Speech is in Dulles, pp. 81–82, Cline, pp. 185–87; Thomas Powers, p. 80. Khrushchev referring reporters to Allen Dulles is in NSK I, p. 351.

On 1956 satellite rebellions and their impact on Khrushchev's political position, see Ulam (2), pp. 262–66; Ulam (1), pp. 572–603; and Crankshaw, pp. 230–44. "When it is a question of fighting": Crankshaw, p. 243. On Anti-Party Coup and its aftermath, see Crankshaw, pp. 245–52; Medvedev (2), pp. 111–23, Ulam, *A History,* pp. 232–34. "My grandsons!": Gunther, p. 486. On Khrushchev's Berlin ultimatum, see Ulam (2), pp. 294–95, and Ulam (1), pp. 619–21. On Berlin crisis generally, see Jack M. Schick, *The Berlin Crisis, 1958–1962* (University of Pennsylvania, 1971), Robert M. Slusser, *The Berlin Crisis of 1961* (Johns Hopkins, 1973), and Alexander L. George and Richard Smoke, *Deterrence in American Foreign Policy* (Columbia, 1974), pp. 390–446. Thompson on nailing down frontiers is in Memcon Pres, October 16, 1959. Berlin as "testicles" of West: Sulzberger (1), p. 860. Eisenhower's responses to Khrushchev's threat are in Ambrose (2), pp. 503–4, 511; JSDE, pp.

213–28; LaFeber, pp. 213–15; Divine (2), pp. 131–39; *Waging,* pp. 332–44. Eisenhower on Khrushchev's "manufactured crisis" is in *Waging,* pp. 332–44. McElroy, Twining, Quarles, Eisenhower on more U-2 flights are in Memcon Pres, February 12, 1959, DDEP. Goodpaster to Twining is in Tel Call, March 4, 1959, DDEP.

Sources on Macmillan include Anthony Sampson, *Macmillan* (London: Allen Lane, 1967); Nigel Fisher, *Harold Macmillan* (St. Martin's, 1982); profile in Gunther, pp. 439–52; and Macmillan's own six-volume memoirs. The author has also benefited from speaking with Macmillan's aide Sir Philip de Zulueta. Macmillan describes his wartime relationship with Eisenhower in his *War Diaries* (St. Martin's Press, 1984). Macmillan's visit to the Soviet Union is described in Macmillan (2), pp. 589–635, and de Zulueta interview. Macmillan on Khrushchev and going home in "affronted dignity": Macmillan (2), pp. 634, 618. Khrushchev on not trying to "pressure" and as "absolute ruler": Macmillan (2), pp. 626, 633–34. Macmillan on Camp David film is in Macmillan (2), p. 645. Eisenhower's worries about Macmillan: JSDE, pp. 228, 230–31; John Eisenhower interview; de Zulueta interview. Macmillan on not subjecting Britain to nuclear attack is in JSDE, p. 229, and John Eisenhower interview.

"As the world is going now": Memcon Pres, April 7, 1959, DDEP. Ann Whitman on Eisenhower's not dwelling on death and in "queer mood" is in her Diary, February 14 and 20, 1959. "Bill, just remember": Mosley, p. 448. Eisenhower to foreign ministers at White House is in *Waging,* p. 398. "I have a special message" and "I couldn't believe my eyes": NSK II, p. 417. Eisenhower's explosion is noted in *Waging,* p. 407. Events leading to the unqualified invitation are in *Waging,* pp. 405–7; JSDE, pp. 235–37; Ambrose (2), p. 535; John Eisenhower, Dillon, Goodpaster interviews. "Someone has failed": Memcon Pres, July 22, 1959, DDEP. "Dad felt he was left": John Eisenhower interview.

Eisenhower on Nixon as no part of negotiating machinery is in Hearst and Considine, p. 197. Nixon's briefing at HTAUTOMAT is in Lundahl interview. Nixon to Cushman, July 17, 1959, is in Nixon Papers. "If RN is looking": Haldeman to Robert Finch, undated, in Nixon Papers. Nixon's preflight meeting with Eisenhower is in Memcon Pres, July 22, 1959, DDEP. "So you will not be astonished": Eisenhower in press conference, NYT, August 4, 1959. Nixon "ready for battle" is in Nixon (1), p. 245. "Moscow Kremlin, here I come" is in Charles Mohr, "Remembrances of the Great Kitchen Debate," NYT, July 25, 1984. Pat Nixon on crowds in streets and being politician's wife is in Jane Thompson interview. Sources on Nixon's Soviet visit include Nixon (2), pp. 206–13; Nixon (1), pp. 246–81; Richard Nixon, *Leaders* (Warner, 1982), pp. 173–93; Milton Eisenhower, pp. 326–34; Hearst and Considine, pp. 187–231; NSK II, pp. 411–15; Toumanoff, Jane Thompson, Milton Eisenhower interviews; Nixon speech at Smithsonian Institution, July 25, 1984. "I could sense": Nixon (1), p. 250. Initial meeting with Khrushchev in Kremlin is in Nixon (2), pp. 207–8. Khrushchev on abstract sculpture is in NSK II, p. 412. "Nixon came out of the TV studio" and "This way to the typical American house": William Safire, *Before the Fall* (Doubleday, 1975), pp. 3–5.

Time on Nixon's "personification" is dated August 10, 1959. Stevenson's view is in Walter Johnson, ed., *The Papers of Adlai E. Stevenson* (Little, Brown, 1977), p. 360. Speedboat trip and luncheon at dacha are noted in Milton Eisenhower interview; Nixon (2), pp. 209–12; Milton Eisenhower, p. 327; Nixon, *Leaders,* pp. 179, 187–191. Dacha perhaps Beria's is in Jane Thompson interview. Nixon's cable to Eisenhower is contained in Thompson to Herter, July 26, 1959, DDEP. Nixon on Khrushchev's "devastating sense of humor" is in *Leaders,* p. 170. Dosimeters are noted in undated document, Nixon Soviet trip file, DDEP. Nixon on offer to Kozlov is in memo to Cushman, July 6, 1959, in Nixon Papers. Nixon's sighting of new missile defense at Sverdlovsk is in *Aviation Week,* May 16, 1960, and Wise and Ross (2), p. 27. Bissell said that Nixon's information would have "added" to the importance of Sverdlovsk as an intelligence target. (Letter to the author, October 9, 1985) "Crowds along the city streets" is contained in Thompson to Herter, July 31, 1959, DDEP. Thompson to Nixon on speech is in Jane Thompson interview. Nixon's behavior at final Spaso House dinner is noted in Milton Eisenhower and Toumanoff interviews. Eisenhower on Roosevelt's alleged drinking is in Ewald, p. 27.

Buckley on Khrushchev's visit is in Mitchell Ross, *The Literary Politicians* (Doubleday, 1978), p. 33, and Ambrose (2), p. 536. "Pray in the streets": Frankland, p. 162. Macmillan on Eisenhower's invitation is in Macmillan (3), pp. 78–79. "I don't think he said": John Eisenhower interview. Eisenhower's attitude on Khrushchev's visit is in *Waging,* p. 557; Memcon Pres, August 5 and 25, 1959, DDEP. Eisenhower on what he wishes Khrushchev to see is in *Public Papers of the Presidents: Dwight D. Eisenhower, 1959* (U.S. Government Printing Office, 1960), p. 576. "I'd been to England"; NSK II, pp. 417–18. Khrushchev on Stalin's opinion of Eisenhower is in NSK I, pp. 220–21. His memory of Eisenhower at Geneva is in NSK I, p. 397. "One can hardly overestimate": Ulam (2), p. 306. "When I woke up": NSK II, pp. 422–25.

8: *Camp David*

WELCOME KHRUSHCHEV is in NYT, September 16, 1959. "Looking out the window": NSK II, p. 425. Eisenhower on Menshikov is in Memcon Pres, September 25, 1959, DDEP. "Tell him he'll do it our way": JSDE, p. 256. "Shortly before this meeting": NYT, September 5, 1959. Khrushchev liked to try to strengthen his hand before meetings with Western leaders with such propaganda events as the *Lunik* launching, which gave at least the illusion of Soviet strength. The bomber surprise on Soviet Aviation Day 1955 occurred a few days before the Geneva Summit. See Chapter Eleven for the *Sputnik* launching before the Paris Summit. Eisenhower's irritation at Khrushchev's statement is in *Waging,* pp. 434–35. "A very solemn moment": NSK II, p. 426. "More like a funeral procession": NYT, September 16, 1959. "No applause" and Goodpaster inquiry are noted in James Rowley to Goodpaster. September 22, 1959, DDEP. *Pravda*'s account is reprinted in SP, XI, 37, pp. 3–4. Khrushchev's arrival in Washington is described in NYT and WP, September 16, 1959; *Time, Newsweek* and *U.S. News,* September 28, 1959; NSK II, pp. 425–27; *Waging,* pp. 434–35; and JSDE, pp. 256–57.

Khrushchev's affliction by Washington heat is in NYT, September 16, 1959. "The fellow might have been sincere": JSDE, p. 257; *Waging,* p. 435; and John Eisenhower interview. Khrushchev's surprise at Oval Office seating is in NSK II, p. 427. Sources on Eisenhower-Khrushchev meetings in Oval Office include *Waging,* pp. 435–38; JSDE, pp. 257–58: Memcon Pres, September 15, 1959, DDEP. Douglas

MacArthur may have been the (perhaps unconscious) inspiration for Eisenhower's appeal to Khrushchev. On a visit to the President-elect in New York in December 1952, MacArthur said, "You have the opportunity to be perhaps the greatest man since Jesus Christ, as only you can dictate the peace of the world. I beg of you to take the initiative with bold action" (as quoted in William Manchester, *American Caesar,* Dell reprint, 1979, pp. 822–33). Like Khrushchev in 1959, Eisenhower was unmoved. Eisenhower on Khrushchev's "sweet words" is in Ann Whitman Diary, September 16, 1959.

Sources on helicopter ride include *Time, Newsweek, U.S. News,* September 28, 1959; NYT, September 16, 1959; *Waging,* pp. 438–39; Salisbury, p. 493; Salisbury and Hagerty oral histories, COHP. "If you are going to be": *Waging,* p. 438. "Decent, fine homes": *U.S. News,* September 28, 1959. Khrushchev on automobiles and helicopter ride is in NYT, September 16, 1959, and Salisbury oral history, COHP. Mamie Eisenhower on the Khrushchevs' attire is in West, p. 184. "Our guest seemed to enjoy": *Waging,* p. 440. "What we should do": NYT, September 16, 1959. "Well, I've never been able to see" is quoted by Richard Nixon in *Vital Speeches,* 1960, p. 485. Khrushchev–Allen Dulles encounter is in *Time,* September 28, 1959. Hoover's complaint is in Parmet, p. 551. White House dinner is described in NYT, September 16, 1959; *Time* and *Newsweek,* September 28, 1959; West, pp. 183–84; JSDE, pp. 258–59; *Waging,* pp. 439–40; John Eisenhower interview.

Khrushchev at Press Club is in NYT, September 17, 1959, and Hearst and Considine, pp. 238–45. Khrushchev and Senate Foreign Relations is noted in Fulbright interview and Committee transcript, September 16, 1959, in John F. Kennedy Pre-Presidential Papers. Khrushchev "impressed" with Kennedy and Embassy report on Kennedy: NSK I, p. 458, and Schlesinger (1), p. 378. Ann Whitman on Sixteenth Street is in her Diary, September 16, 1959. Khrushchev's toast is in NYT, September 17, 1959. Nixon on showing Khrushchev American power and Eisenhower on planning tour are in Memcon Pres, August 5, 1959, DDEP. Khrushchev-Lodge exchanges are in NSK II, pp. 429–30. Lodge's reports to Eisenhower are noted in *Newsweek,* October 5, 1959. Khrushchev's New York arrival is described in NSK II, p. 431; NYT, September 18, 1959; and *Time* and *Newsweek,* September 28, 1959. Harriman reception is noted in NSK II, p. 432–34, and John Kenneth Galbraith's essay, "The Day Nikita Khrushchev Visited the Establishment," in *Harper's,* February 1971. Khrushchev on guests smoking and "like typical capitalists": NSK II, pp. 433, 432. Economic Club banquet is noted in NYT, September 18, 1959, and Hearst and Considine, pp. 247–49. Khrushchev on disarmament at UN is in Divine (1), p. 287. Khrushchev's call on Eleanor Roosevelt is in Joseph P. Lash, *Eleanor: The Years Alone* (Norton, 1972), pp. 272–73. Khrushchev-Rockefeller meeting is noted in Persico, p. 86, and Roberts, p. 161. *Ever Knee-Deep in Blood* was published by Pravda Press, Moscow, in 1957.

Khrushchev's boasts of intercepting American intelligence are in de Gramont, p. 149, and Lodge, pp. 165–66. Khrushchev on Hollywood is in NSK II, p. 436. Reagan's boycott is noted in *New York Post,* March 29, 1984. Marilyn Monroe on her attendance is in Lena Pepitone and William Stadiem, *Marilyn Monroe Confidential* (Pocket reprint, 1980), p. 144. Khrushchev complaint about barring from Disneyland is in Hearst and Considine, p. 260. Sinatra's suggestion to Niven is in WP, August 8, 1983. Sinatra's song and photographers' cries are in *Time,* September 28, 1959, Lodge, p. 164, and NSK II, p. 437. Eisenhower to Lodge on incident is in Lodge, pp. 164–65. Khrushchev on incident is in Whitney, pp. 342–43. Khrushchev's explosion at protest sign is in Lodge, p. 165. Los Angeles banquet is noted in Lyon, p. 803; *Time,* September 28, 1959; and NSK II, p. 440. Gosden to Eisenhower is quoted in Lyon, p. 803. "How dare this man": NSK II, pp. 439–41. "We have decided to manage": Lodge, pp. 168–69. "Poor Eisenhower" and "the plain people of America": Lodge, pp. 179–80.

Chalmers Roberts on Khrushchev's trip is in Roberts, p. 160. Khrushchev on decision to bring family to America is in NSK II, p. 420. Other members of traveling party and Khrushchev's reception are noted in *Time,* September 28, 1959, and Ulam (3), pp. 304–5. *Izvestia, Pravda* and *Literaturnaya Gazeta* are quoted in SP, XI, 37, pp. 3–4, and 38, pp. 5, 7 and 8. The Soviet joke about Khrushchev's visit was told the author by a Soviet refugee, Alex Sigalus. "You have charmed me": *Time,* October 5, 1959. Khrushchev on Reuther and Bridges is in NSK II, pp. 446, 448. On visit to Garst: NSK II, pp. 451–54; Salisbury, pp. 482–96. On Pittsburgh visit: NSK II, pp. 457–58, and Whitney, p. 370. Khrushchev on Americans who came to see him: NSK II, p. 439. "I have no intention of calling you": *Khrushchev in America* (Crosscurrents Press, 1960), p. 148. "We now know he is no buffoon": *Newsweek,* October 5, 1959. Menshikov's reputation in Washington is noted in Dillon interview. Lodge on visit's impact on Khrushchev is in Memcon Pres, September 25, 1959, DDEP.

Khrushchev's original bafflement about Camp David is in NSK II, p. 420–21. *Pravda* on Camp David is in SP, XI, 40, p. 13. Ann Whitman on start of Camp David meetings and Eisenhower feeling "lousy" is in her Diary, September 25, 1959. "It will be difficult to adhere": Memcon Pres, September 25, 1959, DDEP. Khrushchev on flight over golf course is in NSK II, p. 461. Arrival at Camp David is in NYT, September 26, 1959, and *Time,* October 5, 1959. Camp David decoration and Khrushchev's opinion thereof are in West, p. 155, and NSK II, p. 461. Eisenhower and Khrushchev on Westerns is in NSK II, p. 462. Salisbury's dispatch is in NYT, September 26, 1959.

Saturday morning weather problems are noted in Kistiakowsky, p. 89, and Ann Whitman Diary, September 25, 1959. Khrushchev avoiding bugging devices is in NSK II, p. 464. Breakfast is noted in NYT, September 27, 1959; Memcon Pres, September 26, 1959, DDEP; *Waging,* pp. 443–44; JSDE, pp. 260–61; John Eisenhower interview. Nixon on Khrushchev's health: Memcon Pres, August 5, 1959, DDEP. CIA interest in Khrushchev's health is noted in CIA report on August 9 and 11 meetings with Sam Jaffe, CIA/FOI. In 1960, twenty physicians, psychologists and psychiatrists were gathered to assay Khrushchev's health, which they found "superb," and his personality, which they found that of "a chronic optimistic opportunist . . . a product of a gratified infancy" (NYT, September 8, 1968).

State Department talking paper, September 8, 1959, is in DDEP. Morning discussion is noted in *Waging,* p. 444, and Memcon Pres, September 26, 1959, DDEP. Goodpaster's notes, September 26, 1959, are in DDEP. Saturday luncheon is noted in Kistiakowsky, pp. 90–91, and Memcon Pres, September 26, 1959. Nixon on Khrushchev's "inferiority complex" is in Kistiakowsky, p. 91. "Everyone much depressed" is in Kistiakowsky, p. 92. Khrushchev on Eisenhower's farm and smile is in

NSK II, pp. 463, 462. Visit with Eisenhower grandchildren is in JSDE, pp. 261–62; John Eisenhower interview; and conversation with Susan Eisenhower. "If Khrushchev could take us over": JSDE, p. 262. Goodpaster notes Khrushchev's relaxation: Kistiakowsky, p. 93. Eisenhower on Khrushchev and church invitation is in NYT, September 28, 1959. Khrushchev on importing American shoes is in Dillon interview. On Lend-Lease repayment: Dillon interview and NSK II, pp. 427–28. Khrushchev erroneously places his talk with Dillon at the start of his American tour.

Khrushchev on Mao as "lunatic" is in *Saturday Review*, September 7, 1974. Mao on war with West is in NSK II, p. 490. Khrushchev and impending schism with China is discussed in Gaddis (1), pp. 223–24, Gaddis (2), pp. 194–95, Ulam (1), pp. 623–25, Ulam (2), pp. 286–308, and William E. Griffith, *The Sino-Soviet Rift* (Cambridge, Mass., 1964). Khrushchev on nuclear-free zone is in Ulam (1), p. 621. As with the Soviets, U.S. concern about a nuclear China continued. On July 15, 1963, President Kennedy asked his envoy Averell Harriman to inform Khrushchev that he would "work on the French if the Soviets will work on the Chinese" to bring them under a test ban—an interesting twist on Khrushchev's presumed earlier interest in a Germany-China deal. Kennedy asked Harriman to "elicit K's view of means of limiting or preventing Chinese nuclear development and his willingness either to take Soviet action or to accept U.S. action aimed in this direction." (quoted in Seaborg, p. 239) This may have referred to a possible preemptive strike against Chinese nuclear facilities. Eisenhower's awareness of Soviet worry about China is noted in Memcon Pres, November 5, 1958, DDEP. Eisenhower on "foolishness" was quoted by Robert Donovan in NYT, September 16, 1982. Eisenhower and Herter on China is in Memcon Pres, September 24, 1959, DDEP. Eisenhower-Khrushchev talk on China: Memcon Pres, September 27, 1959, DDEP, *Waging*, p. 445.

"When Khrushchev and I were alone": Adams, pp. 454–55. Khrushchev-Eisenhower agreement: Memcon Pres, September 27, 1959, DDEP, and *Waging*, pp. 446–47. Sunday luncheon is in Memcon Pres, September 27, 1959, DDEP. "This ends the whole affair": Memcon Pres, September 27, 1959, DDEP, *Waging*, p. 447, Kistiakowsky, p. 94. Perhaps conflating lunch with his disagreement with Eisenhower over the communiqué, Khrushchev inaccurately recalls the meal as "more like a funeral than a wedding feast" (NSK II, p. 468). Eisenhower and Khrushchev return to Washington and Hagerty's assurance to reporters: WP, September 28, 1959, and *Waging*, p. 448. Khrushchev's television speech text is in NYT, September 28, 1959. Ann Whitman's reaction is in her Diary, September 27, 1959. Khrushchev on "colossal moral victory" is in NSK II, p. 471. Symington on Truman invitation to Stalin is in NYT, September 28, 1959. Eisenhower-Khrushchev exchange on military spending: NSK II, pp. 466–68. Dillon on effect of a Khrushchev complaint about U-2 at Camp David: interview.

9: *"The Great Thaw"*

Khrushchev's return to Moscow and report on his American visit are noted in NYT, September 30, 1959. Films on Khrushchev's tour are noted in Tatu, p. 19; Werth, pp. 26–27; and NSK II, pp. 469–70. The term "chaotic panorama" is used by the Soviet historian Anatoly Gromyko in *Through Russian Eyes: President Kennedy's 1,036*

Days (International Library, 1973), p. xv. *Face to Face with America* is noted in Tatu, pp. 19–20, and Ulam (1), p. 629. *Pravda*'s editorial cartoon is noted in Tatu, p. 20. "Wherever I went in Russia": *Newsweek,* October 5, 1959. Eisenhower to Herter, September 29, 1959, is in DDEP. Gordon Gray on "The Great Thaw," October 9, 1959, is in DDEP, as is Allen Dulles's brief reply, October 19, 1959.

"It would be an overstatement": JSDE, p. 264. *London Evening Standard* cartoon and Khrushchev's Peking visit are noted in *Time,* October 12, 1959; Terrill, pp. 281–82; O. Edmund Clubb, *China and Russia* (Columbia, 1971), pp. 435–37; and Hyland and Shyrock, pp. 4–17. Khrushchev on visit is in NSK I, pp. 472–74, and NSK II, pp. 347–52. "If you are too slow": Werth, p. 27. On Khrushchev's contradictory aims, see Crankshaw, pp. 270–74, and Ulam (1), pp. 605–13. On Khrushchev's enemies, see Thompson to Herter, January 29, 1960, DDEP. Examples of Khrushchev's tributes to Eisenhower are in Werth, pp. 15–20, and Tatu, p. 57n. Khrushchev on Eisenhower "softness" is in NSK I, p. 397. Zorin on summit is in Memcon Pres, October 22–27, 1959, DDEP.

Sources on de Gaulle include his memoirs, Gunther, pp. 464–74, and Don Cook, *Charles de Gaulle* (Putnam, 1983). Louis Halle on de Gaulle is in *The Cold War as History* (Harper & Row, 1967), p. 369. "Nothing saddened me more" is in Cook, p. 26. "I like Eisenhower": Sulzberger (1), p. 86, and Lyon, p. 798 n. De Gaulle on end of age of giants is in Jean-Raymond Tournoux, *La Tragédie du Général* (Paris: Plon, 1967), p. 357, and Sulzberger (1), p. 86. Eisenhower and Macmillan on de Gaulle are in Walters, p. 488, and Drew Middleton, *Where Has Last July Gone?* (Quadrangle, 1973), p. 206. De Gaulle's request for American nuclear aid is in Walters, p. 490. Eisenhower's failure to stop him from delaying Summit is in Halle, pp. 364–71. Eisenhower to Herter on "weariness" is in Memcon Pres, October 27, 1959, DDEP.

On Eisenhower's goodwill trips, see Merriman Smith, pp. 1–187; *Waging,* pp. 485–539; JSDE, pp. 264–69; and DFR, p. 79. Khrushchev nervousness about Eisenhower's reception is in Adams, p. 455; Milton Eisenhower, p. 336; Merriman Smith, pp. 259–61. Menshikov's proposition to Stevenson is in Martin, pp. 471–75. Lodge's talk with Khrushchev is in cable to Herter, February 9, 1960, DDEP. Khrushchev on Eisenhower's Soviet tour is in Thompson to Herter, January 1, 1960, DDEP. Copy of Eisenhower's Soviet itinerary, May 7, 1960, is in DDEP. Khrushchev's answer to Disneyland, golf course and Eisenhower Dacha are noted in Salisbury oral history, COHP; Milton Eisenhower oral history, DDEL; and Sulzberger (1), p. 673. Hagerty's advance trip is noted in his oral history, COHP. List of American journalists, May 3, 1960, and list of gifts, May 13, 1960, are in DDEP. Eisenhower's request to use *Air Force One* in Russia is in letters to Khrushchev, November 28, 1959, and January 12, 1960, DDEP. Khrushchev to Thompson on difficulty in doing this is in Thompson cable to Herter, January 13, 1960, DDEP. Khrushchev on "finally" winning military consent is in letter to Eisenhower, January 13, 1960, DDEP. Eisenhower's reply, January 21, 1960, is in DDEP.

Soviet use of civilian airliners for aerial spying is noted in terHorst and Albertazzie, p. 202. Richard Bissell in interview said that reports of Soviet spying from airliners were "probably correct." Air Force surreptitious photography of Soviet territory was told Eisenhower by Senator Francis Case on May 9, 1960, Memcon Pres,

452   :   *Notes to pages 228–232*

DDEP. *Air Force One* conversion to spy plane is in Bissell interview and terHorst and Albertazzie, pp. 202–5. Bissell notes that this was primarily an Air Force project. Thompson on Russians being "excited" about Eisenhower visit is in Sulzberger (1), p. 667. "We don't know either, but we're sprucing up" and "There's a jazz band in": Toumanoff interview. Soviets telephoning acceptances and queries on Eisenhower third term are noted in McMillan article. Toumanoff on stampeding out of corral is in interview.

Herter-Eisenhower on Berlin is in Memcon Pres, October 16, 1959, DDEP. Eisenhower on promise to bargain seriously is in Memcon Pres, December 18, 1959, DDEP. When Herter warned that the West Germans and French might object to serious bargaining, Eisenhower replied, "If they do, they may be taking on the responsibility for the future of Berliin and West Germany." (Memcon Pres, November 2, 1959, DDEP) Eisenhower's possible reintroduction of Open Skies and other proposals is noted in Herken, p. 127, Memcon Pres, April 25 and 26, 1960. On April 21, 1960, Herter told the Senate Foreign Relations Committee in private that Khrushchev "might be willing to accept a temporary solution" on Berlin "or even let it ride, provided he feels that he is going to make some headway toward . . . the nuclear test proposals in which he seems to have a very keen interest." (DFR, p. 227) Eisenhower's intention to bargain seriously on Berlin and offer other proposals is noted in Goodpaster interview, DFR, pp. 225–43, Memcons Pres, October 16 and 21, November 2, December 18 and 29, 1959, DDEP. Previous historians have tended toward skepticism about the chances for a partial test ban and serious negotiation on Berlin at Paris. This is at least partly due to the fact that they lacked access to the aforementioned documents, all declassified in the 1980s.

Sources on history of disarmament and test ban efforts include Seaborg and Divine (1). Gaither Report on negotiation is in Herken, p. 118. "We now enjoy certain advantages": Eisenhower Diary, October 29, 1957. Allen Dulles agreed (Divine, p. 300). "Why don't you fellows": Herken, p. 118. Thompson on Khrushchev's eagerness for treaty and Eisenhower's reaction are in Memcon Pres, October 16, 1959, DDEP. George Kennan detected "a real sense of urgency in Moscow" to reach arms control agreements, especially because of nervousness about China. (oral history, JFKL) On December 29, 1959, James Wadsworth, chief of the U.S. delegation at Geneva, told Eisenhower that the Soviets "very much want to achieve an agreement." (Memcon Pres, DDEP) During this period, the United States and Soviet Union agreed on an arms limitation treaty for Antarctica, allowing overflights and unlimited other forms of inspection. (*Waging,* pp. 483–85) Another of Eisenhower's motivations for a test ban was to "put a few inspection stations into Russia" and "open that country up to some degree." (Memcon Pres, December 29, 1959, DDEP)

Eisenhower's new approach on test ban and Soviet response are in Ambrose (2), p. 564. and DFR, pp. 183–206. "We must get an agreement": Memcon Pres, March 25, 1960, DDEP. "All the signs": NYT, March 30, 1960. Eisenhower-Macmillan talks on test ban are in Macmillan (3), pp. 188–92, and de Zulueta interview. Eisenhower's proposed warning on Berlin appears in Eisenhower to Macmillan and de Gaulle, undated letter, May 1960 file, DDEP. "All the omens": Macmillan (3), p. 191. Eisenhower and Khrushchev on verge is discussed in Ambrose (2), p. 580, and Macmillan (3), p. 179. Eisenhower's anticipation of possible Paris signing is in Kistiakowsky, pp. 286–88, Ambrose (2), pp. 566, 580, Seaborg, p. 24, Goodpaster interview. Khrushchev on period since Camp David is in NSK II, p. 472.

Dulles to Eisenhower, August 18, 1959, is in DDEP. Eisenhower on U-2, October 26, 1959, is in DDEP. U-2 over French Sahara nuclear sites is in Johnson interview. U-2 over Cuba is in Ambrose (2), p. 557. February PBCFIA meeting is in Memcon Pres, February 2, 1960, and Goodpaster interview.

Eisenhower on leak is in Kistiakowsky, pp. 250–52. Amory's success in persuading Baldwin to kill U-2 story is in Amory interview. Sulzberger made good on his pledge: after the U-2 was downed, Baldwin scored a worldwide scoop by publishing a detailed story on the origins of the program. Reston's and Krock's discoveries of U-2 are in Reston, p. 20, and Arthur Krock, *Memoirs* (Funk and Wagnalls, 1968), p. 181. Leacocos and Roberts are in John Leacocos, *Fires in the In-Basket* (World, 1968), p. 373, and Roberts, p. 171. Knowledge of U-2 as status symbol is in *Waging*, p. 552n.

Model Airplane News item is in March 1958 issue. Oxford students' article is noted in de Gramont, p. 248. After the Bay of Pigs, John Kennedy mused that the failure might have been averted had the *New York Times* run everything it had learned about the impending invasion. (Harrison E. Salisbury, *Without Fear or Favor,* Times Books, 1980, pp. 162–63) It has often been overlooked that as late as 1974, CIA Director William Colby personally persuaded officials of almost all major American media to avoid coverage of the CIA deep-oceanic recovery vessel *Glomar Explorer* with the argument that the ship had yet to make another pass (so he said) at raising an 18-year-old Soviet submarine sunk in the Pacific in 1968. This was despite the fact that parts of the story had already seen print. When the full story broke, Colby recalled the lesson of the U-2 and persuaded the White House to issue no comment. (Salisbury, *Without Fear or Favor,* pp. 557–76)

September 1959 Atsugi incident is noted in Snider interview, FGP, p. 68; de Gramont, pp. 252–53. Suspicions about Turks are noted in Williams interview. U-2 commander on Soviet intelligence against Adana and Atsugi is in Epstein, p. 117. Bissell on same subject is in interview. "Brought me right out of my seat": Epstein, p. 117, and Helms interview. Popov's story is told by William Hood in *Mole* (Norton, 1982). Helms sent friends copies of the book inscribed, "This is the way it was before the advent of technology" (Helms interview). Sources on Oswald include Priscilla Johnson McMillan, *Marina and Lee* (Harper & Row, 1977), and Epstein. Oswald's boast of something "of special interest" is noted in FGP, p. 357. Rumor that Oswald killed guard is in McMillan, p. 64. Sources on U-2 information Oswald might have provided Soviets are McMillan, p. 142; Epstein, pp. 119–22; and a Helms memo, May 13, 1964, considered by the Warren Commission, which says that Oswald may have heard "rumors and gossip" but that there was no reason to believe that he had "factual knowledge" of the plane or its mission (FBI/FOI). "I don't think Oswald": Bissell interview.

Gates on Missile Gap testimony and talk with Eisenhower is in oral history, COHP. Dulles to Eisenhower, January 7, 1960, is in Prados, pp. 87–88. Kistiakowsky on briefing is in Kistiakowsky, p. 219. Request for U-2 resumption and desired targets are in Bissell, Goodpaster, Dillon, John Eisenhower, Lundahl interviews, Ambrose (2), p. 569, Ambrose (3), p. 283, DFR, p. 333. Intelligence needs at time are noted in Laqueur, pp. 148–51. Bissell on lack of flights since Camp David is in interview. Doolittle's appeal to use the U-2 during the February 1960 PBCFIA meeting cited above suggests a lengthy hiatus in the U-2 flights. In his memoirs, Khrushchev also implies a cessation since Camp David. (NSK II, p. 472) Even if there were one or two overflights between October 1959 and April 1960, Khrushchev might well have viewed this as an accident (or so he might have argued to Kremlin colleagues). The two additional flights in the spring of 1960 would have been almost impossible to so rationalize.

Installation of SA-2s is in Prados, pp. 96–97, and Taylor and Taylor, p. 45. CIA estimate on SA-2 is in Bissell interview and Ambrose (3), p. 281. The SA-2's effective ceiling is considered to be 59,136 feet. (Taylor and Taylor, p. 45) Installation of grangers and new engines is in FGP, p. 67, Bissell, Johnson interviews. Routing away from SA-2s is in Miller, p. 29, Bissell interview. Assurances on air defense and pilot and equipment not surviving are in Goodpaster, John Eisenhower interviews. Goodpaster on "prejudicial" flights is in interview. April 9, 1960, flight is noted in Bissell, Dillon, Lundahl interviews, DFR, pp. 315–17, NYT, May 6, 1960.

Khrushchev's reaction to April 9 flight is in NSK II, p. 472. On "terrible headaches" and "war waged by other means": NSK II, pp. 505, 507. Khrushchev's October 1959 plea is in Werth, pp. 226–27. Gromyko and Khrushchev response to April 9 flight is in NSK II, p. 505. Bohlen on U-2 resumption is in oral history, COHP. Bissell considers it plausible that Khrushchev took the U-2 resumption as a signal of an American shift against détente and that his fury was directed at this—not the fact that the U.S. had staged a U-2 flight near the time of the Summit. (interview) There is, of course, no unanimous view among Western scholars about the degree to which there might have been two or more schools of thought in the Kremlin in 1959–1960 about how to deal with the West.

Khrushchev's disappearance from view is noted in Tatu, p. 51. His absence from Lenin birthday is in NYT, April 23, 1960. Khrushchev's tough speeches are in SFRC, pp. 17–19. Herter, Dillon speeches and their impact on the Soviets are noted in Werth, pp. 243, 252, and LaFeber, p. 206. Eisenhower to Khrushchev on leaving Nixon in his place is in Sulzberger (1), p. 668. Sulzberger notes that this "probably wasn't too bright, because we would be a little offended if Khrushchev left Kozlov at the Summit and went off for a few days to Albania." Eisenhower also limited the duration of his presence in Geneva in 1955 and on the prospective tour of Russia, pleading that Congress would still be in session in Washington. Khrushchev on Nixon as goat guarding cabbage patch is in his May 5 speech: NYT, May 6, 1960.

Soviet attacks on American "Cold War circles" are noted in Werth, p. 243, as is *Pravda*'s publication of Stevenson's critique. "Long Live Leninism" and *People's Daily* article are noted in Tatu, pp. 47–48. Soviet military leaders replacement by hardliners is in Tatu, pp. 70–76. Mikoyan's decline is in Linden, pp. 90–94; Tatu, pp. 41–45, 79–83. Khrushchev's speech at Baku is in NYT, April 26, 1960. Eisenhower on Khrushchev failure to protest April 9 flight is in *Waging,* p. 547. "Virtually inviting us": Kistiakowsky, p. 328. Pearre Cabell on new flight's importance is in DFR, p. 335. Herter on reasons to fly U-2 is in SFRC, pp. 57–58. Targets are noted in Kaplan, pp. 286–87, Bissell and Lundahl interviews. Bissell notes importance of seeing missiles under construction and camouflage problem in letter to author, October 9,

1985. Importance of sun angle is noted by Pearre Cabell in DFR, p. 317. He also notes that the chances of finding good weather and sun in both the southern and northern Soviet Union on the same day were very low—as Bissell himself found in waiting weeks in April 1960 for satisfactory weather which did not come until May Day. Allen Dulles and Thomas Gates comments are in DFR, p. 287, and SFRC, p. 136.

10: *"I Would Like to Resign"*

Eisenhower on glassed-in veranda is described in John Eisenhower interview. Rome newspaper is quoted in *Baltimore Sun,* May 9, 1960. Lincoln White besieged and Lyndon Johnson's comment are in NYT, May 8, 1960. May 7, 1960, draft statement is in DDEL. May 7 CIA meeting is noted in Goodpaster interview; Wise and Ross (2), pp. 101–2; Bohlen, pp. 465–66. Herter's return is in Dillon, Goodpaster interviews, and SFRC, pp. 28–31. Herter's displeasure with cover stories is in G. Bernard Noble, *Christian A. Herter* (Cooper Square, 1970), p. 82. "We had to make the decision": SFRC, p. 104.

Sources on Christian Herter include Noble; Alexander, pp. 247–48; Richardson, pp. 162–63; Ambrose (2), p. 323, Christian Herter file, FBI/FOI. "Everyone's picture": JSDE, p. 234. Herter on crutches is noted in Mosley, p. 451. Nixon related his plea to cameramen in a letter to Adela Rogers St. John, May 18, 1959, Nixon Papers. Stassen movement is noted in Parmet, p. 452. Adams lowering boom is in Adams, pp. 240–41. Herter insulted by first job offer is in Noble, pp. 20–21. "Number-two man" is in NYT, February 10, 1959. "I have left this office": Hughes, p. 254. Embarrassing interval is noted in Killian, pp. 226–27, and Noble, p. 2. Hagerty and Henderson on Herter are in their oral histories, COHP. Note taking during Herter's visits is in JDSE, p. 234. Eisenhower on Herter is quoted in Noble, p. 306.

"I liked Allen Dulles": Dillon interview. Kohler's dissent and Bohlen's reaction are in Kohler, pp. 326–27, and Bohlen, pp. 465–66. Herter's verdict is in SFRC, pp. 104–5, and Noble, p. 83. Goodpaster's view is in interview. Herter's call to Dulles is noted in Goodpaster, Dillon interviews; Tel Call, May 7, 1960, CAHP. Other sources on May 7 State Department meeting are Noble, pp. 82–83, and Wise and Ross (2), pp. 104–5. One example of the press's impatience with Eisenhower's calm is T.R.B. in *New Republic,* May 23, 1960. Eisenhower's reluctance to alarm nation is in Goodpaster interview. Herter call to Eisenhower is in Wise and Ross (2), p. 105; Goodpaster interview; and *Waging,* p. 550.

Lincoln White given statement is in Wise and Ross (2), pp. 106–7, and Dillon interview. Text, May 7, 1960, is in DDEP. "Almost instantly": T.R.B. in *New Republic,* May 16, 1960. Ivanov reaction is in Wise and Ross (2), pp. 108–9. Acheson and Truman reactions are in letters to each other of May 23, 1960, and May 9, 1960, Harry S. Truman Post-Presidential Papers. Humphrey, Scott and Capehart reactions are in NYT and CR, May 9, 1960. All American newspapers quoted are dated May 8, 1960. *Chronicle, Daily Mail* and *Telegraph* are quoted in *Baltimore Sun,* May 9, 1960. *Sunday Express, The Times* and *Daily Mirror* quotations are all dated May 8, 1960. *Paris Presse* is quoted in NYT, May 8, 1960. *La Fuistizia* is in *Baltimore Sun,* May 9, 1960. Chinese rally is noted in NYT, May 10, 1960. Moscow reactions are in

McMillan unpublished article and NYT, May 11, 1960. Max Frankel is in NYT of same date. Thompson's report is in cable to Herter, May 8, 1960, DDEP. Reston and Lippmann are in NYT and NYHT, May 11, 1960.

Gates to Herter is in Tel Call, May 9, 1960. CAHP. Eisenhower at church and galled at own silence is in NYT, May 9, 1960, and *Waging*, pp. 550–51. "I'll lie as much": John Eisenhower interview. Eisenhower on losing credibility is in Pinkley, p. 341. On Supreme Commander and responsibility: Lyon, p. 267. D-Day note is in Ambrose (1), p. 309. "He didn't like to blame": Dillon interview. Milton Eisenhower talk with brother is in Milton Eisenhower interview; oral history, DDEL; Milton Eisenhower, p. 335; and *Waging*, p. 553. President to Herter is in Tel Call, May 9, 1960, CAHP, and *Waging*, p. 550. Rationale for admission and May 8 evening meeting are in Goodpaster, Dillon interviews. In June 1960, Allen Dulles noted Presidential acceptance of responsibility for an intelligence operation Daniel Webster "got involved with at the time of the dispute over the boundary of Maine" (DFR, p. 292). As Secretary of State for President John Tyler, Webster negotiated the settlement of the boundary dispute with the British signed as the Webster-Ashburton Treaty in 1842.

Harold Macmillan on U-2 and visit with Murphy are in Macmillan (3), p. 197, and Murphy, p. 537. Bissell later said, "I've often speculated about the feasibility of our adopting the British policy. . . . Washington has never been able to cultivate the 'no comment' response" (Bissell interview). Oliver Powers to Khrushchev and Eisenhower is in FGP, p. 133, and May 10, 1960, letter in DDEP. Bissell call to Kelly Johnson, "That's no U-2" and "My God!" are in Johnson interview and Johnson, pp. 127–28, as is Bissell request to "insult" the Russians. Ann Whitman comment, Eisenhower "depressed" and "I would like to resign" are in Ann Whitman Diary, May 9, 1960. May 9 drafting session is in Wise and Ross (2), pp. 114–15. Johnson's announcement is in NYT, May 10, 1960. Eisenhower at 1959 and 1960 West Point luncheons is in Ann Whitman Diary, January 12, 1959, and May 9, 1960. Eisenhower changing Goodpaster draft is in Goodpaster interview and *Waging*, p. 550. Rough draft, May 9, 1960, is in DDEP. Nixon to Herter is in Tel Call, May 9, 1960, CAHP.

"We're just going to have to take a beating": John Eisenhower interview; Kistiakowsky, p. 321. "Of course, one had to expect": Kistiakowsky, p. 321. "We will now have to endure": *Waging*, p. 552. Officials staying behind is in Kistiakowsky, p. 321. "Fully but without apology": *Waging*, p. 551. Dulles wish to show U-2 photos is in Goodpaster notes, May 9, 1960, DDEP. "Any statement?" is in Wise and Ross (2), p. 116. Herter and Dulles statements are summarized in NYT, May 10, 1960. Lundahl presentation and Dulles mishap are in Brugioni interview. "A rough one": Wise and Ross (2), p. 117. Khrushchev May 9 speech is in Wise and Ross (2), pp. 121–22; NYT, May 10, 1960. Khrushchev cornering envoys and missing Hamit Batu is in *Washington Star*, May 10, 1960. Soviet marshals and Khrushchev to Thompson is in Salisbury, pp. 489–90. State Department May 9, 1960, statement is in DDEP. Most newspapers took the statement to imply future U-2 flights into Russia. State declined opportunities to correct the impression: Wise and Ross (2), pp. 118–19.

AP bulletin is in *Boston Globe*, May 10, 1960. Reston and Lippmann are in NYT and NYHT, May 10, 1960. Alsop is quoted in *Time*, May 23, 1960. *Wall Street Journal* survey is noted in the *Nation*, May 21, 1960, as is the *Nation*'s reaction. *Daily*

Sketch cartoon is reproduced in NYT, May 15, 1960, as is *Stockholm Tidningen* comment. Harold Macmillan's reaction to American statement is in Macmillan (3), p. 201. Dulles on keeping quiet is in George Carpozi, *Red Spies in Washington* (Trident, 1968), p. 238; Andrew Tully, *CIA: The Inside Story* (Morrow, 1962), pp. 127-28; and Dillon interview. At the June 1960 hearings on the U-2, Dulles loyally defended Eisenhower's acceptance of responsibility but pointed out that he had not been consulted on the matter (DFR, pp. 291-92, 295). Mao on waking up "certain people" is in Tatu, p. 48.

Khrushchev's apoplexy is given vent in NSK II, pp. 509-11. "It is pretty clear": Kistiakowsky, p. 324. Eisenhower and Herter on Summit tactics is in Memcon Pres, May 10, 1960, DDEP. Herter cable to Embassy on Powers interview, Herter to Freers, May 11, 1960, is in DDEP. Twining on U-2 mishap is in his oral history, COHP. FBI report is Special Agent Auerbach to J. Edgar Hoover, May 13, 1960, FBI/FOI. *New York Mirror* is May 10, 1960, provided Hoover by his aide Cartha DeLoach, FBI/FOI. Barbara Powers press conference is in NYT and *New York Daily News,* May 11, 1960. Sources on Gorky Park include McMillan article; de Gramont, pp. 269-70; Wise and Ross (2), pp. 124-28; *Reporter,* June 23, 1960; conversation with Carl Mydans. Khrushchev's May 11 press conference is in Wise and Ross (2), pp. 127-30; NYT, May 12 and 13, 1960; McMillan article; SFRC, pp. 203-11. Interference of Moscow censors is noted in NYT, May 12 and 13, 1960. Moscow reactions to Khrushchev statements are in McMillan article.

Goodpaster drafting of May 11 Eisenhower statement and Hagerty to staff are in Goodpaster interview and Kistiakowsky, p. 324. Eisenhower at breakfast is in Memcon Pres, May 11, 1960, DDEP. Hagerty on censorship is in Pierpoint, p. 58. "To hell with slanted reporters" is quoted in Grossman and Kumar, p. 29. Eisenhower admissions are quoted in Deakin, pp. 147-50. "Supposed to set the tone": JSDE, p. 172. "I believe I read in the paper": Lyon, p. 550. "Don't worry, Jim" is from Murray Kempton's "The Underestimation of Dwight D. Eisenhower," *Esquire,* September 1967, an early instance of Eisenhower revisionism. Eisenhower May 11 statement and press conference are in NYT, May 12, 1960, and Wise and Ross (2), pp. 130-31. Time "easily utilized elsewhere" is in *U.S. News,* May 23, 1960. Eisenhower halt on provocations is noted in Goodpaster memo, May 12, 1960, DDEP, and *Waging,* p. 549. CIA on Gorky Park is in Office of Current Intelligence memo, May 11, 1960, DDEP. Thompson's cable to Herter, May 12, 1960, is in DDEP. Eisenhower's reaction and afternoon activities are in Goodpaster interview and Ann Whitman Diary, May 11, 1960.

Stevenson's "rage" and skepticism of Kennedy's diplomatic skills are in Martin, p. 502. "Could it serve": Martin, pp. 495-96. Staff memo, May 23, 1960, is in DDEP. Khrushchev to Shah is in Mohammed Reza Pahlavi, *Answer to History* (Stein and Day, 1980), p. 133. Gromyko summons to envoys is noted in Freers to Herter, May 13, 1960, DDEP. White's reaction is in State Department transcript, May 10, 1960, DDEP. Pakistani reaction is in *Baltimore Sun,* May 8, 1960. Ayub Khan is in NYT, May 14, 1960. Turkish text, May 26, 1960, is in DDEP. Norwegian protest and Herter assurance are in Willis to Herter and Herter's reply, May 10, 1960, DDEP. Shah's denial is in Rockwell to Herter, May 8, 1960, DDEP. Soviet maps provided to Naim and "after arriving in Peshawar": Hannah to Dillon, May 18, 1960, DDEP. Naim talk with Pakistan envoy and Hannah are in Hannah to Herter, May 8 and 18,

1960, DDEP. Kishi and the Japanese security treaty are discussed in Barnet, pp. 182–87. PATRON OF THE BLACK JETS: *Newsweek,* May 23, 1960. Herter to Tokyo is cable to Douglas MacArthur II, May 8, 1960, DDEP. White transcript, May 10, 1960, is in DDEP.

Powers's life in prison is described in FGP, pp 124–36. His sister's telegram to Eisenhower, May 14, 1960, is in DDEP. Eisenhower's departure from Andrews is in John Eisenhower interview; newsreel footage in NA; Wise and Ross (2), pp. 132–33; NYT, May 15, 1960. TerHorst and Albertazzie, p. 197, describe Eisenhower's airborne routine. "Seats far more comfortable": Ann Whitman Diary, August 26–September 7, 1959. Oxygen tanks are noted in Dwight D. Eisenhower FBI file, FBI/FOI. Reston on "things he feared the most" is in NYT, May 11, 1960. Eisenhower's composure is noted in John Eisenhower, Harr, Dillon, Goodpaster, Scoville, Milton Eisenhower interviews. John's talk with father is in interview. Eisenhower reading briefing books and "dreadful clatter" are in John Eisenhower Diary, May 1960, and Ann Whitman Diary, August 26–September 7, 1959.

11: *Debacle at Paris*

Sulzberger in diary is in Sulzberger (1), pp. 668–69. Marina Sulzberger in diary is in C. L. Sulzberger, ed., *Marina: Letters and Diaries of Marina Sulzberger* (Crown, 1978), p. 232. Eisenhower May 15 arrival statement is in NYT, May 16, 1960. Reporters noting missing name and Eisenhower ride into Paris are in Wise and Ross (2), p. 143. Khrushchev's arrival is in NYT, May 15, 1960, and Wise and Ross (2), p. 142. Eisenhower to Herter on private Khrushchev talk in Memcon Pres, May 15, 1960, DDEP. "My visit to the United States": NSK II, p. 511. Khrushchev on efforts to salvage situation: NSK II, p. 509. Mao's invitation to Moscow is in Linden, p. 101. Soviet campaign against "American aggression" is in Tatu, p. 61.

In his memoirs, Khrushchev maintains that it was he, on the flight to Paris, who toughened terms for Soviet participation in the Summit and won consent from his colleagues by radio to Moscow (NSK II, pp. 512–14). Virtually all other evidence suggests that the tough terms were set out before his departure from Moscow and that, if anything, his colleagues feared that he might relax one or more of them to save the Summit. Allen Dulles's information was that Khrushchev's demarche was "carefully prepared in Moscow before he arrived in Paris" (DFR, p. 351).

"With our relations falling to pieces": NSK II, p. 514. Khrushchev at hunting lodge and use of scythe are in Werth, p. 251; Wise and Ross (2), p. 145; NYT, May 16, 1960. *Sputnik IV*'s launching is in *Time,* May 23, 1960. Glennan's comment is in his Diary, May 15, 1960. Malinovsky's background and presence in Paris are discussed in Severyn Bialer's profile in George Simmonds, ed., *Soviet Leaders* (Crowell, 1967), pp. 126–37; *The New Yorker,* May 28, 1960; *Time,* May 30, 1960; NSK I, pp. 548–49; Kistiakowsky, p. 334; Sulzberger (1), p. 670. Khrushchev claims that it was his idea to bring Malinovsky to Paris (NSK II, p. 512). Adam Ulam doubts that Malinovsky was sent to Paris to check on Khrushchev, noting that it was standard practice to send a dour-faced soldier to scare the West and that Malinovsky was hardly in a position to check on his boss. (Letter to the author, August 9, 1985) Khrushchev's March 1960 visit with de Gaulle is in de Gaulle, pp. 224–34. De

Gaulle on Khrushchev's changed identity is quoted by Janet Flanner in *The New Yorker,* June 4, 1960. De Gaulle viewing of U-2 photos in 1959 is in Walters, p. 341. *"Immer Schmidt"* is in Thomas Powers, p. 348. Lundahl's briefing is noted in Lundahl, Brugioni interviews; Sulzberger (1), p. 750. Khrushchev May 15 meeting with de Gaulle is in de Gaulle, pp. 247–48, and NSK II, p. 515. Copy of demarche, May 15, 1960, is in DDEP.

Eisenhower waking from nap is in John Eisenhower Diary, May 1960. Eisenhower's conclusion on Khrushchev using U-2 to scuttle Summit is in *Waging,* p. 559, and Merriman Smith, pp. 259–61. Merchant-Lloyd exchange is in Memcon, May 14, 1960, DDEP. Eisenhower on Summit attendance is in *Waging,* p. 552. Eisenhower May 15 luncheon is in John Eisenhower Diary, May 1960. May 15 afternoon meeting of Eisenhower, de Gaulle, Macmillan, Adenauer, is in Walters, pp. 340–41; de Gaulle, p. 249: Macmillan (3), p. 202; Lyon, pp. 811–14; Ambrose (2), p. 577. Eisenhower May 15 meeting with aides is in Memcon Pres, May 15, 1960, DDEP. Khrushchev May 15 call on Macmillan is in Macmillan (3), p. 202. May 15 evening meeting of Eisenhower, de Gaulle, Macmillan and aides is in Macmillan (3), pp. 203–4; *Waging,* pp. 554–55; Memcon Pres, May 15, 1960, DDEP; Herter to Dillon, May 15, 1960, DDEP. Eisenhower May 15 cocktails and dinner is in John Eisenhower Diary, May 1960. "Dinner quietly at Embassy": Macmillan (3), p. 204. Khrushchev's anger at Eisenhower's failure to attempt to see him is in Tatu, pp. 60–62, and Sulzberger (1), p. 669.

Nixon's interview with Susskind is in Wise and Ross (2), pp. 147–48, and SFRC, p. 75. See also materials in Nixon Papers, May 1960. "Brazen and shameless" is quoted in *Trial,* p. 5. Sources on Gates's alert include Wise and Ross (2), pp. 146–47; DFR, pp. 351, 394; Lyon, p. 813; SFRC, pp. 124, 138. Lippmann on alert is in NYHT, May 19, 1960. Young on alert is in CR, May 18, 1960. "One of the things": John Eisenhower Diary, May 1960. Khrushchev's stroll is in Wise and Ross (2), p. 148; NYT, May 17, 1960. Macmillan-Eisenhower May 16 breakfast is in Memcon Pres, May 16, 1960, DDEP; John Eisenhower Diary, May 1960; Macmillan, pp. 204–5. "After this grueling couple of hours": John Eisenhower Diary, May 1960. Herter to Dillon is May 16, 1960, DDEP. Leaders' arrival at Elysée is in NYT, May 17, 1960; Walters, pp. 342–43: Wise and Ross (2), pp. 149–50; NSK II, pp. 516–17. Charles Bohlen believed that Khrushchev wanted Malinovsky and Gromyko at the Summit table so that they could report favorably back to the Kremlin on Khrushchev's conduct. (Cabinet Meeting Notes, May 26, 1960, DDEP) Khrushchev on his anger is in NSK II, p. 515. Walters's refusal to bring bugging device is in Walters, p. 342. Sources on Summit session include transcript, May 16, 1960, DDEP; Walters, pp. 343–46; Wise and Ross (2), pp. 150–58; *Waging,* pp. 555–56; de Gaulle, pp. 250–52; Macmillan (3), pp. 205–7; NSK II, pp. 517–18; Bohlen, pp. 467–68. Herter's notes, May 16, 1960, are in DDEP. Eisenhower about to choke was noted by Bohlen in Merriman Smith, p. 196.

"Mine is the only red face" and "What kind of apology" are in Wise and Ross (2), p. 159. De Gaulle-Eisenhower exchange is in Walters, p. 346, and *Waging,* p. 556. John Eisenhower on father's return is in his Diary, May 1960. "You might have thought" is in Gerard Smith, p. 12. Eisenhower's harangue against Khrushchev is in Memcon, May 16, 1960, DDEP; Andrew Berding, *Foreign Affairs and You* (Doubleday, 1962), p. 104; Richardson, pp. 174–75; *Time,* May 23, 1960. "Coldest gathering": Merriman Smith, p. 196. May 16 luncheon is noted in John Eisenhower Diary, May 1960. Soviets and Hagerty speak at Palais de Chaillot: NYT, May 17, 1960. NYT and *Rochester Times-Union* comments are May 17, 1960. Dodd on Khrushchev's lecture is in CR, May 18, 1960. Kennedy, Nixon reactions are in NYT, May 18, 1960.

John Eisenhower and father review of letter is in John Eisenhower Diary, May 1960. Draft of letter, May 16, 1960, is in DDEP. Eisenhower's invitation and garden stroll are in John Eisenhower Diary, May 1960. Macmillan on meetings with de Gaulle and Eisenhower is in Macmillan (3), pp. 207–8. Eisenhower May 16 dinner is in John Eisenhower Diary, May 1960. Macmillan May 16 evening meeting with Khrushchev is in Macmillan (3), pp. 208–9. On lamp, *Sputnik* and trousers: de Zulueta interview.

Eisenhower May 17 breakfast is in John Eisenhower Diary, May 1960. Khrushchev May 17 morning announcement is in NYT, May 18, 1960. Western leaders May 17 morning meeting is in *Waging,* p. 556, and Macmillan (3), p. 208. "Ike's object was clear": Macmillan (3), p. 208. Trip to Marnes-la-Coquette is in John Eisenhower Diary, May 1960; Wise and Ross (2), p. 163. Source on Eisenhower draft movement and evening with Jacqueline Cochran is Ambrose (1), pp. 523–24. Eisenhower-Macmillan visit to town hall is in John Eisenhower Diary, May 1960; NYT, May 18, 1960; Wise and Ross (2), pp. 163–64. Herter-Lloyd exchange is in Herter to Dillon, May 17, 1960, DDEP. Khrushchev-Malinovsky visit to Pleur-sur-Marne is in NSK II, pp. 519–23; NYT, May 18, 1960; and Wise and Ross (2), pp. 162–64.

Western leaders May 17 afternoon meeting and Khrushchev replies are in *Time,* May 30, 1960; NSK II, p. 523; Walters, pp. 347–48; Macmillan (3), p. 209; de Gaulle, pp. 252–53; Herter to Dillon: May 18, 1960, DDEP. "You know, poor Hal": Bohlen, p. 469. "De Gaulle unswervingly guarded": NSK II, pp. 518–19. Eisenhower interest in Khrushchev leaving town is in John Eisenhower Diary, May 1960. Mamie's call and explanation of Khrushchev's cancelled invitation is in John Eisenhower Diary, May 1960, and JSDE, p. 262n. John Hay Whitney on Macmillan's pleas and Eisenhower response is in Sulzberger (1), p. 672. John Eisenhower and friends dining out is in his Diary, May 1960. Western leaders May 17 communiqué is in NYT, May 18, 1960. Macmillan on Summit end is in Macmillan (3), p. 211. Doctor's examination is noted in John Eisenhower Diary, May 1960, and *Time,* May 30, 1960.

NYT headline and Reston column are in NYT, May 18, 1960. Eisenhower's May 18 morning activities are in John Eisenhower Diary; NYT, May 19, 1960; Wise and Ross (2), p. 167; and *Waging,* p. 556. Macmillan on May 18 meeting with Khrushchev is in Macmillan (3), p. 211. Khrushchev on their meeting is in NSK II, p. 523. Khrushchev to de Gaulle on Eisenhower and "worry about what might ensue" is in de Gaulle, p. 253. John Eisenhower on May 18 lunch with de Gaulle is in his Diary, May 1960. Sources on Khrushchev's performance at Palais de Chaillot include Whitney, pp. 389–400; *The New Yorker,* June 4, 1960; NYT, May 19, 1960; Smith, pp. 198–99; *New Republic,* June 13, 1960; Wise and Ross (2), pp. 167–68. Eisenhower and Macmillan reactions are in *Time,* May 30, 1960, Macmillan (3), p. 212. "It's a tragedy": Werth, pp. 9–14.

Macmillan May 18 meeting with Eisenhower is in Macmillan (3), p. 213, as is

Macmillan's message to the Queen. Staff telegram to Eisenhower, May 18, 1960, is in DDEP. Eisenhower May 18 dinner is in John Eisenhower Diary, May 1960; JSDE, p. 278. Eisenhower's handling of message from Democratic leaders is in John Eisenhower Diary, May 1960; JSDE, pp. 278–79; *Waging*, p. 557; Martin, pp. 500–501. Herter to Dillon, May 18, 1960, DDEP. Lundahl in safe house is in Lundahl interview. "We never went to bed": Sulzberger, ed., *Marina*, pp. 231–32. Eisenhower Paris departure is in John Eisenhower Diary, May 1960. Arrival at Lisbon is in Merriman Smith, pp. 200–203; Wise and Ross (2), pp. 168–69; NYT, May 20, 1960. Eisenhower "disgusted and fed up" is in Merriman Smith, p. 203; NYT, May 20, 1960. John Kennedy after Bay of Pigs is in Schlesinger (2), p. 292. Stevenson "damned sore" and address on Summit failure is in Martin, pp. 504–5. Farley's comment is in NYT, May 22, 1960. Eisenhower's return to Washington is described in *Time* and *Newsweek,* May 30, 1960, NYT, WP, *Washington Star, Washington Daily News,* May 21, 1960; Arleigh Burke oral history, COHP; Wise and Ross (2), pp. 169–70; *Economist,* May 28, 1960.

12: *Cold War*

Khrushchev attributed the Parisian jeering to the "bourgeois" French press "heaping abuse on me, blaming me for the failure of the conference" (NSK II, pp. 524–25). Khrushchev's arrival and speech in East Berlin are in Tatu, pp. 43–44; Werth, p. 256; McSherry, p. 52; NYT, May 21, 1960; *Time* and *Newsweek,* May 30, 1960; *Pravda,* in SP, XII, 21, pp. 3–7. Edward Freers found at the Soviet Foreign Ministry "deep regret at the breakdown of the Summit and recognition that effort must be made to get on rails again." (Freers to Herter, May 19, 1960, DDEP) Khrushchev's Moscow arrival is in NYT, May 22, 1960. "Yes, we wanted to believe Eisenhower" is in *Pravda,* May 23, 1960, quoted in Tatu, p. 66. Khrushchev's denial of political trouble is in NYT, May 29, 1960, and Tatu, p. 100. "Everything, absolutely everything" is quoted in Tatu, p. 67.

Ann Whitman on Eisenhower's post-Summit mood is in her Diary, June 1960. Eisenhower's explosion at NSC is in Kistiakowsky, pp. 333–36. Glennan's comment is in his Diary, May 17, 1960. Decision to give television speech is in Goodpaster interview, *Time* and *Newsweek,* June 6, 1960; NYT, May 26, 1960. "Nothing more boring for the public" is quoted in James David Barber, *The Presidential Character* (Prentice-Hall, 1977), p. 157. On Eisenhower and television, see Adams, p. 297, and Henry Cabot Lodge, *As It Was* (Norton, 1976), pp. 121–23. Selection of visual aids and text of speech are in Brugioni interview and NYT, May 26, 1960. Soviet reaction and jamming of speech are in NYT, May 26 and 27, 1960.

Eisenhower's May 26 breakfast is in Memcon Pres, May 26, 1960, DDEP; and Wise and Ross (2), pp. 171–72. May 26 Cabinet meeting is in Minutes, DDEP; Glennan Diary, May 26, 1960; Kistiakowsky, pp. 387–88; Gray, p. 273. Macmillan, Gaitskell, Lloyd speeches in House of Commons are in *Newsweek,* May 30, 1960, and *The New Yorker,* June 18, 1960. Eisenhower-Lodge on U-2 debate in UN is in Memcon Pres, May 20, 1960, DDEP. Sources on Lodge include his two volumes of memoirs and William J. Miller, *Henry Cabot Lodge* (London: Heinemann, 1967). Amory on Lodge "disappointment" is in oral history in JFKL. "Eisenhower told me" and "best job in government" are in David Wainhouse oral history, COHP. Dillon's complaint is in Sulzberger (2), p. 856. Murphy on "second foreign office" is in Murphy, p. 448. Eisenhower on Lodge is in his Diary, May 14, 1953.

Sources on legality of U-2 overflights include Quincy Wright, "Legal Aspects of the U-2 Flight," *American Journal of International Law,* October 1960; Spencer Beresford, "High Altitude Surveillance in International Law," 1960, draft in JFKL; McDougall, pp. 134, 185–87, 258–75; U.S. Senate, Special Committee on Space, *Space Law: A Symposium* (Government Printing Office, 1958); Myres McDougal, et al., *Law and Public Order in Space* (Yale, 1963); SFRC, pp. 89–90; DFR, p. 256. Eisenhower on "freedom of international space" is in *Waging,* pp. 210–11. Dulles on high-altitude reconnaissance is in DFR, p. 282. "If there ever was a case" is in Joint Appearances, p. 48. Sources on UN debate on U-2 include *Time, Newsweek, U.S. News,* May 30 and June 6, 1960; NYT and WP, May 23–29, 1960; Lodge, pp. 142–46. Kennan and the bugged American seal is noted in Dulles, p. 69, Lodge, pp. 142–44, and Kennan, pp. 153–56. Lodge-Dobrynin exchange is in Lodge, p. 144.

On Turkish overthrow, see NYT, May 28 and 29, 1960, and Metin Tamkoc, *The Warrior Diplomats: Guardia.s of the National Security and Modernization of Turkey* (Utah, 1976). Mansfield and Goldwater on need for U-2 investigation are in NYT, May 18, 1960, and CR, May 26, 1960. Eisenhower's misgivings and cooperation on U-2 hearings are noted in *Time,* June 6, 1960, and Wise and Ross (2), p. 174. Sources on Fulbright include Fulbright interview; Haynes Johnson and Bernard Gwertzman, *Fulbright: The Dissenter* (Doubleday, 1968); David Halberstam, *The Best and the Brightest* (Random House, 1973), pp. 28–29, 415–20. Use of MacArthur hearings as model is in Fulbright interview. Fulbright on "lying, cheating, murder" is in SFRC, p. 2. Herter on "not to have accidents" is in SFRC, p. 106. "That was a risk": DFR, pp. 276–77. "It has never come up" and "I am ashamed to say": SFRC, p. 103; DFR, p. 261. Herter also told the committee that U-2s based in Japan were never used to overfly the Soviet Union (DFR, pp. 412–13). Dillon on "gobbledy-gook" is in Dillon interview.

Helms's conviction for perjury in 1977 is discussed in Thomas Powers, pp. 298–308. Helms on possible perjury of Herter and other witnesses is in Helms interview. Allen Dulles on value of U-2 is in DFR, p. 282. On what U-2 provided: DFR, pp. 280–86. Russians "far less cocky": DFR, p. 286. "The fact that I was going ahead": DFR, pp. 293–95. "Certain targets that we were afraid": DFR, pp. 322–23. "He loved flying": DFR, pp. 338–39. Fulbright's absolution of CIA is in NYT and WP, June 1, 1960. Dulles to Herter is in Tel Call, June 1, 1960, CAHP. Dryden on U-2 flights is in DFR, p. 371. "We are regarded in one story": DFR, pp. 370–72. Gates on "everyone should be proud": SFRC, p. 162. "Primarily a measure of checking": SFRC, p. 136. "I don't know to my own knowledge": DFR, p. 404.

Censorship of hearings transcript is in Helms, Fulbright interviews; Wise and Ross (2), pp. 174–75. Lausche on "serving the Soviet Union" is in DFR, p. 368. Fulbright's resentment: DFR, pp. 374–75. Aiken on subpoena and Fulbright on "real issue": DFR, pp. 375, 390–91. Wiley and Fulbright on President's "lesson": DFR, p. 275. Capehart on ill-fated flight and Aiken on bum: DFR, pp. 447, 390–91. Fulbright on no good reason to fly so close to Summit: DFR, p. 565. Aiken's wonder who decided to fly on May Day is in DFR, p. 453. Fulbright on starving man is in DFR, p. 555. Final Committee report is U.S. Congress, Senate Foreign Relations Committee,

Events Relating to the Summit Conference (U.S. Government Printing Office, 1960), released June 25, 1960. "I have often wondered" is in *Saturday Review,* January 11, 1975, and Fulbright interview.

Powers shaken by news of Summit collapse: FGP, p. 142. Told of trial for espionage and certainty of execution: FGP, pp. 137–38. Taken to see U-2 wreckage: FGP, pp. 136–37. May 26 letter to Barbara is in Barbara Powers, pp. 84–87. Symington on "humiliating disaster" is in *Time,* June 6, 1960. Democratic Advisory Council comment is in CR, May 23, 1960. Kennedy criticism of Eisenhower in Oregon is in Sorensen, p. 149. Telegrams to Kennedy's office, May and June 1960, are in JFKL. "I'm not prepared to apologize": Sorensen, p. 149. Stevenson on Libertyville talk with Kennedy is in Martin, p. 508.

Japanese political situation and events leading to cancellation of Eisenhower's visit are noted in Barnet, pp. 187–88; Alexander, p. 267; Kistiakowsky, pp. 341–55; Merriman Smith, pp. 213–23; Werth, p. 260; Hoopes, pp. 504–5; Hughes, pp, 306–11; *Waging,* pp. 562–63; DFR, p. 416, Hagerty oral history, COHP. "Ike don't come!": NYT, June 5, 1960. Forged message from Office to U.S. Air Attaché, Tokyo, to MacArthur, May 7, 1960, is in DDEP. On Soviet forgery, see Dulles, pp. 150–51. MacArthur's cable to Herter on Kishi, May 18, 1960, is in DDEP. "The people around Ike": Merriman Smith, p. 216. "Are you so sure": John Eisenhower interview. Kishi's cancellation and stabbing are in Barnet, p. 188. Herter on U-2 withdrawal is in Memcon Pres, July 11, 1960, DDEP. Remainder of East Asia trip is in *Waging,* pp. 564–67; Merriman Smith, pp. 224–40; Kistiakowsky, pp. 355–58. "ONE FIASCO" is quoted in Werth, p. 260. Salisbury on "macabre journey" is in oral history, COHP. Eisenhower June 27 television speech is in NYT, June 28, 1960. "Tragic for the country": WP, June 28, 1960. Soviet walkout at Geneva is in *Waging,* p. 483, and Seaborg, pp. 24–25. Sources on RB-47 incident include *Time, Life, Newsweek,* July 25, 1960; Ambrose (2), pp. 584–86; *Waging,* pp. 568–71; Epstein, p. 121; Macmillan (3), pp. 237–40; Tatu, p. 110; William L. White, *The Little Toy Dog* (Dutton, 1962).

John Eisenhower to father on RB-47 downing is in interview. Eisenhower to Herter on distrust of Russians is in Tel Call, July 11, 1960, CAHP. Reluctance to compromise tracking stations and Dulles interpretation of incident are in Tel Call, July 12, 1960, CAHP, and *Waging,* pp. 569–70. UN's action is in *Waging,* pp. 570–71. President to aides on retaliation is in *Waging,* p. 571. C-47 incident is in Ambrose (2), p. 586. Gray's suggestion is in August 12, 1960, handwritten memo in DDEP. Quantico meeting and anonymous interview are in *U.S. News,* June 27, 1960.

CIA petition on redeployed U-2 operation, July 7, 1960, is in DDEP. Eisenhower on aides "missing badly" and awaiting "more stability": Memcon Pres, July 13, 1960, DDEP. Early development of SR-71 Blackbird is noted in Bissell, Johnson interviews, and Johnson, pp. 133–36. Sources on Eisenhower and development of American spy satellites include Bissell interview; Klass; Ewald, pp. 283–84; Killian, p. 83; Cline, pp. 180–81; Alsop, pp. 220–21; Ambrose (3), p. 291; de Gramont, pp. 489–90; *Interavia,* April 1972. Dulles and Bissell lobbying of Congress for satellite funding is noted in Infield, p. 183. Eisenhower on minimal U-2 use until satellites are ready is in Memcon Pres, February 12, 1959, DDEP.

Lippmann in *Pravda* is noted in Tatu, pp. 63–64. "When the President is no longer in office": NYT, June 4, 1960. Khrushchev's absence from June agriculture conference and its meaning are noted in Tatu, pp. 109-10. Sources on Bucharest meeting include Tatu, pp. 101-106; Linden, pp. 101-104; Ulam (1), pp. 634-35. Khrushchev withdrawal of technical advisers is in Tatu, p. 103; Linden, p. 104; Terrill, p. 282. Khrushchev failure to give main report on Bucharest and its meaning are in Tatu, pp. 110-11. Khrushchev's other problems in summer 1960 are noted in Tatu, pp. 114-22; Linden, pp. 105-16. Khrushchev on U-2 as beginning of fall from power is in Salisbury, p. 489. Eisenhower on Khrushchev's "vituperation" is in *Waging*, p. 560. New Cold War mood in American domestic politics is noted in White, pp. 115-18. "Change of tone in men like Chip": Alsop letter to British friend, July 20, 1960, Alsop Papers. Eisenhower on "stupid U-2 mess" is in Kistiakowsky, p. 375.

13: *Final Reckoning*

Sam Rayburn and John Kennedy at Democratic convention are in NYT, July 12 and 15, 1960. Rockefeller's dissent is in Theodore White, pp. 180-86, and Ewald, pp. 234-36. Rockefeller-Nixon meeting and the Compact of Fifth Avenue are noted in Theodore White, pp. 197-98, 388-90. Goldwater on "Munich" is in Theodore White, p. 199. Eisenhower's anger is noted in *Waging*, p. 595, and Ambrose (2), pp. 597-98. His hasty departure from Chicago is in *Time* and *Newsweek*, August 8, 1960, and Theodore White, p. 308. Powers meeting with Griniev is in FGP, pp. 148-57. Parker and Rogers hiring and briefing by CIA is in Houston interview; Wise and Ross (2), pp. 181-88. Barbara Powers's bad summer is noted in Barbara Powers, pp. 87-94. Oliver Powers acceptance of *Life* offer is in Wise and Ross (2), p. 183; Barbara Powers, p. 93; FGP, p. 197.

Sam Jaffe's notification that he would cover Powers trial is in Jaffe interview. Sources on Jaffe include *Esquire,* March and April 1977; *More,* March 1977; WP, September 9, 1979; and Jaffe interview. On CIA's relations with CBS and other media, see *Rolling Stone,* October 20, 1977; *Broadcasting,* May 3, 1976; *Columbia Journalism Review,* September–October 1974; *New York,* September 26, 1977. Jaffe's briefings by CIA are noted in Jaffe interview; CIA report on August 9 and 11 meetings with Sam Jaffe, CIA/FOI. Jaffe flight with Barbara Powers is in FBI report, September 16, 1960, FBI/FOI; Wise and Ross (2), pp. 190-91; Barbara Powers, p. 95. "How the hell can I stay away" and "She's drinking like hell": Jaffe interview. Barbara on "hating" Powers and "disgusted" lawyers are noted in FBI report, September 16, 1960. "I don't know why you bothered" and call on Griniev are in Barbara Powers, p. 97, and Wise and Ross (2), pp. 193-94. Barbara's telegram and trip to Lubyanka are noted in Barbara Powers, pp. 97-98, and Jaffe interview. "There she told the informant": FBI report, September 16, 1960.

Scene at beginning of trial is described in *Esquire,* May 1966; *Life,* August 29, 1960; de Gramont, pp. 270-72; Wise and Ross (2), pp. 196-99; Barbara Powers, pp. 99-100; FGP, pp. 160-62; Jaffe and Toumanoff interviews. Quotations from trial proceedings are in *Trial,* pp. 22-158. Toumanoff on Powers's calm is in interview. Powers on verge of screaming is in FGP, p. 171. Powers on altitude deception is in FGP, pp. 100-101, 131, 135, 157. Griniev advice to apologize and renounce United States is in FGP, p. 184. Oliver Powers springing to feet and shouting is in FGP, p.

187, and Barbara Powers, p. 105. Scene during reading of verdict is in FGP, pp. 191–92; Barbara Powers, p. 107; Wise and Ross (2), pp. 211–12; NYT, August 20, 1960. Powers meeting with family is in FGP, pp. 193–95; Barbara Powers, pp. 107–8; Wise and Ross (2), pp. 212–13. Hagerty on Eisenhower's regret is in Wise and Ross (2), p. 213. Radio Moscow on "hypocrisy" is in NYT, August 20, 1960, as is "traitor to his country." Marshall, Hutchins, Faulkner comments are in NYHT, August 31, 1960; FGP, pp. 256–57; de Gramont, p. 244.

"Dulles left me with the impression": Sulzberger (1), p. 699. Lyrics to "The Trial of Francis Gary Powers" are in Wise and Ross (2), p. 241n. Final meeting with parents is in FGP, pp. 195–97. Meeting with Barbara is in Barbara Powers, p. 109; FGP, pp. 196–97. Last visit with Barbara is in FGP, pp. 198–99; Barbara Powers, pp. 112–13; Wise and Ross (2), p. 217. Wise and Ross report that during the visit, Barbara asked guarded questions of interest to the CIA and that her husband scratched his answers in her palm. Asked about this, Bissell said, "I don't know anything about that." (interview) This reply may have been intended to conceal an intelligence method. Jaffe's later life is noted in Jaffe interview and WP, September 9, 1979. Khrushchev's decision to attend UN opening session is in NSK II, pp. 526–27. "We shall be looking forward": Nixon to Thompson, September 8, 1960, Nixon Papers.

Khrushchev's voyage is noted in NSK II, pp. 527–31; Shevchenko, pp. 95–106. "Drop dead, you scum": *Economist,* October 9, 1960. Diplomats tugging ropes is in Shevchenko, p. 106. Khrushchev's restriction to Manhattan is in *Waging,* p. 578. Khrushchev's New York activities and UN opening are in Gunther, pp. 487–88; Ulam (2), pp. 312–13; NSK II, pp. 532–34; de Gramont, p. 278. *Economist* on Eisenhower's appearance is October 8, 1960. Khrushchev's attack is in *Waging,* p. 582; NYT, September 24, 1960. Bohlen's advice on summit proposal is in Bohlen, pp. 472–73. Khrushchev's demands, denunciations are in *Waging,* pp. 586–88; U.S. Senate, *Radio and Television Network Newscasts, Presidential Campaign of 1960* (U.S. Government Printing Office, 1961), pp. 477–83, 485, 513. "Khrushchev is trying to promote": Eisenhower to Herter, Tel Call, October 4, 1960; Memcon Pres, October 1, 1960, DDEP. Macmillan's speech and Khrushchev's interruptions are in Macmillan (3), pp. 275–80; U.S. Senate, *Newscasts,* pp. 118–38. *Pravda* on Macmillan is in SP, XII, 40, p. 18.

Kennedy on Khrushchev's change since Camp David is in U.S. Senate, *The Speeches of Senator John F. Kennedy* (U.S. Government Printing Office, 1961), pp. 409–10. Eisenhower's request of Dulles and Dulles's meeting with Kennedy are noted in Dulles to Eisenhower, August 3, 1960, DDEP; Earle Wheeler, Theodore Sorensen and John McCone oral histories, JFKL; Sorensen, pp. 610–13. Jerome Wiesner, one of Eisenhower's science advisers, was "astounded" when the President allowed him to serve Kennedy as a campaign adviser while continuing to counsel the President. Wiesner thought that Eisenhower's intention was that he would give Kennedy the truth about the Missile Gap, although the President asked him to divulge no classified information. (Herken, p. 133) Foreign policy in 1960 campaign generally is in Robert A. Divine, *Foreign Policy and U.S. Presidential Elections, 1952-1960* (New Viewpoints, 1974), pp. 183–287. "Party which gave us the Missile Gap" is quoted in Stephen Hess, "Does Foreign Policy Really Matter?" in *Wilson Quarterly,* Winter 1980.

Nixon on Eisenhower's handling of U-2 and on Kennedy's preparation to deal with the Russians is in U.S. Senate, *The Speeches of Vice President Richard M. Nixon* (U.S. Government Printing Office, 1961), pp. 103, 194–95. Kennedy on Eisenhower Administration's 1958 regrets is in *Joint Appearances,* pp. 148–49. Khrushchev on "circus wrestling match" and "pair of boots" is in NSK II, p. 557, and Laurin Henry, *Presidential Transitions* (Brookings Institution, 1960), pp. 199–201. Khrushchev on Nixon is in NSK II, pp. 557, and Shevchenko, p. 108. On timing of Powers's release: NSK II, pp. 558–60; Shevchenko, pp. 108–9. On "deciding ballot" over Nixon: NSK I, p. 458.

Eisenhower on "biggest defeat" is in Slater, pp. 230–31. Nixon's suspicion of U-2's impact on election results is in Nixon (2), pp. 309–12. He also blamed the recession in the American economy. Nixon's suspicion of CIA effort to help Kennedy and of liberals in CIA is noted in Thomas Powers, p. 201, and Kissinger, p. 11. Operational ICBMs found at Plesetsk is in Kaplan, pp. 286–87, Laqueur, p. 151, Bissell interview. Air Force skeptics persisted, but were worn down as satellite photography, month after month, found no sign of a brisk Soviet missile buildup. (See Herken, pp. 130–31) Quotations from NBC's *The U-2 Affair* are from the transcript noted in Chapter One. Eisenhower's call to Sarnoff is in Scherer interview. Sarnoff's response is in Robert Gray memo, December 19, 1960, DDEP. Nixon's anger about U-2 program and on noncooperation with press are in Ann Whitman Diary, December 27, 1960. Hall's talk with Nixon is in Whitman Diary, December 31, 1960. Khrushchev's New Year's toast is in SP, XIII, 4, p. 26. Eisenhower on return to Gettysburg and "little success" is in *Waging,* pp. 619, 653.

Khrushchev's release and Kennedy's welcome of RB-47 fliers are in McSherry, p. 64, and SP, XIII, 4, p. 27. Powers reaction is in FGP, pp. 244–47. His transfer to Vladimir and assignment to cell with Kruminsh are in FGP, pp. 209–39. "I can never have a future": FGP, p. 250. Menshikov-Bowles talks on Melekh release, Thompson-Gromyko talks on Powers release and Rusk's advice on raising Powers issue are all in State Department Position Paper, "President's Meeting with Khrushchev," May 25, 1961, JFKL. Khrushchev to Kennedy on U-2 and Paris Summit is in Schlesinger (2), pp. 361–62; NSK II, pp. 558–60. "Matter wasn't even discussed" and Powers irritation are in FGP, p. 257. Barbara Powers on "vicious gossip network" is in Barbara Powers, p. 123. Her commitment to clinic is in Houston interview; Barbara Powers, pp. 124–27; FGP, pp. 266–68. Cabell to Rusk letter is November 2, 1961, JFKL. "More and more afraid": FGP, p. 276.

Sources on Rudolf Abel include Louise Bernikow, *Abel* (Ballantine reprint, 1982); James B. Donovan, *Strangers on a Bridge,* Dulles, pp. 101–2, 122. Donovan correspondence with "Hellen Abel" and why the Russians might want Abel back are in Donovan, pp. 297–368; Wise and Ross (2), pp. 234–48; Cabell to Rusk, November 2, 1961, JFKL. J. Edgar Hoover's opposition is noted in November 9, 1961, January 9 and February 21 documents in Francis Gary Powers File, FBI/FOI) Donovan negotiations with Schischkin and East Germans are noted in Donovan, pp. 371–417; Wise and Ross (2), pp. 248–57. John Kennedy's order on briefing Hoover, February 9, 1962, is in Powers File, FBI/FOI. Exchange at Glienicker Bridge is in Bernikow, pp. 247–50; FGP, pp. 281–84; Wise and Ross (2), pp. 3–7, 254–56; Donovan, pp. 418–20. Abel's final years in Moscow are noted in Barron, pp. 77–78; Bernikow, pp. vii–xii, 251–75. White House dinner and release of news in Washington are in Bradlee, pp. 49–52, 55–56; Mohr to DeLoach, February 10, 1962, FBI/FOI; Wise and Ross (2), pp. 5–6. "Imagine a reporter": Bradlee, p. 51. Answering reporters' questions, Dean Rusk minimized the diplomatic importance of the exchange. (NYHT, February 1962, in FBI/FOI) Powers-Donovan flight home is in FGP, pp. 284–92, and Donovan, pp. 420–23. "A couple of weeks ago" and "Powers was a man who" are in Donovan, p. 421.

Powers reunion with parents and Barbara is in FGP, pp. 292–93, and Barbara Powers, pp. 136–37. Powers debriefing is noted in Johnson, Houston interviews; Johnson, pp. 128–29; FGP, pp. 297–99, 303–4; Barbara Powers, pp. 136–37. "Before we start": FGP, p. 298; Johnson interview. "Couldn't help discerning an obvious pattern": FGP, p. 304. "HERO OR MAN WHO FAILED": NYHT, quoted in FGP, p. 294. Wickers, Young, *Newsday* on Powers are quoted in FGP, pp. 299–300. Powers "stunned" by criticism: FGP, pp. 299–303. Morris on Powers as "airplane driver": *Manchester Guardian,* quoted in *U.S. News,* September 5, 1960. Powers visit with Dulles is in FGP, p. 307. Houston on "slightly different stories" is in interview. Board of Inquiry's work is noted in its report, Board of Inquiry to John McCone, February 27, 1962. JFKL. Powers dislike of Board hearings and offer to take lie detector are in FGP, pp. 311–12. Dissatisfaction with public report is in FGP, pp. 314–19.

Powers's testimony before Senate Armed Services is in NYT and WP, March 7, 1962; *Aviation Week,* March 12, 1962; FGP, pp. 312–30. "One of finest pieces of theater": *New Republic,* March 19, 1962. White House cancellation of Powers appointment is in FGP, pp. 311–12. CIA refusal of Fulbright bid to reopen 1960 U-2 hearings is in NYT, February 13, 1962, and *Economist,* March 10, 1962. Quotations are from hearing transcript, U.S. Senate Armed Services Committee, March 6, 1962. Powers as beloved as Glenn is in *Nation,* March 17, 1962. Goldwater note and disbelief is in FGP, p. 330, and Goldwater, p. 79. "Spend it": FGP, p. 330. Disappearance into car is noted in *Time,* March 16, 1962.

14: *Who Shattered Détente?*

Examples of refutation of Khrushchev's claim of Powers downing by Soviet missile at above 65,000 feet include Allen Dulles in DFR, pp. 287–88, 314; Drew Pearson and Jack Anderson, "Pilot Powers and His Secret U-2 Spy Flight," *True,* September 1960; Dulles in Sulzberger (1), p. 678; *Time,* May 23, 1960; *Aviation Week,* May 16, 23, and 30, 1960. In 1985, Bissell said that Dulles had exaggerated the chance that a Pratt & Whitney J-75 engine would flame out. (interview) Dulles told Sulzberger that Powers never broke radio contact, perhaps referring to the "squirt" device mentioned in Notes for Chapter Two. At his May 11, 1960, press conference, Eisenhower said, "There is some reason to believe that the plane . . . was not shot down at high altitude" (NYT, May 12, 1960). At his May 26, 1960, breakfast with Congressional leaders, he said that the "present theory" was that the U-2's engine "flamed out, and that the pilot had to come down . . . to get the plane working again" (Memcon Pres, May 26, 1960, DDEP). On May 7, 1960, Harold Macmillan was told by British intelligence that the U-2 had had "a failure (perhaps of oxygen), lost height and been shot down" (Macmillan [3], p. 195).

Roy and Zhores Medvedev describe the Soviet leadership's embarrassment at having failed to stop the U-2 in *Exterminism and Cold War* (London: Verso Editions, 1982), p. 163. Khrushchev's sensitivity to the charge of having failed to defend his country against the U-2 is suggested by the fact that in his public statements of May 5, 7, 11 and 16, he specifically conceded only two previous U-2 violations—in July 1956 and April 1960. This allowed the Soviet public to conclude that the Soviet military had not downed previous planes because the Kremlin preferred to try stopping them by diplomatic protest—not because the planes were unstoppable. At the time he revealed the U-2 downing, Khrushchev also announced that the Soviet armed forces were "being converted to rocket weapons" and claimed that U-2 pictures recovered from the Powers crash showed that the American spy missions had been "precisely over regions which have no rocket bases," thus trying to maintain his world deception about a vast Soviet ICBM development effort. (McDougall, p. 259) He also claimed that Soviet fighters could reach 28,000 meters (92,000 feet). (*Aviation Week,* May 16, 1960)

On American government motive to convince public that U-2 was downed at lower altitude, see Robert Donovan in NYHT, February 1962, in Francis Gary Powers File, FBI/FOA. Dulles on "no cushion against malfunction" is in DFR, p. 288. "Dulles is sure": Sulzberger (1), p. 678. Powers later thought such stories a "controlled leak" to avoid American anxiety about Soviet air defense missiles. (FGP, pp. 144, 202, 302, 368) KGB pressure on Powers to avow downing by missile at "maximum" altitude is in FGP, pp. 130–31, 134–35, 144. After Powers's trial, his father told reporters in New York that his son doubted that he had been shot down. Three weeks later, the Russians compelled the younger man to write the *New York Times* that his father must have "misunderstood the answers I gave to the questions put to me during the trial." (NYT, September 27, 1960, FGP, pp. 201–2) Kelly Johnson's conclusion is in Johnson interview; Johnson, pp. 128–29; and Johnson to James Cunningham, February 21, 1962, Johnson Private Papers. Johnson's speculation on effect of U-2 granger is in Johnson interview, Ambrose (3), p. 291; Epstein, p. 119.

NSA's protest and conflicting evidence is noted in Thomas Powers, p. 328. Roger Hilsman, Director of the State Department's Bureau of Intelligence and Research at the time of Powers's return to the United States, writes that evidence that Powers was downed at high altitude by a missile was "not conclusive": Hilsman, p. 190. Thomas Powers writes that NSA's finding implies that the U-2 pilot "bailed out under circumstances which would not have prevented him from destroying the plane and its telltale cameras, thus allowing the United States to persist in its cover story" (Thomas Powers, p. 328).

McCone's suspicion of a Powers defection is noted in Houston interview. Bross, Prettyman opposition to NSA findings is in Thomas Powers, p. 328. Board's secret report, February 27, 1962, JFKL, is still partly classified. Public version appears in NYT, March 7, 1962, and FGP, pp. 314–19. The secret version notes that among the NSA findings was an indication "that the Soviets thought the flight of this U-2 continued at the same altitude beyond the point where Powers claimed it fell, that it then descended to a lower altitude and then changed its course by turning in a broad circle back to the neighborhood of Sverdlovsk and disappeared from the observation of the trackers some 35 minutes later." McCone's private briefing on downing at 68,000 feet is noted in *Aviation Week,* March 12, 1962.

Nathan's article in *Military Affairs* is "A Fragile Détente: The U-2 Incident Re-examined," October 1974. Powers denounced the piece in a 14-page rebuttal, which he refused to allow to be published. (See *Village Voice,* December 13, 1976) Selmer Nilsen's claim is in *Counterpoint* and Kaiser, p. 495n. American counterintelligence suspicion of base personnel is in Williams interview. May Day mission approval over open telephone is noted in FGP, p. 356. L. Fletcher Prouty, a retired Air Force colonel who served as a CIA-Pentagon liaison, has written that deliveries of liquid hydrogen used to avoid U-2 flameouts were unclassified and that this might have permitted sabotage of the hydrogen bottle before the May Day flight. (Prouty, pp. 375–76) But there is at least some question as to whether liquid hydrogen was used on the U-2 in May 1960. (Miller, p. 96) The investigative journalist Jack Anderson once noted a report from a "high intelligence source" that a Soviet agent might have equipped the U-2 with "an electronic booby-trap which could be triggered from the ground" and "cause an explosion too small to destroy the plane but just damaging enough to knock it out of commission." (*Parade,* January 7, 1962) Edward Epstein refers to a "sabotage attempt" against Powers's plane in Peshawar "on the eve of his departure, which was foiled by American counterintelligence" (Epstein, p. 118). Asked about this, Richard Bissell said, "That I don't remember." Bissell recalled "little evidence that there were any active sabotage attempts." (Bissell interview) Powers doubt of sabotage is noted in Powers interview with Edward Jay Epstein, February 24, 1976, copy provided the author courtesy of Mr. Epstein. Bissell on Nilsen's charge is in interview.

The *Life* photojournalist Carl Mydans, who took the Gorky Park pictures, has told the current author that two Soviet agents at Gorky Park thought he was photographing the U-2 debris a bit too systematically and threw him out of the hall. Oddly they did not take his film away. (conversation with Carl Mydans) Their suspicions were not ungrounded, for Kelly Johnson obtained the photos, numbered them and used them to deduce what might have downed the U-2. These photos were examined by the author in Johnson Private Papers and in *Life* Archives, New York. Secret State Department report is Bureau of Intelligence and Research, Intelligence Report, June 13, 1960, DDEP. Richard Bissell has suggested that the plane's good condition might be explained by the possibility that much of the fuselage fell to earth in a "flat spin." (interview) American bombers armed with new air-to-ground missiles by 1962 are noted by Robert Donovan in NYHT, February 1962, Powers File, FBI/FOI. Bradlee-Kennedy talk is in Bradlee, pp. 58–59. Bissell finds the hypothesis of a pledge not to contradict Khrushchev's version "too complicated a theory to be very appealing," although he allows that it would have been in the American interest. He argues that the U.S. government "can't shut people up very much." (interview) But presumably this was at least one of CIA's intentions in keeping Powers on its payroll at the CIA and Lockheed after his return. (See Epilogue) Powers believed that President Kennedy implored John McCone to keep him from writing his memoirs in 1962. (FGP, pp. 338–39) Also see Kennedy's comment to Bradlee on withholding Powers's back pay, cited above.

Dulles on U-2 vulnerability to flameout is in DFR, pp. 288–89, 337, 343. See report on Number 360's especial propensity for flameout cited in Notes for Chapter One. *Red Star,* May 10, 1960, reported that Powers told two Soviet officers shortly after capture that engine failure had led to his downing. (Intelligence Report, June 13, 1960, DDEP) The Western agent Oleg Penkovskiy is reported to have told Washington that fourteen missiles were fired at Powers's plane, that shock waves caused it to disintegrate and that one missile accidentally downed and killed a Soviet fighter pilot. (Penkovskiy, p. 271, and Harry A. Rositzke, *The CIA's Secret Operations,* Reader's Digest Press, 1977, p. 69) Penkovskiy's bona fides have been seriously questioned by Western intelligence. (See Chapman Pincher, *The Secret Offensive,* London: Sidgwick & Jackson, 1985, pp. 72–74) Powers later reported seeing a red-and-white parachute in the distance just after he landed in Russia. (FGP, pp. 89–90) Snider on Powers downing is in interview. Dulles on Powers tests is in Wise and Ross (2), p. 18. Bissell does not recall having seen such evidence. (interview) Goldwater on downing is in Goldwater, p. 79. Williams on downing is in interview. Powers notes poker-playing in FGP, p. 76. Powers on downing is in FGP, pp. 82, 101–2, 144, 202, 323–24. Bissell on downing is in interview. Resignation date is in Bissell career chronology in Bissell Private Papers. Bissell lingered at CIA until the end of February 1962, mainly to help write a new budget. (interview)

On the possible effect of U-2 pilot inattention, Miller writes that "at high altitude and heavy weights, the aircraft is operating close to the limit of its capabilities. Under these conditions, the aircraft . . . requires the pilot's full attention. If the aircraft is flown hands off and the autopilot is not engaged, an attitude upset can cause a long period of motion which may be either stable or unstable. . . . Above 60,000 feet, if upset and left hands off, the aircraft will go into a climb or dive and the airspeed will continue to decrease or increase until the pilot corrects the situation." (p. 91) Miller further notes that when one considers the difficulty of flying the U-2 along with the fact that the pilot is for seven to twelve hours "virtually immobilized . . . breathing dry, pressurized liquid or gaseous oxygen . . . it becomes apparent why the aircraft has a poor accident record. The causes of the numerous U-2 accidents are varied. There were recorded instances of instantaneous loss of oxygen supply to the pilot, pilot physiological problems, destruction through enemy action, structural failures brought on by exceeding performance limitations at altitude . . . powerplant failures and, in more than a few accidents, instances of poor piloting technique." (p. 116)

CIA evidence of Soviet overflights is in DFR, pp. 304, 307. On November 1, 1985, the *Daily Telegraph,* London, reported that Chinese fighter planes "scrambled from Shanghai to intercept Soviet reconnaissance planes near the city." Inability of U-2 to survey entire Soviet military complex is noted in Prados, pp. 81–83, Gaddis (1), p. 229, Dinerstein, p. 75. Bissell could not recall an instance in which the U-2 was sent on short notice to acquire tactical intelligence but noted that tactical intelligence needs "might have influenced the priority accorded to particular targets." (Letter to author, October 9, 1985) "Armed with U-2 knowledge": *Waging,* p. 558. Bissell thought SA-2 development was "almost certainly" hastened by the U-2. (February 22, 1966, interview) Possible hastened Soviet receptivity to arms control is in Gerard Smith, pp. 11–12, Barnet, p. 92. "You could see": Transcript of Bissell interview, February 22, 1966, Bissell Private Papers. U.S. ability to announce Soviet developments is noted in DFR, p. 285. Eisenhower on war declaration if Soviet penetration is in Memcon Pres, February 12, 1959, DDEP. U-2 bomb rack is noted in Bissell interview. Kennedy on wholly different meanings is in Schlesinger (2), p. 337. "More infuriated and disgusted" is in NSK II, p. 505, as is Khrushchev on U-2 stampeding Kremlin and "terrible headaches." Eisenhower on "whether the intelligence which we receive" is in Memcon Pres, December 16, 1958, DDEP. Killian on U-2's role is in interview.

Sources on drawbacks of covert decision-making include Schlesinger (1), pp. 452–58; Morton Halperin and Jeremy Stone, "Secrecy and Covert Intelligence Collection and Operations" in Norman Dorsen and Stephen Gillers, eds., *None of Your Business* (Viking, 1974), pp. 105–36; Prados, p. 102. U-2 too secret for 5412 Group is noted in Gordon Gray to Eisenhower, May 12, 1960, DDEP. NSC's 1954 definition of plausible deniability is in Gaddis (2), p. 157. Bissell on plane "pretty much" breaking up and "one chance in a million" is in Bissell interview; Ambrose (3), pp. 279–80. The CIA generally maintained that tightly wound spools could never be destroyed by explosive, although they could be denounced as a Soviet fabrication. (DFR, pp. 310–11) Shortly after May Day 1960, Kelly Johnson equipped a heavier plane, a T-33, with a U-2-style explosive and film and detonated it. He found that the film "came through unscathed." (Johnson interview, photographs and documents in Johnson Private Papers) Other U-2 crashes without killing pilots: Bissell, Snider interviews.

Khrushchev's claim that ejection seat would have blown up plane is in NYT, May 8, 1960, and *Aviation Week,* May 16, 1960. U-2 pilots' suspicion that destruct device was rigged without full seventy-second delay is noted in Infield, p. 175; Wise and Ross (1), pp. 123–24. David Wise noted his own skepticism in conversation with the current author. Passage from *Spectrum* (Viking, 1981) is pp. 163–65. Killian on probability estimate is in Killian interview. Argument that Soviet information might be impossible to obtain after May 1960 is in DFR, p. 322. Cabell on degree of flight's urgency is in DFR, p. 336. Eisenhower on "careless with success," "overconfidence," and reluctance to oppose associates is in Merriman Smith, p. 259; Merriman Smith oral history, DDEL, and Memcon Pres, July 7, 1960, DDEP. Subordinates' not sharing conviction that U-2 backlash would "sweep the world" is noted in *Waging,* p. 546; Goodpaster interview. Eisenhower writes that Bissell was an exception. Bissell later said, "I think it can be said with hindsight that it was bad judgment to take such a risk as to send a U-2 on a mission so close as this in time to the Summit. But it was the President's decision. He made it" (Mosley, p. 456). Eisenhower on flights "within an intelligence policy" and without "any possible bearing on the Summit" is in Adams, pp. 455–56. On need for diverse Presidential advice, see Alexander L. George, "The Case for Multiple Advocacy in Making Foreign Policy," *American Political Science Review,* September 1972.

Khrushchev on flights to show "impotence" is in NSK II, p. 505. See Chapter Eight of the current book for Khrushchev's repeated mention of espionage while in the United States. Khrushchev on "unprovoked demonstration": NSK II, p. 511. "To return the state": Soviet note, May 10, 1960, in *Department of State Bulletin,* May 30, 1960. On warnings about subordinates starting war, see, for instance, NYT, April 24, 1958. "Two-faced policy": NSK II, p. 508. "Didn't realize how high a price": David Wise, *The Politics of Lying* (Random House, 1973), p. 35. Khrushchev on "arrogant" May 9 statement is in NSK II, pp. 509–10. Macmillan on Khrushchev's possible mollification is in Macmillan (3), pp. 201, 215–16, 283–84. He went on to write that Eisenhower "lacked the flexibility of mind to adopt a course that would allow Khrushchev an easy way out."

Bolshakov's service as Cuban Missile Crisis back channel is noted in Schlesinger (1), pp. 499–527, Llewellyn Thompson oral history, JFKL. On 1958 apology, see Chapter Thirteen of this book. Increased American-Soviet talks under Eisenhower are noted in Gaddis (2), p. 189. Eisenhower's suspicions of Russians and concerns about difficulties of democracies are noted in Gaddis (2), pp. 189–97. Eisenhower on "Spirit of Camp David" is in *Waging*, p. 448. Eisenhower on Khrushchev as nearly "absolute dictator" is in Memcon Pres, May 11, 1960, DDEP. Gaddis discusses Eisenhower's acceptance of responsibility and subordination of negotiations in Gaddis (1), p. 230, and Gaddis (2), pp. 189–97. Eisenhower was struck by Khrushchev's reluctance at Camp David to reveal his Berlin concession until he was able to explain it to Kremlin colleagues. (See Chapter Eight.) Llewellyn Thompson had repeatedly advised Eisenhower that Khrushchev's hold on power was not absolute. (see Memcon Pres, October 16, 1959, and Thompson to Herter, January 29, 1960, DDEP), but among declassified documents, there is no evidence that any of the President's advisers gave him a briefing relating this to the pivotal decisions that had to be made about the U-2 controversy. George Kennan later observed that Eisenhower "created a situation" requiring Khrushchev to "scurry for cover by taking a very, very tough line toward us." (oral history, JFKL)

Eisenhower's scientists on test ban is in Ambrose (2), p. 577. Sources on Eisenhower's plans for talks on Berlin at Paris include Goodpaster interview, Memcons cited in Chapter Nine. Dobrynin on 1959–1963 is in Kissinger, p. 113. Kennan on Khrushchev's fall is in Kennan, p. 143. "Can be argued that such a détente": Ulam (2), p. 156. Ulam was referring to 1949–1950. "We showed the whole world": NSK II, p. 511. Soviet presumption that U.S. would not defend South Korea is in Barnet, p. 15, and Ulam (2), pp. 171–85. Khrushchev's underestimation of Kennedy's will is in Ulam (2), pp. 319–21. Kissinger on superpowers is quoted in Arthur Schlesinger, Jr., "Foreign Policy and the American Character," *Foreign Affairs,* Fall 1983. Eisenhower's efforts to more closely engage Americans and Soviets are noted in Goodpaster interview. Also see Barnet, pp. 9–10, and Ulam (2), pp. 243–45. On problems of American-Soviet misperceptions, see, for instance, Barnet, pp. 15–17; Ulam (2), pp. 238, 281–87, Ralph White.

Epilogue: After the Storm

Khrushchev's invitation and Eisenhower's response are noted in JSDE, pp. 293–94, 390–91. Khrushchev's invitation persuaded the former President that the Soviet leader's "anger in Paris was largely spurious" (*Waging*, p. 588n). American-Soviet relations in fall 1961 are noted in Ulam (2), pp. 321–26. Khrushchev's problems are noted in Hyland and Shyrock, pp. 4–18; Linden, pp. 90–116; Tatu, pp. 41–126. His flight from collective leadership is in Crankshaw, pp. 260–65, 270–72; Medvedev (2), pp. 237–44, 314–40. On his motives in moving missiles into Cuba, see Hyland and

Shyrock, pp. 23–63; Tatu, pp. 123–227; Linden, pp. 146–73; Ulam (2), pp. 314–40. American-Soviet relations after the Missile Crisis are noted in Ulam (2), pp. 337–40. Thompson and hot line is in Jane Thompson interview. Khrushchev's ouster is noted in Hyland and Shyrock, pp. 143–97; Medvedev (1), pp. 54–55: Medvedev (2), pp. 235–45; Linden, pp. 174–230; Tatu, pp. 364–428; Page, pp. 11–180. "I'm on holiday": Medvedev (2), p. 236. *Pravda*'s attack is in NYT, October 17, 1964, as is first Chinese atomic test. "Well, that's it": Medvedev (2), p. 245. John McCone said that Khrushchev's ouster "came as a complete surprise" to the CIA (NYT, November 16, 1964). Khrushchev's exile is described in Salisbury, pp. 485–99; Medvedev (2), pp. 249–59; Jerrold Schecter's introduction in NSK II, pp. xi–xx; NSK I, pp. 3–9; NSK II, pp. 1–6. "Granddad cries" and dressing down by Kirilenko are in Salisbury, p. 485, and Medvedev (2), p. 254. Khrushchev on Eisenhower, Paris Summit and U-2 episode are in NSK II, pp. 604–5, 504; NSK I, pp. 200–202. Khrushchev signing formal denial of issuing memoirs is in NSK II, pp. xv–xvi. Khrushchev-Yevtushenko visit is in Salisbury, pp. 496–97. John Eisenhower on Khrushchev's death is in JSDE, pp. 380–81. On Khrushchev's burial, see Kaiser, pp. 228–30. Khrushchev's name unmentioned by Soviet press is noted in WP, January 15, 1984, and January 27, 1985. Closure of cemetery is in Salisbury, p. 498.

Eisenhower on Bay of Pigs and U-2 is in Slater, p. 244. John's proposed statement and father's reaction are in John Eisenhower interview. John's anger about Dulles "falling short" is in interview. Eisenhower refusal to criticize Dulles in memoirs is in Ambrose (2), p. 634, and John Eisenhower interview. Eisenhower and Goodpaster agreed that only Eisenhower would speak about the U-2 during Eisenhower's lifetime (Goodpaster oral history, COHP, and conversation with Goodpaster). Eisenhower on Paris Summit is in *Waging*, p. 558. His certainty that Russians would refuse Open Skies and contrary evidence: DDE oral history, DOHC, and Goodpaster interview. "We kept the peace": Lyon, p. 851. "Had longed to give the United States": Pinkley, p. 373.

Dulles's previous relationship with Kennedy is in Amory, Robert Kennedy oral histories, JFKL. Kennedy on Bissell as successor is in Wyden, p. 96. Cuban invasion leaks plugged: Wyden, pp. 142–45, 152–55. Robert Kennedy on Bissell's view on failure is in Schlesinger (1), p. 443. Dulles on "worst day" of life is in Nixon (1), p. 233. Kennedy to Dulles is in Thomas Powers, p. 115. Murphy's visits and *Fortune* article, "Cuba: The Record Set Straight," September 1961, are noted in Thomas Powers, p. 115. Nixon to Dulles, October 6, 1961, is in Nixon Papers. Dulles's final years are noted in Ambrose (3), pp. 317–18; Mosley, pp. 473–83. Dulles on leaving CIA is in letter to Nixon, October 15, 1961, Nixon Papers. Hunt on Dulles's death is in Ambrose (3), p. 313. Dulles on favorite President is in Bancroft, p. 141. This statement is all the more notable considering that it was under Eisenhower that Dulles and the CIA enjoyed their meteoric rise and that Truman was highly critical of CIA in his retirement. Kennedy to Bissell is noted in John Kenneth Galbraith, *A Life in Our Times*, p. 397. Bissell's later life is in Bissell, Amory interviews. Bissell to Johnson, October 19, 1978, is in Bissell Private Papers. Robert Kennedy–Amory talk on Bissell is in Amory interview.

August 1962 U-2 incident is in *Time,* September 14, 1962. Sources on U-2 and Cuban Missile Crisis include Infield, pp. 180–81; *American Heritage,* October 1977;

Prados, pp. 129–50; *Aviation Week,* November 5, 1962; Dinerstein, pp. 191–93, 228–89. "Always some son-of-a-bitch": David Detzer, *The Brink* (Crowell, 1979), p. 246. U-2 and 1970 Cienfuegos incident is in Kissinger, pp. 635–52; Nixon (1), pp. 485–89. U-2 use over China is in Cline interview; Cline, pp. 201–2, Infield, pp. 178–93, 202; *Aviation Week,* September 17, 1962; *Time,* September 21, 1962. Sources on later use of U-2s include *Air International,* October 1981; WP, December 31, 1984; Infield, pp. 179–80; Bill Gunston, ed., *The Encyclopedia of World Air Power* (Crescent, 1980), pp. 237–38; *Newsweek,* February 17, 1969, January 28, 1977, November 19, 1984; *New Statesman,* September 9, 1983; *Discover,* October 1983; Johnson interview.

Eisenhower founding of National Reconnaissance Office and largest budget by 1975 are noted in James Bamford, "America's Supersecret Eyes in Space," *New York Times Magazine,* January 13, 1985. American concession of spy satellites is noted in Stansfield Turner, *Secrecy and Democracy* (Houghton Mifflin, 1985). On changing Soviet position on legality of spy satellites, see McDougall, pp. 134, 185–87, 258–75; Georgi Zhukov, "Space Espionage Plans and International Law," *International Affairs,* October 1960; and Academy of Sciences of the U.S.S.R., *Space and International Law* (Moscow: Institute of International Relations, 1982). The tortured Soviet reasoning actually led Moscow at one point to claim that *Sputnik* did not violate national sovereignty because it did not fly over countries: the countries themselves rotated beneath the *Sputnik*(!) (U.S. Senate, *Legal Problems of Space Exploration,* Government Printing Office, 1961, pp. 1047–49) Gerard Smith on SALT talks is in Gerard Smith, pp. 11–12. Satellites and verification is noted in Ted Greenwood, "Reconnaissance and Arms Control," *Scientific American,* February 1973, and WP, January 6, 1985.

Sources on SR-71 Blackbird include Johnson, Bissell interviews; Johnson, pp. 133–51; Prados, pp. 175–76; *New Statesman,* September 9, 1983; WP, December 31, 1984; Kelly Johnson in *Lockheed Horizons,* Winter 1981–82. "Perhaps the most enigmatic": Gunston, p. 236. Thousand downing attempts eluded by early 1980s is noted in *New Statesman,* September 9, 1983. Rumors of SR-71 Soviet overflights are in *New Statesman,* September 9, 1983. General George Keegan, former Air Force intelligence chief, writes that American presumptions about the MiG-25 fighter "strongly influenced a national political decision not to overfly the Soviet Union with the SR-71." When the Soviet pilot Viktor Belenko defected with a MiG-25 in 1976, the Pentagon discovered that the plane could not down an SR-71 (John Barron, *MiG Pilot,* Avon reprint, 1980, pp. 180–82). Drone development is noted in Johnson, pp. 150–51. Another aggravation was the Soviet failure to halt a Korean airliner in 1978 before it succeeded in flying a thousand miles into Soviet airspace. (See Ralph White, p. 30.) George Will and Roald Sagdeev discussed the U-2 and Soviet defense on ABC's *This Week with David Brinkley,* transcript, November 10, 1985. Sagdeev spoke in English; I have slightly corrected his syntax without altering meaning.

Diogenes and Eisenhower is noted in Gray, p. 349. RB-47 statements generally accepted: Wise and Ross (2), p. 265. Public speculation after Korean Airlines downing is noted in Dallin and Richard Rohmer, *Massacre 007* (London: Coronet Books, 1984). *Aviation Week* on Cold War incompetence is May 16, 1960. *Marco Polo, If*

You Can was published by Doubleday, 1982. "All's well that ends well": Joachim Joesten, *They Call It Intelligence* (Abelard-Schuman, 1963). Big Stone Gap welcome and Powers work at CIA are in FGP, pp. 332, 336–37; Sue Powers interview; *Ramparts,* April 1967. Divorce is noted in FGP, pp. 334–38; Barbara Powers, pp. 152–70. FBI report on *Spy Wife* is in Francis Gary Powers File, FBI/FOI. David Cort on *Spy Wife* is in *Nation,* January 24, 1966. Powers meets Sue Downey and goes to Lockheed: Sue Powers interview; FGP, pp. 341–42. Marriage and "happiest part of my life" are in WP, October 26, 1963, and FGP, p. 345. Powers's Lockheed work and life in mid-1960s are in FGP, p. 345; *Newsweek,* February 17, 1969; Sue Powers interview; *Esquire,* May 1966, in which Demaris recounts his finally successful efforts to see Powers.

Gates nightmares are in Gates oral history, COHP. Powers irked by Board report and CIA treatment: FGP, pp. 314–19, 343–44. Writing of Powers's memoirs is noted in FGP, pp. 334, 338–40. "A scapegoat, by dictionary definition": FGP, p. 370. Marchetti and Agee books are Marchetti and John Marks, *The CIA and the Cult of Intelligence* (Knopf, 1974) and Agee, *Inside the Company: A CIA Diary* (Stonehill, 1975). Powers dismissed by Lockheed: FGP, p. 374; Johnson, Sue Powers interviews. Johnson on Powers after firing is in cable to "Col. Hartly," September 8, 1971, Johnson Private Papers. Powers on *The Dick Cavett Show* and at North American Rockwell is based on tapes cited in Chapter One. His job search, dreams and call on hypnotist are noted in Sue Powers, Anderson interviews. Effort to reopen U-2 investigation is in Anderson interview. Campaigning and "Frank said he would sit": Sue Powers interview. Anderson on Powers as traffic pilot is in interview.

Powers in mid-1970s is based on Anderson, Sue Powers interviews; *Newsweek,* February 28, 1977. Johnson's inscribed photo is dated February 18, 1975. Television version of memoirs is noted in Sue Powers interview. Hiring by KNBC and helicopter training are in Sue Powers, Anderson interviews. Circumstances of Powers's death are noted in Sue Powers, Anderson interviews; NYT, WP, *Los Angeles Times,* August 2 and 3, 1977; tape of Los Angeles radio news reports, August 1, 1977. "Looked up and saw the helicopter": tape, August 1, 1977. "No evidence of fuel": WP, August 3, 1977. "When he got back" and "Just too good a pilot": Anderson and Sue Powers interview. Rumors on downing are in *Los Angeles Times,* August 28, 1977; Ambrose (3), p. 290. Success in winning Arlington burial is noted in Sue Powers and Anderson interviews. Jimmy Carter on Eisenhower and U-2: conversation with former President Jimmy Carter. Burial is noted in NYT and WP, August 9, 1977. "I want you to meet": Snider interview.

Index

Khrushchev, Nikita S. (*cont.*)
 election of 1960 and, 225, 340–341
 English of, 213, 216
 estates of, 208
 foreigners' impressions of, 30, 163, 164,
  174, 182, 184, 197, 199, 276
 at Geneva Summit (1955), 100–105, 163
 Geneva test ban talks and, 231
 Gorky Park speech of, 262–263, 266,
  274, 280
 in Great Britain, 116, 117–118
 health of, 206–207
 Herter and, 260, 262
 homecoming speech of (1959), 216–217,
  218
 "inferiority complex" of, 208
 Jaffe and, 330
 Kennedy and, 195, 225, 344–345, 383
 Lodge's Moscow visit with, 225–226
 Macmillan and, 173–175, 338–339
 Malenkov and, 168–171
 marriages of, 165
 on May Day (1960), 23–24, 29
 memoirs of, 386–387
 missile claims of, 152
 movies preferred by, 205
 near immigration of, 198
 near overthrow of, in Anti-Party Coup
  (1957), 29, 170–171, 325
 as Nikita the Corn-Grower, 122, 202,
  217
 Nixon and, 178–183, 191–192, 194, 196,
  206
 Nixon's views on, 182, 208, 337
 Open Skies rejected by, 103, 117–118,
  158
 Palais de Chaillot speech of, 299–300
 at Paris Summit, 272–301, 305–307,
  309–310, 376–380, 393
 Paris Summit invitation of, 222
 political fears and risks of, 29, 40–41,
  185, 223, 229–230, 306
 popularity of, 216–218
 Powers's capture announced by, 58–66,
  373
 as propagandist and agitator, 40–45
 psychological profiles of, 163
 Rapacki Plan of, 378
 retirement of, 386–387
 Secret Speech of, 169–170, 171, 194,
  230
 Soviet power blocs antagonized by,
  219–220, 224, 323–325, 374, 385
 Stalin and, 165–168
 Stalin denounced by, 169–170
 Stalin's death and, 71

Khrushchev, Nikita S. (*cont.*)
 State Department U-2 statements and,
  256, 259
 Supreme Soviet speeches of, 43–47, 53,
  54, 58–61, 372–373
 technical advisers withdrawn from
  China by, 324
 "toothache" of, 175, 191
 U-2 flights as viewed by, 123, 238–239,
  371–372, 381
 at UN, 198, 207, 337–339
 underclass image of, 163–164
 U.S. television speech of, 212, 213
 U.S. visited by, 7, 9, 33, 40, 44, 65,
  184–218, 230, 238, 299, 337–339, 371,
  380
 at Vienna meeting with Kennedy,
  344–345, 383
 Virgin Lands idea of, 325
 "We will bury you" pledge of, 184, 195,
  200
 in World War II, 166–167
Khrushchev, Sergei, 201, 387
Khrushcheva, Julia, 165, 201
Khrushcheva, Nina Petrovna, 165, 188,
  199, 201, 223, 228
Khrushcheva, Rada, 201
Khrushcheva, Yelena, 331
Khrushchevland, 227
Khrushchev Remembers, 386
Kiev, 167, 227
Killian, James, 74, 79–80, 81–83, 93, 119,
  123, 149, 152, 366
 on U-2 security, 369–370
Killian Commission (Technological Capa-
  bilities Panel), 74–76, 79–80, 366
Kipling, Rudyard, 13, 174
Kirilenko, Alexander, 386
Kirkpatrick, Lyman, 87
Kirov, Sergei, 166
Kishi, Nobusuke, 144, 268–269, 319–320
Kissinger, Henry, 2, 97, 379, 381
Kistiakowsky, George, 45, 46, 57, 234,
  241, 326
 diary of, 208, 237, 259–260
 on Missile Gap, 237
 on U-2 incident, 259–260
Kitchen Debate, 181
KNBC Television, 400
Knowland, William, 83–84
Kohler, Foy, 190, 244, 246, 254
 at Paris Summit, 278, 283
Koht, Paul, 268
Korea, 98, 319
Korean Airlines incident (1983), 394, 395
Korean War, 14, 18–19, 36, 71, 381

Michael R. Beschloss was born in Chicago in 1955 and educated at Williams and Harvard. He has held appointments at Oxford, the Smithsonian Institution, the Russian Research Center at Harvard and the Brookings Institution. His first book, *Kennedy and Roosevelt,* written when he was 22, was an Alternate Selection of Book-of-the-Month Club and the History Book Club. *Mayday* was a Main Selection of Book-of-the-Month Club and has been translated into five languages. Beschloss lives and writes in Washington, D.C.